Modern Human Relations at Work

Modern Human Relations at Work

ELEVENTH EDITION

National College
of Ireland
Library

KATHRYN W. HEGAR
Mountain View College

SOUTH-WESTERN
CENGAGE Learning™

Australia • Brazil • Japan • Korea • Mexico • Singapore • Spain • United Kingdom • United States

**Modern Human Relations at Work,
Eleventh Edition, International Edition**

Kathryn W. Hegar

VP/Editorial Director: Jack W. Calhoun

Editor-in-Chief: Melissa Acuña

Senior Acquisition Editor: Michele Rhoades

Developmental Editor: Jennifer King

Senior Editorial Assistant: Ruth Belanger

Marketing Manager: Gretchen Swann

Content Project Management:
PreMediaGlobal

Media Editor: Danny Bolan

Senior Manufacturing Buyer: Kevin Kluck

Senior Marketing Communications
Manager: Jim Overly

Production House/Compositor:
PreMediaGlobal

Senior Art Director: Tippy McIntosh

Permissions Acquisition Manager/Photo:
Mardell Glinski Schultz

Permissions Acquisition Manager/Text:
Mardell Glinski Schultz

Cover Designer: Patti Hudepohl

Cover Image: B/W Image: iStockphoto;
Color Image: Shutterstock Images/Octus

Library of Congress Control Number: 2010941474
International Edition:

ISBN-13: 978-0-538-48184-7

ISBN-10: 0-538-48184-6

Cengage Learning International Offices

Asia
www.cengageasia.com
tel: (65) 6410 1200

Australia/New Zealand
www.cengage.com.au
tel: (61) 3 9685 4111

Brazil
www.cengage.com.br
tel: (55) 11 3665 9900

India
www.cengage.co.in
tel: (91) 11 4364 1111

Latin America
www.cengage.com.mx
tel: (52) 55 1500 6000

UK/Europe/Middle East/Africa
www.cengage.co.uk
tel: (44) 0 1264 332 424

Represented in Canada by Nelson Education, Ltd.
tel: (416) 752 9100/(800) 668 0671
www.nelson.com

Cengage Learning is a leading provider of customized learning solutions with office locations around the globe, including Singapore, the United Kingdom, Australia, Mexico, Brazil, and Japan. Locate your local office at: **www.cengage.com/global**

For product information: **www.cengage.com/international**
Visit your local office: **www.cengage.com/global**
Visit our corporate website: **www.cengage.com**

Printed in the United States of America
1 2 3 4 5 6 7 15 14 13 12 11

AVAILABILITY OF RESOURCES MAY DIFFER BY REGION. Check with your local Cengage Learning representative for details.

Brief Contents

National College
of Ireland
Library

Contents

National College
of Ireland
Library

Preface

As always, the original intent of the book remains paramount: to provide an up-to-date textbook for readers who are novices in the area of human relations or for practitioners with little formal training in the subject. Unlike other human relations textbooks, *Modern Human Relations at Work* addresses current topics discussed everywhere, from boardrooms to manufacturing plants to retail outlets, as well as those analyzed in today's newspapers and magazines. Examples are the impact of technology in the workplace, the development of knowledge-based organizations, the use of management tools and techniques for developing and maintaining organizational efficiency and effectiveness, the use of charismatic and transformational leadership in managing a diverse workforce, ways of dealing effectively with cultural diversity, and steps that firms must take to become world-class organizations functioning in an international marketplace.

The purpose of examining these topics is to merge the concepts of human relations theory with human relations practice. Theory explains why things are done the way they are; practice describes what is being done. No study of human relations can be effective without considering both areas.

New to This Edition

As the first decade of the twenty-first century comes to a close, several turbulent years in the world economy as well as changes in technology and rapidly developing trends have all necessitated significant updates to the eleventh edition of *Modern Human Relations at Work*. Specifically:

1. **Updated examples reflect the latest business environment**. Throughout this management textbook, many business people and companies are used as examples to illustrate points and to give validity to the material presented. The business environment is an ever-changing world; CEOs come and go, and acquisitions, mergers, and closures happen. Therefore, it is critical that these examples be reviewed and revised to reflect the latest business environment.
2. **All decisions have consequences**. All decisions have consequences—good or not so good—and employees must learn to deal with their choices and to have a backup plan in case the decision does not work. All decisions effect long-term objectives. To emphasize the importance of this topic, it is integrated throughout the text.
3. **How businesses survive in an economic crisis**. The recession following the collapse of the financial, housing, and automobile markets in 2008 changed the way many businesses operated, resulting in downsizing, layoffs, and in some cases complete closure. These concepts are dealt with throughout the text depending on the topic. For example, the permanent temporary workforce was created and is expected to continue for years to come, changing the employment process. Managing in uncertain times requires risks, creativity, and the willingness to step outside one's comfort zone.

4. **Older and retired employees are filling the gap**. Changes in the economy have required many older and retired people to return to work. Changes in the workforce have created new opportunities and new work schedules allowing older and retired people to have access to meaningful work on their terms. This topic is explored in several chapters.

5. **Dealing with workplace violence**. This topic is discussed throughout the text, emphasizing the necessity for training and having plans in place to protect all employees from potential harm.

6. **Chapter-opening scenarios**. All examples cited connect the latest business operations with topics discussed in the chapter.

7. **Summaries reflect changes in content**. All chapter summaries were revised to reflect changes in content.

8. **Review and study questions**. New questions were added to cover the new material.

9. **End-of-chapter cases**. Several cases are new. Other cases have been expanded, made more complex, or have additional higher-level questions that require more thought and analysis.

10. **Connecting to the Real World exercises**. To assist students in relating the theoretical concepts found in this book to actual work situations, a new exercise at the end of every chapter called "Connecting to the Real World" was created. These out-of-class exercises will help students explore such topics as:

    - What should the professor do?
    - How is recognition used as a motivator?
    - Why are there different values for different occupational groups?
    - How willing are you to take risks in the workplace?
    - How can networking help you?
    - Workplace violence plan?
    - What is wrong? Can I improve it?
    - Why is Joan happy?
    - What is the role of a leader?
    - Getting your degree!
    - Was the message communicated effectively?
    - Change happens!
    - Going overseas—an Internet exercise
    - Creative thinking

11. **Updated examples**. Keeping this edition's content fresh and relevant, new and updated examples feature a wide range of familiar and lesser-known brands and companies, including: HP, the Waidley Company, the Coca-Cola Company, Air France, EX-MAN Company, W.L. Gore & Associates, Inc., Starbucks, Google, BroadwayBank, FedEx, Southwest Airlines, Butler Community College, Hyatt, GE, Walmart, Chevron, Caterpillar, Inc., DecisionWise, Jesclon Group, Space-Management Company, Whole Foods Markets, Burger King, McDonald's, IBM, The Walt Disney Company, GM, Roxling, Inc., Ford, and many more.

12. **New material in each chapter**. In response to feedback from instructors and students alike, we have included new material in every chapter and also expanded a number of topics as follows:

Chapter 1
- Managing Knowledge Workers
- Managing Diversity and Workplace Violence

Chapter 12
- Survival Requires Change (Opening scenario)
- Getting Employees to Change
- Closing Case: What Did Paul Do Wrong?

Chapter 13
- Mickey Has a Human Relations Problem (Opening scenario)
- Table 13.1: Fortune's List of the Top Twenty Most Admired Companies
- Table 13.2: Fortune's List of the Top Twenty Largest MNE Corporations in the United States in 2009
- Reasons for Becoming a Multinational Company
- Outsourcing in Globalization
- Closing Case: Look Out World, Here We Come!

Chapter 14
- Human Relations Ideas Continue to Work (Opening scenario)
- Table 14.1: The World's Top Ten Most Innovative Companies
- The Changing Nature of Work
- Meeting the Cultural Diversity Challenge
- Ethical Trends for the Future
- Workplace Changes Impact Human Relations Management
- Consider Career Switching
- Closing Case: After the Storm, What Next?

How This Book Will Help You

The primary objective of the book is to familiarize you with the field of human relations, pointing out ways this information can be of personal value. For the most part, the text is written from the standpoint of human relations in organizations, as this is the setting in which most adults have the greatest need for such information. However, much of the material is also applicable to your own life. In particular, this book will provide you with four major benefits:

1. **Fact—not intuition**. The information in this book is based on fact. In gathering the material for each chapter, information was drawn from research studies and reports from industry, government, and other major organizations. Although the art of human relations is not overlooked, it is not allowed to interfere with proven, scientific findings.
2. **Comprehensiveness**. This book is thorough in its coverage of the field of human relations. All the major areas of concern to the modern manager, as well as many minor ones, are addressed. The eleventh edition has also been thoroughly updated and revised to include the latest available human relations material.
3. **Applicability**. Information that is too theoretical often has limited value for practicing managers and others who are interested in learning about human relations. In this book, every effort has been made to make the material relevant and show how the information can be applied.
4. **Personal insights**. Each chapter contains short quizzes and exercises that will give you insights into your own personal human relations style or philosophy. The

purpose of these exercises is to supplement the text material and involve you in further analysis of the concepts under discussion, thereby increasing your comprehension.

Some of the information presented here will be of value almost immediately, as in the case of material related to team building and communication technology. Some of the material may be of more value a little later in your career, as in the case of the material related to performance evaluation and appraisal. Yet, regardless of where your career path takes you, the material in this book is designed to help you meet the human relations challenges you will face in the world around you.

Organization and Features

Human relations is a broad field composed of many practices and concepts. *Modern Human Relations at Work* focuses on the most important of these. The organization of the book flows from the human element to the work environment and then considers methods by which one can achieve an effective fit between people and organizational systems. The last section of the book addresses ways in which readers can apply these ideas in the future. In accordance with this flow, the book is divided into six parts as follows:

Part 1 examines the foundation of human relations.
Part 2 focuses on social systems involving individuals, groups, informal organizations, and team building.
Part 3 addresses technical systems, including technology, productivity, and quality improvement.
Part 4 discusses the administrative system and topics such as leadership, appraisal, and rewards.
Part 5 focuses on behavioral effectiveness, including communication and management of conflict and change.
Part 6 addresses human relations challenges in the future.

In Action

In each chapter, a "Human Relations in Action" box illustrates the practical application of chapter concepts. Subjects include how to increase achievement drive, network for effectiveness, become a whole-brain thinker, deal with technology, lead effectively, conduct an effective performance appraisal, become a more active listener, and manage more effectively with fewer resources. Each chapter further addresses in a practical manner key issues facing organizations through another type of "In Action" box: "Cultural Diversity in Action" or "Ethics and Social Responsibility in Action." Each of these boxes examines human relations issues that are emerging challenges in today's business world.

Self-Examination Exercises

A "Time Out" exercise is included in each chapter. These exercises encourage the reader to participate, gain personal insights, and consider key concepts in a more in-depth manner.

"Check Your Understanding" exercises are dispersed throughout each chapter. Some exercises test your knowledge of the essential topics, while others are thought-provoking questions designed to encourage the application of key concepts.

Examples and Cases

In-depth examples and a case are included in every chapter to illustrate the practical and realistic application of its concepts. Each chapter opens with several real-world examples that relate to the main topics in the chapter, and a case that requires the student to apply knowledge learned in the chapter is found at the end of each chapter. The case adds weight to the relevancy of the topics covered in the chapter. The cases are:

1. What Did Carly Do Wrong and Hurd Do Right?
2. Trying to Motivate Everyone
3. A Matter of Personality
4. The New Supervisor
5. A Case of Layoffs
6. So, What's Going On?
7. A Productive Approach
8. The Best Job He Ever Had, but What About Your Current Job?
9. Making Some Necessary Changes
10. Following the Rules
11. Getting Prepared
12. What Did Paul Do Wrong?
13. Look Out World, Here We Come!
14. After the Storm, What Next?

Experiential Exercises

New to this edition is an experiential exercise found at the end of each chapter called "Connecting to the Real World." These exercises require the student to interact with the real world and to explore in greater depth a topic presented in the chapter. The purpose is to learn firsthand how businesses operate. Several exercises can be completed by teaming up with another student; most exercises, however, are to be completed by individual students. The topics are: ethical dilemmas, employee recognition systems, job profile values, risk taking in the workplace, networking, workplace violence, solving problems, job redesign, role of the leader, goal/objective setting, effective communication, dealing with change, preparing for an overseas job, and how to be a more creative thinker.

Career Advisor

The "Career Advisor" in each chapter helps you prepare for and enhance your career-development skills. Topics are:

1. Choosing a Career
2. Develop a Plan of Action for Finding a Job
3. Writing an Effective Résumé
4. The Successful Job Hunt
5. The Interview
6. How to Become an Effective Team Player
7. Developing Your Brand
8. Manage Your Career Effectively
9. Know Your Job
10. Manage Your Time Well
11. Managing Stress Effectively
12. Using a Mentor

13. Organize Your Office Properly
14. Consider Career Switching

Successful careers are a result of constant attention and continuous planning. Few people have the luxury of simply falling into a meaningful and rewarding career. If you are one who has known from childhood what you want to do with your life, you are the exception. Most students do not have a clue. After graduation, they often go from job to job without satisfaction. A good time to begin the process for finding a satisfying career is while you are still in college. The information provided in the "Career Advisor" will help you get started. You are encouraged to keep a journal of the results of each exercise throughout this course. At the end of the course, you will have a wealth of information about yourself and your new career.

NEW Online for Students

Modern Human Relations at Work CourseMate. Cengage Learning's Modern Human Relations at Work CourseMate brings course concepts to life with interactive learning, study, and exam preparation tools that support the printed textbook. Through this Web site, available for an additional fee, students will have access to resources not found in the book, such as flashcards, "You Be the Consultant" exercises, and "Beat the Clock" games, as well as the learning objectives and glossary for quick reviews. A set of auto-gradable, interactive quizzes will allow students to instantly gauge their comprehension of the material, and will refer students to chapter sections so they can review for tests.

    Product Support Web site. The flashcards, learning objectives, and glossary are available for quick reference on our complementary student product support Web site.

Instructor Support Materials

Instructor's Manual with Test Bank

A comprehensive Instructor's Manual and Test Bank, available on the instructor support Web site and on the Instructor's Resource CD-ROM, is provided to assist in lecture preparation. Included are suggestions for class schedules, research papers, research sources, and chapter outlines. The Test Bank includes approximately 100 questions per chapter to assist in writing examinations. Types of questions are true/false, multiple choice, essay, and matching questions.

ExamView

ExamView Computerized Testing Software, located on the Instructor's Resource CD-ROM, contains all of the questions in the Test Bank. This program is an easy-to-use test creation software compatible with Microsoft Windows. Instructors can add or edit questions, instructions, and answers, and select questions by previewing them on the screen, selecting them randomly, or selecting them by number.

PowerPoint Lecture Presentation Software

An asset to any instructor, the lectures provide outlines for every chapter, graphics of the illustrations from the text, and additional examples providing instructors with a number of learning opportunities for students. The PowerPoint lecture presentations are available as downloadable files on the text support site and on the Instructor's Resource CD-ROM.

Instructor's Resource CD-ROM

Key instructor ancillaries (Instructor's Manual, Test Bank, ExamView, and PowerPoint slides) are provided on CD-ROM, giving instructors the ultimate tool for customizing lectures and presentations.

Acknowledgments

Many thanks go to those who offered insights and assistance in writing this book. The author would especially like to thank Dr. Fred Luthans of the University of Nebraska, Lincoln; Dr. Jane Gibson of Nova Southeastern University; Dr. Gary Dessler and Dr. Karl Magnusen of Florida International University; Dr. Regina Greenwood of Kettering University; and Dr. Julia Teahen of Baker College, who provided continuous encouragement in this effort.

The author would like to thank those who read, reviewed, and commented on portions of this text, including Felipe Chia, Harrisburg Area Community College; Terry J. Lovell, Yavapai College; Joseph B. Mosca, Monmouth University; and Ali Naddafpour, College of the Canyons.

Many thanks extend also to those who were involved in reviewing this text in its previous incarnations, including Kenneth Bell, Ellsworth Community College; Joy L. Colwell, Purdue University Calumet; Raymond V. Daniel, Cambridge College; Mark Dannenberg, Shasta College; Les Ledger, Central Texas College; Spencer McCurry, Los Angeles Valley College; R. Michael Traas, Allied College–South; Judy Wood, High-Tech Institute; Kathleen A. Bigelow, Cambridge College; Ronald M. Gordon, Florida Metropolitan University; William M. Lally, Webster University; Bob Redick, Lincoln Land Community College; Jim Murtha, Hartford Community College; Howard J. Klein, Ohio State University; Robert E. Seyfarth, Lock Haven University; Jeffrey S. Hornsby, Ball State University; Gary W. Piggrem, DeVry University–Columbus; Ronald C. Young, Kalamazoo Valley Community College; Edward Valsi, Oakland Community College; John Adamski II, Indiana College; Joy D. Andrews, Indiana Vocational Technical College; Stephen C. Branz, Triton College; J. E. Cantrell, De Anza College; Renee L. Cohen, Southwestern Community College; Lorene B. Holmes, Jarvis Christian College; Marilyn A. Hommertzheim, Seward County Community College; James R. Hostetter, Illinois Valley Community College; Steven Jennings, Highland Community College; Miles LaRowe, Laramie County Community College; Gary D. Law, Cayahoga Community College; Robert O. Nixon, Pima Community College; William S. Pangle, Metro Community College; Carol P. Harvey, Assumption College; Deborah Jones, Hi-Tech Institute; Edward Miller, Kean University; Peter J. Moustatson, Montcalm Community College; and David Murphy, Madisonville Community College.

To the publishing staff who provided assistance and guidance—Melissa Acuña, editor-in-chief; Michele Rhoades, senior acquisitions editor; Gretchen Swann, marketing manager; Jennifer King, developmental editor; Tippy McIntosh, senior art director; and Ruth Belanger, senior editorial assistant—thank you for your hard work.

About the Author

KATHRYN W. HEGAR, PH.D., has taught courses and workshops in management in both the academic and business environments. She earned her M.B.A. and Ph.D. from the University of North Texas. Dr. Hegar has received recognition and awards for her innate ability to teach and create an environment for learning. She has been recognized for her innovation in developing nontraditional courses in management that fit the lifestyle of today's students, who live busy, hectic lives. Her accomplishments include authoring thirty programs for the initial telecourse in business, *It's Everybody's Business*, that was used for more than ten years by colleges across the country and in the military services; initiating the developing of self-paced courses in management at Mountain View College at a time when only traditional methods were being promoted; piloting the first online course in organizational behavior for the Dallas County Community College District, that ultimately resulted in the district offering online degrees; and instructing management courses online from distant locations. Dr. Hegar has authored pedagogical materials for business and management courses for several major publishers.

Prior to her teaching career, Dr. Hegar worked in business and government. In addition, she conducted workshops and training seminars in supervision and management for major companies. She has participated in and held offices in professional organizations at all levels, from local chapters to the president of the USA Chapter of the International Society of Business Education, which holds an international congress in a different country each year. She has traveled throughout Europe and North America.

Dr. Hegar has been the recipient of many distinguished awards. They include "Collegiate Teacher of the Year," "Post-Secondary Teacher of the Year for the United States," "Innovator of the Year," and was nominated for the "Minnie Stevens Piper Professor Award." She is listed in *Who's Who in the South and Southwest*, seventeenth edition; *World's Who's Who in Women*, sixth edition; *Personalities of the South, 1977*; and International Register of Profiles, sixth edition. Dr. Hegar also actively participates in church and community activities.

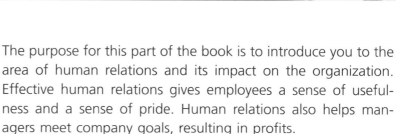

PART 1

INTRODUCTION

The purpose for this part of the book is to introduce you to the area of human relations and its impact on the organization. Effective human relations gives employees a sense of usefulness and a sense of pride. Human relations also helps managers meet company goals, resulting in profits.

Why do people act the way they do on the job? Understanding motivation is fundamental to understanding why people behave the way they do. Motivation is at the heart of human relations; it is how managers get people to do their job. Life on the job can be more enjoyable by making work more meaningful, thus improving performance.

The goals of this section are to:

1. Examine the nature of human relations, trace its evolution from industrialism through scientific management up to the present, examine some of the important human relations studies conducted during the last five decades, examine how the scientific method can be used to solve behavioral problems, investigate the role of behavioral science in promoting better human relations, discuss major challenges and dilemmas facing today's managers, and identify major questions used in conducting a self-evaluation.

2. Study the fundamentals of motivation—movement and motive—identify the basic needs that all people have, explain each of these needs and their importance in the motivation process, study the two-factor theory of motivation and its relevance for the practicing manager, deal with the expectancy theory and its application to motivation, discuss the practical side of rewards and their relevance to motivation, and develop a plan of action for finding a job.

© AVAVA, Shutterstock Images LLC

After reading this part of the book, you should have a solid understanding of the nature of human relations, who the people are who study and investigate human relations problems, and how they go about conducting their investigations. You also should know a great deal about motivation and its role in directing, influencing, and channeling behavior at work. You will know more about yourself, the type of career you might pursue, and how to develop a plan for finding a job.

CHAPTER 1

The Nature of Human Relations

Getting work accomplished in a business environment is a complex process that requires understanding human behavior and the context within which the work is to be done. Human relations is at the heart of that process. Therefore, it is important for managers, as well as for workers, to understand the key role human relations plays in the workplace.

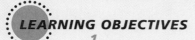

LEARNING OBJECTIVES

1
Explain human relations and its implications for management.

2
Trace the evolution of human relations thinking from industrialism through scientific management to the present.

3
Compare and contrast the traditional model of the worker with the modern human resources model.

4
Discuss the role of behavioral science in human relations.

5
Describe some emerging challenges facing managers today.

6
Discuss the ethical dilemmas facing today's managers.

7
Identify key questions used in conducting a self-evaluation for choosing a career.

The Challenging Workplace

The workplace is constantly evolving. Technology, economic turmoil, financial collapse, global competition, and natural disasters have changed the way businesses operate. Technology—computers, mobile phones, pagers, Internet, and Wi-Fi networks to name a few—has made a big impact on how we do business and where we work. For example, some employees no longer go into an office to work; they work and communicate from their homes, cars, and remote work sites using their computers, laptops, or cell phones. Facebook and Twitter are becoming more than social networks; they are being used as workplace tools. Green technology, using natural and organic materials, also is gaining attention and is expected to be a driving force in changing the way many businesses operate in this decade. As the digital age continues to expand and new technological innovation creates new devices, managers are faced with new challenges in managing employees.

Economic recessions affect employment, how employees do their jobs, and the skills needed to work in the new economy. During the recession of 2008, the worst since the 1930s with unemployment at a 26-year high, layoffs and shut-downs created high unemployment making it difficult to find new work. Retired people also needed to return to work and other people were taking one or more temporary jobs to meet their financial obligations. These actions created a new permanent temporary workforce that is still dominating many segments of the economy and, at the same time, providing new challenges for management. Some companies like Motorola have an appreciation for older workers because "they add a dimension that younger people can't: They have experience and they understand business." Managing employees in any recession is difficult.

The debacle in the housing and financial markets created turmoil, not only in the American workplace, but also around the world. The housing bubble bursts pushed consumer spending down in the United

States, leading to less demand for imports from China causing slower growth in the Chinese economy. Also, the focus of the American consumer turned to value versus prestige, redefining the banking, automobile, housing, entertainment, and publishing businesses. The old system was broken and new strategies and priorities were needed; the business environment had changed. On the positive side, recessions provide opportunities for businesses to change and grow into viable healthy firms; however, dramatically different leadership approaches are needed. The bottom line is that managers must continue to gain new talents and learn new ways to lead.

Directly or indirectly, even natural catastrophes provide challenges for management. Hurricane Katrina, which hit the Louisiana coast, is an example. It not only had economic repercussions because of the increasing oil and natural gas prices that followed, but it also disrupted the shipping industry, causing delays on construction projects around the country. The Gulf of Mexico is one of the world's busiest shipping hubs, serving as a conduit for a range of products from grains to coffee to steel. With refineries in the Gulf of Mexico being shut down due to the hurricane, gas prices rose. Detroit and the automobile industry began to feel pressure; how would increased fuel prices affect car-buying habits? Allstate Insurance Company reported losses in the billions—the biggest losses in its history.

Other challenges come when organizations find themselves locked in a highly competitive battle for market share, sales revenue, profits, and other bottom-line measures of performance. How can they win this battle? The most successful companies are discovering that they need to implement one critical strategy: Hire the right people with the right talent and then give them the opportunity to unlock their full creative potential. Given all the challenges facing management, this may be the greatest challenge of all.

There is evidence that organizations are providing employees a chance to succeed. Pitney Bowes, a multibillion-dollar global provider of informed mail and messaging management, is a strong advocate of diversity and equal opportunity. As far back as the 1940s, the chairman of the board made the decision that the makeup of the company's employees in the manufacturing plant would mirror that of the population in Stamford, Connecticut, where it was located. Pitney Bowes cares about its people and strives to provide a family–workplace balance culture. Fitness rooms give employees an opportunity to stay fit. The company invests in its employees by supporting educational endeavors. Pitney Bowes is not alone in its effort to ensure equal opportunity. Xerox, MasterCard, Goldman Sachs, IBM, AT&T, and Kraft Foods, to name but a half-dozen, all have programs in place to ensure that their workforces are diverse and that women and minorities are given the same opportunities as white men. The complexion of the workforce is becoming more culturally diverse, creating a whole array of challenges for management. It is becoming clear that companies that appreciate differences and capitalize on each worker's potential will enjoy a competitive advantage in a global market.

Wells Fargo is an example of a company meeting challenges in every aspect of its operations. "Wells Fargo won the 2005 Optimas Award for General Excellence for its workforce management strategies that successfully integrated two companies, fostered revenue growth while retaining talent and held employees to high ethical standards." After Wells Fargo and Norwest Corporation merged, their two cultures were successfully integrated to employ the company's vision and values. Mass layoffs were diverted. The company retrained and reassigned two-thirds of the employees whose positions were eliminated in the merger. The company concentrated on growing revenue instead of cutting costs. With success depending on talent, employee development and succession planning received attention at all levels. Wells Fargo also takes ethics seriously. "Its Code of Ethics and Business Conduct details policies and standards for employees, covering everything from maintaining accurate records to participating in civic activities." Dick Kovacevich, CEO, states that "Everything we do at Wells Fargo starts with our people. Why? Because when people are properly rewarded, encouraged and importantly recognized, they provide better service, generate more sales and produce even better business results. This generates more revenue, which results in greater profits." This is an example of human relations at work.

Another way in which organizations are winning the competitiveness challenge is by continuing to invest in employee training and knowledge acquisition. Peter Drucker predicts that knowledge will be the key resource of the Next Society—the era that lies ahead. Online training is growing and is playing an important role in how workers learn about their jobs.

Every day management faces a multitude of diverse and complex challenges. How managers handle these challenges directly affects employees and their performance. Knowing how to employ human relations can make the difference in success or failure.

Explain human relations and its implications for management.

What Is Human Relations?

The process by which management brings workers into contact with the organization in such a way that the objectives of both groups are achieved is **human relations**. The organization is concerned with such objectives as survival, growth, and profit. The worker is concerned with such objectives as good pay, adequate working conditions, a chance to interact with other personnel, and the opportunity to do interesting and meaningful work. Human relations, then, is concerned with four major areas: the individual worker, the group, the environment in which the work is performed, and the leader responsible for seeing that everything is done properly. In this book, we study human relations from the standpoint of the leader or manager who must influence, direct, and respond to both the people and the work environment. Before we begin our study of human relations, however, two points merit attention.

First, human relations implies a concern for the people, but the effective manager never loses sight of the organization's global objectives. He or she must be interested in the people, the work, and the achievement of assigned objectives. Some managers are so interested in pleasing their people that they never get the work done. Others are overly concerned with the work and spend very little time trying to understand the psychological and sociological aspects of the job. An effective manager balances concerns for people and work. In addition, he or she draws on experience and training in deciding how to use many of the ideas presented in this book.

Second, the effective manager realizes that human relations is important at all levels of the organization, but the way the ideas are applied is not always the same. The situation dictates the right way to use human relations ideas.

Much of what we know about people in organizations is a result of careful study. If we were to trace the development of human relations in industry, we would see that two hundred years ago managers knew very little about how to manage their human assets. The

Human Relations in Organizations

The following true–false questions are designed to give you some initial insights regarding your current knowledge of human relations in modern organizations. Read each statement carefully and then choose the correct answer. The key, along with explanations, is provided at the end of the book.

1. When asked what motivates them, most workers put money at the top of their list.
2. In the long run, a work group with high morale and a basic understanding of job requirements will always outperform a work group with moderate morale and a basic understanding of its job requirements.
3. While in physics it is true that opposites attract, in human relations just the reverse occurs—that is, people tend to associate with others who do the same jobs, have the same training, or work in the same unit.
4. The most efficient employees report that they do their best work when placed under high stress.

5. When it comes to getting and giving information along informal lines, managers tend to use the grapevine more than workers do.
6. Most top managers are not very intelligent, but they have terrific personalities.
7. Many managers do not get all their daily work done because the boss overloads them with assignments.
8. The higher up the organization you go, the greater the amount of job-related stress you will encounter.
9. The major reason why workers do not have high productivity is that they are lazy.
10. Most managers say they are very effective two-way communicators, but their subordinates report that the managers seldom listen and are usually interested in only one form of communication—downward.

next section of this chapter examines the evolution of modern human relations and sets the stage for our study of this area. Before going on, however, take the true–false quiz in the following "Time Out" box and see how much you already know about human relations.

Trace the evolution of human relations thinking from industrialism through scientific management to the present.

The Evolution of Human Relations

In industry today, it is common to hear a great deal of talk about human relations and its importance to management. However, concern for human relations is largely a modern development. This should become clearer as we discuss the three major stages through which business has progressed on its way to developing a philosophy for managing human assets:

1. The emergence of industrialism
2. The scientific management movement
3. The behavioral management movement

The Emergence of Industrialism

Industrialism emerged in England in the latter half of the eighteenth century. New inventions enabled wealthy proprietors of this period to invest their money in efficient machinery that could far outpace people doing similar work by hand. For example, no weaver could hope to match the speed and accuracy of the power loom. The age of machine-made goods had begun. These machines were placed in factories, and a workforce was hired to run the equipment. The same pattern emerged as industrialism spread to the United States.

The primary concern of the factory owners was increased output (see Figure 1.1). However, there was a great deal the owner–managers did not understand about this new work environment. For example, they knew very little about machine feed and speed, plant layout, and inventory control. Nor were they very knowledgeable about the management of people. Some tended to use a paternalistic style, in which they told the workers what was expected of them and rewarded those who "toed the line" by giving

Figure 1.1
Rules Posted in 1872 by the Owner of a Carriage and Wagon Works

Starting the New Year Right

1. Office employees will sweep the floors and dust the furniture, shelves, and showcases every day.
2. Each clerk will bring a bucket of water and a scuttle of coal for the day's business.
3. Clerks will fill the lamps, clean the chimneys, trim the wicks every day, and wash the windows once a week.
4. Make your pens carefully. You may whittle the nibs to your own individual taste.
5. This office will open at 7 A.M. and close at 8 P.M. daily, except on the Sabbath, when it will remain closed.
6. Male employees will be given an evening off each week for courting purposes, or two evenings a week if they attend church regularly.
7. Every employee should put aside some of his pay so as to provide for himself in later years and prevent becoming a burden on others.
8. Any employee who smokes Spanish cigars, uses liquor, gets shaved at a barber shop, or frequents pool or public halls will give the employer good reason to suspect his worth, integrity, and honesty.
9. Any employee who has performed his labors faithfully for a period of five years, has been thrifty, attentive to religious duties, and is looked upon by his fellow workers as a substantial and law-abiding citizen, will be given an increase of 5% per day in his pay, providing profits allow it.

them more money than their less cooperative counterparts. Others simply exploited their people in the name of efficiency and profit.

In the United States, the people who helped the factories and industrial establishments develop more efficient work measures for increasing output brought about what is known as the scientific management movement. Today, of course, we can fault them as being shortsighted. However, they simply did not understand how to manage a factory; so they sought to solve the technical (work) problems facing them, which are simpler to resolve than the human (people) problems.

The Scientific Management Movement

The **scientific management** movement in America had its genesis in the post–Civil War era. The scientific managers were, for the most part, mechanical engineers. Applying their technical expertise in factories and industrial settings, they tried to merge people and the work environment scientifically so as to achieve the greatest amount of productivity.

The interest of these managers in people involved identifying the "one best man" for each job. For example, in a task requiring heavy lifting, they would select the person who had the best combination of strength and endurance. If a machinist was needed to feed parts into a machine, a scientific manager would choose the person with the best hand—eye coordination and the fastest reflexes. If someone lacked the requisite physical skills for a job, he would be scientifically screened out.

The scientific managers sought to increase work efficiency by employing such measures as plant design, plant layout, time study, and motion study. By placing the machinery and materials at strategically determined points on the shop floor, they sought to reduce the time needed to move goods from the raw materials stage to the finished products stage. By studying the rate at which the machines were run and the way in which material was fed, they attempted to achieve optimum machine speeds while eliminating excessive time taken and motion used by the machinists.

However, scientific management had its problems. Primarily, these problems stemmed from the tendency to view all workers as factors of production rather than as human beings. Many of the scientific managers saw the hired help as mere adjuncts of the machinery who were to be carefully instructed in how to do the job and then offered more money for productivity increases. Quite obviously, this behavioral philosophy is shallow. Although these early scientific managers may have known a lot about machinery and equipment, they knew very little about human relations in a work setting.

The Behavioral Management Movement

If business and industrial organizations were to continue expanding, investigations of individual and group behavior were imperative. It was obvious that management knew a great deal more about its production facilities than it did about the people staffing them. By the 1920s, breakthroughs began to occur. As scientific management moved into its heyday, an interest in the behavioral side of management began to grow. It was becoming obvious that concern for production brought about people-related problems and that the effective manager had to be interested in both personnel and work.

Many people believe that modern behavioral management had its genesis in the Hawthorne studies. These studies were started as scientific management experiments designed to measure the effect of illumination on output and wound up lighting the way for much of the behavioral research that was to follow.

The Hawthorne Studies. The **Hawthorne studies** were begun late in 1924 at the Hawthorne plant of Western Electric, located near Cicero, Illinois. In all, there were four phases to these studies.

Phase 1. The researchers first sought to examine the relationship between illumination and output. Was there an ideal amount of lighting under which workers would maximize their productivity? The researchers sought to answer this question by subjecting some employees to varying amounts of illumination (the test group), while others kept on working under the original level of illumination (the control group). To the surprise of the researchers, the results of these experiments were inconclusive, because output increased in both the test group and the control group. They concluded that variables other than illumination were responsible for the increases. At this point, Elton Mayo and a number of other Harvard University researchers took an interest in the problem.

Phase 2. To obtain more control over the factors affecting work performance, the researchers isolated a small group of female workers from the regular workforce and began to study them. The women were told to keep working at their regular pace because the purpose of the experiment was not to boost production but to study various types of working conditions to identify the most suitable environment. During this period, the researchers placed an observer in the test room. This observer was chiefly concerned with creating a friendly atmosphere with the operators so as to ensure their cooperation. He also took over some of the supervision, conversed informally with the women each day, and tried to dispel any apprehensions they might have about the experiment. In turn, the women began to talk more freely among themselves and formed much closer relationships with one another than they had in the regular factory setting. The researchers then began introducing rest breaks to see what effect these would have on output. As productivity increased, the researchers believed that these work pauses were reducing fatigue and thereby improving output. Shorter workdays and workweeks were instituted, and output again went up. However, when the original conditions were restored, output still remained high. This proved that the change in physical conditions could not have been the only reason for the increases in output. After analyzing the possible cause of the results, the researchers decided that the changes in the method of supervision might have brought about improved attitudes and increased output.

Phase 3. At this point, the investigators began to focus on human relations. More than 20,000 interviews were conducted in which the interviewers were interested primarily in gathering information about the effect of supervision on the work environment. Although the interviewers told their subjects that everything would be kept in strict confidence, the workers often gave guarded, stereotypical responses. This led the interviewers to change from direct to indirect questioning, allowing the employee to choose his or her own topic. The result was a wealth of information about employee attitudes. The researchers started to realize that both the person and the group members influenced an individual's performance, position, and status in the organization. To study this impact more systematically, another test group was chosen.

Phase 4. In the fourth phase of the studies, the investigators decided to examine a small group engaged in one type of work. They chose the bank wiring room, in which the workers were wiring and soldering bank terminals. No changes in their working conditions were made, although an observer was stationed in the test room to record employee interactions and conversations. During these observations, several behaviors were noted.

- The group had an informal production norm that restricted output.
- There were two informal groups or cliques in the room, and individual behavior was partially dictated by the norms of the groups.
- To be accepted by the group, one had to observe informal rules, such as not doing too much work, not doing too little work, and never telling a superior anything that might be detrimental to an associate.

Results of the Hawthorne Studies.   From their work, the researchers arrived at some conclusions about human behavior in organizations. However, it should be noted that some of their findings were not developed until years later, because more information was needed, whereas other conclusions were only partially accurate.

Major Conclusions of the Hawthorne Studies.
1. Organizations were not just formal structures in which subordinates reported to superiors; they were **social networks** in which people interacted, sought acceptance from and gave approval to fellow workers, and found enjoyment in the work and in the social exchange that occurred while they were doing the work.
2. People will act differently when they know they are being observed.
3. Quality of supervision has an effect on the quality and quantity of work.

Refinement of the Human Relations Theory.   The Hawthorne research generated a great deal of interest in human relations. However, some misunderstandings also arose from the findings of both these studies and subsequent research.

Happiness and Productivity.   Many behaviorists have attacked some of the Hawthorne findings, calling them naive and, in certain cases, erroneous. One of the most vigorous attacks has been made against the supposedly Hawthorne-generated finding that happy workers will be productive workers. This stinging attack has so stigmatized human relations that the term human relations is no longer used in many colleges of business, because it carries the connotation that "happiness automatically leads to productivity." The term organizational behavior is used instead.

IN ACTION

COMMITMENT IS EVERYTHING

One way in which highly successful organizations are developing their human resources is by helping employees cope with both their work demands and family responsibilities. In turn, the firms are finding that these efforts are leading to greater employee commitment—and this is true for both small and large organizations. In fact, a recent survey in *BusinessWeek* found that 42 percent of the respondents said that work had a negative impact on their home life. Yet, at the same time, 51 percent of these individuals reported that their company had high-quality programs for helping them care for their children and elder family members, and this was very important to the workers. Companies offer a wide variety of programs for employees. A few examples are described below.

At the DuPont Corporation, for example, an employee's elderly aunt had a stroke and was unable to care for herself. A company-contracted referral agency helped the employee place the woman in a nursing home, and during the time it took to find the facility, the individual worked only half-days. After that, he and his supervisor developed a flexible work shift that allowed the individual to start work at 6:30 A.M., thus letting him visit his aunt as she awoke, put in a full day of work, and then return to the nursing home to feed her dinner and put her to bed. Commenting on all the help the company gave him, the individual noted, "I feel like I owe something back." As a result, he is deeply committed to the firm.

Yahoo provides an array of personal services to help keep its employees on site and at work. For example, the company provides dry-cleaning pickup and delivery, a masseuse, a dentist who works out of a mobile office, and a gym. Even a Foosball game is available at the coffee bar.

Hewlett-Packard has developed special programs within each business unit for helping its people deal with personal issues. An action plan is designed to identify specific work and family issues of employees. If the unit suddenly faces higher consumer demand and must increase the number of work hours or work shifts, it examines how these new work demands will affect the employees, then reschedules and rearranges the plan so that it will not negatively affect the personal lives of the workers. The company believes this type of planning leads to more effective work output, less employee burnout, and stronger personnel commitment.

At Aetna Life & Casualty, unpaid parental leave has been extended to six months. As a result, the firm cut the rate of resignations among new mothers by more than 50 percent, thus saving it $1 million annually in hiring and training expenses. Aetna's Healthy Lifestyles program is designed to reduce obesity and encourage healthier living for its employees. The program offers many health and fitness initiatives, offers financial incentives for participation in educational courses, and makes use of Web-based health resources, preventative care visits, and workout activities. Employees can earn up to $345 a year. In 2005, the National Business Group of Health honored Aetna with its Gold Award, naming Aetna the best employer for healthy lifestyles.

At a number of Xerox locations, work responsibility for scheduling shifts has been turned over to the employees, resulting in a sharp decrease in absenteeism coupled with higher productivity. Commenting in *BusinessWeek* on these recent developments, one observer has noted:

Slowly, employers are beginning to grasp the importance of providing employees more than just a job. Poll after poll indicates that U.S. workers feel a loss of control over their lives. "Companies are seeing they have all these programs, but people are still really stressed out," says Ellen Galinsky, the Families and Work Institute's director. Certainly, employees bear some responsibility for determining their own family balance, but they need help. When companies recognize the need and adapt work to their employee's lives, they will win workers' loyalty and, with that, a competitive edge.

Sources: News Release, "Aetna Named a `Best Employer for Healthy Lifestyles'," June 21, 2005 (www.aetna.com); Douglas P. Shuit, "That Sartain Touch," *Workforce Management*, August 2003, pp. 42–45; Karen Springen, "Who'll Care For Dad?" *Newsweek*, November 6, 2000, pp. 85–86; Joseph B. White and Carol Hymowitz, "Watershed Generation of Women Executives Is Rising to the Top," *Wall Street Journal*, February 10, 1997, pp. A1, A8; Anne Fisher, "Wanted: Aging Baby-Boomers," *Fortune*, September 30, 1996, p. 204; and Keith H. Hammonds, "Balancing Work and Family," *BusinessWeek*, September 16, 1996, pp. 74–80.

The Role of Participation.   A second misunderstanding revolved around the role of participation. For many of the post-Hawthorne human relationists, participation was viewed as a lubricant that would reduce resistance to company directives and would ensure greater cooperation.

Over the last few decades, this view has changed. Human relationists realize that it is important to allow people to participate, feel important, "belong" as members of a group, be informed, be listened to, and exercise some self-direction and self-control. However, these are not enough. All these ensure that workers will be treated well, but modern human relationists now realize that employees want not only to be treated well but also to be used well. A good example is found in the currently popular use of job autonomy, in which people are given a task and then allowed to do it without interference or unnecessary direction on the part of the manager. The very subtle yet important difference between these two philosophies is that the latter views people as vital human resources who want to contribute to organizational goals and, under the proper conditions, will do so. This is why it has been said that human relations is in a "human resources" era. (See the "Human Relations in Action" box.)

CHECK YOUR UNDERSTANDING

How does the philosophy for managing people differ among the three management movements? Match the management era to its philosophy by drawing a line from the era to the appropriate philosophy statement.

Management Era	Management Philosophy
1. Industrialism	**a.** Individuals and groups influence output
2. Scientific movement	**b.** Concern only for increased output
3. Behavioral management	**c.** Efficiency, one best person for the job

Compare and contrast the traditional model of the worker with the modern human resources model.

The Human Resources Era

The scientific managers' philosophy of management constituted a **traditional model**. Today, this philosophy has given way to a **human resources model** that, in essence, sees personnel as untapped resources containing unlimited potential. Through the effective application of human relations ideas, these resources can be released and used for the overall good of both the organization and the personnel. Table 1.1 provides a summary of the points of contrast between the traditional (scientific management) and the human resources models.

How can modern managers use the human resources model? An answer can be found through an analysis of Rensis Likert's four systems of management, which extend from exploitive autocratic (System 1) to participative democratic (System 4). A brief description of each follows.

System 1: Exploitive autocratic. Management has little confidence in subordinates, as demonstrated by the fact that subordinates seldom are involved in decision making. Management makes most of the decisions and passes them down the line, using threats and coercion, when necessary, to get things done. Superiors and subordinates deal with one another in an environment of distrust. If an informal organization develops, it usually opposes the goals of the formal organization.

System 2: Benevolent autocratic. Management acts in a condescending manner toward subordinates. Although there is some decision making at the low levels, it occurs within a prescribed framework. Rewards and some actual punishments are used to motivate personnel. In superior–subordinate interaction, the management is condescending, and the subordinates appear cautious and fearful. Although an informal organization usually develops, it does not always oppose the goals of the formal organization.

System 3: Consultative democratic. Management has quite a bit of confidence and trust in subordinates. Although important decisions are made at the top of the organization, subordinates make specific decisions at the lower levels. Two-way communication is evident, and there is some confidence and trust between superiors and subordinates. If an informal organization develops, it either gives support or offers only slight resistance to the goals of the formal organization.

System 4: Participative democratic. Management has complete confidence and trust in subordinates. Decision making is highly decentralized. Communication flows not only up and down the organization but also among peers. Superior–subordinate interaction takes place in a friendly environment and is characterized by mutual confidence and trust. The formal and the informal organization often are one and the same.[1]

Table 1.1
Traditional and Human Resources Models

Traditional Model	Human Resources Model
Assumptions	**Assumptions**
1. Work is inherently distasteful to most people.	1. Work is not inherently distasteful. People want to contribute to meaningful goals that they helped to establish.
2. What workers do is less important than what they earn for doing it.	2. Most people can exercise far more creative, responsible self-direction and self-control than their present jobs demand.
3. Few want or can handle work that requires creativity, self-direction, or self-control.	
Policies	**Policies**
1. The manager's basic task is to supervise closely and control his or her subordinates.	1. The manager's basic task is to make use of his or her untapped human resources.
2. He or she must break tasks down into simple, repetitive, easily learned operations.	2. He or she must create an environment in which all members may contribute to the limits of their ability.
3. He or she must establish detailed work routines and procedures and enforce these firmly but fairly.	3. He or she must encourage full participation on important matters, continually broadening subordinate self-direction and control.
Expectations	**Expectations**
1. People can tolerate work if the pay is decent and the boss is fair.	1. Expanding subordinate influence, self-direction, and self-control will lead to direct improvements in operating efficiency.
2. If tasks are simple enough and people are closely controlled, they will produce up to standard.	2. Work satisfaction may improve as a by-product of subordinates making full use of their resources.

Workers from each system display different behaviors, as illustrated in Figure 1.2. For example, workers in System 4 have complete confidence and trust in superiors, whereas workers in System 1 have no confidence and trust in superiors.

Likert has found that the most effective organizations have System 4 characteristics and the least effective organizations have System 1 and System 2 characteristics. A number of organizations have converted to System 4 with very good results. For example, a comprehensive organizational change project involving the Weldon Company, a sleepwear manufacturing firm, has been well documented.[2] In this project, substantial changes were made in the organization's work flow, training programs, leadership styles, incentive and reward systems, and use of employees as a source of expertise. The results were impressive. Improvements in all aspects of the organization's functioning occurred and were maintained over an extended period.

Figure 1.2 The System 4 Approach

Characteristic	System 1	System 2	System 3	System 4
Extent to which subordinates have confidence and trust in the superior	Have no confidence and trust in the superior	Have subservient confidence and trust, such as a servant has to a master	Have substantial but incomplete confidence	Have complete confidence and trust
Extent to which superiors behave so that subordinates feel free to discuss important things about their jobs with their immediate superior	Subordinates do not feel free at all to discuss things about the job with their superior	Subordinates do not feel free to discuss things about the job with their superior	Subordinates feel rather free to discuss things about the job with their superior	Subordinates feel completely free to discuss things about the job with their superior
Attitudes toward other members of the organization	Subservient attitudes toward superiors coupled with hostility; hostility toward peers and contempt for subordinates; widespread distrust	Subservient attitudes toward superiors; competition for status resulting in hostility toward peers; condescension toward subordinates	Cooperative, reasonably favorable attitudes toward others in the organization; possibly some competition between peers, resulting in hostility and some condescension toward subordinates	Favorable, cooperative attitudes throughout the organization, with mutual trust and confidence
Satisfaction derived	Usually dissatisfaction with regard to membership in the organization, with supervision, and with one's own achievements	Dissatisfaction to moderate satisfaction with regard to membership in the organization, supervision, and one's own achievements	Some dissatisfaction to moderately high satisfaction with regard to membership in the organization, supervision, and one's own achievements	Relatively high satisfaction throughout the organization with regard to membership in the organization, supervision, and one's own achievements
Amount of cooperative teamwork that is present	None	Relatively little	A moderate amount	Very substantial amount throughout the entire organization
Extent to which forces are present by which to accept, resist, or reject goals	Goals are overtly accepted but covertly resisted strongly	Goals are overtly accepted but often covertly resisted to at least some degree	Goals are overtly accepted but, at times, with some covert resistance	Goals are fully accepted both overtly and covertly

(Continued)

Figure 1.2 The System 4 Approach *(Continued)*

Characteristic	System 1	System 2	System 3	System 4
Extent to which there is an informal organization present and supporting or opposing goals of the formal organization	Informal organization is present and opposing the goals of the formal organization	Informal organization usually is present and partially resisting formal goals	Informal organization may be present and may either support or partially resist the goals of the formal organization	Informal and formal organizations are one and the same; all social forces support efforts to achieve organization's goals

System 4 management has also been used in a General Motors assembly plant. William F. Dowling, a researcher, reported that the results were improved operating efficiency and decreased grievances and waste.[3] The program involved:

- Training sessions on Likert's theory
- Team-building sessions starting at the top of the organization and moving to lower levels
- Improved information and communication flows to the hourly employees
- Changes in the job of first-line supervisors
- Increased participation of hourly employees in job changes
- New approaches to goal setting

Quite obviously, System 1 represents the traditional model and System 4 represents the human resources model. At present, there appears to be a decided swing toward the use of Systems 3 and 4. Astute managers know that people provide organizations with their competitive edge. If the enterprise cannot keep its people motivated, these individuals will go elsewhere. As a result, modern managers must be keenly aware of the changing attitudes and values of their employees.

 CHECK YOUR UNDERSTANDING

What is the essence of each system in Rensis Likert's four systems of management? Match the following systems to the appropriate statements.

Management Systems
1. Exploitive autocratic
2. Benevolent autocratic
3. Consultative democratic
4. Participative democratic

System Descriptions
a. Complete confidence and trust in employees
b. Rewards and punishments may be used to motivate
c. Employees are consulted; some trust and confidence
d. Managers make most decisions; an air of distrust exists

Discuss the role of behavioral science in human relations.

Behavioral Science and Human Relations

A great deal of what people know about human relations is a direct outgrowth of what they have heard, read, or experienced. Many try to classify this information into the form of rules or principles of behavior.[4] For example, just about everyone knows Murphy's first law: "If anything can go wrong, it will."

Another commonly cited behavioral adage comes from Parkinson, who holds, "The time spent on the discussion of any agenda item is in inverse proportion to the sum involved."[5]

Are these laws scientific or are they generalizations that make for an interesting discussion but little else? Human relations experts opt for the latter view, noting that such rules are too broad in coverage to provide much operational assistance. Furthermore, because nothing is more dangerous than generalizing behavioral findings from one situation to another without systematically studying the facts, modern human relationists prefer to use the scientific method in developing their theories and rules about human relations.

The Scientific Method

The greatest barrier to our understanding of human relations can be found within ourselves. Biases, personal opinions, inaccurate perceptions, and errors of judgment all combine to give us our own views of the world. Sometimes, these factors lead us to see things as we would like them to be rather than as they really are. For example, a manager who dislikes the union may easily regard the shop steward as a mouthpiece for union dissension and may discount anything the steward says as mere "union rhetoric." Practitioners of modern human relations know that they must step outside themselves and study human behavior in the workplace from an objective standpoint. In analyzing behavioral problems, for example, they must rely on the **scientific method**, because, as Kerlinger has noted:[6]

> *The scientific method has one characteristic that no other method of attaining knowledge has: self-direction. There are built-in checks all along the way to scientific knowledge. These checks are so conceived and used that they control and verify the scientist's activities and conclusions to the end of attaining dependable knowledge outside himself.*

The following are generally regarded as the basic steps in the scientific method:

1. Identify the problem. What exactly is the objective of the entire investigation?
2. Obtain background information. Gather as much data as possible about the problem under study.
3. Pose a tentative solution to the problem. State a hypothesis that can be proved to be either right or wrong and that is most likely to solve the problem.
4. Investigate the problem area. Using available data, as well as any information gathered through experimentation, examine the problem in its entirety.
5. Classify the information. Take all the data and classify them in a way that expedites their use and helps to establish a relationship with the hypothesis.
6. State a tentative answer to the problem. Draw a conclusion regarding the correct answer to the problem.
7. Test the answer. Implement the solution. If it works, the problem is solved. If not, develop another hypothesis and repeat the process.

CHECK YOUR UNDERSTANDING

Close your textbook and write down the basic steps in the scientific method. Check your answers. How many did you remember?

Behavioral Research in Human Relations

Obviously, practitioners of human relations do not have time to make a systematic study of human behavior at work. They are too busy being operating managers. However, there are people in academia and industry who do have time for scientific, behavioral research, including psychologists (who are interested in individual behavior) and sociologists (who are most concerned with group behavior). These highly skilled people are known as **behavioral scientists** and are responsible for a great deal of what we know about human relations in industry.

Applying the Scientific Method.   How is the scientific method applied in the study of human relations? There are numerous ways. One way is to set up **test** and **control groups**. A test group is a group that is given some form of "treatment," such as a training course, whereas a control group is a group that is not given any treatment. For example, a company is considering the value of customer-service training for store employees. Will this training be useful? One way to answer this question is by training some of the employees and then evaluating the results. The group to be trained would be randomly selected. This means that each of the employees would have an equal chance of being picked for the training; the company would not send the best or poorest workers, even if it believed that these individuals would profit most from the training. If those with the training were found to be more effective in providing customer service, the behavioral scientist would conclude that the training accounted for these results. If the group members were no more effective than the other employees in providing customer service, the behavioral scientist would conclude that the training was of no substantive value.

Motivating and Leading People.   Behavioral scientists also use their knowledge to help managers motivate and lead people. For example, in recent years, many managers have been taught how to use effective reinforcement to encourage desired behaviors and to discourage undesired behaviors. Through the effective use of rewards, employees are motivated to perform their duties quickly and efficiently. Conversely, by withholding rewards, managers motivate employees to modify their behaviors and to stop acting in ways (such as coming in late, filing incomplete reports, or failing to complete work on time) that are nonproductive.[7]

Using Questionnaires, Interviews, and Surveys.   Behavioral scientists also obtain important human relations information through the use of formal questionnaires: In **structured interviews**, specific questions are asked in a predetermined order, whereas in **unstructured interviews**, the interviewer has questions to be asked but follows no set format, allowing the interview to develop on its own. All these approaches are designed to gather data about workers and working conditions. For example, hospitals and clinics use questionnaires to learn about patient treatment during appointments, and businesses use surveys to learn about how satisfied the consumer is about a service rendered or a product recently purchased. More and more businesses are using the Internet to conduct these surveys. Through analysis of this information and study of the environment in which the subjects work, it is often possible to draw conclusions about factors that affect communication, attitudes, and work habits.

Empirical Data and Pop Psychology

The science of modern human relations is based not on generalizations, hunches, opinions, and "gut feelings" but on empirical information that is systematically gathered and analyzed by trained scientists. Much of what you will study in this book is a direct result of such scientists' investigations. At the same time, some behavioral findings seem to combine research with pop psychology, and it can be difficult to know exactly where to draw the line regarding what is accurate and what sounds good but is incorrect. For example, Frank Sulloway conducted a research on how birth order affects personality.[8] His concept holds that the order in which someone is born helps to determine how this person will behave. As a result, the oldest of three brothers, according to birth-order rank advocates, will be distinctly different from his youngest brother. Here is a sample birth-order rank profile:

Oldest Brother of Brothers.   The oldest brother of brothers is considered to be a good worker when he wants to be. He can inspire and lead others competently, and he often takes the greatest hardship upon himself. He can accept the authority of a male supervisor, however, only if he identifies with that authority. Otherwise, he is likely to look for loopholes in the boss's position and to try to undermine the latter's power. Ultimately, the oldest brother of brothers wants the power for himself.

Youngest Brother of Brothers.   The youngest brother of brothers is seen as an irregular worker, sometimes excellent in his achievements and at other times highly unproductive. He is at his best in scientific or artistic endeavors, where his environment is taken care of by others. He not only accepts authority but also loves it. However, he tends to be careless with his money and often squanders it.

First-Borns.   First-born children tend to be more assertive and authoritarian, dominant, and inflexible. Their natural traits include being conformist, task-oriented, disciplined, and concerned with getting things done right. First-borns are good at executing a plan, following it, and driving others to follow it in a disciplined way. On the negative side, they tend to be concerned about and fearful of losing their position or rank and may find it threatening to bring on partners. They are not good at admitting their own errors.

Second-Borns.   The second-born children tend to be creative, risk-taking, flexible, and more likely to embrace new paradigms than first-born children. They possess many of the traits of successful entrepreneurs. Second-borns are more relationship-focused, more concerned about fairness and justice, less academic, and more interested in the international scene than first-borns. Bill Gates is a good example of a successful second-born child. Often these children start a company then hire someone to run it. Second-born children tend to favor service-type businesses. Because second-born children have siblings on both sides, they tend to be diplomatic and skilled at politics and negotiation, and they are peacemakers and good at mediation and resolving disputes.[9]

Are these descriptions accurate? A recent book by a Massachusetts Institute of Technology research scholar argues that later-born children are indeed more innovative and adventurous than first-born children. In support of his statement, the researcher has identified some well-known business executives and compared their birth-order rank and business behavior. Here are two examples. These people have served as chief executives in one or more companies.

- Louis V. Gerstner: A later-born child, Gerstner makes an effort to learn about his customers rather than dictate to them from a position of technological superiority. Like many later-borns, he identifies with his peer group. He also likes to work with people, and when he was in charge of RJR Nabisco, before going to IBM, he was able to rein in a free-wheeling corporate culture and pay down a stupendous debt load without selling off many assets. Simply put, he is an adaptable individual and uses a leadership style that best fits the situation. In 2003, he assumed the position of chairman of The Carlyle Group, a global private equity firm located in Washington, D.C. In 2008, he retired but remains a senior advisor to Carlyle.

- Albert J. Dunlap: A first-born child, Dunlap likes to dominate, is willing to take charge, and does not hesitate to make difficult decisions. He is best known as a turn-around specialist and downsizer. When he ran Scott Paper, he made sharp cuts in the workforce and then sold the company, making a fortune for himself in the process. At Sunbeam, he downsized the workforce and focused on productivity measures. Clearly, he is a take-charge person.

Of these two leaders, Dunlap is the first-born, and his career has been marked by a willingness to cut the workforce, sell off unprofitable divisions, and make unpopular decisions. The other executive is more human relations oriented. Is this because he is not a first-born child? Answering this question is not easy, because many critics of birth-order rank theory argue that personality and behavior cannot be predicted simply by identifying where one falls in terms of sibling birth order. On the other hand, the theory is interesting if only because it has intuitive appeal—it seems to be accurate, and many people can relate to the general descriptions associated with birth-order rank.

This information may be useful to marketers. For example, "A Dell or a 3M should probably pitch its latest innovations differently to potential first-born buyers than to later-borns. Any innovation-oriented company not testing this first-born/later-born hypothesis in its own marketing initiatives is doing itself a disservice. Sulloway's Darwin-driven insight gives marketers a powerful way to segment and capture customers."[10]

 ## CHECK YOUR UNDERSTANDING

How can scientific methods be used to improve management? Give an example.

Describe some emerging challenges facing managers today.

Emerging Challenges

Over the last decade, human relations concerns have not remained static. New challenges have emerged, increasing the importance of understanding human relations at work. Four major issues now in the forefront are:

- Managing knowledge workers
- Managing diversity and workplace violence
- Addressing ethics and social responsibility concerns
- Adapting to international challenges

These areas are interdependent, but each warrants individual consideration because of its major effect on human relations.

Managing Knowledge Workers

Recruiting Talented Employees.   Many of the most profitable companies in recent years have been those that have successfully managed what are now being called knowledge workers, who produce and distribute ideas and information rather than goods or services. Focusing their recruiting and development efforts on highly creative and talented employees, these enterprises have been able to develop new products and services that have helped to change the way millions of people live. Dell Corporation, for example, has revolutionized the way companies and individuals buy computers. Now customers can go online, customize their order so that their new computer has exactly what they want (and nothing more), and have delivery within a matter of days. At the same time, Dell has significantly increased its sales while sharply reducing its inventory. Yet none of this would have been possible had the company not been able to attract and retain innovative personnel who brought new ideas to the company and were willing to share this knowledge with their associates.

Understanding Knowledge Workers.   Knowledge workers are driven by accomplishment and a need to see results. They have strong beliefs and personalities, are highly mobile, identify themselves with their profession rather than the workplace, and are quick to change jobs. Knowledge workers love a challenge and want to be treated as professional partners. They don't like to be told what to do. Much of their work goes on in their heads and is invisible and hard to measure. Many knowledge workers perform below their potential because companies do not know how to manage them. Just hiring knowledge workers and leaving them alone is not the best way to get the most out of them. Knowledge workers need to receive proper training. For most companies, knowledge workers are the key source of growth and the primary force determining which economies are successful and which are not.[11]

Knowledge workers are complex individuals who bring unique skills, intelligence, and work methods to the workplace, which makes it difficult to create a uniform system for encouraging and rewarding creativity. A. D. Amar, a business professor at Seton Hall University, states that since knowledge workers place a greater priority on individual goals than on group goals, managers must assess and respond to each employee's needs. Organizations must provide knowledge workers with plenty of opportunity for personal and professional growth.[12]

Creating a Knowledge-Sharing Culture.   Once a company has established its direction, it must create an environment that continuously encourages employees to share what they know, as well as be able to sustain a base of knowledge workers. One way is by developing a knowledge-sharing culture. The importance of this strategy has been noted by the Organization for Economic Co-operation and Development, which reports that more than 50 percent of the gross domestic product in major industrial countries is a result of the production, distribution, and use of knowledge and information. Commenting on this, one writer noted that:

> *Today's businesses must position themselves within these new economic realities, and leveraging brainpower through knowledge management is one way to jump-start that process. Intel Corp., the Santa Clara, California-based computer chip maker, for example, has designed its knowledge management initiative to propel the company into a leadership position in the new knowledge era. The program initially facilitated the reuse of knowledge in-house and then expanded the knowledge sharing to business partners. Intel's final goal is to start revolutionary new businesses worldwide to become a leader in its field.*[13]

Another strategy is through interactive learning. For example, at Buckman Laboratories International, Inc., a manufacturer of specialty chemicals for aqueous industrial systems, top management has built a knowledge-sharing, interactive-learning culture. The firm connects all its associates worldwide via the Internet and allows them to take courses from an electronic learning center. As a result of this global knowledge-sharing system, Buckman has significantly increased its "time to market" so that new goods now account for more than one-third of its total revenue, and operating profit per associate has increased by 93 percent in a recent 10-year period. Using interactive learning tools like ShareNet and Case-Based Reasoning allows companies to increase production and reduce expenses often resulting in hiring fewer technical support agents because of the help received from the systems.

Using Training and Development. At the heart of sustaining knowledge workers is continuous training and development. General Electric Company (GE), the largest supplier in the aerospace industry, is capable of providing aircraft manufacturers with one-stop shopping for everything from engines to complex cockpit software. The company has shifted away from manufacturing to providing higher margin services.[14] In the process, GE has placed a strong emphasis on training, education, and development of managers. Today, its knowledge-based workers are among the best in the world. One reason is because the unions agreed that personnel must be continually trained and kept on the cutting edge of technology. In this way, if a GE business does not perform well and ends up being closed or sold to another firm, the workers can take their knowledge base and go somewhere else. They are marketable. GE needs them more than the workers need the firm, because they are knowledge workers who are in demand.

Finding Talented Knowledge Workers. This is not always easy. In 2007, a survey conducted by Manpower, Inc., found 41 percent of 37,000 employers in 27 countries were having trouble hiring the people they needed.[15] It is predicted that by 2015, the average corporation will be left with half the critical leadership talent it needs. One solution is that companies must identify internal talent at an earlier stage and develop prospects much faster, even though the developed world continues to offer superior education for knowledge workers and managers. This process will be complicated by a heightened competition for talent among companies, countries, and regions. The global talent war is well under way but is being ignored by too many corporations.[16]

Because knowledge workers are expensive to train and maintain, companies such as Oracle, Intel, and Microsoft are investing in research and development (R&D) centers in India. The driving force is to obtain talent at a lower price than in the United States. Russia is also emerging as a global center for electronic design. Motorola, Cisco, and Hewlett-Packard have built labs in Russia. Russians have a long tradition of scientific excellence. Another company, Intel, has employed 1,500 Russian researchers who work in labs in Moscow, St. Petersburg, and Novosibirsk, Siberia. Companies spend huge sums on R&D because it powers innovation and growth. However, labor costs account for about 56 percent to 86 percent of R&D spending, according to KPMG studies. Managing knowledge workers provides a critical challenge, especially when it comes to measuring profits.[17] Obviously, effective human relations is going to be of paramount importance to these firms in managing their knowledge-based workers.

Hiring Knowledgeable People. Hiring highly knowledgeable people and facilitating their sharing of information are critical to organizational success. So too is the challenge of getting these workers to remain on the cutting edge so their knowledge can be used in creating a highly competitive enterprise. Yet the greatest challenge may well be that of retaining these employees. Unless organizations know what their knowledge workers want, and are willing to provide it, they can end up hiring and training outstanding talent and then seeing these people leave for jobs with competitive firms. Companies will have to ensure that they are treating all their employees equitably. Firms will also have to realize that when employees are disgruntled, unlike the old days when they would simply quit, they are likely to make things difficult for the company. Some approaches that have been reported include:

- Quitting, but offering to come back as a consultant at three times their former salary
- Telling the human resources department, during the exit interview, negative things about their boss
- Sending an e-mail to senior executives about how bad their boss has treated them
- Asking for an incentive bonus to stay the typically required two weeks and, if they do not get it, leaving immediately
- Recruiting members of their old department to quit and come with them to the new firm
- Going on a break—and never coming back[18]

 CHECK YOUR UNDERSTANDING

1. What are the most crucial issues in recruiting and hiring knowledge workers?
2. Cite an example of interactive learning.

Managing Diversity and Workplace Violence

Multiethnic and Diverse Workforce Issues.   Workforces are becoming more multiethnic and diverse. Figure 1.3 provides government forecasts on the ethnic breakdown of the U.S. labor force between 1995 and 2050. These data reveal that minorities will account for an increasing percentage of the nation's workforce.

Figure 1.3 Overall U.S. Population Growth and Racial Composition

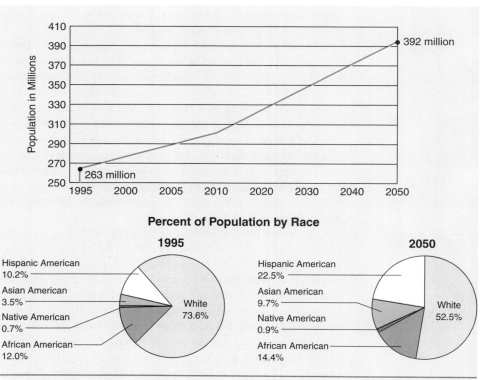

Source: U.S. Census Bureau report, 1997.

These changes are compelling organizations to review their old human relations philosophies in order to answer the following question: How can we prepare ourselves to manage the changing workforce effectively? The days of managing large groups of white men are a thing of the past. Tomorrow's managers must motivate and lead work groups in which women, Hispanics, African Americans, and Asian Americans are being employed in increasing numbers. For example, at DuPont, women and minorities are the primary contact for 12 of the 40 firms that work for the chemical maker. As companies compete in domestic and global markets with an array of cultures and colors of consumers, they also want their supplies to be similarly diverse. According to company officials, this mix stimulates creative thinking and results in better outcomes. In 2008, DuPont named Ellen J. Kullman to be its new chief executive and president. In a new twist, Walmart ended relationships with two law firms because of their lack of diversity. This dramatic action is usually not common. Coca-Cola emphasizes diversity within its own workforce. Coca-Cola does business in more than 200 countries; therefore, to succeed, it must be responsive to diverse markets and sensitive to cultural traditions.[19]

Aging Workforce Issues.   The workforce is aging, creating a challenge for employers seeking to retain topnotch people. "By 2010, the number of workers aged 35 to 44—or those typically moving into upper management—will decline by 19%; the number of workers aged 45 to 54 will increase 21%; and the number of workers aged 55 to 64 will increase 52%."[20]

At the same time, "rather than being an economic deadweight, the next generation of older Americans is likely to make a much bigger contribution to the economy than many of today's forecasts predict."[21] With employees remaining in the workplace well past their sixty-fifth birthday, managers will be managing older workers in greater numbers than in past decades. Will younger managers be equipped to handle older workers? *BusinessWeek* finds that productivity of older Americans could add 9 percent to the gross domestic product by 2045.

Between 2010 and 2030, the baby boomers will hit the traditional retirement age of 65. Will they retire or stay in the workforce? The U.S. Census Bureau estimates that about one in five U.S citizens will be elderly, which may significantly increase the number of elderly in the workforce. The baby boomers are well educated and they want to keep working and continue contributing to society. The majority of the jobs held by the over-65 workforce are professional, managerial, technical, or administrative support jobs.

During the economic recession at the end of the last decade, many workers in their 70s and 80s lost their job. For financial reasons, many of these workers needed a job while others merely wanted the stimulation and challenge of a job. Instead of retiring, they emerged as a new class of workers, making them more visible than ever bringing to light the need for managers to gain skills in learning how to manage the elderly workforce.[22]

A survey by the Society of Human Resource Management and the Commerce Clearing House shows that many companies are aware of the need to manage diversity effectively and are taking steps in this direction. Sixty-one percent of the survey respondents said that the management of diversity was a major obligation of their company, and many of the respondents reported that their firms were hiring women, Hispanics, African Americans, and Asians in record numbers.[23] In turn, this has led companies to consider the following questions: What will our workforce look like in the future? What do we do now to deal effectively with these changes?[24] In some cases, firms are finding that a diversity consultant can be extremely useful in providing advice and guidance.[25] In any event, organizations are discovering that they need to develop policies and guidelines for ensuring equality for their people in the workplace.[26]

Permanent Temporary Workforce Issues.   After the economic collapse in 2008, more people were pushed into part-time work, which changed the nature of part-time work in the United States. More people also held multiple jobs for economic reasons. In the retail industry, the growth of part-time workers slightly outpaced the full-time workers. Women overtook men, benefits were often nonexistent, and pay was typically 10 percent to 20 percent less per hour than comparable full-time work.[27]

According to the *Bloomberg BusinessWeek* magazine, more than 26 percent of America's workforce is classified as "nonstandard." These workers include temps, contract workers, and part-timers. Their pay is low, benefits are vanishing, and no one's job is secure. Will this trend continue? It is forecasted to be the same for the next five to ten years extending into 2020. If so, managers will face new challenges in managing a new larger segment of their workforce, the temporary part-time worker. In times of slow economic growth, companies can more easily lay off unneeded workers and rehire them when times get better. What does this new trend mean for managers? New innovative leadership will be required. What does this mean for workers? "The lack of job security and health-care benefits, as well as social ties to the rest of the workforce, increase stress levels for temps and contractors." As the baby boomers retire, labor shortages may bring some bargaining power back to younger workers, some issues for the next decade. Using temporary workforces is a global practice that is beginning to dominate the American workforce. Companies in Europe, for example, have been using more temporary and part-time workers than in the United States. One big difference is that these workers are covered with government health care benefits and receive pay comparable to permanent workers.[28]

Equal Pay Issues.   Another area in which organizations must examine their human relations practices is that of compensation. The Equal Pay Act was enacted in the United States in 1963 to ensure that women and men were paid the same salary for doing the same job; however in 2008, a woman, on average, still earns only eighty cents for every dollar earned by her male counterpart. Minority women fare even worse: African American women earn approximately 67 percent of what white men earn, and Hispanic women earn approximately 60 percent of what white men are paid. By comparison, black women and Hispanic women had earnings that were around 90 percent of those of their male counterparts.[29]

Although women are more likely than men to work in professional and related occupations, they are not as well represented in the higher paying job groups within this broad category. In 2008, only 9 percent of female professionals compared with 45 percent of male professionals were employed in the high-paying computer and engineering fields. Professional women were more likely to work in the education and health-care occupations, in which pay was generally lower. Sixty-eight percent of female professionals worked in these fields in 2008, compared to 29 percent of male professionals.[30]

In 2002, Senator Hillary Rodham Clinton called for legislation to end alleged pay-scale discrimination against women. She stated that the "wage gap leaves women short-changed and undervalued." One of the biggest civil class action suits ever to be brought against a U.S. private employer, Walmart, alleged the retailer systemically denied promotion and equal pay to female employees. Another lawsuit denying female employees equal pay was filed against Boeing. Both managers and companies can face huge economic consequences for decisions that result in discrimination.

Women in Power Issues.   Another diversity issue is known as the **glass ceiling**, a term used to describe artificial barriers that prevent women from being promoted into the upper ranks of management. No matter how well women perform, in some companies there seems to be an organizational level beyond which they are unable to progress. Recent research reveals that at some of the largest firms in America, women

Rank	Name	Age	Company	Title
1	Indra Nooyi	53	PepsiCo	Chairman and CEO
2	Irene Rosenfeld	56	Kraft Foods	Chairman and CEO
3	Pat Woertz	56	Archer Daniels Midland	Chairman, CEO, and president
4	Angela Braly	49	Wellpoint	President and CEO
5	Andrea Jung	51	Avon Products	Chairman and CEO
6	Oprah Winfrey	55	Harpo	Chairman
7	Ellen Kullman	53	DuPont	CEO
8	Carol Bartz	61	Yahoo	CEO
9	Ursula Burns	51	Xerox	CEO
10	Brenda Barnes	55	Sara Lee	Chairman and CEO

Source: Adapted from "50 Most Powerful Women," *Fortune*, September 28, 2009

hold only a small percentage of managerial positions. However, women in CEO positions are increasing in number. Recently *Fortune* magazine listed 50 of the most powerful women in business, the top 10 of which are listed in Table 1.2. How many names of these women do you recognize?

Hewlett-Packard is making a difference is providing equality and opportunity for women and minorities. It is "committed to building a work environment where everyone has an opportunity to fully participate in creating business success and is valued for their distinctive skills, experiences and perspectives." For years, Hewlett-Packard has actively been creating a diverse, inclusive environment, which the company feels is a journey of continuous renewal. Diversity and inclusion are the key drivers of creativity, innovation, and invention. In the early 1960s, Equal Employment Opportunity (EEO) was the stimulus for Hewlett-Packard to establish a workplace free of discrimination. In the 1980s, the company focused on affirmative action issues, initiating proactive behaviors in making EEO a reality for everyone, and in the 1990s, the focus was on creating an inclusive work environment that values all employees. Today Hewlett-Packard is putting differences to work in the marketplace, workplace, and community. Each step in the process is linked to the previous step and has formed what the company calls a "diversity value chain."[31]

The number of women in corporate-officer positions in 2008 was still low, only 24 percent. Just because a handful of corporate women have made it to the top does not mean the battle for equal opportunity is over. Women must take an active role in breaking down barriers impeding their advancement. One of these barriers is the good old boys' network. Many business deals are made in this network, and women typically are not part of the inner circles of male executives. Women leaders must recognize that businesses still have a long way to go before women can play by the same rules and be judged by the same standards as men.[32]

Another reason for the existence of the glass ceiling is the belief that women tend to place family responsibilities ahead of work; this perception reduces women's chances of being promoted. However, there is evidence that cracks are beginning to appear in the glass ceiling and that things are beginning to improve for some women.[33]

What is the answer to breaking the glass ceiling and being promoted to a top-level position as a women or a minority? The process starts with top management's commitment to equal access to upper-level opportunities. Other things that companies need to consider include: implementation of corporate-wide diversity training and awareness programs, an emphasis on recruitment of qualified women of all races, and a scholarship program that supports technical degrees. Some of the characteristics of an employee wanting to advance to the top level are preparedness, patience, dependability, personableness, teachableness, and able to teach. The employee must understand the values of the company and which behaviors the company rewards. Study the people being promoted, determine their skills, and let your boss know that you want to be promoted. Often it takes more than being qualified, long hours, and hard work to get that promotion.[34]

Sou Wong-Lee, an Asian American woman, began her career in the defense industry over 25 years ago. She was qualified, worked long hours, was personable, and was devoted to the company, but promotions always passed her by. She learned that women and minorities are viewed as not having the qualifications and not being interested in moving up into a particular area of the company and that leadership skills, assertive communication skills, and networking within the company are important factors in seeking and attaining high-profile positions. Instead of stewing about it, Wong-Lee got busy and volunteered for key assignments, especially those that involved several departments. She strived to gain support and recognition throughout the company. She began pushing herself beyond her comfort zone. It worked. She is now the director of the Raytheon Learning Institute, an arm of the defense industry giant, Raytheon, Inc. Wong-Lee is also the vice-chair of the board of directors of Leadership Education for Asian Pacifics, Inc. (LEAP).[35]

In 2009, Raytheon was ranked among the Top 25 Best Places to Launch a Career with entry-level hiring up 13 percent over 2008. This was accomplished in a down economy struggling with the highest unemployment in over 26 years. Then in 2010, Raytheon ranked No. 5 on the list of the Top 50 Employers for Persons with Disabilities. Dave Wajsgras, senior vice president and CEO, stated, "This honor recognizes the company's commitment to creating opportunities for all employees to participate and contribute. Each of us brings diversity of thought and experience into the workplace, and we value these differences."[36] The top 10 best companies to work for in 2009 are listed in Table 1.3.

Few companies that have implemented strategies to manage diversity are discussed next.

Xerox. The ex-chairman of Xerox, Anne M. Mulcahy, most eloquently stated, "I'm convinced diversity is a key to success. Experience tells us that the most diverse companies— companies ruled by a hierarchy of imagination and filled with people of all ages, races, and backgrounds—are the most successful over time." "Somehow, diversity breeds creativity. Maybe it's because people with different backgrounds challenge each other's underlying assumptions, freeing everybody from convention and orthodoxy. Xerox's employee roster is made up of over 30% African-Americans, Latinos, Asians and Native Americans. Xerox has been rated as one of the best companies for hiring minorities."[37]

Avon Products, Inc. Avon Products, Inc., the world's leading direct seller of beauty and related products, has initiated awareness training at all levels of its hierarchy and uses affirmative action to ensure that doors are opened to talented individuals. The company has helped three minority groups—African Americans, Hispanics, and Asians—to form

Table 1.3
Top 10 Best Companies
to Work for in 2009

Rank	Company	Job Growth	U.S. Employees
1	NetApp	12%	5,014
2	Edward Jones	9%	34,496
3	Boston Consulting Group	10%	1,680
4	Google	40%	12,580
5	Wegmans Food Markets	6%	37,195
6	Cisco Systems	7%	37,123
7	Genentech	5%	10,969
8	Methodist Hospital System	1%	10,535
9	Goldman Sachs	2%	14,088
10	Nugget Market	22%	1,536

Source: Adapted from "100 Best Companies to Work For in 2009," Fortune.com

networks that crisscross the company in all 50 states. Each network elects its own leaders, has an advisor from senior management, and has representatives on the company's Multicultural Participation Council, through which management feedback is provided about employee views on diversity issues. The company's efforts have not gone unnoticed. Avon was named among the top 10 companies listed by Minneapolis-based Business Ethics magazine's "100 Best Corporate Citizens," and also was recognized by *Fortune* as one of America's most admired companies.[38]

Andrea Jung, chairman and CEO, was voted among the 50 most powerful women for 2009 and a best manager for 2002 by *BusinessWeek* magazine. In 2004, *Fortune* magazine named Andrea Jung the third most powerful women in business. Andrea Jung stated that "Avon is a company built on a proud heritage of doing well by doing right."[39]

Motorola. Motorola began its initiative toward hiring and promoting women after management took a look at census data and predicted future demographics for workers in such fields as electrical engineering and computer science. The firm then set targets that reflected the increases it wanted to achieve for women, blacks, Asians, and other minorities. The firm also revamped its succession-planning program by focusing first on its senior-level management. Top managers must now supply the names of three people most likely to replace them. The first is the manager who would take their job in the case of an emergency. The second is the individual who could be groomed for the job in three to five years. The third is reserved for the woman or minority closest to being qualified for the position. Today at Motorola, managers are expected to give this third person the opportunities to obtain the experience needed to secure the promotion. As a result, women have now moved into the first or second slots for approximately three-fourths of the company's three hundred most prized jobs![40]

Nissan Motor Company. Recruiting and retaining women were a challenge for Nissan in Japan. This traditionally was not the type of company where women worked. Nissan realized that women made up more than half of its customers and that two-thirds of the buying decisions were influenced by women stated Hitoshi Kawaguchi, Nissan's senior vice-president for human resources, Japan. Nissan got busy and introduced new initiatives to increase the number of women in its workforce. Management began focusing on building a more diverse workforce with its 32,700 employees. Managers were mandated to attend diversity training courses, maternity leave was extended beyond the law, and shorter working hours allowed parents to get home to their children. While Nissan was beginning to see change, the program had its critics and was challenged by the male workers who had dominated the company for so long. After five years, 25 percent of the new hires are women. Currently Nissan is working very hard to develop female supervisors.[41]

Workplace Violence Issues.   The workplace is supposed to be a safe and secure place, but that is not always the case. Violence is a very real almost unpredictable event that can strike anywhere at any time. Workplace violence is the driving force that plagues our workplace and is turning into a number one priority for today's businesses. According to the U.S. National Institute for Occupational Safety and Health, on an average working day, three people will be murdered on the job in the United States. One million workers are assaulted and more than 1,000 are murdered every year. Homicide is the second highest cause of death on the job, after motor vehicles accidents.[42]

Mass murders in the workplace by unstable employees have become media-intensive events. However, contrary to popular opinion, sensational multiple homicides represent a small number of workplace incidents. The majority of incidents that employees and managers have to deal with on a daily basis are lesser cases of assaults, domestic violence, stalking, threats, harassment, and physical and/or emotional abuse that make no headlines. Many of these incidents, in fact, are not even reported to company officials or to the police. What are the costs for this behavior? Estimates from lost work time and wages, reduced productivity, medical costs, workers' compensation payments, and legal and security expenses clearly run into many billions of dollars.[43]

The strangulation death of Yale University student Annie Le led police to arrest a coworker Raymond Clark III, a technician who worked alongside of Le in one of the school's animal research laboratories in September 2009. This is an example of workplace violence that has become increasingly prominent nationwide.[44] In another recent incident, a man in St. Louis who apparently was unhappy about litigation with the company over pension losses entered his workplace and killed three employees and himself and left five more employees hurt.[45] Workplace violence is a real issue for businesses and an inescapable challenge for managers.

 ## CHECK YOUR UNDERSTANDING

1. What are the major discrimination issues confronting today's managers?
2. Have you been exposed to unfair discrimination situations at work? If so, what were they?
3. As a manager, how would you have handled the situation?

Addressing Ethics and Social Responsibility Concerns

Ethics and Social Responsibility.   **Ethics** is the study of standards and moral judgment. **Social responsibilities** are the obligations that a business has to society. In *Fortune's* "100 Most Accountable Companies" for 2008, GE was the only U.S. firm among the top 10 companies. Out of the 100 companies, 31 were U.S. companies.[46] What does that tell you about the importance of social responsibility within U.S. companies?

In today's workplace, managers are continually confronted with ethical and social responsibility issues. Suppose a purchasing manager, for example, lies to a supplier, telling her, "We cannot pay $6 per unit any longer. If you can't provide it for $5.75, we'll have to do business elsewhere." Is the manager guilty of unethical behavior? If the supplier cuts the price, thereby saving the company $27,000, or if the purchasing manager tells the boss, "I saved you $27,000 on these units. I think that entitles me to a raise," has the manager acted unethically? Consider a company president who tells a news reporter that her company is not interested in acquiring Company X, when all the while she is meeting with her investment bankers to plan a takeover bid. And what about the stockbroker who learns that Company X is about to be taken over and quietly buys stock for himself or herself before the news hits the market and the shares rise dramatically? These are all ethical and social responsibility dilemmas.

Scandals and Fraud.   Over the past several years, day after day the headlines in the *Wall Street Journal* and news on television are filled with stories of executives employing a slew of scams to siphon big money out of companies and investors, off-the-book partnerships that concealed millions of dollars, aggressive accounting practices that hid losses and revealed a financially healthy company, and dishonest behavior of CEOs and executives who borrowed millions of dollars they never intended to repay. These activities have resulted in a succession of bankruptcy filings, which ultimately have made history. For example, as a result of unethical behavior and practices, Enron, WorldCom, Adelphia, Global Crossing, and Conseco, Inc., were forced to file for Chapter 11 bankruptcy, impacting both employees and investors. Many employees lost their jobs, benefits, and retirement plans. Company stock in employees' retirement plans became worthless. In the investment sector, Bernard Madoff pulled off the biggest Ponzi scheme in history cheating investors from around the world out of billions of dollars, causing a French financier to commit suicide. Madoff is now serving life in prison. While Ponzi schemes have been around since 1899, it was Charles Ponzi, an Italian immigrant who gave the scam its name. During 1919–1920, he fleeced millions out of investors.[47] In the retail industry, Thomas Coughlin, former Walmart Stores Inc. executive, faced 28 years in prison and $1.35 million in fines for bilking the world's largest retailer. In the aviation industry, the Federal Aviation Administration revoked the licenses of Northwest Airlines pilots when they failed to respond to air-traffic controllers for more than an hour and overshot their destination. In foreign construction, Albert J. "Jack" Stanley, executive of Halliburton, pleaded guilty to orchestrating more than $180 million in bribes to senior Nigerian government officials to win a contract to build a liquefied-natural-gas plant in Nigeria.[48] And the list goes on.

During the economic downturn, fraud was seen as the driver for the wave of mortgage foreclosures in the housing market and the collapse of financial institutions spread across the country. Scams and schemes ran rampant throughout the financial and housing industries. To reverse this trend, managers must take responsible for their decisions and become socially responsible citizens. Decisions should not only have short-term results, they should have long-term consequences as well.

Another type of fraud that is growing is Internet security scams. Most people think of Internet security problems as viruses and spyware, but the most insidious Internet security problems today rely on human gullibility. Con artist scams that can steal identities and empty bank accounts are known as social engineering or phishing. Security software alone cannot always protect people or companies from these scams. In this digital age, management constantly is faced with challenges in keeping company records safe.[49]

The Sarbanes–Oxley Act.   In the weeks after WorldCom initially disclosed its fraud in 2002, the Sarbanes–Oxley Act was passed. The centerpiece of the act is internal controls—checks and balances that make sure public companies record assets, liabilities, and other items accurately on financial statements. It requires companies to establish a confidential system for employees to report malfeasance. If the statements prove to be untrue, companies face stiff civil and criminal penalties. It created a watchdog for auditing firms called the Public Company Accounting Oversight Board (PCAOB), and it forces top executives to certify the accuracy of financial results. The role of board audit committees was expanded and required companies to take "whistle-blower" complaints seriously.[50] Compliance has been expensive for most companies—large and small. Dow Chemical Company, for example, spent more than $12 million and over 100,000 man-hours getting its controls in order.[51]

"There is without question greater accountability in the boardroom," says Thomas Lehner, an official of the Business Roundtable, a Washington group representing big-company CEOs.[52] Critics acknowledge that it has restored investor confidence and helped corporate America move from the epic-size scandals, like Enron and WorldCom, and has spurred companies to take greater responsibility for their decisions and to review their policies and procedures.[53] After almost a decade, many companies are still struggling to comply with the act. One important thing that Sarbanes–Oxley has done is change the way top executives need to manage.[54]

Whistle-Blowers.   What do you do when you see someone else acting out of bounds in your organization? The National Bureau of Economic Research has found that only about one in five workers blow the whistle. And worse yet, when the whistle is blown, more often than not the worker is penalized through being ostracized by fellow employees, being demoted, or pressured to quit. Dyck, Morse, and Zingales reported in their paper, "Who Blows the Whistle on Corporate Fraud?" that 82 percent of whistle-blowers are treated as outcasts, pariahs, and snitches. The authors stated, "In no case is the tension between access to information and lack of incentives to reveal fraud more intense than for employees. However, the career incentives against revealing the fraud are stronger for employees than for any other group. Even according to an advocate for whistle-blowing, consequences to being the whistle-blower include distancing and retaliation from fellow workers and friends, personal attacks on one's character during the course of protracted dispute, and the need to change one's career."[55]

Even with safeguards in place, many workers wait in silence hoping that someone above them will detect the deceit. Ron Crossland, chairman of Bluepoint Leadership Development, encourages corporate leaders to start praising and rewarding whistle-blowers. Maybe over time, this behavior will provide the motivation for workers to report wrong actions by workers and employers.

After the Enron and WorldCom crises, three whistle-blowers were named as "Persons of the Year" on the cover of Time magazine for December 30, 2002/January 6, 2003: Cynthia Cooper of WorldCom, Coleen Rowley of the Federal Bureau of Investigation (FBI), and Sherron Watkins of Enron. They took huge professional and personal risks to come forth and tell their stories. Cynthia Cooper and two other internal auditors took it upon themselves to dig into the accounting practices at WorldCom, which led to the discovery of artificially boosted profits. The U.S. Securities and Exchange Commission (SEC) charged WorldCom with civil fraud and the company declared bankruptcy. Ms. Cooper provided a "wake-up call for this country. There's a responsibility for all Americans—teachers, mothers, fathers, college professors, and corporate people—to help and make sure the moral and ethical fabric of the country is strong."[56]

Coleen Rowley testified before the House and Senate Intelligence Committees about failed operations in the FBI, and Sherron Watkins uncovered a wave of accounting scandals in the Houston-based energy giant, Enron Corporation. Another whistle-blower, Barron Stone, an accountant, warned his bosses at Duke Power that it was overcharging ratepayers. The company agreed to credit $25 million to utility customers in North Carolina and South Carolina and change the company's accounting practices.[57] The government has ruled in favor of whistle-blowers 17 times out of 1,273 complaints filed between 2002 and 2008 with another 841 cases dismissed.[58]

What is the cost for failing to report problems or failing to take warnings seriously? The costs can be very high. An example is the Challenger disaster in NASA's space program. Roger Boisjoly's warning whistle was never taken seriously resulting in the disaster.

Causes of Fraudulent and Unethical Behavior. Why did so much bad stuff happen in the last decade? What set the stage for the rapid outbreak of fraud and unethical behavior? In his speech to the nation, President Bush said, "the 1990s was a decade of tremendous economic growth. As we're now learning, it was also a decade when the promise of rapid profits allowed the seeds of scandal to spring up. A lot of money was made, but too often standards were tossed aside." People lived the good life and believed it would continue. Corporate boards became overly cozy with management and insufficient controls were in place. After the September 11, 2001, disaster, things changed. The economy began to weaken and pressure mounted for executives to meet unrealistic goals, which made it easy for some executives to rationalize putting ethics aside. "And then there was greed. The opportunity to take money to meet your simplest needs or to meet your most extravagant needs is always present," says Carl Pergola, national director of the litigation and fraud investigation practices for accounting firm BDO Seidman in New York.[59] Mostly, we have ourselves to blame. The rash of financial problems, the collapse of the housing market, problems in the auto market, the loss of jobs, and the war with radical Islam came about at least in part due to the neglect of heeding any warnings from around the world and from inside our own country. Our insatiable greed fed by Wall Street and regulators that has undermined the financial system, our self-interest versus what is best for the customers and competition, and the deferral of responsibility by our politicians and government to upgrade and repair our infrastructure and to monitor the financial markets have all impacted social responsibility in this past decade.[60]

Unfortunately, fraud and scandals have been around forever and will continue to occur. Over time, they take different forms and shapes. What can a company do to protect itself? Carl Pergola outlines what companies can do to reduce the temptation to commit fraud:[61]

1. *Set realistic goals.* Setting unrealistic goals and overt pressures to achieve those goals often leads otherwise conscientious and ethical employees to do unethical things. For example, if meeting unrealistic budgets is expected, people will become innovative. Sometimes they believe it is the right thing to do.

2. *Hire competent managers.* Managers must set realistic goals and communicate those goals, agree to listen to their employees, and understand the challenges of their employees. Managers must help employees overcome those challenges as opposed to simply developing unachievable goals and putting undue pressure on them.

3. *Create a positive work environment.* Within the right environment, it is possible to manage a very effective and profitable business by setting realistic goals and giving the people the tools to achieve those goals. Also, management must review what the organization considers to be fraudulent behavior and what the implications are if caught. It might be cheating on an expense report or taking gifts from vendors.

Standards of behavior must be clear and employees should serve as role models for one another. Ethics can be taught and should be taught and talked about. Communication is key to building trust between employees and management. An environment or culture where management's view is "do it, or you're out of here" can lead to fraud.

To help executives manage company ethics, William D. Hall has outlined a series of steps:[62]

- Establish compliance standards and procedures to be followed by all company employees and their agents
- Assign specific individuals at a high level within the organization to oversee standards and procedures compliance
- Ensure that substantial discretion and authority have not been delegated to individuals with a known propensity to engage in illegal activities
- Communicate the standards and procedures to all employees and other agents through training programs and printed materials
- Develop systems to achieve compliance with company requirements such as monitoring and auditing systems
- Reinforce standards consistently through appropriate disciplinary mechanisms
- Respond appropriately to reported offenses and take action to prevent recurrence

Business Ethics Survey.   A recent international workplace survey found that workers want to work for ethical and socially responsible companies. The Kelly Global Workforce Index surveyed about 100,000 people in 34 countries throughout North America, Europe, and the Asia-Pacific region. The survey revealed that nearly 90 percent of the respondents are more likely to work for an organization perceived as ethically and socially responsible, 80 percent would likely work for an organization considered environmentally responsible, 53 percent of baby boomers would forgo higher pay or a promotion to work for an organization with a good reputation, and 48 percent of Gen Xers (ages 30 to 47) and 46 percent of Gen Yers (ages 18 to 29) would forgo higher pay or a promotion to work for an organization with a good reputation. "Employees gain a sense of fulfillment when their employer is focused not only on the bottom line, but also on initiatives and practices which have a connection with the communities in which they operate. There is a great deal of pressure on organizations to meet higher standards of corporate and ethical behavior and to play an appropriate role on issues affecting the environment," says Executive Vice President and Chief Operating Officer George Corona of Kelly Services. The bottom line is that social responsibility is a key to attracting top talent and for sustaining top-quality employees.[63]

Business Ethics Studies.   Practicing good business ethics creates dividends that go beyond avoiding legal disaster. A host of studies have shown that employees who perceive their companies to have a conscience possess a higher level of job satisfaction and feel more valued as workers. The 2000 Ethics Resource Center study canvassed corporations and nonprofits across the country. Among its findings: Managers' efforts to instill good business ethics were welcomed overwhelmingly by workers. "We found a strong connection between employees' perception of their leaders and their own ethical behavior," says Josh Joseph, top researcher in the ethics center. Workers also said their own behavior was influenced by the perceived ethics of direct supervisors and coworkers.[64]

"Ethics is a matter of developing good habits, and it doesn't happen overnight," says W. Michael Hoffman, executive director for the Center for Business Ethics at Bentley

College. "It happens through repetition and a long process of development." Commitment to ethics must start at the top of a company. Most CEOs and executives are ethical and diligent in overseeing major issues. Many, however, have too many things on their plates and are too preoccupied to focus on the ethical consequences of results.

On July 9, 2002, by executive order, President George W. Bush created a new corporate fraud task force headed by the deputy attorney general. Its purpose is to target major accounting fraud and other criminal activity in corporate finance. The task force will function as a financial crimes "SWAT" team, overseeing the investigation of corporate abusers and bringing them to account. President Bush challenged leaders in business to set high standards and clear expectations of conduct, demonstrated by their own behavior. Everyone in a company should live up to high standards, but the burden of leadership rightly belongs to the chief executive officer, who sets the ethical direction for the company. The CEOs set a moral tone by the decisions they make, the respect they show their employees, and their willingness to be held accountable for their actions. They set a moral tone by showing their disapproval of other executives who bring discredit to the business world.[65]

The composition of board members of many companies has since changed. The board now takes accountability serious and "lousy performance won't be tolerated," says Barbara Franklin, who sits on five corporate boards. "Now we're trying to get ahead of the curve and make changes before you have an absolute crisis." For example, the CEO of Dow Chemical was fired after just two years on the job due to disappointing financial performance.[66]

 CHECK YOUR UNDERSTANDING

1. What do you believe to be the major factors in today's society that cause employees to behave unethically in the workplace? What can management do to change the situation?
2. What is your work ethic? How will your attitude about what is ethically right and wrong influence your behavior in the workplace?

Code of Conduct. A **code of conduct** outlines the values of the company and the expected behavior of all employees. If it is to promote ethics, the code of conduct must, however, be meaningful and be communicated to all employees through a planned training program. Before the code can be followed vigilantly, everyone, including the CEO and executives, must understand its contents. There is no standard form to follow in preparing a company's code of conduct. It can be a document of a few pages or a manual that covers every operational relationship inside and outside the business, within the United States, as well as operations in foreign countries.

The purposes of Howard Bank's Employee Code of Conduct are to focus on areas of ethical risk, provide guidance to help employees recognize and deal with ethical issues, provide mechanisms for employees to report unethical conduct, and foster among employees a culture of honesty and accountability. Accordingly, dishonest, unethical, or illegal conduct will constitute a violation of the code, regardless of whether the code specifically addresses such conduct.[67]

A code of conduct contains the business and ethical policies that a company expects its employees to follow, as well as policies regarding compliance with laws. Violations may expose the company, its management, or its employees to criminal or civil liability. In summary, an employee code of conduct sets forth a set of principles describing how

IN ACTION
QUESTIONS TO DETERMINE ETHICAL ACTION

The following questions can help you decide whether or not something is ethical. An ethical action should elicit a positive response to all applicable primary questions listed in the following, and a negative response to each clarification that follows the question.

1. Is it honorable?
   Is there anyone from whom you would like to hide the action?
2. Is it honest?
   Does it violate any agreement, actual or implied, or otherwise betray a trust?
3. Does it avoid the possibility of a conflict of interest?
   Are there other considerations that might bias your judgment?
4. Is it within your area of competence?
   Is it possible that your best effort will not be adequate?
5. Is it fair?
   Is it detrimental to the legitimate interests of others?
6. Is it considerate?
   Will it violate confidentiality or privacy, or otherwise harm anyone or anything?
7. Is it conservative?
   Does it unnecessarily squander" time or other valuable resources?

Sources: Parker, Donn, B., Susan Swope, and Bruce, N. Baker, *Ethical Conflicts in Information and Computer Science, Technology, and Business* (Wellesley, MA: QED Information Sciences, 1990), p. 182

employees, workers, and staff should conduct themselves while performing work for the company. The questions posed in the "In Action" box ("Questions to Determine Ethical Action") can serve as guidelines in determining ethical behavior.

Discuss the ethical dilemmas facing today's managers.

Current Ethical Dilemmas
Downsizing Issues

An interesting human relations–oriented dilemma is how to handle critical problems such as downsizing resulting from reorganization. During the recent recession, many companies cut their workforces and laid off thousands of employees. The unemployment rate rose to more than 10 percent, the highest in more than 26 years. How should these people be handled? How much assistance should management provide? What responsibility does the company have to help these people locate new jobs? What is the company's responsibility to those who remain and must take on the extra work? How does a company recover, regroup, and forge ahead successfully and at the same time build trust among the remaining workers? Forcing employees to take assignments they do not like is not the way to go. Management must find ways to key in on the remaining employee's motivations and adapt management strategies on an individual basis. Managing talented workers is tough during good times, but it is critical during tough times when resources are scarce. One way is to establish clear goals and align the workforce to accomplish them. If layoffs are necessary, view them as a way to keep the best employees and then provide the means for them to grow. Avoid the rumor mills and be transparent, which drives trust and employee engagement.[68]

According to the U.S. Equal Employment Opportunity Commission (EEOC), employers cannot use downsizing as a means for eliminating older employees from their workforce. In 2002, Gulfstream Aerospace paid $2.1 million to 61 former employees who lost their jobs during layoffs.[69]

Reorganization allows companies to reconsider how they do business both inside the company and with outsiders. This process requires knowledgeable people who understand not only processes and systems, but also how people work and how assignments must be carried out. Creativity is often required in designing a system that incorporates the new economic and technological changes that caused the very downturn of the business in the first place. The new organization will need to operate in a new and different way to survive. This may require employees to gain new skills or more training. The dilemma arises in how this will be mastered?

Workplace Discrimination Issues

Another challenge is treating people fairly in the workplace and not discriminating against them on the basis of gender, race, religion, age, physical appearance, disability, national origin, pregnancy, marital/parental responsibilities, language, political affiliation, matriculation, or sexual orientation. Federal, state, and local antidiscrimination laws prohibit workplace discrimination in work-related areas such as recruiting, hiring, job evaluations, promotion policies, training, compensation, and disciplinary action.

In recent years, the U.S. Supreme Court has made it easier for employees to sue because of discrimination on the job,[70] and a growing number of women have filed lawsuits, citing bias by employers,[71] or sexual harassment by employees. In those cases in which sexual harassment has been found, the plaintiffs have been accorded restitution, and in some cases, juries have awarded substantial damages. Moreover, in recent years, some plaintiffs have been trying to extend the coverage they are accorded by the Civil Rights Act to include protection from bullying tactics and obscene remarks by managers and other members of their workforce. However, the courts appear reluctant to extend coverage to these areas, and a number of jury awards have been set aside by appellate courts that feel that the use of workplace vulgarity or bad manners does not, in and of itself, constitute sexual harassment.[72]

This, however, changed on January 20, 2010, when the United States Court of Appeals, Eleventh Circuit, in Atlanta overturned a lower court's dismissal of the case Ingrid Reeves v. C.H. Robinson Worldwide, Inc. A panel of the appeals court ruled in Reeves's favor. Reeves, the only woman working on the sales floor as a transportation sales representative in the Birmingham, Alabama, branch of Eden Prairie, had been forced to listen to profanity and to gender-derogatory language addressed specifically to women as a group, although it was not directed at her. She also was forced to listen to a morning radio show that regularly talked about topics such as the size of women's breasts and elderly people having sex. This decision opened the opportunity for female employees to pursue hostile work environment claims involving vulgarity.[73]

The area of sexual harassment will continue to be one of ongoing debate. However, one thing is certain: Management in effective firms does not tolerate either harassment or bad conduct and will take action against those who engage in such behavior.

The results from a news poll taken in late 2004 by Workforce Week showed that only 63 percent of the companies participating included sexual orientation in their antidiscrimination policies, and 54 percent stated that their company did not provide gender identity or sexual orientation issues in their diversity training. According to these statistics, management must do more to eliminate discrimination in the workplace. It can be done. For example, Denny's, once known as the most racist company in America, has improved its image among African Americans. It now has minority franchisees, female and minority board members, and a diverse senior management team along with training and scholarships.[74]

The EEOC enforces all federal laws prohibiting job discrimination and handles the litigation in court. In September 2009, the EEOC settled a case against Sears, Roebuck and Company for $6.2 million for disability bias. The suit alleged that Sears maintained an inflexible workers' compensation leave exhaustion policy and terminated employees instead of providing them with reasonable accommodations for their disabilities. Sears was in violation of the American Disabilities Act.[75] "A major change under the ADA Amendments Act of 2008 is that an impairment now qualifies as a disability if, when active, it would substantially limit a major life activity, such as hearing, walking or communicating."[76] In another recent case, Tim Dahle Nissan of Sandy, Utah, lost its case to five female employees who were subjected to unwelcomed sexual comments and conduct, including repeated requests for sexual favors and sexually explicit language in the workplace. The women were awarded $455,000.[77] More women are pursuing claims of pregnancy discrimination with the likelihood of that number increasing in the future.

Age Discrimination Issues

Companies must also be careful not to discriminate against older employees who are protected by the Age Discrimination Act, despite the fact that some firms find that these workers make more money than do younger employees. Some recent age-bias lawsuits have awarded thousands of dollars to older employees who were fired because of their age. In one recent case, a television station was found guilty of discriminating against a news anchor person because of his age. The company was ordered to pay more than one year's back wages and to desist from practices that might violate the civil rights of other employees in the firm.[78]

Obesity and Personal Appearance Issues

The EEOC has declared obesity a protected category under federal disability law. This means that individuals who have been obese for a long period now qualify for federal protection and cannot be fired because of their weight.[79] Another area that is becoming a focal point is personal appearance. Do attractive people perform their jobs better than unattractive people? Evidence reveals that attractive people earn approximately 10 percent more annually than do those with below-average looks; these findings carry over to jobs in which personal appearance has no link to job performance.[80]

Technological Issues

Another dilemma facing more and more companies each day is how to deal with ethical and moral issues involving the Internet, e-commerce operations, cell phones, and other technology devices. Decisions must be made about how to handle privacy issues with employees, suppliers, and customers. To what extent will employees' e-mails be monitored and what will be the consequences for engaging in Internet activities not related to company business? For example, a newscaster reported the firing of an employee who failed to follow company guidelines for using the Internet. The debate goes on about invading individual's privacy when companies place cookies on an individual's hard drive to identify each subsequent time the individual visits the company's Web site. There are also ethical issues about using spam e-mails. As more and more personal information becomes publicly available and is stored and analyzed more easily, managers must establish systems for protecting this information in order to retain not only the trust of employees but also that of customers. The use of personal cell phones in the workplace is another issue. As technology changes and the use of Internet increases, managers also must keep pace by developing systems to protect information and sustain the integrity of the company.

Bioscience Issues

Ethical dilemmas are paramount in the medical field. They impact decisions in research firms, hospitals, and clinics. For example, a woman was diagnosed with breast cancer. Her doctors performed a double mastectomy. Within a few days, she learned she did not have cancer. What ethical responsibility does the hospital have in this case? In another situation, ethical issues are being debated over whether—and how—to ban human cloning technology after it was reported that a 31-year-old American woman had given birth to a 7-pound girl who is her own clone. No evidence of the birth has been provided.[81] The debate, however, continues to explore ethical issues concerning human-embryo and stem-cell research.[82]

Knowledge Management Issues

Knowledge is fast becoming the single most important resource any company can own. Knowledge is the central fiber of most business operations. How can all the widespread knowledge, which exists in so many forms and in so many places, be integrated into a single, accessible resource that adds value to the business? Managers must create systems for knowledge sharing. These systems must allow all people access to the information they need regardless of where they work—in the office or in a remote location. Management cannot discriminate against certain individuals in any way. The challenge of knowledge management is to determine what information within an organization qualifies as "valuable" because all information is not knowledge. Knowledge management is ever changing and must constantly be tested, updated, revised, and sometimes even "obsoleted." With the volatile climate in business today, organizations require a faster cycle of knowledge creation.[83] Xerox was one of the first global companies to get involved in knowledge management when the movement emerged in 1996. Today, Xerox continues to work on creating new innovative systems and infrastructure for information to flow faster and to be more automated. Xerox strives to ward off human relation issues by providing information where it is needed in a timely and accurate manner.

Inequality Between Women and Men Issues

On May 16, 2005, the World Economic Forum released its first study that attempted to quantify the size of the "gender gap" in 58 countries. The study measured the size of the gap between women and men in five critical areas—economic participation, economic opportunity, political empowerment, educational attainment, and health and well-being. Sweden, Norway, Iceland, Denmark, and Finland were ranked at the top of the list, while the United States ranked 17 out of the 58 countries included in the study. The Nordic countries seem to understand the economic incentive behind empowering women. Countries that fail to capitalize on women's talents are clearly undermining their competitive potential. This study indicates that management in the United States has not only an ethical dilemma concerning utilizing women's talents in the workplace, but it also faces real challenges.[84]

Migration of American Jobs Issues

The debate is still going on about the consequences of offshore **outsourcing**—contracting with businesses outside the company to do a designated part of the company's work. Although some feared the loss of jobs, the data show that the loss of gross jobs in the United States, prior to the recession in 2008, had been minimal when compared to the size of the U.S. economy. Today outsourcing is a reality; it provides a challenging new dimension to the manager's job.[85] Analyzing a company's needs and determining what can be done by outside sources, as well as researching and selecting the outsourcing company, take a carefully planned process. Offshore outsourcing firms are primarily located in India, China, and Russia.

Why do businesses use offshore outsourcing? Research shows a variety of reasons. For example, Pfizer uses an outsourcing firm in India to create documents, analyze spreadsheets, schedule meetings, and do research.[86] Five Western drug companies have partnerships with Jubilant Biosys, a world-class science laboratory in India, to research for breakthrough treatments that lead to entirely new medicines for diseases such as Alzheimer's, cancer, or diabetes.[87] Initially, many firms used outsourcing to reduce costs. This, however, does not always work out. Stanley Furniture, an 85-year old maker of home furnishing, has moved all its operations back to the United States. Factors such as cheap goods and labor no longer compensate for things like transportation costs, quality control, and intellectual property issues. Jeff Immelt, CEO, has moved parts of GE's aviation components group back to the United States, which he calls "insourcing." [88] Outsourcing also can provide a virtual workforce for firms when operations fail at a particular location due a natural disaster, such as a snowstorm.

Organizations today are finding that they must develop effective strategies for dealing with these ethical and social responsibility challenges. Good intentions are no longer a defense against poor human relations practices. Business firms must formulate codes of conduct and implement well-designed training programs to build an internal response system that identifies biased or unethical behavior and deals with it quickly and firmly.

CHECK YOUR UNDERSTANDING

Which of the current ethical dilemmas do you feel poses the greatest concern for managers today? Why?

Adapting to International Challenges

International Human Relations Issues.   Concerns about diversity, ethics, and social responsibility are not confined to workplaces in the United States. These are international human relations challenges as well, a fact that has been made particularly evident by the changing makeup of the global workforce. Research shows that the world's workforce will become more mobile and that employers will increasingly reach across borders to find the needed human skills. Hiring personnel from nearby countries is a practice that has been used for decades. However, in the future, it will result in workers being hired from around the globe as the world's supply of labor seeks better salaries and working conditions. Today, much of the world's skilled and unskilled human resources are produced in the developing world (China, India, Indonesia, and Brazil),[89] whereas the best paid jobs are generated in the cities of the industrialized world (the United States, Japan, Germany, and Great Britain). This "mismatch" has several important implications for the future:

1. The triggering of massive relocations of people, such as immigrants, temporary workers, retirees, and visitors. The greatest relocations will involve young, well-educated workers who are flocking to the cities of the developed world.
2. The reevaluation of protectionist immigration policies by some industrialized countries.
3. Economic improvement for countries that have a well-educated population but are economically underdeveloped. Examples are Egypt, Poland, Hungary, and the Philippines.
4. A gradual standardization of labor practices among industrialized countries.[90]

Multinational Corporation Expansion Issues.   Another reason globalization is important is that many multinational enterprises continue to increase their overseas expansion. This means that management must be prepared to deal with people from other cultures and learn to adjust to the way business is conducted in those cultures. The belief that there is one universal method of managing that can be exported to other countries is unfounded. People have different values and beliefs, and the way things are done in the United States is not necessarily the way they are done elsewhere. This is particularly clear if countries are examined on the basis of common traits. One researcher conducted statistical analyses on the cultures of various countries and found that there is a series of "cultural allies," the cultures being similar within groups and different among them. For example, Australia, Canada, Great Britain, New Zealand,

Singapore, and the United States tend to be culturally similar. Argentina, Brazil, Italy, Mexico, Spain, and Venezuela constitute a second group. Austria, Belgium, Finland, France, Germany, the Netherlands, and Sweden make up a third.

The ability to deal with a diversity of cultural groups overseas is a major challenge. One primary reason is the values each society places on lifestyles. For example, the Japanese work longer hours than Americans, and they view work as more important to their life than do people in the United States. In contrast, Americans place stronger value on family life and leisure, whereas Scandinavian countries place an even greater value on quality of life. A multinational company doing business around the world must adjust to local concerns. Expatriate managers must be trained properly to fit into overseas assignments.

An area of special challenge is how business is conducted internationally. What are the ethical and social responsibility issues? The way business is conducted in the United States often is sharply different from the way it is done overseas. For example, in such economic powers as Japan and Germany, women are not prominent in the workplace. In most cases, the best they can hope for is an upper-middle-management position, and this usually is not achieved. As one writer described the situation in Japanese firms:

> *While men are hired with the general assumption that they will build careers with their companies, women are still typically separated into one of the categories—ippan shoku (miscellaneous workers or often simply office ladies) and sogo shoku (a career track).*
>
> *The miscellaneous workers, still legion in every Japanese ministry and large company ... are typically women in their 20s who dress in company uniforms or in smart clothing of their own. They smilingly direct visitors to their appointments and serve tea to guests. Some may do clerical work, sales work, or accounting work, but what they generally do not do ... is rise above this lowly status and enter career tracks largely reserved for men.[91]*

In a 2000 lawsuit brought by a Japanese worker against her employer, the woman charged the firm with sex discrimination. She had worked for her company for 6 years before getting her first small promotion and 21 more years before getting another pay raise. Despite the fact that she earned a college degree during these years and continued to perform well, she never advanced in the company. So she brought legal action and the courts awarded her $55,000 in the largest sex discrimination judgment ever rendered in Japan. However, critics point out that such action is unlikely to change the fact that Japanese corporations have a separate-track personnel management system for men and women. Men are often put on the fast track, whereas women are denied such opportunities, even though in 1985 a landmark antidiscrimination law was passed, and in 1999, amendments were adopted to strengthen the law, including sanctions for sexual harassment. Simply put, most women in Japan do not have equal opportunity in the workplace.[92]

Piracy and Counterfeiting Issues. Another area of ethical concern is piracy and counterfeiting. In China, for example, it is common to find small firms copying computer software, books, records, and other proprietary materials. Dealing with these issues is not easy for American firms because many Chinese businesspeople accept copyright piracy as a way of doing business.[93] They do not perceive these practices as wrong. Moreover, the government sometimes turns its back and ignores what is going on. The international firm, then, is left to deal with the problem, which can be complicated because it involves proprietary rights and human relations challenges. Another example is provided in the "Ethics and Social Responsibility In Action" box.

IN ACTION

GIFTS AND KICKBACKS

In Japan, it is common practice for individuals who are doing business with one another to exchange gifts. Often, these gifts are of low value and are merely a way of complying with a social custom. Sometimes, however, large sums of money change hands as a way of ensuring that a business deal goes through without hitches, an illegal practice in the United States. Foreign firms operating in the United States are careful not to engage in such behavior. These firms know that most American companies not only believe in ethical practices but that many of them have codes of ethical conduct that strictly guide their business behaviors. Given this background, Honda Motors of Japan was surprised to learn that some of its American managers were involved in taking kickbacks and bribes.

The illegal activity began in the 1980s when Honda automobiles, particularly Acuras, were in great demand, and dealers found that they could sell these cars at window price or higher. Because of the strong demand, all the company's dealers wanted a steady supply of these cars, but they were unavailable. Consequently, some of the people who were responsible for managing Honda's U.S. sales operations began to accept money from dealers in exchange for ensuring that they were given a steady supply of these cars. Those interested in obtaining Honda dealerships also found that payments were necessary to ensure the success of the deal.

Eventually, the kickback scheme was uncovered. Honda dealers who did not pay money and were not given a steady supply of popular models complained that other dealers were being favored over them. One individual, whose dealership failed, filed a lawsuit claiming that the cause of his failure was an illegal scheme that limited his dealership's ability to compete. An investigation by federal authorities found that many of these charges were accurate. This, in turn, led to the arrest of more than a dozen executives, including a retired senior vice president of the American Honda Motor Company.

Honda expressed its dismay and anger toward the unethical behavior of these executives. The company cooperated fully with the government and announced that it would carefully review its operating procedures and practices to ensure that nothing like this occurred again. In particular, the firm learned that the management of personnel often requires direct, close contact to ensure that company rules and regulations are not being broken.

Sources: Doron P. Levin, "Wide Fraud Linked to U.S. Executives with Honda Motor," *New York Times*, March 15, 1994, pp. A1, C8; Andrew Stark, "What's the Matter with Business Ethics?" *Harvard Business Review*, May–June 1993, pp. 38–48; "Ethics: A New Profession in American Business," *HR Focus*, May 1993, p. 22; and Richard M. Hodgetts and Fred Luthans, *International Management*, 4th ed. (Irwin/McGraw: Burr Ridge, IL, 2000), chapter 14.

Identify key questions used in conducting a self-evaluation for choosing a career.

✔ CHECK YOUR UNDERSTANDING

You are promoted to manage one of your company's overseas operations.
1. What would be your greatest challenge?
2. How would you prepare for this assignment?

Career Advisor

Choosing a Career

The value of human relations is not confined to managing others. It can also be used in choosing a career and succeeding in that choice. When applied this way, human relations concepts can be employed to evaluate yourself accurately and to succeed in a job hunt.

Conducting a Self-Evaluation.   The most important initial step in applying human relations concepts to your career is that of evaluating yourself. What do you do well? What do you do poorly? In conducting this evaluation, some of the most important questions are the following:

1. What do you do best?
2. What do you like to do?
3. What do you dislike doing?
4. Do you work well with others or do you work best by yourself?
5. Do you know your own talents and abilities? What are they?
6. What do you think you would like to do for a living? Has your education prepared you for this career, or is further training necessary?

7. How hard are you willing to work?
8. What are your work habits? Do you work at a steady pace or in short bursts of intensive effort?
9. Have you sought any information or professional advice regarding your career choice(s)? What have you learned?
10. How will you go about beginning your employment search?

These questions require some thought and soul searching. Throughout this course, you will be exposed to concepts and ideas that should give you direction for finding a meaningful career. Some topics include discussions about motivation, personality, values, group behavior, job design, leadership, communication, conflict, and change. Self-analysis is helpful because it provides basic direction in assessing where you are and where you would like to go. Self-evaluation helps to identify both the preparation requirements and the basic skills that are needed for a successful career. Many companies, for example, require applicants for management jobs to have a college degree and in some cases the degree must be in a particular area. Typically, supervisors and first-line managers do not need specialized degrees, although many firms do like to hire business majors for these positions. Salespeople often are hired with all types of degrees, except when the product is highly technical and the firm knows that engineers make the best salespeople. Other jobs require specific training: Accountants must major in accounting; at advertising agencies, advertising majors have the inside track over other applicants; and most human resources departments will give the nod to those who have majored in human resource management.

An understanding of your basic skills is important; it helps to direct both your educational and your career choices. If you are a highly analytical person, you should look for a career in which this trait is a key factor for success. Examples are banking, market research, operations management, and stock brokering. If you have high social and personal or interactive skills, you should consider such career choices as advertising, personal services, sales, and training and development.

In addition, you should think about your career goals. Research shows that 75 percent of college freshmen believe that hard work counts more than luck in succeeding, 65 percent want to do work that offers opportunities to help others, and 57 percent are willing to work more than 40 hours weekly to reach their career goals. Only 33 percent report that they want to earn a high salary.[94] How do you feel about these findings? What other things do you want from your employer?[95] Now is a good time to answer these questions.

Do Not Underrate Your Ability. In your self-analysis, do not underrate your ability. Otherwise you will be selling yourself short. One way of approaching this subject is to keep in mind that you not only possess ability but that you probably have more than enough ability to undertake most jobs. (This idea will be further discussed in Chapter 14.) People often have more ability than is required by the job.

If you feel you are above average in ability, be sure to take this into consideration. What may be an interesting or challenging job for an average person could prove quite boring to you. Try to match your interests and abilities with the requirements of the job. At the same time, remember that you may not have the opportunity to use all your abilities and talents immediately. Sometimes, the first year or two entails a great deal of technical, boring work, and you will not find the job highly rewarding until you receive one or more promotions. You must be willing to persevere if you want the chance to use your ability. In the next chapter, you will use the information learned from analyzing your self-evaluation questions to develop an overall plan of action for pursuing a career.

Choosing the Right Career. A reader writing to Anne Fisher, an editor for *Fortune* magazine, stated, "Whatever you do, don't let anyone else choose your career for you." The more you know about a field, often the better you like it. Trying different jobs would be ideal, but often is not realistic. Another reader commented, "Don't go into any field just because it pays well." You will spend every penny you make consoling yourself for having a job you hate. Life is too short for that. Just remember that everything changes in time and no career decision is set in stone. You can always change career directions.[96]

 CHECK YOUR UNDERSTANDING

1. In a journal, answer the 10 self-evaluation questions on the previous page. What do the results say about you? Summarize the results in a sentence or two.
2. In another self-evaluation exercise, draw a line down the middle of a sheet of paper. On one side, write your "strengths or likes" and on the other side write your "weaknesses or dislikes." Start jotting down ideas. Ask others to give you feedback. Sometimes their answers can reveal things you may not want to know, but can open your eyes to who you really are.

Summary

1 Explain human relations and its implications for management.

Human relations is a process by which management brings workers into contact with the organization in such a way that the objectives of both groups are achieved. Human relations is people oriented, work oriented, effectiveness oriented, based on empirical experience as opposed to relying solely on intuition and common sense, and useful at all levels of the work hierarchy.

2 Trace the evolution of human relations thinking from industrialism through scientific management to the present.

The modern manager must be concerned with human relations if he or she hopes to be effective. When industrialism emerged in the latter half of the eighteenth century, however, the owner–managers were more interested in efficient production than they were in their employees. This concern for efficiency continued through the nineteenth century and was vigorously promoted by scientific managers. Employing their engineering skills in a work setting, these managers studied plant design, plant layout, machine feed and speed, and a host of other factors that could bring about increased productivity. The greatest weakness of the scientific managers, however, was that they knew very little about the management of people.

3 Compare and contrast the traditional model of the worker with the modern human resources model.

As the scientific management movement progressed, an interest in the behavioral side of management began to grow. It was becoming obvious that concern for production brought about people-related problems and that the effective manager had to be interested in both personnel and the work. The Hawthorne studies revealed the work organization to be a social system and pointed to the need for consideration of psychological and sociological aspects of organizational behavior. The Hawthorne studies helped to light the way for much behavioral research. Since then, the behavioral movement has made great progress.

4 *Discuss the role of behavioral science in human relations.*

Even though, today, the human relations model of management has replaced the traditional model of management, there is still a need to use scientific methods. By using scientific methods, behavioral scientists help unravel many of the mysteries of human behavior at work. Scientists can gather data from using tests and control groups. Questionnaires, surveys, and interviews also provide data that can affect communication, attitudes, and work habits. By learning what motivates employees, managers can use effective reinforcement and rewards to modify employee behavior.

5 *Describe some emerging challenges facing managers today.*

Over the last decade, human relations concerns have not remained static. New challenges have emerged, making it even more important for managers to understand human relations at work. Four major issues now in the forefront are managing knowledge workers, dealing with diversity, addressing ethics and social responsibility concerns, and adapting to international and cultural challenges. Issues that managers face in managing knowledgeable workers include recruiting talented employees, understanding their traits, creating a positive work environment, training and developing these workers, and finding and hiring them. Managing diversity and workforce violence requires dealing with issues such as a multiethnic and diverse workforce, an aging workforce, a permanent temporary workforce, equal pay, women in power, and workplace violence. Current ethical dilemmas include issues such as downsizing, workplace discrimination, age discrimination, obesity and personal appearance, technological, bioscience issues, information management, inequality between women and men, and migration of American jobs. Issues of ethical and social responsibility concerns involve scandals and fraud, the Sarbanes–Oxley Act, whistle-blowing, reasons for unethical behavior, and codes of conduct. Lastly, adapting to international challenges involves the placement of global workers, multinational expansion issues, and piracy and counterfeiting issues—primarily copyright piracy. These areas are interdependent, but each merits individual consideration because of its growing impact on the field of human relations. One topic that directly affects these challenges is that of motivation. This subject will be the focus of attention in the next chapter.

6 *Discuss the ethical dilemmas facing today's managers.*

Human relations is at the core of solving problems involving downsizing issues resulting from reorganization and from people not being treated fairly in the workplace. Other ethical issues include age discrimination, obesity and personal appearance issues, technology advancements, bioscience experiments, knowledge management issues, inequality between women and men, and offshore outsourcing. Organizations must develop effective strategies for dealing with these dilemmas. Their codes of conduct must address these issues. Companies must build an internal system that identifies ethical and social responsibility dilemmas quickly and can deal with them firmly.

7 *Identify key questions used in conducting a self-evaluation for choosing a career.*

Human relations plays a big role in choosing a career and succeeding in it. Human relations concepts are also employed in evaluating one's self accurately and in developing a plan for finding a job. A series of questions you should ask yourself include: What do you do best, what do you like and dislike doing, do you like to work with others or alone, do you know your talents and abilities, how hard are you willing to work, what are your work habits, and how will you begin your employment search, just to list a few. Understanding yourself and your basic skills better will help direct your educational and career choices. It is important not to underrate your abilities or you will be selling yourself short. Once the self-evaluation is completed, an overall plan of action should be prepared.

Key Terms in the Chapter

Human relations	Human relations is the process by which management and workers interact and attain their objectives.
Scientific management	Scientific management sought to merge the people and the work.
Hawthorne studies	The Hawthorne studies started the modern behavioral management movement.
Social networks	Social networks are the informal approaches people use for interacting.
Traditional model	The traditional model is the old way of managing people.
Human resources model	The human resources model views people as having untapped potential.
System 1	System 1 managers are exploitive autocrats.
System 2	System 2 managers are benevolent autocrats.
System 3	System 3 managers are consultative and democratic.
System 4	System 4 managers are participative and democratic.
Scientific method	The scientific method is an objective approach to gaining knowledge.
Behavioral scientists	Behavioral scientists are individuals who apply their training to the study of behavior in organizations.
Test group	A test group is a group that is given some form of treatment.
Control group	A control group is a group that is not given any treatment.
Structured interviews	Structured interviews use specific questions asked in a predetermined manner.
Unstructured interviews	Unstructured interviews follow a general direction but no rigidly set format.
Glass ceiling	A glass ceiling is an artificial barrier preventing women from being promoted.
Ethics	Ethics is the study of standards and moral judgment.
Social responsibility	Social responsibility is the obligations of a business to society.
Code of conduct	A guide summarizing the ethical principles and standards for individual behavior.
Outsourcing	Contracting with an outside company to complete part of a firm's work.

Review and Study Questions

1. What is human relations? Define the term in your own words.

2. How much did the owner–managers of factories in the latter half of the eighteenth century know about human relations? Describe the model used by management.

3. What did scientific managers know about human relations? What were their shortcomings in this area?

4. What were some of the principal findings of the Hawthorne studies? Why were these findings important?

5. Are happy workers also productive workers? Explain.

6. How does the traditional model differ from the human resources model? Compare and contrast the two models.

7. How does a System 1 manager differ from a System 2 manager? How does a System 3 manager differ from a System 4 manager? Which of these systems is most reflective of the human resources philosophy? Why?

8. In analyzing behavioral problems, practitioners of modern human relations rely on the scientific method. What is the logic behind this statement?

9. What do managers need to know about managing knowledge workers?

10. Why is the management of diversity so important to the study of human relations? Why is the management of diversity likely to become more important in the next decade?

11. What do you foresee as the trend in managing the permanent temporary workforce?

12. Describe the issues involved in cutting workers wages during downsizing and layoffs during failing economic conditions.

13. What are your thoughts on managing obesity in the workplace? Should personal appearance of employees be questioned?

14. What are two of the major ethical problems with which managers must deal? In what way is training of value in helping managers do this?

15. How can a code of conduct help build an ethical environment?

16. Why are more and more organizations interested in preparing their managers to deal with international and cultural challenges?

17. How can counterfeiting be controlled, especially when this practice is not perceived to be wrong?

18. What types of questions should a person ask when conducting a career-related self-evaluation? List several questions.

19. How can understanding your basic skills help in choosing a career? Explain.

Connecting to the Real World

What should the professor do?

At a local university, Professor Miller administered a major exam to 48 students in one of his management classes. Later in the day, Professor Miller received an email from Jason, a student in his class. Jason appeared to be upset. He felt that three students sitting near him had cheated on the exam. Jason stated that he noticed several times during the exam that Brian, a student sitting near him, was looking at his cell phone and it appeared he was retrieving information. Also, Mark and Travis, sitting directly across the aisle on each side of Brian were continually glancing at Brian's exam paper.

While monitoring the exam, Professor Miller failed to notice any of these activities. Upon examining the three student's test results, the professor noticed that all three of the students missed the same questions. This raised the same question in his mind as that of Jason's. Did these students cheat on the exam?

You may find it helpful to discuss the ethical issues in this case with a classmate. After analyzing this case, prepare written answers to these questions:

1. Identify the ethical dilemmas present in this case for each participant—Jason, Brian, Mark, Travis, and Professor Miller.
2. What are the consequences of Jason's whistle-blowing actions? Discuss the pros and cons.
3. What course of action should Professor Miller take? Why?
4. What are your ethical standards concerning your behavior in completing your college assignments? Do you feel your standards meet or exceed the norm set by other students? Why or why not?
5. How will your ethical standards impact your job and your career?

CASE
What Did Carly Do Wrong and Hurd Do Right?

From 1999 to 2005, Carly Fiorina changed the way management operated at Hewlett-Packard (HP). She did what HP's board of directors hired her to do—turn the sluggish company into a top worldwide competitive company. At first her ideas did not always fit well with all members of the board—after all, she was a young woman, aged 44, who was using too much power to make changes too quickly. Although it was not easy, she managed to successfully complete the controversial $19-billion-dollar merger with Compaq Computer within three years of being hired.

Fiorina's own management style penetrated the entire company. She is direct, articulate, driven, decisive, customer-focused, and successful. Others describe her as unshakable, self-reliant, and impervious to criticism. She is a market-focused executive skilled in major organizational change. She has been described as everything from brilliant and visionary to arrogant and self-serving; but one thing is certain: She expects the very best from her 141,000 employees. Fiorina believes that HP's culture should be based on performance, self-motivation, and high achievement. When she arrived, HP was a flat, decentralized company, with individual departments having a great deal of autonomy. Consensus was how decisions were made. Within the first year, Fiorina aggressively reorganized HP's business units and laid off 6,000 employees, about 7 percent of the workforce, to cut costs. She turned the company into a top-down, do-as-I-say company where most of the important decision making was concerned. She centralized power by reducing the number of business units from 83 to just a handful and consolidating

executive authority through her office. But these movements, along with the merger, failed to raise profit margins.

The consensus-driven style had its problems. Because power was concentrated at the lower levels in the organization, it took too much time to get things done. Now decisions were made more quickly. Before Fiorina, people were reluctant to make decisions until they had all the facts. After Fiorina, it was okay to take risks and go with just 80 percent of the data. Of course, not everyone was happy with HP's new culture. "It's a culture of fear right now," said a former director-level employee. "Nobody believes their job is secure, and it's become habitual to wonder when your number is going to come up. Morale also is suffering in parts of the company where managers who were used to their own empires now have to coordinate their activities."

In the pre-Fiorina days, HP concentrated on innovation and product development. After Fiorina, who came from outside the firm, was hired, the market reigned supreme, with all employees focused on customer needs. It was an environment of finding out what the customer needs, so HP would know what to make next. The new mindset was "people first, technology second." Research and analysis were still important, but so was speed. Employees were held accountable for increasing customer loyalty and having fewer at-risk customers. As well as serving customers more effectively, employees were asked to perform at a higher level. If employees performed poorly, they were given a specific time to improve their performance. The company tried to deal with unacceptable performance in a positive way. During the economic slowdown after September 11, 2001, employees were ranked and were told that people without competitive skills would be terminated. Fiorina believed that employees should be rewarded and promoted based on results, not on longevity or who they know. All of these changes and standards had an impact on the workplace at HP, making it a very different workplace from that before Carly Fiorina was hired.

On February 9, 2005, the board of directors of HP announced that Carly Fiorina had stepped down as chairman and CEO. The board stated that Fiorina had a strategic vision and had put in place a plan that had given HP the capabilities to compete and win; however, the board felt she had failed to execute on her ambitious strategy. Profits were uneven, HP had lost market share, stockholders were unhappy, and the price of HP's stock had fallen by 50 percent. Carly apparently had failed to manage the "HP Way."

HP's board hired Mark Hurd to replace Carly as HP's CEO, and in four years, he lifted the company to the world's biggest technology company and one of the most admired companies. HP has become a benchmark of efficiency in the industry. Mark is a manager obsessed with numbers and execution. Because of his pragmatic, unsentimental personality, he abandoned many of Carly's radical organizational schemes and went back to a simple reporting structure based on product families—getting products out on time, improving quality and service, and increasing profit margins. He is described as a tough guy. He uses many technical terms. Infrastructure and leverage are two of his favorites. When Mark fails to understand the HP Way, he turns to the HP Alumni Association, which is a huge asset for him. He has an uncanny ability to get things done.

Mark Hurd is not merely a cost cutter; he is an unrepentant left-brainer who personally tracks and analyzes his daily tasks using a spreadsheet. These traits make him an ideal CEO during tough times. He is a no-nonsense, competitive, efficiency-driven person and sometimes that means turning down employee requests for using more technology or trimming down the workforce.

Case Questions

1. Does Carly Fiorina subscribe to the traditional model or the human resources model? Defend your answer.
2. Which model fits Mark Hurd? Why did you choose that model?
3. Contrast the differences between the two CEOs. Select the CEO you would like to work for and tell why.
4. How would you describe Fiorina and Hurd in terms of Systems 1 through 4? Which one best fits her approach and which one best fits his approach to managing people? Tell why.
5. What management problems do you foresee for Fiorina as she moves into a new management position? How compatible is her style of management with today's workforce?
6. What kind of company would need Fiorina's talents and expertise?
7. As the workforce changes, what dilemmas do you foresee that Mark Hurd will need to address to continue as HP's CEO?

Sources: Shari Caudron, "Don't Mess with Carly," *Workforce*, July 2003, p. 15; Jesse Eisinger, "Carly Fiorina Fails at Hewlett-Packard after Betting Badly," *Wall Street Journal*, January 26, 2005, p. C1; George Anders, "How the Traits that Aided the Climb to the Top Hurt after She Arrived There," *Wall Street Journal*, February 10, 2005, p. A1; Pui-Wing Tam, "Hewlett-Packard Board Considers a Reorganization," *Wall Street Journal*, January 24, 2005, p. A1; Michael S. Malone, "Opinion: The Weekend Interview with Mark Hurd," *Wall Street Journal*, April 14–15, 2007, p. A9; and Adam Lashinsky, "Mark Hurd's Moment," *Fortune*, March 16, 2009, pp. 91–100.

CHAPTER 2

Fundamentals of Motivation

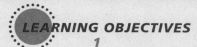

LEARNING OBJECTIVES

1
Describe the two sides of motivation: movement and motive.

2
Identify the five basic needs in Maslow's need hierarchy and differentiate among them.

3
Describe the two-factor theory of motivation and explain its relevance to the practicing manager.

4
Discuss expectancy theory, noting how both valence and expectancy influence motivational force.

5
Explain the value of money, employee satisfaction, incentives, and recognition in the motivation process.

6
Develop a "plan of action" for finding a job.

One of the most important questions in human relations today is: How do you get people to do things? The answer rests on an understanding of what motivation is all about, for it is motivated workers who ultimately get things done, and without such people, no organization can hope to be effective. In this chapter, the fundamentals of motivation are examined.

Maintaining Motivation

The U.S. economy has had its ups and downs over the past decade. The decade started with the tragic events of September 11, 2001, changing forever the way business was conducted. In the following years, businesses began to expand and profits were good. Greed became rampant, driving many business decisions, and stories of fraud began to appear almost daily in the media. Problems were created in the mortgage, banking, and financial industries resulting in the collapse of the housing markets and the downfall of many banks, both creating problems for the automobile industry. As a result, many businesses were forced to shut down or lay off employees, raising the unemployment rate to over 10 percent, the highest in twenty-six years. Managers were faced with some tough decisions on how to motivate the remaining employees. When times are tough, motivating employees is not always a high priority; often it is simply survival.

The best employees are still in high demand and are the ones to help turn around the company. If the organization is not motivating them, they will move on. In the midst of this turmoil, however, one question has remained the same: How can managers more effectively motivate their people? The answer is: Not the way they have been doing so in the past.

Engaging in two-way communication is what really motivates employees, as well as managers. Motivation comes from knowing that employees are being listened to, which gives them a feeling they have a stake in the game. For example, one of Warren Buffett's managers recently stated, "Warren makes us feel like we can do no wrong." Employee motivation programs can be powerful tools that motivate better performance by reinforcing success-building behaviors and boost retention. When reward options are meaningful and desirable, the employee motivation program is on its way to success.

What do employees want from their jobs? After reviewing recent research, Bob Nelson identified six dimensions that any manager or organization can implement to create a more motivating work environment:[1]

1. Create a clear and compelling direction
2. Encourage direct, open, and honest communication
3. Involve employees and encourage initiatives
4. Increase employee autonomy, flexibility, and support
5. Focus continuously on career growth and development
6. Recognize and reward high performance

Not all motivation efforts are based on monetary rewards, however; money still talks, but making recognition personal is on the rise. Globoforce, a designer of corporate recognition programs for clients like Intuit, Procter & Gamble, and Dow Chemical, allows employees to choose a reward they want rather than the company making the choice for them. What types of rewards are being granted? They come in many forms other than the traditional benefits. Examples are stock option plans and stock incentive plans, which are different from employee stock ownership plans and are used to entice executives and CEOs to perform at certain levels. Another strategy is split-dollar insurance policies, whose purpose is to provide tax-free pay and loans to top executives, not life insurance protection. Ownership is another motivator. Employee engagement also is gaining favor. In a recent study, employee engagement was found to be correlated with high levels of quality, productivity, and attendance.

Lincoln Electric Company of Cleveland, Ohio, has been cited as one of the best workplaces in America. Since 1934, Lincoln has been known for its incentive management system. Its benefits are closely aligned with financial performance.

The U.S. Navy won the 2009 Optimas Award in General Excellence for making improvements to its maternity benefits, parental leave, and flexible work options. Likewise, Discovery Communications provides on-site health and wellness clinics staffed with a full-time doctor, a nurse practitioner, and two medical assistants. Free massages and yoga classes are popular amenities. In more cases than not, companies try to motivate their employees with nonmonetary rewards.

Describe the two sides of motivation: movement and motive.

What Is Motivation?

The psychological drive that directs a person toward an objective is **motivation**. The word comes from the Latin word *movere*, "to move." When we see people working hard, we say that they are motivated because we can see them moving. This is as true for a person sitting at a computer typing one hundred words a minute as it is for an executive slowly reading a complex legal document. Yet motivation involves more than just movement. A student staring at some notes on a piece of paper may be memorizing this information, but we see virtually no movement occurring. Thus, motivation involves both physical *and* mental movement. "Motivation is a set of processes that moves a person toward a goal."[2]

In addition, any systematic analysis of motivation must be concerned with both *how* and *why* people act as they do. The former may be easy to pinpoint, but the latter often is not easy to identify. For example, Ralph has been offered time-and-a-half pay to work

What Motivates You?

Many things motivate people. The following list contains ten work-motivating factors. Read the list carefully and place a 10 next to the factor that has the greatest work-motivating potential for you. Place a 9 next to the second most important work-motivating factor. Continue until you have rank-ordered all ten. If you do not currently work, mentally choose a job for yourself and use it in completing the list.

1. _____ Interesting work
2. _____ Job security
3. _____ Up-to-date equipment

4. _____ A feeling of doing something important
5. _____ Good wages
6. _____ Challenging work
7. _____ Effective supervision by the boss
8. _____ A chance for advancement
9. _____ Pleasant working conditions
10. _____ The opportunity to succeed at what you are doing

The interpretation of your answers can be found at the end of the book under "Time Out Answers."

on Saturdays, and he has agreed to do so. We can, therefore, respond to the question "How do you get Ralph to work on a Saturday?" by answering "Money." However, we cannot say with certainty *why* he is willing to work on a Saturday. It may be because he wants to buy a boat, go on a vacation, put aside some money for a rainy day, or help pay some hospital bills for an elderly aunt. The "why" is currently unclear, and if we want to know the reason, we must investigate his motives. Motivation, therefore, has two sides: *movement* and *motive*. The former can be seen, whereas the latter can only be inferred. Before reading on, take the quiz "What Motivates You?" in the "Time Out" box and then read the interpretation of the results at the end of this chapter. This quiz should provide some insights into your own job-related motivation.

The "whys" of behavior are the **motives**. Often, they are defined as needs, drives, wants, or impulses within the individual. Regardless of how they are defined, however, motives arouse and maintain activity as well as determine the general direction of an individual's behavior. Many psychologists believe that there are two types of motives: primary and secondary. Primary motives are unlearned. The needs for food and shelter are examples. In contrast, secondary needs are learned. The needs for power, achievement, and affiliation are examples.

In studying how motives prompt people to action, we must first examine two related topics: motive strength and goals. Motives are *directed toward goals*. For example, a person who needs money (motive) will opt for overtime (goal). An individual who desires recognition (motive) will strive for promotion to the top ranks of the organization (goal).

Of course, an individual often has many motives or needs and cannot actively pursue all of them simultaneously. To determine which motives a person will attempt to satisfy through activity, it is necessary to examine *motive strength*. In Figure 2.1, a diagram of relative motive strengths, Motive 7 has the greatest strength and will receive the most activity. An individual will work hardest to satisfy this motive. On the other hand, Motive 2 has a very low strength and will be given the lowest priority. Finally, once a motive or need is satisfied, it will no longer motivate an individual to seek goal-directed behavior. Therefore, after Motive 7 is satisfied, an individual will direct behavior toward activities to fulfill Motive 3. Once that motive is satisfied, an individual will proceed to seek satisfaction for Motives 5, 4, 8, 6, 1, and 2, in that order.

When an individual is given the opportunity to attain a desired goal, he or she is positively motivated and will pursue that objective. Sometimes, however, an organization will use *negative motivation* because an individual has done something wrong, such as committing a major violation of company policy. In this case, the person may be turned down for promotion or be suspended from work without pay for a predetermined period, such as three weeks. Negative motivation is used to enforce rules and to shape employee behavior.

But before you can improve it, you must first understand the key elements that foster—or ruin—morale

by Benson Smith and Tony Rutigliano

For many companies, 2008 will prove to have been a lackluster year financially. Even historically, low interest rates couldn't produce the much-heralded second-half recovery. To make matters worse, most business news seems focused on threats rather than on opportunities. Competitive threats, economic threats, terrorist threats, the potential impact of war, and a prolonged occupation of Iraq are all contributing to a malaise among businesses. Is it any wonder that so many managers are concerned about their sales forces' morale?

So, how is morale among your salespeople? Perhaps more importantly, how do you know, and what can you do to improve it? Let's look at a scenario that may seem very familiar to you.

Shortly before an upcoming annual sales meeting, the company president asked the vice president of sales a pointed question: "How is morale?" The V.P. hemmed and hawed before admitting that morale wasn't so great.

"I'm afraid our troops are a little down," the V.P. said. "Competition is getting tougher. And with the economy still in the doldrums, many of our customers are feeling the pinch. Orders aren't as robust as they should be. All this has a negative effect on our commission structure, so people aren't as pumped up as I would like them to be."

"So what the heck are you doing about it?" the president barked.

"Well," the V.P. answered, "we're throwing a few extra dollars into the commission pot. We're planning a big first-quarter promotion. And we're going to give away a BMW to the first salesperson who breaks the $2 million mark this year. That should get our troops juiced up and give us something positive to talk about at the upcoming sales meeting."

After the sales meeting, the V.P. came back to the home office and was happy to report that the sales force responded enthusiastically to those changes. "They're all primed and ready to go," he told the president. "You should have seen the looks on their faces when we announced the car contest," he said. "They couldn't wait to get back home and start selling!"

"Really?" the president asked, unconvinced.

Wouldn't you be skeptical, too? Did the V.P. really solve the problem? Or was he deluded? Do these types of programs and gestures actually improve morale?

Before we can answer that, we have to ask an even more basic question: What exactly is "morale" anyway? Sales managers agree that morale is important, but they seem to interpret it in very different ways. Is morale something we can clearly define? Is it something we can measure? Is it something we can improve? Is it even important?

Based on The Gallup Organization's substantial research, we can tell you that the answer to each of these questions is an emphatic *yes*. But our research also reveals some very disturbing facts about morale in most sales forces—facts that every sales manager must understand.

First, let's start with a meaningful definition. Morale is best thought of as the emotional attachment or sense of engagement

If used incorrectly, negative motivation can result in low morale. Morale impacts motivation, which in turn affects production and how things get done. To build a motivated workforce, research suggests that management pay more attention to creating and fostering an environment that promotes good morale. Read "Morale Stinks!" in the "In Action" box and think of things your employer could do to increase morale where you work.

Figure 2.1 Motives and Motive Strength

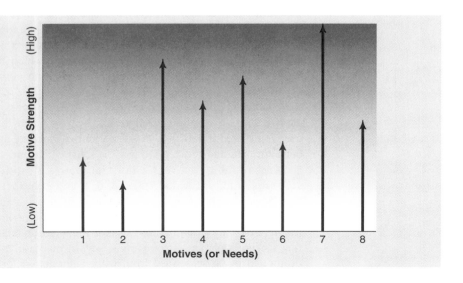

a salesperson has for his or her job. We know that engagement has a direct and meaningful relationship to the results every sales manager gets paid to deliver. Sales teams with high engagement levels are more productive, are more profitable, and develop far more sustainable customer relationships.

So, sales managers and presidents alike are quite right to be concerned about morale. It is too important to leave to guesstimates.

In fact, engagement is so important that sales managers must pay constant attention to improving it within their ranks. But our extensive studies show this is often far from the case. In most sales forces Gallup has studied, we find that as many as two-thirds to three-quarters of individuals in the sales force are operating at engagement levels that substantially inhibit the workgroup's performance.

Research also suggests that short-term fixes, like tweaks in commission plans, new contests, or even giving away BMWs, have very short-lived effects on improving the engagement or morale of sales forces.

Sure, your sales force might act excited at the sales meeting when these tweaks are announced. But most sales forces have been conditioned to react positively at such gatherings. They have been explicitly or implicitly coached to hoot and holler at just the right moments, and they can deliver standing ovations precisely on cue. These outward signs of "good morale" are as credible as the Pavlovian laughter of a sitcom's live studio audience.

In most instances, your sales force's morale is driven much more by local management than by home office policies.

Frontline managers improve morale by setting clear expectations, providing needed resources, focusing sales reps' attention on what they do best, showing frequent appreciation for their efforts, and providing a culture in which they can learn and grow. Those are the key ingredients that create emotional attachment to a company.

When frontline managers pay attention to these fundamentals, engagement improves dramatically and quickly. And improved engagement levels relate to key business outcomes.

Too often, we think that if we simply wait until business gets better, then morale will improve accordingly. A more effective strategy is to focus on improving employee engagement, which can lead to improved business outcomes. This is especially true in tough times when improved engagement levels can be a conspicuous competitive advantage.

Every manager, from the president on down, should rightfully be concerned about the morale or engagement of his or her employees. Our research suggests that it's much too important to leave to guesswork or quick fixes.

Benson Smith is a consultant, speaker, and author for The Gallup Organization and an expert in the area of sales-force effectiveness.

Tony Rutigliano is a senior managing consultant, speaker, and author for The Gallup Organization and an expert in sales-force effectiveness, organizational effectiveness, and talent assessment.

Sources: Gallup Management Journal, January 9, 2003. All rights reserved. Reprinted with permission from gmj.gallup.com.

CHECK YOUR UNDERSTANDING

1. What motivates you?
2. How does movement differ from motive?
3. A primary motive is _____ whereas a secondary motive is _____.
4. Identify three personal motives and rate each one according to its motive strength for you.
5. What kind of motivation fits the statement: "Failure to meet the deadline will be reflected on your evaluation."

Identify the five basic needs in Maslow's need hierarchy and differentiate among them.

The Need Hierarchy

We have examined motives or needs in very general terms. What kinds of needs do people have that, in turn, result in goal-directed behavior? Abraham Maslow, the noted psychologist, has set forth five needs that he believes are universal: *physiological, safety, social, esteem,* and *self-actualization* (see Figure 2.2).

Physiological Needs

The most fundamental of all needs, according to Maslow, are **physiological needs**. Some common examples are food, clothing, and shelter. A person deprived of everything would want to satisfy these basic needs first. Safety, social, esteem, and self-actualization needs would be of secondary importance.

Figure 2.2 Maslow's
Need Hierarchy When
Physiological Needs
Are Dominant

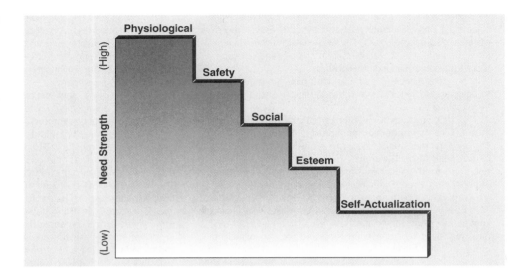

Figure 2.2 Maslow's Need Hierarchy When Physiological Needs Are Dominant

In the workplace, many organizations try to satisfy physiological needs by providing cafeterias, vending machines, adequate ventilation, lighting, heating, and other physical facilities. In addition, the firms pay workers a salary with which they can meet these needs by purchasing food and clothing for themselves and their families. Although many physiological needs exist, the most basic would get prime attention until satisfied and then would be replaced by other physiological demands with greater need strength.

Safety Needs

Once physiological needs are basically satisfied, **safety needs** replace them. These are of two types. First, there is the need for *survival;* this need is so great that many of the laws in our society are designed to protect lives. Second, there is the need for *security;* this need has physical and psychological dimensions. On the physical side, businesses often provide safety equipment and safety rules for protecting workers on the job. They also provide accident, health, and life insurance to help meet employees' safety needs. The psychological aspect of safety is evident in workers' desire for secure jobs in a predictable environment. Individuals who work in government bureaucracies often fall into this category. They want guaranteed employment. Their pay may not be very high, but they are assured of a steady job. Other people find such safety in business bureaucracies where, although it may not pay well, a firm just about guarantees continued employment to anyone who performs even minimally.

Social Needs

When physiological and safety needs are basically satisfied, **social needs** become important motivators. These needs involve interaction with others for the purpose of meaningful relationships. On the job, interaction often occurs among people who work near one another and come into frequent daily contact. Over time, they build up friendships and look forward to the interaction. In their personal lives, people fulfill social needs when they meet their friends and neighbors and socialize with them.

Business firms try to meet this need by allowing workers to interact and talk with one another. On assembly lines, workers know they can do their routine jobs and interact at the same time. In retail and banking firms, there is an increased opportunity for interaction because the workers carry out their jobs by socializing to some degree with the customers.

It is important to note that social affiliation helps to make boring, routine work more bearable. When such interaction occurs, morale is higher and productivity tends to remain at least within tolerable ranges. However, when social interaction is denied, workers tend to fight the system by restricting work output or by doing no more than is required by their job descriptions. By allowing employees to fulfill social needs on the job, negative behaviors are often prevented.

Esteem Needs

When social needs are basically satisfied, **esteem needs** come into play. People need to feel important, and self-esteem and self-respect are vital in this process. Esteem is much more *psychological* in nature than the other three needs we have discussed. We can give a person food, clothing, shelter, protection, and social interaction. However, the esteem with which individuals regard themselves is mostly a function of what they allow themselves to believe. For example, a person who is told by his boss that he does an excellent job will be motivated by this praise only if he accepts the laudatory comments. If the individual believes that the manager is complimenting his work only as a matter of course and is insincere, the praise will have no motivational effect. Research reveals that two motives closely related to esteem are prestige and power.[3]

Prestige.   For many people, **prestige** means "keeping up with the Joneses," or perhaps getting ahead of them. In any event, prestige carries with it respect and status and influences the way people talk and act around an individual. A company president has considerable prestige and is treated with great respect by organizational members. Out on the golf course, however, the company president may have limited prestige among the players, and the country club's golf pro is given the greatest amount of respect. Thus, one's prestige depends on the situation.

Power.   The ability to influence or induce behavior in others is **power**. Power can be of two kinds: positional and personal. *Positional* power is derived from an individual's position in the company. The president has a great deal more positional power than does a middle manager in the same organization, for instance. *Personal* power is derived from an individual's personality and behavior. Anne may have a pleasing personality and an easygoing manner, which results in her being able to cut across departmental lines and gain support for her proposals; Andy, however, is considered hard-nosed and bossy and is unable to secure such cooperation. Within bounds, people like power because it provides them with feelings of self-esteem.[4]

Self-Actualization Needs

When all the other needs are basically satisfied, **self-actualization needs** manifest themselves. Because people satisfy these needs in so many different ways, behavioral scientists know less about them than about the other needs. However, research reveals that two motives are related to self-actualization: competence and achievement.

Competence.   **Competence** is similar to power in that it implies control over environmental factors. At a very early age, children begin illustrating their need for competence by touching and handling objects to become familiar with them. Later on, they begin trying to take things apart and put them back together again. As a result, children learn tasks at which they are competent.

On the job, the competence motive reveals itself in the form of a desire for job mastery and professional growth. An individual begins matching his or her abilities and skills against the environment in a contest that is challenging but that can be won.

Organizations that provide meaningful, challenging work help their people meet the need for competence. In some companies, such as those using assembly lines, such jobs are not in abundance, and the competence motive often goes unsatisfied.

Achievement.   Over the last fifty years, a great deal of research has been conducted on people's desire for **achievement**. One of the leading researchers, David C. McClelland of Harvard University, has been particularly interested in this urge.[5] On the basis of his research, he has set forth the following characteristics of **high achievers**. High achievers:

- Like situations in which they can take personal responsibility for finding solutions to problems.
- Tend to be moderate risk takers.
- Like concrete feedback on their performance so that they know how well they are doing.

Although only about 10 percent to 15 percent of the population in the United States has the desire to achieve, high achievement can be encouraged and developed. McClelland has recommended several methods for individuals who want to become high achievers:

- Strive to obtain feedback so your successes can be noted and you can make them serve as reinforcement for strengthening your desire to achieve even more.
- Pick out people you know who have performed well and use them as models to emulate.
- Modify your self-image by imagining yourself as someone who needs to succeed and to be challenged.
- Control your daydreaming by thinking and talking to yourself in positive terms.[6]

How can you use these ideas? The "Human Relations in Action" box offers some specific steps.

On the job, organizations help create the proper climate for developing high achievement by giving people jobs that provide feedback, increase personal initiative, and allow individuals to take moderate risks. However, although the enterprise can encourage its personnel toward high achievement, to a large degree this drive is something that develops in early childhood. Also, high achievers get things done themselves but often are ineffective in managing others, so organizations do not want all their employees to possess a high achievement drive.

Need Mix

An important premise of the need hierarchy is that as one need is basically fulfilled, the next most important need becomes dominant and dictates individual behavior. Note that we say "basically fulfilled." This is because most people in our society are *partially satisfied* and *partially dissatisfied* at each level. Greatest satisfaction tends to occur at the physiological level and least satisfaction at the self-actualization level. Maslow puts it this way:

> *In actual fact, most members of our society who are normal are partially satisfied in all their basic needs and partially unsatisfied in all their basic needs at the same time. A more realistic description of the hierarchy would be in terms of decreasing percentage of satisfaction as we go up the hierarchy of prepotency. For instance, if I may assign arbitrary figures, … it is as if the average citizen is satisfied perhaps 85 percent in his physiological needs, 70 percent in his safety needs, 50 percent in his [social] needs, 40 percent in his self-esteem needs, and 10 percent in his self-actualization needs.[7]*

IN ACTION

HUMAN RELATIONS IN ACTION

INCREASING YOUR ACHIEVEMENT DRIVE

There are many things you can do to increase your achievement drive. The following are the most helpful.

1. *Put your goals in writing.* This serves two useful purposes. First, it forces you to think through your objectives. Exactly what are you trying to accomplish? Second, it serves as a basis for comparing desired and actual progress.
2. *Make the goals challenging yet attainable.* If the goals are easy to attain, you really are not achieving much. If the goals are too difficult, you will not be able to reach them. Choose objectives that stretch you but are within your grasp. In this way, the goals become learning devices that help you grow.
3. *Be sure your goals are compatible.* If your goals are not compatible, you are working at cross-purposes with yourself. For example, if one of your objectives is to double your sales this quarter, it is unrealistic to have a second objective of cutting travel and entertainment by 30 percent. If anything, this budget will probably go up because you will have to do more traveling and entertaining.
4. *Have specific goals.* Where possible, quantify your goals; for example, you might wish to reduce production costs by 7 percent, increase sales by 9 percent, and increase the number of salespeople by twenty-two. If this is not possible or desirable, write the objective in such a way that progress can be measured.
5. *Establish timetables.* Tie your goals to a timetable, noting when progress will be achieved. This will help you to keep track of how well you are doing. If you start to fall behind, you will be able to identify when and where things are going wrong.
6. *Establish priorities.* Determine which goals must be attained first and which ones can wait. If sales have to be increased as quickly as possible, put this goal high on your list of things to do. If trips to the field to check on your salespeople can wait until next month, schedule them for next month and get back to work on those things that must be done now.
7. *Review and revise your goals.* Look over your list of goals every ninety days and see how well you are doing. Have any of the goals been attained? If so, remove them from the list. Do any of the current objectives need to be changed? If so, change them. Do any new ones need to be added? Put them on the list. This process keeps your goal-directed behavior properly focused.
8. *Reward yourself.* Every time you accomplish one of your objectives, reward yourself. When you close that big sale, treat yourself to dinner or buy that suit you have had your eye on. This work–reward approach will encourage you to keep up your efforts. Remember that successful people are good to themselves. If one of your subordinates did something well, you would reward the individual as a way of encouraging a repeat performance. Be no less kind to yourself.

As a result, Maslow's needs hierarchy cannot be viewed as an all-or-nothing framework. Rather, to understand the fundamentals of human behavior, we should regard the hierarchy as useful in predicting behavior on a high- or low-probability basis. For example, among people who come from abject poverty, the **need mix** pictured in Figure 2.3 probably is highly representative. However, most people in American society are characterized by strong social or affiliation needs, relatively strong esteem and safety needs, and somewhat less important physiological and self-actualization needs; this need mix is illustrated in Figure 2.4. For individuals whose physiological, safety, and social needs are greatly satisfied, esteem and self-actualization are most important. A person born to great wealth would fit into this category, as would a top management executive. The need mix for these people is pictured in Figure 2.5. Of course, these configurations are intended only as examples. Different configurations would be appropriate for different people because, in reality, the need mix changes from one individual to another. Maslow's theory is interesting, but its practical value is limited. To see its application to the motivation of personnel, we must turn to Frederick Herzberg's two-factor theory.

✔ CHECK YOUR UNDERSTANDING

1. List Maslow's hierarchy of needs, starting with the most fundamental of all needs. Give an example of how each need can be met in the workplace.
2. Explain how competence and achievement are relative to self-actualization needs.
3. How does the need mix work?
4. Using Figure 2.4, identify the needs that have the highest strength for you. Why?

Figure 2.3 Need Mix When Physiological and Safety Needs Have the Highest Strength

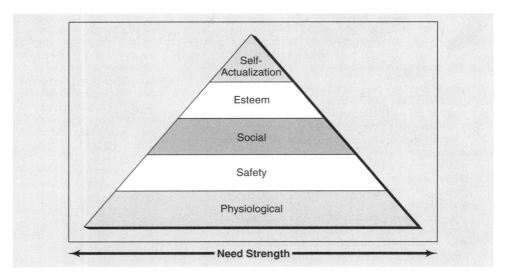

Figure 2.4 Need Mix When Social Needs Have the Highest Strength

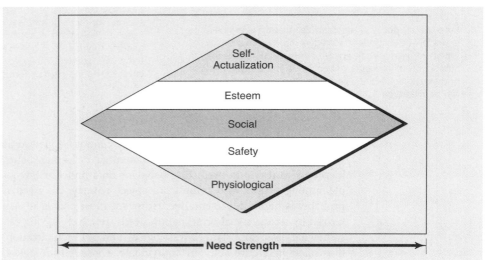

Figure 2.5 Need Mix When Esteem and Self-Actualization Needs Have the Highest Strength

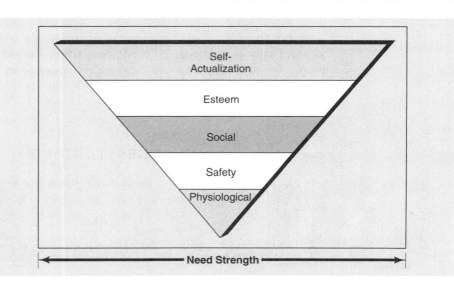

Table 2.1
The Two-Factor Theory

Hygiene Factors (Environment)	Motivators (Work Itself)
Salary	Recognition
Technical supervision	Advancement
Working conditions	Possibility of growth
Company policies and administration	Achievement
Interpersonal relations	Work itself

Describe the two-factor theory of motivation and explain its relevance to the practicing manager.

The Two-Factor Theory

The two-factor theory of motivation is a direct result of research conducted by Frederick Herzberg and his associates on job satisfaction and productivity among two hundred accountants and engineers.[8] Each subject was asked to think of a time when he or she felt especially good about his or her job and a time when he or she felt particularly bad about the job and to describe the conditions that led to these feelings. The researchers found that the employees named different types of conditions for good and bad feelings. This led Herzberg to conclude that motivation consists of two factors: hygiene and motivators (Table 2.1).

Hygiene Factors

Herzberg called the factors associated with negative feelings **hygiene factors**. Illustrations included salary, technical supervision, working conditions, company policies and administration, and interpersonal relations. When the subjects of Herzberg's study were asked what made them feel exceptionally bad about their jobs, typical answers included: "I'm really not satisfied with the salary I'm being paid; it's much too low." "My boss is always too busy to offer me any technical supervision." "The working conditions around here are really poor." All the responses have one thing in common: They relate to the environment in which the work is performed.

Herzberg called these environment-related factors *hygiene* because, like physical hygiene, they prevent deterioration but do not lead to growth. For example, if you brush your teeth (a hygiene step), you can prevent cavities, but your teeth will not become stronger nor will a chipped tooth grow back to its original size. Thus, you have two alternatives: Brush your teeth and prevent further damage, or do not brush your teeth and end up losing them. Analogously, Herzberg felt that if you provide for hygiene factors, you will not give individuals motivation but you will prevent dissatisfaction.[9] Figure 2.6 illustrates how Herzberg believes hygiene can affect performance. Note that when hygiene factors are satisfied, performance does not increase. When hygiene factors are not satisfied, performance drops. Thus, hygiene will not bring about an increase in productivity, but it will prevent a decline.

Motivators

Herzberg called the factors associated with positive feelings **motivators**. Examples are recognition, advancement, growth, achievement, and the work itself. When subjects were asked what made them feel exceptionally good about their jobs, typical answers included: "My job gives me a feeling of achievement." "I like the recognition I get for doing my job well." "The work is just plain interesting." All these responses have one

Figure 2.6 The Result When Hygiene Factors Are Not Satisfied

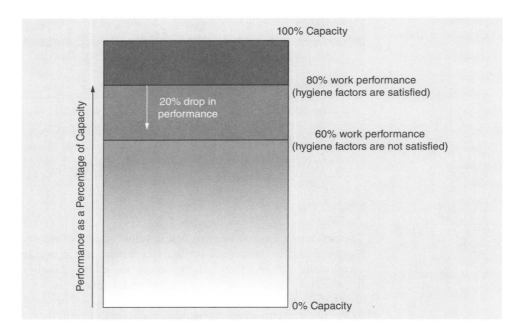

thing in common: They relate to the work itself. Additionally, they are psychological in nature and relate to upper-level need satisfaction. Herzberg termed these factors *motivators* because he believed that they caused increases in performance. Using our own percentages as examples, Figure 2.7 shows the ways in which Herzberg believes motivators can affect performance. Note that the employees represented are performing at 80 percent of their ability. When motivators such as recognition, advancement, and the possibility of growth are used, the employees' performance increases, measuring closer to their potential. The increase in performance is determined in part by the type of motivator used. In short, as performance potential increases, output goes up.

Figure 2.7 The Effects of Motivators on Employee Performance

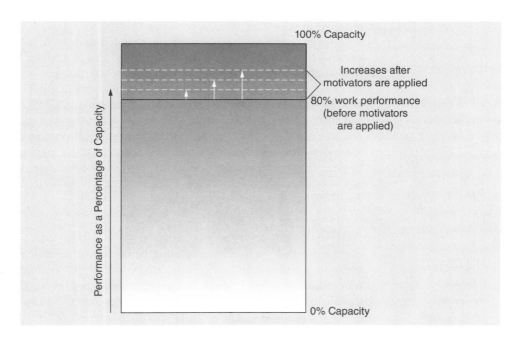

Applying the Motivation–Hygiene Theory

One major reason that Herzberg's two-factor theory has been so well accepted by managers is that it applies Maslow's need concept to the job. For example, Herzberg suggests using hygiene factors to help people attain their lower-level needs. Conversely, he recommends motivators to meet upper-level needs. Figure 2.8 integrates these two concepts. As you can see, Herzberg suggests that physiological, safety, social, and, to some degree, esteem needs can be satisfied with hygiene factors. The remainder of the esteem needs and all the self-actualization needs can be satisfied with motivators.

A second reason for the popularity of Herzberg's theory is that practicing managers agree with it. In a study designed to learn more about work motivations of men and women, 128 managers were asked to rank eight motives for pursuing a managerial career. The results showed that the two top choices—a sense of achievement and challenge—correspond to Herzberg's motivators, illustrating the value of his theory.

A third reason for the popularity of the theory has been revealed by recent research: The most powerful rewards are psychological in nature, a finding that corresponds with Herzberg's research. Hence, organizations are now using approaches such as recognition in a variety of ways to build and sustain motivation.

When employees in a small manufacturing company attained a major safety milestone—one hundred days without a single accident—they felt like heroes. On the morning of day one hundred, it was announced that a catered lunch would be served the next day, if they made it to the 5:30 shift without an accident. At 5:15, anticipation was building. Managers took confetti streamers to the balcony overlooking the shop floor. When the 5:30 whistle blew, there were congratulations all around, confetti flew through the air, and banners were unfurled. It was a great moment for everyone—and one that was not soon forgotten. The recognition value of this celebration was extremely high, although the monetary cost was relatively low.

Highly motivating organizations even celebrate small successes. A health-conscious company distributes fruit bowls to employees' work areas when key personal milestones are attained. Another company uses a more fattening approach: fresh-baked chocolate-chip cookies to say "thank you."[10]

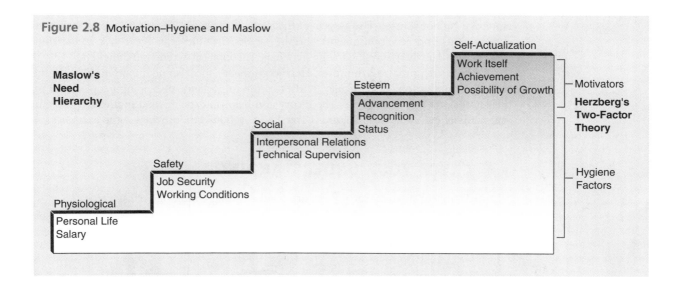

Figure 2.8 Motivation–Hygiene and Maslow

Figure 2.9
Motivation–Hygiene
Continuation

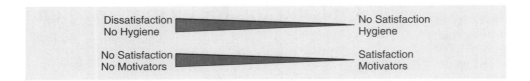

The Motivation–Hygiene Theory in Perspective

Many businesspeople who read about the motivation–hygiene theory are likely to accept it as totally accurate. Certainly, to the extent that it encourages the manager to provide upper-level need satisfaction, the theory is relevant to our study of motivation. However, the theory has several serious shortcomings that merit attention.

First, Herzberg contends that something is *either* a hygiene factor *or* a motivator—the two are independent of each other. Additionally, a lack of hygiene will lead to dissatisfaction, but its presence will not lead to satisfaction. Satisfaction results only from the presence of motivators, as illustrated in Figure 2.9. If you give people hygiene factors, you will not motivate them, but you will prevent dissatisfaction. Thus, hygiene, according to Herzberg, creates a zero level of motivation. Research, however, reveals that some people are indeed motivated by hygiene factors. For example, many individuals say that money is a motivator for them. Some people report that recognition and the chance for advancement lead to dissatisfaction; for them, these are not motivators. Researchers have found that some factors are satisfiers some of the time and dissatisfiers the rest of the time. For example, many people want a chance to achieve but not every minute of every workday. If achievement opportunities are offered too often, workers will be unhappy, believing that too much is expected of them. On the basis of findings such as these, Herzberg's critics claim that his initial theory has not been supported well by further investigation.

A second major criticism centers on the way in which the original data were gathered. The researchers asked accountants and engineers what they particularly liked and disliked about their jobs. Critics say the answers are biased because people tend to give socially acceptable responses when asked such questions. What would you expect people to say they disliked about their jobs? Stereotypical answers would include salary, supervision, and working conditions. Similarly, people could be expected to say that they liked recognition, advancement, and achievement. A close analysis of these two groups of answers shows that things people dislike about their jobs are related to the work environment, a factor the employee cannot control. The aspects of their jobs that people like are related to their own achievements and accomplishments and are factors that they can control. It is therefore possible that Herzberg's methodology may have encouraged stereotypical answers.

Despite such problems, however, Herzberg's theory sheds some important light on the subject of motivation. In particular, it stresses the importance of helping people fulfill *all* their needs, not just basic needs. The theory also helps to explain what motivates people in international cultures. The "Cultural Diversity in Action" box provides some examples.

✔ CHECK YOUR UNDERSTANDING

1. In Herzberg's two-factor theory, are good working conditions considered a motivator or a hygiene factor? What is "work itself" considered?
2. Three reasons managers have accepted Herzberg's two-factor theory are: (1) _____, (2)_____, and (3)_____.
3. Identify two shortcomings of Herzberg's theory.

VIEW FROM ABROAD

Everyone can be motivated, but are the factors that are important in the United States the same as those in other countries? Research shows that there is a considerable cultural impact on achievement, and those motivational factors that are high on the list of workers in one country may be low on the list of workers in another country. This is particularly true when comparing nations that have different political systems. For example, four Far Eastern countries were examined by researchers who wanted to find out the importance of certain motivational variables. The higher the score, the more important the variable. Here is what they learned:

Motivational Variable	People's Republic of China	Hong Kong	Taiwan	Singapore
Cooperative coworkers	635	579	571	624
Need for autonomy	603	512	480	532
Job challenge	515	548	548	571
Good working relations with the manager	483	522	524	551
Salary	454	567	442	552
Job security	450	452	506	437
Work benefits	439	323	363	439
Good working conditions	433	436	407	432
Opportunity for promotion	364	640	630	593
Job recognition	446	487	487	442

The results show that there is considerable cultural impact on the importance of these variables. For example, in China, where the government guarantees everyone a job and the economy is state-run, earnings are not as important as they are in Singapore, which has a free-enterprise system. Similarly, the opportunity for promotion is not very important in China because there are few rewards that accompany the job. In contrast, workers in Hong Kong and Taiwan are highly motivated by such opportunities.

At the same time, however, it is important to realize the many similarities among the four countries examined here. For example, job recognition is of approximately equal importance for all these workers, and they all place similar value on the importance of favorable working conditions.

What, then, can be concluded about motivation in the international arena? The answer is that it varies from country to country, and any generalization about workers in a particular geographical region is likely to be erroneous. Motivation is greatly affected by culture, which helps to create both similarities and differences in work values. The only way to determine precisely how to motivate workers in a specific country is by studying that culture and then fashioning a motivational package that addresses those particular employees.

Sources: Geert Hofstede, *Culture's Consequences: International Differences in Work-Related Values* (Beverly Hills: Sage Publications, 1980); Oded Shenkar and Simcha Ronen, "Structure and Importance of Work Goals among Managers in the People's Republic of China," *Academy of Management Journal,* September 1987, p. 571; and Richard M. Hodgetts and Fred Luthans, *International Management,* 4th ed. (Burr Ridge, IL: Irwin/ McGraw, 2000), pp. 364–366.

Discuss expectancy theory, noting how both valence and expectancy influence motivational force.

Expectancy Theory

Although a study of the needs hierarchy and blocked need satisfaction is one way of examining motivation, there is now a great deal of interest in **expectancy theory**.[11] Developed by Victor Vroom,[12] and based on earlier work by others, expectancy theory has been expanded and refined by such individuals as Lyman Porter and Edward Lawler.[13] Vroom's motivation formula is a simple yet powerful one that can be expressed as follows:

$$\text{Motivation} = \text{Valence} \times \text{Expectancy}.$$

To understand the theory, we must examine the concepts of valence and expectancy.

Valence

A person's preference for a particular outcome or objective can be expressed as a **valence**. A valence describes how much someone likes or dislikes something. The difference can range from $+1$ (highest preference) to -1 (lowest preference). For example, Bob wants a promotion to the New York office. On a scale from -1 to $+1$, his valence

Figure 2.10 Range of an Individual's Valence

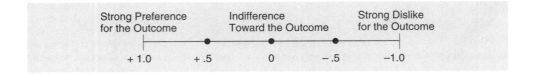

is +1. Suzy, meanwhile, is indifferent to the idea of promotion to the New York office. Her valence is 0. Tom, however, will not take a promotion to the New York office under any conditions. His valence is −1. Figure 2.10 illustrates the valence range.

Note that expectancy theory forces the manager to answer the question: What motivates the individual? By examining the preference of workers for various outcomes, ranging from increased salary to a feeling of accomplishment, the manager is in a good position to offer workers what they want. However, it is important to realize that most managers do *not* know what motivates their workers. Table 2.2 is a list of job qualities for which workers would have varying degrees of preference. This list was given to workers and managers all around the country. The workers were asked to rank the factors from most important to least important. The managers were asked to rank the factors the way they thought the workers would. Before reading further, take time to rank the items on this list by placing a 1 after the item you think workers said was most important to them, a 2 after the item you think they ranked second, down to a 10 after the item you think the workers ranked last. Then compare your answers to those given at the end of the book. You may find that your list was closer to that of supervisors in industry than to that of the workers themselves. Most readers' lists are, because, like many managers, they do not know the valences that workers actually have for various qualities of the work environment.

Table 2.2
What Do Workers Want from Their Jobs?

Job Qualities	Rank (1–10)
Job security	_____
Full appreciation for work done	_____
Promotion and growth with the company	_____
Tactful disciplining	_____
Good wages	_____
Feeling in on things	_____
Interesting work	_____
Management loyalty to the workers	_____
Good working conditions	_____
Sympathetic understanding of personal problems	_____

Source: Reported in Paul Hersey and Kenneth H. Blanchard, *Management of Organizational Behavior: Utilizing Human Resources*, 3d ed. (Englewood Cliffs, NJ: Prentice Hall, 1977), p. 47.

Expectancy

The probability that a specific outcome will follow from a specific act is termed **expectancy**. People at work are motivated to perform because of expectations. Their perception of the value and probability of an outcome will affect the degree of motivation. For example, what is the likelihood that Bob will get a promotion to the New York office if he receives the highest efficiency rating in his department? If Bob thinks that the chances are very good, he will assign to this a very high probability, such as 0.99. If Bob believes the likelihood of the promotion is fair (that efficiency ratings help, but getting the job depends most heavily on how well the boss likes him personally), he may assign it a probability of 0.50. Finally, if Bob believes the high efficiency rating will knock him out of consideration for the New York position (that if he is a good worker, the firm will keep him here rather than let him go away to New York), he will assign it a very low rating, such as 0.01.

Do not confuse valence and expectancy. Although Bob may have a high valence (+1) for a promotion to the New York office, he also may believe that the manager does not like him. So, no matter how high his sales, he assigns the probability of his being promoted to the New York office (expectancy) as very low, for example, 0.10.

Motivational Force

Motivation is a function of both valence and expectancy. One without the other will not produce motivation. This becomes clearer if we apply some illustrations to the expectancy theory formula. Also, let us use the term **motivational force** rather than simply motivation, because force or effort is what we are interested in measuring. The formula then is:

$$\text{Motivational Force} = \text{Valence} \times \text{Expectancy}$$

If either expectancy or valence is 0, the motivational force will be 0. Likewise, if one is high and the other is low, the motivational force will be low. Let us take an example. The vice president of sales has just announced that the salesperson with the best sales record for next month will get an all-expenses-paid trip for two to Hawaii at Christmas. The three top salespeople are Charles, Fred, and Maureen. To determine each one's motivational force, we look at the valence and expectancy each has regarding the free trip.

Charles has a very high valence for this trip (valence = 1.0). He has never been to Hawaii, and he knows his wife would love to go. However, the last time the vice president made a promise like this, he was overridden by the company comptroller, who said the firm could not afford to send two people to Paris for a week. Instead, the winner was given a check for $250. Charles remembers this incident vividly, as he was the winner. As a result, he believes that the possibility of the winner's going to Hawaii is good but not certain (expectancy = 0.5). We can determine Charles's motivational force as follows:

$$\text{Motivational Force} = V(1.0) \times E(0.5) = 0.5$$

Fred would also like to win the free trip to Hawaii. However, as luck would have it, Fred took his wife and family there four months ago for their vacation. Nevertheless, his valence for this trip is still quite high (valence = 0.7). Furthermore, although he also remembers that the vice president was prevented from awarding an all-expenses-paid trip last time, Fred believes that this time the contest probably was cleared with the company comptroller and that the winner will indeed travel to Hawaii (expectancy = 0.9). Fred's motivational force can be calculated as follows:

$$\text{Motivational Force} = V(0.7) \times E(0.9) = 0.63$$

Maureen is the only one who is not delighted with the prospect of the trip. Last week, she and her fiancé decided the date for their wedding would be December 22. They plan to spend the next two weeks honeymooning in Switzerland. The groom's father has a chalet there, right near one of the finest ski resorts in the country. Maureen knows that there is simply no way she can take the trip. As a result, she is indifferent about the prize (valence = 0), although she does believe that the winner will be sent to Hawaii (expectancy = 1.0). Her motivational force can be computed this way:

$$\text{Motivational Force} = V(0) \times E(1.0) = 0$$

Of the three, Fred is the most motivated to attain the highest sales record. A close look at the motivational force computations shows that he had neither the highest valence for the Hawaii trip (Charles did) nor the highest expectancy (Maureen did). However, the *combination* of the two produced a greater motivational force than that for the others.

The Expectancy Theory in Perspective

Obviously, no manager is going to spend time trying to determine the motivational force of each worker for each objective. However, for many reasons, expectancy theory is helpful in understanding motivation.

First, the expectancy model urges us to look at motivation as a *force* or strength of drive directed toward some objective. As a result, we no longer consider *whether* a person is motivated toward doing something but *how great* the motivation may be. Just about every worker is motivated by money, but some workers are more highly motivated by it than are others.

Second, although Maslow's needs hierarchy can be applied to everyone in general, it does not address *individual motivation* and its specific aspects. Expectancy theory does.

Third, the model suggests that people learn what kinds of rewards they like and dislike through *experience*. They also learn to determine the probabilities of their attaining these rewards. Thus, both valence and expectancy are a result of individual experiences, and what highly motivates one person may create no motivational force in another.

Fourth, to a large extent, motivation is determined not only by rewards available but also by their degree of *equity* or fairness. **Equity theory** holds that workers compare their work–reward ratio to that of others in determining how fairly they are being treated. If Tony and Barbara are both receiving the same salary, but Tony feels that he works harder than Barbara, Tony will also feel that he is being treated inequitably. If the organization does not raise his salary above Barbara's, Tony is likely to be dissatisfied and may start doing less work or look for a job elsewhere. Remember that this dissatisfaction is a result of perceived inequity. As long as Tony believes that a lack of equity exists, his dissatisfaction will remain.

Fifth, if we accept the expectancy model, it follows that to motivate an individual to work we can do only two things: (1) increase the positive value of outcomes by increasing rewards and (2) strengthen the connection between the work and the outcomes.

One way of achieving these steps is through effective goal setting, which involves both setting goals and establishing objectives. Goals provide general directions whereas objectives provide specific directions for achieving the goals. Without goals, there is no reason for existence. For example, a goal of a successful business is to provide quality products; another goal is to make a profit. Until clear, specific, attainable objectives are established for each goal, nothing will happen. A goal is a vague statement that fails to provide specific guidance for accomplishing results whereas an objective identifies the strategy, the process, the timetable, and a means of measuring the results of the goal. Through objectives, goals are accomplished. It is also important to provide people with frequent feedback so they know how well they are doing and can make any necessary changes.

 CHECK YOUR UNDERSTANDING

Match the term with the appropriate statement:

Term	Statement
Valence	**a.** perception of probability for a particular outcome
Expectancy	**b.** a motivation force
Equity theory	**c.** preference for a particular outcome
Motivational force	**d.** feeling of fairness
	e. the degree of likes and dislikes for an outcome
	f. valence times expectancy

Explain the value of money, employee satisfaction, incentives, and recognition in the motivation process.

The Practical Side of Rewards

Much of what has been discussed thus far has been theoretical in nature. However, motivation also has a practical side, and financial rewards and employee satisfaction play big roles here. There are three reasons for this.

1. Everyone wants to satisfy his or her lower-level needs, and money often plays a major role in fulfilling this need.
2. Money also can help people attain upper-level need satisfaction. A person who is making 10 percent more than anyone else doing the same job can look in the mirror and say, "Wow, I must be good. Otherwise, I wouldn't be making so much money."[14]
3. Employee satisfaction is important, and rewards—monetary and nonmonetary alike—can influence the extent to which this is present.[15]

When rewards are discussed, most people think immediately of money—and there is certainly good reason for this.[16] Especially at the upper levels of the hierarchy, financial packages are important in attracting and retaining the services of successful managers.[17] It's no secret that CEOs and other high-level managers of publicly traded U.S. companies are well paid.[18] In 2009, aligning pay with performance hit one of its worst years. Major investment banks paid their people 30 percent more than the previous year, while companies slashed the salaries of rank-and-file employees. The public outcry over supersized CEO bonuses given to banking executives caused many companies to review their clawback provisions and policies—requiring executives to return part of their pay under certain conditions. Other companies established **clawback policies**. For 2010, companies on the average budgeted 12 percent of their payroll for bonuses, while base salaries were at a record-low budgeting level. This trend indicated a shift from fixed costs to variable costs since bonuses are given once a year only.[19]

Executives and CEOs are not the only people receiving millions of dollars in compensation; corporate directors are racking in millions of dollars as well. Table 2.3 lists

Table 2.3
Some of the Highest-Paid
Board Members in 2008

Company	Highest-paid Board Member	2008 Pay	Biggest Source of Pay
XTO Energy	Jack P. Randall, founder of Jefferies Group's oil and gas advisory business	$1,561,220	$750,000 that was a 3-for-1 matching gift made in Randall's name to the University of Texas
Freeport-McMoran Copper & Gold	B.M. Rankin Jr., private investor	$1,319,121	$891,001 for consulting on finance, accounting, and business development
Intuitive Surgical	Mark J. Rubash, CFO of Shutterfly	$1,087,428	Options valued at $1,042,928
Stryker	John W. Brown, chairman emeritus and former CEO	$1,036,200	Options valued at $911,200
BJ Services	Don D. Jordan, CEO of Jordan Capital Management	$1,023,512	A $576,439 increase in value of vested pension benefits
People's United Financial	George P. Carter, chairman of the board and president of Connecticut Foods	$930,445	Stock and options valued at $631,905
BMC Software	B. Garland Cupp, private investor; chairman of BMC for most of 2008	$918,643	Options valued at $787,643
Chesapeake Energy	Breene M. Kerr, CEO of Kerr Consolidated until it was sold in 1996	$784,687	Restricted stock valued at $466,040 and personal use of Chesapeake planes valued at $183,647
Apple	Millard S. Drexler, CEO of J. Crew Group	$713,566	Options valued at $639,300
Celgene Corporation	James L. Loughlin, former head of KPMG's pharmaceutical practice	$713,500	Options valued at $622,500

several companies that paid some of the largest sums in 2008 to their directors. Table 2.4 lists the top ten highest-paid women executives in 2008.

Money is often overrated as stated by Daniel Pink in his book, *Drive: The Surprising Truth about What Motivates Us.* Pink contends that given a baseline of compensation,

Table 2.4
Some of America's
Highest-Paid Women
Executives in 2008

Company	Name	Total Compensation (in millions)
Oracle	Safra Catz	$42.4
Wynn International Marketing	Linda Chen	$23.9
Victoria's Secret	Sharen J. Turney	$20.3
Annaly Capital Management	Wellington J. Denahan-Norris	$20.0
Avon Products	Andrea Jung	$19.5
Hewlett-Packard	Ann Livermore	$17.3
Kraft Foods	Irene Rosenfeld	$16.0
Regions Financial	Candice Bagby	$15.2 Left the company in May 2008 and received $14,750,731 in severance pay
Archer Daniels Midland	Patricia A. Woertz	$15.0
Pepsi Company	Indra K. Nooyi	$14.9

Source: "25 Highest Paid Women" www.fortune.com

three other factors matter more than money—a sense of autonomy, mastery over one's labor, and serving a purpose larger than oneself.[20]

How do you keep your best workers? Money is not the sole answer; it is only one of the factors that helps retain employees. Companies also need to be thoughtful when weighing compensation, work–life balance, professional-development programs, employee engagement and other factors that contribute to overall job satisfaction.[21] In recent years, however, other approaches have become increasingly important.

- Stock options, which are tied directly to company performance and, in some cases, not restricted to only senior-level managers.
- Broad banding, which allows managers greater freedom in giving raises to their employees.
- Cafeteria incentive programs, which allow employees to choose the types of rewards that will be most motivational for them.
- Recognition programs of all types.

Stock Options

In recent years, employee salaries in the workforce at large have been increasing by approximately 3 percent annually. However, executive compensation packages have been going up at a much faster rate. One reason is that these managers have been given stock options that allow them to buy company stock at very attractive prices and exercise these options when the stock price is high. During the stock market boom of the 1990s, some executives made millions of dollars by exercising their options, while other CEOs currently hold unexercised options that are worth hundreds of millions of dollars.[22] One of the problems with some of these stock option plans is that they allow the option to be exercised even if the company's performance is poor. For example, before the last recession, the trend in executive options moved toward "pay-for-performance" plans; however, during the recession, the public became outraged at the huge compensation packages and bonuses being given to executives in the banking and financial markets where performance was at its lowest. Some felt that their performance was at the heart of the housing and financial markets collapse.

The Incentive Performance System at Lincoln Electric is one of the oldest "pay-for-performance" systems in the country. It was implemented by James F. Lincoln in the early twentieth century and is frequently used for benchmarking by other businesses. Several features of the system include:

- Open communication with senior management
- Piecework incentive rewards for all production work
- A profit-sharing bonus plan
- Guaranteed employment after three years of service[23]

Though companies offer stock options to executives to keep them highly motivated to improve company productivity and profits, some companies are forcing their executives to assume financial risks if they want to exercise stock options. WorldCom, Inc. provides one such example of pay for performance. WorldCom filed for bankruptcy protection in July 2002 for one of the largest accounting frauds ever. A new chief executive, Michael Capellas, was appointed to take the company out of bankruptcy and turn it into a model of what a company should be. He was given a three-year pay package valued at $20 million. Under the contract, Michael Capellas would receive an annual salary of $1.5 million, a signing bonus of $2 million, and an additional $1.5 million bonus if he met certain performance targets, $12 million in restricted shares, with an additional $6 million in restricted stock only if he met performance targets. In addition, the guaranteed $12 million in restricted stock had a vested period of three years, and if Capellas exercised any stock options, he could sell the WorldCom stock for a twelve-month period. The restricted shares would not become the property of Capellas until he met performance targets. Capellas succeeded in bringing the company through bankruptcy and is presently serving as chairman and CEO of First Data Corporation.

Another example of pay for performance occurred after the board ended Carly Fiorina's rein at Hewlett-Packard (HP) and CFO Robert Wayman was appointed interim CEO. His job was "to make sure that customers stayed comfortable with HP, and that employees remained focused on the task at hand rather than be distracted by the fact that there was a CEO search," said HP spokesperson Michael Moeller. As an incentive, the board agreed to pay him a $3 million cash bonus. The interim lasted fifty-two days, resulting in Wayman receiving $58,000 per day. Was it worth it? HP felt it got its money's worth. This type of pay for performance is increasing as a way to motivate people.[24]

A few companies have already put their CEOs to the test. Level 3 Communications, a network company, "grants options that reward top officers only when Level 3's stock outperforms the S&P 500. But there's little sign that variable options will become the norm. CEOs do not like them because they have to be expensed. And for most executives, the payout would be much less than the riches that fixed options deliver."[25]

In response to new rules issued by the U.S. Securities and Exchange Commission to push companies to treat stock options as expensing, the Dell Computer Corporation cutback on stock options to its senior executives and pays cash bonuses instead. Because the executives are still eligible to receive stock options, the plan is intended to help retain senior executives and to ease Dell's bottom line. The issuing of stock options can expand the company's cash flow and reduce its taxes, but expensing the stock options would reduce Dell's earnings, their bottom line. Expensing requires companies to determine the value of the options when granted and to deduct that amount from profits over a period of years. Counting options as an expense is expected to result in fewer options being offered to CEOs.

Although improvements have been made, pay for performance is still not the standard practice. Some companies are still rewarding their CEOs, who deserve far less, with large amounts of stock options.

With the range of options in pay-for-performance plans, do these plans really work? "The range of opinion about pay-for-performance is broad and deep. Its *proponents* say that rigorous, long-term pay-for-performance systems offer effective methods of helping companies continually improve the workforce while getting and keeping the best people. *Opponents* argue that incentive pay plans tend to pit employees against one another, erode trust and teamwork, and create what critics call dressed-up sweatshops."[26]

Broad Banding

One of the easiest ways for a manager to reward a subordinate who continues to perform well is to recommend the person for a salary raise. However, in many companies, this is not always possible because the individual currently is being paid the highest rate established for the job. For example, an assistant warehouse manager who holds a job with a salary range of $35,000 to $50,000 cannot earn more than $50,000 unless the manager can facilitate the promotion of the assistant manager to a position that commands a higher salary or can convince higher-level management to raise the cap for assistant warehouse managers. Both of these efforts can take a great deal of time and energy.

To overcome this problem, a growing number of firms are turning to **broad banding**, which replaces the number of salary grades with fewer, wider bands and places a larger spread between bottom and top rates of pay. Under broad banding, the assistant warehouse manager's job might now be grouped with a host of other midlevel management positions and have a salary range of $35,000 to $70,000. In this case, it would be much easier for the manager to give the assistant warehouse manager a raise to $55,000.

Why has this approach been gaining popularity in recent years? One reviewer gave this answer:

> *Blame part of it on global competition and the changing nature of work. Companies have cut back their staffs and set up new structures that give them more flexibility to respond quickly to competition. But highly vertical traditional pay systems, with their vast numbers of grades, are out of sync with the new, flatter, team-oriented structures.*
>
> *The solution is broad banding, which makes it much easier to assign workers to different jobs without having to worry about exactly what grade they're moving to. It also allows companies to put workers in traditionally lower-level jobs to learn different skills without demoting them or decreasing their pay.*[27]

Effective Compensation Incorporated, an independent consulting firm in Lakewood, Colorado, summarizes the features that attract firms to broad banding.[28]

- *Efficiency*—Less time is spent on evaluating jobs and defending grade placement decisions.
- *Flexibility*—It is easier to transfer employees between jobs.

- *Decentralization*—Local managers can make and defend pay decisions, which is consistent with many quality-oriented firms.
- *Performance focus*—Supervisors can more easily provide significant rewards within a broad salary range for those who consistently do an outstanding job.

Compensation Resources, Inc., a firm that provides compensation and human resource consulting services, has identified several advantages and disadvantages of broad banding programs.[29]

Advantages:

1. Better accommodate a flat organizational hierarchy.
2. Emphasize skill development rather than vertical promotions.
3. Eliminate need to establish artificial job titles and hierarchy.
4. Provide greater organizational flexibility since the organization is not encumbered by narrowly focused job titles.
5. Simplify salary administration by eliminating promotions that are not *bona fide* changes in duties and responsibilities.

Disadvantages:

1. May not be compatible with the organization's culture and are less successful in highly structured organizations.
2. Loss of control points for salary planning and may result in overpaid employees, requiring greater emphasis on monitoring.
3. Difficult to use as a management tool for determining relationship between jobs.
4. Limit promotional opportunities.

At Sears, managers found that when they tried to recruit a potential employee, the individual's first question was "What is the pay grade?" Applicants did not want to accept a position in which they would soon reach the maximum pay level and, in order to get a salary raise, would have to change jobs again. General Electric has also introduced broad banding because it reduces the bureaucratic red tape associated with salary increases for those who have reached the top of their pay grade, and it allows the company to more easily tie pay to performance.

Broad banding is even used by educational institutions. Boston College, for example, has transitioned from a salary-grade compensation system to a market-pricing broad band compensation system for its office/clerical, technical, and professional/administrative positions. Four bands are used: the first band includes administrative support positions; the second band includes supervisory and individual contributor positions; the third band includes first-level management positions; and the fourth band covers middle and senior management positions.[30]

Cafeteria Incentives

Cafeteria incentives provide employees with a host of choices and allow each individual to select those that best meet his or her needs. The term *cafeteria* is used because choices are similar to those in a cafeteria, in which a diner proceeds down the line and chooses those foods that he or she would like and leaves the others. Employees enjoy the power of being able to choose with cafeteria benefit plans. They are also called *125 plans* because they are covered in Section 125 of the Internal Revenue Service Code. Cafeteria benefit plans make the business more attractive to employees and can be a key to retaining workers. These plans cost nothing, save the business money, as well as save the employee money since the deductions direct to the cafeteria plans area generally not subject to payroll and unemployment taxes.[31]

Cafeteria incentives take a variety of forms. In many cases, the company will put aside a pool of money that each individual can spend on these options, such as $3,000, annually. Then, if one person has a family with two small children and wants to use some of this money for a child-care program, the costs are automatically deducted from that employee's pool of money. Another individual might purchase additional life insurance or medical coverage to meet his or her specific needs. At Lincoln Electric, for example, all payments for worker medical insurance come from the bonus pool. The employees decide what type of coverage they want and the cost is deducted from their bonus.

In some cases, companies also give their lower-level employees a choice between a guaranteed weekly wage and an incentive program that is tied directly to work output. For example, an individual might be given a choice between $600 a week or $6 per unit produced each week. If the person is in good health, feels capable of producing more than one hundred units per week, and wants the opportunity to make more money, she or he will opt for the incentive plan rather than the guaranteed weekly wage.

Another example of cafeteria incentives is the rewards that are offered to individuals and groups that do outstanding work. For example, some firms offer a weekly award to the group that produces the greatest output. Each person in the group can then choose from the available rewards. Examples are a day off with pay, a television set, a dinner for two, two tickets to a play, and a week of reserved parking near the main door to the company. For example, Procter & Gamble gives its ninety thousand employees the choice of two extra days off or the cash equivalent. Research reveals that many individuals like this cafeteria approach because it allows them to match the reward with their personal needs. As a result, they find the programs to be highly motivational. Marriott International designs its incentives to meet a broad range of associates, which include "financial support through family care spending accounts and flexible work policies." Additional programs include "childcare discounts; education and training; on- or near-site child development centers at ten locations; and referral services for child, elder and family care issues."[32]

In each of these cases, the objective is the same: to motivate individuals to achieve higher performance. At the heart of this process, of course, are the ideas that were discussed earlier in this chapter: needs, achievement drive, expectancy, and valence. Indeed, there is a link between motivation theory and motivation practice.

Recognition Programs

Money is an important form of reward, but for a number of reasons, recognition is much more widely used. One reason is that organizations typically have pay systems that are designed to review performance and give financial rewards only once or twice annually. Therefore, if someone does an outstandingly fine job in July, the manager may be unable to give the person a financial reward until after the annual performance review in December. Nonfinancial rewards such as recognition, on the other hand, can be given at any time. Additionally, these rewards can take many different forms, can be given in small or large amounts, and, in many instances, are controllable by the manager. For example, the individual can give an employee increased responsibility, which the latter finds motivational and which results in greater productivity. As a follow up, the manager can then give the individual even greater responsibility. Unlike many financial forms of reward, there is no limit to the number of people who can receive this type of reward. One expert on rewards puts it this way:

> *You can, if you choose, make all your employees ... eligible for non-financial rewards. You can also make these rewards visible if you like, and performance-contingent, and you need not wait for high level sign-offs and anniversary dates, because non-financial rewards do not derive from the budget or the boss and are seldom mentioned in employment contracts and collective bargaining agreements. Furthermore ... if you inadvertently give someone more freedom or challenge than he can handle, you can take it back. Therefore, organizations can be bold and innovative in their use of non-monetary rewards because they don't have to live with their mistakes.*[33]

While recognition programs do not need to be expensive, they often are a major budget item. The Federation Incentive Travel and Merchandise Study in 2007 revealed that organizations in America spent more than $14 billion in 2006 to recognize and motivate their employees. (**www.recognitioncouncil.org**) During the recession in 2009, a Fortune 500 food industry company chopped its employee rewards and recognition budget by half, to $500.000, only to be restated the next year to $1 million, plus $200,000 for retroactive payments to employees whose milestone-setting work had not been recognized during the time the budget cuts were in effect.[34]

Research Findings. Research reveals many types of recognition that can be given to inspire performance and loyalty. One that is receiving increased attention is recognition of the fact that many employees have social and family responsibilities, and when the organization helps them to deal with these obligations, loyalty increases. The Hudson Institute conducted a survey of the attitudes and experiences of workers in business, government, and nonprofit organizations around the United States. The organization mailed 3,075 questionnaires to a cross-sample of organizations and received usable responses from 75 percent of them. The data from the survey revealed the following:

- Only 30 percent of employees feel an obligation to stay with their current employer.
- Individuals who are highly committed to their organization tend to do the best work.
- Workers who are discontented with their jobs are least likely to be productive.
- Employees in large organizations (one hundred or more people) tend to be less satisfied than their peers in small enterprises.
- Lower-level employees are less satisfied than those in higher-level positions.
- The things that the respondents would like their companies to focus more on include being fair to employees, caring about them, and exhibiting trust in them.[35]

Although the last point will come as a surprise to few organizational managers, groups such as Recognition Professionals International (RPI) have concluded that employee recognition is often misunderstood by businesses as a frill—or saved for only monumental events. A simple "thank you" to a coworker can greatly impact the bottom line of a business. That was the message concluded from two companies that received RPI's Best Practices Award.

In 2004, a Northwestern University forum found that "it is an organization's employees who influence the behavior and attitudes of customers, and it is customers who drive an organization's profitability through the purchase and use of its products." The next year, Memorial Medical Center took those findings and made dramatic changes to its culture and was able to show a direct correlation between financial well-being and employee attitudes, behavior, and customer satisfaction.[36]

Surveys conducted in 2002 and 2003 by WorldatWork and RPI show that companies use employee recognition programs extensively to retain their best and brightest employees. According to RPI, recognition is one of the most effective ways to reinforce an organization's culture, support its objectives, and retain top performers. The survey was repeated in 2005, and once again, organizations stated that recognition was important to their success. The results indicated that the top goals of recognition programs are:

- Creating a positive work environment
- Motivating high performance
- Reinforcing desired behavior
- Creating a culture of recognition

Other highlights from that survey include:

- Eighty-nine percent, an overwhelming majority of survey respondents, have recognition programs in place.
- Ninety-two percent of the organizations said that employee recognition was occurring more often than twelve months ago.
- Forty-eight percent were considering adding new recognition programs in the next twelve months.
- Sixty percent of organizations with an employee recognition program have a written program strategy.
- Eighty-nine percent of the organizations identified "Length of Service" programs as the most common type of recognition program offered.[37]

While being recognized for your length of service is nice, is it what really motivates employees on a daily basis? Most employees need short-term recognition. Ideas for developing recognition benefits can be gleaned from Michael Abrashoff, former U.S. Navy commanding officer and author of *It's Your Ship*. He has cited five reasons employees quit a position. Pay and benefits were number five. The other four reasons were:

- Employees want to be treated with respect and dignity—not be treated like children.
- Employees want to be allowed to have influence on their situation—being allowed to improve their environment.
- Employees want to be listened to (managers do not know their own people, their goals, needs, or aspirations) and have their suggestions taken seriously.
- Employees want to be rewarded with greater responsibility and leadership positions.[38]

Implementing a meaningful recognition program can satisfy employee wants and needs. Companies also will save money by retaining good employees, because it is expensive to hire and train new employees.

Creating a Recognition Program

Creating a recognition process need not be sophisticated or time consuming. Recognition and rewards, however, must be timely. A survey conducted by WorldatWork in 2009 found that 65 percent of the sales companies surveyed planned to make changes in their sales incentive plan for 2010, and 80 percent of the companies stated they made changes every two years. The compensation and benefits need to be aligned with company goals/ strategies, and the plan must be simple and not complex.[39] Recognition and reward programs that fail to align with the overall corporate strategies are usually viewed as an expense instead of an investment. Senior management is more likely to support plans that are viewed as an investment rather than an expense. In fact, many firms that are now working to improve their recognition systems use fairly basic and easy-to-implement programs. One expert in the area has recommended the following steps in setting up and managing a reward and recognition program:

- When introducing new recognition procedures and programs, take advantage of all communication tools and other knowledge-sharing networks—let everyone know what is going on.
- Educate the managers so that they use recognition as part of the total compensation package.
- Make recognition part of the performance management process so that everyone begins to use it.
- Have site-specific recognition ceremonies that are featured in the company's communication outlets such as the weekly newsletter and the bimonthly magazine.
- Publicize the best practices of employees so that everyone knows some of the things they can do in order to earn recognition.
- Let everyone know the steps that the best managers are taking to use recognition effectively.
- Continually review the recognition process in order to introduce new procedures and programs and scrap those that are not working well.
- Solicit recognition ideas from both employees and managers as they are the ones who are most likely to know what works well and what does not.[40]

Most employees want to do a good job, make a difference, and be valued for their efforts. Regardless of the situation, the company must take time to determine what employees need. Employee performance is often tied more to personal factors like being appreciated for doing a good job than to money. Recognizing accomplishments in a timely manner by a simple, sincere "Thank You" can go a long way in improving performance. The level of motivation in part will be determined by the time lapse between the occurrence and awarding the recognition. The closer the recognition to the occurrence, the greater will be the motivation, creating a positive environment that fosters improved performance. Really listening to what employees are saying lets employees feel they are contributing, giving them a sense of worth. Recognition in sharing ownership for goals and achievements lets employees know that their work is being valued and is making a difference. The bottom line is that employees who feel valued and trusted are more productive, and they will leave companies that do not value their contributions.[41]

Common Characteristics of Recognition Programs

Today, a wide number of recognition systems are being used by organizations nationwide. Many of these are the result of continual modification, as the enterprises have altered and tweaked their systems to meet the changing needs of their workforce. However, all these programs have two things in common.

First, the programs are designed to maintain worker satisfaction and thus reduce the likelihood that people will leave the firm. Second, they are designed to meet the specific needs of the employees. Simply put, what works in one enterprise may have little value in another. This explains why many firms have used a trial-and-error approach to honing their recognition programs. Moreover, the ultimate programs often vary widely from company to company, and many of them are highly creative.

What Do Employees Want?

Employees want recognition in many forms. Beverly Kaye, chief executive of Pennsylvania-based Career Systems International and coauthor of *Love 'Em or Lose 'Em: Getting Good People to Stay,* practices what she preaches. Every year she asks her key staff members what she can do to keep them for one more year. One employee wanted a job title change; another wanted part of her work delegated so she could work on another company project. Kaye believes that in a small company, it is easier to tailor rewards to individual employees. If something is expected, it is not a reward. Kaye has found evidence that modest tokens of appreciation make a more powerful statement. Ken Siegel, a managerial psychologist and president of the Impact! Group in Beverly Hills, California, suggests that "the smaller the item is, and the more consistently it's applied, the more it's viewed as a significant motivator." An example of a simple but powerful motivator is when a small business rewards employees by hiring a financial advisor to come into the company to provide financial planning advice to employees on an individual and confidential basis. Employees interviewed later stated that it was one of the things that made the company the most special place they had ever worked.[42]

Another type of recognition focuses on pampering and de-stressing employees. According to the results of a workplace survey by publisher CCH Inc., nearly half of the unscheduled absences from work are due to family issues or personal needs, not illness. Jan Goldman, a senior vice president with Mesirow Financial, pampers her team by taking them to a day spa for manicures and pedicures.[43] Research shows that companies do benefit from good employee recognition programs.

Develop a "plan of action" for finding a job.

 CHECK YOUR UNDERSTANDING

1. How are stock options used to motivate employees? What is the relationship between stock options and pay for performance? What is your feeling about how companies use stock options?
2. How does broad banding work? What advantage does it give the company and the employee?
3. How can "cafeteria incentives" serve as a motivator for employees? Identify several cafeteria incentives that would motivate you on the job. Why?
4. How do you personally like to be recognized? Give some examples.
5. As a manager, how would you establish and use a recognition program?

Career Advisor

Develop a Plan of Action for Finding a Job

Once you have completed the self-evaluation in Chapter 1, the next major step is to formulate a plan of action for selecting a job. Begin by answering the following two questions: What career choices match your strengths, talents, abilities, training, and work habits? What type of jobs fit your career choices?

Choosing a Career

For most people, choosing a career is not an easy task. Some people know early in life what they want to do when they grow up; others find it very difficult and a little scary. The exercise in Figure 2.11 can help you get started.

Figure 2.11 Career Preparation Checklist

This exercise helps you to understand what you need to do to prepare for a successful career search. Evaluate yourself in the six areas covered in this program. Use the following scale when responding:

YES! = strong agreement with the statement
Yes = agreement with the statement
yes = slight agreement with the statement
no = slight disagreement with the statement
No = disagreement with the statement
NO! = strong disagreement with the statement

Getting Started	NO!	No	no	yes	Yes	YES!
I know how to manage the emotions I may experience during my career search.	1	2	3	4	5	6
I know what to say and what not to say to people who can help me.	1	2	3	4	5	6
I know the general characteristics that all employers seek when hiring people.	1	2	3	4	5	6
I know what I should be doing *now* to maximize my career potential and satisfaction.	1	2	3	4	5	6
Looking at Options						
I can describe just what I need and prefer from a new job.	1	2	3	4	5	6
I am clear about the skills and abilities I bring to a career.	1	2	3	4	5	6
I am prepared to discuss what I have accomplished with potential employers.	1	2	3	4	5	6
I know how to determine whether a career fits my goals and abilities.	1	2	3	4	5	6
Applications and Résumés						
I am prepared to fill out employment applications.	1	2	3	4	5	6
I understand the different types of *résumé* formats.	1	2	3	4	5	6
I know how to write each part of my *résumé*.	1	2	3	4	5	6
I know how to write cover letters that will catch prospective employer's attention in a positive way.	1	2	3	4	5	6

(Continued)

Figure 2.11 Career Preparation Checklist *(Continued)*

Getting Started	NO!	No	no	yes	Yes	YES!
The Game Plan						
I know how to increase my chances for success when responding to advertisements.	1	2	3	4	5	6
I know how to select and work with agencies and counselors.	1	2	3	4	5	6
I know how to approach companies that are not advertising jobs openings but that may have them.	1	2	3	4	5	6
I know how to develop a network of personal contacts to find opportunities.	1	2	3	4	5	6
Telephone Skills						
I understand the advantages of using the telephone in my job search.	1	2	3	4	5	6
I know how to use the phone to gather information about careers and companies.	1	2	3	4	5	6
I can discuss my strengths on the phone in a way that makes a positive impression.	1	2	3	4	5	6
I know how to use the phone to follow up effectively on correspondence.	1	2	3	4	5	6
Interviewing						
I know how to make a positive first impression in interviews.	1	2	3	4	5	6
I am prepared to answer the typical questions interviewers ask.	1	2	3	4	5	6
I know how to ask questions that convey my interest in working for the company.	1	2	3	4	5	6
I know how to follow up after an interview.	1	2	3	4	5	6

Scoring the Preparation Checklist

Add up your scores for each of the six areas of career management and record them below. Then add your six scores to calculate a total score for the checklist.

Score for *Getting Started* _____

Score for *Looking at Options* _____

Score for *Applications and Résumés* _____

Score for *The Game Plan* _____

Score for *Telephone Skills* _____

Score for *Interviewing* _____

Total Score _____

(Continued)

Figure 2.11 Career Preparation Checklist *(Continued)*

Interpreting Your Scores for Each Area of Job Hunting

≥20 You are quite well prepared in this area. Concentrate on skills that need polishing.

15–19 You are somewhat prepared in this area. Spend extra time on skills that you are weak.

≤14 You are not prepared in this area. Practice each skill with your coach or a friend.

Interpreting Your Total Score

≥120 You are quite well prepared to manage your career. Work through each unit, concentrating on areas that need polishing.

90–119 You are somewhat prepared to manage your career. Work through each unit, spending extra time on areas that you are weak.

≤89 You are not prepared to manage your career. Take each unit seriously, practicing all skills with your coach or a friend. Make the effort to prepare fully and not lose out because you are unprepared. Complete this sentence: "I would describe my level of preparedness as _____."

Complete the exercise, score it, and interpret your answers. What does your score say about you? How much do you know about preparing for a successful career search? From your answers, prepare a checklist of things you need to do to get yourself better prepared. Identify the skills that need improvement and the areas that need to be researched. The checklist serves as a tool to keep you focused. The career center at your college is a good place to get help. The career counselors can provide assistance in your search.

Once you have selected a career, you can focus your energy on finding jobs that fit within that career. Be careful about limiting your career choice to just one. You may be qualified to work in more than one career field. One thing to remember is to find a job you can be passionate about. It is a lot more fun to work at something you enjoy and makes you feel you are contributing to society, than at a job you dislike. In your job search, consider benefits such as training programs, compensation, flexible schedules, approachable and available management, ethics, and mentoring programs.[44] Their value to you will determine their importance when selecting the jobs for which you will interview.

Finding Jobs within Your Chosen Career Field

After choosing a career field, the next step is finding the jobs that fit within the career field. The *Occupational Outlook Handbook* is an excellent place to start your search. It is located online at www.bls.gov/oco. After viewing the career fields and possible jobs, click on "Career Guide to Industries" to find out about occupations in industries, training needs, earnings, expected job prospects, and working conditions. On the www.bls.gov Web site, type into the search box "fastest growing jobs." It should give a list of jobs that have growth potential for the next several years.

Often national employment and wage data can give insight into possible career choices, as well as job titles and positions. The results of aptitude and skill tests can reveal interesting and useful information for selecting job categories and can help narrow the field of jobs that might be suitable for you. The career center and counselors at your college can often administer these tests, which are often free to students.

Once you have chosen a career field and selected several jobs that fit the career field, you are ready to start considering how to present yourself most effectively to prospective employers. Next, comes the task of preparing a résumé that will get the company's attention and will result in an interview. Résumé writing is covered in Chapter 3 and interviewing is covered in Chapter 4.

CHECK YOUR UNDERSTANDING

Record in your journal the results of your research.
1. What career field have you selected?
2. Which jobs interest you the most? Why?
3. What surprised you the most in your career and job search?

Summary

1 Describe the two sides of motivation: movement and motive.

In this chapter, we examined the fundamentals of motivation. We noted that motivation has two sides: movement and motive. Movement can be seen, whereas motive can only be inferred. Yet motives are important, for they constitute the "whys" of behavior. Motives also are directed toward goals. The goal that has the highest motive strength is the one that a person will attempt to satisfy through goal-directed behavior. Having satisfied that goal, an individual will then proceed to the goal with the next highest motive strength.

2 Identify the five basic needs in Maslow's need hierarchy and differentiate among them.

In examining motives or needs in greater depth, we focused attention on Maslow's needs hierarchy. The most fundamental of all needs, according to Maslow, are physiological needs, such as food, clothing, and shelter. When these are basically satisfied, safety needs replace them. Safety needs are of two types: survival and security. Next in the hierarchy are social needs, such as the desire for friendship, affection, and acceptance. The fourth level of the hierarchy comprises esteem needs, such as the need to feel important and respected. Research shows that prestige and power are two motives closely related to esteem needs, and, to the degree that these motives can be satisfied, esteem needs can be met. At the top of the hierarchy are self-actualization needs. Because people satisfy these needs in so many different ways, behavioral scientists know less about them than the other four types of needs. However, research does reveal that there are two motives related to self-actualization: competence and achievement. If individuals can satisfy these motives, they can fulfill their drive for self-actualization.

3 Describe the two-factor theory of motivation and explain its relevance to the practicing manager.

Frederick Herzberg has also found that people desire upper-level need satisfaction. In his famous two-factor theory of motivation, he divided all job factors into two categories: hygiene factors and motivators. Into hygiene factors he placed those things that he found do not motivate people but stop them from becoming unmotivated: salary, technical supervision, working conditions, and interpersonal relations. Motivators include all the factors that motivate people to increase their contribution to the organization: recognition, advancement, the possibility of growth, and achievement. Herzberg contends that hygiene factors do not produce motivation but do prevent dissatisfaction. Conversely, motivators can give satisfaction but not dissatisfaction. Today, the two-factor theory is criticized as incomplete and erroneous. For example, some researchers report that money is a motivator for many people, despite Herzberg's claim that it is a hygiene factor. Similarly, some researchers report that workers regard recognition and the chance for advancement as dissatisfiers. At best, then, the two-factor theory is a controversial approach.

4 Discuss expectancy theory, noting how both valence and expectancy influence motivational force.

The expectancy theory holds that motivation can be expressed as the product of valence and expectancy. Valence is the measure of a person's preference for a particular outcome. Expectancy is the perceived probability that a specific outcome will follow from a specific act. By multiplying the values of valence and expectancy, one can arrive at a motivational force number; the higher the number, the greater the motivation.

Expectancy theory is very helpful in understanding motivation, for several reasons. The expectancy model urges us to look at motivation as a force greater in some people than in others. It also suggests that valence and expectancy are a result of individual experiences, and what will highly motivate one person may create no motivational force in another. Expectancy theory makes it possible to study the issue of equity in motivation among specific individuals as opposed to examining the general motivation of groups.

5 Explain the value of money, employee satisfaction, incentives, and recognition in the motivation process.

Money is a motivator. It helps fulfill both lower- and upper-level needs. Money can take numerous forms, including salary and benefits. In recent years, organizations have begun adapting financial incentives to individual needs through the use of stock options, cafeteria-style plans, broad banding pay systems, and recognition programs. Cafeteria-style plans allow people to choose those rewards that are best for them.

However, organizations also realize that nonfinancial rewards such as recognition are important motivators. These can take a wide number of forms including thank you notes, recognition parties, and publication of achievements in the company newspaper.

6 Develop a "plan of action" for finding a job.

The first step in developing a plan of action for finding a job is deciding on a career field that matches your talents, abilities, aptitude, and interests. An array of jobs is available within each career field. A more complex stage in the process is narrowing the selection of jobs to the ones that are of interest to you and offer the benefits and perks that are important to you. The *Occupational Outlook Handbook*, the *Career Guide to Industries*, your college career center, and college counselors are excellent sources for conducting your research.

Key Terms in the Chapter

Motivation	Motivation is a psychological drive that directs a person toward an objective.
Motives	Motives are the "whys" of behavior.
Physiological needs	Physiological needs are basic requirements, such as food, clothing, and shelter.
Safety needs	Safety needs provide for survival and security.
Social needs	Social needs are satisfied through meaningful interactions with others.
Esteem needs	Esteem needs are those needs for self-importance and self-respect.
Prestige	Prestige carries with it respect and status.
Power	Power is the ability to influence or induce behavior.
Self-actualization needs	Self-actualization needs are those for satisfying one's full potential.

Competence	Competence implies control over environmental factors.
Achievement	Achievement is the desire to attain objectives.
High achievers	High achievers are moderate risk takers who like specific feedback on their performance.
Need mix	Need mix is an individual's need strength at each level of the need hierarchy.
Hygiene factors	Hygiene factors are environmentally related.
Motivators	Motivators are associated with positive feelings.
Expectancy theory	Expectancy theory holds that motivation is equal to valence times expectancy.
Valence	Valence is a person's preference for a particular outcome.
Expectancy	Expectancy is the perceived probability that a specific outcome will follow a specific act.
Motivational force	Motivational force is equal to valence times expectancy.
Equity theory	Equity theory holds that people use a work–reward ratio in determining how fairly they are being treated.
Broad banding	Broad banding replaces the number of salary grades with fewer, wider bands.
Clawback policies	Require executives to return part of their pay under certain conditions.

Review and Study Questions

1. Motives are the "whys" of behavior. What does this statement mean?

2. What are physiological needs? Give some examples of how your job (company) can satisfy your physiological needs.

3. How important are safety needs to people just starting their business careers? How important are they to top executives in large organizations? If your answers differ, what accounts for the difference? Give examples.

4. How do people attempt to meet their social needs? Cite some examples of how a business can meet the social needs of its employees.

5. Research shows that two motives related to esteem are prestige and power. Define these two motives, and explain how people try to satisfy them.

6. One of the ways in which individuals try to satisfy the self-actualization need is through the development of competence. How do they go about doing this? Give an example of how a business can improve an employee's competence.

7. What are the characteristics of high achievers? How can a high achievement drive be developed?

8. In Herzberg's terms, what are hygiene factors and what are motivators? Give some examples of each.

9. According to the two-factor theory, if you give people hygiene factors, you will not motivate them, but you will prevent dissatisfaction. Conversely, if you give people motivators, you may get satisfaction, but you will never get dissatisfaction. Explain the meaning of these two statements.

10. The two major terms in expectancy theory are *valence* and *expectancy*. What is meant by each of these terms?

11. Using the expectancy theory formula, compute the motivational force for Mr. A, whose valence (V) is 0.8 and expectancy (E) is 0.7. Compute the motivational force for three other individuals who had the following respective valences and expectancies: Ms. B, $V = 0.7$, $E = 0.4$; Mr. C, $V = 1$, $E = 0.5$; and Ms. D, $V = 0.9$, $E = 0.5$. Which of the four has the greatest motivational force?

12. Is money a motivator or does it simply prevent dissatisfaction? Explain.

13. The big bank executive bonus payouts in 2009 caused many companies to review their clawback policies and caused other companies to write clawback policies. What are clawback policies?

14. Why is broad banding gaining popularity as a way to motivate employees? Give an example.

15. How does a cafeteria incentive plan work? Describe two of its advantages.

16. Identify two factors that are common to well-designed recognition programs used to motivate employees?

17. What type of rewards do employees want most on the job?

Connecting to the Real World

How is recognition used as a motivator?

As you learned from reading this chapter, businesses use recognition in a wide variety of ways to motivate employees. To get a firsthand idea of how three types of businesses in your community currently use recognition, follow these steps:

1. Select three types of businesses—a retail firm, a restaurant, and a financial institution like a bank or a manufacturing firm—in your community.
2. Interview the owner, manager, or the human resource person of each firm and ask each one the following questions. You are encouraged to add questions.
   a. Does this company use pay to motivate employees? If so, how and in what form? How effectively does it work?
   b. What type of nonfinancial recognition rewards are used to motivate employees? For each type of recognition, what is the primary goal? What is the company trying to accomplish?
   c. If you (the interviewee) had an option of adding additional recognition activities, what would they be and why?
3. Summarize your findings in a report and describe what you have learned from this assignment.

CASE
Trying to Motivate Everyone

The Waidley Company is a food distribution warehouse located in a metropolitan area of over a million people. Jake Jackson started the business forty-five years ago. The company has managed to make a profit every year, even during the slow years in the early 1990s and again during the recessionary years of 2007–2008. The company survived in part because the employees were willing to do their part—work fewer hours and forfeit their cost-of-living raises for two years. After the recession, the company continued to grow and currently is doing extremely well.

Three years ago, the Waidley Company set a sales objective of 20 percent annual growth over the next five years. Sales are up an average of 27 percent per year, and the company's workforce has increased from 126 to more than 500. As a result, the company has expanded its facilities, adding two more warehouses.

The company sells a wide variety of food (sugar, coffee, tea, flour, and butter) to wholesalers and institutional buyers (schools and governmental agencies). The buyers are widespread over the entire metropolitan area. Many of the buyers want their deliveries scheduled at a specific time, making the master scheduling at the warehouses very complex.

Orders are typically placed the day before they are needed, and it is the responsibility of Justin Brown, head of warehouse operations, to see that the food is loaded on the trucks for delivery. Each order is entered in the computer and then sent to the warehouse where it is assigned to a team of workers. This team gathers all the items and loads them on to the assigned truck. Most of this work is fairly simple, as the computer automatically matches up trucks and food orders in the most efficient way possible. The biggest problems are incomplete or slow deliveries. An incomplete delivery occurs whenever an order is filled improperly and the desired merchandise is not loaded. A slow delivery occurs when the driver fails to arrive at the customer's location before the assigned time.

Justin's major problem is keeping his 250 warehouse workers motivated so that they load the trucks quickly and accurately. For many of the workers, the work is fairly boring. The workers constantly listen to music on their iPods, take extra time on their breaks, and congregate in groups to discuss the latest sports events or other headline news. Every day, several employees fail to report to work because of illness.

Justin felt he needed to do something to reduce the number of incorrectly filled orders and the slow orders. He instituted a motivational program that he felt would encourage both accuracy and speed. Since time off is valued by some employees, he chose to give workers an entire day off with pay as one option. The other option was a $100 bonus.

Rewards would be given every month to the fifteen work teams that had the best loading record. The members of each team are allowed to decide whether they each want a $100 bonus or one day off with pay. The program has been in effect for ninety days, and 225 individuals have received awards. Justin has broken down the teams' choices on the basis of gender and age. Here are his findings:

	Chose a Day Off	Chose a $100 Bonus
Men		
18–35	8	32
36–55	29	23
56+	38	2
Women		
18–35	4	25
36–55	19	14
56+	25	6

Problems with orders being filled incorrectly have been reduced and orders are arriving in a more timely manner. So, Justin feels that the motivational program is working well and believes that the company would benefit by using it in the other two warehouses.

Case Questions

1. How important is money in motivating the employees in Justin's department?
2. Of what value are "days off" in motivating the people in Justin's department?
3. How much is the motivation program costing the company per month? Per year? (Use $20 per hour as wages.)
4. What overall conclusion can you draw regarding the value of the motivation program among the warehouse workers? What are the differences among the ages of workers and between male and female workers? What does that tell you about their values?
5. Based on your analysis of the case, which motivational theory is Justin using and why? Give examples.
6. What are your conclusions about improving boredom among the workers? Will Justin's motivational program continue to give improved results?
7. What suggestions do you have for improving the system and reducing the costs of operations?

PART 2

THE SOCIAL SYSTEM

The reason for studying the social system of organizations is to learn why people act as they do. In this section, three major areas will be explored: individual behavior, group behavior, and the informal organization.

The goals for this section are to:

1. Review the nature of individual behavior; study some of its components—values, perceptions, attitudes, and personality; examine ways for managers to improve their understanding of interpersonal behavior; and discuss how to write an effective resume.

2. Examine common types of groups, their stages of development, and their major characteristics—roles, norms, status, and cohesiveness; examine decision making within groups with a focus on ways groups gain power over other groups; explore how managers can resolve intergroup conflict and improve performance; discuss team building; and examine the job-hunting process.

3. Compare and contrast formal and informal organizations, explore grapevine communication patterns within informal organizations, examine the benefits and drawbacks associated with informal organizations, look at ways managers can deal with and use the informal organization to increase employee productivity, and review interviewing techniques.

After reading this part of the book, you should have a solid understanding of human behavior at work. In particular, you should know a great deal about individual and group behaviors in organizations and be aware of how both individuals and groups use the informal organization to accomplish their objectives. You will know more about team building and how different types of teams can be used to get things done. Your career can be enhanced by learning to write an effective resume, to conduct a successful job hunt, and to use proper techniques in the interview process.

CHAPTER 3 — Individual Behavior

At the very heart of human relations is the need for an understanding of human behavior. To be effective, managers need to have an understanding of how and why people act as they do. In this chapter, individual behavior is explored.

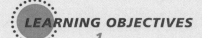

LEARNING OBJECTIVES

1
Identify and describe some of the common values held by all individuals.

2
Describe perception and explain why it is a determinant of individual behavior.

3
Explain how stereotyping can influence a person's view of another's behavior.

4
Define attitude and describe its impact on worker output.

5
Define personality and discuss the major forces affecting personality development.

6
Explain how gender differences influence interpersonal behavior.

7
Describe how assertiveness training can help managers and subordinates improve their understanding of interpersonal behavior.

8
Prepare an effective resume.

Individual Opinions Really Count

Not only do effective organizations believe that their employees are their most important asset, but they also go out of their way to ensure that these individuals feel they are being treated fairly and their talents are being effectively used. A good example is the Texas Nameplate Company, Inc., which makes high quality metallic nameplate products in Dallas, Texas. Since 1946, Texas Nameplate's dedication to performance excellence and innovation has been unmatched in the industry. It is a small company that employs about forty employees who represent the diversity in the Dallas-Fort Worth area. The average tenure of its employees is twelve years. Its organization does not follow the typical hierarchical command structure of authority or power, but rather a round-wheel structure of teams where the contributions of all employees are equally necessary and are treated with equal value. The company has created an environment where the managers trust employees, value their input, and encourage decisions. To keep employees informed and updated on what is happening in every job in the system, a program called "The New Hotrod" was developed. It is referred to as the company's "Pipeline Dashboard." This gives everyone in the company access to all information. As a result, employees can better meet customers' needs by being able to personalize services and provide greater responsiveness, reliability, and flexibility for customers. This puts every employee in charge of decision making.

Employees are encouraged to develop personal Web pages and link them to other work areas within the organization. This gives other employees a chance to know the people on their team. Personal satisfaction also comes through employee recognition of personal accomplishments, whether it is work, family, or community activities. The aim of the company is to encourage employees to be the best, to show respect, and to help others, resulting in a company of appreciated persons. This philosophy helped Texas Nameplate be a two-time winner of the Malcolm Baldrige National Quality Award. Only three companies in history have received this award twice.

The idea of giving more authority to individuals is also being pursued by multinational firms such as Coca-Cola, which has replaced American managers with locals in many of its operations outside the United States. For example Alexander B. Cummings, a West African native, is president and CAO of the African group, and José Octavio Reyes, a native of Mexico, is president of the Latin American group. The reason is that local managers better understand the needs of the local market, and this focus on individual markets is important to Coke, given that it has operations in more than two hundred countries, owns 51 percent of the world market for carbonated soft drinks, and 70 percent of its profits come from outside the United States.

The company also wants to strengthen its relations with its employees in countries where many feel the company has neglected them. In particular, Coke wants to build the company as a host of international markets that are allowed to respond to the needs of their collective niches and not have to take orders from the home office regarding how to run local operations. Simply put, the firm is pushing a new philosophy of "think globally, act locally." This means working more closely with local authorities, local managers, and local customers and giving more authority to local operations.

Coca-Cola continues to use new and innovative ways to seek input from its consumers—individuals whose opinions make a difference in the bottom line of the company. Recently Coca-Cola Fountain and the ICEE Company conducted a nationwide Internet vote to determine the newest flavor, from among ten flavors, to develop as a new product. The grand prize was an all expenses paid trip for four to Universal Studios, Orlando.

Coca-Cola also is involved in bridging the growing "digital divide" between the information and communications technology (ITC) "haves" and "have-nots." Coca-Cola and the United Nations Development Programme created a partnership to pilot a project to bridge the "digital divide" in Malaysia. In this first endeavor for Coke, the goal was to bring e-learning opportunities and ITC training resources to students, teachers, and local communities who can make a difference to others. For Coca-Cola, bridging the information and knowledge gap is an extremely important priority as it moves into the new global knowledge economy. Coca-Cola is built on a deep and abiding relationship and trust with all its constituents: bottlers, customers, consumers, shareowners, employees, suppliers, and the varying communities of which it is an integral part. Another example of how Coca-Cola has made a difference in its employees' lives is the assistance it provided during Hurricanes Rita and Katrina in 2005 and again in 2010 during the Haiti earthquake. Coca-Cola provided an array of products and services, as well as huge amounts of money, to help not only its employees, but also others who were directly impacted by the devastation.

Coca-Cola feels that its greatest assets are its people. It is what grows the business and that is why the company takes a holistic view of rewarding and recognizing its employees. Coca-Cola University (CCU) is designed to unleash the full potential of its employees by offering a one-stop shop for all learning and capability building activities across the entire company. Employees can take classes in a wide range of areas. The CCU conducts best practice research and provides coaching/consulting services to its employees. Coca-Cola values the health and well-being of its employees and provides a variety of market-competitive benefit programs that address employee needs. To ensure that employees receive the benefits that they value, the company regularly assesses the program. Over the past decade, Coca-Cola has won corporate social responsibility awards around the world—China, India, Nigeria, Germany, and Ukraine.

For the first time, in late 2005 Coca-Cola sponsored a symposium for its women employees. It was billed as a "celebration of women in the Coca-Cola Company." It demonstrated the company's commitment to women as employees and highlighted the many ways women are important to the future of the Coca-Cola business. The women were challenged to embrace diversity, grow, become skilled, and find their niche—the place where they could excel in the company. More than one thousand women attended the meeting, which developed as a result of feedback gathered from female employees during the previous year. Coca-Cola is still committed to supporting women and diversity. For example, in 2010, Kathy Waller, vice president and controller, was named among the seventy-five most powerful women in business by *Black Enterprise* magazine. In 2009, *Black Enterprise* magazine listed Coca-Cola among the top "Forty Best Companies for Diversity" after conducting a comprehensive outreach effort to the CEOs of the top one thousand publicly traded companies and the diversity executives of the fifty leading global companies with strong U.S. operations.

The Nature of the Individual

Identify and describe some of the common values held by all individuals.

The individual is a complex being, but this complexity does not stop most people from trying to generalize about human behavior by summing up individuals with a descriptive cliché, such as "people are basically good," or "everybody has his or her price; it's just a matter of how much." Some clichés are totally accurate, some partially accurate, and the rest erroneous. In human relations, however, we need to be much more scientific in our analysis of individuals and to realize that people exhibit many different types of behavior. For example, sometimes people are very rational, and at other times they are highly emotional; sometimes they are controlled by their environment, and at other times they control their environment; sometimes they are interested in economic objectives, and at other times they are more concerned with self-actualizing.

However, in any examination of individual behavior, we must look at the total person. This requires an examination of the major components of individual behavior. The four major components that merit our attention are values, perceptions, attitudes, and personality.

Values

A **value** is something that has worth or importance to an individual. Values are influenced in many ways. Parents, friends, and teachers all play a role; so do coworkers, business associates, and others with whom we come in contact. In fact, learning and experience are the two greatest forces in shaping an individual's values.

One way of examining values is in terms of terminal and instrumental values. A **terminal value** is expressed in terms of a desired goal or an end. An **instrumental value** is the means for achieving the desired goals.[1] Here are some examples:

Terminal Values (Ends)	Instrumental Values (Means)
Self-respect	Honesty
A comfortable life	Independence
Family security	Ambition
Wisdom	Courage
A sense of accomplishment	Helpfulness

Another way to examine values is in terms of a predetermined list and the preferences people have for these values. Eduard Spranger has identified six values common to everyone: theoretical, economic, aesthetic, social, political, and religious (see Figure 3.1).

Different occupational groups tend to have different value profiles. For example, professors of biology tend to be highest in theoretical interests, businesspeople have very high economic values, artists place great significance on aesthetic values, social workers have high social values, politicians have strong political values, and members of the clergy hold high religious values. However, to some degree, each of these values is present within, and important to, each of us. We must remember that what may be important to management is not necessarily important to the "rank and file." For this reason, values are of major importance in the study of human relations.

Figure 3.1
Spranger's Value Types

Theoretical
The overriding interest of the theoretical person is the discovery of truth. In pursuing this goal, the person often looks for identities and differences, trying to divest himself or herself of judgments regarding the beauty or utility of objects. The chief aim in life of this person is to systematize and order knowledge.

Economic
The economic person is basically interested in what is useful. In addition to self-preservation, the person is concerned with the production of goods and services and the accumulation of wealth. The individual is thoroughly practical and conforms well to the prevailing stereotype of the American businessperson.

Aesthetic
The aesthetic person sees highest value in form and harmony. Although the person might not necessarily be an artist, the individual's chief interest is in the artistic episodes of life. For example, aesthetic people often like the beautiful insignia of pomp and power but oppose political activity that represses individual thought.

Social
The highest value for the social person is love of people. This individual prizes other people as ends and, as a result, is kind, sympathetic, and unselfish. The social person regards love itself as the only suitable form of human relationship. This person's interests are very close to those of the religious person.

Political
The political person is interested primarily in power. This individual need not be a politician. Because competition and struggle play a large part in life, he or she will do well in any career or job in which a high power value is necessary for success, whether this be power over people (as in the case of a top manager) or over the environment (as in the case of an engineer who makes the final decision on how to build something).

Religious
The highest value for the religious person is unity. This individual seeks to relate himself or herself to the embracing totality of the cosmos. For some, there is an attempt to withdraw from active association with the outside world (as in the case of monks in a monastery); for others there is some self-denial and meditation coupled with a life of work among local people who attend their church or subscribe to the same religious beliefs.

Source: Allport, Gordon W., and Vernon, Philip E. A study of values. Manual of directions. Boston: Houghton Mifflin Company, rev. ed. 1931. Spranger, Eduard Lebensformen. Halle (Saale): Niemeyer, 1914. Translation by P. J. W. Pigors Types of Men. New York: G. E. Stechert Company, 1928.

Table 3.1
Value Profiles for Different Groups

Spranger Value	Average Male College Student[a]	Average Female College Student[a]	Successful Male Manager[b]	Successful Female Manager[c]
Theoretical	43	36	44	39
Economic	42	37	45	47
Aesthetic	37	44	35	42
Social	37	42	33	31
Political	43	38	44	46
Religious	38	43	39	35

[a]Source: Gordon W. Allport, Philip E. Vernon and G. Lindzey, *Study of Values Manual* (Boston, MA: Houghton Mifflin Company, 1970), p. 11.
[b]Source: William D. Guth and Renato Tagiuri, "Personal Values and Corporate Strategy," *Harvard Business Review*, September–October 1965, p. 126.
[c]Source: Richard M. Hodgetts, Mildred G. Pryor, Harry N. Mills, and Karen Brinkman, "A Profile of the Successful Executive," *Academy of Management Proceedings*, August 1978, p. 378.

Study of Values. The most popular test designed to provide information and insight on individual values is the Allport–Vernon–Lindzey Study of Values.[2] This test is designed to measure one's preference for each of Spranger's values. From the responses, a value profile can be constructed for the individual. In fact, the test has been given a sufficient number of times so as to establish value profiles for different groups. Table 3.1 provides such profiles for the average male college student, average female college student, successful male business manager, and successful female business manager. Figure 3.2 is a graph of these four profiles. Note that the profile of the successful female

Figure 3.2 Value Profiles

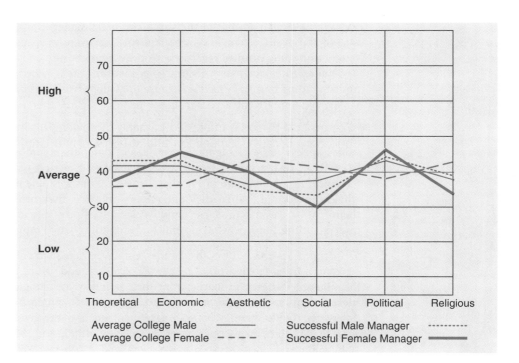

Average College Male ——————— Successful Male Manager - - - - - - - - -
Average College Female – – – – Successful Female Manager ▬▬▬▬

What Is Important to You?

The following quiz is designed to measure how you value certain lifestyles and rewards. Read and then rank each statement using the following scale:

5 = Strongly agree or definitely true
4 = Generally agree or mostly true
3 = Neither agree nor disagree
2 = Generally disagree or mostly false
1 = Strongly disagree or definitely false

____ a. You often take the lead and direct others.
____ b. You believe people should be paid based on how hard they work and what they accomplish.
____ c. You would like to be rewarded in direct proportion to your performance.
____ d. You believe that, in the long run, good people win and bad people lose.
____ e. You would be more motivated by financial rewards than by praise.
____ f. You enjoy being in charge.
____ g. Dishonesty should not be tolerated.

____ h. It makes you angry when you know how to do something but no one wants to listen to you.
____ i. One of your life's goals is to be financially independent.
____ j. Getting ahead should be based on performance and not politics.
____ k. You would enjoy working on a sales commission rather than a straight salary.
____ l. You would like a job that requires hard selling.
____ m. Owning your own business has strong appeal for you.
____ n. Everyone should be treated equally, and favoritism should be discouraged.
____ o. You would enjoy managing a business.

Enter your answers in the appropriate spaces below. Then total each group and divide by five to obtain your average response for each group.

The interpretation of your answers can be found at the end of the chapter.

Group 1	Group 2	Group 3
a. _____	b. _____	c. _____
f. _____	d. _____	e. _____
h. _____	g. _____	i. _____
l. _____	j. _____	k. _____
o. _____	n. _____	m. _____
Total _____	Total _____	Total _____
Average _____	Average _____	Average _____

manager is similar to that of the successful male manager and distinctly different from that of the average female college student. Apparently, successful managers have the same basic value profiles regardless of their gender.

Value tests such as the one provided in the "Time Out" box are useful to understanding human behavior because they identify what is important to an individual. Unless we know what a person holds in high regard, there is little hope that we can motivate or manage the person effectively. (The "Time Out" box provides some insights regarding your own values.) The great problem for today's managers, however, is that values appear to be changing. The values of our fathers and grandfathers are different from those of the modern generation. Raised in a period of affluence and reared on television in a high-technology, digital society, young people have different ideas about what is important. When they enter the workforce, they bring these new values with them. As a result, modern employees' values are an important focal point in understanding human behavior and understanding why employees do what they do.

Employee Values. Over the decades, employee values have changed. Employees of each generation bring to the workplace new expectations and values that they have acquired in their lifetime—drawn primarily from their family values, home and school experiences, friends, and social engagements. Each generation approaches life and employment differently. While there is some disagreement on how the generations are divided, most agree that Matures are those who were born between 1908 and 1945; baby boomers, between 1946 and 1964; Gen Xers, between 1965 and 1979; Gen Yers, sometimes called the

Millennials, from 1979 to 1990; and Gen Zers, between 1990 and 2001. The values each generation brings to the workplace are different. Baby boomers grew up after World War II in very different economic times. They learned to juggle job and family, while Gen Xers move in and out of the workforce to accommodate kids and outside interests. The Gen Yers are hardworking, entrepreneurial, authentic, candid, and upbeat. They have been coddled since birth, and they expect to be continually stimulated at their jobs and to have their feelings and opinions count. Negative feedback can quickly bring tears. Friendship is a strong motivator for them. Gen Yers are not afraid to change jobs, they depend on their digitally handheld devices, and they often work remotely. Volunteering is important to them. To create a cohesive workplace, it is important for older workers to understand Gen Yers and be able to adapt to their values and demands. Today baby boomers make up the majority of U.S. employees, but are increasingly being supervised by Gen Xers, as well as Millennials. Millennials, on the other hand, have a high influence over their parents' purchasing decisions, and love to wear designer clothing, jewelry, and watches. Looking stylish is important to feeling good about themselves. The Internet is where they shop, while baby boomers prefer shopping in department stores. Millennials are highly connected, having had a lifelong use of communications and media technologies such as DVDs; World Wide Web; instant messaging; text messaging; iPods, cellular phones, and smart phones; and Facebook and Twitter social networks. These workers demand productive tasks from the first day of work.[3] The modern generation sees its work and personal lives as much more integrated than previous generations.

Differences in generational values can result in misunderstandings between employees and managers. Senior generations cannot assume the younger generations define job success in the same way as they do. Younger generations want different things from their job. This can cause real challenges for management. One standard way of dealing with all employees usually does not work.

What Do Employees Want?   Princeton Survey Research Associates International conducted a national poll on the benefits that are important to employees when choosing a job. They found that 84 percent ranked health insurance at the very top. Job security and clear policies and procedures were ranked in importance by 82 percent each followed by 76 percent ranking retirement or pension plan as important. A flexible, family-friendly workplace was ranked in fifth place by 71 percent. Pay was ranked tenth on the list. Other things included getting quick decisions on issues, working with talented managers, having the potential for promotions, and being creative and intellectually stimulated.[4] Another survey of technology employees indicated that flexible work arrangements, telecommuting, stock purchase plan, fitness facility, on-site cafeteria, and on-site child care would help them choose one job over another.[5]

In researching the differences among the four generations of employees, Deloitte, a large pubic accounting and consulting firm, found three main dividing lines between the baby boomers and Gen Xers and Gen Yers. Deloitte found that the younger generations rely more heavily on technologies, and their attitudes differ about how and when work gets accomplished and rewarded. The younger generations expect employers to demonstrate exceptional interest in their professional growth. They expect constant challenges and stimulation, which has required Deloitte's managers to learn new ways of coaching, mentoring, and communicating expectations. Deloitte is not alone; companies of varying sizes are grappling with how to address career planning amid momentous demographic shifts in the U.S. labor market. Human relations is at the very heart of this dilemma.[6] To recruit and hire new talent to fit the workplace, management must take the time to learn what their employees want from their workplace and what is important to them. For example, Robert McDonald, now CEO and president of Procter & Gamble,

Gen Xers Workforce	Graying Workforce
Ongoing training, especially in cutting-edge technologies	Pay, benefits, and incentives (long-term care and health insurance, elder-care programs)
Innovative career paths	Avenues for professional development
Floating assignments	Decreased and/or flexible hours
Flex schedules, part-time work, telecommuting, and job-shares that won't affect career growth	Short commutes of 5–10 miles to the job
Performance-based monetary incentives	Computer education classes
Competitive pay	
Increased freedom in the workplace, prefer mentoring rather than a traditional supervisory style	

Source: "Today's Hiring Needs Call for Creative Strategies," http://www.reidlondonhouse.com.

has stated, "We actually recruit for values."[7] This strategy creates a more compatible workplace, reducing problems among workers.

With their savings being depleted during the last recession, older workers are putting off retirement and staying in jobs that otherwise would be freed up for younger workers.[8] These older workers are becoming a major part of what is emerging as the new permanent temporary workforce. As depicted in Table 3.2, "Workplace Needs," the needs and wants of the Gen Xers differ from those of more mature employees in the workplace. Generation gaps between managers and workers bring different values to the workplace. These differences impact the workplace in many ways—recruiting, hiring, coaching, training, and rewarding, to name a few. Even more disturbing is research that shows that the values of many managers have not changed over the last two decades. This means that there is a "values gap" between the way managers run their organizations and the way lower-level employees want the organizations to be run, and this is likely to create major human relations problems in the future. For this reason, many organizations are now developing new approaches to managing their people.

Approaches Used to Meet Workers' Needs. Flextime is growing in importance, with more firms every year offering flexible work schedules. In July 2009, a survey of four hundred employers by the Families and Work Institute in New York found that 81 percent have flexible work arrangements such as telecommuting, compressed workweeks, phased retirement, and voluntary reduced hours. These results show that employers are utilizing flexible programs. To support flexible work programs, Rep. Carolyn Maloney, D-New York, introduced the Working Families Flexibility Act, which guarantees workers they can ask their employers for adjustments in the number of hours, days, and locations required for their jobs.[9] Another growing concept, work sharing, allows employers to reduce work hours instead of jobs. When a company faces a decline in demand for its products or services, it could, for example, trim the hours for all workers by 20 percent instead of laying off 20 percent of its workforce. Work-sharing programs benefit both the workers and the employers. Work sharing is also practiced in Germany.[10] Over the past decade, work-life programs have increasing in popularity among employers who want to retain their talented top employees. In addition to medical leave, some employers are offering employees sabbaticals—extended leaves of absences to pursue personal endeavors. Dana Vandecoevering, manager of the work-life program at Intel Corporation, states that sabbaticals are embedded into the firm's culture. There is evidence in current periodicals that a significant number of employers are looking at this option as a way to attract, engage, and retain talent.[11] Yet another practice is teaming younger and older employees. Randstad, a Dutch company, has successfully teamed younger workers with older workers in its sales department. They work together until the business has grown to a certain size; then new assignments are made. The matching of employees is carefully orchestrated by the human resources department.[12] All these strategies address employees' desires for more control of their lives in the workplace.

Another trend is a move toward reducing meetings and eliminating busy work, so people have more time to relax and unleash their creative potential. At Nestle USA, for example, meetings after 10 A.M. on Friday are prohibited. At Hewlett-Packard, backup people are used to fill in so personnel can take extended vacations. These efforts are all part of a growing trend toward helping employees "unplug" from the office and "get a life."[13] These strategies are designed to also create a stronger employer–employee partnership and show workers that management's values and their own are similar.[14] Of course, to a large degree, these strategies are successful only if employees perceive them as valuable, because perception is a key element in individual behavior.[15]

✔ CHECK YOUR UNDERSTANDING

What Is Important to You?

1. Complete the "Time Out" exercise on page 92.
2. Identify one of your personal values. Tell how it works for you or against you in work situations.
3. What experiences have you had where your generational values have conflicted with the generational values of others?

Describe perception and explain why it is a determinant of individual behavior.

Perception

Perception is a person's view of reality and is affected by, among other things, the individual's values. For example, if a person is a member of a union, he or she may discount much of what management says about declining sales, decreased profit margins, and the need for the union and management to work as a team. Most of this talk may be regarded as an attempt by management to exploit the workforce for its own gain. Conversely, many people in management admit they have a hard time understanding the union's point of view, because they believe it is more interested in "ripping off" the company than in working for the overall good of both groups. This is an example of a common situation in which each person agrees with his or her own group's point of view but regards the other group's point of view as incorrect or biased. Human relations specialists call this selective perception, and sometimes this perception is incorrect. For example, many people believe that the Internal Revenue Service (IRS) is most likely to audit those who make large amounts of money, because the chance of finding errors in their income tax returns is more likely than finding errors in the returns of those who make small incomes, even though the incomes have risen by approximately 30 percent from the last decade. Similarly, many people believe that the U.S. Post Office provides very poor service, but satisfaction surveys report that most respondents are pleased with the service, and they rank the post office ahead of all major airlines and most hotel chains.[16] So selective perception is sometimes incorrect. To understand why individuals perceive things differently, it is helpful to compare sensory reality and normative reality.

Sensory Reality and Normative Reality. Physical reality is **sensory reality**. A computer, an automobile, and a house are all physical objects that people tend to perceive accurately. However, sometimes physical items present perception problems. Before you read further, examine the pictures in Figure 3.3 and answer the question accompanying each.

In Figure 3.3, Section A, the two lines are of the same length, although most people think that the lower line is longer than the upper one. The two diagonal lines at the ends of each horizontal line create this perceptual illusion, which make those lines seem stretched or compressed. In Figure 3.3, Section B, the two lines running across the picture are horizontal, although most people think the lines bend in at the end. This illusion is a result of the diagonal background lines, which appear to be bowing the center parts of the horizontal lines outward. In Figure 3.3, Section C, we are moving away from sensory reality and toward **normative reality**, which is best defined as interpretive reality. In the first two pictures in Figure 3.3, there was a right answer, whether or not you saw it there. You can verify the answers by simply using a ruler to measure the lines or the distance between them. There is more than one right answer in Figure 3.3, Section C, however, and what one person sees, another may not. This is why

Figure 3.3
The Perceptual
Processes

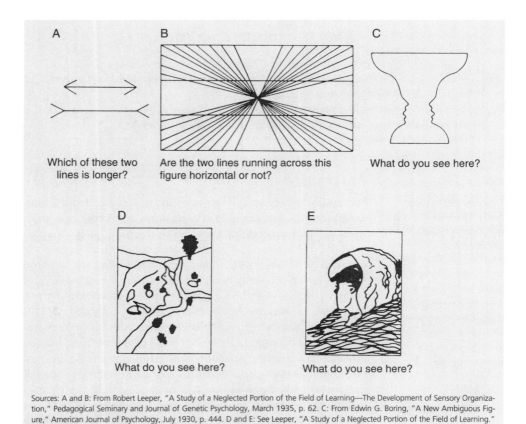

A

Which of these two lines is longer?

B

Are the two lines running across this figure horizontal or not?

C

What do you see here?

D

What do you see here?

E

What do you see here?

Sources: A and B: From Robert Leeper, "A Study of a Neglected Portion of the Field of Learning—The Development of Sensory Organization," Pedagogical Seminary and Journal of Genetic Psychology, March 1935, p. 62. C: From Edwin G. Boring, "A New Ambiguous Figure," American Journal of Psychology, July 1930, p. 444. D and E: See Leeper, "A Study of a Neglected Portion of the Field of Learning." Originally drawn by cartoonist W. E. Hill and published in Puck, November 6, 1915.

Figure 3.4
The Pirate and the Rabbit

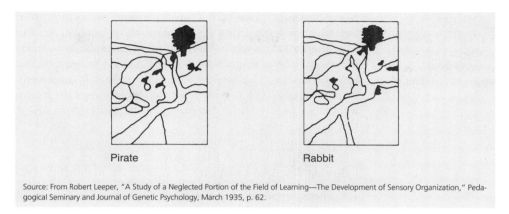

Pirate   Rabbit

Source: From Robert Leeper, "A Study of a Neglected Portion of the Field of Learning—The Development of Sensory Organization," Pedagogical Seminary and Journal of Genetic Psychology, March 1935, p. 62.

Figure 3.5
The Old Woman and the Young Woman

Old Woman   Young Woman

Source: From Robert Leeper, "A Study of a Neglected Portion of the Field of Learning—The Development of Sensory Organization," Pedagogical Seminary and Journal of Genetic Psychology, March 1935, p. 62.

we call it interpretive reality. Some people see a goblet in this picture; others see the facial profiles of twins facing each other.

The picture in Figure 3.3, Section D, is deliberately ambiguous. Some people see a road, a rock, a tree, and some surrounding terrain. Others see the face of a pirate. Still others see a rabbit. Look at Figure 3.4, in which the clear pictures of the pirate and the rabbit can be seen. Note that the ambiguity is reduced if the artist puts more detail in one part of the picture than in the other.

Figure 3.3, Section E, is also a deliberately ambiguous picture. Some people see an old woman; some see a young woman. Figure 3.5 is a clear picture of both. Once again, the artist has reduced the ambiguity by putting in the necessary detail.

What Do You See?   When we examine individual behavior and the impact of perception on that behavior, it is important to remember that people see what they either want to see or are trained to see. Therefore, in terms of human relations, the manager must try to understand the worker's perception of reality. Employees willingly accept management's methods only when they perceive those methods to be in the employees' best interests. Otherwise, they will resort to such perceptual pitfalls as selective perception, which we just examined, and stereotyping. For example, Harvey Lester, a new employee, has been having trouble mastering his new job. His boss, Lois, tells him that if he does not improve, she will have to let him go. Feeling that he is on the verge of being fired, Harvey quits. What Lois saw as a mild reprimand designed to improve output is interpreted as a threat resulting in a resignation. Each party interpreted the action differently.

Explain how stereotyping can influence a person's view of another's behavior.

Stereotyping.   One of the most common perception problems is that of **stereotyping**, which is generalizing a particular trait or behavior to all members of a given group. Too often a stereotype is based on an oversimplified or mistaken attitude, opinion, or judgment. The manager who believes that no union can be trusted has a stereotyped view of unions. The worker who believes that management is always out to exploit employees also has a stereotyped belief. So, too, does the male manager who believes that women are unsuitable for top management positions because they are too emotional and lack aggressiveness.

Every one of us tries to stereotype people, whether it is in the job environment or in a social setting. We even have standard stereotypes for classes or nationalities. Read the following descriptions and try to identify the nationality described.

- These people are loyal to family ties and always look after their younger brothers and sisters.
- These people believe in fair play, are conservative, and keep a stiff upper lip.
- These people are very scientific, industrious, and hard working.
- These people love caviar, Bolshoi dancing, and music by Tchaikovsky.
- These people love pasta, wine, and—most of all—great opera.

Most people say that the first description is that of the Chinese and the second is that of the English. The remaining three are German, Russian, and Italian. To some degree, all these stereotypes are both accurate and inaccurate. For example, in regard to the first description, are not most people loyal to family ties? In regard to the second description, is Britain the only country in which fair play is important? And is Germany the most scientific and industrious of all nations? Research shows that most people of the world attribute these traits not to the Germans but to the Americans! The last two descriptions are also stereotypes because they do not describe one group to the exclusion of all others.

In examining individual behavior, then, it is important to realize that most people employ stereotyping. Stereotyping is very real and is alive in today's workplace. Each generation, for example, has its own perceptions about another generation. If members of one group—baby boomers—believe that members of another group are less flexible, even if they are not, they believe it. Stereotyping is an easy way to generalize about behavior.[17] The effective manager, however, tries to evaluate each person as an individual and to remain aware of his or her own stereotypical beliefs so as to reduce their effect on his or her judgments. For example, what do men have to say about their female counterparts? Successful male managers do not let the old stereotypes influence them. They judge women on the basis of how well they do their jobs. In fact, based on survey responses from more than 6,500 middle- and upper-level male managers, recent research shows that the higher the educational level of the manager, the more likely it is that he has a high acceptance of women in managerial positions. Additionally, men who work for women generally have a higher acceptance of them as managers than do men who have not had such an experience. These findings indicate that stereotypes of women in the workplace are beginning to fade. As more and more women enter the ranks of management, negative attitudes and biases against them continue to lessen. However, there is still a long way to go.

Define attitude and describe its impact on worker output.

Attitudes

A person's feelings about objects, activities, events, and other people are termed **attitudes**. These feelings usually are learned over time and are a major factor in determining individual behavior.

Components of Attitudes. There are three basic components of attitudes: cognitive, affective, and behavioral. Each plays a major role in attitude formation.

The **cognitive component** is the set of values and beliefs that a person has toward a person, an object, or an event. For example, a coworker says, "I don't like the boss. He's out to get me." The cognitive component of this attitude is the belief that the boss is unfair or punitive. The cognitive component creates the basis or reason for the negative attitude. If the worker were to change his mind and believe that the boss was fair, the basis for the attitude would change and the worker would now have a positive attitude toward the boss.

The **affective component** is the emotional feeling that is attached to an attitude. It is the emotion that is felt with regard to a person, an object, or an event. When we feel happiness or anger or disappointment, this is the affective component. When our favorite baseball team loses an important game and we feel sad, this too is a result of the affective component. The affective component is a result of our feelings toward someone or something. The cognitive component influences the affective component. The person who dislikes the boss may feel happy when he learns that the manager has been transferred to another office.

The **behavioral component** is the tendency to act in a particular way toward a person, an object, or an event. For example, when the employee learns that the boss is to be transferred to another location, the employee smiles. When your favorite team comes from behind to win a game in the bottom of the ninth, you cheer. If you enjoy your human relations course, you are likely to show up on time for all classes and participate when asked to do so.

One way to remember the three components of attitude is to think of them in the order they have been presented. This order moves from the cause of attitudes to the results. The cognitive component is the belief that is the reason for the attitude, the affective component is the emotional feeling that results from this belief, and the behavioral component is the tendency to act in a particular way in response to this feeling. Attitude is a combination of cognitive, affective, and behavioral components.

$$\text{Attitude} = \text{Cognitive Component} + \text{Affective Component} + \text{Behavioral Component}$$

Examples of each component are:

Cognitive	Affective	Behavioral
Causes	Emotions	Actions
Values	Feelings	Responses
Beliefs	Happiness	Results
Reasons	Anger	Smiles

A good example of how attitudes affect behavior is found by comparing baby boomers (or boomers for short) and Gen Xers (also called Busters because they are trying to move up in the ranks). Here is a comparison of the attitudes that each holds about the other:

How Boomers Feel about Busters	How Busters Feel about Boomers
They are too cocky and unwilling to pay their dues.	They spend too much office time politicking and not enough time working.
They lack loyalty and commitment to their work.	They lack technical know-how.

They will not go the extra mile.	They have coasted through life by arriving on the scene during the golden age of American business.
They are naive and whine too much.	They are holding down jobs for which younger employees are better qualified.
They have no respect for authority.	They want to control things and not share power.

Obviously, the two groups have different attitudes regarding each other, and the challenge rests in the lap of the Boomers because today they are the managers. What can these individuals do to manage the Gen Xers effectively? One of the first steps is to realize that Gen Xers have grown up in an environment vastly different from that of the Boomers. During the years 1946 to 1964, the Boomers saw both economic growth and recession a number of times. For example, recessions marked the late 1950s, the late 1960s, the mid-1970s—a strong and prolonged recession—and in the late 2000s. At one point, interest rates on loans approached 20 percent and hundreds of thousands of businesses went bankrupt. Growing up and working in this environment, many Boomers were happy to have a job, and they were loyal to their companies. Beginning in the mid-1980s, however, the economy began to regain strength and, except for a downturn in the early 1990s, America enjoyed two decades of economic prosperity. The Gen Xers who grew up in this period saw unemployment drop dramatically, while the importance of knowledge workers increased sharply and traditional work arrangements gave way to new approaches such as flexible work hours.[18] Additionally, many of the Gen Xers' working parents who were thrown out of work because of company cutbacks often found other jobs in smaller, more entrepreneurial firms. This experience led many Gen Xers to believe that company loyalty was a thing of the past, which engendered their willingness to make demands on the company and to switch to other firms if these demands were not met.

How, then, can the young, aggressive workforce be managed? One expert on the subject has recommended that managers understand the needs that Gen Xers have and what they are looking for in their jobs. These include the following:

1. They do not want to do the same thing day after day; they like variety.
2. They are not motivated by money alone; they also want to grow and learn by facing new challenges and opportunities.
3. They are looking for jobs that are cool, fun, and fulfilling.
4. They believe that if they keep growing and learning, that's all the security they are going to need; advancing their skill set is their top priority.
5. They have a tremendous thirst for knowledge.
6. They like to work in a team environment, in contrast to their bosses, who typically like to work independently.
7. They like to learn by doing—and by making mistakes as they go along.
8. They tend to challenge the established way of doing things because they believe there is always a better way.
9. They want regular and frequent feedback on their performance.
10. They are looking to blend their careers with their personal lives.[19]

A comparison of these two groups clearly illustrates why many firms have found attitude to be a major productivity challenge.

Gen Yers. Gen Yers, sometimes called Echo Boomers (born 1979–1990), are the latest generation of workers, who have their own set of attitudes. They are techno-savvy and demand to be treated differently, starting with the interviewing process. Gen Yers are turned off by needless bureaucracy and red tape. The interviewing process must be designed to determine how the values and beliefs of the applicant can be connected to the values and beliefs of the company. This can be done by an assessment test that focuses on the values needed in the job, through well-written interview questions, and in team interviewing. For example, at Southwest Airlines, the interview process consists of several relaxed informal meetings comprising both employees and human relations staff. This gives the applicants an opportunity to learn firsthand about the employees' as well as the company's values and vice versa. The informal setting promotes relaxation and encourages applicants to talk about things that are important to them. Monarch Ski & Snowboard Area in southwestern Colorado uses Gen Yers as first responders to contact applicants and tell them how the job works. This immediately puts the applicant at ease. To find Gen Yers, IKEA uses nonstandard strategies for advertising jobs. For example, it posts ads in local video game stores, Internet cafes, and even handwritten ads on the walls of public bathrooms.[20]

Barbara Moses, an organizational career management expert, speaker, and author of *What Next: Find the Work That's Right for You*, states that "every generation sees the world differently. Their attitudes and expectations are influenced by what was extant during their formative years and when they entered the workplace." Gen Yers' values echo those of their parents and bosses—comfort and a good life with a striving to balance work and personal life. As a whole, this generation is the first that "has not rebelled against their parents' or society's values, or against a work world they saw as withholding opportunities." Barbara Moses suggests some tips for managing Gen Yers.

1. Don't expect them to express ambition (at least not the way you used to).
2. Provide a great workplace that promotes balance.
3. Don't be scared of them (even if you're scared of your kid).
4. Don't assume they are adversarial or don't respect you.
5. Treat them with sensitivity.
6. Communicate in a vivid and compelling way.
7. Provide a compelling value proposition (what accomplishments or skills can the worker expect after twelve months).
8. Give them tons of feedback.
9. Provide stimulating and novel learning experiences.
10. Understand their collegiality (create strong supportive team environments).
11. Don't expect them to be like you when you were in their age (never, and I mean never, start a sentence with "when I was your age").[21]

Civil Behavior.   Human behavior is a reflection of attitude. Managers must make every effort to create a workplace that inspires civil behavior among its workers. According to various studies, people are deeply concerned about behavior toward one another. *U.S. News & World Report* found 89 percent of the respondents described incivility as a serious problem; 78 percent said it had worsened in the past ten years. Another research group, Public Agenda, found that four out of five Americans think that the "lack of respect and courtesy" has become "a serious problem and we should try to address it." For example, airlines have dealt with uncivil passengers on flights across the nation, unhappy employees have shot their bosses, irate parents have harmed coaches, and children have shot their teachers and classmates. These behaviors stem from attitude. Other examples of uncivil behavior in the workplace are verbally harassing someone on a regular basis, withholding resources to guarantee failure, and spreading stories to undermine a person's reputation in the workplace. Uncivil behavior in the workplace affects productivity, as shown in a study by Christine Pearson, a management professor at the University of North Carolina's graduate business school. Her results indicated:[22]

- Twenty-eight percent lost work time trying to avoid the instigator.
- Fifty-three percent lost work time worrying about the incident or future interactions.
- Thirty-seven percent reported a weakened sense of commitment to their organization.
- Forty-six percent thought about changing jobs to get away from the instigator.
- Twelve percent did change jobs—to avoid the instigator.

A question every manager must ask is, "Are my actions creating a kinder workplace, an environment where all people are treated with deep respect day after day?"

Impact of 9/11 and the Recession of 2008 on Employees' Attitudes.   The attitudes of many people were changed forever following September 11, 2001. These new attitudes were carried forth into the workplace and impacted how business was conducted and how employees carried out their work. Dr. Richard A. Chaifetz, chairman and CEO of ComPsych Corporation, observed a renewed emphasis on overall relationship building in the workplace. For example, employees began concentrating on ways to excel at their current jobs instead of looking for new employment. Employees realized that a key ingredient to maximizing their present job was to build strong bonds with their peers and supervisors. Living through the recession of 2008 also impacted the attitudes and values of people across the country. People became penny-pinchers instead of spendthrifts, changing buyer behaviors. They looked for cost-effective ways to live, and these coping mechanisms became engrained. People started saving more. People with jobs found themselves feeling sympathetic for others who had lost their jobs. Value became important both in the workplace as well as in the marketplace. Managers were forced to make changes in business operations and in the way they managed employees.[23] With employee morale, motivation, and productivity taking a nosedive, managers needed new strategies in engaging the remaining employees, for example, letting employees know what is going on and what products are on the drawing board, offering new perks, allowing greater flexibility in working hours, and showing employees that the company appreciates them. Employees who feel appreciated become more engaged in their work and ultimately influence the behavior and attitudes of customers who drive the profitability of the company through their purchases. Attitudes make a difference between success and failure.[24]

Family-Friendly Workplace.   Employees also want a workplace that helps them balance the demand of their work and family lives, rather than forces them to choose one over the other. People quit when rigid workplace rules cause unbearable family stress. Employees want a family-friendly workplace. For example, a manager can promote a family-friendly workplace by allowing employees to change work hours whenever a family crisis arises, such as having to take a sick child to the doctor, or to attend important events at school. Other ideas include:

- Visiting an employee following a death in the family.
- Accompanying employees to their children's ball games and recitals.
- Allowing employees' children to come to work with them occasionally.
- Allowing well-behaved pets into the workplace.
- Researching elder-care alternatives for an employee's parents.
- Sending birthday cards or cakes to employees' family members.
- Getting the company lawyer to help an employee with health insurance problems.

- Allowing family members to accompany employees during weekend travel time.
- Exploring the possibility of employees working from home.
- Giving employees a floating day off.[25]

Attitudes about Generation Os. Each year, Americans, especially children, are growing fatter and more obese. However, new data released in 2010 from the American Medical Association suggest that the rate of increase for obesity in the United States may be slowing. Still, about one-third of adults are obese. It is predicted the next generation of workers will be known as Generation Os. These workers will bring a new set of attitudes, issues, and challenges to the workplace. For example, these workers will require changes in workplace structure and new benefits. The obesity epidemic is considered America's greatest health threat, costing U.S. companies more money than smoking and alcoholism. The results of a survey conducted by the NPD Group showed that three-quarters of those surveyed felt it's OK to be overweight, which is a 45 percent increase over 1985.[26] Attitudes seem to be changing toward obesity and reflecting more positive views. Managers and supervisors have the responsibility to work effectively with all groups of workers and not discriminate among groups of workers.

Ways to Improve Employee Attitudes. SCORE (Service Corps of Retired Executives), which provides counselors to American small businesses, suggests that improving employee attitudes should begin with an examination of the manager's attitudes. Managers must:

- Be genuinely interested in their employees, customers, and suppliers.
- Respect their employees' dignity.
- Be patient, understanding, and helpful to employees.
- Let employees know that they are important to them and to the company.
- Let employees know that performance will be rewarded.
- Help employees identify what makes them feel fulfilled and happy within the job.
- Include employees as team members; ask for suggestions and respect their ideas.
- Give employees credit for their ideas, which are used.
- Listen to their employees.[27]

Attitudes are changing, and one way of dealing with this challenge is to measure it carefully.

Attitude Measurement

One way of measuring attitudes is through the use of an **attitude survey**. Attitude surveys are important for several reasons. First, they reflect current attitudes in an organization. Second, they provide a baseline against which to compare future attitude surveys. (Are attitudes improving or declining?) Third, they serve as a source of information about those areas or issues to which the organization needs to pay greater attention and those areas that are alright.

Attitude surveys are best served when they are designed to fit the specific needs of a company and even better when they reflect the needs of a specific department. Questions should be developed to gain insights into how employees feel, which can directly affect employee behavior and performance. For example, questions can range from how happy the employees are with their jobs, to how they feel about their supervisors and employee morale, to why they come to work each day. A wealth of companies is listed on the Internet that can provide businesses and organizations with design services to help them develop an individualized survey instrument or questionnaire that measures specific

Figure 3.6 Attitudes as an Intervening Variable

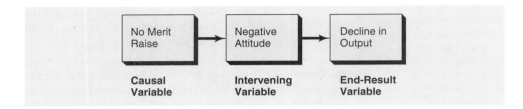

attitudes. Employees are instructed to go online and score the instrument, then feedback is provided to the business or organization. For example, www.surveymonkey.com is a website that Whole Foods uses to conduct surveys that reveal how store employees feel.

Intervening Variable. An organization must realize that attitudes are an **intervening variable**. They are influenced by causal variables and, in turn, affect end-result variables (see Figure 3.6). An individual's attitude will not decline without some cause, such as a change in leadership style, a failure to get a merit raise, or the submission of a poor performance appraisal. This cause brings about a change in attitude—the intervening variable—which then results in a decline in output—the end-result variable.

Conversely, if attitudes improve because a person is given a merit raise or is told how to obtain a merit raise in the future, his or her output increases. The raise (a causal variable) will improve attitudes (the intervening variable) and will result in more output (the end-result variable).

Attitudes Are Internal. They cannot be seen; they can only be inferred through such end-result variables as output and can be measured by means of attitude surveys. Attention to attitudes, therefore, can be one of the keys to increasing productivity because how a person feels about the organization will affect his or her output. For example, research shows that those who think positively tend to be more productive than those who do not. Dr. Martin Seligman, a university psychologist, found that individuals with positive attitudes tend to do better jobs than the average worker. Working with the Metropolitan Life Insurance Company, Seligman gave twenty-minute written tests to new salespeople to determine their attitudes. Within months, the new recruits with positive attitudes were dramatically outselling the new recruits who did not have positive attitudes. The company then used the test to screen prospective employees. During the first year of the program, this new hiring practice increased revenues by $10 million. Seligman's research shows the power of positive thinking. Those who believed that they would succeed were more successful than those who did not. Their attitudes resulted in a number of important behaviors, including:

1. The ability to shrug off bad news.
2. A willingness to take risks.
3. A desire to assume personal control of events rather than just allowing things to happen.
4. A willingness to set ambitious goals and to pursue them.[28]

Workplace Surveys. The first workplace surveys that grew out of the "research era" of the 1940s were viewed as merely opinion polls and, for the most part, were not used in any effective or targeted way. That is no longer the case. In recent years, a growing number of firms have found that attitude surveys are extremely useful in helping to measure morale and improving performance. The Springfield ReManufacturing Group of Springfield, Missouri, discovered that responses from its heavy-duty division personnel were sharply different from what management expected. In particular, 62 percent of the workers said that no one had talked to them about personal development within the last six months; 48 percent said that they did not feel that they had the opportunity to become leaders in the firm; and 43 percent said that their work-related opinions did not count. These responses were particularly surprising to management, because the heavy-duty plant was the firm's most successful operation.

Management decided to find out what was wrong. A worker committee was formed from departments throughout the division and began investigating how to improve employee attitudes. The group quickly found that many workers had been asking for a variety of efficiency-related changes for more than two years, and nothing had been done. The group also discovered that most of the complaints and concerns were a result of small problems that had been allowed to go uncorrected. Using this feedback as the basis for action, the company then began making all the necessary changes. Additionally, the firm now uses attitude measurement surveys every six months to ensure that worker concerns are quickly identified and addressed.[29]

Eaton Corporation, a Cleveland-based industrial manufacturing firm with 55,000 employees worldwide, wanted the straight story. They developed a "global employee survey in 21 languages that gathers information in several areas, including business ethics, values, employee engagement, employee relations, manager effectiveness and strategic vision." The corporate manager of human resources programs says, "the firm achieved a 96.3 percent response rate on its employee survey—despite the fact that many of its employees did not have access to personal computers." Employees could go on company time to take the survey in rooms set up by Eaton. As a result of the survey, he says, "several programs have undergone change, including performance management, rewards and recognition, tuition assistance, training and communication."[30]

In past years, a 65 percent participation rate in completing workplace surveys was considered excellent. Today, with the use of Web-based surveys, participation has climbed steadily, with a few companies managing to hit 99 percent. By developing highly targeted questions, the information gathered can be used to bring greater productivity and economic value to the company. Surveys are considered a necessary tool in creating positive workplaces.[31]

 ## CHECK YOUR UNDERSTANDING

Go to the Internet and type in Seligman in Google. Select Dr. Martin Seligman's Positive Psychology Center. Under the title, "Take Positive Psychology Questionnaires and Get Feedback," you will find a list of questionnaires. Select three of them to complete. Analyze your feedback. What are the results saying about you and your attitude? (www.ppc.sas.upenn.edu)

Define personality and discuss the major forces affecting personality development.

Personality

The relatively stable set of characteristics and tendencies that determine similarities and differences between people is termed **personality**. For example, some people are very outgoing, whereas others tend to be introverted. Some are assertive; others are passive. Every individual has a personality different from the next individual. We can think of personality as a composite of a person's entire behavioral components, which is reflected in how he or she acts.

Figure 3.7 Major
Factors Influencing
Personality

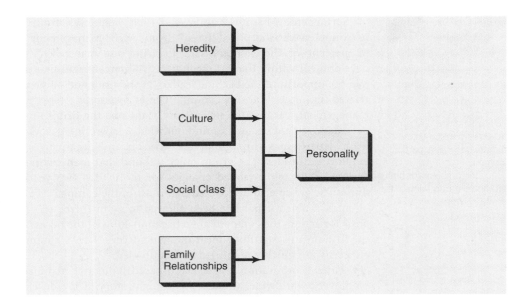

Sometimes we try to generalize about an individual's overall personality by calling him or her aggressive, hostile, kind, easygoing, or warm. These adjectives are all designed to categorize the person in a word or two; although this may be an incomplete way of describing someone, we all tend to do it. Likewise, most of us look at the way a person walks, talks, and dresses in seeking clues to his or her personality. Obviously, personality consists of many factors, making it very difficult to define the term. Psychologists, however, tend to accept certain ideas about personality:

1. Personality is an organized whole; otherwise, the individual would have no meaning.
2. Personality appears to be organized into patterns. These are, to some degree, observable and measurable.
3. Although there is a biological basis to personality, the specific development is a product of social and cultural environments.
4. Personality has superficial aspects, such as attitudes toward a team leader, and a deeper core, such as sentiments about authority or the Protestant work ethic.
5. Personality involves both common and unique characteristics. Each person is different from every other person in some respects while being similar in other respects.

What accounts for differences in personality? Four major forces can be cited as directly affecting personality development: heredity, culture, social class, and family relationships (see Figure 3.7).

1. *Heredity* affects personality because people are born with certain physical characteristics. Intelligence, height, and facial features all are inherited. The person who is highly intelligent may be arrogant toward fellow students; the tall girl may be quiet because she feels awkward; or the short boy may compensate for his size by being aggressive in his dealings with others.
2. *Culture* is important because the values and beliefs of the society in which one is raised help to determine how a person will act. A society that puts great value on money will be different from one in which leisure is emphasized over work.

IN ACTION

WORKING FOR THE JAPANESE

Japanese firms doing business in America are employing more people each year. This trend raises an important question for many Americans: Should you work for a Japanese company? The answer is a result of two interdependent factors: culture and personality. The Japanese tend to bring their culture to the United States and try to get Americans to adapt to it. If an individual has the "right" personality, this is no problem; otherwise, working for the Japanese can be a cultural nightmare. This is particularly true for high achievers and women.

One problem for high achievers is that the Japanese culture promotes group relatedness and activity. This means that when someone does something well, he or she is not individually recognized for it. Instead, the work group gets the praise. A Japanese employee would say, "We are all equal members of the group. So while I may have suggested the idea, it was a product of group interaction." Americans, in general, want to be recognized for their own individual achievements. Conclusion: Individuals who are unwilling or unable to be subsumed into the group are unlikely to do well in Japanese-owned firms.

A second, related problem is that of slow promotion. Japanese firms do not advance their people quickly through the hierarchy as do American companies. Promotions are slow, and those who are in a hurry often find themselves stymied. Conclusion: Individuals who are accustomed to rapid rewards for their efforts will be extremely frustrated in Japanese-managed firms.

Many American women who work for Japanese companies report a great deal of frustration with the way they are treated. Most Japanese have never learned how to cope with high-achieving women. In fact, many Japanese managers believe that women will soon quit the firm to raise a family, so there is little need to be concerned with them as human resources. Conclusion: Women who are looking for a career with a Japanese firm should first talk to other women in that company about how they have been treated.

Another problem is the time demands that are made on employees. A great deal of business is conducted after office hours when Japanese managers go to a bar and drink and discuss decisions that must be made. American managers are accustomed to going home to their families at the end of a workday, not hanging out in bars until the wee hours of the morning. Conclusion: Individuals who want to draw a line between their business life and their family life may find working for a Japanese firm to be highly unrewarding.

However, there is some good news. Many Japanese managers are now becoming aware that their international employees do not work the same way that they do. Hence, a slow change process is taking place as Japanese firms become more Westernized.

Source: John E. Rehfeld, "What Working for a Japanese Company Taught Me," *Harvard Business Review.* November-December 1990, pp. 167–176; Susan Moffat, "Should You Work for the Japanese? *Fortune,* December 3, 1990 pp. 107–120; Richard M Hodgetts and Fred Luthans, *International Management,* 4th ed. (Irwin/McGrawBurr Ridge IL, 2000), chapter 5.

A society in which education is believed to be important will be substantially different from one in which education is not highly regarded. Culture also affects the way managers and subordinates act. The "Cultural Diversity in Action" box provides an example.

3. *Social class* helps to shape personality because an individual's mores are heavily influenced by his or her neighborhood and community life. This social class also affects the individual's self-image; perception of others; and assumptions about authority, work, and money. A manager who wants to understand how people adjust to the demands of organizational life must consider these social class factors.

4. *Family relationships* influence personality by rewarding a person for certain behaviors and not rewarding him or her for others. These actions help to shape a pattern of behavior and serve as a basis for interpersonal relations outside the home.

Each of these four factors influences behavior, and managers have little control over them. This is not to say that managers cannot direct, channel, or reorient an individual's behavior, which can be done by using the motivational concepts discussed in Chapter 2. However, unless managers understand the bases for individual behavior, they will have great difficulty managing it. One approach for helping managers to do this has been training in the area of emotional intelligence.[32]

Emotional Intelligence. The capacity for recognizing one's own feelings and those of others, for motivating oneself, and for managing emotions well in both oneself and one's relationships is **emotional intelligence (EI)**.[33] Research shows that many individuals with very high IQs do not have high EI. As a result, they do not do well in the workplace, especially at the higher levels. Daniel Goleman, one of the leading authorities on EI, puts it this way:

> *IQ has the least power in predicting success among that pool of people smart enough to handle the most cognitively demanding fields, and the value of emotional intelligence for success grows more powerful the higher the intelligence barriers for entry into a field. In MBA programs or in careers like engineering, law, or medicine, where professional selection focuses almost exclusively on intellectual abilities, emotional intelligence carries much more weight than IQ in determining who emerges as a leader.*[34]

Similar findings have been recognized at the lower levels of the hierarchy, where businesses report that a knowledge of technical skills (IQ) is important, but social skills (EI), such as the ability to listen and speak well, adapt to setbacks, generate creative responses to problems, cooperate with others, and exude confidence, are even more important. Simply put, the ability to interact well with others, manage work relationships effectively, and contribute to overall group effort are much more important than the ability to know the technical aspects of one's job. For example, the results of a study of 358 managers across the Johnson & Johnson Consumer & Personal Care Group showed that the highest-performing managers have significantly more "emotional competence" than other managers.[35]

Why do many people lack high EI? One answer is that their personality has been shaped by a focus on values that are not critical to success in the workplace. They put highest emphasis on the tools and techniques needed to do their jobs, but they overlook the importance of building strong social skills. In a growing number of successful firms, managers now are being trained to help their people develop these basic emotional and social (EI) competencies.[36] In particular, these include:

- *Self-awareness*—being able to assess realistically one's own abilities and self-confidence.
- *Self-regulation*—being able to handle one's emotions so that they help rather than interfere with the task at hand.
- *Motivation*—learning how to use one's deepest preferences to move toward desired goals, to improve performance, and to persevere in the face of setbacks and frustrations.
- *Empathy*—learning to sense what others are feeling and to use that information to cultivate rapport with broadly diverse people.
- *Social skills*—learning to handle emotions in relationships; to read social situations accurately; to interact smoothly; and to apply these skills to persuading, leading, negotiating, and settling disputes, thereby increasing cooperation and teamwork.[37]

Goleman suggests we bring intelligence to our emotions. Only with EI can people motivate themselves to persist in the face of frustration, regulate their moods, delay gratification, keep distress from swamping their ability to think, and show empathy. The most successful in life often are those who can develop and maintain intimate relationships and work well with others. Managing one's emotions to overcome chronic anger and anxiety is critical to remaining physically healthy as well. Goleman feels EI skills can be taught and learned.[38]

Since Daniel Goleman published his books, *Emotional Intelligence* in 1995 and *Working with Emotional Intelligence* in 2000, many businesses, the U.S. government, and institutions have adopted EI development programs with great success. "Organizations like American Express, Prudential, Johnson & Johnson and even the U.S. Air Force have reported improvement in performance with EI and the evidence continues to mount."[39]

CHECK YOUR UNDERSTANDING

1. What is your EI Score? Go to http://www.queendom.com. Take an emotional IQ test and learn about yourself. For free you can get a sample analysis of your test results and for a fee you can get a complete analysis. How emotionally competent are you? What do you need to change?

2. What about your personality? Do you need to make changes? If so, what do you need to do? Go to http://www.queendom.com. Take one of the personality quizzes and learn more about yourself. Are you pleased with the analysis? What are your best traits and your weak traits?

3. To learn more about your emotional competencies, use Goleman's list in this chapter. Rate yourself on each competency using a scale of one to ten, with ten being the best. For each competency, write a statement of how you can improve your score.

Interpersonal Behavior

Values, perceptions, attitudes, and personality are all important components of individual behavior. However, no one lives in a vacuum. People interact with other people. In fact, this is how we develop values, perceptions, attitudes, and, to a large degree, personality. Before finishing our discussion on individual behavior, therefore, we should examine interpersonal behavior. We will do so by first looking at the importance of gender differences in interpersonal behavior. We then will examine the value of assertiveness training and the ways in which motivational profiles can help to improve interpersonal behavior.

Gender Differences

Explain how gender differences influence interpersonal behavior.

The number of women in the U.S. workplace has increased sharply over the last two decades. As a result, managers need to know how to interact effectively with both genders. One way is by understanding some of the differences in the way each group behaves. For example, Helen Fisher, an anthropologist, has studied the differences between the genders and found that certain qualities that women have help them to succeed in the workplace by being more effective in terms of interpersonal behavior.[40] For example, women tend to be better than men at articulating their ideas. They are particularly adept at finding the right words to convey what they want to say. They also tend to be better at reading emotions in faces and in deciphering postures, gestures, and vocal inflections. As a result, many women are very effective in reading problem situations and figuring out how to deal with them.

Another area where women tend to excel is in processing information. Fisher has found that men tend to address a problem by formulating a simple, basic solution, whereas women often gather more information and look at a variety of approaches to solving the problem. Here is an example: An employer who could not decide whether to give a raise to a young man or a young woman called both into his office. He said, "Here's a business problem. Which solution would you choose: A, B, or C?" Both went home and thought about it. The following morning the young man walked in and said, "I'd choose solution B." The young woman said she would choose solution A if she wanted to solve problems X and Y; solution B if she wanted to solve problems W and Z; and so on.[41]

As the world of business becomes more complex and problems must be looked at from a variety of perspectives, this type of thinking will be particularly helpful in terms of complementing the linear approach that is used by many men. Women are also very effective in trying to build consensus and getting everyone to work together as a team. Many men in group situations try to win at the expense of others. Women, on the other hand, tend to be more focused on win–win approaches, in which everyone goes away with a positive feeling.

Assertiveness Training

Describe how assertiveness training can help managers and subordinates improve their understanding of interpersonal behavior.

Another way to develop improved interpersonal relations is with **assertiveness training**. The purpose of such training is to teach people how to tactfully and effectively express their preferences, needs, opinions, and feelings in work and social situations. The goals of the training are threefold:

1. The individual is taught how to determine personal feelings.
2. The individual learns how to say what he or she wants.
3. The individual learns how to get what he or she wants.

Assertiveness training can be particularly helpful for those employees who are bottling up too much inside themselves; they become so uptight that, psychologically, they are ready to explode. Often these people do not recognize that their rights are being denied; they simply want to be "nice" and "not cause trouble" but they "suffer in silence" and assume nothing can be done to change the situation. Assertiveness training can help these people recognize that their rights are being denied.[42]

Assertiveness training does not teach individuals to be aggressive and to dominate others; rather, it teaches techniques and strategies for resisting those who seek to dominate and manipulate others. Assertive training helps individuals recognize when they are being abused or maneuvered for someone else's benefit. Still other people take assertiveness training to learn how to persuade people to do as they wish without having to become a bully. Assertiveness training, as a method of personal development, grew in popularity as a means for women to escape from traditional, submissive female roles. While assertiveness training has lost some of its popularity, it certainly has a place in training managers and workers.

Types of Assertive Behavior

Assertiveness training is something of a misnomer because the word "assertive" often conjures up thoughts of pushiness or belligerence. However, this is not what the term means. Actually, in assertiveness training, the objective is to teach an individual how to make a clear statement of personal desires without being obnoxious or abusive. Assertive behavior can be divided into three types—passive, aggressive, and assertive. Passive behavior is exhibited when people do what they are told regardless of how they feel about it. Aggressive behavior is about dominance, with a general disregard for the other person's feelings. Assertive behavior is about finding the middle road. People stand up for themselves, express their true feelings, and do not let others take advantage of them while, at the same time, being considerate of others' feelings.

Consider the case of Mary Harrison, who has been asked to meet an incoming job applicant at the airport first thing in the morning, show the individual around the organization, be sure the person gets to all of his scheduled interviews, and see that he gets back to the airport on time for his departure flight. Mary does not want to take on this assignment because she is snowed under with work. There are three types of interpersonal behavior available to her in responding to the situation: passive, aggressive, and assertive. Here is how Mary can use each response:

- *Passive* Mary is angry and really wants to tell her boss off. However, she grits her teeth, puts her work aside, and makes plans to get to the airport on time.

- *Aggressive* Mary tells her boss, "Hell, I'm not going to do that. I'm up to my nose in work. Get someone else who is not that important. I'm not going to be treated like this, so don't ask me to do it again."
- *Assertive* Mary says to her boss, "I appreciate your thinking of me, but I'm really snowed under with work. I don't have the time to do this. However, I don't think you'll have any trouble getting someone else. There are a number of people in the department who have light workloads this week."

Notice that when using assertive behavior, Mary stood her ground without being rude or discourteous.

Becoming More Assertive

How can an individual increase his or her assertiveness? Over the last decade, many assertiveness training programs have been offered by organizations for their own employees and by professional consultants and trainers for organizational employees and the general public. Although these various workshops employ different techniques for improving individual assertiveness, knowledge of a series of basic steps is essential for every participant. Phrased in the form of questions, the list includes the following:

1. What is my goal? What exactly do I want to accomplish? (Clarify the situation and give specific facts.)
2. How will assertive behavior help me accomplish my goal?
3. What would I usually do to avoid asserting myself in this situation?
4. Why would I want to give that up and assert myself instead?
5. What might be stopping me from asserting myself?
   a. Am I holding on to irrational beliefs? If so, what are they?
   b. How can I replace these irrational beliefs with rational ones?
   c. Have I, as a woman or a man, been taught to behave in ways that make it difficult for me to act assertively in the present situation? If so, what ways? How can I overcome this?
   d. What are my rights in this situation? State them clearly. Do these rights justify turning my back on my conditioning?
6. Am I anxious about asserting myself? What techniques can I use to reduce my anxiety?
7. Have I done my homework? Do I have the information I need to go ahead and act?
8. Can I do the following?
   a. Let the other person know I hear and understand him or her?
   b. Let the other person know how I feel?
   c. Tell him or her what I want?[43]

Assertiveness training is an excellent complement to effective behaviors such as those spelled out in the "Human Relations in Action" box.

Motivational Profiles

Another way to improve interpersonal behavioral skills is to understand what is important to a person. For example, some companies give bonuses such as $1,000 to individuals who do outstanding work, whereas others reward excellent performance by allowing their people to choose from a group of rewards such as a $1,000 bonus, three days off with pay, or reserved parking next to the main entrance for the next twelve months. Although many people choose the bonus, research shows that the

IN ACTION

WHAT YOUR BOSS WANTS YOU TO KNOW

One of the biggest reasons why some people in organizations succeed is that they know what their boss wants them to know. Whether it is explicitly spelled out or learned through experience or intuition, successful people know what the boss is looking for. For example:

1. *Do more than what is expected.* Your boss expects everyone to do his or her job. If you do more, however, you will stand out as a superior performer.
2. *Forget about making up excuses.* The boss expects you to do things right. When you do not, it may cause problems, but it will do you no good to blame someone else. Even if you are right, the boss does not want to hear about it. He or she has more important things to do than trying to assign blame. It is your job to get the work done right the first time. If you did not, work harder to do so the next time.
3. *Anticipate things going wrong.* If you do, you will seldom be disappointed. However, you will be prepared to deal with them before they become too serious. If part of your job calls for getting information from other people and processing it before passing it on to others, anticipate getting the information late or finding that some of it is erroneous. Allow yourself time to check and correct the information.
4. *Remember that punctuality and attendance count.* Do not be late for work or meetings. Even if nothing important happens, you are expected to be on time. If you are continually tardy or absent, your boss will see this as an attitude problem, and it will count against you later.
5. *Get along with your coworkers.* Bosses like to think that everyone in their unit is a team player. If there is internal dissension, the boss will not want to know who is right or wrong. The boss is not there to referee employee squabbles. Everyone involved will have a black mark against him or her. Make it a point to stay on good terms with everyone in the unit.
6. *Be protective of the organization.* Do not say anything that will reflect negatively on the enterprise or anyone who works there. Keep organizational politics and problems within the enterprise, and if you must do anything that reflects on another, go out of your way to minimize its negative effect.
7. *Learn to read your boss.* Listen closely to what your boss tells you and learn to interpret its meaning. If your boss says, "This really warrants our looking into," it may mean that you should drop everything you are doing and start working on the matter he or she has been talking about. On the other hand, if the boss says, "This sounds very interesting," it may mean the matter is a minor one and should be ignored. Every boss has a specific way of communicating. Figure out what your boss is really talking about.
8. *Never lie.* The biggest problem with lying is that it calls your integrity into question. What other lies have you told? What exactly are you up to? Your boss may suspect that you are not as reliable as he or she thought. When this happens, your credibility comes into question and your future with the organization

---

other two rewards tend to be more popular, especially among employees with young families and managers who have been with the company for more than ten years. The latter groups are more motivated by nonfinancial rewards because these best fit their lifestyles.

Research also shows that because people are different, the way in which one person is motivated may vary sharply from that of another.[44] In fact, by understanding personal profiles, it is possible to motivate, lead, and retain individuals more effectively. New employees, for example, tend to fit into one of six profiles listed here (although there is overlap between these in terms of shared characteristics), and when managers understand these profiles, they will be better able to deal effectively with these people.

1. **Independent thinkers** are very entrepreneurial in their approach. These individuals want to be free to choose what they are going to do and how they are going to do it. They tend to be impatient with rules, policies, and procedures and have low loyalty to the organization. They like to create their own way of doing things and are prepared to take full responsibility for their successes and failures. In motivating and leading these people, managers need to focus on individual rewards such as pay-for-performance plans, bonuses, and commissions.
2. **Lifestylers** are particularly interested in their quality of life. The job is important to them, but it is just a means to an end. They want to enjoy their work, but the job is not the most important thing in their lives. People with young children who want to

balance work and family responsibilities often fit into this category. So, too, do young professionals who value their freedom and want to pursue personal priorities and mid-career people who have responsibilities for older relatives who need their help. Lifestylers are prepared to work hard to get the job done, but they also expect the organization to give them flexible work schedules and additional vacation days so they can meet their personal responsibilities.

3. **Personal developers** are interested in jobs that give them the opportunity to keep on learning and becoming more proficient. Individuals who fall into this category are young people who are interested in building a skill base and people who frequently change jobs and need to be on the cutting edge of their field so that they are attractive to new employers. Personal developers evaluate their work in terms of whether they are being challenged and whether they are acquiring new skills. Their primary interest is their career and not the company for which they are working; so if better opportunities come along, they will change jobs. One way that companies are able to retain these people is by continually offering them training that focuses on building skills or updating their skills.

4. **Careerists** are individuals who want to get ahead and are prepared to make the necessary sacrifices to do so. These people have a lot in common with baby boomers, who are loyal to their companies and willing to make a career with a firm. These individuals are ambitious, are motivated by prestige and status, and want to advance continually and finish their careers in the upper ranks of the hierarchy.

5. **Authenticity seekers** are interested in self-expression. They are best represented by the cliché, "I gotta be me." These individuals will not sacrifice their personal expressiveness to play a corporate role nor will they repress their personal values in favor of what is good for the company. At the same time, authenticity seekers can be creative (albeit difficult to manage), and managers must carefully direct their efforts so they contribute to company goals while not losing their personal identification.

6. **Collegiality seekers** like to work with others. They are very social in orientation and are excellent team players. In fact, they identify with their work groups and are extremely loyal to these people. When asked what is important to them, they typically say that it is working with people.[45]

These motivational profiles are useful in helping to explain what is important to individuals. When managers know what motivates their people, they are in a better position to lead them. They also know how and why these people interact with other group members and can use this information to increase group morale and productivity.

✔ CHECK YOUR UNDERSTANDING

1. How assertive are you? Go to the Internet site: www.LifeScript.com. Take the assertiveness quiz titled "How Assertive Are You?"

2. Are you a passive, an aggressive, or an assertive person? Refer to the case of Mary Harrison in the text and assume you are that person. How would you have responded to the boss? Be honest.

3. Using the information in the scenario of Mary Harrison, answer the questions listed under "Becoming More Assertive." What did you learn about yourself? What do you need to change?

© quavondo, iStock

Prepare an effective resume.

Career Advisor

Writing an Effective Resume

After conducting your self-analysis (Chapter 1) and developing a plan for finding a job (Chapter 2), the next step is to write a resume that attracts attention and points you out as someone whom the organization should pursue.

Regardless of the job you are seeking, a resume should always be submitted to the recruiter. A resume is a summary of your qualifications, education, work experience, and training. It is a selling tool that highlights who you are, your accomplishments in previous jobs, and what you have to offer a new employer. The resume tells your story and is your brand. Products have brands and that is what sells them, so think of your resume as your brand. It should sell your skills and abilities in a way that matches what the employer is seeking.

Writing a resume takes time. It starts by brainstorming your educational and work histories. Then, you write and rewrite the resume many times, using job-specific keywords or buzzwords, and by all means, carefully proofread the results. Misspelled words and typos are not acceptable. The employer will quickly delete your resume from the potential list of job applicants.

A resume is typically the first step in the interview process. After reviewing resumes of job applicants, an organization will choose those applicants who look most promising and extend to them an invitation to interview. Without an effective resume, you may never get to the interview stage. If you are just starting out in a career, your resume should be simple, straightforward, and factual. A good rule is to make it only one to two pages long, preferably one page. It is best to gear a resume specifically to the company where you are applying. Otherwise, it can be more general if you are applying to several related companies in the same industry. The following are some of the most important guidelines you should apply in drafting your resume:

1. Group your information into four to six categories, such as personal data, employment objective, education, work experience, special interests, and references.
2. Start writing the resume by listing your name, address, and telephone number at the top of the page.
3. If you have a specific employment objective, state it, but avoid the use of generalities, such as "want a challenging position" or "desire to work with people." These do not tell the reader a great deal. Identifying a job title would be better.
4. Describe your qualifications in a summary, not a full-blown explanation. Be succinct and descriptive. Do not overdo the selling of yourself. Be sure to fit your skills and abilities into what the organization is seeking in applicants. Use terminology appropriate for the job and for the industry. Resumes posted on the Internet are screened using specific industry and job terminology. For example, a manager's job terminology is different from the terminology used by a marketing executive, a warehouseman, or a mechanic.
5. Move on to your education and job experience, listing your most recent degree or job first and working backward.
6. Use a format that is easy to read, has eye appeal, and provides a positive impression about you and your goals. (Remember this is your brand and you want to look good to attract the eye of the screener; otherwise, you will never get an interview.) If you feel it is necessary or useful, underline or capitalize some words.
7. Retain duplicate copies of your resume if you intend to interview with more than a handful of firms; these should be made by a professional printer so that each copy

looks identical to the original. (Caution: Employers do not like to see resumes that look like they have been mass produced. Changing the job objective to fit the company can make a big difference.)

8. If you want to send along a picture of yourself, do so. However, attach it to the resume; do not have it printed as part of the resume. In this way, if the organization is prohibited by state law from requiring pictures or simply does not want a photograph as part of the resume, the picture can be removed.

9. References are optional. If you are just starting out, it is useful to list them. If you have been working for a number of years, you may not want anyone to contact your references without your approval; in this case, simply state that these are available on request.

These nine suggestions all draw on human relations concepts, and they help you to present yourself in a positive light. Figures 3.8 through 3.10 provide examples of resumes that follow these suggestions.

The first, Figure 3.8, is the *chronological resume*, which presents information in descending order, the most recent events being listed first under each heading. This type of resume is easiest to prepare, and it is the most popular and brings the best results.

The second, Figure 3.9, is the *functional resume*, which focuses on skills, aptitudes, and qualities that can be applied in a number of situations. This resume is particularly appropriate for those who have had a variety of jobs or assignments not directly related to their career targets but include relevant functions or responsibilities or have changed jobs often. This form works well for technical jobs.

The third, Figure 3.10, is the *combination resume*, which uses parts of the chronological and functional resumes. The combination resume is often the best choice for people who have a great deal of experience and many jobs or for those who are changing careers.

Skills-Directed Resumes. What do the directors of human resources look for when reviewing resumes? Anna Gray, patient-care director, LifeBridge Health, is interested in how applicants have assisted with some change in their previous job and how they have impacted the organization and made a difference. Stacey Hattle, director of human resources, Scottrade, says she does not want to search for the skill set on the resume. It should be easy to detect. The applicant's objective should focus on the particular position being sought. Lynn Franklyn, HR manager, Wegmans Food Markets, looks at the cover letter first before reading the resume. Ms. Franklyn wants the cover letter to engage her and it should reveal a glimpse of who the candidate really is. Can the candidate clearly define how his or her values and his or her skill set match up to what the organization has to offer?[46]

Attention-Getting Resumes. Over the last few years, attention-getting resumes have appeared. Since most resumes appear very similar, some applicants want to distinguish themselves from the pack by personalizing their resume so that it stands out. For example, a person applying for a marketing manager post recently took along with her a personalized compact disk. On the CD were seven songs that described her work ethic and background, and the accompanying resume appeared in the form of liner notes. The company was impressed with this creative approach. Here is another example:[47]

When … Peter Shankman sought a public-relations job in New York a few years ago, he didn't want to mail out a bunch of resumes. Instead, he printed out his resume on two 4-foot by 3-foot poster boards, sandwiched himself between them, stood on a Manhattan corner on a cold January day, and handed out 1,000 resumes from 6 A.M. until 7:15 P.M.

Figure 3.8
Chronological Resume

MIKE TOWERS   SALES PROFESSIONAL
                                        323-555-1212 mt@support.com

QUALIFICATIONS

Bilingual, customer-focused individual with a proven track record of increasing department and store sales through effective merchandising, superior product knowledge, and comprehensive staff training. Recently honored as *Employee of the Month* at Century Hardware for exceeding company goals by 35% in a weak market. Spearheaded drive for in-store home improvement classes to showcase high-end products, including Andersen Windows, Black & Decker Power Tools, Behr Paint, and Burlington Carpets. Fluent in English and Spanish with excellent communication skills to easily interact with all levels of management, peers, staff, vendors, and customers.

PROFESSIONAL EXPERIENCE   1991–Present

CENTURY HARDWARE, Los Angeles, California
Department Manager/Sales Associate

- Train, schedule, and conduct performance reviews for up to 50 employees.
- Attend manufacturer-sponsored informational classes and review product updates to ensure superior merchandise knowledge for customer satisfaction.
- Maximize customer traffic and increase sales through product displays and promotional events, including the *Deck Days of Summer* that showcased building materials, stains, and sealants.

Accomplishments

- Awarded *Department Supervisor of the Month* for a total of 18 separate months.
- Increased sales 40% by reorganizing the hardware department to market high-end products.
- Boosted garden department sales from $5 million to $10 million+ annually and same store sales by 30% through effective management.

CALIFORNIA HOME CENTERS, Los Angeles, California   1989–1991
Sales Associate

- Educated customers on product brands, rang sales, and maintained merchandise appearance.

Accomplishments

- Doubled department sales by providing personalized customer service.
- Increased store sales, on average, 35% by creating a *shopper-friendly* environment with attractive merchandising and prominent displays.

EDUCATION

STATE UNIVERSITY, San Francisco, California
Bachelor of Arts in Business Administration, Marketing Emphasis, 1988
6689 Ocean Boulevard, #12, Los Angeles, California 90001

Source: http://www.resumeedge.com. Printed by permission of ResumeEdge.com, a Nelnet Service.

The stunt was a raving success. After two hundred phone calls, forty-five interviews, and twenty job offers, Shankman took a job as a director of news media for the New Jersey Devils hockey team. Although he admits his stunt was off the wall, Shankman says

Figure 3.9
Functional Resume

TONI BURNS, MBA

6684 Baca Grande Drive
Albuquerque, New Mexico 87101
505-555-1212/trburns@net.net

QUALIFICATIONS

Business Analyst with superior analytical skills applied to contract negotiations, business processes, data collection and management for major health providers, including *Health First*. Consistently promoted to positions of increased responsibility, advancing three times within a one-year period. Excellent communicator with fluency in English and Spanish. Proven leadership in training employees and conducting formal presentations to all levels of management. Outstanding academic credentials in business, international management, and analytical finance.

SELECTED ACCOMPLISHMENTS

- Completed contracting for 6,000+ providers within 6 months for CHAMPUS contract.
- Improved production 20% through the establishment of department production standards.
- Launched marketing department for the State of New Mexico.

PROFESSIONAL EXPERIENCE
Financial & Business Analysis

- Performed complex analyses for system-wide negotiations, projections, and line-of-business reviews in addition to analysis of population distribution, claims/utilization, and cost.
- Identified, collected, and organized data from multiple sources for input into monthly, quarterly, annual, and ad hoc reports provided to contracting/finance departments and senior management.
- Designed and implemented database applications used in contract rate and risk management analysis as well as the identification and correction of data errors and discrepancies.

Management & Supervision

- Analyzed, interpreted, and resolved claims with authorization for payments up to $75,000.
- Directed activities of 40 claims analysts at a large project site.
- Increased daily with enrollment, claims, utilization/quality management, and customer service to resolve provider issues.

EMPLOYMENT HISTORY
HEALTH FIRST, Albuquerque, New Mexico
Manager, Contract Analysis/Senior Financial Analyst 1997–Present
FEDERAL HEALTH SERVICES, Albuquerque, New Mexico
Manager, Provider Relations 1994–1997
CROSS HEALTH CARE, Albuquerque, New Mexico
Risk Analyst 1993–1994
GROUP SERVICES, Albuquerque, New Mexico
Senior Claims Analyst/Project Manager 1990–1993
EDUCATION
GRADUATE SCHOOL OF BUSINESS, Albuquerque, New Mexico
Master of Business Administration, 1992
NEW WEST UNIVERSITY, Albuquerque, New Mexico
Bachelor of Arts in Business, 1989

Source: http://www.resumeedge.com. Printed by permission of ResumeEdge.com, a Nelnet Service.

Figure 3.10
Combination Resume

JENNIFER RIVERS
1543 Central Park Drive ~ New York, New York 10001
212.555.1212   **pro@news.net**

MARKETING EXECUTIVE
Product Launches ~ Overseas Partnerships ~ Presentations

Accomplished, multilingual Professional consistently recognized for achievement and performance in the fuel industry. Innovative and successful in mining new sales territories and establishing business alliances, including the recent partnership with *MJM Oil* in Korea. Proven leader with special capabilities in building teams, strategizing, and implementing workable marketing plans employing television, radio, Internet, and print media. Fluent in English, Korean, Japanese, and French.

BUSINESS SKILLS

Marketing

- Launch gasoline exports in conjunction with new production plant start-up; target overseas markets.
- Initiate sales of ULS, an environmentally-friendly new product launched in the European market.
- Establish joint venture partnerships in Europe and Far East; implement marketing for aviation fuel and asphalt as a value-added commodity.

Market Planning

- Analyze regional import/export economics and the interregional oil markets.
- Participate in contract negotiations for strategic alliances with major European and Asian concerns.
- Achieved $25 million in revenue by developing offshore storage programs that fulfilled seasonal market trends in the region.

Product Planning

- Optimize production mode by selecting appropriate refinery; research product specification revisions by country.
- Propose and participate in the Plant Operation Committee, a team effort between production and sales.

PROFESSIONAL EXPERIENCE

TTR CORPORATION, New York, New York
Vice President, Overseas Business Division 1993–Present

- Promoted to position in March 1996; selected as one of three employees to attend an MBA course in 2003.
- Named *Employee of the Year* in 1996 based on professional achievements.

FUEL INDUSTRY OF AMERICA, New York, New York 1989–1992
Manager of Marketing

- Provided analysis on fuel industry, drafting report for the White House.
- Awarded the *Honor Prize* in 1992 based on performance evaluations of oil producers.

EDUCATION

UNIVERSITY OF NEW YORK, New York, New York
Bachelor of Arts in Communications, 1988

Source: http://www.resumeedge.com. Printed by permission of ResumeEdge.com, a Nelnet Service.

he was successful because he met people face to face. "At least they could see I was a nice nutcase," says Shankman, who wore a business suit and an overcoat that day. At the same time, it is important to remember that a resume that is too creative may be viewed as inappropriate. Simply put, applicants must be careful about going too far. For example, in one case, a graphic designer seeking a job with a veterinary company sent her resume wrapped in a faux diamond–studded collar with a bone-shaped identification tag that sported her name and title. In another case, a manager in Florida applied for a job up north and, in addition to sending his resume, included a ziplock bag containing sand from the nearby beach and fake gold coins, meant to imply that he was a hidden treasure in need of discovery. In a third instance, an applicant sent out garden spades to employers with a note saying, "hire me and watch your company grow." None of these creative efforts resulted in any interest from the employers. Clearly, creative approaches can end up proving to be worthless.

Weak Resumes.　Weak resumes make job-hunting tougher. JobBound in Chicago identified some common mistakes that college graduates make on resumes. They are:

- Lacking a clear objective
- Using generic job descriptions that omit tangible accomplishments
- Selling short your assets and omitting cutting-edge skills
- Failing to list jobs in reverse chronological order
- Cramming resumes with extraneous information[48]

According to several top headhunters and outplacement specialists, "90% of the resumes they see are riddled with errors or misrepresentations, including 'sales manger' for sales manager, 'skilled in massaging' for messaging and 'on contract with the state' ('in jail')." They suggest you consider hiring a resume "doctor" to help you prepare your resume. In 2003, *BusinessWeek* magazine contacted twenty-one firms to remake a resume. Among those they thought had helped "craft the clearest, most data-filled resumes" were Mike Jeans of New Directions and Jack Downing of WorldBridge Partners. Because the field is unregulated, you must be careful in selecting a firm to help you. It is best to ask for samples of previous work before you make a commitment.[49]

Don't Lie on Resumes.　If you fail to tell the truth, you will probably be found out, and that is not good. In a recent survey, an employer found inconsistencies in work histories and misleading information about educational credentials in nearly half of its job-seekers' resumes. Often what applicants leave off their application and resume causes more problems than what they include. "Fessing up is always better than staying silent."[50]

Gaps in a Resume.　Applicants who have stopped working in order to raise a family or retire early may have gaps in their resumes. In this case, you will need to evaluate your unpaid experiences and decide which ones support the qualifications needed in the position for which you are applying and then list them as skills. If a company you once worked for has merged, then acknowledge both company names. This practice indicates you are keeping abreast of current business changes. Some experts suggest "that re-entry candidates sprinkle a resume with the latest buzzwords for a targeted occupation." Doing so indicates you know what's hot.[51]

By reading classified ads, you can find out the type of employees businesses are seeking. This information is helpful in preparing your resume. For example, in today's newspapers, the popular words are "go-getter, hard-charger, team player, self-starter, multi-tasker, goal-oriented, results-oriented, win-oriented, and 24/7." Only those with these skills and attributes need apply. These ads are indicators of what is important within the business environment, and they also reflect social changes within society.[52]

Strategies for Keeping Your Resume from Being Tossed. Always include a cover letter explaining a few of your qualifications, any gaps in employment, or other information that will entice the employer to read your resume. Use white- or cream-colored paper with black type and a common font like Arial or Times New Roman. Your resume should be no longer than two pages; so you may need to include only your most recent and relevant work history. In your employment history, cite your accomplishments, instead of job duties. Customize your cover letter and resume for each job and employer for which you are going to apply. Do not guesstimate any dates or titles. A background check will reveal all discrepancies. Unless your hobbies relate to your career, do not list them. The same goes for personal information like height, weight, religious affiliation, sexual orientation, or any other facts that could be used against you. Proper grammar is essential; errors can be spotted quickly by recruiters, giving them a negative perception of the applicant. Spell-check cannot catch every typo or misused word; therefore, it is crucial that you proofread several times and have a friend or two give it a final review. This also indicates a concern about the applicant's focus on detail.[53]

Use of the Internet

The Internet is a popular tool for job hunting. For example, Taleo Research found that 94 percent of the top five hundred U.S. corporations solicit online resumes so that their human resources departments can use software to whittle down a huge stack of candidates quickly to a manageable list of finalists. Applicants using job-specific keywords will likely make the final list. Pat Kendall, a career coach, suggests that at least twenty-five keywords that are contextually relevant to the applicant's work history be used.[54] However, accepting only online applications can create legal issues, particularly when computer skills are not required in the job to be filled or if the applicant is covered under the Americans with Disabilities Act (ADA) guidelines. An increasing number of job applicants are posting their resumes on Web sites. In turn, employers can easily access these sites and identify those individuals whom they would like to contact. Likewise, many college and university placement services are creating Web sites that can be accessed by employers who are looking for applicants. As a result, e-mailed resumes are becoming increasingly popular, and many recruiters are finding this to be a convenient and efficient way to handle job applications. The important points that must be remembered by applicants who send their resumes via e-mail is that the resumes must be simple and they must refrain from using symbols, pictures, or other embellishments that can be altered in transmission.[55]

Resume Web Sites. Poorly written resumes result in prolonged job searches and, very often, lower salary offers; therefore, you want to write a resume that is effective. A search on the Internet will reveal many sites that provide information, samples, and assistance in preparing resumes. To help you get started in writing an effective resume, conduct an Internet search on resume writing and examples. You will find a wealth of sites and information, as well as companies that prepare resumes for a fee. Be careful in selecting one of these sites. You may not get a better resume than the one you prepared. With a little time and effort, you can write an effective resume.

Scannable Resumes. The purpose of a scannable resume is the same as a traditional resume. However, the design and format is different, and it is vital that job seekers follow the guidelines for writing a scannable resume that will be prescreened by a machine. Because the technologies involved in scanning and tracking resumes, it is important that the format be simple. Other changes are the size of print, color of paper, headings, the use of industry "buzzwords," and key technical words. The software program can be programmed to weed out resumes based on selected keywords. Always avoid stray marks, graphics, bullets, dashes, italics, highlighting, shading, shadows or underlining, folds and creases, staples, and paperclips, just to name a few. Here again, the Internet is an excellent source for learning about scannable resumes. Conduct an Internet search of "scannable resumes" before starting to write your resume.

Drawbacks.   One drawback of the Internet is that these Web sites often are not very secure. Hence, anything in a resume can be read by anyone gaining access to the site. To protect the privacy of applicants, university placement service personnel now recommend that applicants use a confidential number in lieu of their name and a post office box rather than a home address. In this way, an employer who wants to contact the individual can do so, but the applicant can screen the communication. Additionally, many university placement services have begun charging employers an access fee for the right to review resumes that have been placed at the Web site, thus ensuring that the only people who review the resumes are those seeking job applicants. You should check with the placement office at your college or university to learn what services it has for graduates wanting to find a job.

It is not always easy to find a job online. "The unpleasant truth, according to job seekers, career counselors and even some companies, is that applying for jobs on corporate Web sites is often a complicated and frustrating process, even though it is getting easier." Job seekers often feel their resume has gone into a black hole, never to return, while automated systems scan their resume for certain key words and return an automated response. Some job seekers complain that real-life recruiters do not enter the hiring process often enough.

CHECK YOUR UNDERSTANDING

Writing an Effective Resume

1. Start by preparing several lists:

    - Your *skills* that are needed in the type of job you want.
    - Your *work experiences*, starting with the latest job.
    - Your *training* or *education*.
    - *Key words*—terminology used in the type of industry or job you are seeking.

2. Select the format—type of resume—and determine how it will be delivered.
3. Write the resume and have someone check the accuracy.
4. When applying for a job, file a copy of your resume for future reference. That way, you will not have to look up all the dates, titles, and company information. It will be readily available to you.

Summary

1 Identify and describe some of the common values held by all individuals.

Individuals are complex beings. Nevertheless, many descriptive clichés have been used in trying to sum them up in a word or two. In human relations, we need to be much more scientific in our analysis of individuals and to realize that people exhibit many different types of behavior. For example, sometimes they are rational and at other times they are emotional; sometimes they are motivated by economic considerations and at other times they are self-actualizing. To understand individual behavior more fully, we examined four major components: values, perceptions, attitudes, and personality.

A value is something that has worth or importance to an individual. Values are influenced by a person's experiences and by contacts with other people. Values change over time, creating differences, or what is sometimes called gaps, between generations of people. These differences generate real challenges for management.

People have six values in common: theoretical, economic, aesthetic, social, political, and religious. When examined in a job context, values can be studied in terms of worker satisfaction. Research shows that many employees are dissatisfied with their jobs, feel they do not have equitable promotion opportunities, and are underpaid.

2 Describe perception and explain why it is a determinant of individual behavior.

Perception is a person's view of reality and is affected by an individual's values. There are two types of perception: sensory (physical) and normative (interpretive). Normative perception is particularly important in the study of human relations, because people's interpretations of reality will influence their behavior. In particular, normative perception can result in selective perception and stereotyping, perceptual problems the effective manager tries to avoid. In reality, people see what they want to see or are trained to see. Employees willingly accept an idea, a change, or a method when they perceive it to be in their best interests.

3 Explain how stereotyping people can influence a person's view of another's behavior.

Stereotyping forms an instant or fixed picture of a person or group, which is then generalized to all members of a given group. These impressions may or may not be accurate. It is important to understand most people employ stereotyping because it is an easy way to generalize about human behavior. Effective managers, however, evaluate each person as an individual. As the workplace becomes more diversified ethnically and more women, minorities, and people with special needs are hired, managers must be aware of their negative attitudes and biases and not let stereotyped images influence decisions.

4 Define attitude and describe its impact on worker output.

Attitudes are a person's feelings about objects, activities, events, and other people. Attitudes have three basic components: cognitive, affective, and behavioral. The cognitive component is the set of values and beliefs that a person has toward a person, an object, or an event. The emotional feeling that is attached to an attitude is the affective component, whereas the tendency to act in a particular way toward a person, an object, or an event is the behavioral component.

The differing attitudes among the baby boomers, Gen Xers, and Gen Yers create real challenges for managing employees of mixed generations. Human behavior is a reflection of attitude and managers must create a workplace that inspires civil behavior toward one another. The impact of 9/11 changed attitudes in the workplace forever. Employees want a workplace that balances the demands of their work and family lives. As workers grow fatter and more obese, attitudes of managers must reflect an attitude of responsibility and not one of discrimination.

Attitudes are internal and can only be inferred through behavior. People with positive attitudes tend to perform better than the average worker. It is common to find organizations using instruments such as questionnaires to measure their employees' attitudes because attitudes often are key variables affecting output.

5 Define personality and discuss the major forces affecting personality development.

Personality consists of a relatively stable set of characteristics and tendencies that determine both similarities and differences between one person and another. Some of the major forces affecting personality are heredity, culture, social class, and family relationships. Our physical characteristics, intelligence, height, and facial features, for example, are inherited. The values and beliefs of the culture in which a person is reared help determine how a person will act. Social class helps shape one's personality. Family relationships shape a pattern of behavior and serve as a basis for behavior outside the home.

Emotional intelligence (EI) is the capacity to recognize one's own feelings and those of others, for motivating oneself, and for managing emotions well in both oneself and one's relationships. The emotional and social competencies include self-awareness, self-regulation, motivation, empathy, and social skills.

The manager should also be aware of the available approaches to understanding interpersonal behavior. After all, values, perceptions, attitudes, and, to a large degree, personality are developed through interpersonal relations. An understanding of gender differences helps to explain the challenges managers often have in managing diverse work groups.

6 Explain how gender differences influence interpersonal behavior.

Helen Fisher, an anthropologist, found that women tend to be better than men at articulating their ideas, particularly adept at finding the right words to convey what they want to say, better at reading emotions in faces and in deciphering postures, gestures, and vocal inflections; and therefore are more effective in reading problem situations and figuring out how to deal with them. Women excel at processing information. They gather more information and look at more approaches to solving the problem. Women are better at building consensus and getting everyone to work together as a team.

7 Describe how assertiveness training can help managers and subordinates improve their understanding of interpersonal behavior.

Assertiveness training teaches people how to determine personal feelings, verbalize them, and get what they want without being abusive or obnoxious. Interpersonal behavior includes: passive behavior—the employee does the task with a lot of emotion without verbalizing his or her feelings; aggressive behavior—the employee is very vocal and is not afraid to express his or her feelings; and assertive behavior—the employee expresses appreciation, gives a reason for not doing the job, and suggests an alternative solution. Interpersonal behavioral skills can be improved by understanding what is important to a person. By understanding personal profiles, a manager can deal more effectively with people. People can be profiled as independent thinkers, lifestylers, personal developers, careerists, authenticity seekers, and collegiality seekers. These motivational profiles help explain individual needs and desires and offer suggestions regarding how to manage people on a one-to-one basis.

8 Prepare an effective resume.

A resume is a tool that summarizes your qualifications, education, work experience, and training. It is one to two pages in length, typed on white, standard-sized paper, and uses a simple format. Information is grouped according to the type of format selected—chronological resume, functional resume, or a combination resume. Key words or buzzwords are used to match your skills and experiences to the qualifications required in the job description. A clear objective will give focus to the prescreener and a reason for the submission of the resume. Always check for errors, and most of all, do not misrepresent yourself. Do not leave gaps in your work record.

The Internet is fast becoming the way to send resumes to companies. In fact, some firms do not accept resumes or applications by mail or in person. Sending through the Internet requires resumes to be prepared so they can be scanned. One drawback to the Internet is that some Web sites may not be secure. Applying over the Internet may be a complicated and frustrating process for some people.

Key Terms in the Chapter

Value	A value is something of worth or importance to an individual.
Terminal value	A terminal value is one that is expressed in terms of a desired goal or end.
Instrumental value	An instrumental value is the means for achieving desired goals.
Perception	Perception is a person's view of reality.
Sensory reality	Sensory reality is physical reality.
Normative reality	Normative reality is interpretive reality.
Stereotyping	Stereotyping is generalizing a particular trait to all members of a given group.
Attitudes	Attitudes are a person's feelings about objects, events, and people.
Cognitive component	The cognitive component is the set of values and beliefs a person has toward a person, an object, or an event.
Affective component	The affective component is the emotional feeling attached to an attitude.
Behavioral component	The behavioral component is the tendency to act in a particular way toward a person, an object, or an event.
Attitude questionnaire	An attitude questionnaire is an instrument for measuring attitudes.
Intervening variable	An intervening variable is one that is influenced by a causal variable and that affects an end-result variable.
Personality	Personality is a relatively stable set of characteristics and tendencies that help to describe individual behavior.
Emotional intelligence	Emotional intelligence is the capacity for recognizing one's own feelings and those of others.
Assertiveness training	Assertiveness training teaches people how to assert themselves in work and social situations.
Independent thinkers	Independent thinkers are very entrepreneurial and want freedom.
Lifestylers	Lifestylers are most interested in their quality of life.
Personal developers	Personal developers are interested in jobs that give them the opportunity to continue learning.
Careerists	Careerists want to get ahead and are prepared to make the necessary sacrifices to do so.
Authenticity seekers	Authenticity seekers are interested in self-expression.
Collegiality seekers	Collegiality seekers like to work with others and are excellent team players.

Review and Study Questions

1. What is meant by value? Distinguish between terminal values and instrumental values and give examples of each.

2. How are work values changing in America? Support your answer with examples.

3. How do the characteristics of the baby boomers, the Gen Xers, and the Gen Yers differ? What do managers need to know to manage each group?

4. What are some approaches used to meet workers' needs?

5. How can perception impact a manager's decisions?

6. How does sensory reality differ from normative reality?

7. What is stereotyping? How effective is it in generalizing about behavior?

8. What is attitude? Give an example of the cognitive component, the affective component, and the behavior component of attitude.

9. How can attitude measurement be of value to an organization? Explain.

10. What is meant by personality? What are some ideas that psychologists tend to accept about personality?

11. How do heredity, culture, social class, and family relationships affect personality development? Give an example for each.

12. What is meant by emotional intelligence (EI), and how can people develop their EI competencies?

13. What is interpersonal behavior? Why is it important in managing people?

14. What are some gender differences that help make women more effective than men in interpersonal relations? Describe three.

15. Of what value is assertiveness training to the modern manager? To subordinates? Explain.

16. How do independent thinkers differ from lifestylers? What do managers need to know about managing each?

17. How do personal developers differ from careerists? What do managers need to know about managing each?

18. How do authenticity seekers differ from collegiality seekers? What do managers need to know about managing each?

19. What is the purpose of a resume?

20. What are some suggestions for writing an effective resume?

21. How do chronological resumes, functional resumes, and combination resumes differ? Who should use each style?

22. How can the Internet be used to effectively find a job? What are the drawbacks?

Connecting to the Real World

Why are there different values for different occupational groups?

The purpose of this exercise is to better understand Spranger's value model and to identify value profiles based on an occupation or a career. Follow these steps:

1. Review the Spranger model, Figure 3.1. Be sure you understand the basic characteristics of each value in the model and can identify the differences among the six values: theoretical, economic, aesthetic, social, political, and religious.

2. In the following situation, examine the profile values of the worker in each occupation.

Situation: The following six value profiles are from these individuals: (A) clergyman, (B) industrial engineer, (C) chief executive officer, (D) aerospace engineer, (E) salesperson, and (F) drug counselor.

Theoretical	62	46	49	26	43	25
Economic	51	66	42	44	55	40
Aesthetic	29	27	64	22	34	23
Social	33	30	24	59	23	50

Political	47	49	41	41	66	41
Religious	18	22	20	48	20	61

3. Prepare a written report on why there are differences? Discuss the reasons for the differences in value profiles and how these can affect the way that individual may behave in the workplace. What implications does this theory have for the type of job or career you may be planning?

CASE
A Matter of Personality

Henry Wallace is the manager of ZeeBee's Electronics, an electronic products chain store located in the southwestern part of the United States. He has been with the company for five years, and his store's sales have been rated "below average" in comparison with sales of similar stores in locales with the same general population and per capita income. Wallace's boss, Sue Sutterwhite, has been with the company for twelve years. For five of those years, Sutterwhite was a store manager, during which time her sales were the highest in the region, and her employees rated her "excellent."

Sutterwhite believes that having a good personality is one of the most important characteristics of an effective store manager. She believes that the manager must like people, be willing to listen to customer complaints without taking the matter personally, and express a sincere interest in the well-being of the workers. To Sutterwhite, Wallace seems to lack all these traits. He acts as if he has a chip on his shoulder, and Sutterwhite is afraid that his behavior is likely to lead to the loss of customers.

During her recent visit to Wallace's store, Sutterwhite watched him talk to a customer who wanted to return some merchandise. The woman insisted the merchandise was damaged when she opened the package, and she wanted to exchange it for an undamaged item. Wallace refused to accept the return. "We don't sell damaged goods," he told the woman. "It must have been damaged after you took it from the store." The customer was furious and, in a loud voice, began telling Wallace what she thought of the store and its personnel. Many of the other customers in the store at the time heard the ruckus, and Sutterwhite noticed that most of them left without buying anything.

When Wallace resumed his discussion with Sutterwhite, he explained that the woman had been wrong in saying that the merchandise was damaged and that the store should not be expected to take the loss. Sutterwhite became concerned that he was not following the company's return policy. So she immediately took Wallace aside and explained the return policy, which states that merchandise can be returned with a receipt within ten days of purchase for a full return or exchange for merchandise of equal value. Wallace said he did not agree with the policy and felt that customers too often took advantage by returning merchandise they have damaged themselves by not carefully following instructions in assembly or by carelessly using

the item. Therefore, he did not feel that he should accept the damaged merchandise. After hearing Wallace's side of the story, Sutterwhite tried to help him see the customer's point of view, but she was unable to do so. She dropped the subject and turned to other business matters, including his decline in sales. "Things haven't been going too well since you took over," she told Wallace. "What seems to be wrong?"

Wallace talked about some areas in which he felt there were problems that needed to be straightened out. He felt that all the problems were related to inventory control and the need for more motivated personnel. At no point during the conversation did Wallace indicate that he might be causing any of the problems because of his personality or his leadership style.

Before leaving, Sutterwhite walked around the store and talked to some of the employees. From her brief conversations with them, she learned they did not care much for Wallace as a store manager. One of the workers referred to him as "uncaring," while another said he had "the personality of an army drill sergeant." Sutterwhite decided she would let Wallace run the store for another three months but, if sales kept slipping, she would have to replace him. She documented the information and relayed the information to Wallace before leaving the store.

Case Questions

1. What type of personality characteristics should you expect to find in a successful store manager? Why are each important to the manager's success? Compare them to the personality traits exhibited by Wallace.
2. How is Wallace's personality affecting the attitudes of the workers? What does he need to do to build a better working relationship with his employees? What are his chances of changing in three months?
3. Using what you know about EI competencies, describe how you would advise Wallace about being more effective.
4. Do you think he can succeed? Or do you feel he will be fired? Explain.
5. Describe Sutterwhite's behavior. What personality characteristics did she display and how did she use them in the case?
6. What have you learned about personality and its role in managing effectively?

CHAPTER 4

Group Behavior

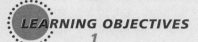

LEARNING OBJECTIVES

1
Describe a group and distinguish among organizational groups— functional, cross-functional, project, virtual, and interest-friendship.

2
Explain the stages of group development.

3
Discuss the importance of roles, norms, status, cohesiveness, and group size to group behavior.

4
Describe how communication and decision-making styles, risk taking, and creativity affect group decisions.

5
List ways in which groups try to gain power over other groups.

6
Identify ways to resolve intergroup conflict.

7
Identify important factors in building effective teams.

8
Explain how to conduct a successful job hunt.

Individuals may act on their own, but the perceptions, values, and attitudes that cause their behavior are often a result of group interaction. People influence those around them. Therefore, we cannot adequately study human relations without considering group behavior. To accomplish objectives, managers use several types of groups, which, even though they all have common characteristics, have their own roles, norms, status, and cohesiveness. It is imperative for managers to understand how decisions are made and how power functions within each group, as well as between groups. Managers from time to time will need to resolve conflict within groups. In this chapter, we examine how people act within groups as well as how groups interact with one another.

Innovative Teams in Action

In recent years, more and more organizations have been creating teams for the purpose of generating creative solutions to business-related problems. For example, British Airways brought together a group of experts to help it with its baggage handling operations. None of these individuals was connected to airline baggage handling, but all knew a lot about moving and reclaiming merchandise. The company established five criteria that were critical to baggage handling:

1. Passengers had to be able to reclaim their baggage within twenty minutes of arrival time.
2. More than 99 percent of all bags at Heathrow Airport had to be routed properly.
3. Dependence on the "human element" in baggage handling was to be decreased.
4. The company had to show a progressive, measurable improvement in baggage handling.
5. Customer confidence and satisfaction in the firm's baggage handling had to be increased.

The expert group was told that the baggage facilities had not yet been built, so the group was free to be as innovative as it wanted.

The group then generated sixty-two actions that the company could take. The company eventually rejected some of the suggestions because their implementation was too costly or difficult. One was the use of a voice-recognition system. The firm found that the system was unable to distinguish between the cockney accents of East Enders and the Scottish brogue of Glaswegians. So bags that were bound for Birmingham would sometimes end up being sent to Bremen. However, the company did accept the bar-code baggage system recommendation, and today, British Airways has one of the world's most efficient baggage handling systems.

In fact, the results were so successful that the firm has begun using innovative teams to help it attack other productivity-related problems in such areas as cargo handling, cleaning of aircraft, and catering operations. In the latter case, the team proposed forty-seven recommendations, of which six were selected for further study and development. One of these dealt with the movement of food from the catering center to the aircraft. This activity is highly labor-intensive and time-consuming. Loads must be assembled on the loading dock and then reloaded into high-lift transport vehicles. The company now is in the process of eliminating an entire section of this routine by introducing demountable swap bodies that can be parked within the catering center marshaling area and then connected to the drive unit for the journey to the plane.

These approaches have resulted in a 67 percent increase in productivity, thus helping British Airways to maintain its reputation as one of the best international airlines in the world. As a result, the company is continuing to use expert innovation teams to help it find new ways of increasing productivity and customer service. The key is the effective use of group effort.

In another example, the management of Air France successfully teamed with its employees to turn a financially strapped airline on the verge of bankruptcy hosting militant, unhappy, employees into a profitable one. Chairman and CEO Jean-Cyril Spinetta convinced his workers and their unions that they had everything to gain as partners with management and everything to lose as adversaries. It was vital to let employees see how opening new markets against increased competition would provide enormous opportunities for everyone. Spinetta said, "It was the moment to really start working together." To do that, Spinetta regularly consulted Air France employees so that they began to feel involved in the airline's management, and he struck labor agreements that would leave American Airlines managers totally bewildered. Spinetta reported that, "Since then, the success of the company has depended on employees understanding our strategy, getting fully behind it and feeling secure knowing that if it all works out, profits from it will be redistributed to them." On January 1, 2009, Jean-Cyril Spinetta became chairman of the board of directors of the profitable Air France airline.[1]

It does not matter whether it is the Pittsburgh Steelers, the New York Giants, Indianapolis Colts, or the Dallas Cowboys; it takes a team of football players, not a group of individual players, to win the Super Bowl. Every player on the team must have the same goal—to win every game in the season, as well as the Super Bowl. And every player must work hard to do what it takes to win. Team players who support each other accomplish more than when individual players strive to be the star of the game. Too often this attitude causes the players to lose the game. It takes time and hard work to build an effective team of players who perform together.

Describe a group and distinguish among organizational groups— functional, crossfunctional, project, virtual, and interest-friendship.

Definition of a Group

Unfortunately, there is no universally accepted definition of the term *group*. However, all groups do seem to have three characteristics in common.

1. A group is a **social unit** of two or more members, all of whom engage, at some time or other, in *interaction* with each other. In work groups, this interaction often occurs on a face-to-face basis, although some groups are geographically dispersed and interact through letters and telephone conversations.
2. Members all are *dependent* on one another. In the pursuit of their objectives, each member realizes the need for the others. In a work setting, an individual is aware that the overall job cannot be done without assistance from other people.
3. The members of the group receive some *satisfaction* from their mutual association. Otherwise, they will drop out of the group. In a work setting, for example, they will ask for a transfer to another department or locale or will simply resign.

Now that we have examined the three major characteristics of a group, let us incorporate them into a meaningful definition. A **group** is a social unit consisting of two or more interdependent, interactive individuals who are striving to attain common goals.

Before examining the nature and activities of groups, it is important to dispel some of the common myths that have sprung up about them:[2]

Myth	Reality
1. The importance of working together has replaced that of individual contributions.	Individual contributions are critical to the overall success of groups.
2. If a group consists of high-performing individuals, the group will automatically become a high-performing group.	Sometimes, the talents and egos of high-performing individuals will reduce the overall effectiveness of a group because of the internal strife that is created.
3. It takes a long time for a group to be up and running.	Many groups can very quickly work out their agendas and interpersonal relationships and be up and running in record time.
4. Decision making by consensus is the best way to make a group work effectively.	Sometimes, group consensus works best, but often, one or two members take the lead and everyone follows.
5. Group accountability means that everyone is collectively responsible for everything.	Although the group is accountable in theory, in practice, everyone has individual responsibilities and is evaluated on her or his ability to meet those obligations.
6. There are no leaders or followers in groups; everyone is equal.	Everyone in a group is equal, but some are more equal than others, as determined by such factors as ability, contribution, and personality.

Many types of groups can be found in organizations. Most of them, however, can be classified as one of the following: functional group, cross-functional group, project group, virtual group, or interest-friendship group.

Functional Group

A **functional group** is composed of individuals performing the same tasks. In a manufacturing firm, for example, it is common to find major functional groups or departments, such as marketing, production, and finance, and further divisions of employees within each group. In the marketing department, for example, there is often an advertising group and a personal selling group. In a personal selling group, there are sales forces for product lines or geographical territories. In all these divisions, functional groups are formed to promote internal efficiency.

Cross-Functional Group

A **cross-functional group** is composed of individuals from two or more different functional areas. For example, in designing and bringing a new product to the market and ensuring its continued, long-run success, companies commonly use the talents of a cross-functional group whose members come from a variety of different areas, including design, development, production, marketing, and finance.[3] In hospitals, cross-functional groups often include people from such areas as radiology, hematology, nursing services, surgical support, and administration. If members of the cross-functional team are chosen carefully and their roles and responsibilities are spelled out clearly, the group can produce extremely effective results.[4]

Project Group

A **project group** consists of individuals from many different areas or backgrounds, drawn together for a specific project or work. The group's purpose is to attain its objective within predetermined time, cost, and quality limits, after which the group is disbanded and everybody goes back to their regular departments. Project groups are used often in building spacecraft, skyscrapers, bridges, and ships. They have also been employed in designing new products and solving particularly complex problems. Whatever the objective, a project group draws employees from many different areas of expertise and combines their talents in the hope of attaining the project goal.

Virtual Group

A **virtual group** is a task-focused group that meets without all the members being present in the same locale or at the same time. Virtual groups use digital communication such as videoconferences, e-mail, and conference calls to exchange ideas and discuss problems. Virtual groups, sometimes called virtual teams, are becoming increasingly common because of advances in communication technology. For example, companies with worldwide R&D groups have found that they can have these teams working around the clock. At the end of its workday, the design group in Germany will forward its daily work progress to the one in the United States, which will pick up where the other group left off. In turn, the American R&D team will forward its work to the company's Japanese R&D group. In this way, groups worldwide will be working on the design. Additionally, the groups use e-mail so they do not have to communicate with one another in real time. As a result of these benefits, a growing number of firms are relying increasingly on the use of virtual groups.[5]

Companies that use virtual groups say they save money, result in more productive and effective use of workers' time, and ultimately generate better products because of the collaborative nature of the groups. Virtual groups allow employees to be fast and competitive in disseminating information.[6] Virtual groups reduce travel expenses and are a cost savings for people not having to meet face-to-face.

Interest-Friendship Group

An **interest-friendship group** is formed on the basis of common beliefs, concerns, or activities. On the job, interest-friendship groups sometimes are found within departments, whereas in other instances, they cut across departmental lines. For example, people who have been in an organization for a long time tend to have many contacts, and they often find it possible to ask friends in other departments to expedite a process or to put a high priority on a particular job. Or they may simply enjoy having lunch together, and sometimes, these people exercise together during the lunch hour.

Interest-friendship groups also function away from the job, as in the case of three members of the accounting department and three members from production who are on the company bowling team. Their primary interest is to win the bowling league title. However, such friendships carry back to the job, and it is not uncommon to find people using their friendships to help attain job-related objectives. Thus, it should be obvious that people are often members of two or more groups.

Explain the stages of group development.

Stages of Group Development

When a group is first formed, initially there is a "feeling out" stage during which the members get to know one another and learn how to interact effectively. As the members become comfortable working together and learn what each can contribute to the group effort, performance begins to improve and may eventually result in a highly effective work group. During this process, the group goes through four stages: forming, storming, norming, and performing.

Forming

The **forming stage** of group development is characterized by efforts to identify carefully what the group should do and how it can get started in this direction. During this stage, group members develop initial interaction; gain insights into one another's values, beliefs, and attitudes; and begin working on role definitions and expectations of each member. Examples of group behavior in this stage are as follows:

1. Everyone is extremely polite to everyone else.
2. Many individuals remain quiet and make minimal contributions to group discussions while trying to determine where they want to fit in the scheme of things.
3. Some initial efforts are made by members to establish bonds and to disclose personal insights.
4. Early efforts are made toward gaining power and building influence in the group.

These behaviors help to create the climate within which the team will function during this early stage. To more quickly move the group to becoming a functioning group, it is important in the first stage of development to provide an opportunity for group members to learn about each other; for example, where do the members work in the company; what are their specific jobs; what are their personalities and attitudes; what are their strengths and weaknesses; and how can their experiences benefit the group? This input will help the group to clarify its vision and find common ground for understanding one another.[7]

Storming

The **storming stage** of group development is characterized by confrontation, questioning of the group's direction and progress, and resistance to task assignments. During this stage, group members believe it is necessary to gain control, and there is often concern that the group has been drifting and lacks a clear sense of focus or direction. Characteristics of group behavior in this stage are as follows:

1. Some members question the group's progress and want the group leader to use a more direct approach to get things done.
2. Some members question the group's goals, assignments, and procedures and want to see changes made.
3. Some participants show frustration because the group's task now appears more difficult than before, and members begin to doubt the group's ability for success.

These behaviors help the group to rethink its approach, make necessary changes, and get on with the job. In carrying out these tasks, the group leader often spends a great deal of time listening to challenges and complaints and calmly responding, renegotiating expectations, and reassigning work based on members' interests and skills. Also common during this phase is the weeding out of ineffective group leaders, who are replaced by more effective members. A group leader may be ineffective because he or she is unwilling to communicate with group members. Alternatively, the leader may be unable to be a team player. Commenting on these types of group leaders, one team of researchers offered the following explanations for the replacement of certain individuals:

> He was not interested in communicating with his team, coworkers, or peers; not committed to sharing and transferring experience, information, knowledge, or process. He tended to be a block in the flow of information, a bottleneck within the company. He was too individualistic. He was not a team player and unable to work with others. A one-man show. He did not accept belonging to a big company.[8]

Norming

The **norming stage** of group development is characterized by agreement regarding the responsibilities of each member, a new sense of cooperation, and a desire to accomplish group goals. The group has now reached the stage at which it knows how to work as a team, and the focus is on getting things done effectively and efficiently. Characteristics of group behavior in this stage are:

1. Effective conflict management by the group leader as well as by the members.
2. Clear identification and prioritizing of problems and action plans for resolving them.
3. A willingness of members to accept responsibility and carry out their tasks as agreed.
4. Effective member interaction resulting in highly effective meetings.

During this phase, group members begin developing negotiation skills, mentoring skills, and the ability to balance differences and similarities. They also learn how to deal with ambiguity and establish common grounds for understanding.[9]

Performing

The **performing stage** of group development is characterized by openness and collaboration among group members and the willingness of individual members to monitor their own performance and make necessary changes. In this stage, the group functions effectively on both an individual and a group level. Examples of such behavior are:

1. The open sharing of problems and solutions.
2. Cooperation on the part of all members.

3. Wide use of recognition and praise by team members.

4. Integration of personal and team goals.

As a result, a sense of unconditional trust exists among the members, and everyone's attitude is positive and productive. This is particularly important because researchers are finding that tomorrow's successful enterprises are more likely to be led not by visionary individuals but by "smart teams." These teams value learning as a core group capability, which allows them to imagine continuously and to give shape to future objectives and the approaches that must be taken to reach them.[10]

Not all groups reach the fourth stage of development. Those that do, however, learn how to achieve the necessary balance between group and individual approaches and become adept at tolerating the creative tension that allows them to reach higher levels of productivity.[11] Regardless of a group's progress, some characteristics are common to all groups.

 CHECK YOUR UNDERSTANDING

For each type of group listed below, write down the name of a group in which you are or have been a member. The group may be at work, at home, or in the community, such as church. Think about each group's current stage of development—forming, storming, norming, or performing. Write down your assessment of its stage of development. Why do you believe the group is in a particular stage? What needs to happen to move the group to the next stage?

Type of Group	Name of Your Group	Stage of Development	Why?
Functional			
Project			
Interest-Friendship			

Discuss the importance of roles, norms, status, cohesiveness, and group size to group behavior.

Characteristics of Groups

All groups have certain characteristics. Some of the most important are roles, norms, status, cohesiveness, and group size.

Roles

A **role** is an expected behavior. In many organizations, job descriptions provide the initial basis for determining one's role. The individual can read this description and obtain a general idea of what he or she is supposed to be doing. Of course, the description does not cover everything, but it will give the person enough general information to begin doing the job.

One of the most serious and most common role-related problems occurs when job duties are unclear either because the job description is vague or because no description has ever been written for the work. This is called **role ambiguity**, because what the individual is supposed to do is uncertain or vague. For example, many workers find that when they are promoted to the rank of supervisor, they are told to "Get out there, manage those people, and get the work done." This statement is too general and does not explain the specific roles the newly promoted workers are supposed to assume. One of the most effective ways of preventing role ambiguity is to have job descriptions that are clear and describe in detail the responsibilities and tasks of the position.

A second major role-related problem is **role conflict**. This occurs when an individual faces a situation in which he or she must assume two roles, and the performance of one precludes the performance of the other. For example, a manager is told to do everything she can to build morale in the department. At the same time, she is instructed to reprimand anyone who comes late to work. In this case, the manager may face a role conflict problem because she feels she cannot perform both of these tasks. If she is to build morale, she will have to be lenient with those who are tardy while working to change their behavior. If she reprimands anyone, she may feel this action will affect morale negatively. Clearly, this represents a role conflict problem.

Norms

The rules of conduct adopted by group members are **norms**. These norms indicate how each group member ought to act. Usually, norms are few and relate only to those areas that have significance for the group. For example, a work group will often have norms related to output (how much you ought to do), participation (whether you should help slower workers), and communication with management (what you should and should not say to the boss). It will not have norms related to where you should live, how you ought to raise your children, or what church you should attend.

Additionally, there are degrees of conformity. For example, you ought to turn out 480 pieces per day, plus or minus 20. There is, thus, an acceptable range, and those individuals who want to remain in good standing with the group will conform to it.

Overall, we can draw some conclusions about individuals and their conformity to group norms.

1. Adults tend to conform less than children.
2. Women, because of our cultural values, tend to conform more than men.
3. Highly intelligent people tend to conform less than people of low intelligence.
4. If all other members agree on something, the remaining person is likely to go along with them.
5. If a person in the group disagrees with the others but receives support from one of them, the person is much less likely to conform. The individual will take heart from the fact that some support has been forthcoming and will often cling tenaciously to his or her original position.
6. If a person does not understand what is going on, he or she is more likely to follow the direction of a group member who does seem to have a grasp of the situation.

Any individual who does not conform to at least the major norms of the group is denied membership. That person is not permitted to participate in group activities and, in some cases, is ostracized or subjected to various forms of harassment by the members.

The manager must be aware of group norms because they play a key role in determining what a group will and will not do. If the group's informal work norm, for example, is much lower than the quota set by the company, the group is likely to have low productivity. The manager's awareness of such informal norms, however, can serve as the basis for developing a change strategy, by which the manager can influence the group to increase its informal work norms. (Change strategies are explored further in Chapter 12.)

Status

The relative ranking of an individual in an organization or a group is **status**. Status can be achieved in a number of ways.

- In our society, a Rockefeller or a Kennedy has status merely through being born into a rich, influential family.
- On the job, people can achieve status through the position they hold. For example, the president of the organization has more status than a vice president.
- Other people achieve status by the job they do. For example, in some firms, the advertising manager has greater status than the purchasing manager.
- Another way to achieve job status is through personality. An individual who gets along with others, is easy to work with, and is always ready to say a kind word is more likely to be given status by the other members of the organization than an individual with whom no one can work because he or she is unpleasant to others.
- Job competence is another work status determinant. The better a person knows his or her job, the more likely it is that the person will be accorded status by members of the peer group. For example, in a group that values high productivity, those individuals who are the highest producers will be afforded the highest status.

Of course, to determine exactly how group status will be accorded, we must examine the specific situation. In some groups, competence (what the person can do) is very important but, in other groups, job title (what position the person holds) is of greatest value in obtaining status. Additionally, if we were to move from one organization to another, we might well find different status determinants. This would be particularly obvious if we were to put five people—two professors, two students, and a bank executive—into three different group settings. As seen in Figure 4.1, the status of these individuals will vary from one situation to the next. Yet, if one were to give them scores—one point for first place through five points for fifth place—in all three group settings, one would find that the overall score per person is about the same. In short, they all have about the same average status across the three groups, but this status varies dramatically within the group. For example, in a university setting, the full professor has the highest status, followed by other faculty, and then students and, finally, members of the group whose occupations are not academic. In a bank, the president has the highest status, followed by individuals knowledgeable in finance, students working toward a master's degree in business administration (MBAs), and then members of the group whose occupations do not relate to finance in any way. Finally, in a bowling alley, the status of each is accorded strictly on the basis of his or her bowling skills.

Figure 4.1 Changing Status

	Academia	Bank	Bowling Alley
High Status			
	Professor of finance	Bank president	Graduating senior in zoology (195 average)
	Assistant professor of biology	Professor of finance	MBA student (180 average)
	MBA student	MBA student	Assistant professor of biology (170 average)
	Graduating senior in zoology	Assistant professor of biology	Bank president (150 average)
	Bank president	Graduating senior in zoology	Professor of finance (135 average)
Low Status			

Status Incongruence.   To understand fully the importance of status within groups, it is necessary to realize there can be problems. The most serious is **status incongruence**, which occurs when there is a discrepancy between a person's supposed status and the way he or she is treated. For example, if all the senior-level managers except one are given new desks, there is a discrepancy between the way this last person is being treated and the way this person's peers are being treated. Unless there is reason for this discrepancy, such as the fact that the manager does not want a new desk and prefers to continue using the old one, the manager's status may be in jeopardy. People will begin to wonder why the manager is not being treated as well as the other senior-level managers. In fact, in some organizations, this is the way managers are told they are "on the way out": They are not given things that are provided to other managers at their organizational level.

Status Discrepancy.   A second status-related problem is **status discrepancy**, which occurs when people do things that do not fit with their status in their group. For example, in an organization where there are bitter feelings between management and the union, members of these two groups do not associate with one another. Anyone who is seen being friendly to a member of the other group is considered a traitor and his or her status will decline. Members of the management team who act friendly toward union representatives may soon find such actions negatively affecting promotion potential. Union representatives who are friendly with management personnel may soon be voted out of office. We can sum it up this way: Status is accorded to people for behaving according to the expectations of those assigning the status rank; and any time people do things that do not fit into this category, they threaten their own status.

Cohesiveness

The closeness or interpersonal attractions that exist among group members are referred to as **cohesiveness**. If cohesion is high, member satisfaction tends to be high, and there is increased cooperation within the group.[12] Conversely, if cohesion is low, there is often dissatisfaction and members will seek to leave the group.[13]

However, cohesiveness does not guarantee high productivity. Individuals may all like one another very much and may also have an informal norm of low output; they may all have agreed to do as little work as possible. Figure 4.2 provides an illustration. Note that Group X has the highest productivity. Everyone in this group is turning out more work than is required by the organizational norm. In fact, all the high producers are in this group. Conversely, all the low producers are in Group Z. Their average is far below than that of the other two groups. However, cohesiveness is very high; everyone in the group is conforming to an informal work norm. Note how little each person's productivity deviates from this norm; this is why we can conclude that it is indeed an informal norm. Otherwise, there would be several high and low producers. For example, in Group X, there is a greater variation between high and low producers, indicating less acceptance of a group norm. In Group Y, the variation is even more significant. We can conclude that Group Z has the greatest cohesion and that Group Y has the least.

Major Challenges of Cohesiveness.   Group cohesiveness presents two major challenges to the manager. First, the manager needs to work closely with low-producing groups to motivate them to increase their productivity norms to the level established by the organization. Many of the ideas presented in Chapter 2 can be used to accomplish this. Second, the manager must protect the cohesiveness of the high-producing groups. Changes in the work or transfer of people into or out of the group can negatively affect cohesion. One of the most famous cases of this has been provided

Figure 4.2 Cohesion and Productivity

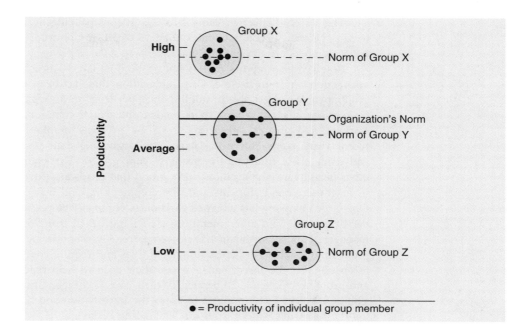

Group X

High — Norm of Group X

Productivity

Group Y

Organization's Norm

Norm of Group Y

Average —

Group Z

Low — Norm of Group Z

● = Productivity of individual group member

by the coal-mining industry in Great Britain, which introduced new technology and procedures into the mines after World War II. Before the change, the miners had worked together in teams, and there was high cohesion within these groups. However, new technology disrupted these arrangements. Many of the small, cohesive groups were reorganized into larger teams, and some of the work previously done by the miners was now done by machines. The restructuring destroyed group cohesiveness, and the coal miners began to slow their production. It became necessary for the companies to reorganize some of their operations again: this time, however, to accommodate the miners better.

Obviously, every organization needs to consider both technology and people. If technology is overemphasized, cohesiveness declines and productivity falls. Conversely, if people are accommodated at the expense of technology, the firm suffers in comparison with other companies that have adopted the latest technological breakthroughs. A balance between technology and people is needed to keep cohesiveness strong among employees and productivity high for the company.

Group Size

Some work groups are quite small (three or four people), whereas others are very large (twenty or more). Research has found that as the size of the group increases, the way in which members interact with one another changes. As group size expands, the time and attention given to creating and maintaining group harmony diminish. This is in contrast to small groups, in which members typically exhibit greater agreement on things and seek one another's opinions more frequently. In large groups, it is common to find the need for group approval also diminishing; people begin focusing more on getting the job done and less on how their coworkers feel about their actions. This behavior is typical in groups, whereas in teams, coworkers seek one another's opinions and are concerned about the feelings of team members, while focusing on team goals.

The secret to effective teams is to keep them small; ideally, a team should have seven to nine people. "If you have more than 15 or 20, you're dead: The connections between team members are too hard to make."[14]

Research also reports that as groups become larger, turnover tends to increase and satisfaction tends to decline. One explanation that has been offered is that in a large group, people are less able to fulfill their upper-level needs, which leads to dissatisfaction. Conversely, in small groups, there tends to be greater cohesion, more concern for fellow workers, and greater satisfaction, resulting in lower employee turnover.[15] In fact, in recent years, some enterprises have been organizing their people into groups of three and using these triads as the primary work groups. For example, some hospitals and other health care organizations have found that triads are extremely effective in helping to diagnose patient ailments and in recommending and delivering the needed services. One large company has assigned each of its regional vice presidents to serve as a member of a triad. The other members are an individual from corporate staff and a field manager. This arrangement has proven extremely useful in helping the firm to identify problem areas that cut across functional lines and require coordinated effort. Moreover, to ensure that the three managers use their triad to help reduce bureaucratic red tape and promote efficiency, 20 percent of their overall compensation is tied to triad responsibilities.[16] Take a few minutes to apply the information you have just read by completing the following "Check Your Understanding" exercise.

 CHECK YOUR UNDERSTANDING

For each of the three groups you named in the previous exercise on page 133, identify your role, status, group norm, group cohesiveness, and group size. Analyze how the three groups differ. What have you learned about group characteristics in analyzing these groups?

Group Name	Your Role	Your Status	Group Norm	Group Cohesiveness	Group Size

Describe how communication and decision-making styles, risk taking, and creativity affect group decisions.

Intragroup Behavior

Communication and decision making are two major activities that impact intragroup behavior.

Communication

The social system within a group helps dictate the way information is communicated internally, as well as externally. The role played by each individual member typically is a result of that individual's knowledge and personality and the needs of the group.

Depending on the size of the group, a varying number of roles may be assumed by the members. In a small group, an individual may assume more than one communication role. In large groups, two or more people may assume the same role, whereas others have no specific communication role. Five of the most common communication roles are the following:

1. The **opinion leader** is often the informal leader of the group. This person typically receives more communiqués than anyone else in the group and is most responsible for determining group goals and actions.
2. The **gatekeeper** regulates the flow of information to other members of the group. If this individual chooses not to tell something to someone, the latter is deprived of the information because the gatekeeper is the only one in a position to provide this information.
3. The **liaison** links the group to other groups. He or she is the contact person who communicates with the other groups and gets information from them.
4. The **isolate** is a person who generally is ignored by the group and receives very little communication. He or she is treated as an outsider, even though the person is a member of the group.
5. The **follower** goes along with whatever the opinion leader or the group at large wants done. He or she is a loyal group member who can be counted on to "stay in line."

Decision Making

How are decisions made within groups? Answering this question is difficult because it is multifaceted. However, we know some things about group decision making that are related to styles, risk taking, and creativity.

Decision-Making Styles.   When making decisions, individuals often display a personal style that reflects how they perceive what is happening around them and how they process information. These decision-making styles are determined by two dimensions: *value orientation* and *tolerance for ambiguity orientation*. Value orientation focuses on the individual's concern for task and technical matters as opposed to people and social concerns. Tolerance for ambiguity orientation measures how much the person needs structure and control (a desire for low ambiguity) as opposed to being able to thrive in uncertain situations (a desire for high ambiguity). These two orientations, with their low and high dimensions, result in four styles of decision making—directive, analytical, conceptual, and behavioral—and are illustrated in Figure 4.3.

Figure 4.3 Decision-Making Styles

	Task and technical concerns	People and social concerns
Tolerance for Ambiguity High	Analytical	Conceptual
Low	Directive	Behavioral

Value Orientation

1. **Directive style** Individuals with a directive style have a low tolerance for ambiguity and are oriented toward task and technical concerns in their decision making. These people tend to be efficient, logical, pragmatic, and systematic in their approach to problem solving. They also like to focus on facts and to get things done quickly. In short, they are action oriented. In addition, they tend to have a very short-run focus, like to exercise power, want to be in control, and display an autocratic type of leadership style.
2. **Analytical style** Analytical decision makers have a high tolerance for ambiguity and a strong task and technical orientation. These people like to analyze situations; in fact, they often tend to overanalyze things. They evaluate more information and alternatives than do directive decision makers. They also take a long time to make decisions, but they respond well to new or uncertain situations. They tend to be autocratic.
3. **Conceptual style** Decision makers with a conceptual style have a high tolerance for ambiguity and for strong people and social concerns. They take a broad perspective in solving problems, and they like to consider many options and future possibilities. These decision makers discuss things with many people in order to gather a great deal of information, and they also rely on intuition. Additionally, they are willing to take risks, and they tend to be good at discovering creative solutions to problems. At the same time, however, they can foster an idealistic and indecisive approach to decision making.
4. **Behavioral style** The behavioral-style decision maker is characterized by a low tolerance for ambiguity and for strong people and social concerns. These decision makers tend to work well with others and like situations in which opinions are openly exchanged. They tend to be receptive to suggestions, supportive, and warm and prefer verbal to written information. They also tend to avoid conflict and be overly concerned with keeping everyone happy. As a result, these decision makers often have a difficult time saying no to people, and they do not like making tough decisions, especially when it will result in someone being upset with the outcome.

Style Implications.   Research reveals that decision makers typically rely on two or three styles, and these will vary by occupation, job level, and culture. For example, analytical decision makers make decisions rapidly, but they also tend to be autocratic in their approach to doing things. Conceptual decision makers are innovative and willing to take risks, but they often are indecisive. These styles also help to explain why different managers will arrive at different decisions after evaluating the same information. In particular, the decision-making styles model is useful in providing insights regarding how and why people make decisions, as well as offering guidelines regarding how to deal with these decisions.

Risk Taking

A number of important findings have been uncovered about risk taking within groups. First, groups are often more effective than individuals in decision making. For example, when faced with the task of evaluating ambiguous situations, groups appear to be superior to individuals. They are also more effective in generating unique ideas or accurately recalling information. However, they are not as effective as individuals in solving problems that require long chains of decisions.[17]

Second, individuals tend to take greater risks when they are in groups than when they are acting alone. This is known as the **risky-shift phenomenon**.[18] Behavioral scientists studying this phenomenon have used measures similar to the questionnaire you will find in the end-of-chapter section, "Connecting to the Real World." The individual is

IN ACTION

UNCERTAINTY VERSUS RISK TAKING

Managers in the United States encourage their people to take risks. This is a socially acceptable behavior. However, in many countries of the world, risk taking is avoided. The term given to this cultural dimension is *uncertainty avoidance*, and it refers to the extent to which people feel threatened by situations that have unclear outcomes or over which they have little control.

In the United States, workers are characterized as having weak uncertainty avoidance. Managers are encouraged to make decisions and learn to live with the consequences. Other countries with weak uncertainty avoidance are Canada, Australia, Hong Kong, Singapore, and Jamaica. At the opposite extreme are those countries whose workers exhibit strong uncertainty avoidance—for example, Portugal, Guatemala, Uruguay, Japan, Korea, and Spain.

Cultures characterized by strong uncertainty avoidance tend to favor group decision making over individual decision making. In this way, the group members are given support by their colleagues, and no one needs to fear that he or she will be responsible for a major mistake. Companies operating in these cultures also tend to have bureaucratic structures so that everyone knows exactly what is expected of him or her and there is no uncertainty regarding work assignments. Employees of such companies have a high need for security, and it is likely that the companies will offer guaranteed employment and provide good health and retirement benefits. Likewise, employees tend to have a high degree of anxiety and stress, and they often exhibit aggressive behavior.

In contrast, companies operating in countries with low uncertainty avoidance are more permissive of mistakes and errors and try to keep job anxiety and stress to a minimum. These companies also shun bureaucratic structures, frown on excessively aggressive behavior, and believe that effective employees have to balance a concern for family and personal life with the demands of the job.

The cultural dimensions of uncertainty help to explain why risk-taking propensity varies from country to country. They also help to explain why multinational corporations often find that the way they do business at home does not work overseas. Willingness to accept or reject risk is heavily influenced by culture, and what is acceptable behavior in one country often is frowned on in another.

Sources: Jane Whitney Gibson and Richard M. Hodgetts, *Organizational Communication: A Managerial Perspective*, 2nd ed. (New York: HarperCollins, 1991); and Richard M. Hodgetts and Fred Luthans, *International Management*, 4th ed. (Burr Ridge, IL: Irwin/McGraw, 2000), p. 117.

---

asked questions and then is placed in a group, which is asked the same questions. The people in groups tend to be greater risk takers. Why is this so? Some explanations for this phenomenon follow:

- *If the decision proves to be wrong, the individual feels less guilt or concern* because other people were involved and responsibility is diffused among all the members of the group.
- *In group discussions, risk-taking people tend to be more influential* than their conservative counterparts. As a result, their viewpoints tend to win out.
- *Risk is a function of knowledge.* The less someone knows about a given area or problem, the greater the risk he or she assumes in trying to remedy the situation. Because group thinking often leads to deeper consideration of, and greater familiarity with, the possible pros and cons of a particular course of action, the risk tends to be reduced. Thus, a high-risk decision for an individual can be a moderate risk for a group.
- *Risk taking is socially desirable in our culture.* As a result, individuals in groups often choose a risk level that is equal to or greater than that risk, which is acceptable to the average person.[19]

We should note, however, that groups do not always encourage higher risk taking. Sometimes they motivate a manager to be even more moderate in setting goals. For example, in many organizations, it is common to find the head of the sales department encouraging the managers to strive for 20 percent higher sales. However, sometimes the individual manager's sales force reports that the market is not increasing and that, at best, a 10 percent rise in sales can be expected; the manager may then be influenced by the sales force to set a more realistic objective for the group. In short, group pressure—toward risky or more moderate goals—influences management behavior.

Culture also affects decision making. Some examples are discussed in the "Cultural Diversity in Action" box under the title, "Uncertainty versus Risk Taking."

Creativity

Sometimes decisions require creative thinking. This process has four phases: preparation, incubation, illumination, and verification.

1. During the *preparation stage*, the group members prepare themselves mentally to make the decision. This phase is characterized by information gathering.
2. During the *incubation stage*, the group often will sit back and let the subconscious mind work on the problem. Often, the result will be a better decision than the one that is forced or made hurriedly. On the other hand, if group members are unable to come up with an effective approach after, say, one week, they will go back to the preparation stage and start the process anew by gathering additional data or reviewing what is there.
3. The *illumination phase* is characterized by the group's realization of the best decision to make. Sometimes the decision will suddenly hit them; other times, it will slowly dawn on them. In any event, they will know what to do.
4. The *final stage* is verification, during which the group modifies or makes final changes to the solution. Often, the decision will need some fine-tuning because of minor problems. Once this is done, the decision can be implemented. For example, when Art Fry invented Post-it® notes, no one understood their value. As he put it, "People had never heard of a 'repositionable note,' and they couldn't conceive of such a phenomenon."[20] However, once they began using the notes, they realized their value and then, as Fry put it, "they became addicted to them."

Research.   Research suggests that a number of factors influence group creativity. For example, although group size seems to have no effect on the overall levels of team innovation, larger groups tend to produce more radically innovative solutions to problems than smaller groups. In addition, groups that have a higher proportion of innovative members tend to generate more creative ideas. Two other critical factors are organizational support for innovation and the willingness of group members to participate in the creative process. It is also important to remember that innovation tends to vary depending on the phase of creative thinking in which the team is operating. One group of researchers put it this way:

> *Individual innovativeness may be most important at the initial stage in determining the quality of ideas available from the pool of individual innovativeness. At the second stage—the proposal, development, and implementation of ideas—group processes may become important in either hindering or facilitating the expression and development of ideas via articulated and enacted support from team members, as well as through participation (interaction, information sharing, and decision making) and constructive conflict processes (task orientation). Finally, perhaps one can speculate that the longer a management team is in position (at least for the relatively short duration enjoyed by the teams), the more the team is constrained to consider the needs of staff when introducing organizational change.*[21]

How to Increase Creativity.   How can individuals increase their own creativity and generate more interesting and profitable solutions? Creativity generally does not happen on its own. It needs an environment where ideas can be generated (born) and nurtured. Management must be supportive and provide the resources to make the ideas work. If not, employees will not waste their time engaging in the process. Therefore, creating an appropriate environment is vital. Changing the environment can begin by something as simple as encouraging employees to improve one thing a day, or week, in their jobs.

When these ideas make a difference in profits for the company, the employees should be recognized and rewarded for their ideas and creativity. More ideas on creativity will be presented in Chapter 14.

Michael Eisner, chief executive officer and chairman of the Walt Disney Company until October 2005, has long contended that creativity is not a "bolt out of the blue" but rather the result of careful thought and examination. In fact, early in his career, one of his bosses wanted to have him fired because every time the boss suggested a new idea, Eisner would ask the manager if he could "think about it and get back to you." The boss was convinced that creativity was based on rapid responses, whereas Eisner believes that creativity is typically a result of careful, deliberate thought, an idea that often is echoed by many successful managers.[22] In fact, Eisner has often said, in contrast to stereotypical views of the creative process, that creativity is a disciplined process. In an interview, he explained his thinking this way:

> *Discipline is good for the creative process, and time limits are good. An infinite amount of time to do a project does not always make it creatively better. The image of an artist being temperamental and acting like a 16-month-old child is usually false. It's a cliché that we've helped perpetrate in the movie business. Artists are always depicted as crazies. But in reality, insane artists are rare. In fact, some of the most creative people I've ever met—Steven Spielberg, George Lucas, I. M. Pei, Frank Stella, and Frank Gehry, just to name a few—are the most organized, mature individuals you'll ever meet. Not many creative people have the urge to cut off an ear.*[23]

Fear is one of the greatest killers of creativity. Fear is a powerful emotion that causes some people to reject the notion of coming up with new ways of doing a job or solving a problem. If their ideas are not accepted, they feel less than okay. Since the employee's ideas may look foreign, strange, or weird, fear can kill them rather than the employee curiously trying to find the value in the ideas and to continue the search for new innovative ways of solving problems. Employees may refrain from speaking in meetings or to their supervisors for fear of being challenged. They do not see the challenge as a way of maturing or changing their perspective. On the other hand, fear can be a motivator for getting the job done. Employees fear the consequences for not doing the job as assigned. Employees have a choice to be afraid or to be curious.[24]

Brainstorming.   The average group member will find it difficult, if not impossible, to be creative on the spur of the moment. However, techniques exist that can help stimulate creative thinking. The most popular is **brainstorming**. A typical brainstorming session begins with the group leader, often the manager, telling the participants the problem under analysis and urging them to be as creative and imaginative as they can. Initial emphasis is placed on generating as many ideas as possible without too much consideration of their realism. As people call out ideas, the others are encouraged to build on them or use them as a basis for developing their own ideas. This approach eventually results in consensus among the group members regarding the best solution(s) to use.

Brainstorming is not a new idea. It has been around for a long time. Socrates and other Greek philosophers sat around brainstorming and debating various issues. Socrates called these principles Koinonia, which means "spirit of fellowship." The basic principles include: establish dialogue, exchange ideas, don't argue, don't interrupt, listen carefully, clarify your thinking, and be honest. These are the same principles used today in modern brainstorming. Einstein and his associates also spent years using these same principles to reach breakthroughs in their work.[25]

Dialectic Inquiry. Sometimes, however, the general consensus approach is supplemented by **dialectic inquiry**, which involves the use of structured discussion and debate in arriving at a final decision. In dialectic inquiry, the brainstorming group is broken into two teams. One develops assumptions and recommendations for action; the other is given this information and asked to develop assumptions and recommendations that are counter to those of the first group. The two teams then meet and hammer out a consensus approach to the problem. Researchers have found that the use of dialectic inquiry results in greater individual acceptance of the final decision and higher member satisfaction with behavior within the group.[26] For this reason, some organizations are now using dialectic inquiry in their brainstorming processes.

Brainstorming is particularly popular when seeking creative solutions to nontechnical problems, such as effective advertising campaigns. Consumer product firms—such as the Campbell Soup Company, which is continually developing new foods based on consumer research and creative packaging concepts—use brainstorming widely. Xerox employs the idea to develop new technology-driven products, such as circuit boards and battery-operated copiers.[27]

In the past two decades, researchers have been experimenting with electronic brainstorming, in which individuals use computers to communicate and share their ideas.[28] This approach has been found to produce more creative ideas than those generated during typical brainstorming sessions. In addition, firms such as Boeing have found that electronic brainstorming eliminates socializing, thus reducing meeting time by as much as 70 percent.

Creative brainstorming techniques go beyond the traditional process for generating new ideas to solve problems. Creative brainstorming techniques can take many forms, such as a random word, random picture, false rules, and role-playing. Sue Barrett has outlined some suggestions for traditional brainstorming.[29]

- Follow Basic Rules

  1. Realize everyone can be creative.
  2. Avoid judgment and think outside the real world.
  3. Let go of your defenses—anything is possible.
  4. No idea is bad—accept all ideas.
  5. Ask provoking questions—how can things be modified, minimized, substituted, rearranged, reversed, combined, or put to other uses?

- Use a Process for Generating Ideas

  1. Break down the problem—be concise.
  2. Set a time limit—say, twenty to thirty minutes.
  3. Write down all ideas—don't worry about how they might work.
  4. Select five to ten ideas you like best.
  5. Decide on five to six different criteria for judging the ideas.
  6. Score the idea on a scale of one to ten using the criteria.
  7. Select the idea with the highest score—it should solve the problem.

Empathic Design Approach. Different firms use different creative approaches. One of these is empathic design, which relies heavily on visual information.[30] The empathic design approach is particularly useful in creating new products because it sidesteps the built-in problem associated with customer feedback. Most customers, when asked what new products they would like, typically respond in terms of the company's current products and suggest that they be made smaller or lighter or less expensive. Customers are notoriously poor in providing useful ideas for new products because their thinking is too closely linked to current products and their everyday uses.[31] Empathic design focuses on observing how people respond to products and services and on drawing creative conclusions from the results. For example, before selecting the type of leather for a new model of car, Nissan Motor Company tested more than ninety samples of leather. Three of those samples were preferred by U.S. car buyers. When Harley-Davidson builds a motorcycle, it adjusts the motor so that it is pleasing to the customer's ears—that is, it sounds like a Harley (and it has sued competitors who have tried to imitate this sound).

By watching how people respond, companies can generate more creative and consumer-pleasing offerings. This can be accomplished in a number of ways. One way is by taking pictures of people using the products. For example, Envirosell, an international research group, takes millions of photos every year of shoppers in retail stores for the purpose of helping answer the question: Who shops here and what do they like? Among other things, the research group has found that shoppers want wide aisles (they do not like to be bumped), good lighting (they like to see the merchandise clearly), and good signage (they want to know where things are located). Companies pay Envirosell large annual fees to provide them with marketing information regarding how to improve their retail sales. Envirosell gets these ideas from analyzing the pictures of shoppers in retail stores.[32] Instead of asking people questions about their decision-making habits, the empathic design approach relies on observation to generate creative ideas and solutions. Table 4.1 provides some contrasts between these two types of approaches.

Table 4.1
Inquiry Survey/Focus Group Approach versus Innovative Observation Empathic Design Approach

Inquiry	Innovative Observation
People often are unreliable when it comes to explaining the types of goods and services that they would be interested in purchasing.	Observers can rely on how people act in drawing conclusions regarding the types of products and services they would be willing to buy in the future.
People often give answers that they feel are acceptable to the questioner.	People give nonverbal clues through body language and spontaneous, unsolicited comments.
People often are unable to recall how they felt about a particular product or service that they received.	Observers can see how well people like a product or service based on the person's reactions.
The questions that are asked can bias the responses.	No questions are asked; all data are based on open-ended observation.
People's routines often are interrupted by someone stopping them to ask questions.	People continue doing whatever they are doing, oblivious to the fact that they are being observed.
When comparing two similar products, respondents often have difficulty explaining why they like one product better than the other.	By giving people an opportunity to use two similar products, observers can determine which is better liked or easier to use by simply watching how people behave.

IN ACTION

DIFFERENT TYPES OF THINKERS

Most people are left-brain thinkers. They are analytical, rational, goal oriented, explicit, and sequential in their approach to decision making. They have been encouraged to think and act this way and, in the process, have failed to develop right-brain approaches characterized by thinking that is spontaneous, emotional, nonverbal, artistic, and holistic. Today, there is a major effort to get people to use both sides of their brain—whole-brain thinking. There are a number of ways of developing this thinking; some are simple and can be used on a day-to-day basis, including the following ways:

Right-Brain Thinking

Doodle, draw, or print on a piece of paper.
Shift the phone to your left ear, allowing empathic listening.
Carry a clipboard, notes, or other comfortable symbols.
Be aware of the colors, space, and sounds around you.
Hum, joke, chuckle with others.

Left-Brain Thinking

Outline things, solve math problems, or do a crossword puzzle.
Shift the phone to your right ear, allowing for analytical listening.
Use a dictating machine, a pointer, or some symbol of authority.
Estimate the value of your net worth.
Ask questions; make puns.

These approaches may seem a little silly, depending on which list you are using; however, this is because you are more accustomed to doing one set of activities than the other. By switching from left to right or vice versa, you enter a mental world that is somewhat strange to you. Yet that is what whole-brain thinking is all about—getting yourself to use the part of your brain that usually lies dormant.

Left-Brain, Right-Brain Thinking. In recent years, attention has been focused on creativity and brain function. Most people are either left-brain dominant or right-brain dominant. The right side of the body is controlled by the left side of the brain, and the left side of the body is controlled by the right side of the brain. This dominance also dictates the way people do things. For example, **left-brain people** tend to be very logical, rational, detailed, active, and objectives-oriented. In contrast, **right-brain people** are more spontaneous, emotional, holistic, nonverbal, and visual in their approach to things. Left-brain people have a preference for routine tasks or jobs that require precision, detail, or repetition. Right-brain people like jobs that are nonroutine or call for idea generation. Left-brain people like to solve problems by breaking them into parts and approaching the problems sequentially and logically. Right-brain people like to solve problems by looking at the entire matter and approaching the solution through hunches and insights.

Most people are left-brain dominant. They tend to be less creative and imaginative than people who are right-brain dominant. In an effort to encourage individuals to use both sides of the brain, some organizations provide their employees with "whole-brain" training, in which the participants learn how to use each side of the brain, as illustrated in the "In Action" box entitled "Different Types of Thinkers." The focus is on making highly rational thinkers more creative and on getting highly intuitive types to supplement their approach with greater emphasis on detail, logic, and procedure. The approach is proving to be an excellent supplement to standard creative-thinking approaches such as brainstorming. Before continuing, take the "Time Out" quiz to find out whether you are more right-brain or left-brain dominant.

A good example is provided in the case of the Hawaiian Telephone Company (HTC). Industry deregulation greatly affected this firm by creating both problems and opportunities. In an effort to deal with these, HTC decided to tap the intuitive skills of its personnel. First, HTC administered a diagnostic test to identify left-brain and right-brain managers. Left-brain managers then were introduced to other left-brain managers, whereas right-brain managers were grouped with other right-brain managers. The firm set forth its objectives for the future. Some of these objectives were best pursued by right-brain managers, some were best pursued by left-brain managers, and some were best

What Type of Thinker Are You?

Are you a left-brain or a right-brain person? Find out by answering the following questions. An interpretation is provided at the end of the book.

1. Do you express yourself well verbally?

   a. _____ Yes b. _____ No

2. Are you a very systematic person?

   a. _____ Yes b. _____

3. Do you enjoy moving the furniture in your room and changing things around so they look different?

   a. _____ Yes b. _____ No

4. When you are learning a new dance, which of the following do you prefer to do?

   a. _____ Get the feel of the music and begin to move to the tempo.

   b. _____ Have someone show you the steps and then imitate them.

5. Are you a goal-oriented person?

   a. _____ Yes b. _____ No

6. When you want to remember directions to a location, how do you do it?

   a. _____ Visualize the information

   b. _____ Write down the information

7. How well do you remember faces?

   a. _____ Not very well

   b. _____ Very well

8. When you are communicating with someone, do you prefer to be the listener or the speaker?

   a. _____ The listener

   b. _____ The speaker

9. Without looking at a clock, can you usually tell what time it is?

   a. _____ Yes b. _____ No

10. Do you like to work alone or in groups?

    a. _____ Alone

    b. _____ In groups

11. Which type of social situation do you prefer?

    a. _____ Planned

    b. _____ Spontaneous

12. Which of the following subjects did you prefer in school?

    a. _____ Algebra

    b. _____ Geometry

13. Do you ever print when you are taking notes?

    a. _____ Often

    b. _____ Never or very seldom

14. Do you like to take risks?

    a. _____ Yes b. _____ No

15. After hearing a song for the first time, which of the following are you able to do best?

    a. _____ Hum the music

    b. _____ Recall the words

16. Do you have frequent mood changes?

    a. _____ Yes b. _____ No

approached by having right-brain managers provide initial suggestions and then having left-brain managers critique and complement these ideas. This "dual" approach to dealing with uncertainty and competitive problems has proven very effective for HTC.

Intergroup Behavior

Intergroup behavior is interactions between or among two or more groups. Sometimes these groups are in the same department; sometimes they are in different departments. In any event, the groups, for some reason, must coordinate their efforts to attain organizational goals. The purpose of intergroup behavior is to achieve high performance. However, sometimes power struggles develop between the groups, and conflict resolution is required.

Achieving High Intergroup Performance

High intergroup performance depends on a number of factors.

- Each group has to know what it is supposed to be doing. *Goals* must be clear.[33] If Group A is charged with building part A, Group B is responsible for constructing part B, and Group C is supposed to assemble the two parts into a finished product, any delay by the first two groups will slow up Group C. Groups A and B must understand how to build the parts and know how much output is required of them.
- There must be *cooperation* among all three groups, because a slowdown or bottleneck in any of them will result in a drop in production.[34] Each group is a vital link in the production process.
- There must be *careful planning* of all interfaces between the groups so that if one group falls behind, the manager knows about it and can start correcting the problem before the situation gets out of control.[35] One way this can be done is through daily monitoring of output. Another way is to designate a liaison or coordination manager, who works out any bottlenecks. For example, if Group A is falling behind because it has run out of raw materials, the coordinating manager checks with the purchasing department to see that the materials are rushed to the group.

Such planning and liaison work can do much to ensure high intergroup performance. However, this is not always enough. Sometimes the problem is that groups are squabbling with each other, a common occurrence when power struggles develop.

 CHECK YOUR UNDERSTANDING

1. How important is creativity in the workplace? Give examples.
2. How does brainstorming work? When should it be used?
3. What can you do to become a whole-brain thinker? Prepare a list.

List ways in which groups try to gain power over other groups.

Power Struggles

Power is influence over others, and although struggles for power can be detrimental to organizational efficiency, they are an inevitable part of intergroup behavior. Sooner or later, one group will try to gain power over others by means of several behaviors, which we identify as follows.

Providing Services

One of the most common ways to gain power over other groups is to provide services for them that they either cannot or will not provide for themselves. For example, many large- and medium-sized businesses in industrial states are unionized. To deal with the union members, each company usually has an industrial relations department, which negotiates a contract with the union and works out the finer points of management–union prerogatives. What type of seniority system will there be to protect the rights of union members who have worked for the company for a long time? If some union people are laid off, in what order must they be rehired? What right of appeal does a member have if he or she is threatened with demotion or dismissal? Most department managers look to the industrial relations department for help in resolving any problem related to these issues. As a result, in the area of labor-management issues, the industrial relations department holds power over others.

Integrative Importance

A second power struggle is directly related to the degree of integrative importance. If a group has an important integrative role in a process involving many groups, the other groups depend on it.

Consider the case of the manufacturing firm that produces a specialized power tool for industrial use. Figure 4.4 is a representation of the production process. The process entails five steps: manufacturing, assembling, painting, quality inspection, and packing. Six major components are manufactured. These then are sent to one of four assembly groups, each of which assembles an identical product. From here, the products are forwarded to the painting groups, each of which is charged with painting one hundred units per day. The products are then sent to the quality inspection group, which has a special machine that checks each for paint quality and determines that the product works properly. If there is some failure in the product, the inspector identifies the problem, writes a ticket on it and, depending on what is wrong, sends it back to the assembly or painting group. If the product passes inspection, it is sent to the packing group, where it is carefully boxed and made ready for shipment. A close study of Figure 4.4 reveals that, of all the groups, quality inspection has the greatest integrative importance.

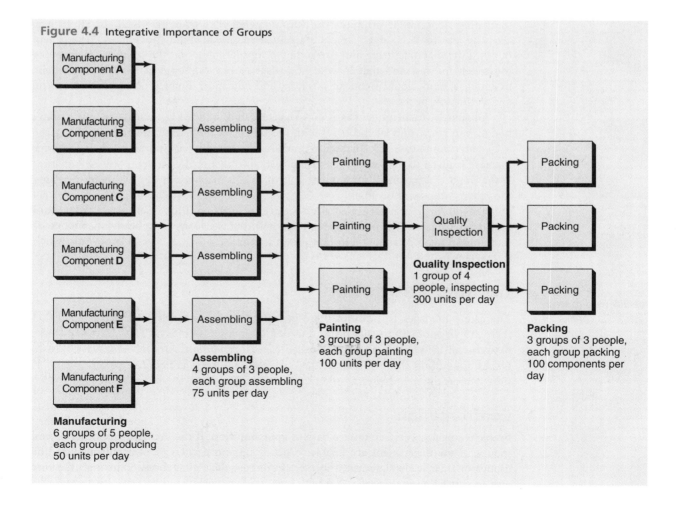

Figure 4.4 Integrative Importance of Groups

There is only one such group, and it performs a very important role: The group can either accept or reject the work of the other groups. Additionally, the other groups are larger, and several groups perform identical tasks. If one of these groups, such as assembly, is short of workers because of illness, the other assembly groups can take up the slack. However, if the quality inspection people slow down, no one is available to help them catch up, and the whole organization can be adversely affected. Therefore, because of its integrative importance, the quality inspection group has a degree of power over the others.

Budget Allocation

A third common power struggle between groups is related to budget allocation. Most organizational groups, especially at the departmental level, would like to increase their budgets. Under favorable economic conditions, when the average annual increase is 10 percent, they will fight for a 15 percent to 20 percent increase. If sales or revenues have not been good and budgets are being reduced by 10 percent, departmental groups will strive to maintain their original allocation.

One of the most effective ways of succeeding in budget battles is to show top management that the department is doing a better job than most of the other departments. For example, the manufacturing group argues that its production costs have dropped and it is turning out more goods than ever before; if the group is given an increase in budget, more machines can be purchased and efficiency can be further improved. The marketing department produces statistics showing that sales per dollar of advertising are way up so its budget should be increased. Meanwhile, the finance department opposes the manufacturing and marketing groups, arguing that the company is spending too much too fast and that it would be wiser to pay off some of the long-term debt, maintain a more liquid financial position, and add more finance personnel for control and evaluation purposes.

Obviously, each group has its own ax to grind, and a big increase in one group's budget can come only at the expense of the others. If the manufacturing group is given a 20 percent increase, the marketing and finance groups will feel slighted. If the large increase is given to marketing, the production and finance departments will be unhappy. If the finance department's argument convinces top management to withhold increases, the other groups will be angry.

This group power struggle arises because of **goal conflict**. Each group must learn that its goal may not benefit other groups and that decisions must sometimes be made that appear to be detrimental to that group's welfare.

Identify ways to resolve intergroup conflict.

Conflict Resolution

The astute manager is aware of these intergroup power struggles but also realizes that there are ways of eliminating or diminishing their negative effects. The individual works to accomplish this through what is called *conflict resolution*. A number of ways exist to resolve intergroup conflict. Four of the most common ways are confrontation, collaboration, compromise, and altering the organizational structure, as illustrated in Figure 4.5.

Confrontation

Problem solving on a face-to-face basis is **confrontation**. If the manager finds that several groups in the department are unable to get along and decides to use confrontation, the groups or their leaders are asked to meet to discuss their differences. Sometimes they are able to express their dissatisfaction with one another quickly and easily; sometimes it is a

Figure 4.5 Conflict Resolution Methods

Conflict Resolution Method	Characteristics of Resolution Method
Confrontation	Face-to-face meeting between groups
	All parties discuss the problem
	All parties agree on a solution
	Create steps to monitor compliance
	Problem is solved
Collaboration	All parties understand the situation
	All parties fully cooperate in resolving the problem
Compromise	Each party reluctantly gives up something
	Problem is temporarily solved
	Problem may reoccur
Altering the Organizational Structure	Transfer workers to new locations
	Change work assignments
	Change the flow of work or supervision
	Rearrange the furniture to separate people
	Move wall petitions to regroup people

long process. In any event, there are some common complaints: "Those guys don't want to work with us. They're always doing something to slow up the flow of operations." "Whenever we're slow with our end of the work, those guys gripe, but if they're slow, they get angry if we say anything." "We don't know what the problem is with that group, but we just don't feel we can trust them, so we don't like working with them."

These standard responses are often the result of misunderstanding among the groups. By encouraging each group to express its objections, the manager usually can cultivate a feeling of harmony among them. Each group begins to see how the other groups view it and obtains a better understanding of its own behavior. Then the groups are asked how they are going to increase their interaction with one another and what steps should be taken to ensure that they do not slip back into their old habits.

This confrontation method is one of the most successful approaches to conflict resolution because it concentrates on solving the problem directly rather than trying to avoid it or to smooth over the issues. Both groups, however, must understand the solution and make a commitment to it or the problem may appear again, meaning that you have only temporarily solved the problem.

Collaboration

Sometimes goals desired by two or more parties cannot be reached without the cooperation of those involved; this is when collaboration can be effective. **Collaboration** calls for all parties to work out their differences and to realize that without full cooperation, all of them will fail. A common illustration is the case of the powerful union that wants a lucrative contract from a company on the verge of bankruptcy. It is obvious that if the union insists on its demands, the firm will go out of business. The only way to resolve the situation is for the union to take less money and to cooperate with the company in working to attain a more profitable position. When the company is stable, the union can resubmit demands for a lucrative contract. In this method, both parties understand the causes of the problem and both parties are willing to give up something to solve the problem. These actions result in a win–win situation for both groups and the problem is solved. With the cooperation of both groups, the chance of the problem recurring is less likely.

Compromise

When each party gives up something and no group is the clear winner, **compromise** occurs. It is a give-and-take situation. Consider the case of the foreman who fires a worker for being late four days in a row. During the ensuing labor-management meeting required by the contract, the union argues that the offense has not justified such a harsh penalty. Both sides, the company and the union, then compromise on the situation: They agree that laying the worker off for five days (without pay) is sufficient punishment. Thus, the worker has not been fired, but he has not escaped punishment for blatant infringement of the rules. In this case, each group gives up something, the problem is not fully solved, and the problem may occur again.

Altering the Organizational Structure

If the manager finds that a particular group cannot get along with some of the other groups, he or she may decide to resolve the conflict by reorganizing the department structure. For example, using Figure 4.4 again, the manager finds that some of the members of the quality control group cannot get along with members of the other groups. He or she may simply remove the people by transferring them to other departments or work assignments and replacing them with more congenial workers. Alternatively, if the manager finds that the assembling and painting departments resent the fact that their work can be sent back to them by quality control people, a supervisor may be appointed to make the final decision regarding what is to be returned as unacceptable. In this way, the manager interposes someone between the antagonist (quality control) and the antagonized (assembly and painting groups). This type of organizational rearrangement has been found to be very effective in cases in which workers object to taking orders from other workers.

 CHECK YOUR UNDERSTANDING

1. Identify three ways to gain power over other groups.

   a. _____
   b. _____
   c. _____

2. Give two characteristics for each method of resolving conflicts.

   a. Confrontation. 1)_____ 2)_____
   b. Collaboration. 1)_____ 2)_____
   c. Compromise. 1)_____ 2) _____
   d. Altering the organizational structure. 1)_____ 2)_____

Identify important factors in building effective teams.

Team Building

So far in this chapter, we have examined groups. We explored several types of groups; the stages of their development; characteristics; intergroup behavior, including decision making, risk taking, and creativity; ways to achieve high intergroup performance and areas of power struggles; and how to use conflict resolution methods to resolve conflict. Now let us take a look at building a team.

A team is a group, and therefore, the same concepts that apply to groups also apply to teams. Teams, however, differ from groups, and turning a group into a team takes planning and commitment.

Teams versus Groups

A group is a social unit made up of two or more people who interact, at some point, with each other. Members depend on each other, and at the same time, they work independently of each other in a competitive environment. Group members work toward individual accomplishments, rather than for the successful completion of the group's goals. Emphasis is on rewarding individuals, not the group. Satisfaction comes from mutual association of members within the group.

A **team** is a group of individuals responsible for the accomplishment of the team's goals. The same characteristics that define groups are also exhibited in teams. A team, however, differs in a number of ways. Members bring to the team a wide range of skills and experiences—technical, problem solving, and interpersonal skills—that are required to accomplish identifiable team goals. All team members are held accountable for accomplishing the team goals and, therefore, are rewarded for the team's accomplishments, rather than for their individual accomplishments. Team members have a sense of commitment to the common solutions developed in the teams. For example, in 2010, the New Orleans Saints functioned as a team to win the Super Bowl. It was the first Super Bowl win in the history of their league. That year, the Saints lost only one game to the Dallas Cowboys. If the Saints had played as a group, it is highly unlikely that they would have won the Super Bowl. Winning the Super Bowl required every player to focus his efforts on the team's common goal—winning every game. Also, it took a lot of hard work, a burning desire to accomplish a challenging goal, the right mix of skills, and the execution of the appropriate plays at the right time.

Turning a Group into a Team

Many workers believe they are working in a team when, in reality, they are working in a group. Turning a group into a team is not an easy task. Many people are not inherently team players. Some people are loners who want to be recognized for their individual accomplishments. To turn a group into a team takes time and effort, requires understanding how to build a team, needs multiple interpersonal skills, and requires a commitment from top management. For example, after surveying customers, the executives at Signicast Corporation of Milwaukee decided to build a new $12-million automated plant equipped with new technology to shorten lead times, improve the reliability of delivery dates, and reduce costs. The process started by asking employees for input. They met as groups, and after a long challenging process, teams began to form. Employees with special knowledge and skills formed teams that worked on specific goals directed at not only saving jobs, but also saving the company. The employees in the new plant would have to do more and have more responsibility than their counterparts at the old plant. The organizational structure would be different—a flatter structure utilizing teams. Employees would be cross-trained to do a variety of jobs. The basic requirements for the employees at the new plant are team orientation, good trainability, good communication skills, and a willingness to do varied jobs over a twelve-hour shift. Signicast would provide all the training. Signicast's success in using teams in developing the new plant led the company to create a team-based and knowledge-based plant. It was more difficult, however, to make the same changes at the old plant. More resources were needed to overcome the reluctance. In the end, Signicast was able to build a new kind of workforce along with a new kind of facility of cross-trained, team-oriented, and empowered employees at both plants.[36] This new team approach was also used successfully to construct an all-new Signicast facility in Hartford, Wisconsin. The company continues to grow, even in times of economic slowdown, requiring more facilities to be built. Since then, Signicast, still using its team approach, has added four additional modules (plants) to its Hartford location.[37]

 CHECK YOUR UNDERSTANDING

Are You a Team Player?

Take a self-test on the Internet to learn whether you are a team player or like to go it alone.

1. Go to http://www.queendom.com. Type "team player" in the search box. For free you can get a sample analysis of your test results, and for a fee you can get a complete analysis. At least, try the sample.
2. Go to http://www.quintcareers.com/team-player-quiz. On this site are several quizzes that you might find helpful in learning more about yourself, such as:

   a. How's Your Team's Spirit?
   b. Team building Skill Assessment: What's Your Team Player Style?
   c. Leadership Quiz

3. After completing the quizzes, summarize what you learned about yourself.

An Effective Team

An effective team needs members with technical skills, problem-solving and decision-making skills, and interpersonal skills, such as good listening, feedback, and conflict resolution. Each team has different needs, and members should be selected on the basis of their personalities and preferences. An effective team has a commitment to a common purpose, which is translated into specific, measurable, and realistic performance goals. The team's end targets are defined by these goals. Teams need leadership and structure to provide focus and direction. A successful team makes its members individually and jointly accountable for the team's purpose, goals, and approach; and its reward system must reflect team performance, such as profit sharing, gain sharing, or group incentives.[38] For example, on a trip to Alaska on Holland America's *Ryndam* cruise liner, the author witnessed work teams in action throughout the ship. The employees were not just workers doing their jobs; they were teams of employees working to fill the needs of every passenger. All employees were introduced to the passengers on the first and last evenings on the cruise. The cruise director recognized the employees for services rendered as individuals or as teams. The expression on the employees' faces always told the story of how they felt. Even gratuities are shared among all employees, not just those who come in contact with passengers, making them feel more connected to their team. Another example of how these employees are connected and work together is through their participation in a variety show of music, song, and dance performed on the last evening in the theatre. It was a fantastic show depicting their many musical and entertainment talents. It was evident the employees felt an important part of Holland America's team.

How did the cruise liner build these work teams and how does it maintain a team spirit? An interview with the cruise director revealed that more than anything, it is the acknowledgment of the little things like a simple "thank you" that keeps workers motivated. The director stated that in creating a team, he:

- Finds a common thread among workers to build cohesiveness among team members. In hiring employees, he looks at personalities as a common thread.
- Provides a training program to train employees to do their jobs.
- Works hard to develop trust among team members and among teams.
- Teaches employees to respect all types of people, regardless of whether the people are employees or passengers.
- Gives team members the authority to solve a wide range of problems.
- Uses one-on-one communication with all employees.[39]

Characteristics of Good Team Building

Team building is a process that works best in a climate that encourages and values the contributions of its members. The contributions of each member are not separated from those of the other members. All members work jointly on tasks of mutual importance. A team's effectiveness is measured by its output, such as: Did the team meet or exceed the expectations of the people who receive the output? A list of the basic characteristics of good team building is shown in Table 4.2.

Table 4.2
Characteristics of Good Team Building

1	High level of interdependence among team members.
2	Team leader has good people skills and is committed to team approach.
3	Each team member is willing to contribute.
4	Team develops a relaxed climate for communication.
5	Team members develop a mutual trust.
6	Team and individuals are prepared to take risks.
7	Team is clear about goals and establishes targets.
8	Team members' roles are defined.
9	Team members know how to examine team and individual errors without personal attacks.
10	Team efforts are devoted to the achievement of results.
11	Team has the capacity to create new ideas.
12	Each team member knows he or she can influence the team agenda.

Source: Arnold Bateman, "Team Building: Developing a Productive Team" (Nebraska Cooperative Extension, June 1990). Adapted from Dave Francis and Don Young, *Improving Work Groups: A Practical Manual for Team Building* (San Diego, CA: University Associates, Inc., 1979).

Types of Teams

Businesses use teams in many ways. **Functional teams** are found in the functional areas of the business. For example, a team can be used in the finance function to deal with budgeting issues; likewise, in the marketing function, a team can solve marketing problems.

Cross-functional teams consist of a mix of specialists who work in horizontal- level positions across the company, such as the vice presidents of finance, marketing, production, and engineering, who meet to solve problems. These teams, for example, can deal with developing strategies for improving profits. Cross-functional teams are horizontal teams including members from several functional areas, whereas functional teams are known as vertical teams in which members come from one functional area.

Project teams can be used to solve problems occurring throughout the company. These teams need members who have the knowledge and skills to make decisions concerning the purpose of the project. In a production plant, for example, a team can be used to find ways to improve the quality of a product to meet customer expectations. Project members come from many functional areas in the company and from several levels of management within the company. Members can also come from quality control, production, marketing, including sales and advertising, finance, and design and can include vice presidents and production workers.

At times, project teams operate outside the organizational structure of a company. For example, Ford Motor Company needed to measure its advertising success and increase its sales leads in the European market. The company wanted to track customer responses and implement a lead-qualifying process to focus sales efforts. With the help of IBM Business Consulting Services, multinational teams were formed in Germany, Spain, and Britain. Their goal was to create and to deploy a standardized European CRM (customer relationship management) solution integrated with key business processes designed to transform simple marketing campaigns into responsive, targeted communications. The centralized approach enabled Ford's main marketing team to better deliver coordinated, cross-border marketing campaigns.[40]

Product development teams are organized to develop new products. Companies that make products, such as Procter & Gamble, General Motors, General Mills, and IBM, use product development teams to identify new products.

Task force teams are short-lived or temporary teams that are assigned a specific objective. For example, an objective might be to implement a recognition program, to solve the congested parking lot situation, or to implement a smoke-free environment policy. When the team's objective is completed, the team disbands. For example, Microsoft used a task force team to look for ways to streamline the company's health care benefits program, while simultaneously making employees more cost-conscious health care shoppers. The team, under the direction of Lee Johnson, selected the program MyMicrosoftBenefits to manage health benefits. As a result, claim costs have been cut significantly. Employees now make better choices and are smarter about their health.[41]

Work teams comprise multiskilled employees, who perform all the tasks previously done by individuals. All members take responsibility for all the tasks assigned to the team—not just what they may have done previously. These teams work well in functional departments such as advertising, maintaining equipment, shipping, or quality control. Team members help each other complete tasks, sort out problems as a group, compliment each other on good work, and share in rewards.

Virtual teams are remote workers who operate away from the main office. The team members may work at home, in another city, or even in a foreign country. Everyone is connected electronically by e-mail, voice mail, fax or whatever digital system the company may be using. It is like being in one central location. Scheduled conference calls and face-to-face meetings allow virtual team members to feel connected to the employees at the main office.

A 2008 study by Nemertes Research, a high-tech think tank, found that 90 percent of U.S. employees work somewhere other than headquarters, and 84 percent work in a different location than their bosses. The percentage jumped over 800 percent between 2003 and 2008. This group includes employees who travel constantly, telecommuters who work from home, and people in one- or-two-person offices spread out all over the globe.[42]

Management of Teams

The type of management a team requires is determined by the type and nature of the team—its purpose and the makeup of members. Some teams are closely controlled by management, whereas other teams are independent work teams, known as *self-managed or self-directed work teams*. Members in management-controlled teams have less authority to plan and to control their work than do members in self-directed work teams. Self-directed teams manage themselves, and they have the authority to plan and to control their work activities. Even though virtual teams require their members to work well independently and with little supervision, managers must spend time communicating with them about such things as work expectations, schedules, and feedback on projects. How does IBM do it?

Today's technology makes it possible to converse with peers and team leaders all over the world. Managers of virtual teams are discovering that technology alone does not build teams. IBM has learned that without a real sense of community, most people just do not do their best work. About 40 percent of IBM's 400,000 employees are working in a virtual environment. To combat the feeling that IBM stood for "I'm By Myself," the company brought back IBM Clubs, an old company tradition that had been allowed to fall by the wayside. The clubs are now active in several hundred cities in thirty countries. Another strategy was to implement a task force called OTTO (Other than the Office) to create social network sites, such as Social Blue, where employees can post photos of and bulletins about topics like their kids, their dogs, their motorcycles, and what they did over the weekend. It is a big hit worldwide, from new entry-level hires to senior vice presidents. The results from IBM employee surveys reveal that being able to work far from colleagues without losing touch has boosted employee satisfaction and makes top talent more inclined to stick around. Social Blue has been a real boon to teamwork and productivity.[43]

It is not enough to tell workers they are a team; the leader must show the members of the team how being a team benefits them personally. The members must believe they are part of a team, or the group will never become an effective working team. A supportive attitude and self-esteem play a big part in the success of the team. To boost self-esteem, members have to feel a sense of satisfaction and accomplishment. Members also must be rewarded for their efforts and experience personal benefits to keep the team viable and functioning.

Process for Building an Effective Team

A company that is thinking about using teams for the first time should spend time researching and studying the concept of using teams, and it should conduct assessments within the company to determine if teams can successfully serve the company's needs. Many questions should be asked and honestly answered. Sample questions are included in the explanation of each step listed below (see Figure 4.6).

Figure 4.6 Steps in the Process of Team Building

- Assessing feasibility
- Identifying priorities
- Defining mission and objectives
- Uncovering and eliminating barriers to team building
- Starting with small teams
- Planning for training needs
- Planning to empower
- Planning for feedback and development time

Source: Warren R. Plunkett, Raymond F. Attner, and Gemmy S. Allen, *Management: Meeting and Exceeding Customer Expectations*, 9th ed. (Thomson Learning, South-Western Publishers, printed in Canada, 2008), pp. 474–476.

Assessing Feasibility.   Companies wanting to establish teams, especially for the first time, should start with a study of the mission, skills, and abilities of personnel, financial resources, and management's commitment to the team building process. Several basic questions to ask are: Will team building work? How long will it take? Does the top management fully support the team? How engaged are the employees?

Identifying Priorities.   An assessment of current concerns, such as customer needs, production process needs, or delivery needs, should identify critical areas where teams can work. Two basic questions to answer are: What are the critical needs of the organization? Where can teams make an impact?

Defining Mission and Objectives.   Before a company begins to build teams, management should be sure that its mission and objectives are well defined and accepted throughout the company. Two questions to be answered are: What is the organization trying to achieve? How can teams help attain those goals?

Uncovering and Eliminating Barriers to Team Building.   The knowledge and skill levels of employees and managers must be assessed. Without adequate expertise, teams will fail. The organizational structure along with the authority and communication channels must be studied. Can teams function within this system and use the processes that are in place? Cultural barriers that run counter to the team approach could cause the team to fail. Are powerful personnel or departments willing to relinquish some power and empower team members? Three basic questions to be answered are: What technical skills are lacking? How will the cultural environment impact working teams? What processes need changing?

Starting with Small Teams.   Start by using a project team whose purpose is to create teams that will work in priority areas—those areas of concern identified to be urgent. Two questions that need answering are: Where can the team approach begin? Which priorities will most benefit from teams?

Planning for Training Needs.   Management should be committed to the idea of using teams and willing to offer training in planning, the effective use of meetings, team dynamics, and group behavior. Members of cross-functional teams will need skills training. Two questions that need answering are: What type of training is needed? What type of guidance is required?

Planning to Empower.   Executives and managers must empower team members if the team is to succeed. The executives and managers must step back and let the team members make decisions, which could involve making mistakes and failing. Two questions the company must answer are: Can managers let go? Are they willing to let people make mistakes?

Planning for Feedback and Development Time. Feedback is vital. In the beginning, team builders need to provide the mechanisms for feedback; later, the team will develop its own system. Launching a team approach takes time and patience. The process can be intimidating and confusing. It often raises unfamiliar issues and procedures. The team approach requires massive changes of individual behavioral habits. Rewards and recognition now focus on team achievements instead of individual contributions. The team leaders become facilitators and coaches instead of being directive in their style. What type and frequency of feedback are needed? Can management be patient? Are workers willing to change their work behaviors?

Hackman's Team Building Approach

J. Richard Hackman, one of the world's leading experts on group and organizational behavior, conducts research on team dynamics and performance for Harvard University, where he is a professor. In his book, *Leading Teams*, he sets out five basic conditions that leaders of companies must fulfill in order to create and maintain effective teams. Hackman believes that it is not the leaders' management style that determines how well a team performs, but how well a leader designs and supports a team so that members can manage themselves. He states that:

1. *Teams must be real.* People have to know who is on the team and who is not. It is the leader's job to make that clear.
2. *Teams need a compelling direction.* Members need to know, and agree on, what they are supposed to be doing together. Unless a leader articulates a clear direction, there is a real risk that different members will pursue different agendas.
3. *Teams need enabling structures.* Teams that have poorly designed tasks, the wrong number of mix of members, or fuzzy and unenforced norms of conduct invariably get into trouble.
4. *Teams need a supportive organization.* The organizational context—including the reward system, the human resource system, and the information system—must facilitate teamwork.
5. *Teams need expert coaching.* Most executive coaches focus on individual performance, which does not significantly improve teamwork. Teams need coaching as a group in team processes, especially at the beginning, midpoint, and end of a team project.[44]

Advantages for Using Teams

Teamwork makes a difference. Teamwork increases production, enhances quality, and improves customer service, all while reducing operational costs, which helps make the company more profitable. When people work together, there is a greater feeling of well-being among employees, and a sense of synergy develops—the whole is greater than the sum of its parts.

Challenges of Teams

A major reason for team failure is the lack of commitment from top management and the lack of understanding of how the team building process works. Another reason for team failure is individual resistance. When an employee's success is no longer measured by his or her individual performance, some employees resist. Using the wrong type of performance measure may lead to individuals competing with each other rather than collaborating and can hinder teamwork.[45] Some employees resist because of their lack of good communication skills. Teams without strong company values will have a hard time succeeding.

Even effective teams can become stagnant over time. Members may suffer from **group-think**—team members who feel their input is not valued as much as another person's may be reluctant to express their thoughts and may become less likely to challenge other team members. Then there are the repeaters who can influence the general opinion of a group. By repeating their position at least three times within a group, they become a powerful force by inferring that it is the opinion shared by everyone. Research indicates that such a person's opinion is 90 percent as powerful as three different people in the meeting affirming the same opinion or point of view.[46]

Problems can also occur in teams when systems and processes designed for simple issues are not changed and redesigned to solve more difficult issues. At this point, management must take initiatives to prepare team members to deal more effectively with issues by providing proper training and motivation.[47]

Norman Shidle summarizes the difference between a group and a team in this way. "A group becomes a team when each member is sure enough of himself and his contribution to praise the skills of others."[48]

✔ CHECK YOUR UNDERSTANDING

Use the same three groups that you used in the previous "Check Your Understanding" exercise to complete this exercise.

1. Indicate which groups function as a team versus as a group. Place a check under team or group to indicate your choice.

Name of Group	Team	Group
a. _____	_____	_____
b. _____	_____	_____
c. _____	_____	_____

2. What suggestions would you propose to turn each group into an effective team? Use ideas presented in this chapter.
3. Recite the steps in the process for building an effective team. Jot them down. How many did you get right?
4. Can you personally tell the difference between working in a group and in a team? Explain the difference.

Explain how to conduct a successful job hunt.

Career Advisor

The Successful Job Hunt

After writing an effective resume, the next thing you have to do is get the resume into the right hands—the company that needs your skills and experience. With a wide range of sources available, you must decide where to start your search. The path can be different for each person. There is no standard starting point. It depends on the level of job you are seeking and the type of job. You may start by visiting the career center on your campus. Other ideas are attending a job fair, searching newspapers or trade journals, seeking recommendations from professional organizations, searching job boards on the Internet, seeking out a professional recruiter, visiting Web sites of corporations, mailing in or taking your resume to companies, and seeking referrals from your employed friends.

College and University Career Centers.

If you are a college graduate seeking your first job, you may want to start by visiting the career center on your campus. Most colleges and universities offer an array of placement and career services, ranging from resume writing and critiquing to self-assessment programs and eRecruiting services—employer-posted jobs. For example, Michigan State University's career center offers summits focused on topics such as how to build leadership skills and how to transition into a career. The University of Alabama's career center has a mentor program where alumni share insight about their careers and offer advice about the "real world."

Periodically throughout the year, college and university career centers offer career fairs, sometimes called job fairs. These fairs give students an opportunity to speak directly with a representative from a company that hires graduates. Some centers are also linked to job banks around the country.

Newspaper and Trade Journal Ads.

A newspaper ad is a good place to look for jobs available in local areas, whereas ads in trade journals focus on jobs available in a particular trade or industry. Some ads identify the firm and describe its job openings, and other ads merely provide a brief description and give a coded box number to which one can send a resume. The ads that seem to describe the opportunities you are seeking are worth pursuing. The others are known as blind ads where companies may be trying to gauge the labor supply in the field or determine salary levels for certain types of jobs, so you may be wasting your time by applying.

Networking.

Networking is the process of interacting with individuals or organized groups. Job referrals can come from members of organizations, such as college clubs, business and professional associations, community groups, and interest groups. Joining a group can have its benefits, particularly where its members hold jobs in businesses in which you are interested in being employed. By interacting with members, you can find a contact person who can help you find the job you are seeking. This is a way to get started networking. It is not too late to start today.

Internet Job Boards.

A search on the Internet reveals a vast number of Web sites where resume writing, resume posting, and employer job posting—eRecruiting— activities are provided for people hunting for a job. Monster and CareerBuilder continue to be the forerunners in the job recruiting field. More and more companies are moving their entire recruiting process online, either on job boards or on company Web sites. Peter Cappelli, professor of management at the University of Pennsylvania's Wharton School, states, "Job boards make it possible for corporations to get lots of applicants, and on the other hand, it has made it easier for people to have access to lots and lots of jobs."[49] Job postings also can be found on niche blogs that specialize in different industries, such as AttorneyJobs.com and SalesJobs.com, or you can simply go to a search engine and type in "marketing jobs."

Barron's, an investment newspaper, analyzed the future of the best-known job board, Monster, and learned that recruiting in general and younger job seekers in particular are increasingly moving from newspapers to the Internet.

Professional Recruiters.

Professional recruiters, sometimes called "headhunters," find people to fill jobs for companies. The recruiter prescreens potential applicants, seeking to match their skills, experience, temperament, and so on to the position requirements. The recruiter presents to the employer those applicants that seem to best match what the employer needs. Professional recruiters usually fill higher-level jobs and not entry-level jobs.

Employment Agencies. Local and state-level employment agencies can fill jobs for companies. Some states have developed job banks where jobs within the state can be posted. For example, the state of Texas has a "Job Bank," with its own Web site that links to the "Texas Workforce Commission Job Listings" and to "Texas Labor Market Information," to name a few.[50]

Organization-Based Recruiting. Companies are using several strategies for recruiting potential applicants, and this is called **organization-based recruiting**. First, they are beginning to sponsor their own job fairs. These fairs usually focus on specific jobs that need to be filled in the company, such as engineering or computer specialist. These fairs are advertised in the local newspapers or television. When you are looking for a job, a job fair is a good event to visit and to get an assessment of what the company is seeking in applicants.

Second, more companies are moving their recruiting process to their Web sites. For some companies, the only way to apply for a job is through their Web site. An example is Procter & Gamble; no paper resumes are accepted. Companies are finding that by using prescreening and tracking software programs, they can speed up the recruiting process, get back to the potential applicant faster, and reduce the total cost of filling positions. In Chapter 2, you prepared a plan of action that identifies potential jobs. Your next step is to locate companies that hire in these occupations, then go to their Web sites and find out how to submit a resume.

Third, other companies are still using newspapers to advertise jobs, receiving walk-ins and mail-ins, using professional recruiters, and accepting employee referrals, as well as using online services.

Internships. Internships can be a great way for students to gain real world experience. According to the National Association of Colleges and Employers, in 2008, almost 70 percent of college interns received employment offers from their internship employer.[51] Some interns are paid a salary, while others are not, which is the downside for those students who need a part-time job that pays money. In either case, the interns must value the real-world experience and opportunities they are getting by working in a real business.

Web Logs or Blogs. The informal nature of these Web sites is catching the eye of many potential applicants, who otherwise might not consider applying. Karina Miller, director of human resources at Impinj in Seattle, feels that the site "goes directly to the right target audience." Last year, the *Boston Globe* launched its own blog site and is receiving ten to twenty million page views per month. To find a blog in a particular industry, for example, type into Google "nursing blog."[52]

Walk-Ins and Mail-Ins. Applicants who personally take their resumes to a company are known as "walk-ins," and resumes mailed to the company are "mail-ins." Before you take your resume to a company, it is best to call the company and talk with the person who accepts resumes to learn whether or not it accepts resumes from walk-ins. For resumes that are mailed in, be sure to address the envelope to the proper person and include a cover letter.

Employee Referrals. When an employee refers the name of a potential applicant to fill a specific job within the company, it is called an **employee referral**. "Employee referrals are by far the most effective source of new hires in terms of the return on dollar invested and quality of hire, especially if you track that 6 or 12 months out," says Bertrand Dussert, vice president of professional services for Recruitmax, an applicant-tracking company that powers corporate career sites.[53] John Girard, CEO of Clickability, says that "we get our best hires through recommendations, noting that roughly 30 percent to 40 percent of the company's new hires come from referrals from the company's employees, contractors or others tied to the firm."[54] Marie Artim, assistant vice president of recruiting for Enterprise Rent-A-Car, the nation's largest rental-car company and the nation's largest recruiter of college grads, states that "forty percent of the company's new hires come about through employee referral."[55]

Research shows that employee referrals are a very important way to fill jobs. As a student, you can enhance your job hunt by starting to actively network and get to know people who work in companies in which you are interested in working, people who work in organizations that make a difference, and people who are leaders in the community.

Tips for Applying Online

Increasingly, employers want applicants to use their Web sites or Internet job boards. Because these online applications go directly into a database, your focus should be on making your application unique. It is important to use keywords, buzz words, or industry jargon to identify your skills, abilities, and experience. Some recruiters report that using up to twenty-five keywords is not too many. Hiring managers enter key words to search the database to find applicants who are best suited for a particular job. You have to include enough keywords so that some of them will match the words the hiring manager inputs.

A survey by the National Association of Colleges and Employers asked employers for their advice on how to make an online application outstanding. Here's what they recommend:[56]

1. Follow directions. Be careful to enter the correct data in the correct field.
2. Ask for advice on completing the application from a company recruiter or an alumnus who may work at the company.
3. Tailor your application information to the position. Don't copy and paste from your generic resume.
4. Use key words, buzzwords, and industry jargon. Use the terms posted in the job ad as your model. Employers search on key words when they are looking for people to fill specific positions.
5. Create a skills-inventory section even if the application doesn't require it. You might put this in a comments section.
6. Provide numbers and statistics if they are available. (Example: Counted five cash drawers daily; responsible for more than $10,000 per eight-hour shift.)
7. Complete all fields—even those that aren't required.
8. If the company offers an optional assessment test online, take it. (One employer recently admitted that students who don't take the optional assessment test are automatically screened out.)
9. Make sure your resume can hold its own in a very simple format. Fancy bullets, text italics, and bold print do not convert well in an electronic application.
10. If possible, spell check and grammar check your application before submitting it. Have an error-free application because this application serves as the employer's first impression of you.

11. Include a strong objective. Ask a career counselor to help you word your objective.
12. Another use for the comments section is to use it to demonstrate that you've done research on the company and the industry.
13. Use quotes from letters of recommendation in your resume or cover letter.
14. Follow up your electronic application with a personal e-mail to the recruiter. A follow-up phone call is acceptable if the ad does not say, "No phone calls."

Where to Start the Job Hunt

With so many recruiting sources available for finding a job, where do you start the search? A basic rule to remember is to start by telling everyone you know that you are looking for a job and the type of job you would like. This can generate possible leads for you, particularly in your local area. If you can get someone to recommend you, you will have a foot in the door, as the saying goes. You may need to think more globally, not just locally. Moving to another city, state, or country can have its rewards and will expand your horizon and job opportunities.

In other cases, you may need to do some research to find out where companies that you are interested in applying recruit for employees. Otherwise, you may want to select several recruiting sources and begin the application process—whether it is sending in a resume or filling out an application form online.

Finding the right job is not an easy task, particularly when economic times are slow and unemployment rates are high. Job hunting requires dedication, commitment, and perseverance. Hunting for a job is equivalent to working at a real job. Once you realize this and put in the time required, you will find that special job that fits your needs and your career goals. The main thing is never to give up.

As you delve further into your job search, you may find you are sending out thirty resumes and receiving fifteen responses, of which only ten or fewer potential employers express any interest. As a result, you may decide to restart the process and send out resumes to new organizations. The important thing to remember is not to despair. Keep a positive attitude. You will eventually find something that will satisfy you.

To find a job, you must sell your capabilities; tired or unenthusiastic salespeople do not make sales. You cannot let the stress of the job hunt lead you to undervalue your potential or restrict your options. There is no logical reason to despair. You know the kind of work you are capable of doing. The big catch is meeting the person who needs someone like you to do a job. Logic says that this will happen sooner or later.

 CHECK YOUR UNDERSTANDING

Prepare a plan for conducting a job hunt.

1. From the list of job sources described in the Career Advisor, select four sources you might use in finding a job. Place the sources in order of importance to you, and tell why your job hunt would progress in that order.
2. Identify several networking sources that could help you find a job in your local community.

Summary

1 *Describe a group and distinguish among organizational groups—functional, cross-functional, project, virtual, and interest-friendship.*

A group is a social unit consisting of two or more interdependent, interactive individuals who are striving to attain common goals. There are five types of groups: functional, cross-functional, project, virtual, and interest-friendship. *Functional groups* are composed of individuals performing the same tasks. *Cross-functional groups* are composed of individuals from two or more functional areas. *Project groups* consist of individuals from many different areas or backgrounds who are gathered together to carry out some task; when the task is completed, the group is disbanded and its members return to their original departments. *Virtual groups* are task-focused groups that meet without all the members being present in the same locale or at the same time. *Interest-friendship groups* are formed on the basis of common beliefs, concerns, or activities.

2 *Explain the stages of group development.*

A productive work group is created through a process that involves four stages of development. The purpose of the group is identified in the *forming stage*. This is the stage where group members get to know each other and learn how they may contribute. The *storming stage* occurs when group members begin to question the direction of the group, certain members take control, and there is resistance to task assignments. When group members take responsibility, have a sense of cooperation, and work to accomplish the group's objectives, the group is in the *norming stage*. A group is in the *performing stage* when its members openly share problems and solutions, cooperate with each other, recognize and praise team members, and have an integration of personal and team goals.

3 *Discuss the importance of roles, norms, status, cohesiveness, and group size to group behavior.*

All groups have certain characteristics. These include roles, norms, status, cohesiveness, and group size. A *role* is an expected behavior; it indicates what a person is supposed to do. Some of the most serious role-related problems are role ambiguity and role conflict. A *norm* is a behavioral rule of conduct that is adopted by group members. Norms dictate how each group member ought to act. The manager must be aware of group norms because they play a key role in determining what a group will and will not do. *Status* is the relative ranking of an individual in an organization or group. There are many ways of achieving job status, including position, the nature of the job, personality, and job competence. Two of the greatest job status–related problems with which the manager must be familiar are status incongruence and status discrepancy. *Cohesiveness* is the closeness of interpersonal attractions among group members. However, cohesiveness does not guarantee high productivity; a group can have high cohesion and low output. *Group size* influences member interaction and satisfaction. Small groups tend to be more satisfied than large groups.

4 *Describe how communication and decision-making styles, risk taking, and creativity affect group decisions.*

The manager must also understand intragroup and intergroup behavior. *Intragroup behavior* consists of behavioral interactions within the group. Of primary interest in this chapter were communication and decision making among group members. Five common communication roles played in businesses are the opinion leader, gatekeeper, liaison, isolate, and follower. *The opinion leader* is responsible for determining group goals and actions. The *gatekeeper* regulates the flow of information to other members in the group. The *liaison* is the contact person who links the group with other groups. An *isolate* is treated as an outsider by group members and is generally ignored by other group members. A *follower* is a loyal group member who goes along with whatever other members want. Each group member plays at least one of these roles, and some may play more than one.

Decision makers use a distinct style of leadership when making decisions. The decision maker who has a directive style focuses on the task to be accomplished, technical concerns, facts, and how to get the job done quickly. The *analytical decision maker* likes to analyze situations, is more autocratic, and takes longer to make decisions. The decision maker with a *conceptual style* takes a broader view of the situation, has concern for people, likes to consider many options, is willing to take risks, and tends to be good at finding solutions to problems. The decision maker who has a *behavioral style* works well with others, creates an open forum for exchange of ideas, receives suggestions, is supportive, and has a difficult time saying no to people.

Groups are often more effective than individuals in decision making, particularly when faced with risk taking in estimating or evaluating ambiguous situations, generating unique ideas, or accurately recalling information. Creative-thinking techniques such as *brainstorming* can also help. Additionally, when making decisions in a group, individuals tend to be greater risk takers, a phenomenon known as the risky-shift phenomenon.

5 *List ways in which groups try to gain power over other groups.*

Intergroup behavior consists of behavioral interactions between or among groups. Managers can achieve high intergroup performance by making group goals clear, obtaining cooperation, and carefully planning all interfaces between the various groups. Low intergroup performance is often a result of power struggles in which one group achieves or strives for some influence over the others. Some of the most common ways of gaining power are providing services for other groups that they either cannot or will not provide for themselves, playing an important integrative role among the other groups, and defeating other groups in budgetary allocation battles.

6 *Identify ways to resolve intergroup conflict.*

Some of the ways for resolving conflicts are confrontation, collaboration, compromise, and altering the organizational structure. *Confrontation* involves solving problems using a face-to-face approach, whereas *collaboration* calls for all parties to work out their differences. This approach requires the full cooperation of everyone. The *compromise* approach asks each party to give up something to reach a solution. The manager can always *alter the organizational structure* to separate individuals and groups.

7 *Identify important factors in building effective teams.*

A *team* is a group of people with an identifiable goal. Members have a sense of commitment to the common solutions developed in the team and are responsible for planning, implementing, and controlling to reach expected results. Every member participates equally in the team rewards. It is not always an easy task to turn a group into a functioning productive team.

Businesses use many types of teams. *Functional teams* are found in one major functional unit of the business, such as finance, marketing, production, and so on. Members in *cross-functional teams* come from several functional areas of the business. *Project teams* are created to solve problems, and its members have expert knowledge and skills and come from many areas of the business. *Product development teams* are organized to develop new products. *Task force teams* are short-lived and are created to make decisions about a single objective. *Work teams* comprise multiskilled employees and usually are used in a single functional area or department. *Virtual teams* work away from the main office in remote locations, such as at home, across the city, in another city, or in a foreign country.

Building an effective team takes time, effort, and commitment by management. The process should start with a company or department assessment to determine feasibility. The assessment should identify critical areas and needs, which must be prioritized. The mission and objectives of the company should be well defined. The assessment should identify the technical skills that are available and those skills that are lacking, reveal the cultural barriers that exist, and determine which processes need changing. Building an effective team should start with a small group and should be built over time into an effective team. Management must be committed to using teams and must be willing to provide proper training, empower team members, and allow teams to make mistakes. Feedback and development time are vital and must be built into the system.

Teams can become ineffective over time. Members can start to resist for varying reasons. Effective teams require constant nurturing and proper use of feedback.

8 *Explain how to conduct a successful job hunt.*

Finding the right company to match a job seeker's skills and experience requires conducting a successful job hunt. The type of job and the job level will determine where the search begins. The most popular sources used in hunting for jobs are college and university career centers, newspapers, trade journals, networking groups, Internet job boards, professional recruiters, employment agencies, organization-based recruiting, walk-ins, mail-ins, and employee referrals.

Keep a positive attitude, even when the process seems to be hopeless. An important point to remember is not to lose hope because there is a right job for you. It may take a little longer than you expect to find it, especially during slow economic times and in times of high unemployment. Don't give up; there is a job for you out there somewhere.

Applying electronically online is fast becoming the only way some companies will accept applications. Your application needs to be unique to set it apart from all the others in the database. It is best to follow directions; tailor your application to the position described in the ad; focus on key words that highlight your skills, abilities, attributes, and experience; take any assessment tests suggested by the company; use the comments section to let the company know you have done some research on the company; and follow up with an e-mail or a phone call.

Key Terms in the Chapter

Social unit	two or more team members interacting with each other.
Group	A group is a social unit of two or more interdependent, interactive people striving for common goals.
Functional groups	Individuals in functional groups perform the same tasks.
Cross-functional groups	A cross-functional group is a group composed of individuals from two or more functional areas.
Project groups	A project group includes members from many different backgrounds.
Virtual groups	A virtual group is a task-focused group that meets without all the members being present in the same locale or at the same time.
Interest-friendship groups	Interest-friendship groups are formed on the basis of common beliefs, concerns, or activities.
Forming stage	The forming stage is characterized by efforts to determine initial direction.
Storming stage	The storming stage is characterized by confrontation, questioning, and resistance.

Norming stage	The norming stage is characterized by cooperation and teamwork.
Performing stage	The performing stage is characterized by openness and collaboration.
Role	A role is an expected behavior.
Role ambiguity	Role ambiguity occurs when the job description is vague.
Role conflict	In role conflict, two roles are mutually incompatible.
Norms	Norms are rules of conduct adopted by group members.
Status	Status is the relative ranking of an individual in a group.
Status incongruence	Status incongruence is a discrepancy between a person's supposed status and the way the individual is treated.
Status discrepancy	Status discrepancy occurs when people do things that do not fit in with their status in the group.
Cohesiveness	Cohesiveness refers to the closeness among group members.
Opinion leader	The opinion leader is typically the informal leader.
Gatekeeper	The gatekeeper controls the flow of information to the group members.
Liaison	The liaison links the group to other groups.
Isolate	The isolate is a person who is generally ignored by other group members.
Follower	The follower goes along with the opinion leader or group at large.
Directive style	individuals with a low tolerance for ambiguity and are oriented toward task and technical concerns.
Analytical style	individuals have a high tolerance for ambiguity and a strong task and technical orientation.
Conceptual style	individuals with a high tolerance for ambiguity and for strong people and social concerns.
Behavioral style	individuals have a low tolerance for ambiguity and for strong people and social concerns.
Risky-shift phenomenon	The risky-shift phenomenon is the tendency to take greater risks in a group than when acting alone.
Brainstorming	Brainstorming is a freewheeling approach for generating creative ideas.
Dialectic inquiry	Dialectic inquiry involves the use of structured discussion and debate.
Left-brain people	Left-brain people are logical, rational, and detailed.
Right-brain people	Right-brain people are spontaneous, emotional, and visual.
Goal conflict	Goal conflict is conflict that arises when one group can achieve its aims only at the expense of others.
Confrontation	Confrontation involves face-to-face problem solving.
Collaboration	Collaboration requires full cooperation of everyone.
Compromise	In compromise, each party gives up something.
Team	A team is a group of people responsible for achieving the team's goals.
Team building	Team building is the process for converting a group into an effective team.
Functional teams	Functional teams work in one functional area of the company.
Cross-functional teams	Cross-functional teams consist of employees from across several functional areas of the business.
Project teams	Project teams work on specific projects. Its members are experts from across the functional areas of the company.
Product development teams	Product development teams work on finding new products.
Task force teams	Task force teams are temporary teams that focus on solving short-term problems.
Work teams	Work teams are found within departments.

Virtual teams	teams of workers who work away from the main office.
Group-think	Employees feel their input is not valued and will fail to challenge other team members.
Networking	Networking is the process of interacting with individuals or organized groups.
Organization-based recruiting	Organization-based recruiting is handled by the company needing to hire people.
Employee referrals	Employee referrals come from employees in the company wanting to hire.

Review and Study Questions

1. Define a group. Identify three characteristics that all groups have in common.
2. What is the difference between a functional group and a cross-functional group?
3. What is the purpose of a project group? How does it work?
4. By what means do virtual groups communicate? How are virtual groups used?
5. Describe an interest-friendship group and give an example.
6. What are the four stages of group development? Give a description of what happens in each stage.
7. What conclusions can be drawn about individuals and their conformity to group norms? Cite at least four.
8. Describe the difference between role ambiguity and role conflict.
9. Identify four ways status can occur in groups.
10. Discuss the difference between status incongruence and status discrepancy.
11. What is meant by cohesiveness? Are all high-producing groups highly cohesive? Do all low-producing groups have low cohesiveness?
12. Describe the role of an opinion leader, a gatekeeper, a liaison, an isolate, and a follower.
13. What impact does group size have on member satisfaction and employee turnover? Explain.
14. Identify four decision-making styles.
    a. Which style makes decisions quickly, is innovative, takes risks, and tends to be indecisive?
    b. Which style uses an open exchange of ideas, works well with others, and is receptive to suggestions?
    c. Which style evaluates information, takes a long time to make decisions, and tends to be autocratic?
    d. Which style is task oriented and uses a logical, pragmatic, and systematic approach to decision making?
15. What is the risky-shift phenomenon? How does it work in groups?
16. What are the four phases of creative thinking? Describe them.
17. How can brainstorming be used effectively in companies?
18. Why would an organization be interested in knowing which of its managers are right-brain dominant and which are left-brain dominant? Explain.
19. What are some of the ways in which groups try to gain power over other groups? Cite and explain at least two.

20. How can a manager go about resolving intergroup conflict? Identify four methods and distinguish among them.

21. What is a team? How does an effective team differ from a group?

22. What are the characteristics of a good team?

23. How can each team be used?
    a. functional team
    b. cross-functional team
    c. project team
    d. product development team
    e. task force team
    f. work team

24. How does the process of team building work? Identify the steps and briefly describe each one.

25. What are some challenges that teams face?

26. Identify nine sources that can help an applicant find a job.

Connecting to the Real World

How willing are you to take risks in the workplace?

The purpose of this exercise is to determine your personal willingness to take risks and to learn how the risks may change when you are in a group situation. This exercise can be assigned as an individual student exercise or a group exercise.

To complete this exercise, follow this procedure:

1. Complete the risk-taking questionnaire below. When you are finished, enter your scores on the answer sheet that is provided and then total them.
2. Select two to four people and collectively complete the same questionnaire. For each statement, there must be agreement among the group members on which alternative to choose. When you are finished, total the scores for the group.
3. In a written report, compare your individual scores to the group scores and explain the reasons for the differences. Are you pleased with your level of risk taking? If you have a low tolerance for risk taking, what do you need to do to increase the level? How will your level of risk taking impact your performance in the workplace?

Situations

Ten situations are presented here. In each case, read the situation and then choose the lowest probability or odds that you would accept.

1. You have just learned you have a serious heart ailment. If you choose not to have an operation, you can live only another ten years. If you choose to have the operation, there is a chance that you will not survive the operation. Should you survive, however, you will have a normal life expectancy. Check the lowest probability of survival you would consider to be acceptable.

    ____ 1 of 10   ____ 3 of 10   ____ 5 of 10

    ____ 7 of 10   ____ 9 of 10

    ____ You would not take the chance.

2. You are playing chess against a much better player. Early in the game, you notice that you have a chance for a quick win, provided your opponent does not see through your strategy. If he does, you are finished. Check the lowest probability you would consider acceptable for the risky play.

    ____ 1 out of 10   ____ 3 out of 10   ____ 5 out of 10

    ____ 7 out of 10   ____ 9 out of 10

    ____ You would not take the chance.

3. You have $5,000 in conservative stock holdings returning 9 percent annually. You have learned from your cousin that she is in the process of selling stock in her new firm. If her company survives the next five years, your stock will quadruple in value. Check the lowest probability of survival you would consider acceptable for investing the $5,000.

    ____ 1 of 10   ____ 3 of 10   ____ 5 of 10

    ____ 7 of 10   ____ 9 of 10

    ____ You would not take the chance.

4. You are thinking about applying to two colleges for admission. College A has a national reputation but also flunks out more than 50 percent of all those admitted. College B has only a local reputation, but the flunk-out rate is less than 2 percent. Check the lowest survival probability you would accept in opting for College A.

    ____ 1 of 10   ____ 3 of 10   ____ 5 of 10

    ____ 7 of 10   ____ 9 of 10

    ____ You would not take the chance.

5. You have a good, steady job at a moderate rate of pay. Your best friend has offered you a job in his firm at a much higher rate of pay. However, his company is small and may not survive the next two years. Check the lowest probability of survival you would look for in this new firm.

    ____ 1 of 10   ____ 3 of 10   ____ 5 of 10

    ____ 7 of 10   ____ 9 of 10

    ____ You would not take the chance.

6. You are thinking about getting married. Your intended is a wonderful person but is also emotional and sometimes very hard to get along with. On the other hand, this individual makes you happier than anyone you have ever met. Check the lowest probability of your marriage surviving that you would accept before going ahead with the wedding.

    ____ 1 of 10   ____ 3 of 10   ____ 5 of 10

    ____ 7 of 10   ____ 9 of 10

    ____ You would not take the chance.

7. You are the coach of a football team. Your team is attempting to win the state title and is a point behind, having scored a touchdown just as the final gun went off. If you allow the team to kick the extra point, you will have a tie. If you try a trick play, you can go for two points. What is the lowest probability of success with the trick play that you would accept?

    ____ 1 of 10   ____ 3 of 10   ____ 5 of 10

    ____ 7 of 10   ____ 9 of 10

    ____ You would not take the chance.

8. You have saved $3,500 over the last two years and are considering buying a bond paying 13.5 percent annually. Your brother, an oil wildcatter, wants you to invest the money with him. If he is successful, you will double your money in one year. If he is not, you will lose it all. What is the lowest probability of success that you would accept for investing with your brother?

____ 1 of 10   ____ 3 of 10   ____ 5 of 10

____ 7 of 10   ____ 9 of 10

____ You would not take the chance.

9. You have the option of taking a steady job in the human resources department, where your future with the firm is just about guaranteed. Another option is to go with the advertising department. It will take five years of hard work before you know whether you will succeed in this department but, if you do, your salary will be almost double that in the human resources department. If you fail, you will have to find another job elsewhere. What is the lowest probability of success in the advertising department that you would be willing to accept?

____ 1 of 10   ____ 3 of 10   ____ 5 of 10

____ 7 of 10   ____ 9 of 10

____ You would not take the chance.

10. You can keep your current stateside job or take one in the Far East. If you stay in your present job, you will receive moderate pay increases and promotions for an indefinite future. If you opt for the overseas assignment and do well, you will be a vice president within five years and will be one of the highest-paid people in the firm. If you do not do well, you will be fired. What is the lowest probability of success in the overseas assignment that you would be willing to accept?

____ 1 of 10   ____ 3 of 10   ____ 5 of 10

____ 7 of 10   ____ 9 of 10

____ You would not take the chance.

Scoring Instructions: Fill in your answers by transferring the numbers you chose in each case. For example, if you chose "1 of 10," put in a 1. If you chose "5 of 10," put in a 5. If you opted not to take the chance, put in an answer of 10. Then total your scores for both the individual and group assignments.

Answer Sheet

Situation	Individual Score	Group Score
1.	____	____
2.	____	____
3.	____	____
4.	____	____
5.	____	____
6.	____	____
7.	____	____
8.	____	____
9.	____	____
10.	____	____
Total	____	____

CASE
The New Supervisor

The EX-MAN Products Company has been in business for thirty-five years, manufacturing a wide array of household products. The company has had its good years and its less-than-good years. Currently, management feels that improvements are needed.

When Gary Paterson was put in charge of the small-products assembly department, output was at an all-time low. Bob Willard, the retiring supervisor, had been in charge of the department for the last ten years, during which time the output had slowly declined.

Bob was an easygoing type of person, who felt that employees were adults who should do what the job required without a supervisor constantly looking over their shoulders. He felt that formal training was a waste of the department's money, and if an employee needed help, he or she would ask for it. In the last couple of years, Bob was spending more and more time thinking about what he was going to do after retirement. Bob found that his job was getting more boring everyday. In fact, he did not look forward to going to work; he simply looked forward to Fridays.

When Willard had first taken over the department, the average worker was assembling 200 units per day, but the company norm was 225. During his decade as supervisor, the firm introduced some technological advances, and the norm was raised to 250 units per day. However, the average output declined to 193.

The management's time-and-motion studies showed that 250 units were well within the ability of the average worker, and the manual dexterity tests given to members of the department revealed that each was physically capable of attaining this objective. Willard, however, explained the situation in terms of changing values. "People are different today," he said. "They no longer want to work hard. They've lost the old work ethic, especially our young people, and that's who works in the assembly department. The average age there has declined from 29 to 23 in the last eight years. I guess lower output is just something we're going to have to learn to live with."

These remarks had Paterson worried. He wondered how he might keep the output from declining even more. After serious thought, he decided to call the department together and talk to everyone as soon as he took over. During this talk, he emphasized three points to the assembled workers.

- First, he told them he wanted them to continue working in their present groups. Because the members of all eight groups knew one another well, he said, there was no sense breaking up satisfied work teams. However, if someone did want to change to another work group, he promised to help

him or her do so, although it would require a mutual exchange of personnel with the other group.
- Second, he urged them all to come and talk with him if they had any problems.
- Third, he asked their assistance in boosting output to 225 units per person per day.

Paterson believed in walking the walk; so everyday he took time to walk through the plant. It was his way to get to know the workers and answer any questions they had. He also complimented those who were doing a good job. He took note of the employees who needed more training and followed through by getting the workers the additional training needed.

During the first three months, Paterson was asked to make a few changes in group composition. He also resolved several job-related technical problems. Overall, however, he found the groups to be congenial and fun to supervise. In addition, output began to move up slowly. At the end of ninety days, the average daily output was 219 units.

One of the women in the department, when asked why production was up, said, "We like this new supervisor. He's a good guy. He talks to us, helps us solve problems, and doesn't keep emphasizing output. He lets us work at our own pace. It's such a change from when Bob Willard was here."

Case Questions

1. What are the problems in this case? Why was production low? Where did Bob Willard go wrong?
2. Are there groups or teams at work in this assembly plant? What is your assessment? What are the differences between these employees working in groups versus working in teams? Support your position.
3. What role is group cohesion playing among the employees? How has group cohesion impacted production and why? After some members changed groups, why did production increase?
4. Why is there a difference between company norms and group norms at this plant? What does the new supervisor have to do to move the group norms in line with company norms? What are your feelings—will the group norms stay, decline again, or move up?
5. What role do the workers want the new supervisor to assume? How did Bob Willard err in this regard? What is Gary Paterson doing right?
6. What does Paterson have to do to build successful working teams? Specifically describe what you would do to start building effective teams of workers.

The Informal Organization

CHAPTER 5

In the last two chapters, we examined individual behavior and group behavior. To complete the discussion of the social system, we now study the informal organization, which engages in both individual and group behaviors. The informal organization operates through the grapevine and is an integral part of the formal organization. The informal organization has its benefits and disadvantages for management. Effective managers learn to deal with and use the informal organization to get things done.

LEARNING OBJECTIVES

1
Compare and contrast formal and informal organizations.

2
Discuss some of the behavioral controls used by members of the informal organization to ensure compliance with its norms.

3
Explain how the informal communication network functions.

4
Identify the primary benefits associated with the informal organization.

5
List some of the disadvantages associated with the informal organization.

6
Cite some of the ways in which a manager can deal with the informal organization.

7
Discuss how to successfully complete an employment interview.

How Work Gets Done

At Yarde Metals, a multi-metal distributor headquartered in Southington, Connecticut, employees are called *associates* rather than employees. An unusual corporate philosophy called *social leveling* gets rid of tension between labor and management. Everyone works together toward one purpose, and peer pressure is used to prevent abuse. Craig Yarde states, "If we can get people working together as a team, we can accomplish anything." He gets his associates to work together by letting them in on the company's financial picture. The books are open to everyone once a month, and the associates are trained to read financial statements so they can understand how the company is doing. This gives the associates an idea of what's going on and how they fit into the big picture. Yarde says, "It shows them that we value our associates as our most important stakeholders." Everyone is responsible for taking care of customers. Because the associates are empowered to understand their roles in the business, they don't abuse their privileges and responsibilities. If an associate abuses privileges, someone will say, "Hey, you're not getting the product out the door." By allowing everyone to feel equal, the company can more readily accomplish its goals.

Employees also are called associates at W.L. Gore & Associates, Inc., a leading manufacturer of thousands of advanced technology products for the electronics, fabrics, industrial, and medical markets, headquartered in Newark, Delaware. The company is listed as No. 13 on Fortune's 2010 "100 Best Companies to Work For." It is one of only a few companies that has been listed for thirteen consecutive years. W.L. Gore recognizes the importance of fostering a work environment where people feel motivated, engaged, and passionate about their work. During the last recession, employees rallied together to make the company stronger than ever. The culture promotes an incredible level of ownership and entrepreneurship that allows associates to channel their talents and interests to produce a continuous stream of innovative, high-value products for customers. The company has created an environment where not only the formal organization is at work but it is supported by the informal organization as well.

Another example of a company using its informal organization to get things done is Trader Joe's, a multibillion-dollar specialty grocery chain. Its success is credited in part to its workforce management practices. It takes the approach that the employee is number one and feels that if it treats employees the way it wants employees to treat customers, odds are that stores will have a better shot at providing a unique shopping experience for people as soon as they walk through the door. A shopper recently commented, "It's a very positive environment, not oppressive, stale, or negative." In fact, Trader Joe's has been cited more than once in *Fortune* magazine as one of the best places to work.

Trader Joe's has created a culture of success where all employees have done each job at one time or another and will work in all positions in the store. It is a place where people's opinions are respected and talents are nurtured, which has resulted in extremely low turnover for the company. Employee autonomy is highly valued; employees are allowed to make decisions about store operations, including produce mix and in-store displays. Employees enthusiastically greet customers as they enter the store, and exchange information and ideas about products and how to use them, as customers move through the store. A retail consultant noted that contrary to employee attitudes that run across many conventional supermarkets, everyone at Trader Joe's, from the captain on down, truly appears to enjoy what they do. Trader Joe's sees its own people as a way to build brand recognition for the store. "The corporate office feels that the people it hires, trains, and promotes are just as important as the low prices and products it carries." Each store operates as a team where individual opinions are valued, rather than an environment where people speak out and are either not heard or have their opinions suppressed. During the last recession, senior managers froze their salaries so that other employees could get raises and the no-layoff policy could be maintained.

UPS is another company that values its employees and the contributions they make to the company. It strives to maintain a spirit of teamwork throughout the organization and capitalizes on the advantages of working together in an informal manner, where advancement is based on individual merit and performance. The managers are held "responsible for creating a workplace of fairness, dignity, and respect for all employees—an environment of inclusion, encouraging participation, and the best effort of everyone." To illustrate this point, on January 26, 2010, 928 drivers, the largest number ever, were inducted into UPS' elite "Circle of Honor" for driving twenty-five years without an accident, bringing the total to 4,793 drivers. Many drivers have safe records for over thirty years and forty years, and one has driven for forty-eight years without an accident.

Compare and contrast formal and informal organizations.

The Nature of the Informal Organization

The informal organization plays a significant role in the dynamics of human behavior at work. As a result, no discussion of human relations would be complete without consideration of this area. In this part of the chapter, we examine the nature of the informal

The Informal Organization: An Initial Appraisal

The following fifteen statements are designed to measure your understanding and use of the informal organization. Assume you are a manager and determine, from that viewpoint, whether each statement is true or false. An interpretation of your answers is provided at the end of the book.

T/F   1. I always work through formal channels.

T/F   2. I don't care how my people get things done as long as they get them done.

T/F   3. Everyone should have a job description and stick to it exclusively.

T/F   4. If I can get things done faster, I cut across formal channels and use whatever means necessary.

T/F   5. All rules and procedures are made to be obeyed.

T/F   6. I use the informal organization to give and get information.

T/F   7. I discourage grapevine activity.

T/F   8. Almost all the grapevine communications are inaccurate.

T/F   9. The grapevine can be influenced by management.

T/F 10. The grapevine is inevitable.

T/F 11. Workers will form into informal groups regardless of what the organization does.

T/F 12. The grapevine's basic objective is to undermine management's efforts.

T/F 13. Most informal communiqués are passed to others on a purely random basis.

T/F 14. The goals of the informal organization almost always conflict with those of the formal organization.

T/F 15. Just about all grapevine messages are started by individuals with an ax to grind.

---

organization by pointing out how it differs from the formal organization. In particular, we direct our attention to four major areas:

1. Interpersonal relations
2. Informal leadership
3. Behavioral control
4. Informal communication

Before reading on, however, take the informal organization quiz in the "Time Out" box and obtain a preliminary evaluation of your use and understanding of an informal organization.

Interpersonal Relations

In a formal organization, relationships among people are clearly defined. For example, all the members of an assembly group are charged with assembling thirty units per hour and placing the completed items on a large table. Everyone is supposed to be doing the same job and turning out an identical number of items. Most organizations, however, do not work this way.

Over time, workers begin to form friendships with one another. This, in turn, results in workers going beyond their job descriptions and helping the workers they like to complete their jobs. Consider the case of the assembly group we mentioned previously. Although each person is supposed to be working independently of the others, we know that in every group there are slow workers and fast workers. Additionally, some of these workers are so well liked that their peers help them with their work. Conversely, some will be disliked and will be ignored by their fellow workers.

Figure 5.1 is an illustration of the degree of assistance that some members of a work group give to others. Note that Jeff is helping two of his coworkers but is not receiving any help in return. This indicates that Jeff is probably a very fast worker. Chuck receives assistance from four of his fellow workers, so Chuck is not a fast worker. However, the other members of the group like him and are therefore willing to assist him in assembling the units. Barbara and Ed help each other. Joe receives help from Barbara but does not reciprocate. Finally, Larry neither receives help from anyone nor does he give any.

Figure 5.1 depicts a **sociogram**, a schematic drawing that shows the social relationships that exist among members of a group. In this case, the relationship is being measured in

Figure 5.1 Who Helps Whom?

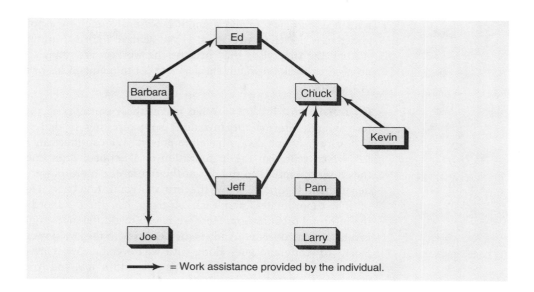

= Work assistance provided by the individual.

terms of who helps whom. Sociograms provide interesting insights to informal group behavior because they help to pinpoint those members who are most popular, those who do all the work, those who get help from others, and those with whom no one interacts.

Research reveals that three types of relationships help to provide insights to informal networks: advice, trust, and communication.

1. The **advice network** shows the prominent players in an organization, on whom others depend to solve problems and provide technical information.
2. The **trust network** tells which employees share delicate political information and back one another in a crisis.
3. The **communication network** reveals the employees who talk about work-related matters on a regular basis.[1]

Sociograms developed by Jacob Levy Moreno are a tool that can be used to understand and evaluate relationships within the context of a particular situation, such as within work teams. They provide communication maps that show general patterns of communication relationships within the group studied. Sociograms can identify informal leaders, social rankings, and isolated individuals within groups. More specifically, they can illustrate the availability and spread of leadership throughout a group or network; the overall level of communication around a specific focus or initiative; cohesive subgroups, cliques, or isolates; and areas that seem to be very strong and those that are not as strongly connected.[2]

Informal Leadership

In a formal organization, management designates the leader, whereas in an informal organization, members of the group choose the leader. If the formal leader does a good job, he or she is often promoted away from the department. If the informal leader does a good job, he or she maintains that position, but if he or she does a poor job, someone else will be chosen who can help the group meet its objectives.

When we compare formal and informal leaders, therefore, we can see that the formal leader has authority and the informal leader has power. **Authority** is the right to command, and it flows from the superior to the subordinate. **Power** is the ability to influence, persuade, or move another person to one's own point of view. The informal leader uses power in two ways: (1) to achieve informal group objectives (such as persuading the supervisor that, because the workers are doing the best they can, there is no need to crack down any harder) and (2) to maintain his or her position of leadership in the group.

Authority and Power. What makes these concepts of authority and power in the formal and informal organizations so interesting is that the person who has the authority may not always have the power.[3] We can illustrate this with Figures 5.2 and 5.3, which represent the organization of a fictional department. In both illustrations, the closer a name is to the top of the figure, the more power the individual has in the department. Figure 5.2 shows the formal organization chart. Note that Harry is in charge of five subordinates, and each of them has three subordinates. Figure 5.3 shows the informal organization. Here we see quite a difference. For example, although Harry is the designated leader, Andy is the person with the real power. For some reason, Harry listens to Andy and goes along with whatever he says. One common explanation for such an arrangement is that Harry is new on the job, and Andy has been around for a long time and is the informal group leader. Realizing he must rely heavily on Andy's help, Harry defers to him on most matters.

The informal organization chart also reveals some other interesting facts. For example, Andy's three subordinates have more power than the other twelve subordinates. (Look how high up in the informal power structure they are located.)

Also, although Mary and Bob are equal in authority (see Figure 5.2), Bob has more power than Mary. Moreover, Charles is supposed to be in charge of Bill, Mark, and Tony, but a close look at Figure 5.3 shows that Bill is giving the orders in the group and Charles has the least amount of power. Finally, although all the subordinates are supposed to be equal, some are more equal than others. A look at Bob's three subordinates—Becky, Dick, and Phil—shows that Dick has the greatest power and Phil has the least.

Company Needs versus Individual Needs. Some people like to define the formal organization as the one the company creates and the informal organization as the one

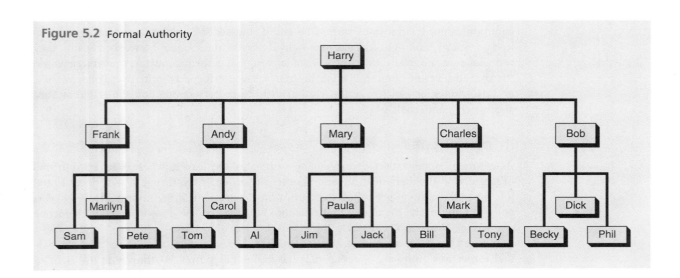

Figure 5.2 Formal Authority

Figure 5.3 Informal Power

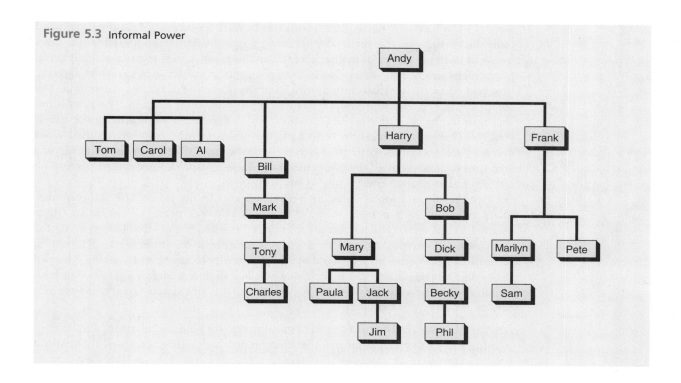

Figure 5.4
Organizational Goals and
Individual-Group Goals

The Organization Goals	The Individual-Group Goals
Good profit	Good pay
High return on investment	Job security
Adequate worker efficiency	Adequate fringe benefits
High-quality goods and services	Challenging work
Strong competitive posture	A chance to achieve
Low tardiness and absenteeism	Work satisfaction
Low turnover	

the people themselves recreate. Certainly, there is give-and-take between the needs of the organization and those of its employees. A company, for example, is most interested in attaining economic goals, such as profit and return on investment. The employees in the business are most concerned with getting good pay, adequate fringe benefits, and doing satisfying work. The company (organization) must strive to make the workers see its point of view, and the workers must persuade top management to understand theirs. Figure 5.4 lists examples of company/organizational goals and individual/group goals. As the lists reveal, the goals of the two groups are very different, thus, setting up a combination of cooperation and competition forces.

Sufficing Behavior.   Who usually wins this conflict between organizational goals and individual group goals? Usually, neither side emerges totally victorious. Each side takes less than it deems ideal, but neither accepts anything less than it regards as minimal. In human relations terms, we say that each side engages in **sufficing behavior** by agreeing to accept adequate or satisfactory payoffs from the other. Let us take an illustration. The company announces that beginning Monday all workers must clock in. The news is not well received by the informal organization, which decides to work around the rule if possible. One way of doing so is to have the group member who arrives first clock everyone else in and to rotate the assignment at the end of the day by having everyone take turns clocking out all the group members. In this manner, the company's rules are obeyed, and the group finds a way to live with them.

Another illustration of sufficing behavior occurs in the case of the company that offers its people a 3 percent increase in salary and a 3 percent increase in fringe benefits. This offer is ideal for management because, if the union accepts it, the company will surpass its goal of a 15 percent return on investment. The union, meanwhile, counters with a demand of 9 percent for both salary and benefits. The two then compromise on 5 percent. Each side gets less than it wanted originally, but both can live with the contract because it provides them with a satisfactory outcome or results that are "good enough."

Politics at Work.   The use of power typically requires political behavior.[4] Rather than running roughshod over someone, the effective manager often uses a well-thought-out political approach. In this way, the manager gets done what he or she wants, while causing the least amount of hard feelings or problems. Research shows that three of the most common organizational political tactics employed by chief executive officers, staff managers, and supervisors are attacking or blaming others, carefully using information, and building support for new ideas.[5] Other political behaviors are designed to upstage the other party or protect one's own position. Common examples are:

- Purse snatching—Stealing other people's ideas and presenting them as one's own.
- Trapshooting—Shooting down ideas, requests, and proposals from others and claiming that these efforts are not worth the trouble of implementation.
- Gatekeeping—Refusing to share useful ideas with others who could profit from this information.
- Perimeter guarding—Protecting one's organizational turf at the expense of company teamwork and overall efficiency.
- Fox holing—Digging in and protecting one's position by not contributing or by doing anything that can result in problems; this is the typical "protect yourself at all times" strategy.
- Fashion modeling—Getting caught up in the latest management fads and using them to find quick answers to complex problems rather than sticking to well-planned, longer-term solutions.[6]

In addition, some defensive behaviors can be used to minimize the effects of these political actions. Examples are playing it safe, passing the buck, pretending to be dumb, stalling, and overconforming. For example, when the market research people at Ford Motor Company investigated the demand for minivans, they found a very large, untapped market. However, the company's finance executives felt that building a minivan was too risky and could endanger the firm's financial status. So, to play it safe and avoid getting in trouble, the finance people rejected the proposed minivan, a market that Chrysler then dominated and that netted that company billions of dollars of profit.[7] Overall, these proactive and defensive behaviors help to create and sustain a political climate in the workplace.

Politics is also employed widely in the appraisal process, as managers use these evaluations to control their subordinates. The following are some of the latest research findings:

1. The higher one rises in the organization, the more political the appraisal process becomes.
2. Because of the dynamic, ambiguous nature of managerial work, appraisals are susceptible to political manipulation.
3. Performance is not necessarily the bottom line in the executive appraisal process. Ratings are affected by the:
   a. boss's agenda
   b. "reputation" factor
   c. organization's current political climate.
4. Senior executives have extraordinary latitude in evaluating subordinate executives' performance; the pitfalls associated with this latitude include:
   a. a failure on the part of superiors to specify meaningful performance goals and standards
   b. a lack of communication between supervisors and executives about the desired style and means of goal accomplishment
   c. the "good-but-not-good-enough syndrome"
5. Executive appraisal is a political tool used to control people and resources.[8]

In dealing with these issues, it is important to know how to play the game. The "Cultural Diversity in Action" box provides some insights regarding how women have worked effectively within the political environment.

The Value of Networking

In informal organizations, one of the most important activities is **networking**, the process of socializing, politicking, and interacting with people throughout the enterprise. Researchers have found that successful managers are promoted much more often than average managers, and these successful individuals also spend a great deal more of their time networking throughout the organization. Most successful managers spend approximately half their time in networking activities, whereas the average manager will spend half that amount of time on networking. As you can tell, networking activities play an important role in the success of managers.

Gender and Ethnicity.   How people network, however, tends to vary based on such factors as gender and ethnicity. For example, research shows that many women tend to be conservative in their networking activities, whereas men tend to be bolder. One reason is that, in some organizations, women who are aggressive in their networking are seen as being too pushy, whereas men who behave similarly are regarded as forceful and confident. Successful women tend to use networks selectively. They quickly learn the organization's norms of behavior and operate within these parameters.

Researchers have also found networking differences between managers in general and minority managers in particular. For example, one researcher studied the networking activities of sixty-three managers: twenty-six white men, twenty white women, and seventeen minorities consisting of twelve African Americans, three Hispanics, and two Asian Americans. She discovered a number of major differences in the way in which minority managers networked. Among these differences were the following:[9]

1. Minority managers tended to have a much more diverse group of individuals in their network, including men, women, blacks, Latinos, and whites.

IN ACTION

KNOWING HOW TO PLAY THE GAME

An increasing number of women now head large organizations. They attained these positions by learning the informal, as well as formal, rules regarding how to get ahead—and, in many cases, the strategies that they have used were more a reflection of their own personalities than of organizational rules. However, many of these women have followed similar approaches in four areas: work experience, personal relationship building, vision, and creativity.

Almost all the women who have risen to the upper ranks of large organizations have had a wealth of experience that provided them important insights regarding how the organization operates, or should operate. A good example is Shirley DeLibero, executive director of New Jersey Transit. In addition to nineteen years in the electronics industry, she spent twelve years as production manager for the reconstruction of trolley cars for the Massachusetts Bay Transit Authority in Boston. By 1990, she had learned all sides of the transportation business and was offered the helm at New Jersey Transit. Her previous experience has helped her to cut almost $1 million annually from the company's energy bill, increase annual revenues by more than $50 million, and create an organization in which empowered employees make critical decisions. During this same period, ridership increased by 14 percent, customer complaints decreased by 40 percent, and the system's overall favorable ratings from customers increased by 18 percent. Shirley DeLibero, one of the most accomplished women in the transportation industry, spent eight years as executive director of NJ Transit before being named president and CEO of Houston Metro (see notes below) where she repeated her accomplishments.

Personal relationship building is another key success factor. Linda Marcelli is the only woman among Merrill Lynch's twenty-nine district directors. Her bailiwick has been New York City; now it is the Tampa Bay complex where she manages a group of about two hundred financial consultants, a support team, and a leadership team who service high-net-worth clients and business owners in growing and managing their wealth. Based on a number of key measures, including total revenues, business growth, and recruitment of new brokers, she ranks first in the Merrill system. How does she do it? In her words, "In order to lead in a man's world, you can't be plain vanilla." And she never has been. She wears loud suits and jewelry that make her stand out from the crowd. At the same time, she also knows how to build personal relationships in a business where building relationships is the key to success. During her early days with the firm, everyone sold stocks by cold calling. She preferred personal meetings. It paid off. People liked her approach to doing business and invested with her.

Vision consists of knowing where one wants to go and then convincing others to accept the same objective. Beverly Harvard, as police chief of Atlanta and the first African American to lead a police department in a major city, is a good example of how successful women use vision to get ahead. Harvard routinely works around the clock at least six days per week and controls a budget of more than $100 million. Commenting on her success, she noted, "The primary job of chief is to provide direction for the department. I think you have to be a visionary. Once you define that vision, you have to show leadership in order to have people follow you to where you want to go." Harvard was able to do this and to get the department behind her. In addition, her initiatives to install microcomputers in patrol cars to give officers instant access to police reports and to combine the department's school detectives and curfew enforcement units in response to concerns about teen crime helped reduce robberies, aggravated assaults, and burglaries.

Successful women also tend to be highly creative and know how to swim against the tide. Roberta Williams is a good example. One evening her husband brought home a computer game. After playing it for a while, she was hooked and began thinking about creating games of her own. The first game she developed was packaged in Ziploc bags by her husband and her in their kitchen. That was more than three decades ago. Over the years, their company Sierra On-Line merged with several companies, but Roberta Williams continued to design for the new business and turn out creative games.

In a field dominated by men, she created games "guys wouldn't think to do." She designed fairy tales instead of Doom-like shoot 'em ups. She did this by first concocting a story and its characters. She then turned it over to a team of engineers, programmers, and artists to create the technical package, working closely with them to ensure that everything is done correctly. As a result, she has become a legend in the industry. Her creativity led to the first game that blended graphics and text, the first three-dimensional animated adventure, and the first adventure involving a female antagonist. Williams and her husband are now retired but still find time to design more games.

Sources: Stephanie N. Mehta, "What Minority Employees Really Want," *Fortune*, July 10, 2000, pp. 181–186; Paula M. White, "Wonder Women," *Black Enterprise*, April 1997, pp. 114–120; Patricia Sellers, "Women, Sex, and Power," *Fortune*, August 5, 1996, pp. 42–56; David Krackhardt and Jeffrey R. Hanson, "Informal Networks: The Company Behind the Chart," *Harvard Business Review*, July–August 1993, pp. 104–111; www.pressrelease365.com; www.onlinepress.trb.org; and www.giant-bomb.com in action.

2. These managers had less-close personal relationships with members in the network.
3. Some high-potential minority individuals tended to balance their network contacts between people from the same ethnic group and those from other ethnic groups, whereas other high-potential minority managers had networks that were dominated by ties to whites.

4. High-potential minority individuals tended to have more contacts with outside groups and less overlap between their social and network circles.

5. In contrast to whites, minority managers saw networks as less useful in providing them career benefits.

Manager's Role in Networking.   Networking can be very useful to managers, but the specific ways in which they carry out this activity will vary. However, one thing does seem to be true for most successful managers: They are very active at networking, typically extending this activity far beyond their own unit or department. Many of them spend a great deal of their time networking inside and outside the organization, getting to know a wide array of people, and often socializing throughout the community. In fact, one group of researchers analyzed data from more than six hundred managers nationwide and found that there are major differences between the ways in which managers and nonmanagers go about networking. In particular, they discovered that managers belong to more clubs and societies than nonmanagers; managers are also more likely to be members of professional or academic societies and service clubs. In terms of core discussion networks, managers have more network members who are colleagues or coworkers, have more network members who are total strangers to one another, have large networks, and also have a greater number of close ties with network members. Furthermore, coworkers represent a large proportion of managers' discussion networks, and close ties make up a greater proportion of managers' relationships with their network members.[10]

Simply put, managers not only spend more of their time networking than nonmanagers, but they also carry out these activities in a very systematic way. They also tend to develop a host of different groups on whom they rely. Successful managers know the value of networking, and they carry it out very effectively.[11]

Virtual Networks.   In recent years, networking activity has become increasingly electronic, particularly in dealing with virtual groups, as seen by the tremendous growth of e-mail and online meetings. Virtual social networks, such as Facebook, MySpace, LinkedIn, and Twitter have allowed virtual networking to explode in the past few years. With new technology in cell phones and handheld devices, virtual networking is rapidly increasing. Some businesses are also finding ways to use a system that is already installed on their computers to network with special groups. In fact, today, many businesses use the Internet to conduct all their business, for example, with their suppliers and customers, often saving billions annually. The drawback to this electronic networking approach is that there is a loss of informal communication. Team members do not have the opportunity to meet face-to-face, and they often miss this ability to chat informally with one another. As a result, it is common to find managers bringing the team members together periodically so that they can share information personally and interact socially. Commenting on this, Leigh Thompson, an expert on team productivity, has written:

> Probably the most-felt impact is the inability to chat informally in the hall, inside offices, and so on. The impromptu and casual conversations that employees have by the water cooler and the coffee machine are often where the most difficult problems are solved, and the most important interpersonal issues are addressed.... Remote group members feel cut off from key conversations that occur over lunch and in the hall. Vince Anderson, director of environmental programs for Whirlpool Corp.'s North American Appliance Group in Evansville, Indiana, oversaw a 2-year project using a virtual team that developed a ... refrigerator, involving the United States, Brazil, and Italy. The team met approximately every 4 months to discuss the project, and it was these informal meetings—a backyard cookout and a volleyball game—that were the most valuable for the project.[12]

CHECK YOUR UNDERSTANDING

How Does the Informal Organization Work at Your Job?

If you have a job, use your place of work. If not, select a group in which you are a member.

1. Prepare a sociogram of the informal organization.
2. Identify who has the authority and who has the power.
3. Identify who executes which political behavior—purse snatching, trapshooting, gatekeeping, perimeter guarding, fox holing, and fashion modeling.

Discuss some of the behavioral controls used by members of the informal organization to ensure compliance with its norms.

Behavioral Control

When people in the formal organization do something right, they are given rewards; when they do something wrong, they are punished. If Barry reduces overhead in his department by 5 percent, he may be placed on a list of "up and coming" young executives. On the other hand, if departmental overhead increases dramatically and Barry is unable to control it, he may be labeled as incompetent and lose the chance of ever being promoted or may even lose his job.

In the informal organization also, rewards and punishments are dispensed to members. These, however, usually take the form of giving or denying need fulfillment. If Paula conforms to group norms, she is included in group activities and provided with social interaction. If she violates group norms or refuses to act "properly," she is ostracized and may even be subjected to pressure and ridicule and made to look foolish in the eyes of the other members. The sociogram depicted in Figure 5.1 illustrated who was helping whom in a department; Larry neither helped anyone else nor was helped by others. From this, we can conclude that he is not a member of the informal group because one of the most common informal norms is that of assisting one's peers.

Dependency. Despite the strength of the informal group leader, the formal leader has a greater capacity for rewarding and punishing personnel. The formal leader can give both physical and psychological rewards to those who obey organizational directives and do things well. Because the informal leader can give only psychological rewards, not everyone conforms to informal group norms. Some people resist because they believe there is more to be gained by not joining the informal group, and not even the most extreme form of ostracism budges them. This was seen clearly a number of years ago in the case of the West Point cadet who was accused of cheating, judged guilty by his peer review board (made up of other cadets), and told to resign his commission. However, the man was found not guilty by those in authority and was allowed to stay at the academy. Because he refused to abide by the decision of his peers, none of them talked to or interacted with him for the remainder of his stay at West Point. Despite such pressures, the cadet remained at the academy and graduated with his class.

Those who agree with the informal group's norms, however, strive for membership and depend on the group for social interaction and support. As a result, there are three subgroups in an informal organization structure.

- First is the **nucleus group**, which consists of full-fledged members of the informal organization who interact with one another.
- Second is the **fringe group**, consisting of those seeking admission to the informal organization. These people are often new members of the workforce who are being screened for membership by the nucleus group.

- Third is the **outer group**, consisting of individuals who have been rejected for membership. These people have failed to measure up to the requirements set for admission to the group. Numerous reasons can be cited for this failure: doing too much work, doing too little work, having an unpleasant personality, and "squealing" to a supervisor about a member of the nucleus group.

 CHECK YOUR UNDERSTANDING

How Do Subgroups Differ?

Using the same group identified in the previous "Check Your Understanding" exercise, list the names of the people who are in each subgroup—nucleus group, fringe group, and outer group—and tell why these people are in each subgroup.

Explain how the informal communication network functions.

Informal Communication

One of the most interesting behavioral aspects of the informal organization is its communication pattern. Commonly referred to as the **grapevine**, this communication network is used to carry information among members of the informal organization. In this section, we examine the pattern of grapevine communication and four of the most likely causes of this activity.

The grapevine arises from social interaction and tends to be an oral, as opposed to written, form of communication. Bud, in engineering, could send a message through the interdepartmental mail asking Doris, in accounting, whether she is going to the party on Friday. However, it is more likely that Bud will either call and ask Doris or wait until they meet later in the day.

Much of the information that is carried by the grapevine deals with matters that are of current interest to employees. For example, the introduction of new work procedures in the metals department, the details of an accident in Plant 2, and the installation of a new computerized accounting system in the comptroller's offices are the kinds of topics commonly discussed via the grapevine. As you can see, these topics are sometimes of interest to people in many departments, so the number of individuals on a grapevine can be extremely large. This is particularly true when the message is viewed with concern or fear. For example, when employees throughout the firm learn about the introduction of new work procedures in the metals department, they may see this as the beginning of an efficiency move by management. If this proves to be the case, various departments would be forewarned, and each will take action to ensure that its efficiency is already as high as can be expected. Meanwhile, if the message proves to be a total fabrication and no new work procedures have been introduced, grapevine activity related to this topic will cease. Because grapevine members begin checking on the truth of a rumor almost immediately, one of these two actions will be initiated very shortly.

Grapevine Networks.   Many people believe the grapevine consists of a long chain of people, with each individual passing the message to the next person in the chain. This type of communication network, known as the **single strand** (illustrated in Figure 5.5), is the least frequently used.

Another way in which informal messages can be communicated is by one person telling all the others. This is called the **gossip chain** (see Figure 5.5). Although more commonly used than the single strand, the gossip chain also is one of the less frequently used grapevine networks.

Figure 5.5 Informal Communication Networks

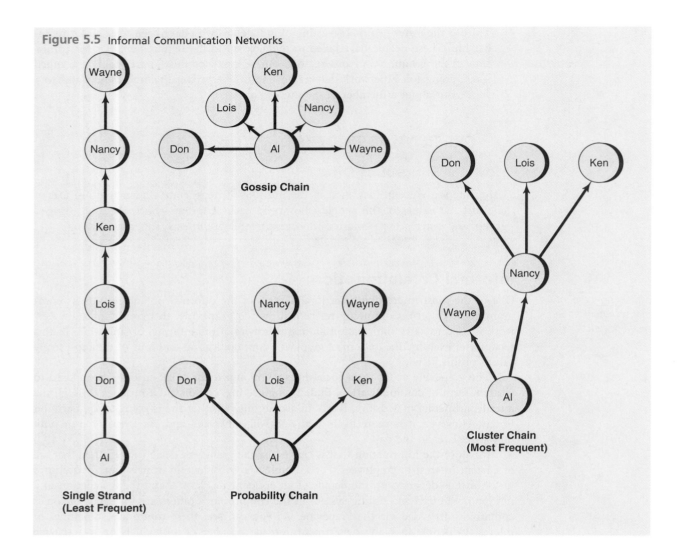

A third way in which information is passed through the grapevine is on a random basis: One person arbitrarily tells another, who goes on and tells one or two others (see Figure 5.5). This is known as the **probability chain,** and, of the three chains we have discussed, it is the most widely used.

However, the most common grapevine network is the **cluster chain**. Using this network, one person tells two or three people who, in turn, either keep the information to themselves or pass it on to two or three other people. As a result, we have one individual passing the message to a cluster of people, and those who pass it on tell it to another cluster. In Figure 5.5, for example, Al tells the message to Wayne and Nancy. Wayne keeps it to himself, but Nancy passes it on to Don, Lois, and Ken. Al and Nancy are the links with their respective clusters.

Carrying this idea one step further, we can conclude that if one hundred people learn of a particular happening, such as the firing of a top manager, it is very likely that only fifteen or twenty people have spread the word. These individuals are known as liaison people because they serve as the links between those who have the information and those who do not. Commenting on the predominance of the cluster chain, Keith Davis has reported that in one company he investigated, a quality control problem had occurred, and 68 percent of the executives knew about it. However, only 20 percent of them had spread the information. In another firm he studied, 81 percent of the executives knew that a top manager planned to resign, but only 11 percent had passed the news to the others.[13]

Selective Communication. Liaison people are very selective in the way they communicate. There are some people to whom they pass information and others whom they bypass. For example, Ed Anderson has just learned that he is to be promoted to vice president of international operations. However, the formal announcement will not be made for ten days. Ed is very eager to tell someone, but he must be selective in leaking the news, for he does not want to tell anyone who will circulate the story back to top management for fear that they might reverse the promotion decision. Ed chooses his best friend, Bob James, to tell about the impending promotion. Bob is delighted and, realizing the confidential nature of the communiqué, passes the information to other people whom he trusts to treat the matter confidentially. Ten days later, the formal announcement is made and, to most people in the organization, it comes as a surprise. Furthermore, even those who knew of the promotion through the grapevine are careful not to let on. If any one of them does indicate prior knowledge, he or she will be bypassed by future grapevine messages.

Bypassing people, however, is not always a sign of distrust or unreliability. The grapevine bypasses those who are not supposed to get a particular message. For example, in one company, the president planned a party for twenty-five top executives. The grapevine learned about the party but did not know for sure which executives were on the list. As a result, only those who they thought would be invited were told about the party by informal communicators. As it turned out, twenty-three executives learned of the upcoming announcement, and, of these, twenty-two were actually on the list. The cluster chain is indeed a selective communication network.

Causes for Grapevine Activity. Some people tend to be very active on the grapevine, whereas others are fairly inactive. However, given the proper situation and motivation, just about anyone will become active on the grapevine. Research reveals that there is little difference between the activities of men and women on the grapevine. If people feel they have cause to be active, they will be. Let us discuss four of the most likely causes of grapevine activity.

First, if people *lack information about a situation*, they try to fill in these gaps via informal channels. Sometimes, these efforts lead to distortion of facts or fabrication of rumors. For example, not long ago, a company president informed a senior executive that his office was to be refurbished. He was to be given a new desk, bookcases, furniture, and a very expensive rug. This was a reward for the successful advertising program he had developed for one of the firm's new product lines. As soon as the man's office was torn up, the grapevine began to hum. Before the afternoon was over, rumor had it that the executive had been fired and that his office was being made ready for a new advertising manager. Also, the employees associated with the manufacture and sale of the new product line all became very concerned, fearing that the next step would be a reduction in their own workforce.

Second, people are active on the grapevine when there is *insecurity in a situation*. Continuing our illustration, people associated with the new product were quick to contact the sales manager to ask whether there was any truth to the rumor. The manager informed them that sales for the product were running 37 percent ahead of projections. After putting these facts together with those about the work being done in the senior executive's office, the workers realized that the executive was being rewarded for the product's success. They then passed this information back through the grapevine, and informal communications related to this development ceased. There was nothing more to talk about.

Figure 5.6
Causes for Grapevine
Activity

- Information is lacking
- Insecurity in a situation
- Personal interest is involved
- Possession of new information

Third, there is grapevine activity whenever *people have a personal interest in a situation*. For example, if Mary and her boss get into an argument over the monthly cost control report, Mary's friends will tend to be active on the grapevine. Likewise, if management decides to lay off fifteen salespeople, the rest of the sales force will be interested in the situation because they have a stake in what is going on. People want to share among themselves any information about what is happening in the part of the world that is important to them.

Fourth, people are most active on the grapevine when *they have information that is recent rather than stale*. Research shows that the greatest spread of information occurs immediately after it is known. When most people learn the news, grapevine activity slows down. Figure 5.6 summarizes the causes for grapevine activity.

Managing the Grapevine.   History tells us the grapevine cannot be abolished, rubbed out, hidden, or stopped. However, some managers believe that if left alone, it will go away. Reality shows that if suppressed in one place, it will pop up in another. If the source is cut off, it merely moves to another one.

By providing a flow of accurate and timely information through the formal communication system about key issues and events that affect employees, management can minimize the negative affects of rumors running through the grapevine. Managers should keep employees informed and learn to listen to what is being said in the rumor. They should gather information about the extent of the rumor, its accuracy, and the level of anxiety it has generated; then prepare a formal response to the rumor.[14]

Managers should identify key communicators in the grapevine. Then the managers can leak important information into the grapevine. Some companies go so far as to create a rumor hotline or a rumor center.

As discussed in this chapter, the informal organization differs from the formal organization in several ways, as illustrated in Figure 5.7.

The Role of Informal Communication Networks.   Research shows that communication among members of the informal organization helps facilitate knowledge exchange within the company.[15] For example, managers receive information from other people far more frequently than from impersonal sources, such as their PC archives,

Figure 5.7
Informal versus Formal
Groups

Informal Groups	Formal Groups
Roles and norms are flexible	Roles and norms are rigid
Membership is voluntary	Positions are chosen
Organizational structure is loose	Organizational structure is formal
Size is smaller	Size is larger
Sentimental and traditional	Utilitarian and functional

Internet, or databases, which asserts the importance of informal networks in organizations. The integration of knowledge contributes to a company's competitive advantage in the global marketplace.[16]

Informal networks by nature are highly dynamic and difficult to identify. Members in informal networks are identified as **nodes**, a central point in the system, that keep networks alive by their links with other nodes. These links are defined by their social or personal relationships with others. In a study, Yukika Awazu identified five roles played by members of informal networks. These roles are:[17]

- Central connectors
- Boundary spanners
- Gatekeepers
- Bridges
- Experts

Central connectors know a lot about their workplace, can identify what knowledge is needed and where the information is located, and can point people in the right direction. They provide shortcuts through the formal system.

Boundary spanners know more than their assigned area of work. They are experts in other areas and often speak more than one language, making them invaluable in international operations. They are good at collecting knowledge outside of their local networks.

Gatekeepers control knowledge. They protect local networks from threats and rumors from the outside by filtering and screening unnecessary information. Gatekeepers monitor knowledge management processes and tools that people use.

Bridges connect people who do not share common backgrounds, skills, or experiences. They are trusted translators for employees who speak another language. They are good at connecting people who have opposite opinions, such as in conflicts where mutual knowledge is missing. Bridges can span this gap.

Experts are very knowledgeable about certain types of products, subjects, or processes, and they tend to have very focused and concentrated experience. Experts learn from experience, and they identify, extract, and provide important knowledge to others in a way that is easy to understand.

Each role is capable of integrating knowledge within the informal organization, which ultimately affects the entire company. The flow of knowledge in the informal network is highly dynamic compared to the formal structure because the links and connections in the informal network are not formally defined. Because these roles can influence the type of knowledge communicated, they can affect the competitive advantage of a company. Companies must constantly implement changes to stay ahead of their competition, and therefore, companies need the support of the informal network. The informal organization provides a number of other benefits.

CHECK YOUR UNDERSTANDING

How Do Grapevine Networks Work?

Draw a diagram of each communication network:

1. Single strand
2. Gossip chain
3. Probability chain
4. Cluster chain

Identify the primary benefits associated with the informal organization.

Benefits of the Informal Organization

Every organization has an informal structure. There must be some very important benefits to be derived from its existence; otherwise it would cease to function. One of the most obvious reasons for an informal organization to exist is that most of the employees—both workers and managers—like it, want it, use it, and benefit from it! In this section, we examine five major benefits to be derived from the informal organization.

1. Getting things done.
2. Lightening managerial workloads.
3. Providing job satisfaction.
4. Serving as a safety valve for employees' emotions.
5. Providing feedback to the manager.

Getting Things Done

One of the primary benefits of the informal organization is that it supplements the formal organization in getting things done. Howard, a supervisor in the components assembly department, needs some help in securing parts from an outside supplier. The company's purchasing department is dragging its feet on the matter. Howard's friend Claire is the comptroller's secretary and a cousin of Greg, who is in charge of purchasing. Howard calls Claire and tells her his problem. Claire contacts Greg, who calls in Eddie, one of his assistants. Their discussion might go something like this:

Greg: How come Howard down in the manufacturing section is having trouble getting parts from outside suppliers?

Eddie: Is he calling to complain again?

Greg: No, I got the message from someone else in the firm. Apparently this order is jeopardizing the production schedule. What is its current status?

Eddie: Well, it's sitting on my desk, but I wanted to get some of my other paperwork cleared up before sending the order to the supplier.

Greg: Forget about sending it. Call it in this afternoon and tell them we need those parts by tomorrow.

Eddie: Okay, I'll get on it right now.

Later in the afternoon, Howard gets a call from Eddie telling him the parts are on the way, and they arrive the next morning.

This flow of communication is diagrammed in Figure 5.8. Note that Howard used the authority of the purchasing manager to help him get the needed parts. However, he worked through the informal organization in contacting Claire, and she used the network in reaching Greg. Without the informal organization, everyone would go through established channels, and it would take a lot longer to accomplish anything. Many of the organization's best workers would leave, and those who remained would simply stop putting out extra effort. After all, who wants to spend all his or her time fighting organizational red tape?

Lightening Managerial Workloads

Another benefit of the informal organization is to lighten managerial workloads. When managers realize the informal organization is on their side, they are more likely to delegate authority and rely on their subordinates to get things done. This results in looser,

Figure 5.8 The Informal Organization in Action

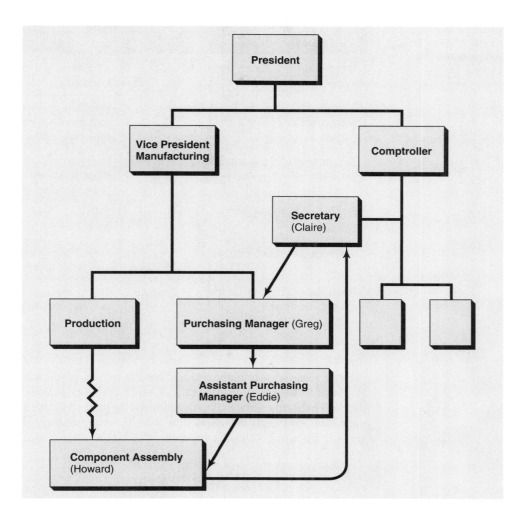

more generalized control and often creates a feeling of trust among the workers, who respond by showing the manager they are indeed reliable. The outcome is higher productivity.

Providing Job Satisfaction

An accompanying benefit is job satisfaction, a term that relates to the favorableness or unfavorableness with which employees view their work. This topic is discussed in greater depth later in this text; however, here we will briefly examine a few of its aspects. Satisfaction is a relative matter in that whether people are satisfied or dissatisfied is determined by how well their expectations fit with what they are given. If Tony has been led to believe that the company stresses imagination and creativity and finds himself instead saddled with rules and procedures, he will be dissatisfied. Conversely, if Dick expects his new job to pay well but to be boring and, to his surprise, he finds the work both interesting and challenging, he will be very satisfied.

Job satisfaction is also related to absenteeism, turnover, and productivity. The higher the satisfaction level, the lower the likelihood of absenteeism and turnover and the higher the likelihood of productivity. When employees find the work satisfying, they

Table 5.1
Formal Working Groups
versus Formal and
Informal Teams

Formal Working Groups	Formal and Informal Teams
The group has a strong, clearly focused leader.	All members of the team share in providing leadership.
Each person in the group is individually accountable.	Each person in the group is individually and collectively responsible for the success of the group's efforts.
The purpose of the group is in total sync with the organization's mission.	The specific purpose for the team's existence is defined by the organization and team members.
Each individual produces work products or outputs.	The group collectively produces work products or outputs.
Meetings are run efficiently.	Meetings involve open-ended discussions and active problem-solving decisions.
The members discuss, decide, and delegate work to be done.	The members discuss, decide, and carry out the work to be done.

derive a sense of meaningfulness and tend to remain on the job. Much of this satisfaction is related to the social environment in which the work is done. Thus, the informal organization helps to create a climate conducive to high productivity. As a result, the participants are not merely members of a working group but are team members in the true sense of the word. Table 5.1 illustrates this idea.

Serving as a Safety Valve

The grapevine also functions as a safety valve for employees' emotions. It lets the workers blow off steam and release some of their job pressures. When people are angry over something, they need some release for their frustration and resentment. The informal organization plays a role in this release. For example, if Don and his boss had an argument and Don told his boss where to get off, Don could be fired. Instead, Don complains to his fellow workers. By sharing his problem with other employees, Don is able to release much of his pent-up anger in a way that does not threaten his job. Also, after he talks about the issue for a while, it is likely to appear minor, and he can turn his attention back to doing his job.

Providing Feedback

Perhaps the greatest overall benefit of the informal organization is that of providing the manager with feedback. The grapevine reflects how the workers feel about the company, the managers, and the work. By tapping the communication flow, the manager can learn what is going on. If a manager makes a bad decision or does not know how to supervise the subordinates properly, this information will eventually be carried back to the boss. What better way to protect one's job than by learning of problems through the grapevine and working to correct them before the boss asks, "What's this I hear about you having trouble with …?" Wise managers use the grapevine to receive and to send information.

CHECK YOUR UNDERSTANDING

Of What Value Are Informal Organizations?
Discuss five ways managers can benefit from using the informal organization.

List some of the disadvantages associated with the informal organization.

Disadvantages of the Informal Organization

Despite its potential benefits, the informal organization has disadvantages. The most common are:

1. Resistance to change
2. Goal conflict
3. Conformity problems
4. Rumor

Resistance to Change

One of the greatest disadvantages of the informal organization is its *resistance to change*. Often, the organization systematically ignores or only partially carries out directives related to such changes as new work procedures or rules. The overriding philosophy of many informal organizations is "live and let live." They do not want the status quo changed. This behavior often is labeled *homeostasis*, which is the tendency of a group to maintain things as they are.

Of course, change is inevitable. Technological innovations, plant redesign, diversity issues, downsizing, and competitive developments in the external environment, as well as global issues, all require the organization to adapt operations to meet these conditions. If an innovative process is developed that will reduce current operating costs by 33 percent, a company must buy it. However, part of this cost savings may be a result of personnel reduction, which explains why the informal organization will fight the change. It does not want any of its members to be fired nor, does the informal organization approve of people being reassigned. If the company breaks up a cohesive group, productivity may decrease.

Another reason that the informal organization resists change is that work standards or quotas often are increased. In many cases, change generates new job demands; in all cases, it brings about higher efficiency (or at least attempts to achieve efficiency). For example, if a company establishes new work procedures, it is usually because a faster way of doing the job has been discovered. If work assignments are changed, it is because the firm has found a way to get more output with the same number of people. The informal organization resists such efficiency moves for three reasons.

First, as mentioned, people like the status quo and believe that any change will disrupt their work environment. DaimlerChrysler is a good example. Before Daimler sold Chrysler it controlled the company and wanted all of its divisions to be profitable. When Chrysler began having problems and incurring great financial losses, the German management put Dieter Zetsche, one of its own managers, in charge of U.S. operations and began a massive restructuring program. One thing was certain: The informal organizations at Chrysler would work to minimize the effects of these actions because the changes upset the status quo. Despite these actions, Chrysler made great strides in improving quality and operating profits.[18]

Second, if employees conform and do more work, management may believe it can introduce change any time it wants, and it may begin regarding employees as mere factors of production who need not be consulted in advance about changes. By resisting, the informal organization ensures that management keeps the human element in mind when introducing change.

Third, many members of the informal organization believe it is unfair for management to introduce efficiency measures and keep all the profit for the company. If employees are going to do more work, they should be paid more money. Keep in mind, however, that this is not always a fair argument. If the firm buys a new machine for $500,000, the cost savings may allow it to pay for the machine and keep costs at a competitive level but may not increase profit. Of course, not being privy to such financial data, the informal organization may simply assume that changes in the work environment always increase profit.

Goal Conflict

Whenever someone is asked to pursue two objectives that work against each other, **goal conflict** occurs. For example, Joe wants to be a member of the informal organization but also wants to meet the work quota assigned by management. The informal organization quota is only 80 percent of the company quota. Clearly, Joe cannot be totally loyal to both.

As we discover later in this chapter, management must carefully cultivate mutual interests with informal groups so as to integrate the goals of both. This is particularly true for young members of the informal group who, according to research, often have very high monetary expectations, a goal that often conflicts with management's desire to control costs closely. A survey by JobTrak.com found that 25 percent of today's college graduates expect to make their first million before they are 30 years old, and another 27 percent believe they will achieve this goal before they reach the age of 40. Only 29 percent of the 2,500 people who were surveyed believed they would never make a million dollars in their lifetime.[19] This is not an area where the firm will ever achieve perfect harmony, as there will always be some differences between the formal and informal organizations, but management must strive to reduce the differences to an acceptable level.

Conformity

Closely related to goal conflict is the problem of **conformity**. Group norms and sanctions are used in persuading members to accept informal goals. Sometimes, these norms and sanctions are so strong that individuals feel compelled to go along with the group despite their own inclinations. More likely, however, the informal organization becomes so much a part of the employees' work lives that they are unaware of its presence. As a result, they conform without consciously weighing the pros and cons of such action; even if their conformity was pointed out to them, they would be unwilling to deviate from these informal norms.

Rumor

The most undesirable feature of the informal organization is **rumor**. Many people believe the word is synonymous with the total product of the grapevine, but this is not so. Rumor is the unverified or untrue part of grapevine information. Communication theorists often define rumor as a product of interest and ambiguity.[20]

$$\text{Rumor} = \text{Interest} \times \text{Ambiguity}$$

The logic behind this equation is simple. First, rumor can exist only if the issue is of interest to someone. You undoubtedly have never heard a rumor about the impact of the

Table 5.2
Benefits and
Disadvantages of the
Informal Organization

Benefits	Disadvantages
Helps get things done	Resists change
Lightens the manager's load	Goal conflicts arise
Provides job satisfaction	Creates conformity problems
Serves as a safety valve	Generates rumors
Provides feedback to managers	

Ice Age on the existence of the penguin. However, you may have passed on a rumor about the type of examination given by a math professor in whose class you were currently registered. Second, rumor is unnecessary if all the facts about a situation are known. If the professor told you the final examination would come from the last ten chapters of the book, ambiguity would be much less than if the questions were to be drawn from all twenty chapters and all class discussion. Ambiguity would be further reduced if the professor gave out a list of fifty equations from which the twenty-five examination problems would be drawn exclusively. Ambiguity could never be totally eliminated (which twenty-five equations?), but it would be reduced.

Rumor is both maintained and magnified through the use of selective filtering and elaboration. **Selective filtering** involves the screening of rumor so that part of the story is maintained and the rest is discarded. Usually, the part that is kept is of greatest interest to the person repeating the rumor. This is then elaborated on; details are added and rearranged to fit the individual's point of view. **Elaboration** thus contributes to the further modification of a rumor.

As you can see, the informal organization plays an important role in getting things done within a company, as well as being a detriment to some managers. The benefits and disadvantages of informal organizations are summarized in Table 5.2.

 CHECK YOUR UNDERSTANDING

How Can Informal Organizations Be a Detriment to Managers?

Discuss each of the following:

1. Resistance to change
2. Goal conflict
3. Conformity problems
4. Rumor

Cite some of the ways in which a manager can deal with the informal organization.

Dealing with the Informal Organization

In dealing with the informal organization, the manager must undertake two major tasks: Recognize the inevitability of the informal network and attempt to influence its direction so that the goals of the formal and informal organizations are in harmony. The manager must also stay abreast of changes within the informal organization and work to create an environment of trust with the members. This is particularly important when trying to retain highly talented employees because there is such a demand for their services by other organizations.[21]

Recognize Its Inevitability

Some managers believe the disadvantages of the informal organization more than outweigh the benefits. As a result, they try to develop means of stamping it out. However, this approach is never completely successful. Using the grapevine as a representative segment of the informal organization, Keith Davis has offered the following explanation of its inevitability:

> In a sense, the grapevine is a human birthright, because whenever people congregate into groups, the grapevine is sure to develop. It may use smoke signals, jungle tom-toms, taps on the prison wall, ordinary conversation, or some other method, but it will always be there. Organizations cannot "fire" the grapevine, because they did not hire it. It is simply there.[22]

Because the informal organization is inevitable, the manager must develop methods for influencing it.[23]

Influence Its Direction

One of the most direct ways for a manager to influence the informal organization is by tapping its grapevine, learning what is being communicated, and countering any negative rumors by getting the formal organization's message into the channel. This can be done by learning who the liaison people in the informal network are and using them as a point of entry. The manager must also work closely with these people and show them that the company is interested in them and views them as important resources. For example, a Gallup Organization study of two million employees at seven hundred companies found that an employee's productivity and length of stay at the company are determined by the employee's relationship with the immediate supervisor. People join companies and leave managers.[24]

Of course, if the manager begins feeding rumors or half-truths back into the grapevine, the liaison people will either modify the message or simply refuse to carry the message. The manager cannot fight rumor with rumor. He or she must determine whether the information in the grapevine is accurate and, when it is inaccurate, must substitute correct information.

Do managers really use the grapevine to influence the informal organization? Research shows they do. Jay Knippen studied the grapevine in a large grocery store and found that although employees knew only 42 percent of the grapevine information, managers knew about 70 percent. Furthermore, while the managers accounted for only a small percentage of the 170 employees, they initiated almost 50 percent of the grapevine information. On average, each manager told eight other people, whereas the typical employee told four. The managers were not waiting to see what information the employees were passing through the grapevine. Rather, they were using this informal channel to get their own messages across.[25] Other research supports these conclusions. For example, the American Productivity & Quality Center conducted a study to determine how the best organizations create an environment that promotes teamwork. They found that one of the most important things management has to do is to share knowledge and keep everyone apprised of what is going on.[26]

Secrets, as well as rumors, are a part of corporate life, and managers should not feel obligated to correct any whispered misperceptions, especially when they might betray the confidences the manager is expected to keep. Kerry J. Sulkowicz, a psychoanalyst, advises

INFLUENCING THE INFORMAL ORGANIZATION

There are a number of ways to influence the informal organization. Most of them relate to how you interact with members of this group. In particular, you have to keep in mind four guidelines.

First, when you communicate with the informal organization, always *convey the fact that the message you are providing has importance*. Do not wait too long, or your listener will begin to wander off mentally, and you will have trouble getting him or her back. For example, if you want to tell Jack something of importance, say it right up front. "Jack, this is something that you'll be interested in. It directly relates to the type of problem you've been investigating in the shipping department." Notice how quickly you have zeroed in on your main point.

Second, *speak authoritatively and with conviction*. Do not end your sentences with a question mark. Phrase them so that they are factual and accurately represent your point of view. If you can make them sound like the other party should also accept them as such, so much the better. Also remember to maintain eye contact as you speak.

Third, *do not give the other person much chance to disagree or attempt to prove you wrong*. This undermines your efforts. For example, if you need to have something done, do not say, "Tim, I think this is a good time for you to handle that cost control report." This sounds too wishy-washy, and Tim may say, "No, I don't think it is." If this happens, you are going to be engaged in an argument regarding whether the time is right. A better way to handle the situation is to say, "Tim, now is the time for you to handle that cost control report." He may still disagree, but you have reduced the chances of this happening. Remember that if you narrow the options, you improve your chances of dealing effectively with the informal organization. For example, instead of asking someone when she would like her vacation, figure out what weeks are available and offer only those weeks: "Mary, would you like your vacation during the first two weeks of August or the first two weeks of September?" This approach saves you time because it eliminates all the other weeks of the year, which have already been taken by people in the unit who have more seniority.

Fourth, *know when to listen*. Sometimes, you can influence the informal organization by listening to others. For example, if you are interested in finding out why so many people throughout the organization are coming late to work, you might ask, "Frank, why is everyone showing up late all the time?" Frank may know the answer, and this information will be useful to you. One company vice president found out why so many people were leaving work early. It was a reaction to his example. Every day, the senior vice president would leave at 4:30 P.M., and the other employees would begin leaving within five minutes. They reasoned that if the senior vice president did not think it was important to stay until 5:00 P.M., why should they? During one of his informal chats with some of the employees, the vice president indirectly learned of the effect that his behavior was having. From that day on, he made it a point to stay until 5:00 P.M. or later. He listened and learned.

In dealing with the informal organization, one must know when to take the initiative and when to hold back. Both can be important strategies in influencing people.

---

that if someone asks if a rumor, regardless of size, is true, managers should be honest about the position they are in. A manager can say "I've been involved in those discussions, and I know it's hard to stay focused with all this uncertainty. But I'm just not free to talk about it." It is true that people who are not in the know try to read between the lines of what you say and do. But still, it is better than lying about whether or not you know what is going on.[27]

The purpose of management-initiated messages should be to smooth the way for more cooperation between formal and informal organizations. The manager's objective should be to create conditions that help align the goals of both groups. When this is accomplished, the manager will find that resistance to change is minimized, rumors are reduced, and overall organizational cooperation is achieved. Several ways that managers can influence the informal organization are discussed in the "Human Relations in Action" box.

Stay Abreast of Changes

The informal organization is continually undergoing change. Some people are dropping out of its ranks, while others are becoming members. Sometimes, this is a result of the membership itself, which accepts and rejects members and thus keeps membership in a state of flux. Often, it is a result of people leaving the company or being transferred to other units or departments. Because transferred people are no longer in the nearby vicinity, they will drop out of the local informal organization and, in all likelihood, be replaced by others. Managers who want to deal effectively with the informal organization have to keep abreast of the changing membership.

Managers must also remember that different problems will bring different informal leaders to the fore. If a university is having a problem with its part-time employees and they are unionized, the shop steward or union spokesperson will probably be the informal leader. This individual is chosen because he or she is perceived as someone who can help the group achieve its goals. This person is seen as able to wield power. If a hospital is having a salary dispute with its nursing staff, the nurse who informally represents the group may be chosen because of her job experience and tenure. She is chosen on the basis of work-related expertise. If a work team on a loading dock sets a goal of loading 10 percent more trucks than any other team, the individual who is the fastest worker may be chosen as the informal leader. This person's informal authority is based on his or her job expertise.

Because informal organizational membership is continually in a state of flux, the manager must continually ask the question: Who is in charge of the informal group and why? The answer will help the manager decide how to influence or deal most effectively with the informal group.

✔ CHECK YOUR UNDERSTANDING

How can managers effectively deal with the informal organization?

1. What does "recognize its inevitability" mean?
2. How can the informal organization be influenced?
3. How can the manager stay abreast of changes in the informal organization?

Discuss how to successfully complete an employment interview.

Career Advisor

The Interview

When you get an interview, you are halfway toward your goal of a job offer. Now you want to be sure that you do not flub your chance. The first thing you should do is learn something about the company.

- What goods or services does it produce?
- How much did it gross last year?
- What is its reputation?
- What qualities is it looking for in applicants?

During the course of the interview, you will want to learn more about the company. Prepare a list of no more than a dozen questions that you can think of before the interview, and that can be grouped into the four categories below. Take these questions with you to the interview.

1. Company questions—market share, projected growth, and new products
2. Industry questions—growth, change, and technology
3. Position questions—responsibilities and duties, travel, and compensation
4. Opportunity questions—potential for growth, advancement, and promotion

If you know about the company, this is likely to impress the interviewer and improve your chances of a job offer. However, do not stop there. Develop some questions that demonstrate your knowledge of your field. Let the interviewer know that you know what you are talking about. Be prepared to go on the offensive.

To a large degree, the success of your interview will depend on your ability to discover the needs of the company and to empathize with the interviewer. In addition to establishing empathy, Bill Radin has identified four intangible fundamentals to a successful interview. They are enthusiasm, technical interest, confidence, and intensity. First, the interviewer will try to learn your level of interest in the job; therefore, your level of enthusiasm may make the difference in whether or not you are selected to fill the position. Often the more enthusiastic applicants are chosen. Second, interviewers look for people who love what they do and like the nitty-gritty of their job. Third, the applicants who are sure of their abilities will most likely be favored. The unsure or negative applicants will not make a positive impression in the interview. And last, you do not want to come across as flat in your interview. There is nothing wrong with being a laid-back person, but sleepwalkers rarely get hired.[28]

Also keep in mind that the interviewer is checking to determine whether personal chemistry might exist between you and the organization. "While degrees, experience and skills count, they are only part of the overall picture. It's a straightforward concept: hire the right people and build a better—and more profitable—organization."[29]

Southwest Airlines, a Dallas-based carrier that employs more than 35,000 people, spares no effort to find the perfect blend of energy, humor, team spirit, and self-confidence. The first step in its hiring process is to take a group of applicants into a room and observe how they interact. Southwest's vice president of people, Beverly Carmichael, might ask a dozen or so participants to tell about a time when their sense of humor helped them or what their personal motto is. Although most responses are not memorable, they provide clues as to how a person thinks and copes. "It's not necessarily the answer, but the way a person answers," she says.[30]

UPS, which has 360,000 employees worldwide, focuses its entire recruiting, training, and internal-promotion process on attitude. Applicants "undergo at least two levels of behavioral interviews that focus on issues such as motivation, commitment and building working relationships."[31]

Other qualities that companies look for in applicants are perseverance, drive, integrity, and good communication skills.[32]

Appearance. How you dress, act, and talk are all important. Upon meeting a person for the first time, research tells us, you have about a minute to affirm or change the opinion that person forms about you. In the first 45 seconds, the new person will form an opinion, and in the next 15 seconds, you will affirm or change that opinion by what you say and do. So, it is important what you wear to an interview and how you act because you are going to be judged. Is a suit always necessary? No, how you dress should vary depending on the type of job you are seeking and the type of industry. For example, an applicant seeking a mechanic's job would dress differently than a person seeking a management position in a financial firm. The applicant seeking the mechanic's job would not come in his or her dirty overalls but in a conservatively dressed manner, such as an open collar shirt, clean pants, and maybe a jacket; whereas, the applicant for the management position would dress in a suit, white shirt, and tie. The applicant should check his nails to be sure they are clean. This is a sign that the applicant tends to details.

People applying for technical jobs usually do not need a suit, says Carole Martin, author of *Boost Your Interview IQ*. A collared shirt and khakis or slacks would work. For higher-level positions, upgrade your attire, and do not forget your hairstyle. For government job interviews, wear a conservatively colored suit; this is applicable for both females and males. Do not be flashy, and keep jewelry to a minimum. You want to show you are responsible, trustworthy, and honest. If, however, you are asked to wear business-casual dress, for example, to an interview, then do it. The company may be testing an applicant on how well he or she can follow the simplest of instructions. Deciding on whether or not to wear pantsuits is often a difficult decision for women. Unless you know that pantsuits are appropriate, it may be safer to wear a suit, dress, or skirt, blouse, and jacket.

Some applicants feel that dressing differently for an interview from the way they normally dress is misrepresenting them and feel it is pointless. What they do not realize is that it shows they do not know how to play the game—the process of getting a job offer. Wearing the appropriate attire on the job continues to be important and, in some companies, can make a difference in whether or not an employee is promoted. Women, in particular, should understand that clothes designed to wear to parties—low neck, tight fitting, sheer fabrics, for example—are not the type of clothes appropriate to wear to the office.

Christina Binkley wrote an article about dressing for interviews for the *Wall Street Journal* and received a number of interesting responses from companies. Some of these responses are: If you want a job, your shoes should be well made; women's shoes should be close-toed and heeled, and men should avoid tassels. Men's suits should be well made, dark-colored, or if tan is appropriate, with a blue shirt, not a white one. Women should avoid pastel and crimson colored suits, French manicures, and wet-looking lip gloss. Men should avoid hair gel, and everyone should avoid fake tans. Avoid low-riding pants and spit out your gum. Sit up straight and make eye contact.[33]

When going on an interview, it is best to dress on the conservative side. With that in mind, Carole Martin has assembled a list of things to avoid, what she calls *fashion blunders*.[34]

1. Your nails should be groomed and neat—no wild nail polish and no extremely long or uncut nails.
2. Do not wear jewelry that jangles; wear only one earring per ear; and wear no nose jewelry and no more than two rings per hand.
3. Wear up-to-date shoes—no mules or slides or open-toed shoes.
4. Stockings should be worn with dresses.
5. Suits should be in style and in good condition.
6. Skirts should be no more than three inches above the knee. Do not wear Capri pants or leggings.
7. Leather jackets are not good for interviewing and neither are turtlenecks for men.
8. Purses should be conservative, inconspicuous, and in good condition and should not be printed or trendy.

Manners.   Positive nonverbal communication messages can be reinforced by your verbal communications. For example, greet the interviewer with a firm handshake, maintain eye contact with the interviewer, use positive voice tones, and demonstrate an interest by showing your attention and enthusiasm. Be sure to listen carefully to what is being asked and answer with clear, concise answers using proper grammar. Be honest and do not exaggerate and by all means do not be negative. It is best to refer to concrete experiences from previous jobs.

The nonverbal messages that you send through your handshake, posture, smile, and eye contact show your level of excitement and your level of confidence. Talking with your hands is very natural, but you need to keep it in moderation. You do not want your hand gestures to distract the interviewer. Some of the most distracting behaviors are playing with your hair, clicking pen tops, tapping feet, or unconsciously touching parts of the body.[35]

Interview Etiquette. Arriving on time to the interview is very important. It sends a signal that you are punctual and indicates responsibility on your part. Introduce yourself before someone has to ask who you are. Always ask for the correct spelling and the exact title of the interviewer. If a business card is available, ask for one. It is best to never use the first name, unless invited to, of the interviewer. Promptly after the interview, write a thank you note to the interviewer. Even after the interview, you should try to impress the interviewer with your skills and talents.[36]

Keep things on a positive note. If you are asked about your ability to interact well with others, talk about your personality strengths. If you are asked why you are leaving your current job, discuss your desire for increased responsibility and challenge. Do not talk negatively about either yourself or your current employer. Such discussion casts a pall over the interview and can result in a missed job offer.

Typical Interviewer Questions. "The guiding principle behind any question to a job applicant is: Can the employer demonstrate a job-related necessity for asking the question?"[37] Legally, employers are prohibited from asking questions that are not job related.

Aside from the information on your résumé, interviewers tend to ask behavioral questions. For example, Chili's Grill and Bar Restaurant has been able to fill manager's jobs faster by using an online interview system. Unlike other online assessment systems, this system includes questions that use a behavioral-interview technique. Applicants are asked to give specific information about past performance and how they have risen to challenges. Chili's asks applicants "to describe the most effective idea they implemented to boost employee morale and create a positive work environment." The applicant is asked to give contact information for verification purposes.[38]

Other typical behavioral questions are:

1. What have you done to prepare yourself for a job with this company?
2. What are you looking for in an employer?
3. Why did you apply with us?
4. After ten years with this firm, what do you hope to be doing?
5. What are your long-range objectives?

The general rule under the Americans with Disabilities Act is that an employer may not ask "disability-related" questions until after it makes a conditional job offer to an applicant. Here are four samples of questions that may be asked during the preoffer stage:

- Is there any setting or equipment that will facilitate the interview process for you?
- Is there any specific technology that you currently use or have used in your previous jobs that assisted you in your work performance?
- Other than technology, what supports did you have in previous jobs? If none, are there any you would benefit from?
- Provide an example of how you use technology to carry out job duties.[39]

For a more complete list of questions, check out "100 Top Interview Questions" on the Web site of Monster.com. At that site, you will find additional articles giving a wealth of information about interviewing. If you are prepared with answers for the most likely questions, your interview is more likely to proceed smoothly. Review the questions and answers posed in Figure 5.9. It offers some additional guidelines for handling interviews, especially difficult ones.

Figure 5.9 Acing a Tough Interview

Any job interview can be tense, but in today's tough job market, more and more executives are using a technique called the stress interview. Their goal is not to verify the claims on your resume—that can be done easily—but to see how you react when you're pressured and to test your professionalism and confidence. Typically, the interviewer sets up the job seeker with softball questions and a friendly manner, then tries to throw her off balance by switching suddenly to much tougher queries. The biggest mistake you can make is to take the probing personally and respond with anger. Instead, phrase your answers in a way that demonstrates positive rather than negative traits, sell yourself to the interviewer, and try to turn the discussion back to the job itself. And take heart: Only top candidates are put through the wringer this way. (The job seeker's words are in screened boxes.)

PROBE FOR WEAKNESS Your resume does a fine job of pointing out your professional strengths and skills, but I'd like to find out more about you as a person. For example, what would you say is your greatest weakness?

POSITIVE "WEAKNESS" I always give 110% to whatever project I'm working on, so I get very frustrated when other members of the team don't pull their weight. I've been trying very hard lately to lead by example rather than express my frustration openly.

FORMER WEAKNESS When I started in sales, I tended to overbook my appointments. Then I realized I wasn't devoting enough time to each call, giving short shrift to some clients. Since then, I've learned not to schedule more calls than I can handle effectively.

JOB-HISTORY PROBE Going over your resume, I notice that you've changed jobs several times in the past few years. Why is that?

LAST-JOB PROBE You've been out of work for a long time. Since you clearly didn't leave your last job for a new one, I assume you were let go. Why?

STAGNATION PROBE You've been with XYZ Company in the same position for five years now. Why haven't you been able to move up?

JOB-HISTORY DEFENSE As you can see, my job moves haven't been lateral; they've all led to positions of greater responsibility. Now that I've gained the experience, I'm looking to settle down with a company that will keep me challenged—like this one.

LAST-JOB DEFENSE Like so many places these days, my company was looking to cut payroll costs and wound up eliminating hundreds of jobs last year. I volunteered for the buyout program because I felt I'd reached the limit of what I could do there anyway.

STAGNATION DEFENSE The new positions that have opened up have gone to employees who have a lot more seniority than I do. That's why I'm looking for a company that offers a real opportunity to move up. What can you tell me about the possibilities for advancement here?

JOB-HISTORY FOLLOW-UP With your history of job-hopping, I'm not sure that you'd be content to stay in one place for long. Would you say you're the kind of person who gets bored easily?

LAST-JOB FOLLOW-UP You've been looking for a new position for several months now, apparently without any luck. What seems to be the problem?

STAGNATION FOLLOW-UP Being in the same job at the same company for such a long time can make you stale. How will you cope with the challenge of a new job in a new organization?

CLOSING JOB-HISTORY DEFENSE Not at all. But I do enjoy being challenged. In fact, what's been most exciting in my previous positions has been finding new ways to keep a product fresh in our customers' eyes. Am I right in thinking that's a crucial part of the job here?

CLOSING LAST-JOB DEFENSE I'm not looking for just another paycheck. My severance was generous enough to allow me to take the time to find a company that's really right for me, where I can make a real contribution. Can you tell me more about precisely what this job entails?

CLOSING STAGNATION DEFENSE It's precisely because I don't want to get stale that I'm looking for new opportunities. From what I understand, your company offers just that. Can you tell me more about the kind of challenges I'd face in this job?

Source: Stephen M. Pollan and Mark Levine, Lifescripts! 1996. Used by permission of the author.

ASKING THE APPROPRIATE QUESTIONS

No matter how much you may want a particular job, some important questions should be asked before you agree to accept the position. In asking these questions, remember that you must be direct while also being friendly. Six of the most important of these questions are:

1. *What happened to the last person to hold this job?* If the person was promoted, ask why. Now you have an idea of what the firm is looking for from the person who holds this job. If the person was fired, find out why. This tells you what not to do.

2. *May I talk to someone who is doing the same basic type of job that I'll be doing?* This will help you to find out what is good and bad about the department. No one knows better than the personnel, and they very often are willing to share this information with new people.

3. *How, and by whom, will my performance be measured?* Find out what the organization expects from you and how the management will determine whether you are doing a good job. To head off confusion later, keep the criteria as objective and measurable as possible.

4. *What is the salary range for this job, and what other compensation do you offer?* This may appear too direct, but most firms like to talk about their financial package. If you are moving from one job to another, this question is particularly important because you should not move for less than a 20 percent salary increase, unless you are very eager to join the company. Additionally, you should find out about any bonuses, perks such as a company car or club membership, vacations, health insurance, pension, and profit-sharing plans. Obtain all the financial data so that you know exactly what you will be getting in terms of remuneration.

5. *If relocation is involved, how much will the company help?* If you are commuting across town, the firm will not give you any assistance. However, if you must relocate, this will take time and money. In many major cities, you will end up paying a fee to secure an apartment. If you have to sell your house and buy another, a broker's commission on the sale and financial points on the new loan will be incurred, as will (in all likelihood) a higher rate of interest. If the firm is unwilling to absorb any of these expenses, you must add them into the cost of taking the job. Often, a move to another location is financially unwise unless the firm agrees to help with costs.

6. *Would you mind putting all of this in writing?* It never hurts to ask for the agreement in writing. This is particularly true if your employment arrangement contains anything other than standard items, such as salary, benefits, and vacation time. In this way, you do not have to worry about some manager later saying, "We never agreed to that. We don't pay those expenses for anyone." You will have the agreement in writing.

Applicant's Questions. Applicants today expect to work for a company with the best technology, the best databases, and the best access to information, as well as have access to coaching opportunities and mentoring. These values should stir a series of questions that need answering before taking a position. A list of questions are discussed under the topic, "Asking the Appropriate Questions," in the "Human Relations in Action" box. Review them and determine how you would answer these questions in an interview. What other questions would you ask?

Handling Salary Questions. How do you answer the question, "What salary do you want?" If possible, sidestep the question by explaining that salary is only one of your considerations and you would prefer to learn more about the job. If you are pushed into an answer, cite a range, such as $30,000 to $35,000, rather than a single figure, such as $33,700. If the employer is willing to pay $33,200 for the job, you are in the ballpark with a salary range but would be too high with a set number. Additionally, because some applicants truly want the job, they may drop their asking price to a lower level, such as $32,700. In this case, these applicants have given up $500, as the employer seldom is inclined to pay more than is necessary.

If you are just starting out, you do not have to be concerned with knowing how much to request. Most employers have a specific salary range for positions, and, if they do not, you can compare starting salaries and job requirements at interviews before deciding which job to take.[40] Also, you can go on the Internet to salary.com or salaryexpert.com and get information regarding how much employers are currently paying for the job that you are seeking.

A basic rule to follow is to never, ever bring up the subject of salary or benefits. If the interviewer asks if you have any questions, then you can discuss your concerns. It is best to focus on what you can do for the company.[41]

Strive for Originality. Most organizations will be interviewing more than one person for each job opening. If you are a typical candidate, you will do all the usual things: write an interesting résumé, dress well, and act properly. However, if possible, try to do something different also. Look for a way to distinguish yourself from the others. Although this requires some degree of creativity, it does not have to be unique. Your level of confidence and your attitude will show in the way you shake hands, greet the interviewer, walk, talk, and sit. Your behavior should indicate that you are eager and ready to help the company meet its goals and objectives. Never display a negative attitude or talk negatively about a previous employer or boss.

Don't Get Discouraged

There are times when it is more difficult to find a job. During these times, you should "relax and realize that you may not be doing anything wrong in your job search." Don't let rejections wear you down. Go to every interview with a positive attitude and a yearning to work for the company. Also, individuals often do strange things that don't help them get the job, such as failing to attach a résumé to an e-mail or cover letter, failing to use correct spelling, failing to address qualifications in the ad, and failing to arrive on time for the interview.[42]

 CHECK YOUR UNDERSTANDING

What are some suggestions for completing a successful interview?

In your career journal, write answers to the following:

1. Make a list of some do's and don'ts of effective interviews.
2. Identify appropriate questions for applicants to ask.
3. Discuss how the question of salary should be handed.

Summary

1 Compare and contrast formal and informal organizations.

The informal organization plays a significant role in the dynamics of behavior at work. A comparison of both organizations shows that the two organizations differ in terms of interpersonal relations, leadership, behavioral control, and dependency. In formal organizations, relationships are clearly defined, whereas in the informal organization, relationships evolve and change continually; so do authority and power. The use of power typically requires political behavior and works in various ways throughout the formal and informal organization. It is important to learn how to use power. Organizational goals and individual worker's goals are not always the same, setting up a combination of cooperation and competition forces, often resulting in sufficing behavior. One of the most important activities that takes place in an informal organization is networking—the process of socializing, politicking, and interacting with people throughout the company. Gender and ethnicity are important factors in how people network.

2 Discuss some of the behavioral controls used by members of the informal organization to ensure compliance with its norms.

In formal organizations, people are rewarded for doing things right and punished for doing things wrong. In the informal organization also, rewards and punishments are dispensed to members. A member will be included in the group for following group norms, but may be ostracized, subjected to pressure, ridiculed, and made to look foolish in the eyes of the other members for not properly acting within the group norms. The formal leader has greater power to reward and punish than the informal leader. Some workers simply resist joining such groups because they believe they have nothing to gain by joining the group. There are three subgroups in an informal organization structure: nucleus—full-fledged members, fringe—those seeking membership, and outer—those who have been rejected.

3 Explain how the informal communication network functions.

One of the informal organization's most interesting behavioral aspects, however, is its communication network. Commonly known as the grapevine, this communication network is used to carry information between members of the informal organization. Four common types of the grapevine network are the single strand, gossip chain, probability chain, and cluster chain. The cluster chain, which involves the selective transmission of messages, is the most common. Liaison people are the links between those who have the information and those who do not. Some people tend to be very active on the grapevine, but others are fairly inactive. However, given the proper situation and motivation, just about everyone will become active on the grapevine. Research reveals that some of the most likely causes for such activity are lack of knowledge about a situation, insecurity, personal interest in a situation, and the possession of recent information.

Managers should learn to manage the grapevine because it cannot be fired, abolished, erased, or stopped. If one source is suppressed, it will simply pop up in another place. Managers should provide a flow of accurate and timely information through the formal structure. Managers can identify key communicators in the informal organization and leak important information into the grapevine. Some companies have set up rumor hotlines and rumor centers.

Informal organizations foster and facilitate the exchange of knowledge within the company. Research shows that managers receive information more readily from others than from formal sources, such as databases, the Internet, or archives. The nodes—central points in the system—keep the system alive. Five roles played by members of the informal organization are identified as central connectors, boundary spanners, gatekeepers, bridges, and experts. Central connectors can point people in the right direction. Boundary spanners have a broad knowledge base and can retrieve information from outside sources. Gatekeepers protect local networks by filtering and screening unnecessary information. The bridges are good at connecting people with opposing views or those who speak a different language. Experts are very knowledgeable and can provide important knowledge in a way that is easy to understand.

4 Identify the primary benefits associated with the informal organization.

Some of the commonly cited benefits of the informal organization are getting things done, lightening managerial workloads, providing job satisfaction, serving as a safety valve for employee emotions, and providing feedback to the manager. The communicators in the informal structure process information faster than through the chain of command. When managers delegate authority and allow workers to get the job done, they create a feeling of trust, and the workers reciprocate by showing they are reliable. The social environment impacts the satisfaction level of employees, and the informal organization can create a climate conducive to high productivity and a high level of worker satisfaction. The informal structure allows workers to let off steam without it threatening their jobs. The grapevine reflects how the workers feel about the company, the managers, and the work. Managers can benefit by listening to the sounds of the grapevine.

5 List some of the disadvantages associated with the informal organization.

Despite its benefits, however, some major disadvantages are associated with the informal organization. They are: resistance to change, goal conflict, conformity, and rumor. Most people do not want the status quo to change. The informal organization can be instrumental in determining the rate at which change occurs in a company. Resistance involves concerns about standards, quotas, unfair management treatment, and profits. Often the goals of the formal and informal groups are different, which causes conflict. Group norms can be so strong that workers feel the need to go along with the group norm. When group norms have been in place for a long time, they may become ingrained in the system and weighing the pros and cons may be difficult. A rumor is the unverified or untrue part of grapevine information; it is a product of interest and ambiguity.

6 Cite some of the ways in which a manager can deal with the informal organization.

In any event, the informal organization is inevitable. It cannot be stamped out; so the manager will do well to understand its presence and, if possible, to influence its direction so that the goals of both the formal and informal organizations are brought into harmony. Some of the most effective ways of doing this are tapping the grapevine to learn what is going on, countering rumor with fact, and creating conditions that help align the goals of both groups. If this can be accomplished, the manager will find that resistance to change is minimized, rumors are reduced, and overall organizational cooperation is achieved. The manager must continually ask, "Who is in charge of the informal group and why?"

7 Discuss how to successfully complete an employment interview.

Before going to an interview, learn as much as you can about the company, its industry, and its position in the marketplace. If you know about the company, it will likely make an impression. Companies look for people with perseverance, drive, integrity, and good communication skills. The interviewer looks for applicants whose personality will fit that of the company. Positive attitude, appropriate appearance, proper manners, and interview etiquette all play key roles in a successful interview. Review key questions that interviewers often ask and be prepared to give positive answers. Do not bring up the question of salary. Let the interviewer bring up salary or wait until after an offer has been given. Prepare a list of questions, and take them with you to the interview—about the company's projected growth and new products or services; changes in the industry's growth or technology; responsibilities, duties, and travel; and opportunities concerning potential growth, advancement, and promotions. Attend each interview with a positive approach and don't become discouraged. There is a right job for you.

Key Terms in the Chapter

Sociogram	A sociogram shows intragroup social relationships.
Advice network	The advice network shows who provides helpful information to whom.
Trust network	The trust network shows who shares delicate information with whom.

Communication network	The communication network shows who regularly talks with whom about work-related matters.
Authority	Authority is the right to command.
Power	Power is the ability to influence.
Sufficing behavior	Sufficing behavior leads to satisfactory payoffs.
Networking	Networking is the process of socializing, politicking, and interacting with people throughout the enterprise.
Nucleus group	The nucleus group contains full-fledged members of the informal organization.
Fringe group	The fringe group members are those seeking admission to the informal organization.
Outer group	The outer group members are those who have been rejected membership by the informal organization.
Grapevine	The grapevine is the informal communication network.
Single strand	The single-strand network passes information along a chain from one person to another.
Gossip chain	The gossip chain involves one person passing on information to all others.
Probability chain	The probability chain involves the passing of information on a random basis.
Cluster chain	The cluster chain involves information being passed on a selective basis.
Node	Node is the central point in a system.
Central connectors	Central connectors provide shortcuts through the system.
Boundary spanners	Boundary spanners collect knowledge from outside their local networks.
Gatekeepers	Gatekeepers protect the local network by filtering and screening unnecessary information.
Bridges	Bridges connect people of opposite sides, languages, and opinions.
Experts	Experts are knowledgeable and can provide important knowledge to others.
Goal conflict	Goal conflict arises when a person pursues two incompatible objectives.
Conformity	Conformity is the willingness to go along with the other members of the group.
Rumor	Rumor is a product of interest and ambiguity.
Selective filtering	Selective filtering is the screening and modifying of rumor.
Elaboration	Elaboration is the expansion and modification of rumor.

Review and Study Questions

1. One of the ways in which the informal organization differs from the formal organization is in interpersonal relations. What does this statement mean?
2. How does the leadership of a formal leader differ from that of an informal leader?
3. How is authority different from power? Which is of greater importance in the informal organization?
4. What kinds of political tactics do managers use? Explain.
5. What is networking? How is networking used in the informal organization?

6. Identify some ways minority managers network differently than managers in general.

7. What are some of the behavioral controls used by members of the informal organization to ensure compliance with its norms? Give examples.

8. What is a grapevine? How does a grapevine work?

9. How does each of the following grapevine networks function: single strand, gossip chain, probability chain, and cluster chain? Explain.

10. When are people most likely to be active on the grapevine? Give four illustrations.

11. Describe how a manager can most effectively manage the grapevine.

12. What is a major role of the informal communication network?

13. Differentiate among the roles played by members of informal networks—central connectors, boundary spanners, gatekeepers, bridges, and experts.

14. In what way does the informal organization help in getting things done?

15. How does the informal organization lighten managerial workloads?

16. Job satisfaction is a benefit of informal organizations. How does it work?

17. How can the informal organization serve as a safety valve?

18. What type of feedback does the informal organization provide to managers?

19. One of the biggest complaints about the informal organization is that it tends to resist change. Is this true? Defend your answer.

20. How does goal conflict differ from goal conformity?

21. What is a rumor? How are rumors and grapevines associated?

22. What are two ways managers can effectively deal with the informal organization?

23. Why must managers stay abreast of changes in the informal organization?

24. What are some things an applicant should know about a company before going to an interview?

25. Identify some common qualities that most companies look for in applicants.

26. What is the significance of attitude, appearance, manners, and interview etiquette? Discuss.

27. Identify some typical interview questions and briefly outline how you might answer them.

28. What type of questions should the applicant be prepared to ask in the interview?

29. How should the issue of salary be handled in the interview?

Connecting to the Real World

How can networking help you?

Networking is used in many ways to gain access to information and knowledge in the workplace. Its benefits can make a vast difference in helping you find a meaningful job, effectively do your job, or gain advancements in your career.

To learn as much as you can about networking and how it can benefit you, research the topic using the Internet. Then, prepare a written report of your findings.

Using the job or career you selected in Chapter 2 under the "Career Advisor," follow these guidelines:

1. Research the topic—networking opportunities in the workplace, in the community, or through professional organizations that can help you advance in your job and your career.
2. Prepare a list of the activities you find. Which networking activities reside within companies, and which ones are found outside the companies?
3. Which of these networking activities can work for you? Tell why? How can you get networking started?
4. Give examples of how networking can help you advance in your career.
5. What is the most beneficial thing you learned from doing this exercise?

CASE
A Case of Layoffs

The rumor mill in Betty Harrigan's department has been in full operation this week. It seems everyone's mind is on the new equipment being installed. The machinery was approved by a management committee more than six months ago and is the result of company efforts to modernize the facilities. The machines are state of the art but, despite their sophistication, still require just as many people to run them as did the old machines. Nevertheless, this has not stopped the rumors about impending layoffs.

In an effort to deal with the situation, Harrigan called a meeting of her staff and explained to them that three months before she became department manager, a committee had approved the purchase of this new machinery. She was unable to explain why no one in the unit knew about the impending purchase, but she assured everyone that there would be no layoffs or cutbacks in the number of hours worked. "These machines are going to help us increase the quality of work, but they will not increase the quantity. We are going to need everyone in the department and will probably have to hire two more people." The group listened quietly as Harrigan spoke. When she was finished, she asked if there were any questions. One of the young men, Fred, in the back said, "Are we the only department getting new equipment?" Harrigan explained that two other units also were having new machinery installed. She then hastened to add, "And like us, neither of them is going to have any layoffs either." With this, the meeting broke up.

As soon as she returned to her office, Harrigan had a call from her boss. "Look, I don't want to panic you," he said, "but I've just had a call from the vice president of administration. The other departments that got new equipment are going to have some layoffs because they were overstaffed to start with. However, you will not have any. You are understaffed, and as we agreed, you will be getting two new people within the month. Unfortunately, none of the people being laid off has the qualifications you need, or we would simply transfer them to your department. The reason I wanted to call was to let you know that you have nothing to worry about." Harrigan thanked him and hung up. Just then there was a knock at her door. Fred who attended the meeting came in and said, "I just heard that people in those other two departments are to be laid off. I was wondering what effect this would have on the new hires in our department. If I'm going to get laid off, I'd like to start looking for a new job as soon as possible." Harrigan asked Fred to stay for a few minutes, which he did. Fred, however, reminded her that the company softball team was having a meeting in 30 minutes. She congratulated Fred on the team's winning streak this year.

Since becoming manager, Harrigan had noticed that some of her staff often left work with people from the other two departments. She did not think too much about it because she felt they were probably having a beer together after work. Harrigan, on several occasions, overheard a couple of her staff laughing about some of the things that had been discussed the evening before. Sometimes they would even share the information with Harrigan.

Questions

1. Why didn't the staff know about the purchase of new equipment in the department? How did Fred find out about the layoffs in the other departments? Explain.
2. Will Harrigan's comment about no layoffs in her department now be regarded with skepticism? Why?
3. What would you advise Harrigan to say to Fred? Explain.
4. What should Harrigan do to maintain her credibility? Tell why.
5. How can Harrigan use the grapevine to her advantage?

PART 3

THE TECHNICAL SYSTEM

The focus of this section of the book is to study the technical system of organizations. The three major components of the technical system are (1) the impact of technology on people at work, (2) a focus on productivity and quality improvement, and (3) job redesign and job enrichment.

The goals for this section are to:

1. Trace the evolution of technology, describe the major characteristics of a postindustrial society, explain the effect of technology on work values, and discuss industrial democracy and the ways in which organizations are now dealing with workplace violence. Discuss how to get ahead in a career by learning to be a team player.

2. Study the nature of productivity and quality improvement, examine total quality management, explain how participative management approaches are improving productivity and quality, examine tools and techniques for increasing quality, explore alternative work schedules and empowerment, and discuss how intrapreneurship attitudes can make a difference in productivity and quality. Explain how developing your own brand can make a difference in your career.

3. Explain job design; discuss how modern organizations can use job redesign; explore job rotation, job enlargement, and job enrichment; describe core job dimensions and illustrate how selected enrichment principles can be used to fulfill these dimensions; and discuss current challenges in job design. Discuss the importance of managing your career effectively.

When you have finished reading this part of the book, you should have a solid understanding of the technical system and how it impacts management decisions, how productivity and quality can be improved, and how job redesign can improve employee productivity. Additionally, you should be aware of the importance of being a team player in getting ahead in your career, and that developing your own brand can make a difference in career advancement.

CHAPTER 6

Technology and People at Work

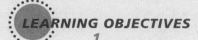
An organization must respond to many factors, one of which is technology. As technology advances, the organization finds itself bombarded with change. The relationship between technology and people at work is known as *sociotechnical systems*, and modern managers are finding that they must pay increased attention to this technology–human interface.

People and Technology: Working as One

As technology changes the way we work and the way we live, human relations must constantly be at work within organizations. It is vital that we understand how to integrate these changes into our work and into our lives to be productive and satisfied. Technology is exploding exponentially and, over the past two decades, has changed the design of work and the rhythm of our lives. It seems that almost daily a new product or system is announced that changes how we retrieve, process, or send information; how we manufacture and market products; and how we learn in our public schools, colleges, universities, and company training programs. Technology is also changing how we pay our bills, how we get examined at the local clinic, the type of fabrics we wear, and the equipment we use to stay slim. Our military, space, and Olympics programs all use advanced technology to complete their missions. Even organizational structures are being affected. Technology has impacted our basic assumptions about how to work and where to work. We now can engage in conversations, shopping, learning, and working anywhere, any time. This was not possible a few years ago.

World-class companies are finding that by blending the abilities of their employees with the capabilities of technology, they can offer new products and services to a growing number of customers. A good example is Dell, a personal computer manufacturer headquartered in Round Rock, Texas. In 2010 Dell launched a program with AT&T for delivering communications solutions for wireless operators and their dedicated customers located in China and Brazil. Dell and AT&T also collaborated on one of the first Android-based smart phones to run on AT&T. For Dell, smart phones are an extension of its strategy to develop intelligent and more mobile products that meet the needs of operators and customers.

The team at Dell can find solutions for many different types of business operations. For example, Papa Gino's Holding Corporation, a company behind New England's leading quick-service Italian restaurant chain and the premier regional sub sandwich chain, needed to reduce risks, improve security, and increase workplace efficiency. Dell came to the company's rescue and installed several systems to solve the problems. The 7-Eleven Company is another firm that has reduced its management costs by 81 percent by using Dell's products and services. And at the same time, as Dell competes with Hewlett-Packard for the top position in sales, it forces Dell to work more diligently with customers to design and build new products and services. The goal is to provide gains in quality, productivity, and performance while, at the same time, reducing the costs of technology.

Technology also plays an important role in the funeral industry. In a sleepy, historic, tourist town of Salado, located along the old Chisholm Trail in Central Texas, is the Broecker Funeral Home, owned and operated by Dave and Pat Broecker. The funeral home offers personal services designed to meet the client's wishes, regardless of budgetary preference. Broecker, however, does not carry an inventory of caskets. So how can Broecker get the needed casket in a timely manner? It relies on technology. After the client selects the desired casket from a computer screen that lists many styles and types of caskets, Dave Broecker sends the order by email, fax, online order form, or phone to the Aurora Casket Company in Indiana, where the information is processed and transferred to a distribution center in Austin, Texas, located near the Broecker Funeral Home. The distribution center matches the information to the casket location in the warehouse, to personnel needed to process the order, and to the truck and driver needed to deliver the casket to Salado. Unless the casket requires special details, it takes no more than four hours to complete the process, from the time Dave Broecker places the order with Aurora to delivery of the casket. The computer system in Aurora keeps track of the inventory in each distribution center located throughout the United States. When inventory needs replacing, it automatically places orders with the manufacturing plant.

When transporting a body for embalming, cosmetology, dressing, and casketing, Pat Broecker depends on an electronically operated scoop attached to a set of tracks installed in the ceiling. Otherwise, it would be impossible for a small person to lift the body, especially a large and heavy body. This technology helps protect Pat Broecker's back and legs.

Another company, Netflix, the world's largest online and mail-order DVD movie rental service, located in Los Gatos, California, provides more than 11.1 million subscribers access to more than 100,000 DVD titles. Netflix relies on high technology and a staff of trained employees to provide one-day service and to answer customer's questions. Reed Hastings, the founder, leads his company from a customer-centered perspective. For example, Cinematch, a one-to-one, mass customized software system, urges customers to go through a rating exercise to find the movies they will like. "Friends," a growing network of Netflix users, lets customers peek at what their friends are watching. It's another way to more deeply engage customers in its customer service loop. RSS, a feedback system, automatically sends customers updates on new releases or account changes. Netflix has the capability to stream the movies immediately onto a customer's computer. Reed Hastings, the owner, is negotiating with Hollywood to gain greater access to that market.

Because warehouse employees do not interact with customers, the Web site must be the most personalized Web site in the world, according to Hastings. To keep cost low and further speed up shipping times, Netflix improved its already high-tech distribution centers to make video-on-demand services available. Netflix effectively uses technology to meet customers' expectations, as evidenced by *Fast Company* magazine naming Netflix as its annual Customers First Award winner in 2005.

Snyder Salvage, an automotive recycler in Holland, Texas, has combined technology with teamwork to grow from a single owner into a multimillion-dollar business. Each year Snyder continues to grow, and currently the company falls within the top 2 percent of the largest independent automotive salvage businesses in the United States. Dan Snyder, the general manager, believes in giving the customer two things: excellent customer service and quality products. "If you focus on these two things, the rest will come." To provide faster customer service, Snyder had to find a better way to track its inventory. As a result, a new inventory bar-code tag system created by CMSI Technologies was installed. The technology, called thermal transfer tag printing, works with the CheckMate, Hollander, and Powerlink 1 inventory systems. The durability of its tags has increased productivity and eliminated the need for someone to write up the tags by hand, which often faded and were unreadable or were missing because they had blown away. The system allows the salespeople immediate access to the inventory and to the number of parts that are available for shipment to body shops and insurance companies. Customers get quality customer service and quality products in a timely manner.

The Evolution of Technology

Trace the evolution of technology from the handicraft era to the cybernated technology stage.

One of the most dramatic events of the twentieth century has been the dynamic development of technology. Today, people are traveling faster than ever before, residing in houses made of material that was unavailable twenty-five years ago, using home appliances and tools that make their lives more enjoyable, and, as a result of improvements in medical technology, living longer. However, technology has had its price. Many people are now living at a very fast rate, being subjected to what Alvin Toffler called **future shock**—the effect of enduring too much change in too short a time.[1] How has our society arrived at this advanced state of technology? We attempt to answer this question by examining the eras of technological development through which humankind in general and the United States in particular have progressed.

Handicraft Era.   The first phase of technological development was the **handicraft era**. During this period, people made things by hand. They built their own houses, made their own clothes, and developed their own medicines and herbs to combat illness. In short, they were self-sufficient. Examples of specialists during this era were carpenters, cobblers, and tailors, who provided the local population with their services and, in turn, received goods or money with which to buy food, clothing, and shelter. However, these craftsmen were to be found only in larger towns where their services were required. In outlying areas, such as farm communities, there was little need for a tailor or a cobbler, although a blacksmith might be able to eke out a living. In any event, specialization was minimal at this time; almost everyone was a jack-of-all-trades.

Mechanization Era.   Next came the **mechanization era**, in which machine labor replaced human labor. One of the most significant developments of this era was job specialization, by which workers were assigned a limited number of tasks that were to be repeated. During this period, humankind began to harness energy and use it to drive machinery; the spinning jenny and the power loom are examples of machinery of this era. Hence, mechanization increased on two fronts: the workers and the machines. Each was seen as a complement to the other. Humans and machines working together increased productivity dramatically. The age of mechanization was upon us.

Mechanistic Technology. A further increase in the use of machines and job simplification was represented by the era of **mechanistic technology**. Eli Whitney, best known for his invention of the cotton gin, introduced standardized interchangeable parts in his production plant and was soon turning out muskets and clocks in greater quantities and at a lower cost than ever before. A century later, this basic idea was extended further through the development of the modern assembly line, such as that used by Henry Ford in building his Model T. By this time, the pace of technology was increasing and the role of the worker was diminishing. The number of tasks a person had to perform was decreasing, as was the amount of skill required.

Automated Technology. In many organizations, **automated technology** has replaced mechanistic technology. Automated technology involves linking together and integrating assembly-line machines in such a fashion that many functions are performed automatically without human involvement. Some people have contended that this development represents the beginning of a second industrial revolution. Modern auto assembly lines are an excellent example, as well as office computer systems that are linked to one another, thereby allowing managers using a microcomputer to interface with a giant mainframe. Technology is not confined to office or manufacturing environments. For example, oil companies now use undersea robots for deep-water dives to repair oil platforms or perform other hazardous tasks that were earlier carried out by human divers.[2] Honda has developed Asimo, a four-foot humanoid robot, designed to help older people live a better life at home. It not only can walk, but also can run, climb steps, and even carry a tray or push a cart. Advances in technology have allowed Honda to develop several mobility devices to help people with movement problems.

Cybernated Technology. At present, a fifth era, that of **cybernated technology**, also known as the **digital age**, is evolving into many forms. To cybernate is to automate operations using computers and electronic tools. Today, digital technology is used in business operations around the world. It is almost impossible to compete in the fast-paced technological world without integrating technology into business operations. Technological changes are occurring in manufacturing processes, marketing operations, office and management functions, and training programs, just to name a few.

1. **Manufacturing** Computers are used throughout many manufacturing processes that were once handled by humans. Computers are also used to monitor the temperature throughout plants and buildings and to order the heating and air-conditioning units to turn off or on as needed. This form of environmental control helps reduce costs throughout industries. Using robotics is another way to reduce costs. Robotics is fast becoming a necessary tool in manufacturing processes, business operations, National Aeronautics and Space Administration (NASA), entertainment, and household products. For example, robots were used to stop the flow of oil in the Gulf of Mexico during British Petroleum's oil well disaster in 2010. The NASA program also uses robotics. NASA plans to launch the Curiosity Rover, the Mars Science Laboratory, in the Fall of 2011. It will be larger and heavier than the two rovers already on Mars. In another example, on May 26, 2010 the Field

Museum in Chicago, Illinois, launched its first interactive robotics exhibit. Robo-SUE, a robotically animated recreation of the famous Tyrannosaurus rex skeleton, is outfitted with cameras, sensors, and artificial intelligence, giving each visitor a different experience. Robotics is not just for manufacturing, business operations, or the space program. The robot vacuum cleaner is also used in our personal lives to clean our houses.

The usage of GPS (global positioning systems) technology for such purposes as tracking employees in the field or shipments across the country is also rapidly expanding. For example, truck drivers are constantly monitored as they deliver goods across the country and around the world. With advancements in digital technology, manufacturing companies will experience more changes to their operations.

2. **Marketing** Computers not only are a major component in manufacturing operations and in operating businesses, they also serve a major role in marketing—the way products and services are bought and sold. Research shows that more and more people are depending on the Internet for purchasing products and services. E-commerce has emerged as a vital sector in marketing and a necessary component for the survival of many businesses. Companies are starting to realize how crucial quick, friendly, and efficient customer service on the Internet has become. As a result, they are beginning to improve their customer service and deliver high-quality assistance.

Digital technology is changing how products are advertised. For example, Adidas rewards consumers for sharing online advertising. It created a highly interactive advertisement to promote Adidas' lightest-ever footwear and apparel lines. The 30-second spot encourages viewers to visit its Web site and YouTube channel, where they can access more content of an NBA player that will gradually unlock to reveal more content of the player the more times it's shared. Adidas is the first marketer to tie access to content to the number of views of the video.[3]

3. **Office Management Functions** Net-based forms of communications, such as e-mail, instant messaging, videoconferencing, cell phones, and laptop computers, have sped up both work and business decisions. This can lead to stressed employees. Greg Welch, a researcher from the University of North Carolina at Chapel Hill, has been busy developing technological products that help ease this stress. For example, he has designed desk chairs that can sense when you are stressed and, perhaps, tell your boss to offload some of your work; computers that can figure out where you have seen a particular name; and desktops that can transform themselves into computer monitors to help facilitate discussion during a roundtable meeting.

Wireless network technology is growing at a rapid pace. It can be found in every facet of life, from cars and homes to office buildings and factories, and is changing the definition of the modern office and the way we live. Many offices today depend on Wi-Fi (Wireless Fidelity) to conduct their operations. The next generation wireless technology is WiMAX (Worldwide Interoperability for Microwave Access). This technology will expand Internet access to those who currently are not able to obtain high-speed wireless Internet access. WiMAX will greatly enhance the Internet experience for all users.[4] Wireless providers currently are rolling out services to make it possible to know exactly where a person is at a particular time. This allows employees working in remote locations to be tracked and managed from a distant site. It is also used to manage employee records and payroll, issue checks, make deposits, and manage various operational systems within the business. Videoconferencing is another convenient tool used in conducting meetings among managers located in different locations. It reduces the costs of travel and saves time that can be better used within each location.

4. **Training** E-learning uses computers to deliver training to employees. It works well when combined with other forms of training. For example, IBM "conducts 48 percent of its training electronically," says Ted Hoff, vice-president, Center for Learning and Development.[5] To reduce the time employees spend learning in a classroom, Capital One, a financial services company, purchased three thousand iPods with podcasts (digital recordings) for its employees' training program.[6] In businesses faced with high turnover, such as retailers, e-learning has been proven to boost sales. Nike, for example, developed and implemented SKU—Sports Knowledge Underground—an e-learning training program. Nike experienced a 4 percent to 5 percent increase in sales, and the e-learning program helped set a standard of learning for diverse workforces among Nike stores. This also proved to be true for Cingular Wireless when it acquired AT&T Wireless. E-learning was used to ensure that all employees could follow the same procedures in all store locations.[7]

As the twenty-first century progresses, technology will change, and it will continue to be a vital part of business operations and will make the difference between success and failure for many business owners.

Research and Development, Knowledge, and Technology

How has humankind been able to accomplish such tremendous breakthroughs in technology? One way is through the billions of dollars invested annually in research and development (R&D). These expenditures are bringing about the development of all sorts of new products. The results can be seen in any large retail store, where one can find more goods than ever before. But it does not stop there. As a result of research breakthroughs, we have supersonic transports, telecommunication satellites, and computers for medical research. In short, at work or at home, the employee is surrounded by technological innovation. Furthermore, there is no going back. Technology is speeding up, and the modern organization is being forced to accommodate many breakthroughs. For example, the large drug companies are reinventing their labs to boost productivity. Pfizer, Merck & Co., Abbott Laboratories, and Wyeth have hired new people with strong biotechnology and genomics expertise to find answers to complex conditions such as cancer, diabetes, and Alzheimer's disease. The trade group Pharmaceutical Research & Manufacturers of America says that the R&D expenditure of its big drug company members soared to $50.3 billion in 2008, and industry-wide, it rose to a record $65.2 billion. According to the drug companies, it takes over $800 million in R&D expenditures and fifteen years of research on average to develop a new drug.[8] What is the basic cause of this accelerated technological thrust? The answer is found in knowledge, technology's fuel.

The rate at which information has been gathered has been spiraling upward for 10,000 years. The first great breakthrough occurred with the invention of writing. The next great leap forward did not occur until the invention of movable-type printing by Gutenberg in the fifteenth century. Prior to this event, Europe was producing approximately one thousand book titles annually, and a library of 100,000 titles took nearly one hundred years to turn out. In the years after Gutenberg's accomplishment, a tremendous acceleration occurred such that, by 1950, Europe was producing 120,000 titles per year. What had once taken a century now required only ten months. Today, the world's output of books is more than 5,000 titles per day.

Naturally, not every book will lead to a technological breakthrough, but the accelerated curve in book publication crudely parallels the rate at which humankind discovers new knowledge. Advances in science support this statement.

For example, before the invention of the movable-type press, only eleven chemical elements were known, and it had been two hundred years since the last one—arsenic—had been discovered. The twelfth element was discovered while Gutenberg was working on his invention. Subsequently, more than seventy additional elements were discovered, and since 1900 scientists have been isolating new elements at the rate of one every three years.

Much of this advance must be attributed to the fact that 90 percent of all the scientists who ever lived are alive now, and new discoveries are being made every day. This is evident from reading local newspapers and magazines. Some of the latest technological developments and research breakthroughs are included in the next section.

New Products Are Continually Emerging

Scientific discoveries are being brought to fruition at a faster rate than ever before. For example, in 1836, machines were invented that mowed, threshed, and tied straw into sheaves and poured grain into sacks. The machine was based on technology that even then was twenty years old, but it was not until 1930 that such a combine actually was marketed. The first English patent for a typewriter was issued in 1714, but another 150 years passed before typewriters were commercially available. Today, such delays between ideas and application are almost unthinkable. It is not that we are more eager or more ambitious than our ancestors but that we have, over time, invented all sorts of social devices to hasten the process. Thus, we find that the time between the first and second stages of the innovative cycle—between idea and application—has been cut radically.

Technology in Automobiles.   Hybrid auto engines developed in the last few years now provide a combination of gas and electric power, thus allowing autos such as the Honda Insight to travel 66 miles per gallon and the Toyota Prius to travel 650 miles between gasoline fill ups, according to claims found on these companies' Web sites. The original hybrid, the Honda Insight, continues to be rated as the most fuel-efficient car in its class in America. In 1970, Honda introduced its first lightweight, fuel-efficient car, the Honda N600, in America. Since then, Honda has continued to be an innovator of new vehicle technology. In 2001, Honda introduced its first fuel cell car, the Honda FCX, which is government-certified for everyday use. Honda worked with the Cities of Los Angeles, New York, Las Vegas, and San Francisco under a two-year lease agreement. City employees used these vehicles on a day-to-day basis and provided Honda with valuable, real-world feedback on the use and operation of fuel cells. In 2004, the second-generation 2005 Honda FCX debuted. It is designed with a fuel cell stack capable of starting in temperatures as low as −208°C (−48°F). Honda began leasing hydrogen-powered fuel cell cars in Japan and the United States in 2008. Honda is planning for mass production of the car by 2018. Toyota also has introduced its second-generation fuel cell hybrid vehicle, the FC HV-5, and has developed a fuel cell hybrid bus, the FCHV-BUS1. It is actively developing fuel cell hybrid systems for public transport buses in an effort to find ways of improving urban air quality and reducing urban noise. "Hydrogen-powered fuel vehicles hold great promise for future clean air vehicles, while at the same time reducing our global dependence on oil," said Tom Elliott, executive vice president, American Honda Motor Company, Inc.[9] Honda believes it has a responsibility to advance technology that moves toward a cleaner environment.

To support the automobile industry, two U.S. companies, Ener1 and A123, are busy developing lithium-ion battery technology for plug-in hybrid vehicles. The T-shaped lithium-ion battery for the Chevrolet Volt is due out in 2011 and will contain two hundred cells. Several other companies around the globe also are spending money on developing batteries for the plug-in hybrid market. For example, BYD Auto in China, one of the world's top battery makers, has a $22,000 plug-in hybrid that it hopes to sell in the United States very soon.[10]

Technology in the Military.   Technology is at the core of the equipment being built for the U.S. military. For example, the drone, an unmanned aerial vehicle, is equipped with GPS tracking maps and is under the constant control of an operator or pilot through radio links in a remote location. Drones have been used in the Iraq and Afghanistan wars for reconnaissance or surveillance of enemy activities, target acquisition, relay of friendly communications, and jamming enemy communications.[11]

Another example is ceramic technology. It is critical to American troops, who carry heavy loads of equipment and armor. "Elite American units such as the Delta Force have been wearing ceramic armor—about half as heavy as the metal variety—since the mid-1990s. Now more U.S. ground forces will get it." Not only is it lightweight, it also provides protection in close-up combat. Ceramic technology is used to shield Patriot missiles, used in helicopters, and used in tracked vehicles that glide across water and climb over rough terrain. Through the development of ceramic technology, General Dynamics Corporation, Japan's Kyocera Corporation, and Lockheed Martin Corporation are helping transform the U.S. military into a quicker, lighter, and more lethal force.[12]

Technology in Sports and Medicine.   Computerized engineering and materials science have become an integral part of sports. For example, space-age technology was applied to the equipment Lance Armstrong used in mastering the Tour de France title for the seventh time in 2005. His altimeter, built into a titanium-coated wristwatch, was engineered by Nike and Seiko; his eyes were protected by sunglasses from Oakley, precision molded to thousandths of an inch for aerodynamic efficiency and equipped with optical lenses so clear a laser beam can pass through them without noticeable diffraction. Armstrong's super-strong carbon fiber-epoxy bicycle frame was built to cut the wind with teardrop-shaped tubing and weighed in at a pixiesque 2.27 pounds.[13]

The figure skating sport also needs technological changes. During the 2006 Winter Olympics in Turin, Italy, the number of fractures in the legs and spines of skaters as young as ten years old and the number of routine surgeries to repair hips were revealed. Orthopedists and physiologists believe the skate boot is the reason. Although technology has made a difference in other sports, the skate makers have not changed their designs, partly because "it's an old, classical sport without a lot of motivation to change," says Mahlon Bradley, chairman of the U.S. Figure Skating Association's Sports Medicine Committee.[14] This is an opportunity for R&D to make a difference in the lives of skaters. When will this happen?

Wii games are being used for rehab therapy, called Wii-habilitation. The usual stretching and lifting exercises required for patients to recover can become boring. Patients using Wii games, however, become engrossed mentally, and they almost become oblivious to the rigor. It does have a downside, a condition called "Wii-itis" when patients spend too much time using Wii games.[15]

Motion capture technology is making inroads in medicine. It can improve treatment quality for disorders from cerebral palsy to arthritis. Motion capture technology is also making a difference in advertising (bringing pedestrians into the ads on flat screens), in market research (using eye-tracking screens), auto safety (drowsiness detection system that sounds an alarm), mobile phones (users tilt, shake, or flick their phones to play games), and security system (detects a person's gait on security cameras).[16]

Technology in Debit and Credit Cards.   Jim Keyes, CEO of 7-Eleven, has not only spent lavishly on training, upgrading technology, and setting up a distribution system for fresh foods, he has also spent heavily on enhancing 7-Eleven's prepaid Vcom cards, developed by Alliance Data Systems. The "prepaid everything card" allows customers to make ATM transactions as well as buy money orders, transfer funds, cash checks, and eventually pay bills. Convenience needs have changed, requiring a more convenient alternative method of payment. With Vcom cards, there is no interchange fee.[17] Breakthroughs in counterspy technology for surveillance and security equipment are making it harder for crooks to steal credit card numbers and bank account passwords.

Technology in Education. E-learning starts with students in elementary schools and continues on through college and into the workplace. Online courses, for example, have emerged as an acceptable way to take a class and to earn credit toward a degree. Today, colleges and universities across the country, such as the University of Phoenix, offer a wide array of courses and degrees online. As the twenty-first century advances, e-learning will continue to be an important learning strategy. New technologies and teaching techniques will change how e-learning is delivered. Technology continues to bring students and teachers together to enable learning.

Technology has changed the way books, textbooks, and magazines are printed. The printing industry now uses digital technology with electrophotographic and formatted data technologies. Will the introduction of Stephen Jobs' iPad in 2010 change the way people read books? If so, digital technology will play another role in getting the copy into the proper format for delivery.

In the newspaper industry, Digital Technology International worked with *Boston Herald* and BostonHerald.com to develop an integrated system to create multimedia content for multiple channels and build a broader audience for the *Boston Herald*. This unified content management process manages both the print and Web content.[18]

To save costs, colleges and universities with remote campuses are moving away from face-to-face meetings and are embracing digital technology through videoconferencing systems for a range of faculty and staff meetings. Research shows that videoconference meetings are not as good as in-person gatherings when it comes to building trust. To remedy this problem, researchers are working on improving personal interactions by developing holograms and stand-in robots. These robots mirror the movements of the person controlling it—turning its head as the human operator moves. The key is eye control—looking people in the eye helps build trust. Robert Ubell, vice president of Enterprise Learning at NYU's Polytechnic Institute, states that "with improving technology and dropping costs, videoconferencing will be a key technology for encouraging more teamwork in the classroom and in research."[19] These are just a few examples of how digital technology is making a difference in people's lives.

Technology in Consumer Products. In addition, the number of consumer goods is increasing so rapidly that the time between introduction and decline is diminishing. Cheaper, better quality, or more useful goods are being produced. This is true, in part, because a growing number of firms are now spending more and more money on R&D to develop new-age products. One good example is the Gentex Corporation, a leader in the global auto-dimming mirror market and camera-based active safety systems. Gentex has invented a car rearview electrochromic mirror with interfaces and displays that turns on the headlights at dusk and turns off the lights at dawn, in addition to adjusting the air-conditioning, detecting the presence of rain and automatically turning on the wipers, and providing a button to summon emergency assistance. A video display located in the rearview mirror shows a real-time panoramic view of the rear of the vehicle.[20]

Spurred on by tire recalls and the belief that underinflated tires can lead to accidents, Gentex developed a tire pressure monitoring indicator that warns the driver when one or more of the vehicle's tires becomes underinflated. Sensors located in each tire or from the vehicle's antilock braking system send information to the interface located in the rearview mirror, which alerts the driver. Gentex has also developed a microphone located in the rearview mirror that is specifically designed for the harsh, noisy automotive environment. Gentex prides itself on being a technology company.[21]

"We are moving toward a time when physical objects around us will be made of active materials than can change shape, heal themselves and have a built-in computation," said Christine Peterson, president of Foresight Institute, a nonprofit think tank. The researchers are not far off from designing materials, such as plastics, metals, and even cement, that can mend themselves. They also are working on developing power fabrics that make energy and devices that generate electrical power from the swing of a walking person's knee. Researchers hope to construct buildings and bridges with stronger, more flexible steel and to pave a road with cement that mends itself at the first sign of a crack.[22]

Radio frequency identification (RFID) tags were recently implanted in two workers at CityWatcher.com, a video surveillance company that serves businesses and governments. The chips were surgically embedded just beneath the skin on the forearm. The technology, advocates say, will replace employee keycards or electronic security badges. The chips can be used as a tracking device. Also, telephone calls can now track your whereabouts and can be used for clocking in from distant locations, especially in construction and related industries. Galaxy Technologies, which sells time-and-attendance products to large companies, is giving its customers the option to use telephones or cell phones as time clocks.[23]

Technology in Communications.   Wi-Fi has penetrated the corporate world. It is a radio signal that beams Internet connections out three hundred feet. These are called *hot spots*. "Its super fast connections to the Web cost only a quarter as much as the gaggle of wires companies use today."[24] WiMAX is the new generation of technology for wireless services. It is more powerful and can extend beams over a larger area and provide faster and more efficient service to customers.

Wireless technology is being used for mission-critical jobs in factories, trucks, stores, and even hospitals. For example, UPS has equipped its worldwide distribution centers with wireless networks at a cost of $120 million. "As loaders and packers scan packages, the information zips instantly to the UPS network, leading to a 35 percent productivity gain." IBM is developing Wi-Fi powered systems to monitor equipment ranging from potato fryers at restaurants to air conditioners in computer labs. Boeing is scheduled to equip one hundred of its jets with speedy wireless technology. General Motors Corporation has developed Wi-Fi in ninety manufacturing plants. Although Wi-Fi technology is growing and is being used by more companies worldwide, security is still a problem. Until improved security techniques are developed, many companies are reluctant to use Wi-Fi in sensitive areas of the company where privacy is crucial.[25]

Simply put, technology is changing the way we live. Every year, more people are connected to cable or satellite television, have access to more cell phones, have more personalized Web pages for their investment portfolios and personal use, get more financial news from wireless devices, join more social networks such as Facebook and MySpace, and participate more in iMessaging, blogging, and twittering. This trend is certain to continue. Moreover, the current emphasis on R&D is unlikely to decline, given that research shows that companies with in-house R&D programs are achieving faster growth and better gross margins than are those that either outsource R&D or do not have such a program.[26] The state of the economy, however, does impact budgets and where money is spent. During the recession of 2008, many corporations reduced the amount of money budgeted for R&D.

Hence, the United States has entered a postindustrial society in which changes in the external environment are bringing about an entirely different set of internal values. In short, technology is changing America in general and employees in particular.

 CHECK YOUR UNDERSTANDING

1. How is technology changing your life?
2. Identify ways you use electronically operated equipment each day.
3. Make a list of new things that have been developed in the last five years. How surprised are you at the list?

Identify and describe the four major characteristics of a postindustrial society.

Postindustrial Society

In more than fifty years, the United States has progressed from an industrial society to a **postindustrial society**. This transition has involved four major changes:

1. A more service-oriented workforce.
2. An increase in the number of professonal and technical workers.
3. An increase in the importance of theoretical knowledge.
4. The planning and controlling of technological growth.

A Service-Oriented Workforce

Unlike the workforce in other countries, the majority of the U.S. workforce is no longer engaged in manufacturing or agriculture; it is engaged in services. Workers in transportation, utilities, trade, finance, insurance, real estate, and government now constitute approximately two-thirds of the total workforce. The remaining one-third is in agriculture, forestry, fisheries, mining, construction, and manufacturing. To release such a large number of people from manufacturing and yet maintain our production output, we had to make great technological advances. The result has been a dramatic change in the work environment.

An Increase in Professional and Technical Workers

Another characteristic of postindustrialism is the dynamic growth in the number of white-collar workers in the managerial, professional, technical, service, and sales occupations. In contrast, the number of blue-collar workers in occupations such as production, installation, construction, and farming is declining. According to the latest statistics from the U.S. Department of Labor, in January 2010, white-collar workers constituted approximately 79.7 percent of the labor force and blue-collar workers approximately 20.2 percent. These statistics reflect the high unemployment rate still in effect from the economic recession during 2008–2009. From 2004 to 2010, the blue-collar rate fell by 7.6 percent.

Increase in Importance of Theoretical Knowledge

The third characteristic of a postindustrial society is an increase in the importance of theoretical knowledge. Industrial societies are interested in the practical side of things. They concentrate on what works and ignore the rest. A postindustrial society, however, is concerned with more than just this short-run, heavily pragmatic view. For example, in hospitals today, a great deal of research is being conducted. Medical institutions are collecting all sorts of data on their patients: What is the patient's height, weight, age, gender, and religion? From what ailment is the person suffering? Can the patient's condition be traced to any variable? If so, can we make any generalization about how people with this condition might be cured? In many cases, though the data are analyzed, no answer is found. Nevertheless, medical personnel retain this information in a computer; they do not need to find a short-run value for it. Possibly, in the future, researchers will have collected sufficient data from which to postulate a theory regarding the causes of and cures for a given ailment. This theoretical knowledge is accumulated to serve as a foundation for projecting and planning for the future. A postindustrial society is more future-oriented than its predecessors.

Planning and Controlling Technological Growth

The fourth characteristic of a postindustrial society is an attempt to plan and control technological growth. When we examine the first three characteristics of a postindustrial society, we realize that it is an environment totally different from anything we have seen. It is a society in which highly educated people work in "think jobs" and in which a tremendous amount of money is spent each year on R&D, with much of the new knowledge being stored for future use. What will the year 2015 look like? The prospect scares many people and helps account for the fact that planning and control have now become important considerations. After all, if we fail to attend to monitoring our technological environment and deciding how we want it to grow, humankind will face a truly uncertain future.

 CHECK YOUR UNDERSTANDING

1. How will technology change the workplace, the marketplace, or how you live? In five years? In ten years? Can you even predict that far out?
2. What would you like to see changed? Why?
3. What do you think will change? Why?

Discuss the effect of technology on organizational culture.

Technology at Work

As the external environment changes, the environment within organizations alters as well. Technology permeates the organization's boundaries, affecting not only the structure but also the employees. It has an effect on people at work for two reasons. First, technology is causing a change in people's values, which workers bring with them to the workplace. Second, technology is leading to changes in the work environment, from the machines people use in creating output and making decisions to the way in which employees' offices and workstations are designed.

In analyzing this people/work environment/technology interface, we will consider four areas:

1. Changing organizational cultures.
2. Alienation in the workplace.
3. How workers feel about their jobs.
4. The quality of one's work life.

Before reading further, however, take the quiz in the "Time Out" box. The quiz is designed to measure the effect that the technological surroundings of your job have on you. What were your results? How do technological surroundings impact you?

Your Job and You

This quiz is designed to examine the relationship you have with your job. How comfortable do you feel doing your work? What role is played by technology? After you read each statement, try to be as candid as possible in your answer. Interpretations are provided at the end of the book.

	Highly Disagree	Disagree	Indifferent	Agree	Highly Agree
1. Although you have certain things you have to do every workday or workweek, you set the pace at which you work; management simply judges you on whether you have reached your overall objectives.	_____				
2. Basically, you do the same thing day after day, and the work is downright dull.	_____	_____	_____	_____	_____
3. Your job is mentally challenging; it requires rigorous thought.	_____	_____	_____	_____	_____
4. Your job is meaningless; anyone could do it, and to be quite frank, you are embarrassed when someone asks what you do for a living.	_____	_____	_____	_____	_____
5. On your job, you feel extremely tense and anxious, even though you may not know why.	_____	_____	_____	_____	_____
6. There is virtually no chance for you to socialize on your job.	_____	_____	_____	_____	_____
7. No matter how fast you work, there is always more to do; you can never finish.	_____	_____	_____	_____	_____
8. Your work environment is a very comfortable, enjoyable place; it is relaxing and encourages high productivity.	_____	_____	_____	_____	_____
9. Your job requires a variety of skills, and people in the organization admit that it takes real talent to do what you do.	_____	_____	_____	_____	_____
10. Face it; on your job, you are a small cog in a big machine; if you cannot master the latest technology, the organization will find someone who can.	_____	_____	_____	_____	_____

Changing Organizational Cultures

When new technology is introduced to an enterprise, some change in the organization's culture often occurs. **Organizational culture** is the environment in which people work. When this environment changes, people must learn to adapt. For example, a decision by a manufacturing firm to bring in robots and streamline production will have an effect on employees. Even if no one is let go, some people will have to learn new jobs, and the overall manufacturing process will change the way many workers interact. Technological change often affects the cultural match.

Cultural match is the similarity between individual and organizational culture. **Individual culture** is the norms, attitudes, values, and beliefs that a person brings to the job. These can vary from the type of work philosophy to which one adheres (how hard people should work) to his or her willingness to take risks (high, moderate, or low) and to his or her desire for power and control (high or low). Effective enterprises exhibit a cultural match between the organization and the individual culture. Simply put, people fit into the enterprise. However, when new technology is introduced, a mismatch between the organizational and individual cultures can occur.

Table 6.1
Organizational Culture Profiles

	Tough-Guy, Macho	Work Hard–Play Hard	Bet-Your-Company	Process
Risk assumed	High	Low	High	Low
Feedback from decision	Fast	Fast	Slow	Slow
Organizations that often have this kind of culture	Construction, TV, radio, management consulting	Retail sales, auto distribution, real estate	Capital goods, aerospace, investment banks, military	Banks, insurance companies, many government agencies
How successful people in this culture behave	Have a tough attitude, are individualistic, can live with all-or-nothing decisions	Are friendly, supersales types, work well in groups	Can stand long-term ambiguity, are technically competent, check and recheck their decisions	Are very cautious, always follow accepted procedures, are good at taking care of details
Strengths of successful people in this culture	Can get a lot done in a short period	Are able to produce a great deal of work quickly	Can generate high-quality inventions and major scientific breakthroughs	Bring order and system to the workplace
Weaknesses of successful people in this culture	Are short-run in orientation, ignore the benefits of cooperation	Look for quick-fix solutions, are more interested in action than in problem solving	Are slow in getting things done, cannot adjust well to short-term changes	Initiative is discouraged, lots of red tape, work is often boring
Habits of successful people in this culture	Dress in fashion, live in "in" places, enjoy one-to-one sports such as tennis	Avoid extremes in dress, prefer team sports such as softball	Dress according to hierarchical rank, enjoy sports such as golf in which outcome is unclear until the end of the game	Dress according to hierarchical rank, enjoy process sports such as swimming and jogging

Source: Terrence E. Deal and Allan A. Kennedy, *Corporate Cultures* (Reading, MA: Addison-Wesley Publishing Co., 1982), chapter 6.

A good way of explaining this problem is by first examining typical organizational culture profiles. Table 6.1 describes the four most common cultures. Notice that organizational culture can be described in terms of two characteristics: risk taking and feedback. In some organizations, success depends on the ability to take risks, whereas in others, success is achieved with low risks. In some successful organizations, feedback on results is very rapid, whereas in others it is very slow. Individuals who work in an organization for an extended period learn to adjust to its culture.

One of the most important cultural issues facing corporations globally is the recruitment and retention of valuable employees, regardless of the economic outlook. Instead of being human resources responsibilities, recruitment and retention are moving into boardrooms. Linda Rabbitt, chairman and CEO of Rand Corporation, spends a great deal of time trying to create a culture where employees can enjoy their jobs and can get fulfillment out of what they are doing. To retain talent in today's workplace, a company must develop a culture where employees are enthusiastic about executing the strategy in an environment where they know where they are going and how they are going to get there.[27]

Banks and Insurance Companies.   Technological modifications that cause a change in the need to assume risk or obtain feedback can cause problems for employees. For example, many banks and insurance companies have faced increased competition in recent years. As a result, they have been forced to assume increased risks. Those individuals who do not like increased risk have been compelled to leave the enterprise. Similarly, technology in these organizations has increased the amount of feedback regarding the outcome of decisions and thus changed the culture. The old way of doing business is becoming outdated, and employees must adjust to a new culture.

Google.   Corporate culture can mean so many different things. So then, what makes a great culture and what makes a less desirable one? That, of course, depends a lot on the employee's wishes. For example, the culture created by Google in its home office located at Mountain View in the Silicon Valley includes a wide array of perks, such as free meals at the Googleplex, free dry cleaning, free birthday massages, special parking spots for expectant moms, a state-of-the-art gym with swimming pool, child care, and car services, and employees can bring their dogs to the office. And the list goes on.[28] Benefits are important, but even more than that is the flow of information within the organization.

Oregon Health & Sciences University.   Providing information to the appropriate people when needed is vital in many companies. For example, Oregon Health & Sciences University (OHSU) in Portland, a leading teaching hospital and dental clinic, converted data from two hundred different software application packages, many of which were unable to communicate with each other, into Oracle's simplified, streamlined software program. The Oracle system provides more timely patient information wherever and whenever needed within OHSU. The job of the hospital's chief information officer is to keep track of the patient's records from the time of admittance through billing. With the new system, the patient's records are available in the department where the patient is being examined. Streamlining the business software for OHSU has been a complex and costly process. Such data integrations and software simplifications are changing the environment and culture in businesses.[29]

Oracle.   The way products are developed and the way business is conducted have changed dramatically at Oracle. The company has reduced its products from 150 to 1. A team's success is now measured in terms of how well integrated its product is with what the customer wants, not on how many different products the team can develop. According to the latest CIO survey by Morgan Stanley "every CIO is looking to reduce the number of vendors they work with." Oracle feels this message plays to its strength. Oracle willingly changes its culture to meet market needs.[30]

Starbucks.   Corporate cultures must be managed carefully or they can go astray. In 2008, when Starbucks customers were no longer receiving a superior experience and business began to slow, Howard Schultz, founder of Starbucks, took back the reins to address the challenges and to get the company back on track to the things that had made Starbucks successful in the first place. Some challenges are ethically sourcing and roasting the highest quality coffee in the world, focusing on customers and their experiences while in the store, building trust with the company's employees, and engaging in entrepreneurial risk taking through innovation and creativity, all of which were former hallmarks of its success. Starbucks strives to hire the right people, to keep lines of communication open, and to reward and retain employees with attractive compensation packages. Key to employee retention are the practices and the culture that the company has developed from its strong mission and values statement, which emphasizes creating a respectful and positive work environment. Technologically, communications plays an important role in creating the small-company feeling.[31]

Eli Lilly & Company.   The Eli Lilly & Company has a "culture that looks at failure as an inevitable part of discovery and encourages scientists to take risks."[32] For drugs that fail, Eli Lilly assigns a team of scientists to study the failures, in hopes of finding new ways to use the drugs. This risk taking has resulted in a pipeline of new drugs that has helped keep Eli Lilly's price-to-earnings ratio consistently at the high end of the drug industry.

Southwest Airlines.   At Southwest Airlines, changes in management and growth are influencing its culture. For example, for a short time, a new CEO disapproved of the company's annual Halloween celebration. Dressing up in costume and doing comedy sketches did not seem productive, but he came to see that the party preparations were a model of teamwork and employee bonding. Some new recruits who have never had a job before misunderstand the culture at Southwest and see it as one big party. In fact, the culture is based on an ethic of hard work and quick response; if something isn't working out, the employees do not let it drag on. The success of Southwest Airlines is based on its employees' dedication to quality customer service.[33]

Ford Motor Company.   The Ford Motor Company has been working to change its culture and become more productive. In doing so, the firm is trying to influence its managers to act more like owners and entrepreneurs and to make decisions that will cut costs and increase output. Although Ford is cutting costs, the company is learning how difficult it can be to change "old ways" to "new ways" and operate in an ever-changing environment to satisfy customers' wants and needs. Karen Yvonne Hardin, a Ford truck owner, after experiencing problems says that, "Quality must be job one. Saying it isn't enough."[34] Toyota has for decades promoted itself as a manufacturer of quality products, but recent cases of significant quality failure resulting in massive recalls have damaged the company's credibility and reputation. How will the recalls affect the culture at Toyota? Will the company need to establish a new culture or will the old culture work? History tells us that Toyota will need to make changes to survive in the years to come. The biggest challenge for most firms is being able to alter their culture and thus deal with environmental changes. Researchers have found that companies that are able to do this often achieve significant bottom-line results. For example, Kenexa has found that turnover among managers who feel pride in their company is 21 percent lower than those who do not.[35] Another group of researchers reported that over an eleven-year period, firms with cultures that accommodated change performed significantly better than did their counterparts who did not accommodate change, including the following accomplishments:

1. Increasing revenues by an average of 682 percent, as compared with 166 percent for other firms.
2. Expanding their workforces by 282 percent, versus 36 percent for the others.
3. Achieving stock price increases of 901 percent, versus 74 percent for the others.
4. Improving net income by 756 percent, versus 1 percent for the others.[36]

Enterprises that introduce technology to stay competitive must also ensure that the organizational culture will accommodate these changes. Otherwise, the employees are likely to feel alienated by what is happening around them.

✔ CHECK YOUR UNDERSTANDING

1. Using the information in Table 6.1, identify the type of culture you work in at your present job, or a previous job.
2. Describe the type of culture you would like to work in. Tell why.

Identify and describe four ways employees feel alienated by technology.

Technology and Alienation

Of all the behavioral implications of technology, the most important seems to be that of alienation. This concept incorporates powerlessness, meaninglessness, isolation, and self-estrangement.

Powerlessness.   Many workers, particularly assembly workers, feel they are at the mercy of technology. Their sense of **powerlessness** can lead to alienation. Workers on an assembly line, for example, remain at their stations and the work comes to them. If the line is moving very quickly, they must work faster to accommodate it. At the Westinghouse Air Brake Company's factory, a shrill buzzer erupts every two minutes and twenty-six seconds, a signal that the conveyor that carries parts down the line is about to move and everyone must hurry to keep up. Moreover, every worker at the plant is motivated to hustle because there is $1.50-per-hour bonus if the plant makes its daily production quota. Therefore, although the workers may feel they are powerless, they are willing to accept this condition because the bonus can mean an additional $3,750 annually. Another example is older workers who may feel stressed when new equipment is installed and they are required to learn how to operate it.

Meaninglessness.   Many employees are unable to determine what they are doing or why they are doing it. Individuals who put a bolt on a widget, assemble two minor parts of a major system, or test a component that will be placed in a giant machine feel no relationship with the finished product. Technology helps to create this **meaninglessness** through its emphasis on job specialization, as in assembly-line work. How do workers adapt to these conditions? Some simply fail to show up for work. It is not uncommon to find assembly plants with staff shortages when the hunting season opens. Those who do show up for work often spend a large percentage of their workday playing mental games or daydreaming.

Isolation.   On the job, people cannot run away from technology. If only to keep up with the competition, it is a part of their work life. Here, then, the individual is locked in, forced to cope with technology. However, **isolation** still occurs in many cases, for the person is often confined to one locale, as in the case of a worker on an automobile assembly line who must remain at a particular place on the line for the entire workday; a computer operator who must stay near the machine, checking on jobs being run and remaining alert for any machine malfunctions; a press operator who is confined to the general area of the printing press, constantly observing the speed and feed of the paper, prepared to adjust or stop the machine should something go awry; or an individual working at home who has no opportunity for face-to-face contact with coworkers or customers. All these people are isolated within a given area and, depending on the specific situation, isolated from other workers. At best, the technology allows them to interact only with those in their immediate vicinity; at worst, the demands of the job sometimes prevent them from associating with anyone for extended periods of the workday. This is particularly true for those workers who are continually on the road. These "mobile workers" report that it is difficult to balance work demands and home demands.

Self-Estrangement.   **Self-estrangement** occurs when the worker can no longer find intrinsic satisfaction in what he or she is doing: The work becomes merely a means to earn a living. No fun or challenge is associated with it. If another job offered more money, the worker would quit. Technology can create self-estrangement by reducing the scope and importance of the work itself. As we saw in Chapter 2 when we discussed Herzberg's two-factor theory, the things people liked best about their jobs were related to the work itself: Intrinsic motivators, such as achievement, responsibility, and the possibility of growth were part of the job. Technology can eliminate many of these. Technology requires finding new ways to gain intrinsic satisfaction on the job.

 CHECK YOUR UNDERSTANDING

1. Has technology ever made you feel alienated? If so, describe the situation.
2. Give an example of each type of alienation: powerlessness, meaninglessness, isolation, and self-estrangement.

Explain how technology impacts an employee's quality of work life.

How Workers Feel about Their Jobs

Today, workers no longer have as strong a fear that machines will replace them as they had more than a decade ago. Earlier, new technology introduced into the workplace created problems and human relations issues among employees. This fear was typical among people who were not highly skilled or who performed paperwork functions, such as checking forms, filling out structured reports, or entering data in accounting ledgers. Although advances in technology are inevitable, methods exist for dealing with it from a human relations standpoint. The "Human Relations in Action" box describes some of these methods.

Despite the feelings of alienation that workers have in their jobs, the effect of technology can be effectively addressed. In the late 1980s, *Inc.* magazine conducted a national survey and found that more than 70 percent of the respondents were either satisfied or extremely satisfied with their place of employment; the highest percentage was found in small firms. This number has been steadily declining over the years. In 2010, the Conference Board reported that fewer than half (45 percent) of U.S. workers are satisfied with their jobs, the lowest level in 22 years, despite big improvements in the work environment. The findings revealed that workers younger than 25 were the most unhappy in their jobs.[37]

Phil Rosenzweig, in his book *The Halo Effect*, raises the question of whether satisfied employees drive performance or high performance drives employee satisfaction. He has concluded that high-performing companies lead to employee satisfaction more than employee satisfaction leads to high-performing companies.[38]

Current issues, such as inflexible work arrangements and employee engagement, are the main reasons why employees leave an organization; it is not the fear of technology. However, this does not mean that all workplace issues related to technology have been resolved. In fact, quality of work life (QWL) issues continue to be a major challenge facing organizations.

The Issue of Quality of Work Life

A major sociotechnical issue is the quality of work life. QWL is concerned with the overall work climate, with specific emphasis on the effect of the work environment on

IN ACTION

DEALING WITH TECHNOLOGY

Technology is making many jobs easier. At the same time, it may cause concern among employees who are convinced that computers, robots, or some other form of advanced technology will replace them. Nothing can be done to prevent the advance of technology. However, some human relations steps can be followed to help with the employees' challenge. Five of the most useful steps follow:

1. *Become familiar with the jobs your people are doing.* This has two benefits. First, if new technology is to be introduced, you will have a fairly good idea of what it can do. Second, most workers object to any changes that are likely to lead to their being displaced. If you understand how their jobs work, you are in a better position to help them confront this problem.

2. *Be aware of the negative impact technology can have.* When people become adjuncts of the machines they operate, their self-esteem and job satisfaction often drop. You cannot help your people deal with this problem until you realize it is a common response to technology. It does no good to tell a person that his or her job is interesting if he or she does not see it that way. Try to empathize with those who are most affected by the impact of technology. Then you will be better able to help them to adjust.

3. *Get worker input regarding how to use technology.* This is one of the most effective ways of introducing work changes. The workers often have good ideas for using new machinery and equipment; after all, they are the ones who do the job. If any shortcuts can be worked out, the workers will find them, or if any problems arise in making the machine do what it is supposed to, the workers will fix them. There is no better source for evaluating job technology than the workers themselves.

4. *Keep your people apprised of what is going on.* If you and your boss have been talking about putting in new automated machinery, tell this to the workers as soon as the decision is made. If you wait until the machines are delivered, the impact of the change will cause panic. You need to introduce change slowly. Sure, some of the workers may accuse you of trying to undermine their jobs and may threaten to quit. However, most of the workers know that it is your job to maintain high productivity, and if new machines are needed, they will have to be purchased.

5. *Be honest with your people.* Some workers will be displaced by new technology. This is particularly true of those who do simple jobs or those who are unable to learn new work procedures. In many cases, these people will be able to obtain work elsewhere in the organization. If this is not possible, be open with them and tell them they are going to be laid off. No one likes to give people this kind of news, but it is better to be honest with them so that they can make plans than to keep them in the dark until the last minute. The way you treat workers who are being let go will influence the morale and trust of those who remain in the department. Honesty is always the best policy.

organizational effectiveness, health, safety, and worker satisfaction. The concern for reducing ergonomic-related injuries and illnesses in the workplace has generated attention at the Occupational Safety & Health Administration (OSHA) and the National Institute of Occupational Safety and Health (NIOSH).

One of the primary areas of attention is **ergonomics**, which is concerned with designing and shaping the physical work environment to fit the physical abilities and characteristics of individuals. In the past few years, many businesses are redesigning work spaces to make accomplishing tasks easier. In an office environment, ergonomic concerns include the type, shape, and color of work surfaces; workstation heights; and chair sizes and heights. For example, one ergonomics expert has noted that office chairs should be tested carefully to ensure that they are comfortable and do not limit productivity. In choosing the best chair, she suggests that each person test the following features before purchasing a chair.

1. Seat height adjustability allows the user to adjust the chair so that his or her feet are on the floor.
2. Seat depth adjustability changes the front-to-back depth of the seat. Smaller people need a shorter seat pan, while taller people need a deeper one.
3. Backrest angle adjustability allows the chair to support different degrees of recline, lightening the load on the lower back's intervertebral discs.
4. Chair recline or tilt changes the angle of the entire seat relative to the floor. A recline chair transfers some upper-body weight to the backrest of the chair.
5. Seat pan angle adjustability refers to changing the forward-back angle of the seat. The purpose is to open the angle between the trunk and thighs, inducing lordosis and reducing disc pressure.

6. Armrests support the arms, reducing the work of the shoulders and possibly the upper arms.

7. Height-adjustable armrests help avoid the problems of too-high armrests, which result in elevated shoulders and pressure on the undersides of the elbows and forearms.

8. Width-adjustable armrests change the distance between armrests. Armrests that are too close can cause the wrists to bend to the side during keying.

9. Padded armrests can avoid uncomfortable pressure on the undersides of the forearms and elbow.

10. Lumbar support is intended to prevent the flattening of the lumbar spine that occurs in most people when seated.

11. Backrest height adjustability refers to a change in height of the lumbar support area of the chair backrest.

Lumbar depth adjustability affects the size and sometimes the firmness of the lumbar support curve in a chair's backrest.[39] A growing concern of ergonomics is the prevention of work-related *musculoskeletal disorders*, which are costly illnesses in the workplace. An example, carpal tunnel syndrome, caused by a repetitive motion and overuse of extremities, often involves the wrist and can be related to the use of the computer keyboard. For this reason, attention should be paid to the type of computer, monitor, keyboard, and computer accessories, such as wrist rests, copyholders, and footrests, which are being used in the office.

Another ergonomics-related issue is the amount of time people spend in front of *video display terminals* (VDTs) in the workplace. Some municipalities now have guidelines that regulate the workplace and are designed to prevent such problems as VDT-attributable diseases and injuries associated with continuously striking computer keyboards. Until recently, San Francisco companies with more than fifteen employees were required to make the workplace more ergonomically correct. Employees using VDTs were to be given a fifteen-minute break or transferred to another job after working at their terminals for two hours. The San Francisco law, which also mandated that certain kinds of furniture and equipment be supplied to workers to aid them with ergonomically related problems, was struck down in court. Nonetheless, ergonomics continues to be a QWL issue.

Still other areas of concern are *lighting, heating, and ventilation, as well as office layout*. In each case, the focus is on designing the workplace so that it is comfortable and conducive to productivity. Some companies now allow their employees to wear an iPod so they can listen to music while they work. Especially for workers whose jobs entail repetitive tasks, such as mail sorting or simple assembly, the music provides a way of dealing with the boredom.[40]

Another QWL issue is the amount of authority and participation workers have in the decision-making process. For example, employees who work with large-batch or mass-production technology have the highest reported levels of alienation. However, these workers also seem to be at a loss in determining what can be done.

When managers and workers have formed QWL committees, employees have not been very actively supportive of the committees' work. Many workers distrust these types of joint committees, believing that, in the long run, the only change will be to speed up the assembly line. A number of managers also believe that these committees are of no real value.

What, then, is the answer in dealing with sociotechnical problems? One part of the solution is the use of job enrichment and other redesign techniques, which are discussed in Chapter 8. Another part of the answer must be found in the industrial environment

SELLING THEM ON IT

Technology can have negative as well as positive effects on employees. For this reason, management has a social responsibility to employees to ensure technology-based changes are introduced properly. Although a wide variety of steps can be taken, five of the most important are listed here:

1. *Let everyone know about the new technological changes that will be taking place.* If new machinery is going to be introduced, explain why these machines are important, and stress the fact that employees will be trained to use these units. This step involves "telling and selling."

2. *Introduce the system to the right people first.* When new technology or systems are introduced in companies, it often is more effective first to acquaint middle management with the new changes. Then, with middle management solidly behind the new system, introduce the changes to the staff and workers. If there is any friction regarding the change, middle management will voice its support and work to sell its people on the need for the new technology and the changes.

3. *Be sure the new technology works as promised before introducing it.* If a manufacturer says the new computers can all be linked to the company's mainframe and used for analysis of centralized records, be sure these claims are backed up. If something goes wrong after the system is installed, convincing people to accept the technology after the corrections have been made will be much more difficult.

4. *Once the new system is up and working, get rid of the old system.* Some companies that have introduced new pieces of digital equipment started out by making them available for use while leaving the old systems in place. However, they have also given everyone training and set a deadline for scrapping the old system. As they begin to master the new technology, employees voluntarily abandon the old system, although it is there in the beginning should the workers encounter problems and need to fall back on a system they understand. Once the old system is scrapped, there is no going back. From that point, only the new system is used.

5. *Be sure the training is hands-on and useful.* Sometimes training involves the teaching of theory, but this should not be given precedence over teaching employees how to use the machines for day-to-day operations. Once the workers master the new technology, they will use it. It's all a matter of getting them to see the value of the new system.

---

itself. In many European countries, industrial democracy is used, while in the United States, participative management is more prevalent. Both offer possibilities for meeting the sociotechnical challenge.

Meeting the Sociotechnical Challenge

Discuss how knowledge-based organizations, industrial democracy, and participative management can aid in integrating technology and the organization's personnel.

The dysfunctional effects of technology can be traced, in large part, to the fears it creates among employees. Human relations management requires that the employees' interests be considered and protected by management. (See the "In Action" box, "Ethics and Social Responsibility in Action.") Workers need to feel confident that ultimately they will gain from technology. In other words, a supportive climate must exist between employees and management. If this climate can be created, workers will be more receptive to the changes being thrust on them by technology. This concept is now leading to the development of knowledge-based organizations and the use of industrial democracy and participative management, as well as the creation of programs designed to deal with workplace violence.

Development of Knowledge-Based Organizations

Technology is radically changing the way organizations are managed. In the past, organizations provided the tools and equipment and some on-the-job training, and the workers were expected to do the rest. Today, technology is making far greater demands on both groups, and each must be prepared to change. Many employees have limited skills and training for meeting current job demands. Resource-based organizations are now being replaced by knowledge-based organizations, requiring managers to change their approach to leading the employees. A **knowledge-based organization** is viewed as a group of knowledge workers who are interconnected by a computerized infrastructure. The main features are local workstations, support centers, communication paths, and knowledge databases.

One way in which organizations are meeting the sociotechnical challenge that faces employees is by retooling these workers. Some of this training in manufacturing, for example, is technical in nature and includes such subjects as just-in-time production, reliability engineering, and statistical sampling. Some of it is behavioral in content and focuses on ways of dealing more effectively with others. In both cases, the training is heavily practical and hands-on, and is designed to equip the worker with tools and techniques that can be used for dealing with day-to-day problems.

While some companies faced shrinking training budgets during the last recession, the American Society for Training & Development in Alexandria, Virginia, reported that, on average, companies spent $1,068 per employee on training and devoted 36 hours of training per employee. Due to decreased training dollars, a shift began to occur; instead of offering mass training, some companies became more selective in deciding which employees would receive training. More emphasis was placed on leadership training, as companies began searching for a way to survive the recession.[41]

In the past decade, virtual training has gained acceptance in the workplace and is continuing to grow each year. In 2009, roughly one-third of formal learning was delivered online, up by 24 percent from the year before. One of the main reasons for an increase in virtual learning is a shift in demographics from the older, book-bound workers near retirement to a more tech-savvy cadre of people who are entering the nation's workforce. They are eager to use online tools to aid professional growth and development. Another reason is that more workers entering the labor force need training.

One of the fastest developing learning technology tools is collaboration and decision making that requires the learner to become engaged in the learning process. Collaboration technology allows learners to enter a simulated work situation where they make decisions related to the challenges they face on their job. For example, Southwest Airlines uses the Paradigm Learning game, called *Zodiak*, to develop adaptive thinking. The employees work in teams to create and build a mythical company. Then facilitators work with the teams on applying what they have learned to similar challenges and surprise scenarios at Southwest. Employees at Southwest Airlines must constantly adapt to new security rules and roles, changing online reservation requirements, volatile fuel prices, and weather conditions. So proper training is very important at Southwest Airlines.[42]

As you can see today, technology is an important and growing part of learning. In the past, colleges and universities provided a great deal of this training. A production worker would be sent to a local community college to study basic electronics, a middle manager would attend a nearby university and learn some of the latest techniques of just-in-time inventory control, or a senior-level manager would be sent to Harvard University's thirteen-week advanced management program to learn about new management developments. Today, however, many firms are bringing their training in-house and creating their own colleges and universities. For example, General Electric has a corporate university in Crotonville, New York, where managers from throughout the firm attend specially designed courses taught by in-house personnel and outside consultants. Motorola University in Schaumberg, Illinois, annually trains thousands of corporate employees, suppliers, and vendors in a wide variety of technical and managerial subjects. In some cases, people do not go to a training site; rather, the training comes to them.

FedEx employees faced another technology adjustment after Federal Express and Motorola united to develop the FedEx PowerPad, designed to enhance customer service by providing 40,000 FedEx couriers with online, near real-time, wireless access to the FedEx network. The FedEx PowerPad enhanced and accelerated "package information available to customers by enabling couriers to wirelessly send and receive near real-time information and updates from any location." This replaced the handheld courier FedEx Supertracker.[43]

Such developments are helping to ensure that workers are able to adjust to the new high-tech environment. At the same time, managers are adapting their approach to meet emerging changes. Whereas managers once functioned in a **resource-based organization**, in which the company provided the necessary tools, equipment, and direction and the employees used these resources to pursue predetermined goals, today managers are operating in a knowledge-based organization, in which information sharing, teamwork, trust, and empowerment are key characteristics. Table 6.2 contrasts these two organizations and helps to illustrate why a knowledge-based management orientation is necessary in today's workplace. In this knowledge-based environment, industrial democracy and participative management are playing increasingly important roles.

Table 6.2
Resource-Based Organizations and Knowledge-Based Organizations

Job	Resource-Based Organizations	Knowledge-Based Organizations
Overall direction	Set by top management	Set by top management but shared by all employees
Planning and decision making	Top management sets the plan and everyone else works on implementing it	Planning and decision making take place at all levels in a well-coordinated, teamwork fashion
Problem solving	Employees analyze the situation, formulate a solution, and then convince others to accept their approach	Through the use of collaboration, cooperation, and the integration of diverse points of view, a solution is formulated that is acceptable to all involved parties
Conflict resolution	The person with the most power bends the others to his or her way of thinking	There is a dialogue and integration of many points of view in deciding how to resolve the conflict
Motivation	Managers get things done by offering rewards that are desired by employees	Managers get things done by offering challenges that are personally acceptable to the employees
Leadership	Top leadership creates a vision for the organization and sells it to the employees	Top leadership creates a vision for the organization that incorporates employee values and beliefs, and the personnel willingly accept and follow this vision
Organizing	Management designs a structure that ensures that everyone knows his or her job and has the necessary authority for carrying out these tasks	Management empowers employees with sufficient resources and knowledge so that they fulfill their jobs with the least amount of bureaucracy or red tape
Controlling	Management sets up checkpoints to monitor employee performance and prevent problems from getting out of hand	Management trains the employees to use self-control to monitor their performance and ensure that work output meets all quality standards

Use of Industrial Democracy and Participative Management

Two major trends in management-worker relations over the last twenty-five years are those of industrial democracy and participative management. Both involve shared decision making between workers and management. However, despite their similarity of intent, fundamental differences exist between the methods of each of these trends. **Industrial democracy** is a formal and usually legally sanctioned arrangement of worker representation in the form of committees, councils, and boards at various levels of decision making. **Participative management**, on the other hand, is an informal style of face-to-face leadership in which management and workers share decision making in the workplace. It is sometimes called shop-floor democracy. Some countries of the world make more use of one method than the other.

In Germany, for example, companies with more than five hundred workers have supervisory boards that set company policy. These boards are made up of two-thirds shareholder representatives and one-third worker representatives. Firms with more than two thousand employees have 50 percent worker representation on these boards. By law, industrial democracy is a way of life in Germany. German workers also have much more operating authority than do American workers. For example, the workers are allowed to rotate jobs to prevent the work from becoming boring. Some firms even allow their workers to vary the number of hours they work throughout the year. They can work less hours during some months as long as they work more hours during other months.

One of the primary reasons for the high degree of participative management in Germany is that the unions and management have a much more cooperative relationship than in the United States. The two sides try to work out their differences in a way that is beneficial to both.[44]

In the Scandinavian countries—Norway, Sweden, and Denmark—statutory requirements are established for worker representation on governing boards. For example, for almost forty years, Sweden has required that companies with more than fifty employees maintain work councils made up of representatives of both management and labor who meet regularly to solve problems and exchange information.

However, Scandinavians also lead the way in terms of shop-floor democracy. In some of their factories, autonomous work groups have been introduced. These groups have decision-making discretion that allows them to determine for themselves how to do their jobs. Their range of authority often extends from the receipt of orders to final inspection. These groups consist of councils and committees that have been formed to encourage employee involvement in identifying and implementing changes that will improve workplace ambience and help sustain high morale and positive employee attitudes.

In the United States, both participative management and industrial democracy have developed. Participative management—if only because of the American traditions of individualism and democracy—has always been very popular. However, industrial democracy is also gaining in importance.

One of the primary reasons for these developments is that they help organizations tap the brainpower of their employees by getting people involved in planning and implementing new ideas. For example, in Motorola's engineering, manufacturing, and marketing departments, people work together to design and build new products and deliver them to market. As a result, the total time needed for bringing many products to fruition has been reduced from seventy-two months to eighteen months.

In another example, scientists at Pioneer Hi-Bred International, a leading developer and producer of seed products for agriculture in the world, breed special strains of corn for disease resistance, high yield, or specific attributes such as oil content. A decade ago, such work ate up hundreds of acres of farmland and consumed untold numbers of worker hours. These days, the plant's DNA is manipulated in a petri dish. Apart from the cost savings, the company expects to knock two years off the seven to ten years that it takes to develop a new hybrid. This trend is continuing with the introduction of Roundup Ready brands of alfalfa and corn designed to help control weeds.

Empowerment.   At the heart of participative management and industrial democracy is the concept of **empowerment**, the process of giving employees control over decisions and policies that directly affect them. One reason empowerment tends to work is because it increases motivation. Even if people have power, they must feel they have the power or there is no gain. "People must feel they control their own destiny if they are to be part of a change effort, provide excellent service, or take risks."[45] Over the past ten years, this idea has become very popular. The basic components of empowerment are:

- Giving employees greater authority to make decisions.
- Maintaining an open and decentralized communication system.
- Utilizing people from many different departments to solve complex organizational problems.
- Rewarding and recognizing those who assume responsibility and perform well.

The Dancing Deer Baking Company in Boston is an example of empowerment in action. What began as a hobby investment in 1994 has evolved from small café accounts to a high-end wholesale market and a mail-order business. It has maintained 20 percent to 30 percent in annual growth. Patricia Karter, president, credits her success on what she calls an *innovative management philosophy*. All workers are stakeholders, with ownership in the company's profitability. Workers have empowerment in their jobs and can push the boundaries of creativity. Everyone wants quality on all levels and wants to create a brand that stands for something. The employees are passionate about food, nature, and aesthetics. Karter's toughest job as the company continues to grow is to hold the team together and maintain an exceptional culture of respect and passion, excellence, and working values.[46]

A survey conducted by the Gallup Organization for the American Society for Quality found that workers in small businesses feel they have more authority (more empowerment) to take action than those at large companies, and are more likely to believe management would approve. More workers in small businesses would take action to stop work in progress to correct a problem than workers in larger businesses.

CHECK YOUR UNDERSTANDING

1. Select a business you are familiar with. Use the information in Table 6.2 to decide the type of business it is. What did you find?
2. In which type of business would you like to be employed? Why?

Discuss workplace violence and how managers are dealing with it.

Dealing with Workplace Violence

Workplace violence is violence or the threat of violence against workers. It can be any physical assault, threatening behavior, or verbal abuse that occurs in and around the workplace. In recent years, there has been an upsurge of such violence, some of which is directly attributable to technology. Moreover, workplace violence is much more common than many people realize and is a growing concern for employers and employees nationwide. Sometimes this violence results in homicide.

Some two million American workers are victims of workplace violence each year. It can strike anywhere, and no one is immune. Some occupational fields are more prone to workplace violence than others. For example, health care, retail trade, law enforcement and security professions have high cases of workplace violence. Domestic violence brought to the workplace by angry spouses has also impacted the level of workplace violence.

Some workers, however, are at an increased risk. They are workers who exchange money with the public; deliver passengers, goods, or services; or work alone or in small groups, during late night or early morning hours, in high-crime areas, or in community settings and homes where they have extensive contact with the public. This group includes health-care and social service workers such as visiting nurses, psychiatric evaluators, and probation officers; community workers such as gas and water utility employees, phone and cable TV installers, and letter carriers; retail workers; and taxi drivers.[47]

All one has to do is visit the Web site of the U.S. Bureau of Labor Statistics to learn the extent of workplace violence. Its most extreme form, homicide, is the fourth leading cause of fatal occupational injury in the United States. Most common violent acts were simple assaults followed by aggravated assaults, rapes and sexual assaults, robberies, and homicides.

Other examples of workplace violence are:[48]

- Verbal threats to inflict bodily harm, including vague or covert threats.
- Attempting to cause physical harm, striking, pushing, and other aggressive physical acts against another person.
- Verbal harassment, abusive or offensive language, gestures, or other discourteous conduct toward supervisors, fellow employees, or the public.
- Disorderly conduct, such as shouting, throwing or pushing objects, punching walls, and slamming doors.
- Making false, malicious, or unfounded statements against coworkers, supervisors, or subordinates, which tend to damage their reputations or undermine their authority.
- Inappropriate remarks, such as making delusional statements.
- Fascination with guns or other weapons or bringing weapons into the workplace.

For the first time since the Census of Fatal Occupational Injuries program was implemented in 1992, the total fatal work injuries recorded in 2008 were down slightly from the previous year. Economic factors likely played a role in the fatality decrease, as well as decreases in government budgets that support the compilation of the data. Fewer people were working during that recessionary period as unemployment rates were the highest in over two decades.

What can Employers Do?

Businesses have a responsibility to provide a safe place for employees to work. Employees expect the workplace to be a safe environment where they can go to make their lives better, a place to make careers for themselves. Violent acts can be extremely upsetting to those who feel that their rights in the workplace are being violated. One would think that today most businesses would have policies and procedures in place to protect their employees, but that is not the case. It is shocking to find that over 70 percent of the U.S. workplaces do not have a formal program or policy that addresses workplace violence according to the U.S. Bureau of Labor Statistics. Of those companies reporting having a workplace program or policy in place in 2006, 82 percent of them experienced coworker violence during the year.

While many violent acts do not make the national news, some do. For example, in 2009, a Yale University student Annie Le was allegedly killed by a research lab technician Raymond Clark III, and her body was found hidden in a wall. In January 2010, in St. Louis, Timothy Hendron killed four workers and himself at an ABB, Inc., transformer factory. Then, barely a month later, a University of Alabama professor, Amy Bishop, opened fire on three colleagues, fatally wounding them. And then, within two weeks, Andrew Joseph Stack III, an irate tax protester, flew a plane into a building housing an Internal Revenue Service (IRS) office in Austin, Texas, killing himself and an IRS agent. Violent acts of all magnitudes keep happening, and no business or no one seems to be immune. These reports simply heighten the importance of having a workplace violence program and policies in place to protect employees. Without them, companies expose themselves and their employees to greater liability. Organizations must take proactive steps to reduce and, it is hoped, eliminate this problem. OSHA has recommended some engineering and administrative controls to help prevent and mitigate the effects of workplace violence. They are:[49]

- Physical barriers, such as bullet-resistant enclosures and shields, pass-through windows, and deep service counters
- Alarm systems, such as panic buttons, GPS, and radios ("open mike switch")
- Convex mirrors at elevated vantage points to provide clear visibility of service and cash register areas
- Bright and effective lighting
- Staffing an adequate number of employees
- Room design; for example, arranging furniture to prevent entrapment
- Money safeguards, such as using cash-handling controls and drop safes
- Height markers, which mark heights on exit doors
- Emergency procedures, such as developing procedures to use in case of a robbery
- Training; for example, training all employees to identify hazardous situations and in how to respond appropriately in emergencies
- Video surveillance equipment; for example, installing in-car surveillance cameras and closed-circuit TV cameras
- Establishing liaison with local police

An effective violence prevention program should include postincident response and evaluation. All workplace violence programs should include providing treatment for victimized and traumatized employees and witnesses. The types of assistance may include trauma or crisis counseling, critical incident stress debriefing, or employee assistance programs to assist victims.[50]

Behavior of Individuals

One way in which enterprises are trying to reduce workplace violence is by screening people during the job selection process or the probationary period that follows. Although identifying the behavior of those who are prone to violence is sometimes difficult, many tend to exhibit specific types of behavior. Some of those behaviors are described in Table 6.3.

These behaviors often are very costly to employers. They can result in substandard production, poor morale, excessive labor problems, unnecessarily high labor turnover, and excessive absenteeism. The behaviors can also affect other employees, who do not want to be around these individuals and who find that they cannot get their work done efficiently because of the environment that is created by the emotional problems of these individuals. When individuals become violent, where do you begin the investigation? A series of steps to take is outlined in Figure 6.1.

Table 6.3
Behaviors of Violence-Prone People

Behaviors	Descriptions
Belligerence	Walking around with a chip on one's shoulder, ready to argue or quarrel with others at the slightest excuse
Excessive moodiness	Spells of the blues or feeling down in the dumps a great deal of the time
Exaggerated worry	Continuous anxiety about small matters that are blown entirely out of proportion
Suspiciousness and mistrust	A persistent feeling that the world is full of dishonest, conniving people who are trying to take advantage of them
Helplessness and dependency	A tendency to let others carry the burden, while exhibiting problems with making decisions
Poor emotional control	Exaggerated emotional outbursts that are inappropriate or out of proportion to the cause
Daydreaming and fantasy	Spending a good part of the day imagining how things could be rather than dealing with them the way they are
Hypochondria	Worrying a great deal of the time about minor physical ailments or experiencing imaginary symptoms of illness

Source: Romould A. Stone, "Homicide in the Workplace: Crisis or False Alarm?" *Business Horizons*, March–April 1995, p. 6.

Figure 6.1 Investigating Workplace Violence: Where Do You start?

Here's a Ten-Step Game Plan

Issue: You've just received the unsettling news that one of your employees physically attacked another employee, causing him serious injuries. You want to initiate an investigation, but you're not sure where to begin or what the investigation should entail. What do you do?

Answer: The short answer is to conduct an investigation that is thorough, well documented, objective, prompt, confidential, and well organized. Ultimately, however, you need a game plan—a good strategy that will ensure you've covered all the bases. To that end, consider the following ten steps:

1. Decide who should conduct the investigation.

This is a critical decision that requires several issues to be considered, and should be made well in advance of any incident. The investigator should be objective, experienced in investigations, and should make a credible witness in case the incident results in legal action.

2. Review company policies.

In the scenario described above, the company's workplace violence policy should be consulted. Be sure to follow any procedures and safeguard any rights established in the policy.

(Continued)

3. Identify any potential witnesses.

This aspect of the investigation can be a bit murky, as both parties may request that you interview numerous witnesses to buttress their positions. List all potential witnesses in order of priority, beginning with eyewitnesses and supervisors.

4. Gather and review documents.

Documents to look for in an inquiry may encompass a number of written materials, including previous complaints, incident reports, company policies, police reports, witness statements, personnel files, time cards, and even expense reports. In short, review all relevant documents.

5. Identify the issues to be investigated.

The person conducting the investigation must ask, "What are we talking about here?" In the scenario above, the answer is straightforward: workplace violence. However, the investigator should keep in mind that new issues may arise as the investigation progresses. Be sure to follow up.

6. Prepare your investigation strategy.

A good strategy involves structuring the interviews in a way that will maximize the amount of information you discover. Ask yourself, "Who do I want to talk to first—and why?" Generally, the person bringing the complaint and the person accused are good places to start in a workplace violence case. The investigator should also consider beginning with the person who is most likely to "spill the beans."

7. Take interim steps.

It is perfectly acceptable to suspend someone pending an investigation, especially in cases where the employer suspects a threat to the health and safety of other employees. The person allegedly posing such a threat should be suspended.

8. Prepare interview questions.

The investigator should always prepare the questions in advance. Know what questions you want to ask and how you want the interview to develop. The interviewer should begin with broad-based questions to put the person at ease and gradually get around to asking the critical questions.

9. Anticipate questions.

The interviewer should also try to think of any questions that will arise from the other person's perspective.

10. Prepare opening and closing statements.

The advantage to having a prepared opening and closing is to be sure that certain areas are covered with each person interviewed. You want to remind each person of the company policies involved, that the allegations are taken seriously by the company, and that the company will conduct a thorough and prompt investigation. You also want to "keep the door open"—let each person know to come back and see you if anything new comes up.

Source: A presentation given by Charles L. Thompson IV, a partner with the San Francisco law firm of Hanson, Bridgett, Marcus, Vlahos, & Rudy, September 3, 1999. Reference source: www.workforce.com/archive/article/22/05/75_printer.php. Used by permission.

Dealing with the Issue

Companies are now developing a variety of programs to help them deal with workplace violence.

- One such initiative is *to place all workers in positions that best employ their skills.* In this way, the individuals will feel that they are doing meaningful work and will be an important asset to the organization.
- A second program calls *for providing clear job descriptions and supportive supervision* so that everyone knows what she or he is supposed to be doing and receives any help and guidance required. This approach is particularly beneficial in reducing the anger and hostility that result when people become frustrated or stymied on the job.
- A third initiative is *to recognize and value cultural diversity among employees at all levels of the enterprise* so that each person feels that he or she is a part of the group rather than an outsider.
- A fourth approach is *to conduct periodic reviews of job performance and to recognize and reward work output,* thereby assuring all employees that when they do a good job, the organization will show its appreciation.
- A fifth program calls *for providing reasonable job security,* which affords workers the peace of mind of knowing that they will not be arbitrarily terminated, and if a cutback is needed, they will be given ample advance notice.[51]

In addition, organizations that experience high incidents of workplace violence often provide training to their people regarding how to handle various situations, such as identifying those workers who seem to be getting out of control. Employees are taught techniques on how to diffuse the situation before it escalates. Also, a series of checklist procedures can guide employees when problems occur. In most cases, workplace violence is not life threatening, and if managers and coworkers know how to handle the situation, it can be diffused without incident. The following are some steps that managers can take when dealing with an angry person:

1. Avoid an audience. This makes the individual feel special and will avoid agitating others who may be angry.
2. If possible, have a second employee in the room. This gives you a witness to what occurs, and it may deter an attack.
3. Establish the dispute boundaries. Initially, ignore any comments that are not related to the problem. Reduce anxiety by keeping to the subject.
4. Listen patiently, attentively, and actively to all parties to the conflict.
5. Speak slowly, softly, and clearly. Slow your speech to reduce anxiety. The other person usually will mirror your pace.
6. Focus on behaviors, not personalities.
7. Make eye contact and give the angry person your full attention.
8. Specify acceptable behaviors, and if possible, involve the conflicting parties in the problem resolution.[52]

Tips on How to Prevent Workplace Violence

The Crisis Prevention Institute, Inc., has compiled a list of tips on preventing workplace violence. Many of these tips are commonsense procedures that must be addressed in the workplace violence program and policies.

1. *Assess Your Work Environment.* Critically examine all areas of your work environment, including parking lots, entry ways, reception areas, work areas, and offices.

Is the lighting adequate? Are there convenient escape routes? Do you have a method to summon assistance?

2. *Pay Attention to the Warning Signs.* Many people who become violent communicate their intentions in advance. Threats from customers, coworkers, or third parties should be reported immediately.

3. *Promote Respect.* The best way to prevent violence in the workplace is to foster a day-to-day attitude of respect and consideration in your work environment.

4. *Eliminate Potential Weapons.* Take a mental inventory of objects available in your immediate work area that could be potential weapons. Remove or secure objects that could be thrown.

5. *Know Your Violence Response Procedures.* Violence response procedures are simple plans designed to minimize injury during a violent incident. These procedures should include a plan to summon assistance and move people to a safe area.

6. *Trust Your Instincts.* Do not ignore your internal warning system. If you sense impending danger, react accordingly.

7. *Use a Team Approach.* If you are in a situation where hostility could occur, use the "buddy system."[53]

Domestic Violence in the Workplace

Violence in the home does not remain a domestic issue. Domestic violence affects employees at all levels in the organization. Too often the domestic violent offender can enter the employee's workplace, call the employee at work, stalk the employee going to or from work or at lunch, and even make detrimental or threatening comments to the employee's employer. This is even worse when both people work for the same company. Offenders can use workplace resources, such as e-mail, telephone, and vehicles, to further their cause. Employers, however, have occupational health and safety, criminal, and even civil obligations to take steps to reduce the risk of violence. There are instances where partners in domestic disputes have murdered their partners, as well as colleagues, in the workplace. While employers do not have the right to interfere in their employees' private lives, they have a responsibility to help manage and prevent domestic violence in the workplace. Examples of actions that an employer can take are developing work-based safety plans, providing secure car parking, allowing special leave, changing a person's duties, workstation, phone number, and e-mail address, instituting work-based restraining orders, and implementing an awareness program.[54]

Employees involved in domestic violence directly or indirectly often cannot concentrate and have lower performance and productivity levels as they struggle to separate the trauma of their personal life from their work life. They can be physically and emotionally exhausted, stressed, and depressed to the point of absenteeism or to the point of having to stop work for periods of time. This is costly for both the employee and the employer.[55]

Stressed Employees

Stress has been found to promote violence, and recent research demonstrates that a growing number of workers suffer from stress. For example, a survey by Northwestern National Life Insurance found that 40 percent of the workers report their job is "very or extremely stressful." A survey by the Families and Work Institute found that 26 percent of workers report that they are "often or very often burned out or stressed by their work," and a survey by Yale University reports that approximately 30 percent of workers feel "quite a bit or extremely stressed at work."[56]

The nature of work is changing at whirlwind speed. Perhaps now more than ever before, job stress poses a threat to the health of workers and, in turn, to the health of organizations. What is job stress? **Job stress** is defined by NIOSH as the harmful physical and emotional responses that occur when the requirements of the job do not match the capabilities, resources, or needs of the worker. Job stress can lead to poor health and even injury. The concept of job stress should not be confused with challenge. They are different. Challenge motivates workers to learn new skills and master new jobs, makes workers feel good after jobs have been completed, and is an important ingredient for healthy and productive work.

NIOSH suggests that job stress results from the interaction of the worker and the conditions of work, but views differ on the importance of worker characteristics versus working conditions as the primary cause of job stress. Some believe individual characteristics such as personality and coping style are most important, whereas others suggest that certain working conditions, such as excessive workload demands and conflicting expectations, are stressful to most people. Some believe that job redesign can be a primary prevention strategy. More on job redesign will be covered in Chapter 8.

"St. Paul Fire and Marine Insurance Company, now known as the Travelers Companies, Inc., conducted several studies on the effects of stress prevention programs in hospital settings. In one study, the frequency of medication errors declined by 50 percent after prevention activities were implemented in a seven-hundred-bed hospital. In a second study, there was a 70 percent reduction in malpractice claims in twenty-two hospitals that implemented stress prevention activities. In contrast, there was no reduction in claims in a matched group of twenty-two hospitals that did not implement stress prevention activities."[57] The U.S. Bureau of Labor Statistics reports that workers who must take time off work because of stress, anxiety, or a related disorder will be off the job for about twenty days. Stress management training can help workers deal with job stress. It is reported that approximately "one-half of the large companies in the United States provide some type of stress management training for their workforces."

Low morale, health and job complaints, and employee turnover often provide the first signs of job stress, although at times there are no signs, particularly if workers are fearful of losing their jobs. Figure 6.2 identifies some causes for workplace stress. NIOSH suggests ways to change an organization to prevent job stress.[58]

Figure 6.2 Causes of Workplace Stress

1. Heavy workload, infrequent rest breaks, long work hours, and shift work; hectic and routine tasks that have little inherent meaning; do not use workers' skills; and provide little sense of control.
2. Lack of participation by workers in decision making, poor communication in the organization, and lack of family-friendly policies.
3. Poor social environment and lack of support or help from coworkers and supervisors.
4. Conflicting or uncertain job expectations, too much responsibility, and too many "hats to wear."
5. Job insecurity and lack of opportunity for growth, advancement, or promotion; rapid changes for which workers are unprepared.
6. Unpleasant or dangerous physical conditions, such as crowding, noise, air pollution, or ergonomic problems.

Source: National Institute of Occupational Safety and Health, *Stress ... At Work*, NIOSH Publication No. 99–101, 2000, p. 9 (http://www.cdc.gov/niosh).

- Ensure that the workload is in line with worker's capabilities and resources.
- Design jobs to provide meaning, stimulation, and opportunities for workers to use their skills.
- Clearly define worker's roles and responsibilities.
- Give workers opportunities to participate in decisions and actions affecting their jobs.
- Improve future employment prospects.
- Provide opportunities for social interaction among workers.
- Establish work schedules that are compatible with demands and responsibilities outside the job.

NIOSH's research identified four characteristics associated with low-stress work and high levels of productivity in so-called *healthy organizations*—ones that have low rates of illness, injury, and disability in their workforce and are also competitive in the marketplace. The characteristics are:

- Recognition of employees for good work performance
- Opportunities for career development
- An organizational culture that values the individual worker
- Management actions that are consistent with organizational values

In dealing with stress-related problems, companies are now formulating a number of different approaches. Some companies are encouraging their employees to schedule an aerobics class at 3:00 P.M. or a brisk, daily walk capped off with a cappuccino. Managers help in this process by examining the amount of work their people are doing and shifting workloads when they find an imbalance. They also try to match tasks to those most capable of doing the work and communicate regularly with their people to ensure that workloads do not become onerous. Flexible work arrangements is another way for employees to work within their family and personal time restraints, reducing stress and improving productivity. In fact, it is reported that more top talent employees leave their jobs because of inflexible work arrangements than because of their relationships with their bosses.

 ## CHECK YOUR UNDERSTANDING

How Violent Is Your Workplace?

1. Identify behaviors at your workplace that could lead to violence. If you don't work, then prepare a list of behaviors that could potentially lead to a disruptive workplace.
2. Describe the measures that have been implemented at your workplace to avoid violence. If you don't work, then describe the measures that should be in place to prevent a violent workplace.
3. How does domestic violence impact a workplace?
4. What role does stress play in workplace violence?

© Daniel Laflor, iStock

Explore how to become an effective team player as a new employee.

Career Advisor

How to Become an Effective Team Player

Now that you have landed that perfect job, what's next? In today's workplace, being a team player is an expectation. Regardless of whether you are a new employee to the company or have been promoted to a new position within the company, your success in the job will be affected by how well you perform as a team player. How do you begin the process of becoming an effective team player in a new job? It all starts with orientation.

Orientation

Orientation is the process of introducing new employees to their jobs and to the company. It is the first look inside the company—its mission, values, and policies, and how things are organized. As a new employee, you should be interested in learning how the company is formally organized and who holds key positions in the company and especially in areas of the company where you will be working. You should show interest in meeting these people—ask for introductions, if they are not included—and by all means remember their names, even if you have to write them down. Identify someone who might become a mentor to you, or simply ask for the name of someone from whom you can receive help. Mentors can play an important role in your success; they can show you the ropes and give you insider tips.

Company values reveal what is important to the company. By knowing the company's values, you can better understand how you can fit into the organization. Understanding the importance of recognition and rewards can help you to set realistic expectations. During training on the job, which should occur even for people being promoted, performance expectations should be established.

Training on the Job

As a new employee, you willingly should take advantage of all internal and external education and training activities. Exhibiting a positive attitude about learning new vocabulary and knowledge shows that you want to be a team player. When cross-training assignments are offered, accept them with enthusiasm—more knowledge and experience can be a valuable asset as a team player. Always be sure you understand your performance expectations and how the company expects you to achieve them. Now that you are doing your job, what else needs your attention? It is the norms operating in the company and in your assigned group. Norms in groups were discussed in Chapter 4.

Norms in the Work Group

Even though you may be able to do your job and work within the group, you may not be considered a team player. You may have to adapt your behaviors to meet the expectations of the group before you will be accepted as a team member. By closely observing the group and asking questions, you can learn how to fit in. For example:

- How do you address your coworkers? Is the first name used or a more formal way used?
- How do you dress on the job? Is it a uniform, casual wear, business casual, or business suit? Is facial jewelry aside from earrings acceptable?
- What are the social obligations? Who goes to lunch together and where?

- What is important to group members? What kind of hobbies and interests do they have?
- What type of attitudes do group members display? Are they positive or negative?
- How do group members deal with performance goals? Are performance goals restricted by group members or do the members strive to exceed performance expectations?
- Who are the informal leaders? Who has power in the group?
- What type of power do group members have? How does decision making work?
- What pettiness and jealousy surround the group? What is at the core of these actions?

Even after adapting your behaviors to fit in, you may not be accepted as a team player. Sometimes it can be one's personality and physical appearance that can restrict a person from being accepted as a team player. There are federal laws that address this issue, but still it is the attitudes and opinions of the group's members who ultimately make the decision of whether to accept you.

Understanding the informal organization can move you closer to being an acceptable team player.

Understanding the Informal Organization

Often it is through the informal organization that things get done in a timely manner. An effective team player will not only know the formal organization, but will understand the informal organization as well. As a new employee, mentors can be most helpful in this area and can teach you how to maneuver through the system to get things done. Getting to personally know key people within the organization can make a difference in your success. It takes extra time and energy to learn how the informal organization works. Learning how to be a team player takes a concerted effort on your part.

Being a Team Player

To be a team player, you must first clearly understand the goals and expectations of your company, department, and group. Being an effective team player requires a lot of you. Some important behaviors to being a team player are:

- Be willing to take on new responsibilities, learn new tasks, and always strive for excellence.
- Work at developing relationships by listening to coworkers and finding something good to say to everyone every day.
- Demonstrate a personal commitment to continuous improvement by continuing to learn and upgrade your skills.
- Understand how individual work impacts the department's success.
- Promise only what you can deliver on time to both internal and external customers; answer e-mail in a timely manner.
- Recognize and take responsibility for your own failures.
- Engage in risk taking after being properly informed.
- Accept and support team members' decisions after individual views have been expressed.
- Resolve disagreements within and between work teams by doing what is best for the company.
- Contribute to the success of others by helping to solve problems, meet deadlines, and work effectively.
- Understand and appreciate the contributions others make to the team.

- Treat people as you would like to be treated—with respect, fairness, and trust.
- Accept criticism graciously and be careful about criticizing others. Always strive to use constructive criticism.
- Be willing to negotiate, compromise, and share relevant information with others.
- Give credit to the appropriate team members.
- Strive to maintain a work area free from harassment.
- Exhibit a positive attitude, smile often, and be happy.
- Display confidence, optimism, and energy, which indicates to others that you are likable and sociable.

Becoming an effective team player requires your time and effort. It is not always easy. You must remember that changing your behaviors at the expense of your ethical system may not work for you and that a particular job may not be the one for you. For most people, however, adjustments in behaviors are possible.

 CHECK YOUR UNDERSTANDING

What does it take to become an effective team player?

1. Describe how you can become a more effective team player.
2. How can you learn about the informal organization in a company?

Summary

1 Trace the evolution of technology from the handicraft era to the cybernated technology stage.

Technology has encountered five stages. The first was the **handicraft era**, in which people made things by hand. Next came the **mechanization era**, characterized by machine labor replacing human labor. This was followed by the **mechanistic technology** stage, as seen in the case of the early automobile assembly lines. Next came **automated technology**, in which assembly line machines were linked together in such a way that many functions were performed automatically. Currently a fifth stage, **cybernated technology**, known as the digital age, has emerged and is evolving into many forms. Cybernated technology is used in manufacturing processes, marketing operations, office functions, and training programs, just to name a few.

These technological breakthroughs have been possible because large amounts of money are being spent annually on R&D and because more and more members of society are attaining higher levels of education. When these R&D funds and highly educated people are brought together, the result is an accelerated thrust from which more and more goods and services can be produced at an ever-increasing rate.

Technology is changing the automobile industry with the development of its fuel efficient hybrid vehicles. Technology is protecting our soldiers and athletes. It helps our Olympian athletes bring home medals for the United States. Technology is used to pay bills and send information. Technology is changing products and how they are used. Technology is the vehicle through which people communicate. Technology is changing our lives.

2 Identify and describe the four major characteristics of a postindustrial society.

The United States has entered the stage of postindustrialism, which is characterized by (1) a service-oriented workforce, which makes up approximately two-thirds of the labor force; (2) a dynamic increase in the number of professional and technical workers; (3) an increase in the importance of theoretical knowledge, not just the practical side of things; and (4) the planning and controlling of technological growth.

3 *Discuss the effect of technology on organizational culture.*

In the workplace, technology has some specific effects on employees, which explains why it is important to have a cultural match between the organization and the people. A cultural match is based on similarities between an organization's culture—the shared beliefs, customs, traditions, philosophies, and norms of behavior of the organization—and an individual's culture—the norms, attitudes, values, and beliefs that a person brings to the job. Technological modifications that cause a change in the need to assume risk can cause problems for employees. Companies that introduce technology to stay competitive must also ensure that the organizational culture will accommodate these changes. Otherwise, employees are likely to feel alienated by what is happening.

4 *Identify and describe four ways employees feel alienated by technology.*

Technology can cause alienation in the workplace in the form of powerlessness, meaninglessness, isolation, and self-estrangement. When workers feel they are at the mercy of technology, they feel powerless. Offering incentives can help workers gain a sense of worth. Individuals have a need to know what they are doing and why they are doing it. Technology can take that away from workers and make the work seem meaningless. Unless a company strives to inform employees about their work, the employee may simply fail to show up for work or not strive to do his or her best on the job. Technology can isolate people. Individuals are social beings and have a need to interact with other people. It is important for companies to provide ways for employees to interact at work. This is especially true of people who are continually on the road. Technology can cause an employee to feel estranged from work. Self-estrangement occurs when the employee can no longer find intrinsic satisfaction in what he or she is doing. The work itself should provide a means for employee achievement, responsibility, and the possibility of growth.

5 *Explain how technology impacts an employee's quality of work life.*

Additionally, advances in technology cause some workers to fear that machines will replace them. This is particularly true among those who are not highly skilled or who are performing paperwork functions that can be handled by computers.

Despite these feelings, many workers find life in a modern factory quite livable. In particular, they like the pay and benefits and, to a large extent, seem unclear as to how the QWL could be improved.

OSHA and NIOSH have been instrumental in researching safety issues. A primary health issue in the office environment is ergonomics, which is concerned with designing and shaping the physical work environment to fit the physical abilities and characteristics of individuals. Carpal tunnel syndrome caused by repetitive motion and overuse of extremities, often involving the wrists, is an example of an ergonomic-related problem. Other ergonomic factors include video display terminals, lighting, heating, ventilation, and office layout.

6 *Discuss how knowledge-based organizations, industrial democracy, and participative management can aid in integrating technology and the organization's personnel.*

The sociotechnical problem is being addressed through the development of knowledge-based organizations, the use of industrial democracy, and the implementation of participative management practices. Technology is drastically changing the way organizations are managed. Knowledge-based organizations are retraining workers to use technology, as well as to work in teams, share knowledge, trust, and use empowerment. Much of this training is being done in-house using technology-driven educational programs. Some companies are establishing their own colleges and universities. In this emerging environment, industrial democracy and participative management are important. In industrial democracy, there is a formal sanctioning of worker representation in the decision-making process, and in participative management, there is an informal style of face-to-face leadership in which workers share decision making.

In Germany, industrial democracy is a way of life, whereas in the Scandinavian countries, participative management predominates. In Britain, there is a movement toward more participative management. In the United States, both styles of management have developed. At the heart of this movement is empowerment, a process of giving employees control over decisions that directly affect them.

7 Discuss workplace violence and how managers are dealing with it.

Unfortunately, violence in the workplace is growing. Workplace violence creates safety and health issues, which sometimes result in homicide. Some examples of workplace violence are verbal threats and harassment; pushing; striking; disorderly conduct such as shouting and throwing things; making false, malicious, or unfounded statements against others; inappropriate remarks; and bringing weapons into the workplace.

Organizations try to reduce workplace violence by developing workplace violence programs and policies and by screening people during the job selection process and placing them in positions that best employ their skills. Other programs dealing with workplace violence are providing clean job descriptions and supportive supervision, recognizing and valuing cultural diversity among employees at all levels of the enterprise, and conducting periodic reviews of job performance, as well as recognizing and rewarding work output.

Behaviors that lead to violence can be costly to employers. To deal with workplace violence, companies are now developing a variety of programs, including training on how to handle various situations. Not only is technology a cause for workplace violence, but stress has also been identified as a cause. To help companies with workplace violence issues, NIOSH has created a list of ways organizations can reduce stress in the workplace. It is estimated that approximately half the large companies in the United States provide some type of stress management training. Effective managers strive to match tasks to those most capable of doing the work and communicate regularly with their people to ensure appropriate workloads. Seven tips that can prevent workplace violence are: assess your work environment, pay attention to the warning signs, promote respect, eliminate potential weapons, know your violence response procedures, trust your instincts, and use a team approach. Violence in the home can be more than a domestic problem. It can bleed over into the workplace and interfere with an employee's productivity and safety at work. This is costly for both the employee and the employer.

Job stress can result from interactions between workers and the conditions of work. Job redesign can be a solution for reducing stress. Low morale, health and job complaints, and employee turnover are often the first signs of job stress. NIOSH has provided some solutions for reducing job stress, such as giving recognition for good work performance, providing opportunities for career development, creating an organizational culture that values the individual worker, and implementing management actions that are consistent with the organization's values.

8 *Explore how to become an effective team player as a new employee.*

The process for learning to be a team player in a new job starts with orientation. This is where you find out about the company's mission, values, policies, and formal structure, and meet key personnel within the company, especially in the areas where you will be working. In training, you become acquainted with the performance expectations, gain knowledge, and learn to speak the language required to do the job.

Every company, department, and group has its own set of norms—behaviors that are expected of everyone. By observing closely and asking questions, you can soon learn about the norms. In some cases, you may need to adapt your behaviors to meet those of the group, if you expect to be accepted as a team member. The informal organization helps get things done in an organization. It is the responsibility of a new employee to explore how that works within the organization.

Being an effective team player requires that you become involved in many ways, including understanding the organization; taking responsibility; listening and developing relationships; commitment to improvement; keeping promises; accepting criticism; understanding individuals; engaging in risks; resolving disagreements; contributing to the success of others; treating people with respect, fairness, and trust; and giving credit to others. It also means striving to maintain a work environment free from harassment, exhibiting a positive attitude, and displaying confidence, optimism, and energy.

Key Terms in the Chapter

Future shock	Future shock is the effect of enduring too much change in too short a time.
Handicraft era	The handicraft era was characterized by self-sufficiency.
Mechanization era	The mechanization era saw the use of machine labor.
Mechanistic technology	Mechanistic technology brought the assembly line.
Automated technology	Automated technology modernized the assembly line.
Cybernated technology	With cybernated technology, machines run other machines.
Digital age	The age of using computers and electronic tools to accomplish work, run business operations, communicate, and be entertained.
Postindustrial society	A postindustrial society is characterized by four major changes.
Organizational culture	Organizational culture is the environment in which people work.
Cultural match	Cultural match is the similarity between individual and organizational culture.
Individual culture	Individual culture is the norms, attitudes, values, and beliefs that a person brings to the job.
Powerlessness	Powerlessness is a feeling of being at the mercy of technology.
Meaninglessness	Meaninglessness is the feeling of doing work that has no personal value.
Isolation	Isolation occurs when people are confined to one particular work locale.
Self-estrangement	Self-estrangement is characterized by a lack of intrinsic job satisfaction.
Ergonomics	Ergonomics is concerned with redesigning the physical environment to meet the needs of personnel.
Knowledge-based organization	A knowledge-based organization relies on information sharing, teamwork, trust, and empowerment.

Resource-based organization	A resource-based organization focuses on providing needed physical assets.
Industrial democracy	Industrial democracy is a formal sanctioning of worker representation in the decision-making process.
Participative management	Participative management is an informal style of face-to-face leadership in which the workers share decision-making authority.
Empowerment	Empowerment gives the employees control over decisions and policies that directly affect them.
Workplace violence	Workplace violence is any physical assault, threatening behavior, or verbal abuse occurring in the work setting.
Job stress	Job stress is the harmful physical and emotional responses that occur when the requirements of the job do not match the capabilities, resources, or needs of the worker.

Review and Study Questions

1. How does the handicraft era differ from the mechanization era?

2. Differentiate between the mechanization era and the mechanistic technology era?

3. Compare the mechanistic technology era with the automated technology era.

4. Contrast the automated technology era with the cybernated technology era.

5. How has technology changed manufacturing and marketing operations?

6. How is technology being used in the automobile industry to conserve the U.S. oil and gas reserves?

7. What is WiMAX and how is it used?

8. Describe the impact that R&D has had on technology.

9. What are the four characteristics of a postindustrial society? Describe each.

10. How does a tough-guy, macho culture differ from a work hard–play hard culture? Compare and contrast the two.

11. How does a bet-your-company culture differ from a process culture? Compare and contrast the two.

12. What do individuals need to understand about cultural match? How can the basic idea be used effectively? Explain.

13. How can technology cause powerlessness, meaninglessness, isolation, and self-estrangement? Discuss each condition separately.

14. How does technology lead employees to fear replacement by machines? Explain.

15. What is ergonomics? How does ergonomics affect QWL? Identify several examples and tell how you, as a manager, would deal with each issue.

16. The major step that the modern organization must take in integrating technology and people is to determine the effects that technology is likely to have and to develop a plan for reducing its dysfunctional effects. What does this statement mean?

17. In managing the sociotechnical challenge, what role can be played by the knowledge-based organization? Explain.

18. Compare industrial democracy to participative management. What roles can industrial democracy and participative management play? Explain.

19. For each country listed, describe the predominant style of decision making: Germany, Scandinavia, and Britain.

20. What is empowerment all about? Why is it important in managing the sociotechnical challenge?

21. Identify workplace violence behaviors.

22. How can organizations deal more effectively with workplace violence? Offer two suggestions.

23. What is job stress? Identify several causes of job stress at the workplace.

24. Discuss ways to change an organization to prevent job stress.

25. Identify the steps in the process for investigating a workplace violent act.

26. Where and when do you begin the process of becoming a team player as a new employee?

27. Describe a team player's behavior in orientation and training.

28. Why is it important to understand the norms of your work group?

29. Identify effective behaviors of team players in the workplace.

Connecting to the Real World

Workplace Violence Plan?

As you learned in this chapter, workplace violence is more common than most people realize and appears to be a growing issue among businesses. Unfortunately, only few companies have addressed the issue by having policies or procedures in place.

Your assignment is to help a business develop a plan for dealing with violent acts that might occur at its place of business. No one or no business is immune from facing an irate person for whatever reason. It is best to be prepared. Follow the steps in preparing your assignment:

1. Select a small business in your community that does not have a written plan for dealing with workplace violence. The business can be one where you work or a restaurant, a retail store, a beauty salon, a repair shop, a service business of some type, a financial service, a service station, a manufacturer, and so on.

2. Meet with the manager or owner and discuss the topic "workplace violence," and point out some situations where the business may face violence, such as encountering an angry customer, an upset supplier, employees who have conflicts among themselves, workers who feel their contributions are not being appreciated, employees who are involved in domestic violence at home, a jealous spouse who stalks the workplace or one who keeps the phone lines tied up by continuously calling, or an upset employee who was recently fired.

3. By using the ideas presented in this chapter, assess the work environment and identify those things that need changing or things that need to be implemented to make the workplace safer. Develop procedures for dealing with perpetrators.

4. Prepare a written plan and present it to the business manager or owner and to your professor.

CASE
So, What's Going On?

Where in the world is it? Travis Cobar thought as he scanned the files in the office. *I know it must be here somewhere.*

Travis walked around his office then looked out the window to a cloudy, rainy day, wondering how he was going to finish his report for a Monday afternoon presentation before the senior management of BroadwayBank. He was working on LasColinas, an important project for the bank. BroadwayBank had been trying for months to land the LasColinas project as a client.

Travis recently moved from the research department to the investment banking division. This was his first presentation, and he wanted to make a good impression. It was Friday, and Travis was desperate to finish the report before the weekend, but it did not look hopeful at this point. He needed information from the master file, which seemed to be missing. At this point, he needed a lifeline. He thought Randi, his new colleague and teammate on the LasColinas project, might know where to find the file. In fact, Travis suddenly remembered seeing Randi with the file earlier in the week, but where was Randi now? She was nowhere to be seen. Another colleague told Travis that at the moment Randi was probably in a plane over Europe and could not be reached until Monday morning. Becoming concerned, Travis looked around her office but failed to find the file he needed.

Travis smiled as he recalled being immensely impressed with Randi, when he first met her. Dressed in her designer suit, she was quick to show him around the office and introduced him to all the senior managers in the division. She helped Travis get acclimated, and she seemed astute and focused, every bit the competent executive. Randi offered her assistance in the future. She indicated that, although she was extremely busy, she wanted them to be a good team. She even invited Travis to lunch to fill him in on the messy story of his predecessor.

Depressed over not finding the file, Travis sank down into his desk chair and loosened his tie. He could hear the Friday night cleaning crew down the hallway. All of a sudden, he remembered Robert Beasley, the head of corporate strategy at LasColinas, who was a family friend. After all, Robert had been instrumental in helping Travis get the job at BroadwayBank almost ten years ago and also encouraged Robert to transfer to the investment banking division. Their relationship, although warm, had never blossomed. Travis opened his e-mail and began typing a message to Robert, but paused thinking that it might not be such a good idea. He closed the e-mail and clicked on his presentation and contemplated a half-created slide.

Monday morning, Travis stuck his head into Randi's office and asked, "How did the trip go?" "Great, thanks, I'm a little tired. It was an awfully long flight." She, however, did not look it. She asked Travis about his weekend. "Well, I spent most of the weekend looking for the file on LasColinas, but ultimately couldn't find it. So, I just put something together." "Oh, that's not good," said Randi as she opened a desk drawer and offered Travis a piece of Swiss chocolate. "I know that file is somewhere."

Even though Travis knew Randi was probably inundated with work, he asked her to look over the slide deck before the

presentation to be sure that it looked all right. "Just give me a minute," she said. Travis returned to his office to rehearse his portion of the presentation. He decided to focus on LasColinas' past acquisition patterns. By 11:30 A.M., Randi still had not responded, which made Travis extremely nervous. As he walked by her office on his way to get a sandwich for lunch, he noticed she was on the phone with her glass door shut. When he returned, Travis noticed Randi looking at her monitor. She called out, "It looks great. I think it will make a good impression. I will see you in a few minutes."

Travis was surprised when Randi dimmed the lights and began her presentation. She progressed slowly and deliberately through her portion of the slide set, and Travis began to feel impatient. Randi clicked to a slide that Travis had never seen. It was an organization chart. She stated that LasColinas is considering reorganizing and this is what the new organization is going to look like. Austin, the senior manager of the investment banking division, noticed that the new structure was much flatter than the old structure. Everyone began talking at once. Randi hushed the group and began answering questions one by one. Travis knew he should interject, but his mind was in a whirl. This was exactly the information that he had been looking for. Travis wondered why Randi had the file and why she hadn't shared it with him. Austin ended the meeting, declaring they would reconvene later in the week.

Travis began getting mad. He just could not understand Randi. What type of teammate was she? In the hallway, Travis overheard Austin telling Randi, "Great sleuthing." About an hour later, Austin entered Travis' office and remarked that he believed that Travis needed more insight on what is going on politically at LasColinas and suggested that he contact Robert. Travis did not respond immediately because he felt uncomfortable about doing such a thing. Austin insisted that they have lunch together. Before Austin left the office, Travis was on the phone to Robert to set up a luncheon date to talk about LasColinas. "Funny you say that" remarked Robert, "because just last week I received an e-mail from a colleague of yours, Randi, who was rather insistent about a meeting." Travis hung up and immediately marched down the hallway to Randi's office. Travis told Randi that Austin had asked him to meet privately with Robert "since he is my friend." "Why are you contacting him?" Randi became a little red-faced, stood up, and stated, "There is no way you are going to meet with Robert if I'm not there." Randi said she had been working on the project for a long time, and then said, "If you think you're going to take that away from me, you've got another think coming." Travis decided to be direct. "I see, you want to grab all the credit." Randi admitted she wanted the credit as she turned the corner and walked down the hallway. Travis stood speechless as he watched her walk away.

Travis' mind was reeling as he walked into Austin's office and asked, "Do you have a few minutes?" "Sure," said Austin. Travis stated that he needed some perspective on working with Randi. "What is the problem?" asked Austin. Travis related what had happened between him and Randi. Travis went on to describe his surprise at Randi's presentation. He felt like a little boy running to his headmaster to rat on a bully. Travis was concerned about Randi's behavior and expressed it to Austin. Austin, being a bit irritated, offered to intercede and talk with Randi. Travis declined the offer, stating he simply wanted Austin to know about what was happening. Austin was glad to hear it. "Randi is an ambitious young woman, and you need to learn to respect her results; I have," said Austin as Travis left the office.

Questions:

1. What is going on? Is Travis being sabotaged or is he sabotaging himself? Why?
2. What does Travis need to do to work more effectively with Randi so that their relationship does not turn violent? How can Randi's professional jealousy be turned into something positive and not into something ugly? As a team, what are their roles and how can they be defined? Will Travis and Randi ever be able to work successfully as a team? How?
3. How important is technology in this case? Was it used properly? How could technology have been used more effectively to wane off the problem in the first place?
4. How well does Travis understand the divisional culture and norms? What type of leader is Austin? What does Austin value?
5. What does Travis need to do to repair the relationship between him and Austin?
6. Should Austin have a role in dissolving this situation? If so, what?

Sources: Adapted from Bronwyn Fryer, "When Your Colleague is a Saboteur," Harvard Business Review Case Study, *Harvard Business Review*, November 2008, pp. 41–52.

Productivity and Quality Improvement

CHAPTER 7

Two major objectives of modern organizations are to increase productivity and to improve quality. Today, these are important challenges facing businesses in America, especially in a time when economic growth is slow. Increasing productivity and improving quality also are issues facing many competing companies located in other countries. Finding ways of attacking these problems requires a commitment from top management. Some participative management approaches can improve productivity and quality. In many businesses, philosophical approaches, such as empowerment and intrapreneurship, are being considered in management's overall effort to achieve productivity and quality improvement.

Merging Technology and People

Many companies have found that the easiest way to increase their productivity is to downsize. This helps them to reduce their payrolls so that, if they can maintain their sales revenue, they have more profit at the end of the year. More effective organizations, however, realize that downsizing can be fraught with problems, including loss of employee morale and failure of the remaining employees to keep up with work demands. Some enterprises are taking a different approach. They are developing methods to reduce the time needed to do the work by effectively merging technology and people.

A good example is the Yamaha Corporation of America. Just a few years ago, the firm found that its customer hotline was so congested that one-third of all callers hung up before getting through. This was when Yamaha turned to a specialized software company to develop a package that would automate and monitor customer service calls. Now, when a person calls the hotline, the system not only logs in the individual's name but keeps track of the problem and how long it takes to resolve the situation. As a result, Yamaha is now able to identify those problems that occur most often and focus on ways of resolving them quickly and effectively.

One of the keys to the success of Yamaha's program is a well-trained workforce that knows how to follow the primary rule of total quality management: Do things right the first time. By empowering employees to make the decisions that are needed to ensure that things are done right, companies like Yamaha are finding that customers are more willing to buy their products. In addition, customers

LEARNING OBJECTIVES

1
Describe the current status and future direction of management efforts to improve productivity and quality.

2
Discuss how total quality management programs are increasing productivity and quality, and identify the steps in total quality management.

3
Explore the strategic intent, organization, and training efforts in a total quality management program.

4
Explain how Pareto chart analysis, cause-and-effect diagrams, customer-value-added programs, and benchmarking reduce errors and increase quality.

5
Relate the value of alternative work arrangements and empowerment to increased productivity and quality.

6
Define the term intrapreneurship and relate its value to improved organizational productivity and quality.

7
Explain the importance of developing intrapreneurship strategies.

8
Explore how to develop your own brand as an employee.

know that if they have a problem, they can always get through on the hotline and receive the assistance they need.

Another good example is provided by Wendy's, the third largest hamburger chain in the United States behind McDonald's and Burger King. One of the keys to success in this industry is rapid drive-through service, and according to the latest statistics, Wendy's is the fastest. The average time from the menu board to departure is 2 minutes and 30 seconds, which is 17 seconds faster than McDonald's and 19 seconds faster than Burger King. Given that two-thirds of the sales of most of these fast-food units come from drive-through business and projections show that, over the next decade, drive-through sales are likely to increase three times faster than in-unit sales, rapid service is the key to profitability. In fact, a 10 percent increase in drive-through efficiency will bolster sales by more than $50,000 annually.

Realizing that whatever it does will be copied by the competition, Wendy's continually strives to improve its efficiency. For example, Wendy's uses a combination of timers to keep track of how long it takes to deliver the food, kitchen choreography that is designed to eliminate unnecessary movement, and wireless headsets that let all workers hear customer orders as they come in. The units that use this system have increased their sales by 3 percent to 4 percent more than units that have not introduced the system. Wendy's objective is to reduce the time from menu board to departure to 100 seconds because, at this rate, customers are able to perceive the rapid service and are more likely to return. Wendy's has also implemented an aggressive marketing and advertising campaign that focuses on its target market, the slightly older consumer. Simply put, the company's success depends on how well it can merge technology and people.

Opening more new restaurants and becoming bigger each year does not always bring in more sales. So McDonald's is taking a new tactic "to get better" rather than bigger. A nationwide campaign was launched to make the restaurants "more relevant to customers" by tailoring the décor, style, and offerings to their local environment and consumer base, said Bill Whitman, a McDonald's spokesman. Along with providing Internet access, the company has improved menus to meet consumers' changing dietary needs, and technology has helped to speed up the delivery of customer service. To keep improving productivity, McDonald's continues to change as it battles its competition. For example, after Wendy's and Starbucks improved their breakfast menus, sales at McDonald's, a longtime dominant fast-food breakfast restaurant, began to fall. To fight back, McDonald's introduced a more robust blend of coffee, and in some restaurants, lattes, cappuccinos, and a variety of flavored coffees are offered. To help change the image that its food is unhealthy, McDonald's has introduced a variety of salads, such as a fruit-and-walnut salad. Most recently, the one-third-pound Angus burger was introduced, a premium sandwich, to compete with the heavyweight cheeseburgers of Burger King. Technology continues to merge with people to increase productivity and improve quality.

Describe the current status and future direction of management efforts to improve productivity and quality.

Productivity and Quality Challenges

Productivity is typically measured by the equation: output/input. Beginning in the mid-1970s, the United States began to feel the effects of the increasing productivity from foreign competition. The Japanese and Germans, in particular, began making more effective use of their labor and other resources and thus produced output at a lower cost per unit than could many American firms. Japanese manufacturing companies, for example, were able to produce automobiles at $2,000 to $3,000 per car below the cost of their American competitors. In the international services arena, increased productivity was evident in the form of lower prices and better service in the airline, hotel, and restaurant industries. Obviously, the United States was falling behind in terms of productivity growth. America needed to focus more attention on increasing output (goods and services) or lowering input (salaries, wages, benefits, materials, machinery, and equipment).

At the same time, quality became a major issue. Auto firms found quality was more important than price in consumer purchase decisions, and American companies were having problems. In manufacturing at large, executives were admitting that their firms were losing their place as world-class manufacturers. Airlines were developing an awareness that equipment safety and on-time arrivals, two major quality issues, were critical factors for customers deciding which airline to fly. Hospitals found high-quality service was becoming critical in meeting patient expectations and competitive pressures from other health care outlets. Similarly, restaurants were discovering that service often was more important than price. During this same period, one major research study found that businesses that increased their quality over the competition gained both market share and profitability.[1] Obviously, something had to be done.

Current Status

Currently, the United States is working hard to increase productivity growth and quality. However, because the competition is doing the same, this means the United States must continue its efforts. To date, America has made some significant progress. For example, beginning in the mid-1990s, the economies of Japan and Germany encountered recessions, whereas that of the United States began to grow significantly. Productivity in the United States had increased, at best, by around 2 percent annually and was expected to remain at 2 percent. During the next five years, the productivity rate not only met its goal of 2 percent, but it also exceeded that amount. From 1999 to 2004, the rate fluctuated between 2.8 percent and 4.6 percent. Those were the days of plenty—a time when people were working and overspending on bigger and better homes, cars, and electronic gadgets. However, in 2005, things began to change. By 2008, the housing and financial markets began to collapse, and the automobile industry experienced massive losses. Buying slowed to a crawl causing businesses to lay off employees and in some cases to shut down. The productivity rate dropped to 1.7 percent and continued on a downward spiral until 2009, after which the rate rose to 2.9 percent.[2] The surprise is that productivity did not drop in this recession to the extent that it normally does.

Some people believed the United States was in the middle of the worst financial crisis since the Great Depression, yet businesses were able to produce more with fewer workers. They aggressively squeezed out waste and boosted efficiency to keep production moving and at the same time were able to keep prices low. By laying off workers as well as many professionals, companies were able to keep output per hour up. But what does this mean for the future? Professionals, for example, are the ones who do the research, new product development, and training for necessary innovation and future growth.[3] Will laying off professionals stunt growth in the future as in Russia?

Russia's productivity rate lags behind that of the United States by 17 percent to 26 percent, depending on the sector. For example, in Russia, it takes three times as many workers to produce a ton of steel as it does in the United States. Inefficiencies are the main reason for Russia's lower productivity rate. Russia has one of the lowest productivity rates among industrialized nations. Why? Russia has built very few big companies in the last twenty years, so technology is old. Some people suggest it is the ineffective business processes and organization that keep Russia's productivity rate low. Also, the lack of competition provided little incentive to innovate or improve quality.[4] In contrast, up-to-date technologies and a plentiful labor force keep China's productivity rate higher.

Meanwhile in retailing, Home Depot, the world's largest home improvement chain, is redesigning the way it ships merchandise to stores, answers customers' questions, and showcases its wares on the Internet. The goal is to improve productivity and expand profits by revamping a slew of business practices that have not changed since the 1980s. It is phasing out antiquated practices that, in some cases, are upsetting customers, but the company believes it has found the path to greater profits. Home Depot is trying to regain the customers it lost to lousy customer service during Robert Nardelli's reign as CEO.[5]

The reliability of American vehicles has improved, but still lags behind that of Japanese vehicles. For example, in the 2010 Consumer Reports list of the top ten best vehicles in reliability, value, and performance, six were Japanese made, while only two were U.S. made, the Chevrolet Silverado and the Chevrolet Traverse. So you can see that the United States still has a ways to go in improving its quality in the automobile industry. However, in 2010 the quality issue of Japanese cars changed when runaway acceleration problems on Toyota vehicles were reported by the ABC Investigative Team. Brian Ross and Joseph Rhee first revealed how Toyota had for years ignored complaints from hundreds of its owners about cars suddenly accelerating out of control. The story was aired on *ABC News Nightline, Good Morning America*, and *World News with Charles Gibson*. It uncovered a rebellion of angry Toyota owners and helped prompt the company to acknowledge defects, shut down sales and manufacturing, recall almost nine million cars, and apologize to its customers. How badly will the reputation of Japanese cars be tarnished by this massive recall? Will Toyota be able to recover and regain the confidence of its customers? How long will it take? It is interesting that in 2009 Toyota received ten of J.D. Power and Associates' Initial Quality awards for the best vehicles in a segment, more than any other automaker.[6] Additionally, U.S. manufacturers are finding themselves under scrutiny by the National Highway Transportation Safety Administration. Research in the area of vehicle crashes continues as new makes and models of vehicles are introduced. But Detroit still continues to be plagued by quality issues.

The United States continues to increase its productivity by effectively linking technology and worker effort. Manufacturing firms are now identifying the skills and knowledge needed for specific jobs and bringing them together with the most effective technology in the factory to make products most efficiently. R&D efforts and innovation are important to efficiency and to moving businesses into the next decade.

Future Directions

Despite these successes, however, research shows that, in many areas, U.S. management must do a better job if productivity is to continue growing. A recent study of more than 10,000 American workers has found a large gap between what workers believe they need to be productive and what managers are providing. In particular, workers say that conditions for collaboration, commitment, and creativity must be improved. They want the chance to work more closely with others, including management, and to break down the barriers that reduce productivity. They also want to feel that the work they are doing is important and want management to appreciate their efforts. Finally, the workers want the opportunity to do interesting, creative work in a friendly environment.

Specifically, they feel that management must:

1. Value people as human beings and develop policies and procedures that treat employees better.
2. Develop a support system for recognizing and rewarding good performance.
3. Create an atmosphere of trust and show that it has confidence in the workers.
4. Give employees an opportunity to influence events in the workplace.
5. Provide employees an opportunity to carry out relevant, meaningful work.
6. Develop a shared sense of purpose and commitment among all employees.
7. Create a work environment in which people learn to rely on one another and develop and share creative work ideas.
8. Create a spontaneous, fun, collaborative social environment in which innovation is recognized.
9. Develop a dynamic problem-solving process, the goal of which is to achieve high-quality, productive, and relevant output.[7]

Absenteeism and Presenteeism. Absenteeism and presenteeism are two issues that directly affect productivity rates. A study published in the *Journal of Occupational and Environmental Medicine* found that "**presenteeism**—when employees are present at their jobs but unable to perform at full capacity—creates a greater drain on company productivity than employee absence." Proper training, use of appropriate technology, and adequate organization and workplace space are not the only issues impacting productivity rates; one more issue is dealing with unhealthy employees. Five of the most costliest medical conditions causing absences are depression, obesity, arthritis, back/neck pain, and anxiety. The study found that these losses were as prevalent among executives and managers as among the rank-and-file workers. Another study of 60,000 Australian workers found that workers who did not have symptoms of mental health problems were the most productive on the job. The results suggest that "addressing employee mental health increases employee productivity in the workplace with the potential for a positive return on investment from an employer's perspective."[8]

Stress is another condition that affects absenteeism and presenteeism. The 2009/2010 North American Staying@Work report found that most employers are doing very little to relieve the stress that many employees experience because of long hours at work, a lack of work/life balance in their lives, and the fear of losing their jobs. While a little stress is good, it has grown beyond the level of being motivating.[9] With employee productivity down by 5 percent, employers must begin addressing these issues in their productivity management programs, as well as do a better job of cutting costs.

The remainder of this chapter examines some of the major human relations approaches that are proving to be effective in handling the productivity–quality challenge.

✔ **CHECK YOUR UNDERSTANDING**

1. Productivity is measured by the equation: _____/_____
2. Identify important changes that management must undertake to improve workers' productivity and quality of work.

Management of Quality and Continuous Improvement

One way to increase productivity and improve quality is to implement a total quality management (TQM) program. The idea originated in the 1950s, and it steadily became more popular, peaking in the 1980s. With the introduction of the ISO 9000 (International Organization for Standardization) standards, TQM was revived and is currently being used to measure quality in companies against ISO standards.

Total quality management is a people-focused management process that aims at continual increases in customer service at a continually lower cost. Its focus is managing quality. TQM is a philosophy that must continuously be a way of life in a company. What does TQM stand for? *Total* is the involvement of everyone and all activities in the company, while *quality* is directed at meeting and exceeding customer expectations, and *management* means that quality can be and must be managed.[10]

In the past, many firms argued that it was impossible to increase quality without also increasing cost. As an example, they contended that if a company made 10,000 television sets and 1,000 were defective, the cost of eliminating all these defects would significantly run up the product's overall cost. As a result, they argued that firms should learn to live with these mistakes to keep down the price and, where possible, try to eliminate some of the most glaring production mistakes. Over the years, however, more and more organizations have learned that the cost of eliminating defects more than often pays for itself. It usually is less expensive to produce things properly the first time than to correct mistakes later.

For example, consider the company that must spend $50,000 to eliminate all mistakes in order to produce defect-free televisions. Consider also that each defective TV costs the firm a total of $200 in reworking costs and another $200 in shipping and customer service costs. If the firm is producing 10,000 television sets each year and 10 percent are defective, the cost of correcting these mistakes is $400,000 ($400 × 1,000). Clearly, it is better for the firm to produce the sets correctly the first time than to remedy the mistakes later. In fact, by dividing the $50,000 that the firm must invest in correcting its production facilities by the $400 average cost to repair and replace each TV, we can see that once the firm produces 125 defective sets ($50,000/$400), it is paying more for repairing these units than it would cost to prevent these mistakes in the first place. This is the **first principle of TQM**: Do it right the first time.

One reason that many firms are now able to do this is that they have changed their beliefs about the nature of quality and have come to accept new ideas. The following are four of these ideas:

1. The quality output of goods and services is everyone's job.
2. The thinking that quality is "good enough" must be replaced by the belief that quality must be continually improved.
3. Work can often be done faster without loss in quality.
4. Everyone associated with the organization needs to be part of the quality effort, including top managers, low-level workers, outside suppliers, and customers.[11]

Table 7.1 provides a contrast between the old way of viewing quality and the way in which highly productive organizations now do so.

Today, thousands of U.S. firms are implementing TQM programs designed to provide better products and services at lower prices than ever. In carrying out this strategy, they are relying on a host of critical steps, including:

1. Formulating strategic intent.
2. Designing organization structure and training efforts.

Table 7.1
The Nature and Role
of Quality

Myth	Truth
Quality is the responsibility of the people in the quality control department	Quality is everyone's job
Training is costly	Training does not cost; it saves
New quality programs have high initial costs	The best quality programs do not have up-front costs
Better quality will cost the company a lot of money	As quality goes up, costs come down
It is human to make mistakes	Perfection—total customer satisfaction—is a standard that should be vigorously pursued
Some defects are major and should be addressed, but many are minor and can be ignored	No defects are acceptable, regardless of whether they are major or minor
Quality improvements are made in small, continuous steps	In improving quality, both small and large improvements are necessary
Quality improvement takes time	Quality does not take time; it saves time
Haste makes waste	Thoughtful speed improves quality
Quality programs are best oriented toward such areas as products and manufacturing	Quality is important in all areas, including administration and service
After a number of quality improvements, customers are no longer able to see additional improvements	Customers are able to see all improvements, including those in price, delivery, and performance
Good ideas can be found throughout the organization	Good ideas can be found everywhere, including in the operations of competitors and organizations providing similar goods and services
Suppliers need to be price-competitive	Suppliers need to be quality-competitive
People are the problem	Processes are the problem
Marketing is concerned with customers and purchasing handles suppliers	Everyone has a customer and a supplier
Problems can be easily fixed	Problems must be prevented
Quality cannot be measured	Quality can be measured
Quality control is random	Quality must be continuous
Expectations can be negotiated	Expectations are requirements
Quality happens	Quality improvement must be planned

Source: Adapted from Richard M. Hodgetts, *Measures of Quality and High Performance: Simple Tools and Lessons from America's Most Successful Companies* (New York: American Management Association, 1998), p. 15.

3. Using common tools and techniques.
4. Focusing on customer value added.
5. Using benchmarking and continuous improvement.
6. Measuring performance results.

The following sections in this chapter examine each of these steps.

✔ CHECK YOUR UNDERSTANDING

1. What is TQM?
2. What do the words *total, quality,* and *management* mean in a quality management program?
3. Identify the critical steps in a TQM program.

Explore the strategic intent, organization, and training efforts in a total quality management program.

Formulating Strategic Intent

Strategic intent is the company's vision. Basically, strategic intent sets forth an organization's overriding ambitions or desires that, in turn, create the basis for the organization's mission and help to drive its strategy. Organizations state their strategic intent in a variety of ways. Here are three examples.

- **Eastman Chemical:** To be the world's preferred chemical company and to be the leader in quality and value of products and service with a responsible care commitment to improve health, safety, and environmental performance.
- **Xerox Corporation:** To help people find better ways to do great work by consistently leading in document technologies, products, and services that improve work processes and business results.
- **Ames Rubber:** To focus on developing new elastomeric compounds to exactly fit a customer's needs, and then defining and developing the best process for creating and applying these compounds to produce an exceptional product. Ames is known for its exceptional attention to process quality control, which it has integrated into daily operations, assuring its customers that they will receive the best possible products and services.

Strategic intent provides an overriding picture of what the organization wants to accomplish. In the process, it also helps to identify those changes that must occur. When Motorola decided in the late 1970s that it needed to increase its quality to world-class levels, the firm asked the question: What do we have to do to correct the current situation? For example, it first had to acknowledge that quality needed to be sharply improved. Then, in the 1980s, Motorola named a corporate quality officer, established the Motorola Training Center, began establishing total-defect-per-unit measurements in the communications sector, and adopted a Six Sigma goal of 3.5 defects per million. Six Sigma is a methodology that uses data and statistical analysis to measure and improve performance. It seeks to improve the quality of a process by identifying and removing the causes of defects. In the 1990s, Motorola developed customer satisfaction metrics and refined their measurements. Over the years Motorola has continued to expand the use of Six Sigma into other areas of its operations. Today, the Motorola University has replaced the Motorola Training Center and training in the Six Sigma business management strategy continues. Training classes are also offered online. Motorola has changed over the years and today Motorola has ultimately become a world-class organization.

In an effort to increase its market share in Asia, Hewlett-Packard's (HP) decision to move away from its traditional approach of selling through stores to selling directly to its customers provides another example of strategic intent. The direct-sales method "is definitely a key element to our strategy if we are going to grow our share in the market," according to Adrian Koch, the senior vice president of HP's Personal Systems Group for the region.[12]

Another example is Chrysler. It has embarked on a new strategy of outsourcing that is intended to reduce the cost of producing cars. "Instead of developing cars from scratch, as it has done for 75 years, it is leaning on partners like Mercedes and Mitsubishi, as well as on outside suppliers, to provide everything from intellectual capital to assembly-plant paint shops." It is a whole new way of doing business. Its first product, Crossfire sports car, was driven off an assembly line in Germany. It went from design to market in twenty-four months at a budget price of $280 million.[13]

After making a thorough analysis of its environment, Xerox has concluded that to remain a leader in the global market, it has to focus on providing document services that enhance business productivity. In the process, the company identified five areas that are critical to its success:

1. Increasing customer satisfaction and loyalty.
2. Increasing motivation and satisfaction of company personnel.
3. Building market share.
4. Increasing the return on assets.
5. Increasing productivity.

Xerox then began pursuing these concepts by identifying specific goals that had to be achieved. In document outsourcing, four goals were identified:

1. Help businesses develop online document archives
2. Analyze how employees can most efficiently share documents and knowledge in the office.
3. Operate in-house print shops or mailrooms
4. Build Web-based processes for personalizing direct mail, invoices, brochures and more.[14]

These goals are helping Xerox to create an agenda for becoming both a leader in the global document market and one of the most productive companies in the world. At present, its two major targets are to become more market driven and to maintain leadership in digital technology. Over the years, Xerox has received many top industry awards. In 2010 it received the J.D. Power and Associates' Certification for "Outstanding" Customer Service, which indicates it has stayed on target. In the same year, Xerox was also named one of the "World's Most Ethical Companies," ranked 38th on the "Best Corporate Responsibility Citizen's List," and was ranked in No. 4 position in the computer industry in Fortune Magazines' annual ranking of the "World's Most Admired Companies." The awards recognize Xerox's superior quality, affordability, and reliability in its color and black-and-white network printers, fax machines, and digital multifunction systems.[15] At the same time, the firm is focusing on ways to increase its productivity, including empowering the workforce and developing more efficient processes. These developments are designed to help Xerox attain new levels of productivity, market share, and sustainable, profitable growth. The company is doing this by using strategic intent to drive the process forward. Advanced technology gaves the printing company a competitive advantage in quality of print, speed in completing jobs, and customer satisfaction.

Strategic Intents Can Change. For example, in the NASA space program, the tragedy of the space shuttle Columbia on February 1, 2003, raised some painful questions about the space program and its strategic intent. The Columbia tragedy, however, can be a brave beginning for NASA as it determines its strategic intent for entering the second Space Age.[16] The Bush administration's goal is to land humans on Mars by around 2030. By 2020, a base is to be set up on the moon to act as a staging area. To accomplish these goals, NASA must revisit its strategic intent.

As of 2010, the Mars program is still on target; however, the Space Shuttle mission program is on its countdown, and the last mission is to be launched in 2011. At the same time, the Constellation program is being canceled. So what is happening? NASA's new strategic approach will spawn exciting developments in R&D that will make future spaceflight more affordable and sustainable, inspire a new generation of Americans, and increase our knowledge of the solar system and the universe of which we are a part. NASA emphasized that it is not ending its ambitions to explore space; it is just launching a vigorous new technology development and test program that will pursue game-changing technology development to take us further and faster and more affordably into space.[17]

Designing Organization Structure and Training Efforts

Companies organize their TQM efforts in a number of ways. It is common to create a **quality council**, a group of individuals who oversee the quality initiative and make decisions regarding the projects to be undertaken and the funding to be provided. This group often is assisted by one individual who is placed in charge of quality and is given the authority for coordinating these projects and serving as the full-time quality person in the organization.

Initial quality efforts are directed toward identifying problem areas and creating quality improvement teams to deal with them. These problem areas typically are identified through an analysis of feedback from customers and from attitude surveys of employees. In this way, the organization knows the types of changes its clients and workers would like. Armed with this information, quality improvement teams of five to ten individuals are then formed and assigned projects. Typical examples of project goals are:

- Reducing the time needed to produce from one-and-a-half hours to fifty-five minutes.
- Reducing delivery time from twenty-four hours to twelve hours.
- Making recommendations on how service in the employee cafeteria can be improved.
- Improving customer service to online customers.
- Building customer trust by increasing security measures for online transactions.

Sometimes, these quality improvement teams consist of members from just one department, but in many cases, they are cross-functional teams with members from many different departments.

After the team analyzes the problem assigned to it, the group will reach conclusions regarding what needs to be done and will present its findings to the quality council. The quality council will then decide whether the members agree and, if so, the type of follow-up action that should be taken. In most cases, the council will agree with the quality team and vote to implement the recommendations.

Partnerships. To help reduce costs for developing or improving a major component, some companies are signing agreements to work together and share the costs. These agreements have many potential benefits not only for the companies themselves but also for their shareholders and customers. For example, Ford Motor Company and General

Motors Corporation (GM), the world's two largest automakers, have worked together to develop a high-volume, front-wheel, six-speed automatic transmission with improved fuel economy. Ford has a Green Partnership with the U.S. Department of Energy to help accelerate the development of advanced technologies for better fuel efficiency and emissions. And GM and the University of Michigan Institute of Automotive Research and Education are partners in delivering world-class research on the reinvention of the automobile through new technology solution in the areas of lithium-based batteries, assembly welding, forming, manufacturing systems, and engine systems. GM has also entered into partnerships with Suzuki Motor Corporation and Isuzu Motors Limited of Japan, as well as Chrysler LLC, Daimler AG, BMW AG, and Toyota Motor Corporation. Working together serves the needs of both parties, advances the industry, reduces costs, and better serves the customers.

Training.   Research reveals that quality improvement teams cannot function effectively unless they are trained in how to gather and analyze data and how to work together as an effective team. This typically is provided by offering training in both quantitative and behavioral techniques. At Eastman, for example, all employees are trained to gather complaint information and enter it into a companywide database. In addition, many firms establish the necessary budgets to support these efforts. Some do this by setting aside a percentage of overall sales, such as 3 percent, that is to be spent exclusively for training, whereas others establish a specific amount, such as $2.5 million for the year. A supplemental approach is to express training requirements in terms of hours per year. In another example, Motorola has renewed its former learning policy by replacing prior emphasis on hours of training per employee, with a new learning policy that emphasizes maximizing learning investments by aligning employee development with Motorola's business strategies.[18]

The American Society for Training & Development estimates that U.S. organizations spent nearly $130 billion on employee learning and development in 2006. Another research firm found corporate training spending approached $58.5 billion for 2007. Regardless of the amount, a lot of money is being spent on training. One of every three hours of training is now being delivered via some form of technology. E-learning is becoming more prominent for several reasons—higher fees being charged for instructor-led classes and the reluctance of having employees miss work to attend training.[19] In spite of a push for e-learning, by 2009, nearly 60 percent of employee learning was still being led by traditional instructors in physical classrooms. A trend that is becoming popular among corporate learning is collaborative online learning.

Graniterock Company of Watsonville, California, a small construction materials company, has won many awards over the years for its outstanding quality, due in no small part to its outstanding TQM training. Employees average around forty hours of training annually, which is thirteen times more than the construction industry average. As part of the firm's effort to reduce process variability and increase product reliability, employees are trained in statistical process control, root-cause analysis, and other quality-assurance and problem-solving methods.

At Solectron, an electronics firm and a Baldrige winner, all employees receive a minimum of 160 hours of training each year. This training is broad in scope and encompasses a wide variety of general training, as well as operations-focused offerings. To identify and address training needs, an advisory committee reviews the firm's strategy and business plan and then conducts a needs analysis among employees. In the process, the committee examines current worker skills and analyzes the company's technology requirements. After this, training needs are prioritized, and the required programs and seminars are developed.

CHECK YOUR UNDERSTANDING

1. What is the role of strategic intent, organizational structure, and training in managing quality improvement?
2. Give an example of a strategic intent for an airline company.
3. What is a quality council and how does it work?
4. Give examples of quality management goals for a restaurant.

Explain how Pareto chart analysis, cause-and-effect diagrams, customer-value-added programs, and bench-marking reduce errors and increase quality.

Using Common Tools and Techniques

Organizations use a wide variety of tools and techniques to increase productivity and quality. One of the most common types of training is to teach the participants how to collect information by answering such questions as:

- What do you want to know?
- How can the necessary information be collected?
- When and where do the data need to be gathered?
- How can the information be displayed so it can be easily totaled and evaluated?

A **Pareto chart** is an example of a tool that displays information in an easily inter-preted form. It is a special vertical bar graph that helps to identify problems and the order in which they are to be addressed. Figure 7.1 provides an example of a Pareto chart that was constructed based on customer complaints. A close look at the chart shows that 60 percent of all customer complaints relate to delivery time, so the quality

Figure 7.1 A Pareto Chart of Customer Complaints

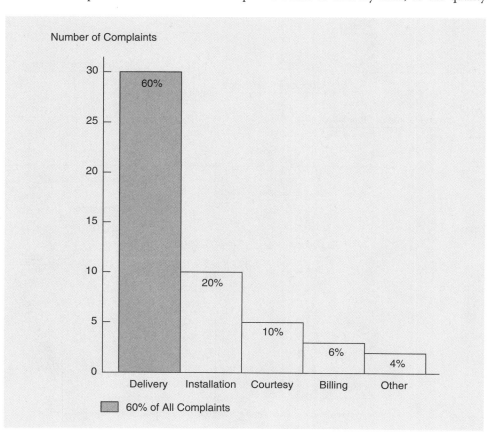

improvement team would want to analyze why delivery time is a problem for customers. Another common approach is the cause-and-effect diagram.

Cause-and-effect diagrams, often used as a follow-up to Pareto charts, are designed to help identify reasons for the problem. The approach consists of four specific steps:

1. The quality team will conduct a brainstorming session and identify the most likely causes for the problem.
2. These causes will be broken down by category.
3. The team will vote for the most likely group of causes.
4. Based on this decision, an action plan will be created and implemented.

Figure 7.2 provides an example of a cause-and-effect diagram for dealing with the problem of cleaning up the work area more quickly. Four major causes have been identified—materials, methods, machinery, and workforce—and the reasons for each cause have been listed. Now the team will decide which of these is the major cause of the problem and will begin working to resolve the issue.

Research shows that a number of other TQM tools are available. They all, however, function in the same way: to help the team identify and deal with quality-related problems. In addition, team members commonly receive training in how to be effective group members, how to lead a quality improvement team, and how to facilitate team analysis. As a result, team members learn how to work well together and how to collectively identify and solve quality-related problems.

Figure 7.2 A Cause-and-Effect Diagram

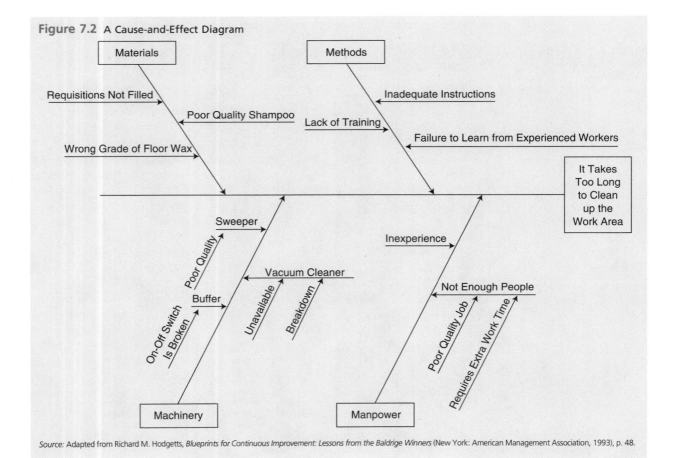

Source: Adapted from Richard M. Hodgetts, *Blueprints for Continuous Improvement: Lessons from the Baldrige Winners* (New York: American Management Association, 1993), p. 48.

Focusing on Customer Value Added

Organizations are improving their quality and productivity by finding out what the customer wants and finding a way to provide it. Researching and understanding customer needs and expectations lead to increased revenue, higher market share, and a greater effectiveness in the use of the organization's resources. This approach is known as customer value added. Briefly defined, **customer value added** (CVA) is providing products and services that offer greater value than is available from the competition. There are copious examples of firms offering CVA. Sony, for example, created the first Sony Walkman in 1978 because it realized that people want to listen to the radio while they exercise. In response to this demand, the company designed and built a small unit with earphones that allowed a person to walk or jog while listening to his or her favorite radio station. The technology was not new, but its application was, because it focused on adding value for the customer.

Today, handheld computers, such as personal digital assistants (PDAs), BlackBerry™ devices, iPods, and iPads along with instant messaging, are adding value to customers. GPS (global positioning systems) devices provide directions (adding value) for employees working in all kinds of industries from the transportation industry, delivery services, and travel agencies to individuals trying to find the nearest restaurant. The same is true for personal services. When a customer asks for directions in the Ritz-Carlton Hotels, the staff member will stop whatever he or she is doing and walk the individual to the location. This ensures that the guest does not get lost. Again, the emphasis is on customer service.

Another example is provided by General Electric Company (GE), which has an arrangement with Home Depot. Customers who buy a GE appliance at Home Depot have their purchase delivered and installed by GE. In an effort to add value to this purchase, GE began looking at ways that it could better serve the customer and, to its surprise, the firm learned that many of its ideas regarding CVA were incorrect. For example, GE believed that if it delivered the appliance to the customer's home within twenty-four hours, the buyer would be impressed and more likely to buy a GE product in the future. However, this perception turned out to be incorrect. A survey of customers revealed that they were indifferent about twenty-four-hour delivery. The company also learned that if the product was delivered late or was damaged in transit, customers did not become upset as long as the delivery people had a professional, soothing demeanor. As a result, GE now contacts buyers and tells them when the product will be delivered and then works to meet this target. At the same time, the firm has been giving people-skills training to its installers and deliverers, so that they are able to interact effectively with customers.[20] This plan has worked so well that GE now delivers all of Home Depot's appliances to its customers.[21]

GM and Ford provide examples of CVA. Both companies are trying to radically reduce the amount of time needed to build and deliver a car that is "made to order." Unlike the computer industry, in which Dell Computer can deliver a custom-made machine to the buyer in a matter of days, GM required forty-five to sixty days to build a car to buyer specifications and deliver it to the buyer. Few buyers were willing to wait this long, and so automakers lost these sales. To keep from losing sales, a salesperson arranged a "dealer trade" from another dealer that has in stock what the customer wanted, giving CVA to the customer. GM and Ford, however, are now beginning to look closely at the process and to develop a strategy for attracting customers who want to have their cars built specially for them. The current plan is to take the order, fill it, ship it, and have the car in the buyer's possession within fourteen days.[22] If GM and Ford can do this, they are likely to find a growing number of customers for whom custom-made cars constitute a CVA.[23] Currently, it still takes six to eight weeks from the time an order is placed for a vehicle until it is delivered to the customer. GM has not met its goal yet.

In design improvements, GM, in the last few years, has decreased the time it takes to develop a new car from nearly four years to twenty months. A committee was used to cover the entire process rather than have the design pass through marketing, engineering, and then manufacturing. No American or European automaker has come close to the twelve months it takes Toyota to go from the design table to building a new Corolla-class car. Other automakers are reportedly aiming to cut their development cycle to less than thirty months, but Toyota is shooting for a ten-month cycle. Advances in digital technology are allowing automakers to produce vehicles faster and in greater quantity.

In providing CVA, organizations now realize that perceived value is often the key to success. Alcatel-Lucent, for example, has created a quality-driven strategy based on four basic beliefs:

1. People buy on perceived value.
2. Value is a function of quality relative to price.
3. Quality includes all nonprice attributes.
4. Quality, price, and value are all relative measures.

Research by the company has revealed some interesting links among perception, quality, price, and profit. For example, Alcatel-Lucent found that customers who see themselves as receiving higher quality also are more willing to pay higher prices. Hence, perceived superior quality earns price premiums. Moreover, higher quality does not always mean higher costs. In fact, Alcatel-Lucent found that as quality increases, costs tend to decline and then slowly increase and, overall, the cost of the increased quality remains significantly less than the price paid by the customer. Thus, superior quality drives up both profitability and market share.

Using Benchmarking and Continuous Improvement

In ensuring that they maintain their quality and productivity gains, many firms now rely on benchmarking and continuous-improvement strategies. These two approaches complement each other.

Benchmarking. **Benchmarking** is an ongoing process of measuring products, services, and practices against those of competitors or organizations that are recognized as industry leaders.[24] Aside from the pressure of doing things better and faster, global competition is currently a major force causing companies to measure how well they are doing compared to their competition. By using benchmarking processes, a company can learn its effectiveness. Quality awards also actively encourage businesses to compete and defend markets internationally. These awards require self-assessment, of which benchmarking processes are a key component. The purpose of comparing a company's performance against the practices of other leading companies is to improve performance.

The general process does not vary much from organization to organization. The steps presented in Figure 7.3 are fairly universal. However, four different types of benchmarking can be used: internal, competitive, functional, and generic. Each of these contributes to improvement but some are more important than others, as can be seen in Table 7.2.

Benchmarking has been particularly useful in helping organizations to reduce their error rate and drive up quality-related factors, such as customer satisfaction and "time to market." For example, Ames Rubber has used the process to reduce the defect rate

Figure 7.3 The Benchmarking Process

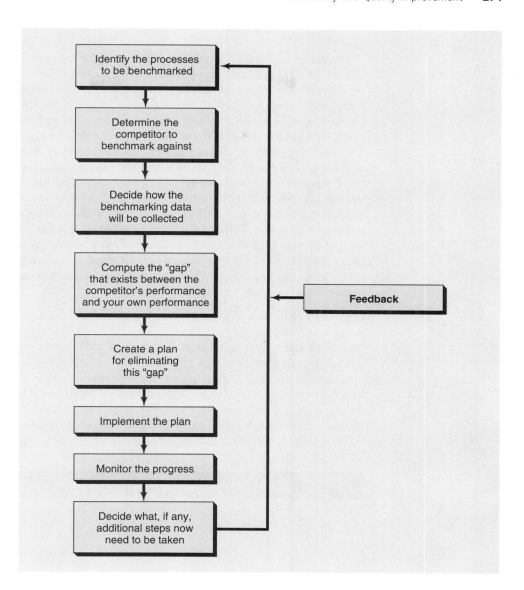

for its largest customer, Xerox, from more than 30,000 to 11 parts per million. As a result, Ames is now the "benchmark" producer of fuser rollers for the very highest-speed copiers. At the same time, delivery performance for Ames's top customers is well above the industry average, and productivity, as measured by sales per teammate, has increased sharply.

Table 7.2
Improvement Gained through Benchmarking

Type of Benchmarking	Activity Performed	Amount of Improvement (%)
Internal	Compare similar processes within the company	10
Competitive	Specific competitor-to-competitor comparisons	20
Functional	Compare similar functions to industry leaders	35
Generic	Compare unrelated practices or processes	>35

Another example of benchmarking is provided by GTE Directories, which uses a host of different information sources to help it carry out benchmarking activities. These include industry comparison data; customer satisfaction feedback; internal and external competitive analysis of both products and services; information from other GTE business units for business and support services, as well as employee and supplier performance data; and industry studies for operation and support services benchmarks. The company employs these efforts to compare current processes to those of other world-class companies and then sets and validates world-class targets of its own. Using these processes, the firm's leadership council then determines gaps and identifies the quality improvement opportunities that can have the greatest impact on customer satisfaction. In addition, the firm continually provides process management tools and training to its people, empowering them to make an ongoing assessment of opportunities for quality improvement and to take appropriate action. In fact, benchmarking is the primary vehicle used for information gathering and analysis, and in refining these efforts, GTE Directories has reduced the number of steps in its own benchmarking process from eleven to six.

Continuous Improvement. Closely tied to benchmarking is continuous improvement, which helps organizations to maintain their productivity and quality improvement success. Continuous improvement relies on two developments: consistent, incremental gains and occasional innovation. This approach is critical to TQM because it puts strong emphasis on the value of small improvements that are achieved on a continual basis. When this happens, employees continue to focus on productivity improvements every day rather than devote all their time to making major breakthroughs. Table 7.3 provides a comparison of constant improvement (small gains) to innovation (large gains).

Table 7.3
A Comparison of Constant Improvement and Innovation

	Constant Improvement	Innovation
Results	Long-term and long-lasting but fairly undramatic	Short-term but very dramatic
Progress	Many small steps	A few large steps
Time frame	Continuous and incremental	Stop-and-go and nonincremental
Rate of change	Gradual and constant	Abrupt and volatile
Personnel involvement	Everyone in the organization	A few people who are involved in bringing about the major breakthrough
Organizational approach	Group efforts	Individual efforts
Focus of effort	Development of people to carry out the improvements	Heavy reliance on technological breakthroughs
Advantage	Very useful in slow-growth economies	Very useful in fast-growth economies
Evaluation of progress	How well small changes are leading to better quality	Profits

KEEPING THE FOCUS TEAM ALIVE Every organization would like to increase the quality of its goods and services. Getting the effort started is often the easy part. Keeping the focus on quality is much more difficult. Here are five steps that are particularly useful in ensuring that quality teams maintain their focus.

1. *Do not expect too much immediately.* Many TQM teams begin by attacking a major problem and find that, after a couple of months, they have not solved the problem and the commitment of the team members is beginning to wane. A better approach is to start with an easy target that will not take too much time and effort. Then, motivated by this early success, the quality team can set its goals a little higher and try again.

2. *Conduct weekly meetings and keep minutes.* To ensure that quality teams remain active, it is important to have weekly meetings during which the members discuss what they have done since the last meeting, what still needs to be done, and what each person should do by the next meeting. Minutes should be kept of these meetings so that everyone is aware of the group's progress and future objectives.

3. *Choose the team leader and facilitator carefully.* Each quality team should have a leader and a facilitator. The leader's job is to direct the meeting; the facilitator's job is to ensure the discussion remains focused on the relevant issues. The leader and the facilitator are critical to the effective performance of a quality team. To the extent that these people are carefully chosen, the team's potential for increasing quality will increase.

4. *Collect quantifiable data.* Quality teams should collect information that can be quantified. For example, if a team is studying the reasons for low productivity and believes one reason is high rates of absenteeism and tardiness, the group should collect information on how many people have been absent or late during the period under study. If possible, this information should be broken down by day of the week (perhaps more people are absent on Mondays and Fridays than on any other days) or hour of the day (perhaps people are late coming to work on Mondays and Fridays and many are also late in coming back from lunch on Tuesdays, Wednesdays, and Thursdays).

5. *Motivate the participants.* To ensure that everyone on the team remains an active participant, they must be motivated. One simple motivational approach is to acknowledge those who do a good job by calling it to the attention of the other members. For example, the team leader might note, "Betty did an excellent job in gathering the absenteeism data from the shipping department, and Tim's thorough analysis allowed us to see clearly that Wednesdays are the biggest problem day for this department. I'd like to thank both of you for a job well done." If the group has been allocated funds for use in carrying out these tasks, it is always a good idea to set aside some of these monies for a small party (for example, coffee and cake) after the group has completed its project, and to use this time to thank all the participants for a job well done.

Research reveals that some of the highest quality firms in the United States report an increase in quality of output, greater competitiveness, and higher profitability as benefits from their emphasis on incremental, small improvements. Employees actively participate in the decision-making process, and they use this information to set realistic, attainable goals.

Most important, a continuous-improvement strategy ensures that employees maintain their focus on increasing the quality of goods and services, and they do not stop once a particular productivity goal has been achieved. One way some companies ensure that this happens is by having the quality improvement teams develop lists of problems and improvements that they want to investigate. At AT&T Universal Card Services, these teams have "hit lists" of ten target areas; when a group resolves one of the problems, it is taken off the hit list and another replaces it. In this way, the team never runs out of projects or problems to resolve. At Honda, managers work closely with suppliers to identify small, simple changes that will increase performance. As a result, the company has been able to raise the productivity of its suppliers.[25]

In a continuing effort to provide world-class service to shippers, FedEx Freight has improved transit times in six U.S. markets involving sixty cities. Reducing transit time supports FedEx's customers who use just-in-time and regional distribution models. FedEx continues to strive for further enhancements to give its customers a competitive edge, while also increasing its own efficiency.[26]

The "Human Relations in Action" box provides additional insights into some of the strategies that companies use in ensuring that the TQM effort continues.[27]

IN ACTION

MANAGING THE PRODUCTIVITY EFFORT WITH A PEOPLE FOCUS

Controlling productivity and improving quality require far more than the collection and analysis of operating data. Consideration must also be given to the employees and the "tools" required to keep them motivated and committed to their work projects. The following five steps can be helpful in keeping employees focused.

1. **Keep everyone openly informed.** Employees must be kept informed regarding the company's objectives and plans for the future. Revising operating procedures and improving efficiency require a great deal of commitment from employees. Therefore, they should be told up front what management wants to do and why. Employees are often the ones best equipped to figure out shortcuts and ways to cut waste and inefficiency. Therefore, their support must be obtained from the outset, and this is where open communication enters the picture.

2. **Find out which skills everyone possesses.** Also, you should identify the skills employees need to increase productivity. Then create the necessary training program to provide workers with the expertise to move to this next higher level of skill performance. This is particularly important when organizations decide to purchase new technology.

3. **Teach the employees how to focus on the root causes of problems.** Employees need to know how to quickly isolate the reasons for these problems and the steps that need to be taken to resolve them. Be sure to empower the workers so they do not have to check back continually with a higher-level manager for approval to proceed. If the employees are competent and well trained,

they will know what to do, and it is a waste of organizational resources to monitor them too closely.

4. **Create autonomous work groups.** Encourage these work groups to look continually for ways of improving performance. This continuous-improvement effort is critically important in ensuring that productivity and quality gains are not lost. In this process, place a great deal of emphasis on the generation of suggestions for improvement. In some American companies, management has been able to generate one practical idea per week, which has helped to turn these companies into world-class competitors.

5. **Create a reward system.** Share productivity gains with employees. For example, if productivity increases by 10 percent and this generates $100,000 for the company, have a predetermined system for giving part of this money to the workers. Additionally, share these gains on a frequent basis, such as quarterly. Research shows that if these gains are distributed only once or twice annually, their motivational impact tends to diminish. However, if employees are given productivity bonuses on a more regular basis, they tend to be motivated to continue their efforts toward increasing output and maintaining high quality levels.

The key to productivity success is a well-trained, well-motivated workforce. Of course, having state-of-the-art technology is also important, but in the final analysis, it is the employees who make the system work. Thus, the role of human relations in the productivity equation cannot be overstated.

Source: Adapted from Richard M. Hodgetts, Measures of Quality and High Performance: Simple Tools and Lessons from America's Most Successful Companies (New York: American Management Association, 1998), chapters 6 and 7.

Measuring Performance Results. The purpose of measuring performance results is to evaluate how well things are going and to make any necessary changes. This activity can be accomplished in a number of ways. The "Ethics and Social Responsibility in Action" box provides insights into the human relations challenges presented by this activity.

At AT&T Consumer Communications Services, for example, customer-related feedback data are analyzed and correlated with other types of information, such as operational performance. In this way, the company can determine how well customer needs are being met. Then, based on the results, appropriate action can be taken. The firm also carries out extensive marketing research to determine customer satisfaction and to track its own performance against that of the competition.

Another good example is provided by FedEx, which is committed to providing outstanding quality customer service. To measure how well the company is doing, it developed a series of service quality indicators (SQIs) that are used to measure customer satisfaction and service quality. Some of the SQIs that have been used by FedEx are:

- *Abandoned calls*—any phone calls in which the caller hangs up when his or her call cannot be answered within ten seconds of arrival.
- *Complaints reopened*—any customer complaint reopened after an unsatisfactory resolution of the initial complaint.

- *Damaged packages*—all packages that contain visible or concealed damage, including weather or water damage.
- *Invoice adjustments requested*—the number of packages for which customers request invoice adjustments, whether or not they are granted, because the company feels that such requests indicate that the customer perceives a problem.
- *Lost packages*—both missing packages and packages that arrive with missing contents.
- *Late pickups*—package pickups made after the customer's requested time.
- *Missing proofs of delivery*—invoices that are not accompanied by proof-of-delivery paperwork, which is something that the company promises to its customers with each bill.
- *Overages*—packages that arrive at a U.S. clearance port without being listed on Customs' clearance documents.
- *Right day, late deliveries*—all packages that are delivered after the commitment time (no matter how small the time error) but on the day on which delivery was promised, according to exceptions noted in the terms and conditions of service (such as an incorrect address on the package or an extreme weather–caused delay).
- *Wrong day, late deliveries*—all packages delivered after the day on which delivery was promised, according to exceptions noted in the terms and conditions of service (such as an incorrect address on the package or an extreme weather–caused delay).
- *Traces*—proof-of-performance requests from customers that cannot be answered through data in the company's computer tracking system because an employee failed to scan the package's identifying bar code electronically into the computer at each point in the delivery process.
- *International*—a composite score of SQIs that includes many of the other eleven indicators just listed as well as other indicators that are international in focus, such as customs clearance delays.

Each of these SQIs is assigned a relative weight; so FedEx not only tracks its performance for each of these quality indicators, but also uses the weighting system in arriving at an overall evaluation of how well it is serving the customer.[28]

FedEx also provides quality customer service in ways other than the delivery of packages. For example, in 2010, FedEx teamed up with ProFlowers to deliver flowers and gifts on Sunday, February 14, 2010, Valentine's Day. This was an exclusive arrangement, and it was the first time in its history that FedEx had worked with another company to deliver on a Sunday. In 2009, FedEx conducted a year-long study with Florida University to determine the best solution for shipping fresh flowers from Colombia, the major exporter of cut flowers, to the United States. FedEx wanted to find the best way to ship to extend the vase life of the flowers and retain as much freshness as possible. FedEx even ships passengers. On February 4, 2010, it flew two special passengers—pandas Tai Shan and Mei Lan—back to China.

In 2010, FedEx will begin using a SenseAware device on its shipments, especially those carrying health care and life sciences products. Some of the things it will monitor are: temperature readings, the exact location of the shipment, and when a shipment is opened or if the contents have been exposed to light. This is another example of how FedEx puts its customers first. Not only is the company's concern for customer satisfaction important to FedEx's success, so also is the work environment for its employees. For twelve of the past thirteen years, FedEx has been honored as one of the best companies to work for.[29]

 CHECK YOUR UNDERSTANDING

1. What is the purpose of a Pareto chart?
2. Explain how a cause-and-effect diagram differs from a Pareto chart.
3. Discuss how Walmart can add customer value to its merchandise.
4. Identify a company that would be a good benchmark for Walmart.
5. Compile a list of SQIs that Walmart can use to measure its customer satisfaction and to track its performance.

Relate the value of alternative work arrangements and empowerment to increased productivity and quality.

Participative Management Approaches

Some approaches to improving productivity and quality are based on getting employees more involved in the effort by giving them greater authority in the workplace. The most popular approaches are:

1. Alternative work schedules.
2. The use of empowerment.
3. Development of intrapreneurship attitudes.

Alternative Work Schedules

An alternative work schedule is a variation in the times at which employees begin and end work each day. This can be done a number of ways. The three most common are the compressed workweek, flextime, and shift work.

Compressed Workweek.   The **compressed workweek** allows an individual to work a shorter workweek than the typical five-day week. The arrangement might involve four ten-hour days (4/40) or three twelve-hour days (3/36). A common arrangement is the 9/80 schedule. Employees work nine hours for eight workdays and eight hours for one workday during a biweekly pay period, and receive one day off biweekly; all basic work requirements apply. When work is compressed into four days, it is typical to find people working Monday through Thursday or Tuesday through Friday. Younger employees, who are concerned about their careers and also want a greater balance between work and their personal lives, may choose a day within the week. Because Mondays are usually characterized by more activity, employees concerned about career advancement should consider another day, such as Wednesdays, which would allow time to pause from heavy workloads, allowing employees to get more control over their personal lives. Although Fridays tend to be a slower day, employees need to keep in mind that supporting working relationships are vital to career advancement.

Firemen have long used a four-day arrangement. So have some manufacturing firms, which have found that a four-day workweek reduces cleanup and start-up time and cuts back on three to five paid holidays per year. In industries such as petroleum and chemicals, many people work a three-day, thirty-six-hour schedule.

Some of the major reasons cited for adopting a compressed workweek are that it:

- Increases employee leisure time
- Increases work quality and production
- Decreases employee tardiness, turnover, and accidents

- Lowers setup and cleanup cost
- Improves employee satisfaction and morale
- Extends service hours
- Aids in recruitment and retention

In recent years, European companies have tried to overcome high national unemployment by compressing the workweek and reducing work hours. For example, Volkswagen cut employees from a five-day, thirty-six-hour week to a four-day, twenty-nine-hour week in an effort to hire more people.

Is the compressed workweek a good idea? Research reveals that most employees favor it and that it takes only about a month to adjust to the fatigue factor. However, this arrangement does not work well for employees who are carrying out heavy physical or taxing mental work. In these cases, many employees have opted for flextime.

Flextime.　Flexibility is a must for companies working toward becoming more globally competitive. Giving employees the opportunity to make greater use of flextime helps them to achieve a desirable work–life balance and, at the same time, increase their productivity. A number of different versions of **flextime** exist, but all require employees to be on hand during certain times known as core hours.

- One of the most common arrangements calls for everyone to be at work by 10:00 A.M. and not to leave before 3:00 P.M.: these are the core hours. Those who choose to come in later in the morning can arrive at 10:00 A.M. and go home at 6:00 P.M. Those who prefer to arrive at 7:00 A.M. can leave at 3:00 P.M.
- Under another common arrangement, employees can take their lunch period any time during the core hours.
- A third arrangement is to allow the employees to work as many hours in a day as they like just as long as they are present for all core hours and work their total number of hours per week.
- A fourth arrangement is to use the same approach as the third plan except that each employee's hours are checked for completeness on a monthly instead of a weekly basis.

In firms that employ a large number of people, work scheduling often is handled by a computerized system. This system matches employee work preferences with the demand for workers so that the necessary number of employees is on hand at all times. Computers and cell phones give employees who work off location, such as at home or on a job site, a direct connection to those in the office. Face-to-face contact is not always necessary, as long as the customer is served.

Many enterprises have had success with flextime. Workers, as well as employers, like the flexible schedules. Some of their reasons for liking flexible schedules are listed in Table 7.4.[30]

As far back as 1985, in a study of nine hundred firms, three hundred each in the banking, insurance, and utilities industries, researchers focused on the benefits of flextime among clerical workers. They found some of the major advantages included increased worker satisfaction, higher work quality, greater efficiency, reduced tardiness, lower absenteeism, and less overtime.[31] Overall, the researchers reported that 83 percent of the utilities, 85 percent of the banks, and 97 percent of the insurance firms believed that flextime, in comparison with fixed hours, increased effectiveness.

The latest figures from the U.S. Bureau of Labor Statistics report that 27.5 percent of full-time wage and salary workers had flexible work schedules. Men (28.1 percent) were more likely to work flexible schedules than women (26.7 percent). Flexible schedules were most common among managerial occupations, with 45.8 percent of executives, administrators, and managers able to vary their work hours. Although more than one in

Table 7.4
Reasons for Using Flexible
Work Schedule

Worker's Reasons	Employer's Reasons
Gives personal control over schedules	Expands business hours for local customers
Experiences less traffic congestion and less delays	Enhances ability to work with other time zones
Opportunity to work at personal peak times	Offers flexibility to workers who need different schedules
Flexibility to take care of personal business	Increases ability to attract new employees
Opportunity to adjust work schedules to meet personal needs	Provides additional cost-free benefit
Decreased stress	Reduces tardiness and absences
Increased job satisfaction	Decreases employee turnover
	Improves productivity and morale

four workers can work a flexible schedule, only about one in ten are enrolled in a formal, employer-sponsored flexible program. Workers in management, professional, and related occupations were among the most likely to have a formal flextime program (14.2 percent). Workers in production, transportation, and material-moving occupations were the least likely to have a formal flextime program (5.9 percent).[32] Many of these workers are considered nonexempt workers who work for wages and not a salary. A recent study by WorldatWork and Work Design Collaborative revealed that 45 percent of the firms surveyed reported they include nonexempt employees in their flexible work programs. The researchers expected to find only 15 percent.[33]

Management has found it difficult in setting up flexible work schedules to include nonexempt workers because nonexempt workers are paid overtime wages for time worked over 40 hours in a week as stated in the rules under the Fair Labor Standards Act. In 2009, the United States Court of Appeals for the Ninth Circuit addressed this issue by approving an overtime pay plan for nonexempt workers on flexible schedules. In essence, it states that employers may implement an alternative pay schedule so long as employees continue to earn approximately the same salary at an hourly rate that meets or exceeds the minimum requirements of the Fair Labor Standards Act.[34]

Many organizations have found that in deciding whether to implement a flextime approach, it is advisable to begin by putting a small number of employees on flextime, work out any problems with the program, and then extend it to include more people. The approach often used in implementing a flextime program is as follows:

1. Get top management's support.
2. Solicit involvement from employees at all levels.
3. Appoint someone who will have the respect of management and workers to oversee the entire program.
4. Set up a committee or task force to coordinate work assignments, hold meetings to explain the procedures necessary to implement the program, and keep two-way communication channels open.
5. Train the management staff by acquainting them with how flextime works, its advantages and drawbacks, and what they need to know about managing their people under this work arrangement.

6. Conduct a pilot test of the program to pinpoint any problems that need to be overcome before the arrangement is carried to the organization at large.

7. Formulate guidelines for handling problems that may arise.

8. Set up procedures for monitoring work schedules.

9. Evaluate the results.

Shift Work.   Most enterprises use **shift work**, with 8:00 A.M. to 5:00 P.M. or 9:00 A.M. to 5:00 P.M. being the most common shifts. Some industries have round-the-clock shifts because of the demand for output. Manufacturing firms with a large backlog of orders are likely to go to a second, and perhaps a third, shift until the backlog is eliminated. Police, fire, and hospital units, however, maintain round-the-clock shifts everyday of the year.

Shift work offers a number of advantages.

1. The pay usually is better for those on the second and third shifts.

2. Commuting time is usually shorter due to less traffic for people on these shifts.

3. These shifts are often less hectic and allow the worker more job autonomy.

Employees like to work shifts for several reasons. Figure 7.4 lists four common reasons. Is shift work, however, a good idea? Many organizations feel it is. In some cases, no alternative exists. Police and fire departments, for example, have no other way of providing twenty-four-hour protection. In other enterprises, management has found that people soon adjust to their new work shifts, and as their seniority increases, they are able to switch to other shifts that better meet their social and personal preferences. For these reasons, shift work will continue to be an important alternative work schedule.

Flexible Retirement.   Many employers are aware that the baby boomer generation is getting older and getting closer to retirement, but few have implemented any strategies for dealing with the issues it will create. By 2015, the number of workers aged 55 and older will hover around 30 million, which will be 20 percent of the work force. A Merrill Lynch survey reports that "76 percent of baby boomers say they want to continue working in some capacity after they reach retirement age—but it will have to be on their terms." What does this mean for employers? They will need to make adjustments if they want their businesses to continue running smoothly. Management will need to devise new work opportunities, such as more flexible schedules, enhanced opportunities for newer challenges, and improved workplace ergonomics. A shortage of workers is expected, and those coming into the labor force will lack the experience, talents, and skills of those retiring, making it more important for the companies to find ways to keep the older workers.

It has been proven that older workers fare very well on the job. There are some myths about younger workers versus older workers, but the facts prove otherwise. For example, while younger workers may work faster, they make more mistakes than older

Figure 7.4 Reasons for Working Alternative Shifts

Reasons	Percentage of Responses
Nature of the job	54.6
Personal preference	11.5
Better arrangements for family or child care	8.2
Better pay	6.8

workers. Younger workers may not have the health issues of older workers, but younger workers hurt themselves more often on the job. And younger workers job hop more often than older workers, so investing in retraining older workers has a greater return. Also, when looking at the obesity, drug dependency, and anxiety levels of young people, it is not easy to make a case that young people are more physically fit than older workers.

"The baby boomers like the idea of working after retirement." They do not want to work as many hours and may not want to do the same thing. So this is where flexible retirement comes into play—working out a schedule that fits both the employer and the retired worker. Several companies—IBM, HP, and Apple Computer—are ahead of the game. They are already creating the next generation of flexible retirement programs.[35]

Future of Flextime.   To cut costs during the last recession, some employers were forced to reduce work hours of their employees, forcing them to work flexible hours, while others were allowed to work at home or to telecommute. In time, what employers found was that the flexible work arrangement was something that could help their organization and, at the same time, save the company money. Will the flexible work arrangement be a future trend? It is well on its way. What has emerged is a permanent part-time workforce, changing the traditional ideas of when and where people work. This trend fits well into balancing work–life issues of today's workforce.[36] For some employees, however, flexibility is more than they can handle. While many people yearn for the freedom to decide when to work or where to work, in reality it is too confusing for them. They need a traditional work schedule to maintain their sanity. Flexibility work arrangements are not for everyone.

Despite the recession, a study conducted in 2009 by the Family and Work Institute (FWI) found that 81 percent of the U.S. employees maintained their flexible work programs and 13 percent increased their flexibility offerings during the recession. This was accomplished despite high unemployment and widespread cost cutting. In many ways, the recession caused employers to improve their workplaces. FWI has compiled a book of 260 ideas on how employees can make a difference in a down economy. It is called *2009 Guide to Bold New Ideas for Making Work Work.* All the employers who contributed to the book were 2008 winners of the Alfred P. Sloan Awards for Business Excellence in Workplace Flexibility.[37]

Use of Empowerment

Empowerment is the process of giving workers autonomy over the way their jobs are performed and holding them accountable for the results. Throughout history, empowerment leadership was implemented when "getting the job done" had priority over control. For example, the Chinese brought empowerment leadership styles to California during the 1850s gold rush and in 1864 during the construction of the railroad from Sacramento, California, into the Sierra Mountains. Empowerment gave full control and responsibility of the project to frontline workers. The empowerment concept was so successful that most railroad construction companies adapted it. This, however, was not true of the operations of the railroad, where power and control were paramount.[38]

The Panama Canal project in the early 1900s is another example where empowerment leadership made a difference in completing the project. The first chief engineer, John Wallace, had a command-and-control leadership style that meant his workers were treated as machines and the project was failing. The second chief engineer, John F. Stevens, knew how to organize work environments that energized and motivated workers, which allowed the project to be completed as scheduled even though he resigned after realizing his railroad engineering experience was no longer sufficient to complete the project.[39]

TIME OUT

Is Empowerment Necessary?

Identify a company and use it to answer the following questions with "yes" or "no."

_____ Is your organization lean and mean, like so many others, after years of downsizing?

_____ Is your span of control larger than ever, and are the expectations from above constantly increasing your workload and pressure?

_____ Do some of your employees seem apathetic or less than eager to show up on Monday mornings?

_____ Are many of your employees still waiting to be told what to do every step of the way?

_____ Is the competition nipping at your heels?

_____ Have you lost any of your talented team members because they were bored or needed a new challenge?

_____ Do your stars (employees) have more options outside your organization than they have in recent months or years?

Analyze your answers by comparing them with the answers in the "time out answers" at the end of the book.

Source: Adapted from Sharon Jordan-Evans and Beverly Kaye, "The 'E' Word…. Again," _Fast Company,_ March 2005.

The empowerment trend gained significant ground in the 1990s and today is one of the primary causes of quality improvement in the workplace. Not only are workers becoming more empowered in the workplace, they are also more empowered as consumers. As online customers, they are shaping online business models by demanding that Web sites respond to the security and privacy preferences of the e-commerce consumer. Consumers are willing to share information with sites in exchange for services, but there is still the issue of trust.[40] Meg Whitman, former CEO and president of eBay, believed that by extending power to the buyers and sellers, a form of empowerment is created. This empowerment seems to be the prime motivator for people to keep coming back to eBay.[41]

Empowering employees is not always an easy process, and in many workplaces, true empowerment is rare. The process involves sharing information, training, and allowing employees to manage their jobs, which can be complicated. Empowerment cannot be forced on employees; management must first create an environment where employees can manage their jobs, be valued for their ideas, and be able to think for themselves.[42] Some companies simply create an illusion of empowerment. For example, one reason the American Idol television program is so popular is that it creates the illusion of consumer empowerment—Americans have an opportunity to vote on their choice of best musical presentation for the week. Research, however, indicates that having an opportunity to vote is actually the least engaging aspect of the show.[43]

"Is empowerment necessary?" is a question often asked. To answer that question, complete the exercise in the "Time Out" box.

How to Start Building an Empowered Organization.

The first place to start the process of empowerment is to ask employees more questions instead of giving them step-by-step directions. This allows employees to build self-confidence and to develop a trusting relationship with management, making employees more creative problem solvers. Second, employees need to be encouraged and praised as they struggle to produce outstanding, creative solutions and new approaches. Third, giving employees the freedom to do it their way can be risky and there will be failures. Managers must collaborate with the employees to learn from their mistakes and not instantly instill punishment. Fourth, empowerment means sharing the stage and the applause with team members, not taking unearned credit. A micromanaged environment will not allow empowerment. Empowered employees will have good ideas and they need space to solve problems their way.[44] Empowered employees get

IN ACTION

EMPOWERMENT RULES IN ACTION

NINE RULES FOR EFFECTIVE EMPOWERMENT TEAMS

These nine rules are based on the belief that the level of elementary problems controls efficiency, quality, and cost. If there are many elementary problems, productivity will be negative; likewise, a low level of problems puts productivity in the positive column. In the typical workforce, there is no recognition for people who spend time on elementary problems; big problems receive all the attention. Yet big problems start as minor and there are people around who are aware of them. Because of leadership attitudes, employees develop the habit of ignoring problems until they explode, at which time they become big problems, and the leaders want to go on record for being problem solvers. Empowered teams correct this attitude. They focus on getting the job done while solving or preventing problems.

1. *Priority 1—Get the job done!!!* In many work environments, the top priority is cost control, which limits the ability to get the job done. While it takes money to control project costs, the focus should be on "getting the job done" and what it takes to finish the job, not on what it costs.

2. *Consider employees as an investment, not as a cost.* In any work environment, employees' skills and abilities will reflect the attitude of their leaders. If leadership considers employees a cost, the quality of employees will suffer; likewise, if leadership considers employees an investment, then both sides will be motivated to increase skill quality. Greater efficiency is the result.

3. *Employee attitudes are by-products of leadership style.* If subordinates' attitudes are negative toward the company, it is because of leadership style. If they are positive, it is because of leadership style. If attitudes need changing, it must start with the leaders.

4. *Sharing knowledge inspires motivation.* People who have an opportunity to share knowledge feel they are a part of the team. Team members want to impress by their ability to contribute valuable information, and this motivates the desire to seek information. It maintains a desire to excel, accept challenges, and reject the status quo.

5. *Coach, not control.* People who only follow orders do not assume responsibility, are not motivated, and do not have a desire to excel. Coaching is inspiring people to find solutions to problems. Finding solutions is a motivating force; it also becomes a habit. Coaching is sharing knowledge.

6. *Team responsibility.* Being responsible for results is a highly motivating force. Also, a group of three or more, focused on a common goal, becomes a highly intelligent force. Such a group is aware of minor problems and has the authority to manage them. The team is recognized for its ability to prevent problems while getting the job done.

7. *Supply quality resources.* Efficiency is as effective as available resources (tools, supplies, and work environment) to complete tasks. Teams will work hard to get jobs done, but they need quality resources to be efficient. Resources influence pride, which affects output quality.

8. *Opportunity to learn.* Repetitive tasks kill the desire to learn, an attitude that rejects change and accepts the status quo. There is always a better way of doing a task, including a repetitive task, and better ways are found in empowered teams. Challenges motivate people to learn, and the desire to learn is based on opportunity for challenges.

9. *Wages.* Effective, empowered teams require above-average wages. Empowerment is no substitute for low wages. High wages force leaders to manage in an efficient way. Low wages promote sloppiness. Wage level influences attitudes and output quality.

Source: Robert L. Webb, "Motivation Tool Chest," 2000, http://www.motivation-tools.com. Used by permission.

things done, while focusing on solving and preventing problems. To see how this works, see the "In Action" box for nine rules for effectively empowering teams.

Empowerment in Action. The Ritz-Carlton Hotel chain empowers, and even encourages, any employee at any of its properties to "fix" any guest problem on the spot. "Employees are empowered to implement or create any customer satisfaction solution that will cost under $2,000." Customer service at the Ritz radiates from every employee. In another case, Mike Abrashoff created an environment where employees were empowered and encouraged to help tweak a ship, the U.S.S. Benfold, the worst ship in the Pacific Fleet, into a winner of the prestigious Spokane Trophy. This award is given to the ship with the best combat readiness in the fleet.[45] Dow Chemical Company and Johnson & Johnson are two more examples of companies that believe in using empowerment to build a world-class organization.

Xerox is well known for its document equipment, services, and solutions. Xerox is able to stay competitive and lead the market with innovative products and services by using quality principles in all areas of its business. It operates under the guidance of six core values, one of which is valuing and empowering employees.

In one case, a team of virtual sales executives from an eBusiness/Teleweb division formed a graphic arts team on that segment of the marketplace. This North American Teleweb graphic arts team found there were varying degrees of sales skills and product knowledge, and very little industry-specific knowledge among the team members. Because of specialized market segments, information and training were not available from the immediate Teleweb support team. The newly formed graphic arts team effectively used quality tools, including employee empowerment, to identify and set improvement goals, to determine and prioritize solutions, and to guide the implementation of the team's solutions. It successfully developed the skills and processes for sales, solutions management, and issue management, thereby enhancing the relationships with graphic arts customers. The team put its own training and support mechanisms in place to enable the members to meet increased Teleweb coverage, excel in their jobs, grow revenue, and maximize customer satisfaction. Most importantly, the customer and solutions developed for the customer were the focal point of all team activities.

The team's achievements have been measured in the form of increased sales revenue. It has consistently achieved more than 100 percent of its total revenue goal and expects a 400 percent increase in fulfilled revenue year after year.[46,47]

CHECK YOUR UNDERSTANDING

1. How can flextime improve productivity and quality of work? Give an example.
2. What is empowerment, and how does it work to improve productivity and quality?

Development of Intrapreneurship Attitudes

Define the term intrapreneurship and relate its value to improved organizational productivity and quality.

An **intrapreneur** is an entrepreneur who works within an enterprise. During the 1970s, Norman Macrae predicted "that dynamic corporations of the future should simultaneously be trying alternative ways of doing things in competition within themselves." During the 1980s, Gifford and Elizabeth Pinchot took the work of Macrae and developed their own concept of an intracorporate entrepreneur. They coined the word "intrapreneur." Under the early model, the intrapreneur would initially have to risk something of value, such as a portion of salary. The intrapreneur would then sell the completed project for both cash bonuses and intracapital, which could be used to develop future projects. Finally in 1992, the word *intrapreneur* was added to the American Heritage Dictionary.

Sometimes, the individual is known as an *in-house entrepreneur*. In any event, many organizations realize that intrapreneurs are critical in an organization's efforts to increase productivity and quality. Steven Brandt, in the early 1980s, made the following comments, which are still true today:

> *The challenge is relatively straightforward. The United States must upgrade its innovative prowess. To do so, U.S. companies must tap into the creative power of their members. Ideas come from people. Innovation is a capability of the many. That capability is utilized when people give commitment to the mission and life of the enterprise and have the power to do something with their capabilities. Non-commitment is the price of obsolete managing practices, not the lack of talent or desire.*
>
> *Commitment is most freely given when the members of an enterprise play a part in defining the purposes and plans of the entity. Commitment carries with it a de facto approval of and support for the management. Managing by consent is a useful managing philosophy if more entrepreneurial behavior is desired.[48]*

Pinchot has some advice for intrapreneurial employees. He suggests that the intrapreneur be courageous, take moderate risks, be frugal and flexible, and at the same time

TIME OUT

Are You An Intrapreneur?

Many people have intrapreneurial desires and would enjoy working in a job that allows them to fulfill these ambitions. Are you an intrapreneur? To find out, answer the following questions. An interpretation of the responses is provided at the end of the book.

Y/N 1. Are you a high risk taker?

Y/N 2. Do you enjoy taking the ideas of others and working to improve them?

Y/N 3. Do you prefer to work alone rather than with others?

Y/N 4. Are you effective at networking with others?

Y/N 5. Do you like to work around rules and regulations by figuring out how to get things done despite all the red tape?

Y/N 6. Would you be willing to risk losing your job to develop or improve a product that could make a great deal of money for the company?

Y/N 7. Are you loyal and true to those who work with you?

Y/N 8. In terms of what motivates you, is money near the top of the list?

Y/N 9. Do you believe luck is a critical factor in the success of most individuals?

Y/N 10. Are your ethics and morals higher than those of the average person?

Y/N 11. Do you like to roll up your sleeves, dive in, and get involved in accomplishing things?

Y/N 12. Do you like to have your boss set goals for you rather than do it yourself?

Y/N 13. Do you believe that to get ahead you often have to do things that are illegal or unethical?

Y/N 14. Are you extremely self-confident?

Y/N 15. Do you like to gather information and examine the facts before you jump into something, as opposed to getting in quickly and going to work on a project?

Y/N 16. Do status symbols such as a big office, a company car, and a key to the executive washroom strongly motivate you?

Y/N 17. Are you good at persuading people to do things?

Y/N 18. Do you often dislike the organizational system but overcome this dislike by working out ways of manipulating the rules and regulations to your own advantage?

Y/N 19. Do you enjoy following orders from above?

Y/N 20. Are you good at generating fresh ideas?

be creative. Intrapreneurs must do what is needed to make the project work, regardless of their job descriptions. They must share credit wisely. Sometimes, it is easier to ask for forgiveness than for permission. Most courageous of all is to come to work each day willing to be fired. Building a team of the best people, who are willing to be a quiet coalition for your ideas, is important. Also, never forget to honor the sponsors of the project.[49]

Intrapreneurs have been credited with increasing the speed and cost effectiveness of transferring technology from research and development to the marketplace. Because intrapreneurs are risk takers, they are often considered to be inventors—people who come up with new products.[50]

The invention of the Post-it™ notes by Art Fry, a scientist, of the 3M Corporation is one of the most well-known examples of intrapreneurism. Art Fry turned a failed product—a repositionable adhesive—into a marketable product that changed people's communication and organization behavior forever.[51]

Do you have intrapreneurial desires? Take the "Time Out" quiz and find out. Additional insights into intrapreneurship are provided in Table 7.5. A close reading of these characteristics, along with the information provided in the "Time Out" quiz, reveals that intrapreneurs provide an interesting blend of behaviors that complement and extend the thinking of traditional managers and entrepreneurs. This helps explain why many firms are interested in promoting an intrapreneurial way of thinking to increase productivity and improve work quality.

Creating the Right Climate.   Many approaches can be used to create and nurture an intrapreneurial climate. Four steps that many enterprises have taken are:

1. Setting explicit, mutually agreed-on goals so employees know what is expected of them.
2. Providing feedback and positive reinforcement so people know how well they are doing and are encouraged to continue their efforts.

Table 7.5 Intrapreneurs: A Comparative Look

Characteristic	Traditional Manager	Entrepreneur	Intrapreneur
Primary motives	Wants promotion and other traditional corporate rewards; power-motivated	Wants freedom; goal-oriented, self-reliant, and self-motivated	Wants freedom and access to corporate resources; goal-oriented and self-motivated but also responds to corporate rewards and recognition
Tendency to action	Delegates action; supervising and reporting take most energy	Gets hands dirty; may upset employees by suddenly doing their work	Gets hands dirty; may know how to delegate but, when necessary, does what needs to be done
Attitude toward courage and destiny	Sees others being in charge of his or her destiny; can be forceful and ambitious, but may be fearful of others' ability to sabotage him or her	Self-confident, optimistic, courageous	Self-confident and courageous; many are cynical about the system but optimistic about their ability to outwit it
Attitude toward risk	Cautious	Likes moderate risk; invests heavily, but expects to succeed	Likes moderate risk; generally not afraid of being fired, so sees little personal risk
Decision-making style	Agrees with those in power; delays making decisions until a feel for what bosses want is obtained	Follows private vision; decisive, action-oriented	Adept at getting others to agree with private vision, somewhat more patient and willing to compromise than the entrepreneur, but still a doer
Attitude toward the system	Sees system as nurturing and protective; seeks position within it	May rapidly advance in a system; then, when frustrated, may reject the system and form his or her own company	Dislikes the system but learns to manipulate it
Problem-solving style	Works out problems within the system	Escapes problems in large and formal structures by leaving and starting over alone	Works out problems within the system or bypasses them without leaving

Source: Adapted from Gifford Pinchot, *Intrapreneuring* (New York: Harper & Row, 1985), pp. 54–56.

3. Placing emphasis on individual responsibility that builds confidence, trust, and accountability.

4. Giving results-based rewards that encourage risk taking and high achievement.

Other ideas for creating an innovative environment are:

- Encourage action.
- Use informal meetings whenever possible.
- Tolerate failure and use it as a learning experience.
- Be persistent in getting an idea to market.

- Reward innovation for innovation's sake.
- Plan the physical layout of the enterprise to encourage informal communication.
- Expect clever adaptations of other employees' ideas.
- Put people on small teams for future-oriented projects.
- Encourage employees to circumvent rigid procedures and bureaucratic red tape.
- Reward or promote innovative employees.[52]

 CHECK YOUR UNDERSTANDING

1. Who is an intrapreneur? How can intrapreneurs increase productivity and promote quality improvement?
2. Describe the type of company environment that fosters intrapreneurism.

Explain the importance of developing intrapreneurship strategies.

Developing Intrapreneurial Strategies

Intrapreneurial strategies are designed to create an environment in which creative, innovative employees flourish. In this environment, the manager often assumes a number of roles, including those of coach, teacher, and mentor. The employees, meanwhile, are encouraged to develop ideas that will result in higher productivity and quality, without concern about making mistakes and losing their jobs. "Very simply put, intrapreneurship is entrepreneurship practiced by people within established organizations." Intrapreneurs "tend to be motivated by the dream of things that conventional wisdom says can't, won't, or shouldn't be done."[53] Intrapreneurship is about making business better. It is not a system, but a process that evolves by using creativity to bring about change. It is not a solo activity; it is a team effort where credit is shared widely. Jobs are done regardless of the job description. An intrapreneurial organization seeks change and responds to it.[54] Intrapreneurial organizations often supplement their strategies with rewards that encourage effort and commitment. Examples are bonus plans, stock incentive plans, stock option plans, and profit sharing.

Intrapreneurial Intentions. Even though intrapreneurship has many different interpretations, two intents seem to persist: growth and innovation. As a corporate growth strategy, intrapreneurship might include continuous improvement to bring new or improved products to market to generate new revenue, whereas innovation strategies require breakthrough thinking and action, like being different and creating evolutionary change. The results of a survey of corporate executives conducted by Daniel F. Twomey and Drew L. Harris of Silberman College of Business, Fairleigh Dickinson University, indicate a high correlation between corporate entrepreneurial strategies and intrapreneurial outcomes of employees.[55] Companies willing to promote internal entrepreneurism and foster innovation have their own ideas of intrapreneurism and how it works within the company. For example, Thermo Electron, HP, 3M, and Deere & Co., each have their own ways of fostering intrapreneurism. For the 3M Corporation, Post-it notes were a legendary billion-dollar idea that the company tried to kill. It survived under a "skunkworks" innovation experiment. "Skunkworks" allows a committed individual to continue working a bit on a project even after the company has decided not to pursue it.[56]

Phases of an Intrapreneurship. Intrapreneurial strategies often have two phases. The first phase creates the necessary environment, whereas the second gains participant support. During the first phase, top management will determine the types of entrepreneurial ideas in which it is interested and the rules that will be used in managing intrapreneurs. This includes developing the necessary vision and communicating it to employees. Management will also use this time to identify potential intrapreneurs and target them for attention. The second phase is dedicated to convincing these people to formulate and implement intrapreneurial projects and to helping them do so. GE is a good example.

Intrapreneurship in Action. The company carefully selects young, high-technology people with only a few years' work experience, and often no formal management education, and literally sets them up in businesses. Basically, GE gives these new entrepreneurs a product line and a time period and then asks them to make the company grow. They must compete against each other for allocation of funds and resources, and they must learn to assess markets and prioritize and deploy resources. This process is enhanced through the active support of the supervisors, who regularly meet with their intrapreneurs. Finally, at the end of the time period, these venture managers are assessed by how well they have attained their objectives and how much money they have made. Compensation is related to this contribution.[57]

There are three foundations of intrapreneurship:[58]

1. Innovation—the ability to see things in novel ways.
2. Calculated risk taking—the ability to take calculated chances and to embrace failure as a learning experience.
3. Creativity—the ability to conceive of multiple possible futures and to proactively create the one you most desire.

The intrapreneur. The intrapreneur is typically the person who challenges the status quo and fights to change the system and who is inclined to act first and ask for forgiveness rather than to ask for permission before acting. A good example is Howard Schultz of Starbucks. He traveled to Italy and saw the power of the barista and wanted to bring that experience back to America. He presented his idea to Starbucks, but was rejected multiple times. Finally, he was given permission to try it on a limited basis. He even worked without a salary for a while to stave off threats of his vision going under. Howard Schultz had what is called adaptive persistence, a characteristic of many intrapreneurs.[59]

Regardless of the specific steps taken by them, all organizations have similar patterns. They seek a proactive change in the status quo and a new, flexible approach to the management of operations. They also tend to undertake the following steps:

1. Encourage individuals to assume the challenges of intrapreneurship.
2. Give intrapreneurs the authority and freedom to do the job their own way.
3. Let the individuals see their ideas through to completion.
4. Fund intrapreneurial efforts.
5. Have many intrapreneurial projects going on at the same time.
6. Encourage risk taking and tolerate mistakes.
7. Stick with intrapreneurial ideas long enough to determine whether they will work.
8. Encourage people from different departments and areas of interest to pool their interdisciplinary skills.
9. Allow the formation of autonomous teams that have full responsibility for developing their ideas.
10. Let intrapreneurial teams have authority to use the resources of other divisions and outside vendors if they choose.

CHECK YOUR UNDERSTANDING

1. Intrapreneurship is based on the foundations of: a. _____, b. _____, and c. _____.
2. Describe several key strategies for making intrapreneurialism work in a company.

© Sean Locke, iStock

Explore how to develop your own brand as an employee.

Career Advisor

Developing Your Brand

What is your **brand** and how can you effectively use it in your career? This is a question that some of you may not have ever asked yourself. Most people think of brands as being used only in terms of products and companies. For example, a brand can identify a product—Kleenex tissues, Libby's whole green beans, or Crest toothpaste; or identify a company—Ford Motor Corporation, Disneyland, or Sara Lee. A brand expresses and reinforces the underlying values and personality of the service, product, or organization it represents. It is a promise of value you will receive. Successful companies understand the importance of using good brands. They go to great lengths to develop a brand that gives them a distinctive visual identity, which is usually displayed in a logo. Understanding and developing your brand can be an important vehicle for career advance.

Building a Brand in the Workplace

You start building your brand by first understanding that you live in a branded world, and there is no escaping it. The type of car you drive, the symbol on your sneakers, the coffee cup you carry, the type of music you like, just to name a few, all reflect who you are, what you value, and the things you believe to be important in your life. How you spend your time and how you treat others all reflect your brand. You are a reflection of your self-image, creating a personal brand for you. But is that the brand you want to be known for at your job?

Successful employees figure out how to deliver value, whether it is to the manager, to the company, or to the customer. For example, they take the initiative to learn new skills, volunteer for new projects, or strive to improve service to customers. If you are really smart, you will figure out how to distinguish yourself from all the other very successful people and learn how to sell your sizzle. You will figure out a distinctive role for yourself, and create a message and a strategy to promote you—your brand.[60]

Your brand is not your job title, your company name, or whether you are an employee, a staffer, or a worker. It is you and who you are. A brand can be long lasting, but it can be changed. To develop your brand, start by identifying the qualities or characteristics that make you distinctive from your peers and coworkers. What is your greatest and clearest strength? What is your most noteworthy personal trait? Companies use branding to articulate their core values and to project into the world who they really are. The same is true of individuals. Your brand should say to the world who you are, and it should set you aside from the rest of the employees. Developing an effective personal brand takes exploring yourself and identifying what is important to you because that is what other people in the workplace will see in you.

Build Recognition.   One of the first things you must do is figure out how to become more visible in your workplace. Visibility is vital to creating an identity—your brand. You must find a way to use your expertise beyond what is expected in your current job. If you are good at writing, for example, write an article for the local newspaper or volunteer to write the copy for a new product manual. If you like speaking, serve on a panel discussion for the local school district or offer to be the spokesperson for your team at the next top management meeting. Participating in the activity alone is not enough; it is a matter of substance—what you have to say, how well you get it said, and your style of delivery.

Network.   Your network of friends, colleagues, clients, and customers is your most important marketing vehicle for creating and promoting your brand. It boils down to what they say about you and your contributions. That is what the market—your boss and others in your workplace—will ultimately gauge as the value of your brand.

Power.   If you want your brand to grow, you must come to terms with your own power. Getting and using power intelligently and responsibly are essential skills. In the workplace, you can begin in a small way. If your team is having a hard time organizing productive meetings, you can volunteer to write the agenda for the next meeting. Not only are you contributing to the team, you get to decide what is on the agenda. When it is time to write a postproject report, ask for the chance to write the report. Your report can write and/or, in some cases, reshape the organization's history. Power is a matter of perception. If you want people to see you as a powerful brand, then act like a credible leader. Your position on the organizational chart will not always indicate your authority as a leader. You need to exercise your leadership.

Performance.   The truth today is that we live in a project world. Most work is organized in bite-sized packets, whether it is production, measurements, or deliveries. This makes it easier for you to assess the strength of your brand and to boost your power. What you have delivered will reflect your brand, not your title.

Passion.   Donald Trump says that "if you don't have passion, you don't have energy, and if you don't have energy, you have nothing." What are you passionate about? Only after you identify what you truly are passionate about can you expect others to go along with you. People like to associate with a winner, so look like a winner.

Trustworthiness, Confidence, and Competency.   Do you come across as trustworthy, confident, and competent, and do you captivate your listeners? As a salesperson, how would your presentation to a potential customer reflect these characteristics? What would your brand say to the potential customer?

Loyalty.   Being loyal is not dead. Today, it is more important than ever before. In years past, being loyal to the company was an expectation. Too often, it was measured only by the length of time a person had worked for the company. Today, loyalty involves a much deeper sense of commitment, which includes being loyal to your colleagues, to your team, to your project, to your customers, and most of all to yourself.

Body Language.   What does your body language say about your brand? A self-confident, competent, and honest person will usually stand or sit tall, hold his or her head up and maintain eye contact at least 80 percent of the time, and have a warm, agreeable smile. Some people question the use of hand gestures in communicating face-to-face. Research has shown that it is acceptable to use your hands. David McNeill, University of Chicago, learned from his studies of body language that complex hand gestures reflect complex thought. These movements are a reflection of clarity in thinking—a "window to their thought process." Hand gestures can instill confidence in listeners.

Appearance and Dress.   Your wardrobe does matter. What does dress say about a company's brand, as well as your brand? The way a person dresses is a symbol that indicates that person's value and ultimately a company's value. That is why employees often are expected to wear clean, pressed uniforms and collared shirts with logos. You should choose clothes that fit your job and the environment in which you work. Professional clothing or business casual clothes are appropriate for most office environments. A wardrobe of low-cut necklines, mini skirts, or see-through fabrics is meant for party attire, not office wear. Your dress will indicate your values. To improve your brand image, figure out what type of wardrobe is appropriate for your position; then, as an old adage goes, dress like the position you would like to hold. In today's checkerboard pathway through companies, that position is not always the next higher one. Looking like the position you want gives the impression that you are ready to tackle a new challenge.

Stay Current.   As technology changes, jobs also change and the skills required to do the jobs will change. Employees must keep up, or they will be left behind in their careers. People who are curious about the world in which they live and work usually are given challenges beyond the ordinary. Companies are more likely to invest in the people they like and feel good about. Does your brand say that about you?

What Should Your Brand Look Like?

When your brand has a clear and cohesive vision that is visible, your brand sets you apart from other employees. Self-branded people are a tremendous value to all kinds of workplaces, especially now that the economy is striving for recovery. What is different today versus ten years ago, when Tom Peters first mentioned personal branding, is the rise in social technologies that allow people to make themselves more visible, which means that developing the kind of brand that you feel is worthy of yourself is more important than ever. A negative perception is not what is going to land you that top-of-the-line job.

Today, even customers take into account not only the company's values and the value of its products, but also the salesperson's values when purchasing products or services. Here is where a person's brand will make a difference in success and failure. You have to deliver what your brand promises. Building a strong brand is one thing, but delivery is another matter.

Engagement is critical to brand success. After all, others are influenced by what they see, more than what they hear. Brands communicate values. Your brand should form deep emotional connections with others; for example, your family and friends, your employer, your supervisor, your job, your clients or customers, and so on.

A company that has implemented a strong employment brand is Robert Half International, a global leader in professional services. It recruits people who embody the core values of the company. Job seekers meet with several of Robert Half's employees who talk about the culture, which is a fast-paced growth-oriented environment. Behavioral interviewing also is used to get candidates to talk about how they handled various situations in previous jobs. How they solved problems gives clues into their core values.

Mistakes in Branding

Often people fail to invest time in learning about what's in their best interests; they simply assign themselves a brand by saying, "I'm simply like this or like that." That's not good enough. You must figure out what you want to do for the rest of your life, setting goals, writing down a vision and personal brand statement (what you do and who you serve), as well as creating a development plan. If your goal is to be a leader (manager), you have to set the tone, and your behaviors (arising out of your values) should be the influencing factors that your employees will imitate. Think about how you want your followers to perform, and then set the example through your brand.[61]

Growing Your Brand

A way to grow your brand is to take on a steady diet of more interesting, more challenging, and more provocative projects. By writing your own mission statement—a guide to where you want to go with your career and a statement of your personal definition of success in terms of money, power, and fame—you are on your way to developing a brand that is exciting, futuristic, and broad enough to reflect what you want in a career. What will your brand name be?

Tom Peters suggests four things you need to measure yourself against. You must be:

1. A great teammate and a supportive colleague.
2. An exceptional expert at something that has real value.
3. A broad-gauged visionary—a leader, a teacher, and a farsighted "imaginer."
4. A businessperson—you must be obsessed with pragmatic outcomes.

Tools that Give Greater Visibility

Dan Schawbel, author of *ME2.0: Build a Powerful Brand to Achieve Career Success*, has identified several ways you can highlight your brand and allow people to see what you're about.

1. **Use business cards** with your picture and your personal brand statement. Create an online business card through mydropcard.com or BusinessCard.com.
2. **Take your résumé online** and add features to make it the ultimate social media résumé, promoting your personal brand.
3. **Prepare a portfolio** to showcase what you have done in the past.
4. **Create a blog or Web site** that aligns with your name in some way.
5. **Set up a LinkedIn profile** to advertise your search for a job or to meet new people by posting your résumé, cover letter, and reference documents.
6. **Create a Facebook profile** by posting a professional picture, inputting your work experience, and disabling the ability for people to tag your pictures and videos.
7. **Set up a Twitter profile**, using an avatar carved out of your Facebook picture and used in your LinkedIn profile.
8. **Prepare a short video résumé** of yourself explaining why you are the best candidate for a particular position.
9. **Wear an appropriate wardrobe** to look your best. Never forget how you look. Your appearance is important as we stated earlier.
10. **Establish an e-mail address** that is significant to your brand. It is suggested you use "firstname.lastname@" in the address.

CHECK YOUR UNDERSTANDING

What is your brand?

1. How would your coworkers or friends describe your brand? Ask several people to describe your brand.
2. How would you describe your personal brand?
3. What do you need to change? Compare the answers and determine how you might improve your brand.

Summary

1 Describe the current status and future direction of management efforts to improve productivity and quality.

Two major challenges facing organizations today are those of increasing productivity and improving the quality of goods and services. *Productivity* is measured as a relationship between output and input. During the last decade, American productivity has been declining vis-à-vis such foreign competitors as the Japanese and Germans. The same is true for quality. To improve productivity, workers say that conditions for collaboration, commitment, and creativity must be improved. The work needs to be important and management needs to appreciate the workers' efforts. Workers want an opportunity to do interesting, challenging work in a friendly environment. They want an opportunity to influence events in the workplace and to be recognized for good performance.

2 Discuss how TQM programs are increasing productivity and quality, and identify the steps in TQM.

One step being taken to attack the problem directly is the introduction of total quality management (TQM) programs. *TQM* is a people-focused management system with the objective of meeting and exceeding customer demands while trying to keep costs as low as possible. The underlying assumptions of TQM are: (1) the quality output of goods and services is everyone's job; (2) the thinking that quality is "good enough" must be replaced by the belief that quality must be continually improved; (3) work can often be done faster without loss of quality, and (4) everybody associated with the organization needs to be part of the quality effort, including top managers, lower-level workers, outside suppliers, and customers.

Today, thousands of U.S. firms are implementing TQM programs through the use of six steps: (1) formulating strategic intent; (2) designing organization structure and training efforts; (3) using common tools and techniques; (4) focusing on customer value added; (5) using benchmarking and continuous improvement; and (6) measuring performance results.

3 Explore the strategic intent, organization, and training efforts in a TQM program.

Strategic intent focuses on the company's vision and forms the basis for the organization's mission or its reason for being in business. A *quality council* is a group of individuals who oversee the quality initiative and make decisions regarding the projects to be undertaken and the funding to be provided. Quality efforts are directed toward identifying problems and creating improvement teams to deal with them. The structural design, therefore, should allow quality efforts to identify, analyze, and resolve problems. These teams cannot function effectively unless they are trained properly in quantitative and behavior techniques. Establishing budgets for training is necessary.

4 *Explain how Pareto chart analysis, cause-and-effect diagrams, customer-value-added programs, and benchmarking reduce errors and increase quality.*

A wide variety of tools and techniques are used, such as surveys, charts, bar graphs, and cause-and-effect diagrams. A *Pareto chart* is a special vertical bar graph that helps to identify problems and the order in which they are to be addressed. *Cause-and-effect diagrams*, often used as a follow-up to Pareto charts, are designed to help identify reasons for the problem. Cause-and-effect diagrams use four basic steps: (1) conducting a brainstorming session to identify the most likely causes for the problem, (2) breaking down the causes into categories, (3) voting for the most likely group of causes, and (4) creating an action plan and implementing it.

Another way of improving quality is to find out what the customer wants and provide it. This is called *customer value added* (CVA). CVA programs determine what customers want and follow up by giving them the products and services they are seeking. To ensure that quality is maintained, companies use *benchmarking,* an ongoing process of measuring the quality of products, services, and practices against those of leading competitors in the industry. *Continuous improvement* relies on consistent, incremental gains and occasional innovation. The emphasis is on small improvements achieved on a continual basis. Continuous improvement focuses on increasing the quality of goods and services. The last step in the TQM is to measure performance results to evaluate how well the organization is doing and to make any necessary changes. Each of these tools is a strategy for improving quality and maintaining a competitive position in the marketplace.

5 *Relate the value of alternative work arrangements and empowerment to increased productivity and quality.*

An approach that encourages participative management is using alternative work arrangements, which allow people some control in determining when they will come to work and when they will go home. These include such work schedules as the compressed workweek, flextime, shift work, and flexible retirement. A *compressed workweek* allows employees to work a shorter workweek than a five-day week. *Flextime* requires employees to work a set core of hours and make adjustments to their starting and ending times. *Shift* work involves round-the-clock work hours. *Flexible retirement* allows older workers to reduce their work hours before officially retiring or to return to work part time after retirement.

Empowerment is the process of giving workers authority over the way their jobs are done and holding them accountable for the results. This process is used by a large number of successful firms, resulting in cost cutting, increased productivity, and higher-quality output. Empowerment starts by allowing employees to solve problems, not by constantly giving step-by-step instructions. Employees must be given the freedom to do the job their way and must be praised for their accomplishments. Empowerment means sharing the stage and applause with team members.

6 *Define the term intrapreneurship and relate its value to improved organizational productivity and quality.*

Another major approach in improving productivity and work quality is the introduction of a new philosophical approach known as *intrapreneurship*—the encouragement of entrepreneurial activity within the enterprise. Intrapreneurs have been credited with increasing the speed and cost-effectiveness of transferring technology from research and development to the marketplace. Creating and nurturing an intrapreneurial climate involve setting explicit, mutually agreed-on goals so employees know what is expected of them; providing feedback and positive reinforcement so people know how well they are doing and are encouraged to continue their efforts; placing emphasis on individual responsibility that builds confidence, trust, and accountability; and giving results-based rewards that encourage risk taking and high achievement.

7 *Explain the importance of developing intrapreneurship strategies.*

This usually takes two steps. First, the right climate is created. Second, employees who are designated as having intrapreneurial potential are encouraged to engage in intrapreneurial activity and rewarded for their efforts. These steps seek a proactive change in the status quo and a new, flexible approach to the management of operations. The basic foundations of intrapreneurialship are: (1) innovation; (2) calculated risk taking; and (3) creativity. Employees must be encouraged to assume the challenges of intrapreneurship, be given the authority and freedom to do the job their own way, be allowed sufficient time to see the project through, and have funds provided for their intrapreneurial efforts.

8 *Explore how to develop your own brand as an employee.*

Your brand expresses and reinforces your underlying values and personality. It is a reflection of who you are and what you represent. It is how your coworkers describe you. Your brand should set you aside from the rest of the employees. Your brand is reflected in your behavior—your performance, your passion, your trustworthiness, your confidence, your competence, your loyalty, your body language, your trust, and the way you treat others. Your appearance and dress are symbols of your brand logo. Your brand needs to grow and change and, therefore, needs nurturing over time. Staying current, as technology changes, and taking on new and challenging assignments provide two ways to grow your brand.

Your brand should have a clear and cohesive vision that is visible to others. Today, the creation of new social technologies allows people to be more visible with their values and beliefs than they did ten years ago. People want to see engagement—that's what influences others to imitate them. This calls for deep emotional connections with others. Building the brand is one thing, but delivery is another matter. Developing a personal brand is not always successful. Often people fail to invest sufficient time in learning about themselves. Your self-impression is how people perceive you. Dan Schawbel has identified several tools for giving people greater visibility and promoting their brand. They are: using business cards; uploading résumés online; using portfolios; creating a blog or Web site; setting up a LinkedIn profile, a Facebook profile, and/or a Twitter profile; preparing a short video résumé; paying attention to your appearance; and using an e-mail address appropriate for your brand.

Key Terms in the Chapter

Productivity	Productivity is the relationship between output and input.
Presenteeism	Employees are present at their jobs but unable to perform at full capacity.
Total quality management	Total quality management seeks to increase customer service and reduce cost.
First principle of TQM	The first principle of TQM is: Do it right the first time.
Strategic intent	Strategic intent is the company's vision.
Quality council	A quality council is a group of individuals who oversee the quality initiative.

Pareto chart	A Pareto chart is a vertical bar graph used to identify and rank-order problems.
Cause-and-effect diagram	A cause-and-effect diagram is designed to help identify reasons for a problem.
Customer value added	Customer value added is the providing of products and services that offer greater value than those of the competition.
Benchmarking	Benchmarking is an ongoing process of measuring products, services, and practices against those of competitors and industry leaders.
Compressed workweek	A compressed workweek has longer individual workdays.
Flextime	Flextime allows workers to decide when they want to stop and start their workday.
Shift work	Shift work is assigned on the basis of time shifts such as 8 A.M. to 5 P.M.
Empowerment	Empowerment is the process of giving workers autonomy over the way that their jobs are performed and holding them accountable for the results.
Intrapreneur	An intrapreneur is an entrepreneur who works within the confines of an organization.
Brand	A brand expresses and reinforces underlying values and indicates what is important.

Review and Study Questions

1. What is meant by productivity? Of what importance is productivity to American enterprise?

2. Is productivity and quality improving or declining in the United States? Defend your answer.

3. What must management do to improve productivity and quality?

4. How does presenteeism differ from absenteeism?

5. What is TQM and how does it work?

6. What are some ideas on how the first principle of TQM, "Do it right the first time," should be implemented?

7. How does a formulation of strategic intent help an organization increase its productivity and quality?

8. How can training be used to improve quality? Give some examples.

9. What is a quality council, and how can it be used most effectively?

10. What is the purpose of a Pareto chart? Give an example of how to use it.

11. How can a cause-and-effect diagram be used to promote quality?

12. How are businesses using the CVA approach to improve their services to customers? Give examples.

13. What is benchmarking?

14. What are the basic steps in benchmarking? Of what value is this process in increasing productivity and quality?

15. How can the results from measuring performance be used?

16. Why is continuous improvement critical to the success of TQM efforts?

17. How does each plan work: compressed workweek, flextime, shift work, and flexible retirement? Give an example of each.

18. In what ways do alternative work schedules help to increase work productivity and quality? Defend your answer.

19. What is empowerment, and why is it such a powerful management tool? How can managers empower employees?

20. Why are more companies using empowerment? Identify and discuss two reasons.

21. What is an intrapreneur? How can organizations encourage intrapreneurship? Cite five examples.

22. How can an intrapreneurial climate be created and nurtured? Discuss at least four ideas.

23. Why would organizations seeking to increase their productivity and work quality be interested in encouraging intrapreneurship?

24. What are two phases in developing intrapreneurial strategies?

25. What are three basic foundations of intrapreneurship? Discuss each one.

26. What are the steps in undertaking the intrapreneurial strategies?

27. What is your brand, and why is it important to your career?

28. What should your brand look like? What are some key things that identify your brand?

29. What are some mistakes that people make in developing their own brands?

30. How can you develop and grow your brand? Prepare an outline that applies to your own brand development and growth.

31. What are the ten tools that can be used to give greater visibility to a person's brand?

Connecting to the Real World

What is Wrong? Can I Improve It?

This exercise can be completed by one or two students. Your professor may want to assign another student to work with you on this exercise or you can do all the work yourself. Get approval from your professor before beginning the assignment.

The purpose of this exercise is to apply ideas presented in this chapter to improve the quality of a situation that directly affects you and other students. Follow the steps:

1. **Select an activity.** Select an activity at your college or university that directly affects you. It may be the long lines at the cafeteria or at the bursar's office. It may be the service at the library or some other type of campus activity—such as checking out equipment in a laboratory, using a piece of equipment in a designated area, having computer access, a sporting activity, a dorm activity, and so on.

2. **Research the cause(s).** You are responsible for researching the cause(s) for the problem. Prepare a list of things you can do to find out why there is a problem, such as interview personnel who are directly involved, conduct surveys of students using the facility, make observations and record the results, or brainstorm with other groups of students on campus.

3. **Carry out the work.** Based on the list prepared, proceed with the interviewing, conducting surveys, observing, questioning other students, researching the Internet for

new ideas, and so on. If you are not familiar with some of the personnel at your college or university, ask your professor for help.

The idea is to improve the situation; so be sure you dig hard to find the cause(s). Remember that what you see is not the cause, but the results of the cause. So look below the surface to find what you need to change to improve the situation.

4. **Analyze your data.** Here again, your professor is a good source for getting some additional ideas. You want your plan to be as practical as possible, keeping in mind the need to improve quality, reduce costs, and increase revenue. An effective plan will include cost savings and/or additional profits.

5. **Prepare a plan.** Write up your recommendations for action and submit them to the appropriate university or college official and to your professor.

CASE
A Productive Approach

Karl Landis, a young financial analyst, decided he wanted to do something different with his life. His job at the bank was not giving him the kind of satisfaction he needed. One day, while attending a baseball practice with his son, he overheard a friend of his complaining about being harassed by a collection agency over a small overdue account at a major department store in the local mall. He thought "How rude! I would never treat people that way." He thought about it and became intrigued with the idea of owning his own collection agency. Karl thought that would be interesting work. He liked the idea of being able to make the decisions, but was a bit scared about trying to start a new business. He pursued the idea and eventually bought The Collection House.

The Collection House handles bills that are turned over to it by organizations that believe these debts are uncollectible. The Collection House receives 40 percent of all monies collected. The agency also does bill collecting for the county. A large number of parking tickets go unpaid each year, even though residents are denied renewal of their licenses if they have any outstanding violations. Many of these people will not pay until they are forced to do so. However, the county does not want to wait for its money, and so it has hired The Collection House to collect the fines.

Collection work can be very time consuming and costly. The work can generate a lot of stress especially when dealing with unhappy people who feel they do not owe any outstanding balances. The collection agent must have strong negotiation skills and an even temper, and must not be one who easily gets upset. The agent also needs skills that can calm and console unhappy people.

The Collection House relies almost exclusively on telephone collection. This method is fairly effective given the fact that most people would like to pay their bills but are financially strapped. What Landis found was that most people will pay their overdue bills if they are put on a time payment plan. They just need someone first to coax them into agreeing to it and then to follow up to ensure that they are sticking to the agreement. In the case of overdue parking tickets, most people are surprised to get a call at home and often pay the bill within ten days. The secret of success in the business is to find the person's telephone number and get through to that person. Sometimes, the person has no phone at home or uses only a cell phone; other times, it is unlisted; still other times, the person answering the phone will say the person who is needed is not at home. In the collection business, experienced bill collectors are vital to success. To maximize his agency's income, Landis has taken five steps.

First, he uses a computer software program that keeps track of the names, addresses, and phone numbers of every person from whom his agency is trying to collect. This program also keeps track of those who have agreed to pay their bills and how much they have paid. The system provides the collection agency employees with accurate information on when they need to do a follow-up call on slow-paying customers, or whether they need to make a visit to their homes.

Second, after a one-week training program on how to collect, Landis turns the employees loose on their own. He gives each employee full authority to handle the collection process. He does not interfere with his people.

Third, he allows his employees to set their own hours collectively. Among the group of fifteen full-time people who work for him, some employees prefer to come in around 1:00 P.M. or 2:00 P.M. Landis does not care when his employees come and go, just as long as they get the work done.

Fourth, Landis requires each person to be on the phone talking to a customer or placing a call at least fifty minutes of every hour. Research shows that one successful collection should occur every fifty minutes; so Landis knows that each employee should succeed in obtaining collections from eight people per day.

Fifth, anyone who is responsible for collecting more than $1,000 in any day is given a 5 percent bonus for all sums in excess of this amount.

Since Karl introduced these five steps, the collections have increased by 55 percent per week. Additionally, he has not lost any employees, although the turnover is extremely high at most other collection agencies. In fact, there is a waiting list of job applicants for The Collection House.

Questions

1. How is technology improving productivity at the agency? How can Karl better use today's advances in technology to improve productivity?
2. What type of alternative work arrangement is Landis using? Explain. Is it the best, or would you recommend another arrangement? Defend your position.
3. What impact has the training program had on employee retention? Explain the relationship between training and productivity at the agency.
4. How is Landis encouraging productivity among his people? Give an example.
5. How is Landis implementing the concept of CVA?
6. Outline the ways that empowerment is involved in this case.
7. Why is there a waiting list of potential applicants who want to work for Landis's agency? Identify the key factors that make this company attractive to applicants.

CHAPTER 8

Job Redesign and Job Enrichment

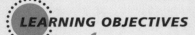
How can modern organizations deal with the challenge of technology and the ever-changing effects it creates? One of the primary ways is to redesign jobs and enrich them with psychological motivators, such as increased autonomy, feedback, and task variety. In this chapter, we study how this can be done, as well as examine some of the current challenges in job design.

Out of Sight, But Not Out of Mind

The technology revolution has not only changed the way employees do their jobs, but also where they work. While some companies turn to job redesign, empowerment, and enrichment, other companies allow their employees to telework or telecommute from their homes. With today's high-tech computers, cell phones, and other wireless devices, it is no longer necessary to come into the office to do the job. Work can be completed away from the office and transmitted to the appropriate location, when and where needed. On-site job reporting can be completed electronically without having to physically report to a central location to complete the paper work. Being out of sight does not mean that the employees are not doing their work. It simply means that a new system must be designed to report the on-site work results, to monitor employees on the job, and to assess their work.

As costs of new technology have risen, some companies have found ways to improve productivity and maintain quality without investing in newer high-tech machinery and tools. Earthstones of Temple, Texas, a granite and marble fabricator, is an example. Marty Janczak, president, states that the aim of Earthstones is to offer a better quality of service and products than its competitors. To fulfill its aim and to meet the demands of Earthstones's growing business, Janczak is using worker empowerment in the production plant. By giving his workers the authority to make decisions about their work and to solve problems on the spot, Janczak has found that his workers are more committed to their work and they take a greater pride in the finished product. The time required to complete their jobs has decreased, while the quality of their finished products has improved, creating more satisfied customers.

As the business continues to grow, Earthstones strives to keep its hiring to a minimum. Instead, it redesigns its office and management positions to fit the needs of the growing company. This practice creates a better-trained workforce where employees can fill in to do whatever job is needed at the time, without having to hire additional employees. At the same time, the company can quickly respond to customers' needs. Janczak states that, "it's important for the company to do what it tells its' customers it will do."

A growing number of employees are now working at home or other locales outside the office. These individuals, known as *teleworkers* or *telecommuters*, are electronically linked to the office and go on-site only periodically to attend meetings or to have a face-to-face conference with their bosses or coworkers. The number of firms that are employing teleworkers is continuing to increase annually.

A good example is Georgia Power. The company first implemented its telecommuting effort back in 1992 by having fourteen people work from home. The program was part of a citywide effort to help cut air pollution by reducing the number of vehicles on the road. In the process, the firm found that it saved more than $100,000 in annual leased space expenses, as it no longer needed to provide offices for these telecommuters. Today, Georgia Power has approximately 250 employees who telecommute on a casual or full-time basis. Each situation is different and is dependent on the type of work done, management discretion, and the equipment provided. Employees can now access the company's network with an Internet connection, and it is as if they were sitting at their own desks at the company office. This gives employees and managers more flexibility in dealing with a more diverse workforce.

Another benefit of teleworking is that it helps organizations maintain their employees by allowing them to balance family and work responsibilities more handily. Consider Janna Tess, a former buyer for Smith & Hawken, a multimillion-dollar garden store. When her child was born, Tess would have taken maternity leave so she could stay at home with him. However, because of teleworking, she was able to log onto her computer and go to work every day without ever leaving home. When Tess's husband was transferred to Europe for two years, Tess was able to continue working, and the company did not have the added expense of having to find a replacement.

Technology has redesigned today's workplace and changed how employees work. Employees can live in another state or even in a foreign country and continue to work for a local company. The boundaries go beyond the four walls of an office or plant building. Redesigning jobs can provide employees with challenging work that lets them balance personal time with work.

Work in America

When workers admit they are bored with their jobs, feel no challenge, or have no desire to do a particularly good job, what can management do? There are four alternatives:

1. Management can do nothing.
2. The workers can be offered more money for accepting these dull, repetitive, uninteresting jobs.
3. The workers can be replaced with technology (computerized machines).
4. The work can be redesigned so that it has meaning for the employees.

The most important of these alternatives in the study of human relations is the last. Workers today want a job that provides them with more challenge and the opportunity to do an entire task, an opportunity to use advanced skills and to grow in the job, and a chance to contribute their ideas in a meaningful way. This philosophy represents a positive change in the manner of doing business. In America, many businesses still have a long way to go before reaching this level of employee involvement. In Europe, for example, job enrichment concepts have been employed for decades.

The Nature of Job Redesign

Explain what job redesign is all about.

Activities aimed at making changes to work with the purpose of increasing the quality of a worker's job experience or improving a worker's productivity are known as **job redesign**. Under this term can be included such commonly used job redesign techniques as job rotation, job enlargement, and job enrichment. Job redesign is a unique way of improving organizational efficiency. This is true for four reasons.

First, job redesign alters the basic relationship between the worker and the job, which has long been a human relations problem. The scientific managers tried to deal with the problem by blending the physical requirements of the work with the physical characteristics of the workers and by screening out those who did not measure up. When behavioral scientists entered industry, they attempted to refine this process by improving the selection and training of the workers. As with the scientific managers, however, the concentration of effort was still on the people doing the job. The work was treated as a fixed commodity that could not be altered. Job redesign breaks with this tradition and is based on the assumption that the work itself can be a powerful influence on employee motivation, satisfaction, and productivity.

Second, job redesign does not attempt to change attitudes first (such as inducing workers to care about work results in a zero-defects program that is designed to reduce, and then to eliminate, all product errors) but assumes that positive attitudes will follow if the job is redesigned properly. Initial attention is given to determining how the job ought to be performed. Once this is worked out, the individual doing the work will be persuaded to change his or her old behavior and, it is hoped, will like the new arrangement so much that attitude toward the job then will be positive.

Third, job redesign helps individuals regain the opportunity to experience the "kick" that comes from doing a job well. There is more here than just satisfaction; there is a sense of competence and self-worth in which people feel they are stretching and growing as human beings.

Fourth, sometimes when an organization redesigns jobs and solves people–work problems, other opportunities for initiating organizational change are presented. For example, technical problems are likely to develop when jobs are changed, offering management the opportunity to smooth and refine the entire work system. Interpersonal issues also are likely to arise, often between supervisors and subordinates, providing the organization a chance to undertake developmental work aimed at improving the social and supervisory aspects of the work system.

Job redesign is a very important tool for it provides a basis for developing and using the organization's resources. Some experts like to say that it is a way for the enterprise to work smarter rather than harder. In the next section, we examine three job redesign techniques commonly used in this process.

Describe how job rotation, job enlargement, and job enrichment work.

Job Redesign Techniques

Job redesign techniques are methods used to change work procedures and, depending on the situation, to increase or decrease work demands. These techniques are very useful in dealing with morale problems caused by boring or meaningless work. When employees do not feel challenged by their jobs or believe their work is of little importance, morale tends to decline. Conversely, if these individuals feel challenged by the work and are convinced that their jobs are important, morale tends to rise and remain high. Job redesign techniques often, although not always, are used to improve morale. The three popular job redesign techniques are job rotation, job enlargement, and job enrichment.

Moving a worker from one job to another for the purpose of reducing boredom is termed **job rotation**. For example, six workers are charged with assembling, soldering, testing, painting, and packaging a piece of sophisticated machinery. As seen in Figure 8.1, the first person assembles components A, B, and C; the second assembles D, E, and F; and each of the other workers performs a specific function on the unit. The arrows in the figure illustrate how job rotation works. Each person moves to the task immediately following the one he or she has been doing. The person assembling components A, B, and C now assembles components D, E, and F; the worker soldering the unit and putting it into a casing now tests the unit to be sure it works; the individual packaging the unit now moves to assembling components A, B, and C. Continually moving all the workers in this manner can often keep them more interested in their work than if they each did the same thing day after day. Another benefit of job rotation is the perspective it provides the individual as to how his or her activity fits into the overall work flow. A third benefit is that the individual's identification with the final output increases. A fourth benefit is that job rotation turns workers from narrow specialists who can do only one task into broad generalists who can do many. All these benefits can help to increase work motivation.

Giving the worker more to do is **job enlargement**. Usually, this new work is similar to what the person has done before. For example, if Joe is wiring, Ralph is soldering, and Mary is testing the product, the three of them may have their jobs enlarged by allowing each to perform all three functions. One way in which this job redesign can result in efficiency is through the time saved by not having to pass the product from one person to the next. Additionally, a psychological reward is associated with completing a unit as opposed to performing just one small task on a large product. Some researchers have reported that the main advantages of job enlargement appear to be increased job satisfaction and improved quality of work.

Figure 8.1 Job Rotation

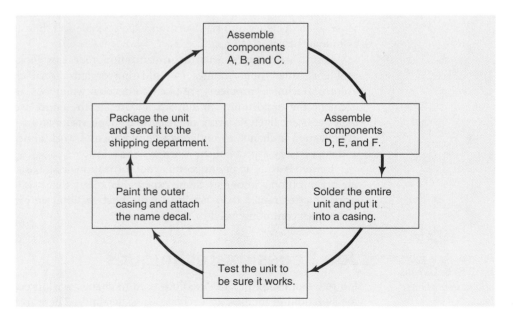

A technique that is more behaviorally sophisticated than job enlargement is **job enrichment**, which attempts to build into the job psychological motivators, as described by Herzberg's two-factor theory. In particular, job enrichment programs attempt to give the worker more authority in planning the work and controlling the pace and procedures used in doing the job.

Industrial research reveals that a number of firms have had success with job enrichment, including AT&T Corp., Campbell Soup Company, and Travelers Indemnity Company. At AT&T, for example, employees who were handling insurance correspondence with stockholders were chosen for a job enrichment program. Using a test group and a control group, the researchers enriched the jobs of the test group by permitting the group members to sign their own names to the letters they prepared, encouraging them to become experts in the kinds of problems that appealed to them, holding them accountable for the quality of their work, and providing them with expert assistance in carrying out these duties. After six months, the group's quality, attitudes, and productivity had increased, and the tardiness, absenteeism, and work costs of group members had declined. The control group's performance on these factors, meanwhile, had remained the same. However, job enrichment is not without costs, and those who do not approach it with enough determination to do it properly often will fail. This is especially true if they fail to consider core job dimensions.

CHECK YOUR UNDERSTANDING

1. Job redesign can be defined as _____.
2. Match the terms to the statements:

Terms		Statements
a. Job rotation	_____	Adding more tasks to the job.
b. Job enlargement	_____	Learning to do new tasks.
c. Job enrichment	_____	Giving workers more authority and control.

Describe the five core job dimensions and illustrate selected enrichment principles that help to create these dimensions.

Core Job Dimensions

Why do redesign techniques such as the three discussed in the previous section often lead to increases in productivity and higher satisfaction among employees?

The answer rests not only in the physical changes that take place in the work environment but also in the psychological changes that take place within the employees. In particular, it has been found that certain dimensions can be built into the work that will bring about higher output, lower absenteeism, higher quality, and greater internal work motivation. Research reveals five **core job dimensions** that are extremely useful in enriching jobs: skill variety, task identity, task significance, autonomy, and feedback. These core dimensions typically are a result of redesigning jobs so that they are more psychologically rewarding and result in higher morale and job satisfaction. Research shows that when these core job dimensions are present, morale and job satisfaction tend to increase and, when they are not present, morale and job satisfaction will often decrease.

Skill Variety

The degree to which a job requires the completion of different activities, all of which involve varying talents and capabilities, is **skill variety**. The two most common types of skills are motor skills and intellectual skills. Motor skills help one with performance tasks, whereas intellectual skills are used with "thinking" tasks. If a job can draw on both, it will provide greater variety than if only one type of skill is needed.

Bob Williams, for example, is a salesman for a large machine manufacturer. The machine he sells is very complex and requires a technical sales pitch. Advertising is also very important in gaining customer attention and arousing initial interest. The typical sales strategy is to mail an advertising brochure to potential customers and then to follow up by sending a salesperson to meet with those who express interest.

Williams had been the company's number one salesman for three years and had been thinking about quitting because the challenge of selling was losing its excitement. He had begun to feel that the requisite technical sales presentation did not allow him to exercise his creativity. He decided to stay on, however, after the vice president of sales asked him to help write the advertising brochure.

"We need some input from you regarding how to make the initial pitch to the customer," the vice president told him. "You know how these people think; we'd like to put your ideas into the brochure." Delighted with the chance to do some "think" work, Williams dropped his plans to leave the company.

Task Identity

The degree to which the job requires completion of a whole or identifiable piece of work is **task identity.** The more an individual does on the job, the more likely he or she will identify with the task. Assembly-line employees who put a bolt on a car or weld part of the structure have little task identity. Those who complete a major part of the car (working as a member of a group) have much greater task identity.

Jane Copeland is an assembler–packer for a consumer goods manufacturer. A year ago, Copeland used to assemble two parts of a seven-part consumer product. Then, following a job redesign program, she was given all seven parts to assemble, as well as the responsibility of packaging the product. As a result, in Copeland's group, there was a 90 percent decline in absenteeism and turnover and a 7 percent increase in output.

Task Significance

The degree to which a job has a substantial impact on the lives or work of other people is its **task significance**. When employees are able to see how the work they do influences others, they tend to be more motivated to do a good job.

Alice Bodelyn is a manuscript editor for a college textbook publishing firm. Generally, Bodelyn is assigned two manuscripts at the same time, and for the next two to three months, she reads the material, edits it for grammar, recommends style and substantive changes, and then sends it back to the respective author in batches of three to four chapters for the author's comments. As the edited manuscript reaches completion, Bodelyn discusses the content of the book with a member of the design department, who will work up a cover for the text. Finally, the author visits the publishing house, meets Bodelyn and the cover designer, and spends a few days with them and the marketing people who are putting together the advertising campaign.

Bodelyn has been a manuscript editor for four years, and she has received a personally autographed copy of each book from its author. When asked what she likes best about her work, she says, "I feel an integral part of an important team. When I look at the finished book, I see part of myself in it."

Autonomy

The degree to which the job provides the worker freedom, independence, and discretion in scheduling the work and determining how to carry it out is **autonomy**. As people begin to plan and execute their assignments without having to rely on others for direction and instructions, they develop feelings of strong personal responsibilities for job success and job failure and are motivated to do the best job possible.[1]

Dick Jackson is a life insurance agent for a large company based in New York. Jackson usually begins his workday at 10:00 A.M., calling on one or two prospective customers and taking a third to lunch. Then he returns to the office to prepare material for people whom he will be meeting later in the day. From 4:00 P.M. to 6:00 P.M., Jackson talks to customers in the office, and three days weekly, he works evenings. Last year, Jackson was again a member of the million-dollar club, having sold $1.92 million of life insurance.

When the district manager asked Jackson whether he would like to leave his current job and become an office manager, Jackson replied, "What for? I've got freedom in my current job. Who wants to be tied down to a nine to five office schedule?"

Feedback

The degree to which the work required by the job results in the individual's receiving direct, clear information about the effectiveness of his or her performance is **feedback.** Feedback allows people to monitor their own work rather than depend on someone else to do it for them.

Group A is charged with wiring the panels for a complex telecommunications satellite. The incorrect wiring of these panels could result in a malfunction of the entire system during or after launching into Earth's orbit. To prevent such an occurrence, a few simple tests can be conducted on the panels. Owing to the complexity of the wiring, however, it is not uncommon for each panel to have three or four incorrectly placed wires. When this occurs, errors are caught by the test group and are noted on an error chart. The panel then is returned to Group A for partial rewiring.

Group A has recently protested this procedure, claiming that it is virtually impossible to wire a panel correctly on the first try. They argued that there are bound to be a few errors, and the group is embarrassed when a panel is sent back by the test group. The members of Group A have asked management to redesign their work and incorporate testing as one of their functions while, of course, maintaining a small test group to make a final check of the panel. The company agreed and, over the past four weeks, none of the forty panels sent to the test group has been returned. "Once we know there's an error," said a member of Group A, "we can correct it before sending it on. This type of feedback from our own group reduces tension and helps us to do a better job."

 CHECK YOUR UNDERSTANDING

1. Identify a job and determine its five core job dimensions.
2. Match the terms with the statements:

Terms		Statements
a. Skill variety	_____	The importance of work.
b. Task identity	_____	Using varied talents and capabilities.
c. Task significance	_____	Responsible for doing the entire job.
d. Autonomy	_____	Receiving information about quality of work.
e. Feedback	_____	Relating to specific components of a job.

Explain the significance of motivating potential score (MPS) and job profiling charts.

The Motivating Potential Score

Researchers have used the five core job dimensions described in this section to develop a **motivating potential score** (MPS)

$$MPS = \left(\frac{\text{Skill Variety} + \text{Task Identity} + \text{Task Significance}}{3} \right) \times \text{Autonomy} \times \text{Feedback}$$

Although we do not need to get into the mathematics of the formula, one overriding conclusion can be drawn from it. If an organization wants to redesign jobs so that its employees are motivated, it must build in autonomy, feedback, and at least one of the three remaining dimensions. This last statement becomes clear when we observe that if autonomy or feedback is lacking, the MPS will be zero, because these two dimensions are multiplicative. Likewise, if all three other dimensions are zero, the MPS will be zero. Testing of these core job characteristics has provided some breakthroughs in job design. In particular, researchers have found that if these dimensions are present, individuals with high growth needs will be more motivated, productive, and satisfied than if they work on tasks without these dimensions.

Job Profile Charts

In addition, it is possible to construct **job profile charts** so that enrichment programs can more effectively be designed. For example, in Figure 8.2, Job 1 is low on skill variety, task identity, and task significance. Job 2 is low on task significance, autonomy, and feedback. Job 3 is low on skill variety, task significance, and feedback. The first question the organization must answer is: Can the particular job be enriched? That is, can Job 1 be redesigned so that it has greater skill variety, task identity, and task significance? If the answer is yes, then the people charged with the redesign program know where to begin. If the answer is no, the employees must be made to realize that there is nothing that can be done to restructure the job.

Figure 8.2 Profile Chart of Core Job Dimensions for Three Jobs

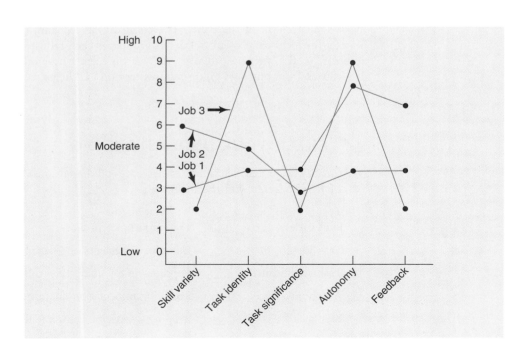

How You View Your Work

This quiz is designed to provide insights into how you view your work. If you do not currently work full time, refer to your last full-time job in answering the questions. If you have not had a full-time job, think of one you would like to have (be reasonable in your choice), and use it throughout the quiz. Interpretations are provided at the end of the book.

A. Read the following job-related questions carefully and decide how accurate each is in describing your job. Then answer each using the following scale:

    1 = None
    2 = Very little
    3 = A little
    4 = A moderate amount
    5 = Some
    6 = Quite a bit
    7 = A lot

_____ 1. To what degree does your job allow you to do an entire series of different things, employing a variety of skills and talents in the process?

_____ 2. To what degree does your job allow you to complete an entire piece of work, in contrast to just a small part of an overall piece of work?

_____ 3. How much significance or importance does your job have?

_____ 4. How much freedom do you have to do your job your way?

_____ 5. To what degree does the job itself provide feedback on how well you are doing?

_____ 6. To what degree does your boss or coworkers let you know how well you are doing?

B. Determine how accurately each of the following statements describes your job. Use the following scale to record your answers:

    1 = Highly inaccurate
    2 = Mostly inaccurate
    3 = Slightly inaccurate
    4 = Uncertain
    5 = Slightly accurate
    6 = Mostly accurate
    7 = Highly accurate

_____ 1. Your job is simple and repetitive.

_____ 2. Your boss and coworkers never give you feedback on your work progress.

_____ 3. Your job provides you no chance to use personal initiative or judgment in carrying out tasks.

_____ 4. Your job is not really very important.

_____ 5. Your job provides independence and freedom in doing the work your way.

_____ 6. Your job provides the chance to completely finish pieces of work you begin.

_____ 7. How well you do your work really affects numerous other people.

_____ 8. Just by the way the work is designed, you have many opportunities to evaluate how well you are doing.

_____ 9. Your job calls for you to use a lot of complex or high-level skills.

_____ 10. Superiors often let you know how well you are performing your job.

_____ 11. Your work is set up in such a way that you do not have the chance to see an entire piece of work through from beginning to end.

_____ 12. Your job provides few clues regarding how well you are performing your tasks.

Before closing our discussion, we must be very clear on an important point: Some jobs cannot be enriched. There may be no way of increasing the task significance of a dishwasher's job, nor can American automakers' assembly lines, under present conditions, provide a person with skill variety. In some cases, the individual must conform to the work pattern because the work pattern cannot be altered.

How many of these core dimensions can you find in your own job? One way of answering this question is to take the "Time Out" quiz, and analyze your work by using the information at the end of the chapter. Which job core dimensions would you redesign in your job? What results would you expect from the change?

 CHECK YOUR UNDERSTANDING

1. What is an MPS? Why is it important in job redesign?
2. In Figure 8.2, identify the job core dimensions for Job 3 that need redesign. For Job 2, which job core dimension needs redesign? For Job 1, which job core dimension needs the most attention?

Job Enrichment Principles

*Discuss five job enrich-
ment principles.*

Many ways exist to enrich jobs so as to provide more meaningful work. In this section, we examine five job enrichment principles:

1. Forming natural work units
2. Establishing worker–client relationships
3. Combining tasks
4. Loading jobs vertically
5. Opening feedback channels

We study how each principle can be used in redesigning work. Figure 8.3 illustrates how each principle is tied to one or more of the core job dimensions.

Forming Natural Work Units

In many organizations, the workers all contribute to providing a product or service but do not have any basis for identifying with the work. An administrative assistant may do all the word processing and reports assigned by the supervisor. On a given day, there may be letters from five or six departmental managers as well as part of a speech for the vice president of human resources. After a while, all the work blurs together, and the administrative assistant identifies with none of it. He or she is simply a producer of word processed material. This situation also holds for a person on an automobile assembly line who is installing upholstery. One car looks like another. The job has no real meaning.

One way of enriching jobs such as these is through the formation of natural work units, in which the employee obtains some ownership of the work. For example, responsibility for all the work requested by a single department or person could be assigned to one administrative assistant, instead of processing only one part of a large report. Over time, the employee begins to identify with the task and sees how the material is of value to those who receive the finished product. The formation of natural work units contributes to two core job dimensions: task identity and task significance (see Figure 8.3).

Figure 8.3 Example of the Relationship between Selected Job Enrichment Principles and Core Job Dimensions

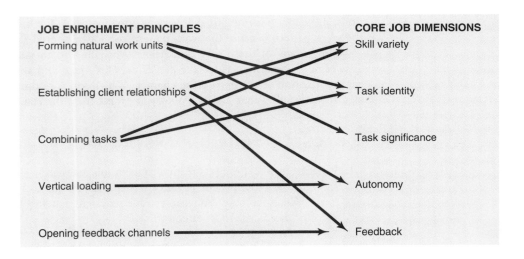

Establishing Worker–Client Relationships

Workers seldom come in contact with the ultimate user of their product or service. If such a relationship can be established, however, job commitment and motivation will usually be enhanced. Three steps go into establishing worker–client relationships:

1. Identify the client.
2. Determine the most direct contact possible between the worker and the client.
3. Set up a system by which the client can evaluate the quality of the product or service and convey the judgments directly to the worker.

Establishing worker–client relationships can contribute to three core job dimensions: skill variety, autonomy, and feedback. Skill variety increases because the worker has the chance to exercise interpersonal skills in managing and maintaining the client relationship. Autonomy increases because the person is given responsibility for deciding how to manage the client relationship. Feedback increases because the worker has the opportunity to receive praise and criticism for his or her output.

Combining Tasks

The principle of combining tasks is based on the assumption that higher work motivation can result when a series of simple tasks is combined to form a new and larger work module. For example, several years ago, a plant of Corning Incorporated, manufacturer of glass and ceramics, redesigned the job of assembling laboratory hot plates by combining a number of tasks that had been separate. The redesigned job called for each operator to assemble an entire hot plate. Costs declined and motivation increased as a result of this redesign effort. The combining of tasks contributes to two core job dimensions: skill variety and task identity. The enlarged job requires a greater variety of skill, and as the individual begins turning out finished products, task identity increases. The assembler can see the unit taking shape as the various pieces are affixed and soldered.

Loading Jobs Vertically

When the gap between the "doing" and "controlling" aspects of the job is reduced, **vertical loading** occurs. In particular, responsibilities that formerly were reserved for management are now delegated to the employee as part of the job. Some ways of vertically loading jobs are as follows:

- Give the worker responsibility for deciding work methods and for advising or helping to train less experienced workers.
- Provide increased freedom to the worker, including decisions about when to start and stop work, when to take breaks, and how to assign work priorities.
- Encourage the workers to do their own troubleshooting and manage work crises rather than immediately call for a supervisor.
- Provide workers with increased knowledge of the financial aspects of the job and the organization, and increased control over budgetary matters that affect their work.

When a job is vertically loaded, autonomy increases and workers begin feeling personal responsibility and accountability for the outcome of their efforts.[2]

Opening Feedback Channels

In most jobs, there are ways of opening feedback channels so that each worker can monitor his or her own performance. One way, discussed already, is to establish direct worker–client relationships by which the individual can learn what the client likes and dislikes about the product or service being provided. Another is to place as much control as possible in the hands of the worker. For example, rather than having quality checks performed by people in the quality assurance department, let the worker do the checking. Such a move ensures immediate feedback and allows the individual to exercise self-control. Placing quality control functions in the hands of workers can result in higher quantity and quality of output. This principle helps to overcome one of the main human relations problems—failure to tell people how well they are doing.[3]

 CHECK YOUR UNDERSTANDING

Select the job enrichment principle that can enhance each core job dimension.

Core Job Dimension		Job Enrichment Principle
a _____	Skill variety	Vertical loading
b _____	Task identity	Establishing worker–client relationships
c _____	Task significance	Opening feedback channels
d _____	Autonomy	Forming natural work units
e _____	Feedback	Combining tasks

Cite some illustrations of job enrichment in action.

Job Enrichment in Action

Numerous firms have successfully applied the job enrichment concepts discussed in this chapter. Perhaps the best-known company is Volvo, the Swedish car manufacturer. Job enrichment has been equally effective in many other organizations, ranging from manufacturing firms to insurance companies. Let us examine some cases of job enrichment in action.

General Electric Company

One of the foremost companies in job enrichment is General Electric Company (GE), which continues to rely heavily on change and innovation. The focus of many of GE's efforts is to tap employee brainpower by reducing the role of the boss and giving more authority and responsibility to the workers. This is accomplished in a number of ways. One is through the use of "workout," an approach in which the employees are given the opportunity to identify problems and then organize themselves into teams and attack the issues. There is no concern over the fact that these matters are in management's domain. At GE, they are everyone's business, and if there is an easier way to get the job done or if reorganizing can save money, workout sessions allow the employees to get involved.

A typical workout session lasts two to three days and involves forty to one hundred people from all ranks and functions in the company. The session usually begins with a talk from the boss, who roughs out an agenda, such as thinking up ways of reducing meeting time or eliminating inefficient procedures. A facilitator breaks the employees into groups, then into five or six teams, each of which tackles part of the agenda. When the group is finished (usually a day or two later), the boss returns and the team spokespeople tell the boss what they would like to do. In one case, for example, a group insisted that the company give it the opportunity to bid against an outside vendor to build new protective shields for grinding machines, based on a design an hourly worker had sketched on a brown paper bag. The group was given the authority to do so and ended up bringing in the job for $16,000 versus the $96,000 bid by the vendor.

Workouts are also used with customers and suppliers in an effort to get their ideas for improving overall productivity and quality. For example, the locomotive paint shop in Erie, Pennsylvania, was having trouble with the color and consistency of its paint bought from two suppliers. To remedy this problem, a team of workers, along with a chemist, wrote new standards, which resulted in reducing the shifts to complete the paint job from twelve to ten. In another case, the company has been able to reduce the time needed to change production and switch from one product line to another as well as reduce inventory for the products. In the appliance division, for example, GE has cut changeover time from four hours to fifteen minutes and has reduced inventory by more than 20 percent. The cost of making these changes was less than $3 million, and the changes have already saved the company more than $300 million. Clearly, by allowing the workers to redesign their jobs, the firm is finding it can achieve dramatic bottom-line results.

A large part of this success is a result of GE moving into what it calls a "rearchitecting stage," which is characterized by:

- A flatter structure with fewer hierarchical levels and more incentives that are broadly shared by employees throughout the organization.
- A closer cooperation between departments and product groups, which share ideas and information and help one another.
- A closer cooperation between the company and its suppliers, customers, stakeholders, and competitors, as reflected through supplier and customer teams and alliances with other firms.

As a result, GE has made strides in changing its technical, political, and cultural environments to adapt to the challenges of a global competitive marketplace. In the strategy area, for example, the company is aiming only for high-growth businesses, is seeking synergy across the hierarchy, and is encouraging employees to act like entrepreneurs. In meeting these goals, the organization structure is being flattened, employees are being empowered, and everyone is being encouraged to share a common vision. The motivation for all this is being provided through changes in human resources management, including new incentive systems, ongoing training, and the creation of a boundaryless organization.

For the past century or so, GE has continually set the agenda of management ideas and practices that other companies follow. Almost everyone in business realizes this. GE is admired for its ability to change direction "unabashedly." Although employees respect GE's past history, they do not let it bog them down; instead, they focus on how to move forward and to grow the business, which is extremely important. It is hard to find any other organization that so enthusiastically allows employees to destroy its own creations. GE has a track record of developing people, evaluating them, and acting on the results.[4]

These transformations help to explain why GE continues to be a leader in its industry and to be one of the most admired companies in the world. The approaches used by a firm in implementing job enrichment are often similar to those of other firms. See the steps for implementing job enrichment discussed in the "Human Relations in Action" box.

Southwest Airlines

Southwest Airlines has consistently been rated as one of the best airlines in the country. Its on-time departures and arrivals, baggage handling, and customer satisfaction reports are the envy of the industry. In addition, the company is consistently profitable. One of

IN ACTION

IMPLEMENTING JOB ENRICHMENT

Many firms have successfully implemented job enrichment programs, but some companies' efforts have failed. The reasons some programs have been unsuccessful can often be linked directly to one of the five critical steps in implementing a job enrichment program. Those five steps are as follows:

1. **Be willing to make changes in jobs.** The first step in any job enrichment program is willingness to change work procedures or job requirements to increase the motivational potential of the tasks. Unless an organization is willing to make such changes, there is no chance for a job enrichment program to succeed.

2. **Get the workers involved.** No one knows more about a job than those who are doing it. If the work is boring, excessively demanding, or poorly organized, the workers are aware of this. By getting them involved in redesigning the job, an organization increases the chances that the new work will be more motivational or will result in increased productivity.

3. **Stay the course.** Will a newly designed job result in increased output or improved service? It may, but the results often take time; the company must be willing to wait and see how things turn out. If a job is totally reorganized, for example, the workers may like the new arrangement but need a couple of months to master the new procedures and techniques. Only then can management draw valid conclusions regarding the overall effect of the program.

4. **Be prepared for more changes.** Sometimes changes in one job result in the need for changes in other jobs. For example, if assembly-line workers are given greater authority over their tasks, supervisors' jobs may become less challenging and need to be redesigned as well. This ripple effect may be felt throughout the entire department or plant and result in the need for job redesign in many areas.

5. **Know how to measure the results.** The organization should know how it will measure the results of any redesign effort. Typical examples are productivity, service, and personnel-related results, such as absenteeism, tardiness, and turnover. Is efficiency increasing? This is commonly measured by comparing the amount of output with the cost of producing the goods. Is service improving? This usually is measured in terms of customer feedback. Are absenteeism, tardiness, and turnover decreasing? These typically are measured through time cards, supervisory feedback, and personnel records.

---

the reasons for its success is that the airline has created a high team spirit by putting the employees, not the customers, first. Additionally, although the airline is unionized, it has been able to negotiate flexible work rules that enable it to meet its rapid flight turn-around schedule. As a result, pilots helping flight attendants clean the airplanes or assisting the ground crew in loading baggage is not an uncommon sight. In fact, many employees are trained to fill in on other jobs so that there is never a shortage of workers to get things done. One way the company has been able to do this is by "hiring for attitude and training for skill." Southwest deliberately looks for applicants with a positive attitude who will promote fun in the workplace and have a desire to "color outside the lines." The firm also has a culture committee that regularly visits all stations across the country, infusing the corporate culture, reiterating the company's history, and motivating the employees to maintain the spirit that has made the airline so successful.

Herb Kelleher, one of the founders of Southwest Airlines, believed that giving people flexibility empowers them to do what is right. Managers cannot anticipate all the situations across the system; therefore, employees must handle them the best way possible. When employees have the freedom to do their job the way they think it should be done, they will work hard. "Southwest has made living legends of employees who went above and beyond the call of duty to offer exceptional customer service." As proof of exceptional service, Southwest Airlines has consistently maintained, since 1987, the fewest overall customer complaints, as published in the U.S. Department of Transportation's Air Travel Consumer Report. Among Southwest's recognitions in 2009 alone are: Best Value Airline, Best Consumer On-Time Estimates, Best Luggage Policy, Best Blog, and 2009 Corporation of the Year. It was also listed as one of the Top 50 Companies Recognized as Leaders in Corporate Social Responsibility, took top honors in nine out of twelve categories in SmarterTravel.com's second annual Readers' Choice Awards, and is one of *FORTUNE* magazine's Most Admired Airlines.[5]

To stay ahead in the industry, Southwest Airlines implements technology and restructures jobs to fit current needs. For example, it was the first airline to establish a home page on the Internet, which has saved the company many dollars over the years and has helped keep Southwest profitable.[6]

Current Challenges in Job Design

Discuss four current challenges in job design.

Job design is a very important issue in human relations. After all, designing work so employees achieve a sense of task identity and task significance and are provided with skill variety, autonomy, and feedback stimulates motivation. However, some additional challenges are becoming prominent. These relate to both job design and job enrichment and include new workplace designs, the increasing use of permanent part-time workers and teleworkers, the increasing number of workers choosing flextime schedule arrangements, the challenge in dealing with contract workers, and managing hard-to-keep employees (see also the "Ethics and Social Responsibility in Action" box).

New Workplace Designs

A year-long survey by Tom Davenport, professor of management and information technology at Babson College, found that three factors determine the performance of white-collar workers: management and organization, information technology, and workplace design.[7]

In an effort to motivate their employees and create a more conducive work environment, a growing number of organizations are introducing new workplace designs. Procter & Gamble's (P&G) 13 million-square-foot building just north of Cincinnati is a good example. The building's design facilitates teamwork by project groups. For example, file cases are mounted on wheels so they can be easily moved, and office walls can be reconfigured to increase or decrease the enclosed space. Likewise, instead of elevators, escalators move people from floor to floor, because this form of transit encourages the easy flow of communication among individuals, in contrast to elevators, which tend to discourage communication during transit. The building also has "huddle rooms" strategically placed where teams can come together to brainstorm, as well as electronic whiteboards in the lunchrooms and lounges that can be used to convert scribblings and notes into e-mail messages.

P&G is also among those companies using design to help dual-career families while still boosting productivity. When planning its new building, the company specifically designed in a dry cleaner, a shoe-repair shop, a fitness center, and a cafeteria that prepares food for employees to take home at night.

Small firms are also discovering that careful workplace design can increase productivity. For example, at Inhale Therapeutic Systems, a Palo Alto, California, firm that works on novel drug-delivery technology, the president found that everyone was obsessed with having an office close to his. No one wanted to feel left out of anything, so the company redesigned its office layout and now everyone, including the president, sits in large cubicles with four other people of various ranks and functions. There are no walls or barriers of any kind between them. This forces everyone to talk to one another all the time. Moreover, the lack of private space limits gossip, reduces the need for memo writing, and gets top managers scattered among the rest of the employees. Periodically, the president shuffles the workplaces and assigns people to different cubicles. This approach helps maintain morale and productivity.

New-age technology is changing the workplace and how customers place orders inside McDonald's. On a pair of kiosks bolted to the floor near the front door, customers

IN ACTION

ETHICS AND SOCIAL RESPONSIBILITY IN ACTION

IT PROVIDES A COMPETITIVE EDGE

Job enrichment involves more than just giving people greater autonomy and feedback in their jobs. Many firms are finding that they need to address the personal concerns of their employees or risk losing them to competitors who will address these concerns. One primary way that organizations are accomplishing job enrichment is by creating a balanced work-life environment that allows employees to meet both their work and family responsibilities. In past years the boundaries between work and home were fairly clear, but that is no longer true. Today, work is likely to invade your personal time. Maintaining a work-life balance is no simple task. When a firm creates a work-life balance environment, research shows, workers tend to be more productive and businesses increase their profits.

Laura Berman Fortgang, author of *Now What? 90 Days to a New Life Direction*, says that figuring out what really matters to you in life and getting your priorities clear are the first and most essential steps toward achieving a well-balanced life. By making a list of your priorities, you can begin dropping any commitments and unnecessary activities that do not make the top five on your list. It is equally important to protect your private time. One thing you can do is stop checking your email and cell phone so often. If your work consistently interferes with your personal time, then discuss the matter with your boss and make changes in your work assignments. It is up to you to create boundaries that keep work from intruding on family time. You cannot always do it alone. Allow yourself to rely on others, such as your partner, family, or friends to help with household chores and babysitting. Do not forget that fun and relaxation are an essential part of living a well-balanced life. Greater satisfaction in both work life and your personal life should bring greater productivity and more creativity.

When your work-life balance and personal life are out of balance, your stress level is likely to soar. The staff at the Mayo Clinic has developed a list of strategies for juggling the demands of a career and personal life. They are:

1. Track your time and decide what is important and what satisfies you most. Cut out activities or delegate them to others.
2. Take advantage of your options by asking for flex hours, a compressed workweek, job sharing, telecommuting, or other scheduling flexibility.
3. Learn to respectfully say no to those requests that are not meaningful in your life.
4. Leave work at work. Make a conscious decision to separate work time from personal time.
5. Manage your time by organizing household tasks efficiently, using a family calendar to record family events, and keeping a daily to-do list. Do what needs to be done and let the rest go.
6. Bolster your support system by joining forces with coworkers who can cover for you when family conflicts arise and enlist trusted friends and family to pitch in to help with child care or household responsibilities when you need overtime or travel.
7. Nurture yourself by eating healthy foods and including physical activity in your daily routine, and by all means, get enough sleep.

Everyone needs help from time to time. When life feels too chaotic to manage, it may be time to seek professional counseling. Creating a work-life balance is a continuous process, not a one-shot deal. Also remember that the right balance for you today will probably be different for you tomorrow. There is no perfect, one-size-fits-all work-life balance for all employees.

Sources: Sherry Rauh, "5 Tips for Better Work-Life Balance," WebMD Community, August 1, 2010, www.webmd.com and Mayo Clinic Staff, "Strike a Better Work-Live Balance," *Work-Life Balance: Tips to Reclaim Control*, May 29, 2010, www.maycoclinic.com

---

use a touch screen to order their Big Macs and Happy Meals exactly the way they want them. With amazing results, McDonald's is quietly putting self-ordering computers in their restaurants. This self-service technology has swept through the airline industry, changing the workplace of its employees.[8]

Another recent development in workplace design is to give people more control over their physical environment. For example, the West Bend Mutual Insurance Company of Wisconsin had a system installed that allows employees to adjust the temperature, fresh air, and noise in their cubicles. Researchers have found that these workers are 3 percent more productive because of their ability to control their environment, and the novel workstations have become an asset in both recruiting and retaining workers.

Not all workplace design benefits employees. Kmart, Kroger, A&P, and Home Depot have replaced their human cashiers with machines. The "scan-it-yourself checkout lines" are designed to give customers faster checkout service, and they generally pay for themselves in nine to twelve months. A&P labels its machines as "Express Yourself" lanes. Today the majority of grocers use "scan-it yourself checkout lines" for part or for all checkout stations.

Yet another recent development in workplace design is provided by Herman Miller Inc., a firm famous for its creation of cubicles in the work area. The firm created a system called "Resolve" that offers employees a wide number of workplace options. For example, workers can raise or lower a table so that they can work seated or standing. Additionally, if workers use a flat-screen monitor, they can raise or lower the apparatus that holds it, and the table on which the computer sits is wheeled so that it can be rolled to other locations, thus allowing the workers to come together in teams. One designer for the company explained some of the new configurations this way:

> Some workstations have a curved screen that extends from the floor over the desk and connects to the center pole, sort of like a giant leaf. The screen's wheels let workers reposition it to reduce glare on their terminal, to block an air-conditioning vent, or simply to cover their backs for privacy—all solutions to routine complaints. These adjustments may seem minor … but for someone who works all day at a terminal, they represent major control over the environment.[9]

Miller is rethinking both the cubicle and the office landscape and plans to unveil new designs in the near future. Its engineers are experimenting with a signal light that could connect from your phone—or a word document—to the name tag on the "workstation." It would glow red if you do not want to be interrupted. It is also working on sound-muffling technology to give workers more privacy when dealing with confidential information.[10]

Butler Community College, a very forward-thinking institution, is always looking for ways to serve its students. It feels that getting students involved in their learning is a key factor in their success. Butler felt that it needed to create spaces for students that would encourage collaboration and build a real sense of community, which cannot always be done successfully in a traditional classroom. Based on the latest research, Miller helped Butler College develop the Learning Studio Research Program, which started with two general education classrooms and two nursing classrooms. The program involved redesigning the classrooms and furniture, acquiring technology support, and installing programmable electrical and data infrastructure.[11]

In another case, Miller worked with the Hyatt Reservation Center to create a space that would be inviting to employees, six hundred agents, as well as a space that exhibited the quality of the Hyatt brand. The eighteen-year-old facility—dark, dated, and dreary—needed more light, less clutter, better collaboration areas, and a roomier feeling. This space was not the best environment for employees to eagerly promote the Hyatt brand. The redesigned space helped Hyatt compete more effectively with brand new call centers and gave the employees a new sense of pride in encouraging guests to stay at the Hyatt Hotel.[12]

Dell, Inc., formerly sold its PCs only on the phone and over the Internet before it redesigned its marketing model to include retail store sales. Dell installed kiosks in shopping malls and launched a trial store-within-a-store with Sears, Roebuck & Co. in Austin, Texas, to allow customers to try out the computers before placing an order. This new workplace design reflected a drive to increase sales amid a weak economy, which is another example of what motivates companies to make workplace changes.[13]

Increasing Use of Telework

Closely linked to new workplace designs is the use of telework, virtual teams, and global teams.

Telework.   Telework (also called telecommuting) is the ability to do your work at a location other than your "official duty station." With wireless technology, high-speed telecommunications links, and ever-present pocket cell phone devices, many employees today can work almost anywhere at least some of the time. Telework, telecommuting, virtual teams, and global teams fall under the umbrella of flexible work arrangements and are recognized as a fundamental component in organizational restructuring. According to the latest survey conducted in 2004 by the U.S. Bureau of Labor Statistics (BLS), 13.7 million wage and salary workers did some work at home. About 3.3 million, or one in four, had a formal arrangement with their employer to be paid for the time they put in at home.[14] Teleworkers often come to the office only for special meetings or to check in and discuss important matters with their bosses or subordinates. Otherwise, they operate out of their homes or work on the road while remaining in electronic contact with their offices.

People in every major occupational group have at-home work arrangements. The prevalence of telework, however, continues to grow in the federal government. The workforce of the majority of federal agencies participates in telework to some extent.

Global and Virtual Teams. Virtual and global teams are boundaryless, with participants linked by telecommunications and technology across organizations, functions, and geography. The advances in satellite technology have given global access via the Internet and the cell phone. **Global teams** represent the extreme example of working as a telecommuter. Successful management of these teams requires mutually defining the culture and values applicable to the particular situation, which often are exaggerated by ethnic differences. **Virtual teams** tend to be geographically dispersed, time dependent, and project based. Research has found that they work best if members have learned virtual collaborative skills, virtual socialization skills, and virtual communication skills.

Two of the major human relations challenges that telecommuting presents to firms are those of carefully choosing who will be telecommuters and determining who will supervise these individuals. Research has revealed that managers typically look for people who are self-motivated, have a high level of job knowledge, and are flexible. While the job qualifications of teleworkers are the same as traditional workers, teleworkers often need additional qualities, such as the ability to work reliably without supervision. They need to be self-disciplined and enjoy working alone for long periods of time. Typically, teleworkers are better educated and earn higher incomes than most employees. Because the person will be working away from the office and not having social interaction with employees on a regular basis, the teleworker must have a low need for face-to-face contact with others. A successful teleworker must be a team player, be willing to take responsibility, and be reliable.[15]

Are you a good candidate for telework? The U.S. Office of Personnel Management has provided some guidance on this question. See the "In Action" box: "Am I a Good Candidate to Be a Teleworker?"

Researchers have discovered that, although many employees would like to volunteer to be teleworkers, certain behaviors and work habits are critical to success. In particular, when people work from home, they must be able to put the work first and limit the number of distractions or interruptions caused by family members or personal matters. Organizations that look for individuals who can work effectively from home want to feel that these employees are indeed committed to their jobs. In the case of people who have been working at the office and would like to become teleworkers, some of the best suggestions for becoming a successful teleworker are:

- **Establishing a routine:** Once you start teleworking, you will have twenty-four-hour access to work. You may be tempted to work longer hours. However, working too much can cause stress and stress-related illnesses. Knowing when to stop is essential for effective performance. One way to get around overwork is to implement specific business hours. Set firm starting and stopping times, and communicate these to your manager and coworkers. At the office, there are routines that structure your time. If you work at home, it may help to establish your own routine so that you do not overwork.

IN ACTION

AM I A GOOD CANDIDATE TO BE A TELEWORKER?

All or parts of many jobs are appropriate for teleworking, however, usually 100 percent of a position is not appropriate for teleworking. Teleworkers usually perform part of their jobs at their official duty stations, while the rest of the job can be performed elsewhere. Teleconferencing is a tool that can be used to communicate directly without requiring the teleworker to make a trip to an official duty station. There will be times when the teleworker must personally travel to the official duty station for meetings and other special activities.

What type of work is best for telework? Telework is feasible for work that requires thinking and writing (data analysis, reviewing grants or cases, and writing decisions or reports); telephone-intensive tasks (setting up a conference, obtaining information, and following up on participants in a study); and for computer-oriented tasks (programming, Web page design, data entry, and word processing).

Telework is not suitable for employees who need to be in the office to learn the organization, who require on-the-job training, who need close supervision, or who thrive on interaction with coworkers and would suffer from the isolation of working alone.

To be a successful teleworker, you should be an organized, disciplined, and conscientious self-starter who requires minimal supervision.

Your teleworking should not adversely affect either your own performance or that of your coworkers. Thus, if your job involves frequent interaction with your coworkers or customers, you will be expected to be available at the same times as when you were at work for this interaction via e-mail or the telephone.

Although telework will give some employees more time for their family responsibilities, you may not use duty time for providing dependent care or any purpose other than official duties.

You must have a safe and adequate place to work off-site that is free from interruptions and that provides the necessary level of security and protection.

Source: Office of Personnel Management, "Featured Questions," www.telework.gov.

- **Establishing goals:** Develop a list of goals and assignments for the days you telework. At the end of the day, go over the list and see how much you have been able to accomplish. It is helpful to start the list a couple of days before you are teleworking. This helps you to plan for all the resources you will need to support your activities at home.

- **Setting deadlines:** While teleworking, follow the same rules for deadlines as if you were in the office. If you are mailing reports to the office, send them so they arrive the day they are due or earlier. If you are sending your work electronically via a computer, it should also arrive on time.

- **Avoiding distractions:** Avoid teleworking on days when there may be friction at home, such as family quarrels or problems. If you have an elderly family member, an infant, or a toddler needing care, it will be difficult to telework and complete any work. Telework is not a substitute for child care or elder care.

- **Maintaining regular communication with your manager:** As a teleworker, you will need to keep your supervisor informed about the status of the programs you are working on, your progress, and any difficulty encountered. Think of your manager as a client who needs information on a timely basis.

- **Being accessible:** Be sure to stay in touch with the office during teleworking days. Set up a system (mobile telephone, voice mail, e-mail, answering machine, or pager) so that you can be reached easily.[16]

Other suggestions for being a successful telecommuter are maintaining communications with the office. Let people know you are working. Strive to talk with your supervisor on a regular basis and e-mail or fax messages to illustrate your work. One disadvantage of telecommuting is that it may negatively impact your chances for advancements because you are not seen working in the office. To show that you are not isolating yourself from other workers and are committed to the workplace, find a reason to turn up at the office at least once monthly. Keep up your contacts with the people you work with in the office. Additionally, make it a point to schedule lunch with them every couple of weeks and let your boss know you are staying in touch with them. Always be flexible and show up when a meeting is called in the office. It will look bad if you miss the meetings. On the other hand, be careful about being too flexible, or your boss will think you are not working very hard at home.

The Manager's Skill Requirements.   Researchers have also found that managers need to have a series of skills and abilities that allow them to manage their telecommuting work group effectively. The five most important traits are the ability to:

1. Set goals and communicate plans to employees.
2. Identify resources and structure the organization.
3. Motivate and develop people.
4. Foster cooperation and resolve conflicts.
5. Monitor performance and evaluate work.

Managers and supervisors play a key role in the success of a company's telework program. They must identify eligible positions and employees, set performance expectations and parameters for telework arrangements, and monitor productivity. This may require establishing new ways to evaluate teleworkers.[17]

Managing Job Sharers

Job sharing is a work arrangement in which two or more employees are responsible for the duties and tasks of one full-time position. It allows an employee to cut back on work hours and still get the job done with the help of another employee. The employees usually coordinate their schedules. Each employee will work at times and days that the other employee does not work. Often, these employees are allowed to keep half of their benefits of a full-time job.

For job sharing to be successful, the participating employees need similar work habits and complementary strengths and skills. Being able to communicate with the partner is critical. Since the BLS does not collect data on job sharing, it is difficult to know just how many job sharers there are.[18]

Dealing with Contract Workers

A related challenge is dealing with contract workers. Some of these workers are hired on an hourly basis while others are hired to perform a job, often for a specified time or task. Over the last decade, a growing percentage of the workforce has consisted of contract workers or hourly employees. One advantage of this arrangement is that it helps many workers to meet specific objectives. For example, an increasing number of retired people are interested in supplementing their social security or organizational retirement benefits and are happy to contract for twenty hours per week for a specific amount. The same is true for some college students who are going to school part time and financing their education by contracting to work four to five hours per week or on Saturdays and Sundays.

The Home Shopping Network (HSN), a global multichannel retailer, had its sales volume growing so rapidly that it had a hard time staffing its call centers. The senior vice president of customer care met the challenge by drawing on a new labor pool—people with full-time jobs who wanted to earn additional money. These were "qualified workers, who could work an extra 10 to 25 hours per week." This strategy provided HSN with plenty of qualified applicants and helped maintain flexibility and diversity within its workforce.

As Baby Boomers begin to retire, there will be a shortage of experienced workers. According to the BLS data, the pool of workers aged 35 to 44 will shrink by 7 percent between 2002 and 2012. Along with that information and a study of the demographics of its customer base, Borders, a retail book store, moved toward creating a formal hiring initiative aimed at older workers. Currently, 16 percent of its workforce is over the age of 50. According to the senior vice president for human resources, the turnover rate for workers over the age of 50 is ten times less than those under 30, and it has seen its turn-over drop 30 percent since it began its effort to recruit older employees.[19]

Another practice to filling positions is called temp-to-perm. For example, T-Mobile acquired a new cell system from a competitor and needed to hire a large group of work-ers. The director of engineering and operations for Northern California met the chal-lenge by filling the positions with temporary workers. What started out as a strategy for filling a vast number of positions turned into a very beneficial hiring tactic. It gave those who were interested in full-time work a chance to see if they were a good fit for the company. It carries the philosophy "try before you buy." The temp-to-perm hiring pro-gram has become quite popular among companies.[20]

In contrast, though, individuals who depend solely on part-time work find that making a living can be very difficult. An employee, who works at UPS, was able to earn $30,000 in one recent year by working forty hours weekly. However, the next year, his shifts were trimmed and he worked only twenty-five hours per week, cutting his annual income by $11,000. This is not enough to support his wife and two children. Stories like these indicate the challenge that organizations face when they hire part-time employees and rely on them to help keep down costs. Eventually, something must be done to address the problems of part-time workers. This issue will become more critical as the permanent temporary work-force, created by the economic crises of 2008–2009, increases.

The contents of the contracts between a company and its union workers can high-light some of the problems that management faces as it seeks to deal with the human relations challenges associated with managing part-time employees. Not only does the work often carry low pay, but also the jobs are not designed to be motivational. They are simply opportunities for individuals to make moderate incomes. However, in the years to come, management is going to find that part-time employees need many of the same types of motivation that are provided to full-time workers: interesting and chal-lenging work, an opportunity for advancement in the organization, and medical and retirement benefits that ensure the future well-being of the workers. For the moment at least, these challenges have remained unmet. In light of the surge of part-time workers during the last recession, a new phrase "permanent part-time workers" was coined. Will this be the trend for the future and what does it mean for redesigning work?

Managing Hard-to-Keep Employees

In addition to telecommuters, job sharers, and contract workers, there are a number of other groups that present challenges to today's organizations. These include single mothers, nonconformists, and the talented high performers—those who can make signif-icant contributions to the firm if they are managed properly.

Single Mothers. The 2005 statistics from the U.S. Department of Labor and the U.S. Census Bureau report that 69.1 percent of single mothers are gainfully employed compared to 65.87 percent of married mothers.[21] Many of these women, especially those who have never been married, are not highly educated and, as a result, tend to hold fairly low-paying jobs. This, in turn, can create a problem for management because companies offering better compensation packages are likely to lure such workers away. As a result, many firms are now creating job enrichment programs that are designed to complement their pay packages. Examples, some of which were discussed in Chapter 7, are flextime, shift work, and other job-related arrangements that allow employees to coordinate their work with the needs of their children. Many companies now allow single mothers to come to work in midmorning so that they can drop their children off at school. These employees make up the time later in the day by working until 6:00 P.M. and then pick up the children from the day care center on the way home. In addition, managers are being trained to interact more effectively with these workers both to encourage productivity and to maintain high levels of job satisfaction, so that they do not leave the organization.

Nonconformists.   Another group of hard-to-keep employees are nonconformists. These individuals tend to exhibit a number of different needs and attitudes. For example, nonconformists like to set their own work hours. Coming in at 6:00 A.M. and leaving at 2:00 P.M. is a common work arrangement and one that many nonconformists like because they feel they are most productive early in the day. Other nonconformists like to work long hours and enjoy being at work six or seven days a week, putting in eighty or more hours. The challenge for management is to balance these personal needs with organizational requirements.

Talented High Performers.   A third group of hard-to-keep employees consists of those who are highly educated and experienced and make major contributions to both productivity and profit. These individuals are continually being sought by the competition. In an effort to avoid what is commonly called a brain drain, companies are now taking a number of steps to lock in this talent with carefully formulated job redesign and job enrichment programs. Research shows that in addition to compensation packages, companies are offering flexible work schedules, increased job training so that these individuals can qualify for promotion or more challenging work, and job assignments that allow employees to work at home. These strategies help to address the most common reasons that high-performing employees leave their jobs, including feeling undervalued by the organization, having insufficient opportunity for advancement, and having a job that provides insufficient challenge.[22]

The International Arena.   American firms are also looking at how companies in the international arena deal with this problem and are copying some of the ideas they find. For example, in Europe, the labor market is becoming tighter, and one of the best ways of attracting new talent is to lure it away from the competition. In an effort to prevent this from happening to them, companies are now designing new retention strategies. Laboratoires Boiron, a maker of homeopathic medicines in Lyon, France, establishes an annual fund to help employees realize some of their personal desires. As a result, one warehouse worker received nine months off and enough euros to help finance a voyage around the world with her husband and two children. In another instance, the company gave euros to a telephone order taker to finance a sculpture and painting studio.

European firms also are altering work schedules to fit the personal needs of their employees. For example, the MFI Furniture Group PLC, a British manufacturer and retailer of full kitchens and other big-ticket household furnishings, instituted a program to reduce turnover among its sales staff. To make the job more attractive, MFI stripped out the work responsibilities that were not sales related and beefed up technology training so that the salespeople could focus on their primary responsibilities and not be bothered with peripheral chores.[23]

Retaining Employees.   In addition to these types of changes, a growing number of companies are putting strong emphasis on providing personal recognition to employees who do exceptional work. A good example is Stew Leonard's, which started in 1969 as a small dairy store and is now the world's largest dairy store, with locations in Norwalk, Danbury, Newington, and Hartford, Connecticut, and Farmington, New York. Stew Leonard's is known for its outstanding customer service and quality. Customers know that Stew Leonard's is a fun place to shop. With its amusement park atmosphere, combined with its farm-fresh foods and outstanding customer service, Stew Leonard's has been recognized as one of the "100 Best Companies to Work for in America" by

Fortune magazine. Opportunities for growth, camaraderie, and community service are a few of the reasons why it is a good place to work. Not only are its managers accountable for personally recognizing employees' efforts, the company also supports:

- A philosophy of promoting from within
- An employee profit sharing program
- A "mom's program" that provides working mothers with flexible hours

In 2005, 88 percent of the managers were promoted from within the company. With new stores on the horizon, Stew Leonard's has instituted a number of new training programs to give team members the opportunity to take on managerial positions that the additional locations will create. Dating is usually taboo in the workplace and couples are not allowed to work together, but at Stew Leonard's, couples contribute to the family-caring atmosphere. In fact, 30 percent of the workforce is composed of families and married couples. Some advice given by two couples are: "treat each other with respect," "work together as a team to be stronger as a couple," and "a positive attitude brought to work will permeate the entire department." Stew Leonard's uses feedback from employees in developing its recognition program, to celebrate seniority, and to add training classes to continue to grow team members.[24]

Stew Leonard's passion for quality customer service includes two basic rules. Rule number one is, "The customer is always right." Rule number two is, "If the customer is ever wrong, reread rule number one." And Stew Leonard's management philosophy is: "Take care of your people and they in turn will take good care of your customers." Coupled with that philosophy is the belief that, "You can't have a great place to shop without first making it a great place to work." Stew Leonard's goes out of its way to recognize employees' efforts on a daily basis. Handwritten notes are just one of the ways employees are recognized for doing an excellent job.[25]

Stew Leonard's is not alone. A growing number of businesses are developing programs aimed at retaining employees. Macy's West, a division of Macy's Inc., in San Francisco has a program for assigning mentors to new managers and telling all managers that 35 percent of their compensation will be linked to how well they retain the people who report to them. At the International Paper's plant in Moss Point, Mississippi, morning training sessions are devoted to teaching managers how to give positive reinforcement to their people.[26] The reasoning behind these programs is that satisfied employees are more likely to stay with the firm, and managers play a key role in this process. As one person put it, "People come on board because they want to join a company, but when they quit they do so in order to leave a manager." Thus, to the extent that managers are able to treat their employees well, the likelihood of these employees leaving is sharply reduced.[27] For obvious reasons, job redesign and job enrichment programs will continue to be important in meeting the human relations challenges of the new century.

✔ CHECK YOUR UNDERSTANDING

1. Discuss how redesigning a workplace can impact productivity and the quality of work.
2. Describe how a company might use teleworkers to control costs and to increase productivity.
3. Outline ideas for retaining employees and at the same time improve customer service.

© Jason York, iStock

Career Advisor

Manage Your Career Effectively

After you have secured employment, your challenge becomes one of managing your career effectively. The most successful people do not allow their career paths to develop randomly. They take steps to ensure that things go their way, and when they do not, these people know how to adjust their career course.

Explain how to manage your career more effectively.

Career Planning

Until recently, career planning was a vehicle for gathering "information about skills, strengths, and developmental needs" to prepare employees for senior management roles. With the surge of Baby Boomers into the workplace, mergers, and downsizing, a flatter organization was created, which provided fewer opportunities for vertical advancement. As a result, career planning emerged as a way of helping employees advance by moving in a zigzag pattern through the organization. Career planning is a strategy for maintaining motivation and gaining commitment rather than a way to support employees. Organizations now "recognize that the only way to gain the benefits of motivation and high performance is to respond to the individual's careers concerns." In today's fast-paced world, employees are constantly dealing with stressful competing demands on their lives both at work and at home. To deal with these issues, career planning is being expanded to help employees cope with change and manage their complicated and overcommitted lives. For example, chronic uncertainty in today's world, as well as in the workplace, is another complex issue causing employees concern and an issue that companies are addressing. Effectively using your company's career planning resources is only one way to manage your career. Using coaching and mentoring are two more ways.[28]

Coaching

A growing practice in firms today is that of coaching. So, how does coaching differ from mentoring? They are related, but different. Coaching involves a more formal structure with an informal conversational tone that focuses on improvement in the employee's job. Measurable goals are established; personal talents, personality, and soft skills are assessed; and periodic meetings are conducted with the boss/supervisor. Mentors work in a more informal setting and are more concerned with an employee's career development.

Most employees want to move up in this competitive world, and often, they need the guidance of someone who knows the ropes. Never be afraid to seek advice from those who can help you navigate through the system. Be proactive in seeking advice; do not wait for your supervisor to notice and offer you a promotion. That may never happen.

Using Mentors

According to Barbara Moses, an organizational career management expert, being mentored is one of the most important predictors of a successful career. Managers today are too stretched to give their staff proper feedback. Employees need someone "who can tell them how to navigate through organizational politics or deal with an obnoxious co-worker or jerk boss." Employees will hear the truth from a good mentor. In formal mentoring programs, mutual respect is important, whereas in informal mentoring, chemistry, that is, how you feel about the person, is more important. Good mentoring is determined by finding the right match. In fact, it would be wise to find more than one mentor. For example, find a mentor for "expertise issues" and another for "life issues." Do not limit the search; mentors are often found outside the area where you work. You must understand how to work with mentors and to respect the boundaries. It is important not to abuse the relationship by expecting more than the mentor is willing to give. Mentors also like to know how they are doing and you should not forget to show your appreciation.[29]

Effective mentoring programs should supplement coaching programs. Mentoring programs should be positioned to make both the business and the employees more successful. Mentors need to have a coaching attitude and the ability to work with each employee differently. What works great for one person may not work for another. Examples of some areas where mentors can be helpful are: providing the best ways to maneuver the political waters of an organization, providing advice about strategies for the best way to accomplish work goals, and supporting and advising employees on career development. Mentors work with employees in face-to-face meetings at lunch or dinner or in a casual setting; whereas in coaching, bosses/supervisors meet with employees in a more formal setting on the job.

A recent study revealed that companies are getting more serious about implementing mentoring programs to capture and share key organizational information as veteran leaders approach retirement. Mentoring and coaching are great ways to teach people and transfer intellectual capital before it leaves the organization.[30] Coaching and mentoring do matter in managing your career successfully.

Networking

Outside contacts are important in managing your career. Start by joining a professional organization, a community group, or a networking group. These people can not only help with work-related questions, but also can be a stepping stone to advancement in your career. Most people are hired as a result of a recommendation, and the more contacts you develop and nurture, the more chances you will have for learning about job openings in the future. Who you know is always more important than what you know. Effectively managing your career is often a matter of knowing the right people.

Line Jobs

Being hired into the right job in a company can affect your career, and in some cases, not being in the right job can make it difficult to advance. Line jobs that deal directly with the functions of the business are viewed as making more important contributions to a company than staff jobs that advise or assist line positions. The work in line positions is more highly prized, giving you a step up from other employees and making it easier to manage your career.

Short-Term Rewards

Do not be lured by long-term rewards that will not materialize for twenty years. Consider the shorter run. Achieving short-term goals will help maintain your motivation and your desire to produce quality work. Reaching short-term goals will give you a chance to experience how the company views employees' accomplishments and how the company implements its reward system. If the rewards do not meet your satisfaction, you can start investigating new opportunities. You should always be prepared to leave so that, if things go badly in the organization, you will have a plan of action.

Organizational Size

With millions of companies operating in the economy, do not limit yourself to just the largest industrials. Many smaller firms offer attractive employment packages and opportunities for advancement. They can provide the experience that is required to qualify for jobs in larger firms. Managing your career is a matter of knowing where you want to go and figuring out how to gain the experience and knowledge to qualify for the job. It is a matter of moving ahead in small steps.

Behavioral Changes

Whether you agree or not, your behaviors will affect your career. If not managed properly, your behaviors may, in fact, kill your chances of succeeding in your chosen career. Barbara Moses has identified the following egregious behaviors that you may need to change.[31]

One of the first things you need to do is to understand your behaviors and how they affect other people. Here is where you must be brutally honest with yourself. You also may need to consult with someone who will be completely honest with you. Begin by asking, "Are my behaviors irritating?" "Do I constantly interrupt those who are speaking because I am bored or I think I know what the speaker is trying to say?" "Am I completely self-focused, and when someone tries to change the topic, do I bring the topic back to me?" Before sharing another story, ask yourself, "Does that person care?" If not, turn your attention to the other person and do not interrupt. Eye contact lets the other person know you care and are listening.

Some people have an "insatiable need for positive feedback." If you do, try to understand why you need constant feedback and why the approval of others is so important. In today's workplace, self-management is expected; neediness can be an irritant. Are you boring? Do you constantly tell the same old war stories, regardless of whether anyone is listening? Try making an effort to ask listeners about themselves. Do you operate as a robot? Do you focus so much on what you are doing that you fail to show any emotion in your work? Why not try smiling and doing something totally spontaneously?

How judgmental are you? Do you have strong opinions on many matters? Before giving an opinion, be sure of the facts, then soften the delivery of your opinion. People will listen harder and will respect you more. Do you alienate your coworkers by not accepting responsibility? When you try to drown others in detail about how something is not your fault, you lose trust and respect from your coworkers.

Can you imagine yourself in the shoes of others and behave accordingly? How perceptive are you of body language? It is often a key to something deeper that might be happening. How sensitive are you to others who may be having a difficult time in their life and may need your help? Sometimes you need to extend an extra helping hand and to respect the needs of others, regardless of how you might feel personally.

Are you too pushy? Do you want your way every time? If so, pretty soon no one will want to work with you. Coworkers have areas of expertise, and they also want to contribute. You may be proud of your accomplishments, but constantly reminding others is not the way to manage your career. There is a time and place to review your accomplishments.

Finally, a simple "thank you" can go a long way to reaching your career goals. It starts with sending a "thank you" note after each employment interview. People like to know that their efforts are appreciated. Telling someone "thank you" sets you apart from others and writing a note will move you higher on their list of respected people. People want to work with people who care. Your courtesies will be remembered and will make a difference in managing your career.

Tips for Working Your Way Up

Peter Harris of Snelling Staffing Services offers the following tips to help you make the most of your career opportunities.[32]

1. ***Keep up with industry trends and technology.*** Employers want top-caliber performers. One way to wow your boss is to demonstrate the extent and timeliness of your expertise.
2. ***Stay marketable.*** Take classes, workshops, courses, and seminars to keep abreast of what is happening in your field. Also, volunteer for projects. Always keep an up-to-date résumé ready.
3. ***Be proactive.*** Ask for feedback and what you need to do to move forward toward a promotion. Chart your productivity and quality goals.
4. ***Adopt a mentor.*** This is one of the best things you can do. A great mentor can boost your confidence, provide valuable insight, and help you set attainable goals.
5. ***Avoid the office rumor mill.*** Nothing can hurt your credibility more than perpetuating negative or sensitive office buzz.

 CHECK YOUR UNDERSTANDING

1. How can you use the information in the Career Advisor to manage your career more effectively?
2. Which items do you need to work on that will make a difference in your career?

Summary

1 Explain what job redesign is all about.

Many workers are bored with their work, feeling no challenge or desire to do a particularly good job. What can management do about this? Various alternatives are available, but the most practical is that of redesigning the work so that it has meaning for the employees. Job redesign alters the basic relationship between the worker and the job. It assumes that positive attitudes follow properly redesigned jobs, creating a sense of competence and self-worth in which people feel they are stretching and growing as human beings. Job redesign is an important tool for initiating organizational change and a way to work smarter rather than harder.

2 Describe how job rotation, job enlargement, and job enrichment work.

There are a number of ways to accomplish job redesign, including job rotation, job enlargement, and job enrichment. **Job rotation** is a technique for moving workers from one job to another, basically to reduce boredom, whereas **job enlargement** involves giving workers more to do, allowing them to complete more tasks on a particular job. The quality of work improves and the workers receive greater satisfaction. **Job enrichment** is a technique that attempts to build into the job psychological motivators, such as giving workers more authority in planning the work and controlling the pace and procedures for doing the job. Job enrichment is the most commonly used approach.

3 Describe the five core job dimensions and illustrate selected enrichment principles that help to create these dimensions.

How does one go about enriching jobs? Some of the latest research reveals that five core job dimensions are extremely useful in this process: skill variety, task identity, task significance, autonomy, and feedback. **Skill variety** is the degree to which the job requires a worker to perform a variety of tasks requiring different skills and abilities. Motor skills are used to perform manual or mechanical tasks, and intellectual skills are used in "thinking" tasks. **Task identity** is the degree to which the job requires a worker to perform a whole or completely identifiable piece of work. **Task significance** is the degree to which a job affects the lives of other people within or outside the organization. **Autonomy** is the degree to which a job provides the worker with freedom in carrying it out. **Feedback** is the degree to which the work provides the worker with information about his or her performance. Researchers have used these five core job dimensions to develop a motivating potential score (MPS) by which to evaluate a job.

4 *Explain the significance of MPS and job profiling charts.*

The MPS formula shows that to redesign jobs so employees are motivated, the work must offer autonomy, feedback, and at least one of the other three core job dimensions. A profile chart illustrates which core job dimensions are the weakest and which ones are the strongest. Redesigning the job to increase the weak areas can increase worker motivation. Some jobs cannot be enriched and workers must conform to the work pattern.

5 *Discuss five job enrichment principles.*

The common job enrichment principles that can be used to obtain these dimensions are forming natural work units, establishing worker–client relationships, combining tasks, loading jobs vertically, and opening feedback channels. One way of enriching jobs is through the formation of natural work units, in which the worker obtains some ownership of the work. The worker then begins to identify with the job and begins to see how clients value the job.

Job commitment and motivation are usually enhanced when workers establish a relationship with the clients. The steps are: identifying the client, determining the most direct contact possible between the client and the worker, and setting up a system for feedback from clients. Combining a series of simple tasks to form a new work unit can provide worker motivation. Assembling a whole unit provides greater satisfaction than doing repetitive work.

Vertical loading closes the gap between "doing" and "controlling" aspects of the job. Autonomy increases and workers begin feeling personal responsibility and accountability for the outcome of their efforts. Opening feedback channels allows workers to get direct feedback from clients. People have a need to know how well they are doing and the workers need to know this information as quickly as possible.

6 *Cite some illustrations of job enrichment in action.*

GE and Southwest Airlines are two companies that successfully apply job enrichment. GE uses "workouts" as a way for employees to identify problems and then organize themselves into teams and attack the issues. Workouts are also used with customers and suppliers to get their ideas for improving overall productivity and quality. A part of GE's success comes through implementing a flatter organization, closer cooperation between departments and product groups, and a closer cooperation between the company and its suppliers, customers, stakeholders, and competitors. The motivation is provided through human resources management changes, including new incentive systems, ongoing training, and the creation of a boundaryless organization.

Southwest Airlines has created a high team spirit by putting the employees, not the customers, first. It is the job of the employees to put the customers first. The company's flexible work rules and training allow all jobs to get done quickly, which gives the airline a fast turnaround time record. Employees are encouraged to "color outside the lines." A culture committee infuses the corporate culture throughout the company. Employees are empowered to make decisions at the point of operations. Recognition is an ongoing process for the employees, as well as for the company.

7 Discuss four current challenges in job design.

The first challenge in job design is creating new workplace designs that facilitate teamwork, the flow of communication, and employee interaction. A second is the use of telework or telecommuting, which is a type of flexible work arrangement that creates new challenges for both the organization and the employee. Special skills and attitudes are needed to be a teleworker or telecommuter and to be a manager of these employees. A third challenge involves ways of dealing with job sharers and contract or part-time workers, many of whom receive neither medical nor retirement benefits. An advantage to this arrangement is that it helps many workers to meet specific objectives, such as spending more time with the family, conducting personal business, or attending college classes. A fourth is designing strategies for managing hard-to-keep employees. Married and single mothers often need special arrangements to take care of family matters. Nonconformist employees have a different set of needs and attitudes. They often like to work nontraditional hours, such as 6:00 A.M. to 2:00 P.M. Hard-to-keep employees are highly educated and experienced, and need challenging work and job assignments that allow them to work at home. They make major contributions to the productivity and profit of the company. The international arena brings another set of problems and the need to redesign jobs to retain these employees. Personal recognition is important in motivating and retaining employees. People join a company because they want to, but they quit because of their manager.

8 Explain how to manage your career more effectively.

Successful people take steps to ensure that their careers go their way. Managing your career will require adjustments from time to time. Managing your career should start with using the career planning resources that are available at the company where you work. Hopefully, coaching is available and conducted on a regular basis. It can provide a source for resolving issues and learning about opportunities, which is useful in managing your career. If the company does not have a formal mentoring program, then identify one or more people who can show you the ropes and give you honest information about things in the company and in your job. Outside contacts and networking are important in managing your career. These people can open the door to other employment opportunities and can be a sounding board for work-related problems. Line jobs have more potential for advancement and career development than staff jobs. Do not be lured into seeking long-term goals when shorter-term goals can provide faster feedback on how the company views accomplishments and how it implements its reward system. Smaller firms can provide opportunities for advancement, as well as the experience for landing jobs in larger companies.

Your behaviors will make a difference in your career advancement. You need to understand how your behaviors affect others. You may need to change some behaviors to have a greater chance for success in your career. For example, you should be a good listener and not interrupt someone else who is speaking. Although you need positive feedback, be careful of how much you request. Do not tell old war stories over and over again. Ask questions and show an interest in what another person is saying. Do not act like a robot; instead smile and show some emotion. Be careful about being too judgmental in expressing your opinions. Find out the facts first then use an acceptable tone of voice in expressing your ideas. In times of need, extend a helping hand to others, regardless of how you feel personally. You cannot have your way all the time. Allow others to give their ideas and show an interest in their work and ideas. And last, but not least, show that you appreciate other people's efforts by telling them "thank you" and writing "thank you" notes.

Tips that can help advance your career ladder are keeping up with industry trends and technology, staying marketable, being proactive, adopting a mentor, and avoiding the office rumor mill. It takes hard work to develop a successful career; unfortunately for most people, it just does not happen automatically.

Key Terms in the Chapter

Job redesign	Job redesign refers to any work changes that increase work quality or productivity.
Job rotation	In job rotation, the worker moves from one job to another.
Job enlargement	Job enlargement gives the worker more to do.
Job enrichment	Job enrichment gives the worker more authority in planning and controlling the work.
Core job dimensions	Core job dimensions are characteristics that make work more motivational.
Skill variety	Skill variety is the degree to which jobs require a completion of different activities.
Task identity	Task identity involves the degree to which a job requires completion of an identifiable piece of work.
Task significance	Task significance is the degree to which a job has a substantial impact on others.
Autonomy	Autonomy is the degree to which a job provides the worker with freedom in carrying it out.
Feedback	Feedback is the degree to which the work provides the worker with performance information.
Motivating potential score	The motivating potential score measures the presence of core job dimensions.
Job profile chart	A job profile chart helps to identify core job dimensions.
Vertical loading	Vertical loading closes the gap between the doing and controlling aspects of the job.

Review and Study Questions

1. Define job redesign.
2. Identify four benefits of job redesign.
3. Explain how each of the following job redesign techniques works: job rotation, job enlargement, and job enrichment.
4. Describe what is meant by each of the following core job dimensions: skill variety, task identity, task significance, autonomy, and feedback.
5. How are the five core job dimensions used in developing an MPS formula? What does the score mean?
6. What is a job profile chart and how can it be used in job redesign?
7. Discuss each of the five job enrichment principles and tell how each works.
8. For each core job dimension, identify a job enrichment principle that can be tied to it. Explain, using a figure or drawing to relate each principle to its respective core job dimension(s).
9. How have GE and Southwest Airlines used job enrichment to redesign jobs and increase productivity?
10. How has Southwest Airlines used job enrichment to keep it a profitable company in the shadow of the other major airlines losing money and filing for bankruptcy under Chapter 11?
11. What are the current challenges in job redesign? Describe them.

12. How are new workplace designs helping organizations to increase job enrichment? Give an example.

13. In what ways is the increase in teleworkers or telecommuters creating job redesign and job enrichment challenges for managers? Give two examples.

14. Explain some of the issues in dealing with contract and part-time workers.

15. What are some techniques that managers can use to retain hard-to-keep employees?

16. How do the needs and attitudes differ among the three groups of hard-to-keep employees?

17. Discuss how companies in the international arena are dealing with managing hard-to-keep employees.

18. Discuss the role of "employee recognition" in retaining employees and keeping them motivated and productive.

19. How can career planning resources help you manage your career?

20. Why do you need a mentor? How can a mentor help you?

21. Why is networking beneficial to your career?

22. Identify some behaviors that can be detrimental to your career.

23. What are some tips for advancing your career?

Connecting to the Real World

Why is Joan happy?

The purpose of this exercise is to compare the five core job dimensions of the newly redesigned job to the original job as described in the situation below.

Procedure

1. Analyze the original job duties and responsibilities and the newly redesigned job duties and responsibilities of Joan's job.
2. Use Figure 8.2 to illustrate the profiles of each set of duties and responsibilities using the five core job dimensions.
3. Identify the dimensions that needed improvement in the original job description.
4. How effectively were the weak core dimensions addressed in the redesigned job description?
5. What else would you suggest to make the job even better and more motivating?
6. Is this a case of job enlargement or job enrichment? Support your answer.

Situation

When Joan Mitchell was hired at the Ogleby Plant, she was brought in as a small products assembler. Specifically, Mitchell was given the job of putting together some of the inner assembly of a handheld power drill. Ogleby makes a number of different versions of the machine, and all of them are sold to other, better known firms that, in turn, market the units under their own labels.

Ogleby has to turn out one thousand of these units everyday. Mitchell is responsible for performing partial assembly on thirty of them per hour. The job is basically boring, but she generally daydreams her way through the workday, and the money is good; so Mitchell does not complain. However, last month, the company decided to reorganize the assembly jobs, and the assemblers each put together an entire unit. Now Mitchell sits in the middle of a U-shaped table with the parts of the machine placed around the table. She assembles the unit moving from left to right, and when she is done, she tests the product to ensure that it works properly. If it does, Mitchell then places the unit on a tray at the end of the table. If it does not, she disassembles the unit, finds the error, corrects the mistake, and then retests the machine. Mitchell never has any trouble finding the error; usually, it is a loose wire or an improper connection.

Mitchell was recently asked how she likes the new arrangement. She said she enjoys the work much more now. "I like assembling the entire unit and feeling that I'm personally responsible for the whole machine. I also like the fact that as long as I assemble eighty complete units per day, I can work at my own pace. The fact that I am averaging eighty-four units per day and the company pays a $4 bonus for every unit over eighty is an additional incentive to work fast."

CASE
The Best Job He Ever Had, but What About Your Current Job?

When Emile Varas was in college, he worked part time for a small accounting firm. His duties were highly routine. Varas would clock in at 4:00 P.M. and clock out at 8:00 P.M. every weekday. During these four hours, he was responsible for taking phone messages and processing the outgoing mail for the day.

Varas found the work to be boring, but at $7.25 an hour, he knew it would be impossible to find a higher paying job that required so little mental effort. Additionally, he knew that once he graduated, he would find a job that would be more psychologically rewarding and start him on a meaningful career.

Eight months ago, Varas finished his undergraduate degree in English and landed a job as a copy editor at a publishing house that specializes in trade books. Varas's job is to read and copyedit books for the business market. Typical titles include *30 Steps to More Effective Negotiating*, *Building Confidence in 5 Minutes a Day*, and *Creating Excellence in Your Own Company*. These titles appeal to those interested in how-to-do-it books. They are very popular with businesspeople, especially with young managers and entrepreneurs. It is common to find the author being interviewed on radio talk shows and television programs, while the publisher works hard to support the sales effort through newspaper advertising and mail brochures.

Although most authors believe their book can stand on its own merits, Varas's company understands the importance of everyone on the sales team knowing the message the author is trying to convey. For this reason, the publisher will invite the author to its headquarters to meet those who will be working on the project, from the copy editor and the designer to the chief of advertising and the head of the sales force. These individuals listen to the author explain what he or she is trying to convey in the book, and then they have an opportunity to ask questions. Once everyone understands the basic message of the book, it is much easier to produce and market. The advertising people have a firmer idea of the book's unique features, and the salespeople know the right "hooks" that they can highlight in reinforcing why a bookstore should carry the title. Even Varas has found that by listening and talking to an author, he can gain valuable

insights for copyediting purposes. "Anyone can copyedit a book," he told his mother. "But to copyedit it with a slant toward the author's message, that is the difference between an average book and a best seller."

In addition to meeting the author, Varas is assigned to a work team that consists of all in-house employees who are responsible for turning out the book. This group makes all the decisions associated with its publication. Typically, Varas is asked to copyedit a book within twenty working days. The rest of his time is spent discussing the cover with the design artist and the promotion program with the advertising people. When recently asked what he likes about his job, Varas said, "This work really gives me an opportunity to be creative and show what I can do. I love helping turn out a completed project and then watching its release and sale to the public. I feel like I'm helping create something rather than just reworking words on a page. This is the best job I've ever had."

Case Questions

1. Which of the core job dimensions are present in Varas's current job? Identify and briefly describe each. Use Figure 8.2 to graph the results.
2. How does Varas's current job differ from his previous job? Compare the core job dimensions of the two jobs.
3. Which core job dimensions still need changing to make them a more motivating force in Varas's current job?
4. If you have a job, use it, or interview someone who has a job. Get as much information about the job as you can. Analyze the job and determine the values of its core job dimensions. Use that information and graph it along with Varas's current job on Figure 8.2.
5. How does your job differ from Varas's current job?
6. What have you learned about using core job dimensions in designing jobs? How can you use this information to analyze your jobs in the future? What can you do with the information?

PART 4

THE ADMINISTRATIVE SYSTEM

The administrative system of organizations is about providing effective leadership and developing, appraising, and rewarding the organization's employees for doing their jobs.

The goals of this section are to:

1. Examine the nature of leadership, review some of the leadership and personal characteristics and skills that effective leaders often possess, and examine the assumptions many leaders hold regarding the nature of organizational personnel. This section also investigates four contingency leadership approaches, studies four leadership behavior models, reviews emerging challenges in developing internal leaders who can deal effectively with difficult employees, and explores how to function effectively in your job to get ahead in your career.

2. Study what personnel development is all about and how a leader appraises and rewards performance, explore orientation and training programs, examine the performance appraisal cycle, review appraisal tools commonly used in employee evaluations, look at some of the problems associated with performance appraisal and ways of dealing with appraisal problems, discuss ways for rewarding performance, examine ways of linking performance and rewards, examine discipline and methods of employing it, and learn how to manage time more effectively in your job.

When you have finished reading this part of the book, you should have a solid understanding of the administrative system in modern organizations. In particular, you should know the role the leader must play in the organization and the ways in which performance can be measured, rewards can be given, and discipline can be carried out. You will have a better understanding of how to get ahead in your career.

CHAPTER 9

Fundamentals of Leadership

Leaders direct activities in organizations, but it's their leadership skills that determine an organization's level of success. Leadership is a process of influencing people toward achieving results. In this chapter, the nature of leadership is examined, leadership behaviors are studied, and contingency leadership models are investigated. The characteristics and personal qualities of effective leaders are examined, along with basic managerial assumptions of leaders. Also, getting ahead in your job is explored.

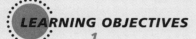

LEARNING OBJECTIVES

1
Describe the characteristics and skills related to managerial effectiveness.

2
Compare and contrast Theory X with Theory Y.

3
Distinguish among four styles of leadership behavior.

4
Explain the concept of "self-leaders" and the basic rules of behavior.

5
Describe the two major dimensions of leadership—concern for people and concern for work.

6
Distinguish among the four contingency leadership approaches.

7
Describe several challenges of leaders in the next decade.

8
Identify ways of developing internal leaders and dealing with high-potential employees who have bad work habits.

9
Discuss how to function in your job to get ahead in your career.

New Leaders Are Emerging

When businesspeople are asked to name the best business leader in the last half of the twentieth century, the overwhelming choice is Jack Welch of General Electric Company (GE). However, at the beginning of the millennium, GE was faced with a leadership challenge. Jack Welch retired in 2001 and was replaced by Jeffrey Immelt, who continues to hold that position. He has a very different leadership style than Welch. When Jack Welch took the reins in 1981, he spent a good deal of his time getting rid of managers who could not meet their goals. In fact, he soon was dubbed "neutron Jack," because like a neutron bomb, he got rid of people but left the buildings and machinery intact. As Welch began replacing these managers, however, performance began to increase. Stockholders were delighted with his performance.

Immelt's leadership style is different from Jack Welch's style. A security analyst who tracks GE stock and operating performance very closely has described Immelt as a person who has "tenacity, intellectual sharpness and has a results orientation" but, unlike Welch, "is easier to get along with." Immelt has proven to be an effective leader for GE. He believes that having the best people in every single position provides an infinite capacity to improve. Managerial talent at GE is the driving force to its success. By empowering its employees and breaking down boundaries, the employees can use their energy innovatively in solving problems.

During the last recession, Immelt told his managers, who had been preparing detailed reports explaining the declines in their businesses, that he did not need that information because he already knew it. He wanted to know what the managers were going to do to make things better and move the business forward. Immelt said,

"Just forget about waiting for normal to return. This is the new normal." Immelt also changed the way people communicate within the company. He hired people from different backgrounds to teach the employees how to communicate better with their investors and with their own people.

Certainly, Immelt has had a proven track record as a leader. His previous assignment was head of GE Medical Systems (Gems), now named GE Healthcare, a job he held for four years. In his first year at the helm, Gems took in $4 billion, and by the end of the fourth year, it was grossing $7.5 billion. Much of this success was a result of Immelt's working closely with his people to set goals and help them develop their abilities. In particular, Immelt earned a reputation as one of the company's champions of diversity. When he took over at Gems, fewer than twenty women, Hispanics, or African Americans were found in the top ranks. Four years later, there were seventy-five, and Immelt had set up a system by which fast-track minorities and women were to be formally mentored.

Increasing the number of women, in particular, may well be one of Immelt's best strategies given that recent research reveals that female executives tend to outshine their male counterparts in almost every measure. In one study, 425 high-level executives were each evaluated by twenty-five people, and female executives had higher ratings on forty-two of the fifty-two skills that were measured. In a second study, women ranked higher than men on twenty-eight of thirty-one measures. In a third and massive study of 58,000 managers, women outranked men in twenty of twenty-three areas. In a fourth, evaluations of 2,482 executives from a variety of companies were examined, and it was found that women outperformed men on seventeen of twenty measures. In particular, these studies found that female leaders tended to be superior to their male counterparts in motivating others, fostering communication, producing high-quality work, and listening to others. On another note, the debate continues on who is better at multitasking—men or women. "Our society and culture expect women to do it all, so we do," writes Margaret Gottlieb, managing director, Foster Partners Executive Search, Washington. Some employers prefer to hire women on the belief they can get "two-fers or even three-fers" who can multitask. One individual explained the situation this way:

> Twenty-five years after women first started pouring into the labor force—and trying to be more like men in every way, from wearing power suits to picking up golf clubs—new research is showing that men ought to be the ones doing more of the imitating. In fact, after years of analyzing what makes leaders most effective and figuring out who's got the "right stuff," management gurus now know how to boost the odds of getting a great executive: Hire a female.

Whole Foods Market believes that the critical decision of whom to hire should be made by those who will be most directly impacted by the consequences of the decisions. Unprecedented in retailing is Whole Foods' small, empowered work groups that have a degree of autonomy. Each store has eight teams that oversee various areas of the business, ranging for example from seafood to produce to checkout. After a four-week trial, teammates vote on an applicant's fate. The new employee needs to win two-thirds majority vote to win a full-time spot on the team. This peer-based selection process is used for all new employees, including those at the headquarters.

W.L. Gore & Associates, a chemical company famous for GORE-TEX, has no management levels and no organization chart; few people have titles and no one has a boss. The core operating units are small self-managing teams that have two common goals: "to make money and have fun." Some associates, however, have earned the recognition of "leader" by their peers. Employees are granted a half-day a week of "dabble time," which they can devote to an initiative of their own choosing.

Google found that the typical bureaucratic supervisory structure did not work. Such structure was putting a damper on innovation. Today, roughly half of Google's ten thousand employees work in small teams of three to four. Each team has a leader who rotates among the team members depending on the project.

How can these companies with so much freedom manage to meet budgets and delivery deadlines? These teams are assessed against monthly profitability targets, and when they meet the goals, team members receive a bonus in their next paycheck or some meaningful reward. Since each team's performance is visible across the entire company, there is more incentive to work hard and stay focused.

Describe the characteristics and skills related to managerial effectiveness.

The Nature of Leadership

Leadership is the process of influencing people to voluntarily direct their efforts toward the achievement of some particular organizational goal(s). Good leaders have visions of where they want the organization to go, and they have the ability to create enthusiasm among their followers to pursue their goals. Some managers are highly effective leaders, but most are, at best, only moderately successful. What accounts for this difference? Some people believe the answer rests in **leadership characteristics,** such as drive, originality, and tolerance of stress, which, they say, are universal among successful leaders. If you have these qualities, you will do well in leading others; if you lack them, you will be ineffective in the leadership role.

Others argue in favor of **personal characteristics**, such as superior mental ability, emotional maturity, and problem-solving skills. They claim that no universal list of leadership characteristics exists, and so we must turn to personal characteristics that interact with one another to produce the desired outcomes. Only through an awareness of how these characteristics influence managerial effectiveness can we truly understand the nature of leadership. To begin our study of this subject, we examine both approaches— leadership characteristics and personal characteristics—and then address the importance of managerial assumptions regarding the nature of organizational personnel.

Leadership Characteristics

Leadership studies have pointed out the importance of environmental influences on leadership effectiveness. They indicate that, regardless of the situation, certain characteristics favor success in the leadership role.

From 1920 to 1950, the study of leadership characteristics, known as **trait theory**, sought to isolate those factors that contribute to the effectiveness of a leader. This approach assumed that such attributes as initiative, social dominance, and persistence were the primary factors in leadership success and failure. Unfortunately, the research studies conducted during this period failed to produce a universal list of traits. Additionally, in most cases, no consideration was given to the possibility that different situations might require different characteristics or that a specific situation might demand so little of the leader or might be so unfavorable that leadership characteristics would be of little, if any, value. Despite the arguments for situational leadership, however, Ralph Stogdill, one of the leading authorities in the field, concluded that a select group of characteristics does, in fact, differentiate leaders from followers, effective from ineffective leaders, and high-echelon from low-echelon leaders.

The leader is characterized by a strong drive for responsibility and task completion, vigor and persistence in pursuit of goals, venturesomeness and originality in problem solving, drive to exercise initiative in social situations, self-confidence and a sense of personal identity, willingness to accept consequences of decision and action, readiness to absorb interpersonal stress, willingness to tolerate frustration and delay, ability to influence other persons' behavior, and capacity to structure social interaction systems to the purpose at hand.[1]

The greatest problem with trait theory, however, is that no common list has been forthcoming. Some traits appear important, but their value is situationally determined. As a result, many researchers have turned their attention to the personal characteristics of effective leaders.

Personal Characteristics

Many personal characteristics appear to be related to managerial effectiveness, but an exhaustive list is beyond our current needs. We will, however, examine some major personal characteristics that contribute significantly to leadership effectiveness. They are superior intelligence, emotional maturity, and motivation drive. Basic skills of effective leaders are problem-solving skills, managerial skills, and leadership skills.

Superior Intelligence.   Research reveals that effective managers tend to have superior intelligence. There is a minimum level of mental ability below which we are unlikely to find successful leaders. Conversely, there may well be a ceiling above which we are, again, unlikely to find effective leaders. Some researchers, for example, report that the intelligence quotient (IQ) of successful leaders typically falls in the range of 115 to 130.[2]

Keep in mind, however, that intelligence is a relative matter. Some geniuses are excellent leaders, whereas some people with IQs in the 115 to 130 range lack the personality to manage effectively. Additionally, one can have a superior intellect and be in the wrong job. For example, a person with high verbal skills and abstract reasoning ability and low quantitative ability might do poorly in an accounting firm or a bank, and an individual with low verbal skills and high quantitative abilities might be a total failure as a human resources manager. Yet both have high IQs, and their mental abilities are comparable.

Emotional Maturity.   Successful leaders are emotionally mature. They are self-confident and capable of directing their subordinates in a calm, conscientious manner. If a subordinate makes a mistake, the effective leader tries to use the experience as an opportunity to teach and counsel the person so as to prevent recurrence of the problem. The leader realizes that little is to be gained from bawling out the subordinate, especially if the person really wanted to do the job right. Effective leaders also have a sense of purpose and meaning in life. They know who they are, where they are going, and how they are going to get there. They are practical and decisive and have confidence in their own abilities. Additionally, the goals they set for themselves are often challenging but realistic.

Finally, because they are emotionally mature, successful leaders are neither ulcer prone nor workaholics. They know how to deal with stress, to delegate work that is either minor in importance or is best handled by someone more technically skilled, and to handle the challenges of the job without resorting to alcohol or drugs. Because they know and understand themselves, they are able to cope with the demands of both their business and personal lives. For example, the divorce rate among successful leaders is no greater than that in the general population.

Motivation Drive. Effective leaders have a high motivation drive. In particular, they seem most motivated by the opportunity to achieve the chance for power or control over a situation and by the need to self-actualize. Additionally, as we noted in our discussion of money in Chapter 2, they are motivated by increased personal income, because it is a sign of how well they are doing. Effective leaders often measure their progress in quantitative terms: how much money they are making, how many promotions they have had, and how many subordinates they control.

Additionally, we know from research that successful leaders tend to have subordinates who are also interested in fulfillment of self-actualization and esteem needs. Average leaders have followers who are most concerned with esteem and social needs. The least successful leaders have subordinates who are most interested in safety and physiological needs. In short, successful leaders tend to attract a particular type of subordinate, as do the average and least successful leaders, and these subordinates have need drives similar to those of their superiors. In large measure, highly motivated leaders attract or develop highly motivated subordinates.

Skills Required of Leaders

Problem-Solving Skills. Effective leaders also possess **problem-solving skills**. They see a problem as both a challenge and an opportunity to prove their managerial abilities. As such, these skills are closely related to high motivation drives, for without such motivation, leaders might be unwilling to assume the risk that comes with problem solving. These individuals also have a great deal of self-confidence. Conversely, average leaders and, especially, ineffective leaders tend to shun problem solving because they either are unprepared to deal with the issues or have learned through experience that they are not up to the task.

Managerial Skills. Effective leaders, especially at the upper levels of the hierarchy, have managerial skills: technical, human, and conceptual.

- **Technical skills**—the knowledge of how things work. These skills are very important for lower-level managers, such as foremen. This is where the technical work gets done.
- **Human skills**—the knowledge of how to deal with people. These skills are equally important for all levels of managers. Without a solid understanding of such behavioral areas as interpersonal communication, motivation, counseling, and directing, managers would be ineffective in leading their subordinates.
- **Conceptual skills**—the knowledge of how all parts of the organization fit together. These skills are very important to top-level managers. They cover many activities, from formulating organizational objectives, policies, and procedures to developing techniques for handling office work flow and to coordinating a host of seemingly unrelated functions that enable the enterprise to operate as an integrated unit.

As shown in Figure 9.1, the leader's place in the hierarchy determines the degree of managerial skill that he or she must possess. As managers prove their effectiveness and begin moving up the ranks, they need to learn more about conceptual skills. In the final analysis, conceptual skills make the difference between leaders who will head the organization and leaders who must be content to manage at the intermediate and lower levels.

Figure 9.1 Skills Needed at Different Hierarchical Levels

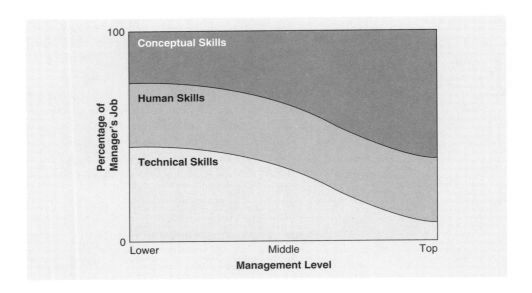

Table 9.1 Summary of Leadership Skills

Stogdill's Task-Related Characteristics	Stogdill's Social Characteristics	Gallup Organization's Leadership Talents
Initiative	Administrative ability	Goal orientation
Need to excel or achieve	Interpersonal skills	Energy
Task orientation	Tact and diplomacy	Ability to help people grow
Drive for responsibility	Ability to enlist cooperation	A desire to win
Responsibility in pursuit of objectives	Social participation	Willingness to accept challenge
	Cooperativeness	
	Attractiveness	

Leadership Skills.   Although effective leadership style depends on the situation, some personal characteristics seem to contribute to the leadership skills of managers. Some of these characteristics are task related, whereas others are more social in nature. The task-related characteristics of effective leaders, as isolated by Stogdill, are initiative, need to excel or achieve, task orientation, drive for responsibility, and responsibility in pursuit of objectives. Some of the social characteristics of effective leaders are administrative ability, interpersonal skills, tact and diplomacy, ability to enlist cooperation, popularity, social participation, cooperativeness, and attractiveness.[3] The Gallup Organization has identified a host of key leadership talents or themes possessed by effective leaders, which include goal orientation, energy, the ability to help people grow, a desire to win, and the willingness to accept challenge.[4] Table 9.1 summarizes the leadership skills of Stogdill and the Gallup Organization.

In an interview with *Gallup Management Journal*, Robin Gerber, a national commentator and speaker on leadership, defined leadership as "motivating others toward a common, ethical purpose." She also discussed leadership skills and believes everyone can develop them. Some of the leadership skills she discussed were having the ability to communicate; having strong convictions; having the ability to collaborate; and being courageous, persistent, rational, strong, and assertive. The ability to communicate is an important leadership skill necessary in motivating, influencing, and inspiring people. Leaders must also have a strong conviction in what they believe and have the courage to live up to those convictions. Leaders just do it; they persist and do not give up. Leaders are rational people who have an innate ability to collaborate with others. They are strong, assertive and, at times, aggressive.[5]

The profile of a typical twenty-first-century CEO leader is a male, fifty-six years old, who has been with the company for eighteen years. As a group, they are well educated—37 percent of them have Masters in Business Administration (MBAs). These leaders understand numbers and the inner workings of their companies. Some 22 percent have come through finance and another 14 percent have worked in operations. They operate in a complex, imperfect world, often balancing the chore of knowing one thing and having to say another, which creates a public debate about whether they know right from wrong. At the top of the organization, they operate alone. There is a lot that cannot be shared, which puts them on a razor's edge in how they choose to act and to manage the organization. However, a new type of leader is emerging. The corporate scandals of 2002 changed the old CEO epic hero image.[6]

 CHECK YOUR UNDERSTANDING

What are the personal characteristics of effective leaders?
Identify the managerial skills that are important to each level of management.

Level of Management	Managerial Skills Needed
Lower	
Middle	
Top	

Compare and contrast Theory X with Theory Y

Assumptions about Employees

Leadership characteristics and personal characteristics provide insights regarding who leaders are. However, it is also important to understand why leaders act as they do. Part of this explanation can be found in the opinions leaders have about their people. Are the subordinates content with satisfying lower-level needs, or do they also strive for esteem and fulfillment of self-actualization needs? How important is money to them? As managers begin to answer these questions, they express their assumptions about the nature of the organization's employees. The research conducted by Douglas McGregor has provided management with a set of basic assumptions. He called these assumptions *Theory X* and *Theory Y*.[7]

Theory X

Theory X is based on assumptions that people are basically lazy and that often it is necessary to use coercion and threats of punishment to get them to work. McGregor summarized the assumptions this way:

1. People, by their very nature, dislike work and will avoid it when possible.
2. They have little ambition, tend to shun responsibility, and like to be directed.
3. Above all else, they want security.

4. To get them to attain organizational objectives, it is necessary to use coercion, control, and threats of punishment.[8]

From this summary of their attitudes, we can arrive at two conclusions regarding Theory X managers. First, they like to control their subordinates because they feel such control is in the best interests of both the organization and its employees. Second, they believe that people work to satisfy their lower-level needs (security above all else) and that upper-level need satisfaction is not very important. Additionally, because lower-level needs are satisfied with physical rewards, such as money, job security, and good working conditions, Theory X managers will withhold these rewards if the workers do not comply with organizational directives.

Theory Y

Modern behavioral research has provided the basis for formulating assumptions for an alternate theory of management, which McGregor called **Theory Y.** It assumes that:

1. The expenditure of physical and mental effort in work is as natural to people as is resting or playing.
2. External control and the threat of punishment are not the only ways of getting people to work toward organizational objectives. If people are committed to objectives, they will exercise self-direction and self-control.
3. Commitment to objectives is determined by the rewards associated with their achievement.
4. Under proper conditions, the average person learns not only to accept but also to seek responsibility.
5. The capacity to exercise a relatively high degree of imagination, ingenuity, and creativity in the solution of organizational problems is widely distributed throughout the population.
6. Under conditions of modern industrial life, the intellectual potentialities of the average human being are only partially used.[9]

As you can see, Theory Y presents a much more dynamic view of employees in the organization. They now are seen as interested in both lower-level and upper-level needs satisfaction and as having untapped potential. This theory urges management to reevaluate its thinking and to begin focusing attention on ways of enabling employees to attain their upper-level needs. Motivation is viewed as a problem that must be solved by management. No longer can the leader hide behind Theory X assumptions, claiming that workers are by nature lazy and unmotivated.

Before continuing, however, we should answer one very important question: Is a Theory Y manager always superior to a Theory X manager? Although we have presented Theory Y as a modern, superior view of the workers, it is not without its critics. Some point out that Theory Y can be dangerous because it allows too much freedom to the workers, many of whom not only need but also want close direction and control. Additionally, Theory Y assumes people want to satisfy their needs while on the job. However, many satisfy their needs off the job, as in the case of workers who want a shorter workweek so they will have more leisure time.

Therefore, to put these two theories in perspective, we must acknowledge that some people respond better to Theory X management than to Theory Y management. However, many managers tend to underrate the workers, subscribing much more heavily to Theory X than to Theory Y.

Your Assumptions about People

Read the following ten pairs of statements. In each case, show the relative strength of your beliefs by assigning to each statement a weight from 0 to 10. The points assigned to each pair must total 10 points. If you totally agree with one statement and totally disagree with the other, give the first one a 10 and the second a 0. If you like both statements equally, give each 5 points. The interpretation of your answers is provided at the end of the book.

1. Most employees are fairly creative but often do not have the chance to employ this ingenuity on the job. _____ (a)
   Most workers are not creative at all, but the job does not lend itself to creativity so nothing is lost. _____ (b)

2. If you give people enough money, this will greatly offset their desire for interesting, challenging, or meaningful work. _____ (c)
   If you give people interesting, challenging, or meaningful work, they are less likely to complain about money and fringe benefits. _____ (d)

3. Workers who are allowed to set their own goals and standards of performance tend to set them higher than management would. _____ (e)
   Workers who are allowed to set their own goals and standards of performance tend to set them lower than management would. _____ (f)

4. People want freedom to do work the way that they believe is correct. _____ (g)
   People want to be told what to do; freedom actually makes them nervous. _____ (h)

5. The better an individual knows his or her job, the more likely it is that the person will work just hard enough to produce the minimum amount acceptable to management. _____ (i)
   The better an individual knows his or her job, the more likely it is that the person will find satisfaction in the work and try to produce at least as much as the average worker in the organization. _____ (j)

6. Most workers in a modern organization are not up to the intellectual challenge presented by their jobs. _____ (k)
   Most workers in a modern organization have more than sufficient intellectual potential to do their jobs. _____ (l)

7. Most people dislike work, and if given the chance, they will goof off. _____ (m)
   Most people like work, especially if it is interesting and challenging. _____ (n)

8. Most employees work best under loose control. _____ (o)
   Most employees work best under close control. _____ (p)

9. Above all else, workers want job security. _____ (q)
   Although workers want job security, it is only one of many things they want, and it does not rank first on all lists. _____ (r)

10. It increases a supervisor's prestige when he or she admits that a subordinate was right and he or she was wrong. _____ (s)
    A manager is entitled to more respect than a subordinate, and it weakens the former's prestige to admit that a subordinate was right and he or she was wrong. _____ (t)

What are your basic beliefs regarding these two theories? You can answer this question by taking the "Time Out" quiz. Do you agree with your results? Why?

Distinguish among four styles of leadership behavior.

Leadership Behavior

Leadership behavior is the way leaders actually carry out their jobs. Four styles of leadership behavior are authoritarian, paternalistic, participative, and laissez-faire. On a continuum, they range from high concern for work and people to a general lack of concern for work and people (see Figure 9.2). As subordinates have greater input, leadership behavior generally changes to that of helping subordinates rather than supervising them. Depending on the situation, any one of these styles can be ideal.

Figure 9.2 Continuum of Leadership Behavior

Task Oriented			People Oriented
Authoritarian	Paternalistic	Participative	Laissez-Faire
On this end, subordinate's input is small or not wanted			On this end, subordinate's input is large and is expected

Authoritarian Leadership

Leaders who engage in **authoritarian leadership** tend to be heavily work centered, with much emphasis given to task accomplishment and little to the human element. Such leaders fit the classic model of management in which the workers are viewed as factors of production.

These individuals can be very useful in certain situations. For example, when a crisis occurs and the organization needs a "get-tough" leader, the authoritarian manager is often ideal. Attention is focused on objectives, efficiency, profit, and other task-related activities, and this is just to the manager's liking. A good example is Jurgen E. Schrempp, chief executive of DaimlerChrysler. After the two companies merged, he began instituting a strategy to make Chrysler operate more like Daimler. Chrysler's top management opposed this approach, and most of the top managers ended up either leaving the company or being fired. As a result, Chrysler began experiencing major losses. However, this did not stop Schrempp from continuing to try and force his operating system on Chrysler.[10] After spending years defending his trouble-prone empire, Schrempp was asked to step down at the end of 2005, more than two years earlier than planned. His "Schrempp curve" management principles that had steered him through some wrenching restructuring of Daimler Benz were not working. He had worked his employees to the limits.[11]

In few instances is an authoritarian manager superior to all others, although a fairly large number of such managers are at work in industry today. These people have authoritarian personalities, often developed because their parents were also authoritarian. They were taught early in life to be submissive toward superior authority and, in turn, have used this parental model to dominate those who hold positions subordinate to theirs. As a result, they tend to be "yes men" when talking to their bosses and to demand the same type of behavior from their own employees.

Paternalistic Leadership

Leaders who practice **paternalistic leadership** are heavily work centered but, unlike authoritarian leaders, have some consideration for employees. They tend to look after their people the way a father does his family. Their basic philosophy, far out of step with the needs of most employees, is "work hard and I'll take care of you." This style of management was prevalent in the late nineteenth century, when some businesses went so far as to provide the workers with lodging, medical services, a company store, and even churches for religious worship. The Pullman Palace Car Company, famous for the Pullman railroad sleeping car, was such a company, and like other firms that built company towns, it eventually found the workers fighting its paternalism. We know from human relations studies that people do not want to be treated like children or feel that the company owns them.

Many managers in the United States are paternalistic leaders; they believe their subordinates want someone to look after them and provide job security, cost-of-living raises, insurance programs, retirement plans, and other extrinsic rewards. Actually, these leaders are confusing management with manipulation. In terms of Theories X and Y, they are soft Theory X managers. Although they do not believe that people are totally lazy or security oriented, they do feel that workers tend to act this way. By playing the role of the parent, these leaders believe they can get the most productivity out of their people. However, most workers resent this type of leadership, although some like it. Employees who have been smothered with affection and security by their parents often welcome a boss who acts the same way. They now have a surrogate parent who takes care of them when they are on the job. However, these people are exceptions to the rule; most workers dislike paternalism.

Participative Leadership

Leaders who have a high concern for both people and work are engaged in **participative leadership**. They encourage their subordinates to play an active role in operating the enterprise, but they reserve the right to make the final decision on important matters. In short, they delegate authority but do not abdicate in favor of subordinate rule. Some management experts have contended that no manager can perform effectively over an extended period without some degree of employee participation. This is certainly true of U.S. managers, for it is an accepted norm in this country that workers have a voice in what goes on.

One way that participative leadership is commonly exercised is through delegating authority to the lowest possible organizational level. A second way is through encouraging feedback from the subordinates. While an authoritarian manager is busy telling the employees what to do, the participative leader is getting information on what is going well and what is going poorly. From this feedback, the manager is able to decide what should be done next. No leader can be truly effective without the support of the subordinates, and feedback is a key indication of such support. Finally, participative leaders discuss objectives with their people and then give them the opportunity to attain these objectives. This is in contrast to authoritarian leaders, who keep objectives to themselves, distrust their subordinates, delegate very little, and try to do too many things themselves. The participative manager builds esprit de corps by sharing objectives and providing the chance for subordinates to fulfill their esteem and self-actualization needs. Employees, in turn, like this approach and work harder for the leader.

Laissez-Faire Leadership

Laissez-faire is a French term meaning "noninterference." As we move across the continuum from authoritarian to participative leadership, the subordinates begin playing an increasingly larger role. If a leader continues this transition, however, he or she will come very close to abdicating the leadership position. Figure 9.3 diagrams the comparisons among leadership behaviors that we have discussed. Note that the subordinates in the **laissez-faire leadership** diagram are interacting with one another to get the work done. The leader is merely checking in on occasion to see how things are going.

Although this style is effective for some, such situations are not very common. University professors are an example. Very seldom does the department chairperson check up on a professor to see whether the individual is having any problems, meeting classes on time, or conducting appropriate research activities. The chairperson usually meets with the professor prior to the beginning of the academic year to discuss objectives and assignments and relies on him or her to fulfill these obligations by the end of the school year. This approach works for highly skilled professionals in any area. The office manager of a research and development (R&D) laboratory leaves the scientists alone to get their work done. Only occasionally does the manager check in to see that everything is running smoothly. In a business setting, some managers employ a laissez-faire style with their outstanding employees, and a board of directors uses it with a president who has led the company into a new period of prosperity. In each case, the subordinates play a tremendous role in running the show. Keep in mind, however, that although the laissez-faire leadership style can work effectively with some people, it does not work well with most. On average, the participative style tends to be most effective.

Figure 9.3 Leader–Subordinate Interactions

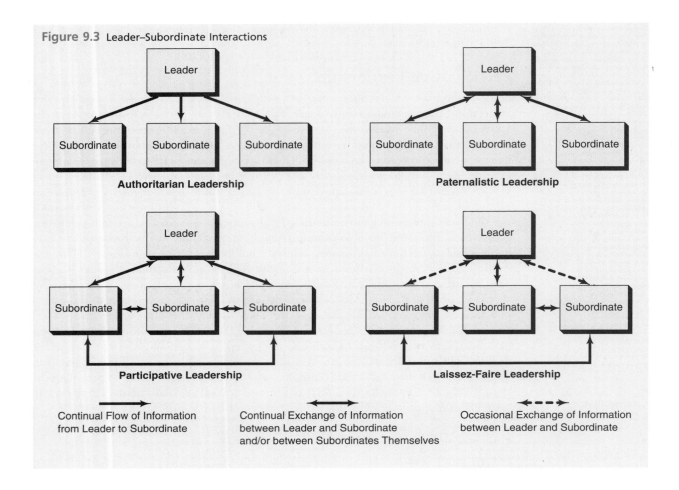

Continual Flow of Information from Leader to Subordinate

Continual Exchange of Information between Leader and Subordinate and/or between Subordinates Themselves

Occasional Exchange of Information between Leader and Subordinate

---

 CHECK YOUR UNDERSTANDING

Match each style of leadership with each statement.

Style	Statement
a. Authoritarian	_____ Encourages feedback.
b. Paternalistic	_____ Leader's role is minimized.
c. Participative	_____ Subordinates have little voice in decisions.
d. Laissez-Faire	_____ A care-taking environment is created.

Explain the concept of "self-leaders" and the basic rules of behavior.

Common Leadership Behaviors

To understand effective leadership, it is important to realize that effective leaders try to do a number of things to influence and direct their people. First, they strive to get their subordinates to become "self-leaders"—that is, to learn to motivate and direct themselves. This reduces the amount of time that the leader must spend on direct supervision.[12]

Leaders also support their subordinates with assistance and guidance as needed. In this way, a mutual exchange takes place between the two that is rewarding to both parties. In fact, some researchers have concluded that organizations that promote extraordinary

IN ACTION

WOMEN LEADING THE WAY

Over the last decade, the U.S. economy has become stronger than ever. Not only is America the most competitive nation in the world, but it is also the most productive, and a large portion of this economic resurgence and growth can be directly attributed to the fact that an increasing number of women are moving into leadership positions. As a result, companies are finding that they have been overlooking a large pool of highly talented individuals who are capable of both growing the firm and increasing the bottom line. Additionally, research reports that, on average, women outscore men in leadership skills. Lawrence A. Pfaff and Associates, a Michigan-based human resource consulting firm, reports that female managers—as rated by their bosses, themselves, and the people who work for them—scored significantly better than their male counterparts. In addition to having better communication, feedback, and empowerment skills, the women were also rated higher in such areas as decisiveness, planning, and setting standards. This study was the second one conducted by Pfaff and Associates, and although the overall results were the same, the differences were significantly better for women this time around. In short, the management and leadership skills of women are even better than those reported in the first study. These latest data led the head of the consulting firm to note that "the statistical significance of these data is dramatic. In two successive studies, men were not rated significantly higher by any of the raters in any of the areas measured."

These findings are not a surprise to most women, especially those who are successful leaders. For example, Stacey Lawson is currently a lecturer and advisor on entrepreneurship at the Center for Entrepreneurship & Technology at the University of California, Berkeley. Formerly, she was senior vice president of product marketing strategy at the Parametric Technology Corporation in Waltham, Massachusetts. After graduating from the University of Washington with a chemical engineering degree, she went to work for IBM in semiconductor processing. However, she did not like her technical job, so she applied to Harvard's MBA program and was accepted. While there, she followed up on an idea she had had at IBM: building content libraries for digitized three-dimensional industrial components, which are needed by companies such as Boeing, John Deere, and Ford to create digital models of their machinery. When she graduated from Harvard, she founded her own company, InPart, with an IBM colleague. Soon thereafter, she agreed to sell the company to Parametric Technology, which was working on similar technology. The purchase included jobs for all her employees and made her a senior vice president of product marketing strategy. Today, she serves as executive chairman for Chelsey Henry, Inc., is an active board member of Catalog Data Solutions, CET, Social Fusion, and the Institute of Noetic Sciences. She sits on the board of advisors for Ahuma Institute, Claremont Creek Ventures, Pharmacopis, and Tripura Foundation.

Before Anne M. Mulcahy stepped down in May 2010 from serving as chairman of Xerox, she told a group of women managers that great business leaders have a "paradoxical blend of personal humility and professional will. Great leaders are self-effacing." After four years of piloting a widely admired turnaround at Xerox, she announced that Xerox had missed its earnings forecast in the first half of 2010. During the previous year, however, Mulcahy had made some fundamental progress even though it was not reflected in the financial statements. Ninety-five percent of its product line has been redesigned. Revenue in inks and toners, the biggest source of profits in the printer industry, finally rose. Her strategy has been to promote color printers, which use more ink. Much of Mulcahy's success is attributed to aligning employees around the company's customers, which gives the company the flexibility and nimbleness to move quickly and make a huge positive impact on customers. Mulcahy is making sure that Xerox provides an exceptionally favorable environment for women managers. "Eight of its 32 corporate officers, or 25 percent, are women, up from 20 percent when she took over. Below that level, about 30 percent of its 800 middle managers are women."

Nancy Lublin was a first-year law student at New York University when she received a $5,000 check from the estate of a relative. She used the money to realize her vision of finding a way to get professional clothing to low-income women seeking employment. When her nonprofit company, Dress for Success, opened its doors, it generated such a positive response from companies such as Avon, Coach, and Garfield & Marks that she dropped out of law school to tend the organization full time. As executive director, her job is to bring in big sponsors. For example, Avon gives the company jewelry and stockings, Coach donates shoes, and Garfield & Marks contributes suits. Today, Dress for Success has employees and locations in more than seventy cities across the United States as well as in Vancouver and London. In each city, local social services networks—homeless shelters, domestic violence groups, job training, substance abuse programs, and unemployment agencies—refer job applicants eager for a new look and a new life. In its latest year, the company suited more than fifteen thousand women. After six years, Lublin relinquished her role as executive director and took the job of turning around a youth organization called DoSomething. She speaks to groups throughout the nation about activism and advocacy, and because of her interest in organizational management and behavior, she has become an adjunct at New York University.

Sources: Mark Sappenfield and Julie Finnin Day, "Women, It Seems, are Better Bosses," Research and Articles, Madison MacArthur Executive Search, www.mmsearach.com; Stacey Lawson, Industrial Engineering and Operations Research, University of California, Berkeley, www.ieorr.berkeley.edu; News release, "Xerox Turnaround and Transformation," Accenture, www.accenture.com and www.news.xerox.com; "Nancy Lublin: CEO of DoSomething.org & Founder of Dress for Success," www.speakers.ca; and William M. Bulkeley, "Running the Show," *Wall Street Journal*, October 31, 2005, p. R4.

employee relations actually function like an extended family. For example, members of strong families gather periodically to communicate, share, celebrate, resolve problems, and enjoy one another's company. The same is true for effective organizations that routinely have meetings and social get-togethers. Additionally, as in families, everyone is accessible to everyone else; there is an open-door policy throughout the company. Another similarity is trust. As in families, effective enterprises trust their people to do the right things and to be honest and fair in their dealings with others.[13] Leaders also tend to follow basic rules that have proven effective in the past. The following are some examples:

1. Be decisive; do not operate on assumptions alone.
2. Do not promise what you cannot deliver.
3. Praise employees in front of others for a job well done.
4. Reprimand workers in private when they have made a mistake.
5. When possible, promote from within.

As seen in the "Cultural Diversity in Action" box, these leadership behaviors are reflective of successful managers, regardless of gender.

In an interview with *Fast Company Magazine*, Jeffrey Immelt, a proven leader, revealed his list of ten keys to great leadership that he teaches to up-and-coming leaders at GE's management development center. They are things that effective leaders do.[14]

1. **Personal responsibility.** "Enron and 9/11 marked the end of an era of individual freedom and the beginning of personal responsibility." You lead today by building teams and placing others first. It is not about you.
2. **Simplify constantly.** "Every leader needs to clearly explain the top three things the organization is working on. If you can't, then you're not leading well."
3. **Understand breadth, depth, and context.** "The most important thing I've learned since becoming CEO is context. It's how your company fits in with the world and how you respond to it."
4. **The importance of alignment and time management.** "There is no real magic to being a good leader. But at the end of every week, you have to spend your time around the things that are really important: setting priorities, measuring outcomes, and rewarding them."
5. **Leaders learn constantly and also have to learn how to teach.** "A leader's primary role is to teach. People who work with you don't have to agree with you, but they have to feel you're willing to share what you've learned."
6. **Stay true to your own style.** "Leadership is an intense journey into yourself. You can use your own style to get anything done. It's about being self-aware. Every morning, I look in the mirror and say, 'I could have done three things better yesterday.'"
7. **Manage by setting boundaries with freedom in the middle.** "The boundaries are commitment, passion, trust, and teamwork. Within those guidelines, there's plenty of freedom. But no one can cross those four boundaries."
8. **Stay disciplined and detailed.** "Good leaders are never afraid to intervene personally on things that are important. Michael Dell can tell you how many computers were shipped from Singapore, yesterday."
9. **Leave a few things unsaid.** "I may know an answer, but I'll often let the team find its own way. Sometimes, being an active listener is much more effective than ending a meeting with me enumerating 17 actions."
10. **Like people.** "Today, it's employment at will. Nobody's here who doesn't want to be here. So it's critical to understand people, to always be fair, and to want the best in them. And when it doesn't work, they need to know it's not personal."

✔ CHECK YOUR UNDERSTANDING

1. Compile a list of behaviors that effective leaders possess.
2. As a leader, identify the behaviors that you need to acquire.
3. Which behaviors do you need to improve? How will you change the behavior?
4. Which behaviors do you need to get rid of?

Describe the two major dimensions of leadership—concern for people and concern for work.

Leadership Dimensions

Each of the four leadership styles we have just examined contains some degree of concern for work and concern for people. These two **leadership dimensions**—concern for work and concern for people—have been found to be independent dimensions. This means, for example, that someone can be high in one of the dimensions without having to be low in the other. As a result, there are four basic leadership behaviors:

- High concern for work, high concern for people
- High concern for work, low concern for people
- Low concern for work, high concern for people
- Low concern for work, low concern for people

Figure 9.4 is a leadership grid incorporating these behaviors. Although effective leaders have a preferred style of leadership, at times each of these four basic styles will be used. For example, a high concern for work and people typically is employed when the leader wants to develop high teamwork, wants to set challenging goals, or must act decisively. A high concern for work and low concern for people is often used when the leader strongly needs to control employees, must have strict compliance, or is faced with an emergency that must be quickly resolved. A low concern for work and high concern for people is often used when the leader is eager to help, is sympathetic because of a personal problem facing a worker, or wants to praise someone for doing a good job. A low concern for work and people is often used when the leader feels that a situation will work itself out without personal intervention, as when a new worker has been told how to do a job and must now be left alone to accomplish the task. Although the leader may want to help, he or she may feel that the best approach is to allow the new worker to carry out the task without interference or assistance. Later, the leader and the worker can evaluate the situation and decide what needs to be done. For the moment, however, a low concern for the work and the people is the preferred leadership style.

Let us examine some specific examples of each style and place them in the grid (see Figure 9.5), keeping in mind that any one of these can be an effective leadership style. First, let us take the supervisor on an assembly line. The supervisor is charged with seeing that the workers keep up with the line. The most effective style for such a person is usually one that stresses high concern for work, for this is where the emphasis is needed, and low concern for people. After all, what can a supervisor do for the workers, as the entire operation is automated?

Figure 9.4 A Leadership Grid

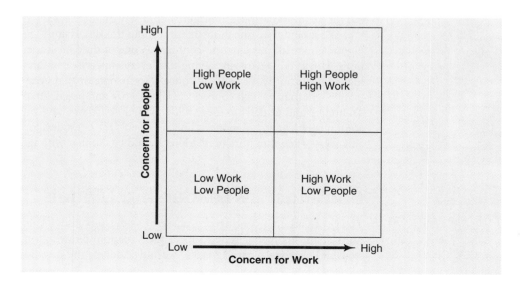

Figure 9.5 Contingency Leadership Styles Applied to a Leadership Grid

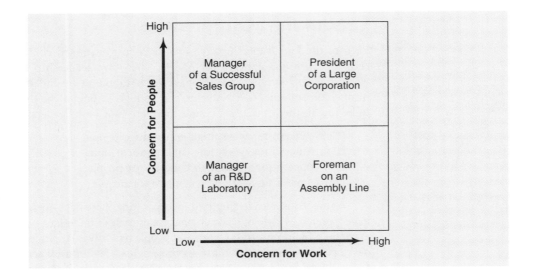

Conversely, the manager of a successful sales group has little need to be concerned with a work emphasis. The people are doing the job and sales are very high. The leader can therefore concentrate his or her attention on praising the salespeople and encouraging them to keep up the good work. This manager needs a style with high concern for people and low concern for work.

The president of a large corporation, meanwhile, has to have high concern for work and for people. This individual must be concerned with long-range planning, budgets, and programs and must be friendly, approachable, and willing to look out for the personal welfare of all the employees.

Finally, in the lower-left corner of Figure 9.5 is the manager of an R&D laboratory. This individual has highly competent employees; so there is no need to be concerned with production. These workers are self-motivated. Likewise, there is no need for the manager to praise them for a job well done, because they are skilled scientists who receive intrinsic satisfaction when their peers praise them. Such praise from their boss means very little to them, because the manager of such a laboratory usually is not a scientist and so would be less able to value their work. As a result, the most effective style for the leader is low concerns for both people and work. The manager should be prepared to help them if called on, but for the most part, the manager should stay out of the way.

We should keep one thing in mind about this discussion. The examples we have used in Figure 9.5 are all presented to conform to one of the four leadership dimension combinations. However, we are not saying that every supervisor on an assembly line should have high concern for work and low concern for people or that every president of a large company ought to have high concerns for both work and people. It all depends on the situation. To understand leadership more fully, many researchers have turned to an investigation of contingency leadership models. This represents the latest development of leadership theory, and every student of human relations should be familiar with it.

Distinguish among the four contingency leadership approaches.

Contingency Leadership Models

Today, we are in a contingency phase of leadership study. The human relations manager must adapt his or her style to meet the situation. Drawing on our discussion of leadership and personal characteristics, we now address the question: "What specific style of leadership is best in which type of situation?" To answer this question, we need to match styles with environmental demands. In this section, we examine three contingency approaches:

1. Fiedler's contingency model
2. The managerial grid
3. Charismatic and transformational leadership

Fiedler's Contingency Model

The best-known contingency model of leadership effectiveness was developed by Fred Fiedler and his associates.[15] **Fiedler's Contingency Model** represents a significant departure from earlier trait and behavior leadership models, because Fiedler contends that group performance is contingent on both the motivational system of the leader and the degree to which the leader can control and influence the situation. The theory postulates that there is no one best way to lead; the style of leadership is determined by the situation. To classify leadership styles, Fiedler and his colleagues developed the least preferred coworker scale.

The **least preferred coworker (LPC) scale** uses a questionnaire asking the leader to describe the person with whom he or she can work least well. From the responses, an LPC score is obtained by adding the item scores. This score reveals the individual's emotional reaction to people with whom he or she cannot work well.

Fiedler found that a leader with a high LPC score describes an LPC in favorable terms. The individual tends to be relationship oriented and tends to obtain great satisfaction from establishing close personal relations with the group members. Conversely, a leader with a low LPC score describes his or her LPC in unfavorable terms. The individual tends to be task oriented and obtain much satisfaction from the successful completion of tasks, even if it comes at the risk of poor interpersonal relations with the workers.

Situational Variables.   In addition to administering the LPC test to each individual, Fiedler sought to determine the major situational variables that could be used to classify group situations. He discovered three:

- **Leader–member relations** are very important. The leader who is trusted by the subordinates can often influence group performance regardless of his or her position power. Conversely, the leader who is distrusted by the members must often rely solely on position power to get things done.
- **Task structure** is the degree to which the leader's job is programmed or specified in step-by-step fashion. If the job is highly structured, the leader knows exactly what is to be done, and if there are any problems, the organization can back the leader. If the job is highly unstructured, no single correct solution to the problem is identifiable, and the leader will have to rely on personal relationships to get the group to do things his or her way.
- **Leader position power** is the authority vested in a leader's position. For example, the president has more power than the vice president, and the division head has more power than the unit manager.

Fiedler's Findings.   Fiedler then brought together the LPC scores (which identified leadership style) with the situational variables to find what leadership style works best in each situation. Figure 9.6 illustrates all the variables in the model. At the bottom of the graph are the eight possible combinations of situational variables (leader–member

Figure 9.6
Identifying the
Effective Leader

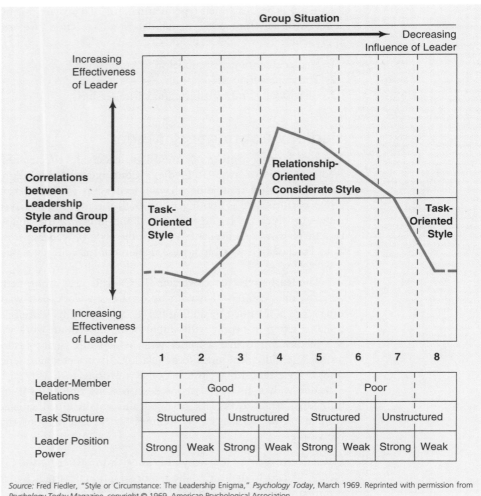

Source: Fred Fiedler, "Style or Circumstance: The Leadership Enigma," *Psychology Today*, March 1969. Reprinted with permission from *Psychology Today Magazine*, copyright © 1969, American Psychological Association.

relations, task structure, and leader position power). Note that in Situation 1, on the left, things are very favorable for the leader; the leader–member relations are good, the task is highly structured, and leader position power is strong. Meanwhile, in Situation 8, on the right, things are very unfavorable for the leader; leader–member relations are poor, the task is unstructured, and the leader's position power is weak. As we move across the continuum from the first to the eighth situation, things get progressively worse for the leader.

What type of individual does best in each of these eight situations? As can be seen from the model, a task-oriented leader does best in very favorable situations (1, 2, and 3) or very unfavorable situations (7 and 8), and a relationship-oriented leader does best in the moderately favorable and moderately unfavorable situations (4, 5, and 6). Fiedler explained it this way:

> The results show that task-oriented leaders perform best in situations at both extremes—those in which they have a great deal of influence and power, and also in situations where they have no influence and power over the group members.

Relationship-oriented leaders tend to perform best in mixed situations where they have only moderate influence over the group. A number of subsequent studies by us and others have confirmed these findings.

The results show that we cannot simply talk about good leaders or poor leaders. A leader who is effective in one situation may or may not be effective in another. Therefore, we must specify the situations in which a leader performs well or poorly.[16]

Fiedler's Theory.   Fiedler's theory offers several important alternatives for improving human relations. First, *the organization, as well as the leader, is responsible for the latter's success* because a leader can be effective or ineffective depending on the situation. Many human resource psychologists and managers tend to view the executive's position as fixed and turn their attention to changing the person's basic leadership style. However, this is the wrong approach. To change a leader's style, the leader must want to alter his or her personality. This can take from one to several years; a few lectures or some brief but intensive training will not do it. What, then, should be done? The answer is to first develop training programs that provide leaders with the opportunity to learn in which situations they can perform well and in which situations they are likely to fail.

Second, *engineer the job to fit the leader.* This recommendation is based on the fact that it is a lot easier to change the leader's work environment than to change his or her personality. Any one of the three situational variables can be altered. For example, the leader's position power could be improved by giving the leader a higher rank, or be reduced by forcing the leader to consult with the subordinates rather than make unilateral decisions. Similarly, the leader's task can be made more explicit or can be changed to be more vague.

Finally, *leader–member relations can be altered.* The group can be made more homogeneous or more interdisciplinary, or the leader can be reassigned to a group that gets along well or one that is continually engaged in squabbling.

Applying these recommendations to Figure 9.6, we can move the leader back and forth on the grid depending on our objectives. For example, a task-centered manager operating under the conditions in Situation 5 will not be very effective; a relationship-centered leader would do better. However, if we can do something to change leader–member relations from poor to good, we will have moved the leader to Situation 1. You can verify this by comparing the three major variables for Situations 1 and 5 and noting what happens when the leader–member relations are changed. Likewise, a relationship-oriented manager operating under the conditions in Situation 8 will be ineffective. However, the same person would do well in Situation 4. This can be arranged simply by working to improve the leader–member relations from poor to good. Again, you can prove this by comparing the three major variables for Situations 8 and 4 and noting what happens when the leader–member relations are modified. If leaders are aware of their strengths and weaknesses, they could try to change the group situation to match their leadership style. In addition, leaders can profit from the ideas presented in the "Human Relations in Action" box.

The Managerial Grid

The grid approach is most closely associated with Robert Blake and Jane Mouton.[17] The **managerial grid** consists of two dimensions: concern for production and concern for people. As can be seen in Figure 9.7, nine gradients or degrees are associated with each dimension, resulting in eighty-one possible combinations of concern for production and concern for people. The number 1 represents low concern for the dimension, and 9 represents high concern.

IN ACTION

LEADING EFFECTIVELY

A great deal of research has been conducted on leadership. Drawing together much of this information from a human relations standpoint, we find there are four things managers should know in their quest to lead effectively.

1. **Know your biases**. Are you a Theory X person? A Theory Y person? A combination of the two? If the latter, do you lean more to the X side or to the Y side? If you can answer these questions accurately, you know something about your leadership biases. This is important because, like it or not, you eventually resort to that leadership style with which you feel most comfortable.

2. **Know the situations in which you function best**. Do you do well when there is a crisis? Are you good at handling situations that are out of control? Or are you best when things are on an even keel? In answering these questions, think of a time when you have done extremely well as a leader. Then think of a situation when you performed poorly. What was the difference in the two situations? Your answer will help you to understand your "best" environments.

3. **Understand the leadership preferences of your people**. What leadership style do your subordinates like best? Your answer will undoubtedly include a range of behaviors, but group them all under one of the four basic styles: authoritarian, paternalistic, participative, and laissez-faire.

4. **Match your style with the situation and the people**. Pull everything together: your style, the demands of the situation, and the needs of the subordinates. Do the best you can to lead from your strengths by employing that style with which you have had the most success. You may have to alter this style a bit, but stay within the leadership parameters you know best. Use Fiedler's ideas to change the environment to suit your style rather than vice versa. Also, remember that in the short run, you may have to use a style you do not prefer. Be flexible and adapt to this brief inconvenience while working to get things back to where you can enjoy your most effective style.

Rather than trying to direct attention to all eighty-one combinations, grid development practitioners tend to focus on five crucial combinations. The combinations are usually referred to by number, and when people become familiar with the grid, they know what the numbers mean. Although they are briefly described in Figure 9.7, let us examine each combination in more detail.

The **1,1 managerial style** is used to describe the *do-nothing manager.* This individual tends to put people in jobs and then leave them alone. He or she does not check up on their work (concern for production) or try to interact with them by offering praise and encouraging them to keep up the good work (concern for people).

The **9,1 managerial style** describes the *production pusher.* This manager has a high concern for production and a low concern for people. He or she plans the work and pushes to get it out. Little interest is shown in the workers; if they cannot keep up, they are replaced by others who can.

The **1,9 managerial style** has been called *country-club management* because of a high emphasis on concern for people's feelings, comforts, and needs. The manager is interested in obtaining loyalty from the subordinates and tries to motivate them to do their work without putting pressure on them.

The **5,5 managerial style** typifies the *organization manager.* This person assumes that an inherent conflict exists between the concerns for production and people. Therefore, he or she tries to compromise and balance the two dimensions.

The **9,9 managerial style** is used by the *team builder.* The 9,9 style is regarded by many as the ideal style, the one that both managers in particular and the organization in general should employ. This style focuses on people's higher-level needs, involves subordinates in decision making, and assumes that the goals of the people and the goals of the organization are in harmony. As a result, the 9,9 manager believes that maximum concern for both dimensions will result in the greatest overall efficiency.

Which of these basic styles is best? The answer will depend on the needs of the subordinates, the manager, and the organization. *There is no such thing as one ideal style for*

Figure 9.7 The Managerial Grid

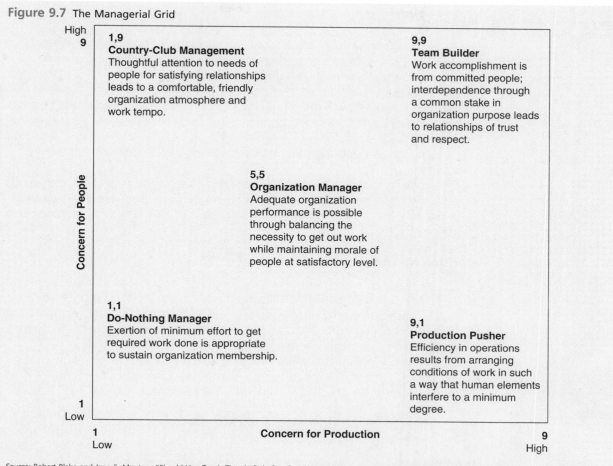

all situations. This can be made clear by giving you the opportunity to choose a leadership style on your own.

Identifying Your Style.   A modern manager must perform many functions. Four of the most important are planning, decision making, leading, and controlling. In carrying out these functions, various degrees of concern for both people and work can be employed. In Figure 9.8, we have listed for each of these functions five leadership behaviors that can be used to implement them. Read the five behavior descriptions that accompany each function and place a 1 next to the behavior that you feel is most descriptive of you. Put a 2 next to the second *most* descriptive behavior, and so on, to a 5 for the *least* descriptive. If you are not currently a manager, imagine that you are in a managerial position while taking the test.

When you have finished assigning numbers to all the behaviors, write your answers in the columns at the bottom of Figure 9.8. Be sure to enter the numbers properly. If you assigned a 3 to alternative b in the planning part of the figure, put a 3 in column I in the

Figure 9.8
Management Style
Identification Test

Planning

a. _____ I sit down with my people, review the whole picture, and get reactions, ideas, and commitments from them. Schedules, goals, responsibilities, and control points are developed during this interaction period.

b. _____ I plan the work for each of my people after discussing such things as targets and schedules with the person involved. I then make individual assignments but also ensure that each person knows to check back with me whenever further assistance is needed.

c. _____ I suggest steps and offer assistance to my people in arranging their activities.

d. _____ I let my people have planning responsibilities for their own parts of the job.

e. _____ I plan for my people, set quotas where they are needed, and assign steps to be followed. I also establish checkpoints that can be used for measuring performance.

Decision Making

a. _____ I make decisions, and after they are made, I stick with them.

b. _____ My decisions follow the thinking of my boss; I think as he or she does.

c. _____ I discuss decisions with those who will be affected by them, give them the facts from my point of view, and, in turn, get facts from them. After evaluation of alternatives, decisions are reached based on mutual understanding.

d. _____ I sit down with each person who is affected by the decision and listen to the person's point of view. Then I make the decision and communicate it to those who will be affected, along with my reasons for making that particular decision.

e. _____ I try to get a picture of what the subordinates want and use it as a basis for my decision.

Leading

a. _____ Once assignments and plans have been clearly explained, I keep up with each person's performance and review their progress with them. If someone is having difficulty getting the job done, I lend assistance.

b. _____ After assignments have been given to the people, I prefer to take little on-the-spot action. I think it is best for people to solve their own problems.

c. _____ Once upcoming assignments are discussed, I keep in touch with my people to show I am interested in how each is getting along.

d. _____ Once plans have been determined, I keep up with the progress of the subordinates. I contribute time and effort as required by defining problems and removing roadblocks.

e. _____ After I have set out plans and instructions, I keep a close eye on the subordinates' work performance and make changes as necessity dictates.

Controlling

a. _____ As work progresses, if any problems or changes need to be made, I make them on the spot. When the job is completed, I evaluate everyone's performance, correct those who have done a poor job, and recognize those who have performed well.

(Continued)

b. _____ I sit down with my subordinates and review progress in detail, and, when the job is totally finished, I study how the entire operation was handled. Correct decisions, good work, errors, and misjudgments all are noted and examined in detail so that the former can be reinforced and the latter can be prevented in the future. When deserved, recognition for contribution is given on both a joint basis and an individual basis.

c. _____ When I receive a reaction to their work, whether it is praise or a complaint, I pass this information on to the respective subordinates.

d. _____ I compliment my subordinates when they do a good job and invite their suggestions for improvements. I believe that criticism tends to arouse tension and make people defensive.

e. _____ I point out weaknesses as well as strengths to each subordinate. Each person then gets a chance to introduce his or her own suggestions for improvements.

	I	II	III	IV	V
Planning	b. _____	d. _____	e. _____	a. _____	c. _____
Decision making	d. _____	b. _____	a. _____	c. _____	e. _____
Leading	a. _____	b. _____	e. _____	d. _____	c. _____
Controlling	e. _____	c. _____	a. _____	b. _____	d. _____
Total	_____	_____	_____	_____	_____

table. If you gave a 5 to alternative d in the planning part, put a 5 in column II. Then add each column and put the total on the bottom line of each. The short survey quiz is designed to determine the type of leadership style you use in carrying out each of the four functions we discussed. Which overall leadership style is your favorite? That will depend on the total scores of the columns. Remember, the *lower* the total, the *higher* your support for that leadership style. (You assigned a 1 to your favorite choice and a 5 to the least preferred one.)

Column I reveals your preference for the 5,5 style; column II measures your preference for the 1,1 style; columns III, IV, and V measure preference for the 9,1 style, the 9,9 style, and the 1,9 style, respectively. Which is your most preferred style? Which is your least preferred style? Could you have predicted this, or are the findings a surprise to you?

The grid is important in the study of human relations because it offers the opportunity to close the gap between one's current and ideal leadership styles. The current style is the one identified in the management style test. The gap is the difference between the current and ideal styles. For example, if a person feels that the 9,9 leadership style would be most effective but currently is relying most heavily on the 5,5 style, that person must become more people and work oriented. On the other hand, if the person's current style is 1,9, he or she must become more work oriented.

Charismatic and Transformational Leadership

In recent years, many human relations experts have concluded that the contingency theory of leadership does not fully explain the nature of leadership. As a result, attention is now being directed toward charismatic and transformational leadership.

Charismatic Leadership

Charismatic leaders are those who lead by the strength of their personal abilities. Researchers characterize these leaders as self-confident, ideological, confident of their subordinates, having high expectations of subordinates, and leading by example. Followers of charismatic leaders identify with the leader and his or her mission, are loyal to and have strong confidence in the leader, emulate the leader's values and behaviors, and derive personal esteem from their relationship with the leader. Here are three examples of commonly cited charismatic leaders:

- Herb Kelleher, founder and former CEO and president of Southwest Airlines, a chain-smoking, bourbon-loving maverick, inspired employees to break the rules and have fun. His enthusiasm helped make the airline a success.
- Oprah Winfrey, Harpo Entertainment, whose telegenic charm and empathetic personality have helped make her America's hottest businesswoman. She manages employees the same way she does her audience—with emotion and intimacy.
- Michael Dell, Dell Computer, a highly innovative individual who has surrounded himself with skilled employees who have a strong grasp of the industry. He is also highly optimistic and able to capture the imagination of both employees and customers.[18]

There is a link between charismatic leadership theory and Fiedler's contingency theory in that charismatic leaders often perform best in crisis situations or when followers are dissatisfied with the status quo. However, more research on the theory is needed before we can understand fully the nature, scope, and value of charismatic leadership. Additionally, some researchers have suggested that this type of leadership is actually just one of other, broader-based emerging theories of transformational leadership.[19]

Transformational Leadership

Transformational leaders are visionary agents with a sense of mission who are capable of motivating their followers to accept new goals and new ways of doing things. In contrast to the charismatic leader, the transformational leader gets followers to change rather than follow. During his reign as CEO of IBM, Louis Gerstner used his transformational leadership skills to bring the company back to its previous prominence. He changed a culture that was preoccupied with itself rather than its customers. David Glass, another transformational leader, used his style to maintain Walmart's dominance in the retail industry by successfully creating more than seven hundred Sam's Clubs worldwide and pioneering the development of the first supercenter, which is now the company's dominant retail format.

Transformational leadership begins with the development of a vision, a view of the future that will excite and convert potential followers. Leaders then sell their vision by convincing others to climb on the bandwagon. Transformational leaders actively move the process forward, always staying visible and being accountable. They are models of how everyone else should behave. They are people oriented and believe that success comes first. One fault of transformational leaders is they often do not seek detail, only the big picture. They need followers who can take care of the details. A transformational leader will be frustrated if an organization does not need transforming or if employees are happy and do not feel the need to change.[20]

Erik Rees writes about seven principles of transformational leadership. He calls for a critical mass of transformational leaders who will commit to creating a synergy of energy within their circles to influence new levels of social, economic, and organizational success. His principles are:[21]

1. **Principle of Simplification.** It is the ability to articulate a clear, practical, transformational vision that answers the question, "Where are we headed?"
2. **Principle of Motivation.** It is the ability to gain the agreement and commitment of other people to the vision.
3. **Principle of Facilitation.** It is the ability to effectively facilitate the learning of individuals, teams, and other reliable and reputable resources.
4. **Principle of Innovation.** It is the ability to boldly initiate change when needed because the leaders have built trust and fostered teamwork.
5. **Principle of Mobilization.** It is the ability to enlist, equip, and empower others to fulfill the vision. They start with small steps to enlist larger participants.
6. **Principle of Preparation.** It is the ability to never stop learning about themselves, with and without the help of others. Leaders are learners.
7. **Principle of Determination.** It is the ability to finish the race. Leaders depend on their stamina, endurance, courage, and strength to finish each day.

Transformational leaders are distinct from most other leaders, who are best defined as transactional leaders. A **transactional leader** exchanges rewards for effort and performance and works on a something-for-something basis. Table 9.2 compares the characteristics and approaches of transformational and transactional leaders. This comparison illustrates why transformational leaders often head organizations that are superior, whereas transactional leaders often head mediocre organizations. In the future, it is expected that researchers will continue their efforts to understand fully why

Table 9.2
Transformational and Transactional Leaders: A Comparison

Transformational Leader	Transactional Leader
Provides a vision and a sense of mission to followers	Sets goals and encourages employees to pursue them
Attempts to instill pride, respect, and trust in employees	Uses reward and punishment systems to generate compliance
Communicates high expectations and expresses important purposes in simple ways	Lets everyone know the objectives
Promotes rationality and careful problem solving	Is interested in results rather than problem-solving process
Gives employees individual attention, coaching, and advising	Carefully spells out rewards for accomplishing objectives
Is a courageous change agent	Tends to support the status quo
Is able to deal with complexity, ambiguity, and uncertainty	Avoids complexity and uncertainty by delegating responsibility to subordinates
Leads by example	Watches for mistakes or deviations from rules and regulations and then takes corrective action
Is a lifelong learner	Relies on past knowledge to deal with future problems

Source: Adapted from Bernard M. Bass, "From Transactional to Transformational Leadership: Learning to Share the Vision," *Organizational Dynamics*, Winter 1990.

transformational leaders are effective and how this knowledge can be incorporated into organizational training programs, thus helping to create a larger pool of transformational leaders.

Another current area of leadership inquiry is the role of transformational leaders as sponsors, facilitators, and individuals who encourage teamwork by breaking down organizational barriers. In this role, leaders share information, focus on results, and view themselves more as internal consultants and coordinators than as directive managers. Transformational leaders are also able to take time off, reflect, and think about where their organizations are going and the roles they need to play. In this process, researchers find these leaders to be objective, continually learning new things, self-confident, prepared to assume personal responsibility, able to deal with uncertainty and ambiguity, and prepared to take action. In the future, greater attention will be focused on understanding how and why leaders do these things.

Universal Leadership Behaviors

In drawing together all the current information on leadership, it would seem reasonable to ask: Are there some leadership behaviors that are more effective than others? A research by Bernard Bass reveals that there are. After gathering leadership data from around the world, Bass has grouped leadership behaviors into five categories. The first category, which Bass calls the "4 Is," is a series of interrelated factors that help to define a leader's charisma:

1. *Idealized influence* results in followers admiring the leader and having pride, loyalty, and confidence in the leader's vision.
2. *Inspired motivation* is the ability of the leader to articulate the vision and provide a sense of meaning regarding what needs to be done.
3. *Intellectual stimulation* is the ability to get followers to view the world from new perspectives and paradigms.
4. *Individualized consideration* is the ability to address personally the needs of the followers.

These **4 Is** are presented in Figure 9.9, top right box. As can be seen, they represent the most effective leadership behaviors. Next in importance (again see Figure 9.9) are **contingent reward (CR) behaviors**, which are widely used by transactional leaders. The CR leader clarifies what needs to be done and exchanges both psychic and material rewards with followers who comply accordingly. Third in importance is what Bass calls the **active management-by-exception (MBE-A) leader**, who monitors followers' performance and takes corrective action when deviations from standards occur. The next leader, ineffective in performance, is the **passive management-by-exception (MBE-P) person**, who intervenes only when standards are not met. Finally, the least-effective leader is the **laissez-faire (LF) individual**, who avoids intervening or accepting responsibility for followers' action. Commenting on his findings, Bass reports:

> According to a higher-order factor analysis, the eight factors can be ordered from lowest to highest in activity: 4 Is, CR, MBE-A, MBE-P, LF. Correspondingly, the eight factors can be ordered on a second dimension—effectiveness. The 4 Is are most effective; CR, second-most effective; MBE-A, next most effective; MBE-P, even less effective; and LF leadership, least effective (or most ineffective).[22]

Bass has found that transformational leaders also use transactional leadership to supplement their approach. Hence, both the 4 Is and the CR leadership style are important to them, as shown in Figure 9.9. Less-effective leaders tend to use styles that do not

Figure 9.9
An Optimal Profile of Universal Leadership Behaviors

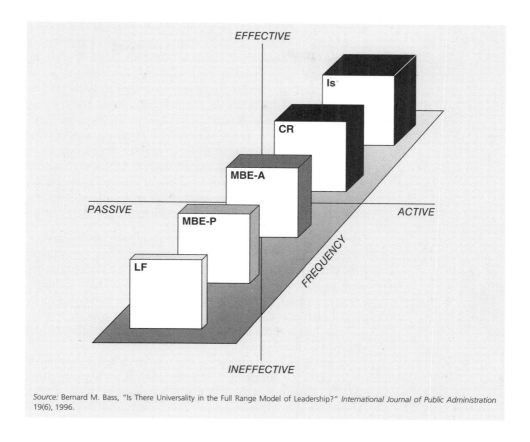

Source: Bernard M. Bass, "Is There Universality in the Full Range Model of Leadership?" *International Journal of Public Administration* 19(6), 1996.

include the 4 Is and may use CR leadership only cursorily. Additionally, Bass reports that various modifications of these findings are extant, depending on the culture of the country. For example, in some nations, leaders employ the 4 Is in an autocratic manner, whereas in others, the leaders use a more participative approach. For example, he reports that transformational leaders in India and Japan tend to be more participative than those in Pakistan and Taiwan.

These findings help to bring together much of what is currently known about leadership. In particular, they point out the importance of charismatic behaviors in the leadership process.

Management versus Leadership

What is the difference between management and leadership? While some people might suggest they are the same, others disagree. "Rather, management and leadership are two distinctive and complementary systems of action. Each has its own function and characteristic activities." Management is about coping with complexity within the organization by bringing order to the process of providing quality products/services and, at the same time, creating a profitable company whereas leadership is about coping with change. As the marketplace becomes more global, more competitive, and more volatile, and as technology advances, major changes are necessary to survive and to compete effectively in the new environment.[23]

Managers (management) are the ones who do the planning and budgeting, organizing and staffing, and controlling and problem solving. Leaders (leadership) set the direction by developing a vision of the future along with strategies for producing the changes needed to accomplish the vision. Leaders communicate their new visions to people who can create coalitions that understand the vision and are committed to its achievement. Leadership keeps people motivated, inspired, and moving in the right direction.

Managers and leaders have different roles in organizations. Managers react according to their role (position) in the company; focus on how to get things done; strive for win–lose or win–win situations; and serve as regulators and monitors of an existing order of affairs from which they receive rewards, compensation, and benefits. Their job is to promote stability within the organization. Leaders show more empathy and are more intuitive. They are concerned with ideas, focus more on what the decisions mean to participants, and seek opportunities for change. Since leaders function at a conceptual level, determining where the company is going and how to get there, they often feel separated from their environment rather than being a part of the environment.

Trust.　Trust is the foundation that supports all leadership efforts. Without trust, a leader will never get passionate engagement from employees. Trust is critical to the effectiveness of leadership. Building trust is an ongoing process that leaders can never leave to develop on its own. Results from a study published in the Edelman Trust Barometer show that 66 percent of the people surveyed trust corporations, and only 39 percent have a high regard for and widely admire top leadership. These statistics indicate that leaders need to spend more time building trust with employees, and also, within the community.

Leaders can start building trust by developing relationships. Trust begins when a leader takes a genuine interest in employees and appreciates their uniqueness. Leaders look for ways to acknowledge and honor all of those around them. They project an excitement about the future and do not shy away from the unknown. Leaders face their fears head on. They understand the power of effectively communicating to employees, the investors, and the community.[24]

Characteristics of Leadership.　Lee Iacocca in his book, "*Where Have All the Leaders Gone?*" compiled a list of "Nine Cs of Leadership," by which he says all presidential and CEO candidates should be judged. These are the characteristics that Iacocca feels comprise a successful leader.[25]

1. **Curiosity.** A leader listens, reads, and steps outside his/her safety zone.
2. **Creative.** A leader is willing to try something new and different. Leadership is about change, "think outside the box."
3. **Communicate**. A leader faces reality and tells the truth, regardless of the consequences.
4. **Character.** A leader knows the difference between right and wrong and has the guts to do the right thing.
5. **Courage.** A leader commits and willingly sits down to negotiate the roughest deals.
6. **Conviction.** A leader has passion, fire in his/her belly, and a deep desire to get things done.
7. **Charisma.** A leader is charismatic and has the ability to inspire.
8. **Competent**. A leader knows what he/she is doing and is surrounded by people who know what they are doing.
9. **Common sense.** A leader understands the reality of the real world, not a fabricated world, and knows the difference.

Another important C related to leadership is crisis. That is when leadership is forced to reign. Crises are inevitable. Every organization at some time will find itself in disarray. It may be easy to do nothing, but it is another thing to lead when your world is tumbling down.

CHECK YOUR UNDERSTANDING

1. How does Fiedler's contingency model differ from the managerial grid?
2. How does charismatic leadership differ from transformational leadership?
3. How is a transformational leader different from a transactional leader?
4. What are the 4 Is of universal leadership behavior?
5. How do managers differ from leaders?
6. Can you remember at least six of the nine Cs of leadership?

Describe several challenges of leaders in the next decade.

Leaders in the Next Decade

Patrick McKenna of McKenna Associates, Inc., Edmonton, Canada, and David Maister, experts on management professional services, believe that "today's leaders have to be kinder, gentler, more empathetic—and able to show genuine interest in whatever their charges are trying to achieve." They argue that executives must move past outdated notions of what makes a good leader and move toward genuine affection and empathy as essential management tools. Another argument is that professionals develop confidence and achieve peak performance at the office through a leader's inspirational techniques. McKenna and Maister present five questions that can inspire employees:

1. Do you show a genuine interest in what each of your group members wants to achieve with his or her career? (This is a critical part of any group leader's role.)
2. Do you show an interest in the things that mean the most to your people in their personal lives?
3. Are you there for your people in their times of personal or professional crisis?
4. Do you informally "check in" with each of your people every now and then?
5. Do you offer to help when some member of your group clearly needs it?[26]

Inspiration comes from within, and it is the job of the leader to create an environment that inspires others. Study after study shows that it is the intangible variables that motivate employees, such as "full appreciation for a job well done, being a part of decisions that affect them, open communications, interesting and meaningful work, and having good relationships at work."[27] What is interesting is that these require "little if any money, but rather simply some time, thoughtfulness and creativity" on the part of the leader. Successful leaders today take time to show genuine interest in their employees. It is the leader's role to treat people well and to help employees understand the end results of a project and why it will be better than it is now. If people know you champion their cause, they will buy into your cause and line up on your side, but it can't be done long distance. It takes a lot of time to meet with people, to look them in the eye, and to listen to what they have to say. People also will watch what you do and say and will act accordingly.[28]

Regardless of the type of employee recognition and acknowledgement given, Bob Nelson, author of *1001 Ways to Reward Employees*, states that three guidelines must be followed:

1. **Match the reward to the person.** Ask employees what they value and how they like to be recognized for their accomplishments, and then follow through with their wishes.
2. **Match the reward to the achievement.** The type of reinforcement should be in proportion to the significance of the achievement and the length of time and money spent on the project.
3. **Be timely and specific.** Awards and recognition should be given as soon as possible after the achievement or change in behavior.[29]

To help keep employees motivated and engaged in their work, many companies sponsor activities and events. For example, Southwest Airlines in Dallas runs a Halloween costume contest, a design contest for the December newsletter, and an annual chili cook-off. Truck drivers from FedEx Freight West in San Jose participate in truck-driving championships and maneuvers. Winners receive special recognition and opportunities for all-expense-paid trips and other prizes. Domino's Pizza, Inc., in Ann Arbor holds an annual company-wide "Olympics" in events ranging from accounting to dough making, vegetable slicing, truck loading, dough catching, and tray scraping. The awards range from $4,000 in each category to a free vacation for the team leader who supervises the most "gold medalists."[30]

Leading Virtual Teams

As we learned in Chapter 8, teleworking is growing. These individuals and groups need leadership just like those working in an office environment. Managing teleworkers has its own set of issues and problems. Caroline Davis, president of Worth Collection, a women's clothing company, has surrounded herself with a stellar team of teleworkers. Her suggestions for managing long distance are:

- **Hiring process**—Hire people who work independently and who do not need supervision. She uses a written "personal profile" test to gain insight into a prospective employee's work habits.
- **Communication**—Connect everyone digitally by using systems, such as e-mail, iPhone, social networks, and so on, that allow communication to flow much as it would in a single location. Davis also has weekly conference calls with all levels of management and requires managers to meet in New York every ten to twelve weeks for additional long-term strategic planning.
- **Culture**—"We pay more attention to our corporate culture than if everyone were in one place and we took it for granted," says Davis. To help keep people connected, a company newsletter goes to everyone on a regular basis.[31]

Multitasking Skills

Leaders are constantly being asked to do more with less, make more decisions, and get more done with fewer people and fewer resources. As an economy slows down, leaders are asked to do more with less, often creating impossible expectations. Feelings of being overworked and overwhelmed have set in. How do leaders remain sane? They must become very good at multitasking. Effectively using technology and communications is important to successful multitasking. For example, voice mail, conference calls, e-mail, Web cast, advanced voice mail functions, face-to-face meetings, and instant messaging all provide a means for accomplishing several tasks at the same time and in several locations around the world at the same time. The fast-paced world of the twenty-first century requires leaders to be connected and to be fast paced as well.[32]

Is multitasking always the answer to greater productivity? According to a study published in the *Journal of Experimental Psychology*, "it takes the brain four times longer to recognize and process each item it is working on when multitasking than when it is focused on a single job." Other studies have revealed that work quality suffers when multitasking. More often it is best to do one thing at a time. If something comes up, make a note of it, then proceed to complete the task already started.[33]

People who multitask feel they are getting more done in a shorter period of time, but that has not been proven to be true. Scientists have proven that the brain can process only one thing at a time. Doing a task draws on a specific set of cognitive operations. When several tasks are being done at one time, the pool of resources is being drained; therefore, some tasks will suffer. Even switching back and forth between tasks takes the brain time to reorient. Laura Stack, author of *Leave the Office Earlier*, states that "multitasking is really an act of procrastination" and is essentially a bad habit.

Some research suggests that the more intelligent have a more difficult time at multitasking; they tend to focus more on one thing at a time. Teens more often can multitask better than more mature people, which has gotten many of them into dangerous situations, especially when text messaging or talking on the phone while driving. Sometimes multitasking may be necessary, but it is best to complete one task at a time.[34]

Emerging Leadership Challenges

Over the last two decades, the U.S. economy has seen unparalleled growth, due in part to the explosion of global activity. This, in turn, has created a demand for leaders, whose greatest challenge is to manage the complexity of the emerging social/economic environment. The second challenge is managing diversity. And the third challenge is managing uncertainty. Leaders need global emotional intelligence and specialized knowledge about fundamental issues that separate the cultures. Leaders in the world today are lacking in the ability to coach effectively and the ability to deal with conflict. Too many leaders try to avoid conflict rather than get creative or innovative in trying to solve the problem.[35]

Today, large and small firms alike are facing the challenge of both attracting and developing leadership talent. Moreover, given that the pool of such talent is smaller than the demand, more and more organizations are now working to hire and develop leaders through careful training and mentoring. What abilities and skills will these individuals need? According to a survey conducted by Accenture, over the next decade, the best leaders will have to do the following:

1. Create a shared vision for everyone in the firm.
2. Ensure customer satisfaction.
3. Live the values that are critical to the company.
4. Build internal teamwork and external partnerships.
5. Think globally.
6. Appreciate cultural diversity.
7. Develop and empower people.
8. Be able to anticipate opportunity.
9. Learn how to achieve competitive advantage.
10. Embrace change.
11. Share leadership.
12. Demonstrate personal mastery of the job.
13. Show technological savvy.
14. Encourage constructive challenge.[36]

Blending Work and Family Issues

The ten-hour workday that is typical in many companies has increased the need to blend professional and personal tasks. For example, while attending their children's school events, employees use their digital handheld devices to answer colleagues' questions, proof reports, and make appointments with clients. For managers, this overlapping of work and personal life presents several new challenges. Many managers recognize that because employees are expected to be available 24/7 with their cell phones and e-mail, they must give employees more freedom, but they must also set some limits. How can managers deal with employees who abuse this new flexibility? Managers are handling this challenge in different ways. For example, an executive vice president of Grey World-wide, an advertising firm, expects workplace productivity to increase by allowing employees to conduct some personal business at work. They can also do some work at home. All the company cares about is that the employees get their work done.[37]

Some managers have established guidelines for doing personal business at work. Other companies that allow employees to conduct personal business on work time are offering equipment and services to help keep employers at work longer with fewer inter-ruptions, such as dry cleaning services, ATMs, health and beauty aids, massages, washers and dryers for doing your laundry at work, and fitness centers. Google offers its employ-ees at the Mountain View, California, headquarters free lunches and dinners cooked by a gourmet chef. Managers feel that by blending work and life needs, employees are happier and do better at weathering life crises.[38]

Managerial Mistakes That Lead to Litigation

It is employee anger arising from perceived unfair treatment that fuels lawsuits. Managers and supervisors often engage in behaviors that, unwittingly, lead employees to feel misled, lied to, or otherwise unfairly treated. Leaders should make sure they do not engage in behaviors that can potentially lead to lawsuits. Maxine Neuhauser has compiled a list of ten common mistakes that increase the likelihood of employee law-suits. They are:[39]

1. **Forget about training.** Managers and supervisors need training, as well as workers. What managers say and do represent what the company says and does.
2. **Disregard company policies.** Company policies provide guidance for both employ-ees and managers. They are rules to follow. Following policies ensures consistent treatment of employees.
3. **Shoot from the hip.** Firing employees without notice may occasionally be appropri-ate, but rarely. Employees need to be aware of the consequences of misconduct and the discipline process.
4. **Motivate poor performers with raises and bonuses.** Giving undeserved raises and bonuses does not spur poor performers to improve. Rather it reinforces poor performance.
5. **Criticize the person.** Very few jobs lend themselves to purely objective evaluation. Subjective criteria nearly always come into play; therefore, it is crucial that the focus is on the work and not on the person. To avoid such pitfalls, companies should encourage and assist managers in establishing measurable goals and create standards against which to evaluate employee performance.
6. **Ignore problems.** Failing to address performance issues has the practical effect of lowering performance standards and leads employees to believe their work is satis-factory. Accepting poor performance makes it more difficult to fire an employee later for poor performance.
7. **Put nothing in writing.** Without written records documenting employee perfor-mance, employers are left with little concrete evidence to prove a history of poor performance as a reason for discharge. Performance evaluations, counseling, and warning notices must be in writing.
8. **Condone any type of discrimination or harassment.** A hostile work environment is not acceptable, whether it is sexual harassment or harassment based on age, dis-ability, or race. Jokes, e-mails, and passing comments can be used to show pervasive misbehavior that has converted a professional workplace into an uncomfortable environment. Managers must take action to stop the misconduct.

9. **Lie.** When management fails to tell the truth, employee disgruntlement inevitably follows, along with potential liability. Employees see lies as a pretext to hide other factors that may be important to them.

10. **Cover-up.** Repeatedly, experience shows that a cover-up carries worse consequences than the initial misdeed. When confronted with a bad situation, it remains true that honesty is the best policy.

A number of approaches are proving particularly helpful in dealing with these challenges. One is to develop an internal cadre of leaders who can meet the varied challenges being confronted by their organizations. A second is to learn how to lead high-potential employees who need careful direction.

Identify ways of developing internal leaders and dealing with high-potential employees who have bad work habits.

Developing Internal Leaders

Every successful company identifies the results it needs to achieve. The challenge, then, is to get the leaders to reach these goals. At Cisco Systems, Inc., for example, senior-level executives carefully spell out the results that are expected from the managers. In this way, the managers know what they have to do as leaders. Additionally, they know how they are going to be evaluated, as their performance is tied directly to their compensation.[40] At the same time, leaders at Cisco work to develop leaders in their group so that, as the company grows, it has leaders to help handle the new business. This sometimes is labeled *managing the law of explosive growth.* John Maxwell, a world-renowned expert on leadership, explains the logic this way:

> Leaders who develop followers grow their organization only one person at a time. But leaders who develop leaders multiply their growth, because for every leader they develop, they also receive all of that leader's followers. Add ten followers to your organization, and you have a power of ten people. Add ten leaders to your organization, and you have the power of ten leaders times all the followers and leaders they influence.[41]

Firms such as GE, Motorola, Walmart, IBM, and Hewlett-Packard, among others, use this approach to meet the impending shortage of leaders. This was not true years ago when companies were able to hire leaders from other firms by offering more attractive compensation packages. Today, however, the best leaders often are unwilling to leave because their current employers are giving them generous compensation as well as challenging jobs that are personally fulfilling. As a result, a growing number of firms are now training their managers to develop leaders from their work groups so that the firm can handle its needs on an internal basis. The old approach of developing followers now is being replaced by a strategy of developing leaders. Table 9.3 illustrates the differences between these two approaches.

Leading High-Potential Employees

Many organizations have employees who are innovative, highly skilled, or strongly motivated but who, at the same time, are creating problems for other employees because their approaches to doing things are disruptive. The challenge for the leader is to help these people overcome their bad habits while still remaining high performers. Waldroop and Butler, two psychologists, have identified six patterns of behavior—hero, meritocrat, bulldozer, pessimist, rebel, and home-run hitter.[42]

1. The *hero* is an individual who works long and hard everyday. This person continually pushes himself or herself as well as those in the work team. The problem is that

Table 9.3
Developing In-House
Talent: Followers versus
Leaders

Leaders Who Develop Followers	Leaders Who Develop Leaders
Develop the bottom 20 percent of their people	Develop the top 20 percent of their people
Focus on the weaknesses of their people	Focus on the strengths of their people
Have a need to be needed	Have a need to be succeeded
Hoard power	Give away power
Spend time with others	Invest time in others
Grow by addition	Grow by multiplication
Affect only people they touch personally	Affect people far beyond their own reach
Treat all their people the same in order to be fair	Treat their leaders differently to allow them to make an impact on the organization

Source: Adapted from John C. Maxwell, *The 21 Irrefutable Laws of Leadership* (Nashville, TN: Thomas Nelson, 1998).

many of these team members do not like the continual stress that is created by the hero, and they feel that this individual does not consider their needs. The hero is interested in maximum effort and wants everyone to contribute to this goal regardless of his or her personal situation. In dealing with this person, leaders must do three things.

a. First, express appreciation for all the hero's accomplishments and then note the negative effect that this maximum effort is having on the workers.

b. Second, discuss the importance of the hero paying closer attention to the workers and noting when they are being worked too hard.

c. Third, encourage the individual to focus more attention on long-range projects and stop emphasizing short-run goals, because this is what often causes problems for the other team members.

2. The *meritocrat* believes that recommendations, ideas, and suggestions will be accepted based on their merit. What the person fails to realize is that sometimes even the best ideas need to be sold, negotiated, or shaped to meet political and organizational realities. In leading this individual, the manager needs to support the person's ideas while also helping the meritocrat to understand that often new ideas must be sold to others, which means that networking and politicking are necessary. Often the manager will ask the meritocrat, "Do you want to be right or do you want to be effective?" Once the individual realizes that good ideas do not always sell themselves, he or she is often more willing to add realism to the situation and begin seeking support from others for these ideas.

3. The *bulldozer* is a person who runs roughshod over others in a quest for power. This individual typically intimidates and alienates others in an effort to get his or her ideas accepted. In dealing with this person, the leader must be equally blunt in making the individual aware that he or she is not liked by many of the people in the organization and that the person's confrontational style must change—or the leader will have to replace him or her. Once the person realizes this, the leader must then work with the individual to mend fences.

4. The *pessimist* focuses on the downside of things and worries aloud about what could go wrong if changes are introduced. The leader's objective must be that of getting

the pessimist to look at the positive side of things by pointing out where this individual's fears were unjustified in the past. The leader must then help the pessimist to evaluate better the risk associated with change so that the individual realizes that some changes are going to work just fine and others have a small degree of risk and should be accepted. In this way, the pessimist begins to take a more realistic view of things and abandons the continual negative attack on all proposed changes.

5. The *rebel* automatically fights against authority and convention. The leader's role here must be that of co-opting the individual and getting him or her to stop making negative comments and become a team player. One of the most popular initial approaches is to have the individual spend a week or two noting the way people in the department go about interacting with one another, how they align in groups, and how decisions are made. The rebel then is assigned to write up this information in a report for the manager. Once the rebel has gathered that information, ask him this: "If you were a real revolutionary fighting somewhere against a dictatorship, would it be better to stand out or to blend in?" The answer is clear, so push the rebel to the logical conclusion. "You have a choice. You can work to change things here or you can follow your old pattern and just be an irritant. If you choose the latter, your career will stall and your influence on the organization will never amount to much. I hope you make the other choice, because you're right—this place isn't perfect, and we need people like you to help improve it."[43] This approach typically gets the rebel to see how he or she can be more effective. As a result, the individual often drops the negative attitude and begins turning his or her energies toward constructive criticism. This does not happen immediately, but the ultimate result is often beneficial for both the organization and the pessimist.

6. The *home-run hitter* tries to do too much too soon and, as a result, often ends up failing. This type of individual is like a baseball player who always swings for the fences. He or she hits a fair number of home runs but also strikes out often. In getting this person to slow down and focus on doing less, the leader needs to work with the home-run hitter in setting smaller goals that can reasonably be accomplished. The leader also needs to encourage the individual to work more closely with others and to remind this employee that a successful career track in the company often begins with slow progress (hitting a lot of singles) that adds to the bottom line. Then, as the individual begins to make headway in achieving these small goals, the leader must continually praise the employee and show him or her how this progress will contribute to career success.

 ## CHECK YOUR UNDERSTANDING

Match the behavior to the statement:

Behavior	Actions
a. Hero	_____ Makes negative comments, fights authority
b. Meritocrat	_____ Intimidates and alienates others
c. Bulldozer	_____ Is interested in maximum effort
d. Pessimist	_____ Needs to set smaller goals and work closely with others
e. Rebel	_____ Believes ideas will be accepted on merit
f. Home-Run Hitter	_____ Looks at the downside; worries about change

These approaches to dealing with individuals with bad habits can be very helpful to leaders in getting everyone to contribute as a team member. They are also useful in developing productive team members.[44]

© quavondo, iStock

Career Advisor

Know Your Job

In every job, a basic set of skills must be mastered. For engineers, these skills are technical in nature; for human resources specialists, they are behavioral in content; and for managers, they are a combination of technical and behavioral skills. Discover which skills are most important to your job and learn and master them as quickly as possible. A good example is found in the case of individuals whose careers require them to have some international experience. Research shows that a working knowledge of a second language can be particularly helpful. The "Cultural Diversity in Action" box explains why.

Discuss how to function in your job to get ahead in your career.

Know How You Will Be Judged

Most people are judged on two types of criteria: formal and informal. Formal criteria tend to be measurable and often take such forms as volume of work output or productivity, sales increases, or profit. Those who do well in these areas receive greater raises or faster promotions than those who do not.[45] Your performance on formal criteria is measured by some document or evaluation instrument. If you are determined to win the career promotion game, you must concentrate on doing well on these formal criteria.

On the other hand, if you find that the formal criteria also include qualitative criteria such as personality, interpersonal skills, leadership styles, and work attitudes, you must broaden your attention and address these criteria as well. In some companies, you may find that most people do well in pursuing the quantitative objectives and that it is the qualitative objectives that separate the most promotable employees from the others. In this case, concentrate most of your attention on qualitative criteria, as this is where your career progress in that firm will be decided. Informal criteria are more difficult to describe, because your boss often determines them. Typical examples are the way you dress, whether you seem interested in your job, and whether you fit in as a member of the work group. The best way to meet these challenges is to watch successful members of your department or group and emulate how they function.

Keep a Hero File

The formal evaluation system is used by the organization to reward you for your contributions. However, at some point during your career, you may decide to move to another enterprise. How will you be able to show your new prospective employer how good you are?

- One way, of course, is by pointing to your past promotions and current salary.
- A second way is by having your boss write a letter of recommendation for you (assuming he or she would comply).
- A third way, and best of all, is to keep a hero file that contains all your accomplishments.

Typical examples are memos congratulating you on your work, awards given to you by the organization, and samples of your work (a major report you wrote, an

IN ACTION

A MATTER OF BILINGUALISM

Many people today are finding that if their job requires them to work overseas or with international clients, knowledge of a second language can be very helpful. Of course, English will continue to be the primary language of international business. However, training in the host country's language can be particularly useful, and those who are willing to learn another language often find that their career opportunities improve.

One of the most popular languages is Spanish. A large percentage of the world's population speaks this language, including most people in Latin America. A second popular language is French, which is widely spoken in Europe, as well as in certain areas of Africa and Asia. Learning both these languages is fairly easy for Americans, as the pronunciation and rules of grammar are not as "foreign" as are those of Russian and Chinese.

Students in other countries often are taught a second language at both the high school and college levels, with English continuing to be the most popular. In China, for example, more people speak English than any other language, because there are so many variations of Chinese that people from one part of China are unable to understand those from another part. Similarly, it may be difficult initially for people from the Midwestern United States to understand people from Scotland (who also speak English) because of their pronunciation, but this problem will be overcome once Americans become attuned to the accent.

Americans must become bilingual so that they can communicate with others around the world and will not have to rely on other nationals to speak English. In business operations, for example, many international clients like doing business with individuals who speak their language, even if the person does not demonstrate fluency in this language. Specifically, businesspeople often feel that fewer misunderstandings ensue if the participants in a professional pursuit all speak the same language, and they feel most comfortable using their native tongue. Hence, those Americans who have learned a second language have a distinct advantage when it comes to career opportunities because, during the next decade, more and more firms will be increasing their international operations. Those who can communicate fluently in the language of the country where the firm does business will have an advantage over other job applicants.

Another reason that companies prefer individuals who can speak the language local to their international enterprises is that it helps the firm to monitor the competition. Multinational firms often locate near their major competitors, because new developments by these firms are most likely to be reported in local newspapers and other sources. For the cost of a subscription, it often is possible to learn more about what a competitor is doing than one could ever find out if the investigation were conducted from headquarters. For this reason, many foreign multinational organizations employ personnel who read and speak English fluently and can peruse the *Wall Street Journal*, the *New York Times*, and American industry publications on a daily basis and compile folders on the strategies of their U.S. competitors.

Of course, not every job applicant is going to be bilingual. However, those who are not can always learn a second language after they are hired. The important thing to remember is that as multinationalism increases, bilingualism is going to become a more important asset for those who are seeking increased career opportunities.

---

advertisement you designed, or a financial analysis you conducted) that show the quality of your performance. Remember, modesty has its place, but sometimes it pays to blow your own horn!

Develop Alliances

Very few loners succeed in modern organizations. You must be able to get along with others if you are going to advance. This requires the development of alliances. In developing alliances, begin with your subordinates by creating an effective work relationship with them. This will show others that you are qualified in your job and will begin to open doors at the management level. Next, you should begin developing peer group relationships with others who occupy the same level in the hierarchy as do you. Finally, you should seek ways of developing work relationships with higher-level managers.

If you violate this "from the bottom up" approach, you may find it very difficult to develop meaningful alliances. Your peers will regard you as an apple polisher or someone who is trying to succeed at their expense; when possible, they will look for ways to undercut your performance and your reputation. Your subordinates will look on you as someone who is more interested in his or her own career than in helping them to get things done. They will retaliate by giving you minimum performance and helping create a reputation for you as someone who is not very effective in managing work teams. Because both of these groups can be just as harmful to you as they can be helpful, it is best to win their support and create an alliance with them as soon as possible. Learn to be a team player.

"Networked people are smarter people. The reason they get smarter is that they talk to each other, sharing the benefits of past experience." The onset of the Internet provided workers with the tool to increase their knowledge and expertise in every area of operations. This has resulted in companies treating employees with more respect and has impacted the age-old adversarial relationship that has existed between labor and management. The bottom line is that corporate behavior is beginning to change from control to being a partner.[46]

Show That You Are a Star

Strive to prove that you are a star on the rise. You can do this by turning in a top-notch performance. When your work is outstanding, word gets around, and people begin to notice you.

A second way of proving that you are star material is by realizing the truth in the cliché that great performance is 99 percent perspiration and 1 percent inspiration. In modern organizations, most people succeed because of hard work; it is still the key to great performance.

A third way is by making yourself a crucial part of the work team. The more your boss relies on you, the greater are your chances for success. As your supervisor goes up the chain of command, he or she is likely to take you along. Of course, you may find that your boss is at a dead end; a classic example of the Peter Principle where he or she has risen to his or her level of incompetence. In this case, get out; find another position in the organization or look elsewhere. Your mobility is limited. How do you know when your boss is no longer a fast-track manager? Simply compare the average time between promotions for other managers and for your boss. Typically, managers are promoted every three to five years. If your boss has been in the same position for seven years, he or she is probably not going anywhere. If you remain in the department, the same will be true for you.

A fourth way of demonstrating that your star is rising is by getting continuous feedback on how well you are doing. Stay alert to comments from your boss on what you are doing well and the areas in which you need improvement. Treat this feedback as a source for personal action. Sure, it may hurt when the individual tells you, "Your report was incomplete," or "Jones tells me that you were late for the meeting yesterday afternoon," or "I want you to start paying closer attention to the cost data I'm sending you; your work group's efficiency is falling down." However, you can use this feedback to improve your performance. Accept it in a positive light and use it to help correct your shortcomings.

A fifth way is by standing out from the crowd. How do you distinguish yourself from others? What is your brand? This is what marketers try to accomplish in every advertisement—to sell products. You must take the initiative to sell your skills, talents, and accomplishments. Your leaders—bosses—are too busy promoting their own career to focus on your career. How do you make a difference and set yourself apart from the average employee? Do something that sets you apart. Take an assignment that provides you the opportunity to present your findings to the board of directors. Agree to serve on a committee that has representatives from all management levels and go out of your way to impress them. Volunteer for extra assignments that you feel you are qualified to handle and no one else wants. Gain exposure by giving talks to outside groups and writing articles in magazines and journals, thus establishing yourself as an expert in a management-related area.[47] As you try to separate yourself from the crowd, remember that your strategy has its risks. If you fail, your career may be jeopardized; so be somewhat conservative and do not bite off more than you can comfortably chew. Additional ideas about developing your own brand were discussed in Chapter 7 under the topic "Developing Your Brand."

Train Your Replacement

If you are a rising star, your promotion will leave a void unless you have a replacement. In some cases, your promotion may be delayed until there is someone to take your place. You can speed up your career progress by training your replacement early. If you are being promoted to another department or unit, your boss will be reluctant to let you go because he or she will be left without adequate assistance—hence, the need for a replacement.

Leadership Aspirations

What level of leadership do you aspire? If you have aspirations of becoming a manager or leader, then you should ask yourself three questions to assess your own leadership potential.[48]

1. **How far do you want to go?** Leaders continuously make choices that affect other people's money and lives. They are constantly in competition with others for higher-level positions. A useful exercise: Look at your immediate boss's job and ask yourself if you could do it as well, or better—honestly. You might even go a level higher, learn what that person does, and ask the same question.
2. **What are you willing to invest?** Given your limitations, how much effort are you willing to invest to develop the skills needed to do the job? Leadership requires business smarts, technical capabilities, and cultural sensibilities, but above all, it is about power. A leader must gain, exercise, and retain power. For some people, this is distasteful and not pleasurable. "As a leader, you must take people where they have never been—in thought and action—often against their initial preferences."
3. **How will you keep it up?** How will you be able to keep going when you are not rewarded or recognized for your performance, and when you must deal with criticism, resistance, setbacks, and people disliking you or for what you are asking them to do. Will you be able to find ways for maintaining your physical vitality and your emotional flexibility? The reality is that it is difficult to continuously manage novel situations especially under extreme circumstances. Are you willing to deal continuously with new challenges?

Slacking on the Job

Just how much slacking on the job is permissible and how many personal chores are acceptable at work? Recently, the line between personal and work time has blurred considerably in some companies. But what are not acceptable are personal conversations that interfere with your coworker's work. Because employees have lives outside of work, sometimes they need to make personal calls during working hours to handle situations. It is best to find out the company's rules and then follow them.

What do you do if a coworker is a slacker? It is best to look the other way. You don't want to look like a tattletale. After all, that person could be doing some work at home. Only if it becomes disruptive should you report it. Slacking will show up in performance reports. Your manager usually will give a cue on when slacking is permissible and when it's time to get back to work.[49]

Appearance

In Chapter 5, we talked about the importance of appearance when going for an interview. That continues to be true. If you want to advance in your career, never forget the importance of looking your best. Always dress appropriately for the kind of work you are doing. You should wear clean, up-to-date clothing, have your shoes clean and/or polished, wear your hair in a becoming style, and keep your body clean. There is nothing worse than a coworker who has body odor.

Enthusiasm

Your attitude toward your work, your coworkers, and your company will impact how effectively you get things done. Enthusiasm, optimism, and a sense of efficacy will translate into positive reactions. They are feelings that help build relationships through which things get done. People have a desire to belong and be a part of something important. Employees become engaged in their work. The opposite feelings can be described as depression, which can spell disaster for performance. Just remember that enthusiasm can make the difference in where you go with your career.[50]

Periodically Reassess Your Career

As you begin to learn your job and show those around you that you are capable of higher-level tasks, continue to reassess your career. Sometimes, opportunities for you to be promoted in your current organization are minimal. If your boss is five years younger than you are and it appears that he or she, in all likelihood, is content with the organization, you are not going to be promoted over him or her. You are going to have to go around him or her by finding a job elsewhere in the organization, or you must seek employment in another enterprise.[51]

Career reassessment can help you to decide exactly what you should do. Set some objectives for yourself, and, if you do not attain them, consider moving. The following are examples of typical objectives:

- If I do not receive two promotions in the first five years, I will leave.
- If I do not receive a raise of more than five percent each year for the first three years, I will leave.
- If I am not in a middle-management position, with a group or unit of at least seven subordinates within five years, I will seek employment elsewhere.
- If I feel that I am not going to be in top management by the time I am age forty-five, I will leave.

None of these examples is meant to serve as a definitive guideline; however, all are representative of the types of goals high-achieving people set for themselves in reassessing their careers.[52]

It also is helpful to examine where you are in your career and what lies ahead. For example, many people start out on a very fast track but after receiving a series of promotions, their careers plateau. Can they get back on a fast track, or is it time to move on? This requires careful analysis of where the company is heading and what role you will play. Often the best initial strategy is to sit down with your boss and discuss what your future looks like. If you like the scenario that is presented, you can stay. Otherwise, start looking around to learn what other opportunities are available either within the organization or in another firm. Perhaps your career field is no longer a growing one. Table 9.4 provides a list of some of the occupations that are anticipated to be most in demand between 2004 and 2014.

Table 9.4
New Jobs for the New Economy: The Ten Fastest-Growing Occupations (in thousands of jobs)

Occupation	Employment		Change	
	2004	2014	Number	Percentage
Home health aides	624	974	350	56.0
Network systems and data communications analysts	231	357	126	54.6
Medical assistants	387	589	202	52.1
Physician assistants	62	93	31	49.6
Computer software engineers, applications	460	682	222	48.4
Physical therapist assistants	59	85	26	44.2
Dental hygienists	158	226	68	43.3
Computer software engineers, systems software	340	486	146	43.0
Dental assistants	267	382	114	42.7
Personal and home care aides	701	988	287	41.0

Source: U.S. Bureau of Labor Statistics.

One final note: If you do decide to leave for new employment, do so at your convenience and on a good note. Furthermore, regardless of why you leave, stay on good terms with everyone. Bosses tend to remember your last days on the job more vividly than they do most other days. If you need them to say something about you in the future, you want them to give positive and complimentary responses.

 ## CHECK YOUR UNDERSTANDING

In your journal, write your thoughts on what you need to do at work to get ahead in your career.

Summary

1 Describe the characteristics and skills related to managerial effectiveness.

Leadership is the process of influencing people to voluntarily direct their efforts toward the achievement of some particular organizational goals. What makes a leader effective? Some people believe the answer rests in **leadership characteristics**, such as drive, originality, and the tolerance of stress. The greatest problem with this trait theory approach, however, is that it does not take the situation into account. A leadership style that is effective in one situation may not be effective in another.

In an effort to address the situational nature of leadership, many people have turned to **personal characteristics**. Some of the most commonly cited personal characteristics of leaders are superior intelligence, emotional maturity, motivation drive, problem-solving skills, managerial skills, and leadership skills. The degree and importance of each are determined by the situation. For example, some situations require the leader to rely heavily on human skills, but others demand conceptual skills.

Intelligence is a relative matter, but there is a minimum level of mental ability below which successful managers are unlikely to be found, as well as a ceiling above which effective leaders are generally not found. Successful leaders are **emotionally mature**, self-confident, and capable of directing their subordinates in a calm, conscientious manner. They have a sense of purpose and meaning in life, know how to deal with stress, delegate work, and handle the challenges of the job. Effective leaders have a high **motivation drive**. They like money, power, and control and measure success in quantitative terms. Effective leaders possess **problem-solving skills** and see problems as both challenges and opportunities to prove their **managerial skills**. They have technical skills, human skills, and conceptual skills. Their **leadership style** depends on the situation. Some leader characteristics are initiative, need to achieve, task orientation, drive for responsibility and the pursuit of objectives, interpersonal skills, tact and diplomacy, ability to enlist cooperation and help people grow, desire to win, and willingness to accept challenge.

2 Compare and contrast Theory X with Theory Y.

To lead employees effectively, one must also form some opinions about the employees. Some managers are adherents of the **Theory X** philosophy, which holds that people are basically lazy and that, to get them to work, it is often necessary to use coercion and threats of punishment. Other managers support **Theory Y,** which holds that people are interested in both lower-level and upper-level needs satisfaction, have untapped potential, and, if given the right rewards, exercise self-direction and self-control in attaining organizational objectives.

3 Distinguish among four styles of leadership behavior.

Leadership styles vary. Some situations require authoritarian leadership behavior, but others call for a paternalistic leader; some are best handled with a participative leadership style, and others require a laissez-faire manager. **Authoritarian leaders** are work centered and task directed, with little emphasis on the human element. They are good in crisis situations and when tough leaders are needed. **Paternalistic leaders** are also work centered, but they have some consideration for employees. **Participative leaders** have a high concern for both work and people and encourage subordinates to play an active role in operations. They delegate to and seek feedback from subordinates. Under **laissez-faire leaders**, subordinates play an increasingly larger role. The subordinates are highly skilled professionals requiring their leaders to provide resources and to check on the progress of the job.

4 Explain the concept of "self-leaders" and the basic rules of behavior.

Self-leaders motivate and direct themselves, reducing the amount of time required for supervision. These leaders support their employees and provide them with assistance and guidance as needed. Examples of the basic rules that leaders follow are: be decisive; do not promise what you cannot deliver; praise people in front of others for a job well done and reprimand them in private when they have made a mistake; and when possible, promote from within. Ten basic rules of behavior for effective leadership are: being personally responsible for building teams and placing others first; simplifying and clarifying the important things the organization is working on; understanding the breadth, depth, and context of how your company fits into the world and how you respond to it; understanding the importance of setting priorities, measuring outcomes, and rewarding employees in a timely manner; learning how to teach; staying true to your own style of leadership; setting boundaries of commitment, passion, trust, and teamwork; staying disciplined and detailed; leaving some things unsaid; and most of all, liking people.

5 Describe the two major dimensions of leadership—concern for people and concern for work.

Each of the four leadership behavior styles can be described in terms of two dimensions: concern for work and concern for people. Every leader exercises some degree of each and, because these dimensions are independent, the individual can exercise a high degree of one style without having to sacrifice another style. A person can exercise a high degree of both styles or, for that matter, a low degree of both.

6 Distinguish among the four contingency leadership approaches.

Today, we are in a contingency phase of leadership study. The best-known **contingency model** is that of Fred Fiedler, who has found that task-centered leaders do best in very favorable or very unfavorable situations and relationship-oriented leaders are most effective in situations that are moderately favorable or moderately unfavorable. He recommends matching the leader to the situation rather than trying to change the individual's personality to fit the job. The situation will determine the degree of the leader's success.

The **managerial grid** approach is well liked by practicing managers. It consists of two dimensions: concern for production and concern for people. It is useful in helping participants to understand the five basic styles of leadership and to close the gap between current and desired leadership styles. The 1,1 managerial style is described as the do-nothing manager. The leader lets people do their job. The 9,1 managerial style is described as the production pusher, who is more concerned with production than with people. The 1,9 is called country-club management because of a high emphasis on concern for people's feelings, comforts, and needs. The 5,5 managerial style typifies the organization manager who compromises and balances concern for production and concern for people. The 9,9 managerial style is used by the team builder and is regarded as the ideal style. It focuses on employees' higher-level needs, involves subordinates in decision making, and assumes the goals of employees and the goals of the organization are in harmony.

Current attention is also being directed toward better understanding of charismatic and transformational leadership. **Charismatic leaders** use the strength of their personal abilities to get things done. **Transformational leaders** are visionary agents who have strong confidence in their employees and who encourage them to accept challenges and do things in new, more effective ways. Seven principles of transformational leadership are: simplification, motivation, facilitation, innovation, mobilization, preparation, and determination. This is in sharp contrast to transactional leaders, who give rewards in return for effort and performance. Researchers today are studying the roles of leaders as internal consultants, coordinators, and advisors who reflect on their roles and deal effectively with uncertainty and ambiguity. Bass found that the 4 Is—idealized influence, inspired motivation, intellectual stimulation, and individualized consideration—are important to transformational leaders. Effective leaders tend to use them.

Management and leadership are distinctly different; they, however, complement each other. Each has its own function. Management is about coping with the complexity of activities within the organization, while leadership is about coping with change—creating a vision. Managers are the ones who deal with management functions—planning, organizing, directing, monitoring, and controlling—and leaders are the ones who set the direction for the organization and deal with the changes necessary for management to be success. Without trust, neither managers nor leaders will be able to engage employees.

Lee Iacocca's nine Cs of leadership are: curiosity, creative, communicate, character, courage, conviction, charisma, competent, and common sense. Another important related C is crisis.

7 *Describe several challenges of leaders in the next decade.*

Leaders must be kinder, gentler, more empathetic, and show genuine interest in what each team member wants to achieve, as well as what the team members want in their personal lives. Leaders must support team members in times of personal crisis, check in on their progress, and offer to help them. Employees expect leaders to appreciate a job well done, allow them to be a part of decisions that affect them, use open communications, assign interesting and meaningful work, and have a good working relationship.

Regardless of the type, a recognition or reward should be something meaningful to the employee, should be proportionate to the significance of the achievement, and should be timely and specific.

Many leaders will manage virtual teams or teleworkers, which requires dealing with issues and problems different from in-office workers. To accomplish many tasks simultaneously in a fast-paced global world, leaders use multitasking skills. Communications technology helps leaders successfully complete several tasks in several locations at the same time. Voice mail, e-mail, and instant messaging are just three examples of how to stay connected. Leaders live in a 24/7 world, where the workplace has expanded to include more than an office at the official headquarters. Leaders will manage workers in many locations, many at a distance.

As the economy changes, so do the needs for leadership skills. Hiring qualified people and developing them through training are constant challenges. Abilities and skills needed in the future include being able to create a shared vision for everyone in the firm, ensure customer satisfaction, live the values that are critical to the company, build internal teamwork and external partnerships, think globally, appreciate cultural diversity, develop and empower people, be able to anticipate opportunity, learn how to achieve competitive advantage, embrace change, share leadership, demonstrate personal mastery of the job, show technological savvy, and encourage constructive challenge. To meet the shortage of leaders, many firms are training their managers to develop leaders from their work groups. The new approach to leadership is to develop leaders instead of followers.

Blending work and family issues will become more important and will create a greater challenge for leaders. Guidelines will be established to provide the boundaries. As litigation becomes more prevalent, leaders must not engage in behaviors that potentially can lead to lawsuits. Some appropriate behaviors are providing training for leaders as well as workers; following company policies; not firing employees without notice; providing raises and bonuses only to deserving employees; when criticizing employees, focus on the work and not the person; taking care of problems as soon as possible, and not ignoring them; keeping written records, especially of disciplinary actions; maintaining a fair, friendly workplace free from harassment; telling the truth because lies create mistrust; and regardless of how bad the situation, not covering it up.

8 Identify ways of developing internal leaders and dealing with high-potential employees who have bad work habits.

Some of the latest trends in leadership are strategies for dealing with high-potential employees who have bad habits that must be changed. Six types of these behavior patterns are hero, meritocrat, bulldozer, pessimist, rebel, and home-run hitter. The **hero** works long and hard everyday, causing stress among team members. The **meritocrat** believes that recommendations, ideas, and suggestions will be accepted based on their merit, but fails to realize that ideas have to be sold, negotiated, or shaped to meet political and organizational realities. The **bulldozer** seeks power and typically intimidates and alienates others in an effort to get his or her ideas accepted. The **pessimist** focuses on the downside of things and worries about what can go wrong if changes are introduced, instead of looking at the positive side of things. The **rebel** automatically fights against authority and convention and must be trained to be a team player. The **home-run hitter** tries to do too much too soon, often ending up failing. With the proper training and development, these individuals with bad habits can be productive team members.

9 Discuss how to function in your job to get ahead in your career.

Learn which skills are needed to do your job then master them. In today's global marketplace, speaking a second language can be very valuable. Knowing how you will be judged will dictate your behavior. Will you be evaluated only on achieving your work objectives, or will you be judged on other subjective criteria, such as how well you fit into the team, how you dress, or whether you seem interested in your work? Keep a hero file of your rewards, letters of congratulations, and accomplishments. They can be used with prospective new employers to show your accomplishments. Develop alliances with your subordinates by creating an effective work relationship with them. Networked people are smarter people because they share knowledge. Perform your work like a star by turning out top-notch performances. Word of good work gets around in organizations. Seek continuous feedback on how well you are doing. That way you can improve your performance before an appraisal period. Distinguish yourself from others by developing your own brand. In some organizations, you will never be promoted unless you train a replacement.

What level of leadership do you aspire to attain? Answering three important questions can provide some guidance: How far do you want to go? What are you willing to invest? And how will you keep it up?

Never get too comfortable in your job; always have an open mind toward finding another job. Set some objectives for when you might want to leave a firm and find another job. It is best to leave on your terms and not those of the company.

Key Terms in the Chapter

Leadership	Leadership is the process of influencing people to direct their efforts toward particular goals.
Leadership characteristics	Leadership characteristics are those possessed by effective leaders and include drive, originality, persistence, and tolerance of stress.
Personal characteristics	Personal characteristics are personal attributes often possessed by effective leaders and include superior mental ability, emotional maturity, and problem-solving skills.

Trait theory	Trait theory is an attempt to isolate those factors that contribute to leader effectiveness.
Problem-solving skills	Problem-solving skills help an individual determine the causes of why the acquired results fail to match the desired results.
Technical skills	Technical skills help an individual determine how things work.
Human skills	Human skills help an individual interact with other people.
Conceptual skills	Conceptual skills help a manager understand how all parts of the organization or department fit together.
Theory X	Theory X holds that people are basically lazy.
Theory Y	Theory Y holds that, under the right conditions, people will work.
Authoritarian leadership	Authoritarian leadership tends to be heavily work centered, with little attention to the human element.
Paternalistic leadership	Paternalistic leadership tends to be heavily work centered but has some consideration for the personnel as well.
Participative leadership	Participative leaders have high concern for people and work.
Laissez-faire leadership	Laissez-faire leadership is characterized by a lack of concern for either the people or the work.
Leadership dimensions	Leadership dimensions entail a concern for people and a concern for work.
Fiedler's Contingency Model	Fiedler's Contingency Model holds that leader effectiveness is determined by leadership style and situational variables.
Least preferred coworker (LPC) scale	The LPC scale describes the individual with whom the respondent can work least well.
Leader–member relations	Leader–member relations are determined by how well the two parties get along.
Task structure	Task structure is the degree to which the leader's job is laid out in advance.
Leader position power	Leader position power is the authority vested in a leader's position.
Managerial grid	The managerial grid addresses concern for production and concern for people.
1,1 managerial style	The 1,1 managerial style shows a low concern for both people and work.
9,1 managerial style	The 9,1 managerial style shows a high concern for work and a low concern for people.
1,9 managerial style	The 1,9 managerial style shows a high concern for people and a low concern for work.
5,5 managerial style	The 5,5 managerial style shows a moderate concern for both people and work.
9,9 managerial style	The 9,9 managerial style shows a high concern for both people and work.
Charismatic leaders	Charismatic leaders lead by the strength of their personal abilities.
Transformational leaders	Transformational leaders are visionary agents who motivate people to do things differently.
Transactional leader	Transactional leaders exchange rewards for effort and performance.

Review and Study Questions

1. How do leadership characteristics differ from personal characteristics?

2. Which leadership characteristics appear to account for success in the leadership role?

3. Why are superior intelligence, emotional maturity, and motivation drive important to the success of a manager?

4. In terms of motivation drive, how do *successful* leaders differ from *least-successful* leaders?

5. Identify the characteristics related to the problem-solving skills of effective leaders.

6. Differentiate among the three managerial skills that every leader must have? Which skill is more important to top managers? Why?

7. What are the basic assumptions of Theory X and Theory Y? How accurate are they?

8. Is a Theory Y manager always superior to a Theory X manager? Explain.

9. Compare authoritarian leadership with paternalistic leadership. Compare participative leadership with laissez-faire leadership. Compare authoritarian leadership with laissez-faire leadership.

10. Who are "self-leaders"? Why is the concept important to successful leadership?

11. Identify five basic rules that have proven effective in leadership. Why do they make a difference in leadership?

12. Discuss Jeff Immelt's ten keys to great leadership. If you had to choose, which item would you say is the most important? Why?

13. The two leadership dimensions—concern for work and concern for people—have been found to be independent dimensions. What does this statement mean?

14. What type of leader would do best in a situation requiring high concern for work and low concern for people? High concern for work and people? Low concern for work and people? Explain your answers.

15. According to Fiedler, in which types of situations are task-oriented leaders most effective and in which types of situations are relationship-oriented leaders most effective? Be complete in your answer.

16. In what way is Fiedler's theory useful in the study of human relations?

17. What is meant by each of the following: 1,1 management, 9,1 management, 1,9 management, 5,5 management, and 9,9 management?

18. Of what value is the managerial grid in the study of human relations?

19. How do charismatic leaders lead their people? Give two examples.

20. How do transformational leaders differ from transactional leaders? Discuss three differences.

21. Identify seven principles of transformational leadership and describe each.

22. Identify the 4 Is that define a leader's charisma.

23. What is the difference between management and leadership?

24. What role does trust play in leadership?

25. Identify Iacocca's nine characteristics for successful leaders.

26. Describe a leader in the next decade. Identify the skills that will be required and tell how they differ from skills used by leaders two decades ago.

27. Identify some emerging leadership challenges. How can developing internal leaders meet these challenges?

28. What are some behaviors of leaders that can fuel lawsuits from employees?

29. How can effective leaders deal with hard-to-manage employees, such as heroes, meritocrats, bulldozers, pessimists, rebels, and home-run hitters?

30. What are some things you need to know to get ahead in your career?

31. How can developing alliances help your career?

32. How can you show you are a star? Why are these things important in promoting your career?

33. What can developing your own brand do for your career?

34. Identify some career assessment objectives that can serve as guidelines for deciding when to quit your job and seek new employment.

Connecting to the Real World

What is the role of a leader?

The purpose of this assignment is to better understand leadership. You are to interview a leader in your community or go online and find a CEO to research. This exercise will provide firsthand knowledge about leaders and leadership.

Procedure

1. Select a manager to interview who has at least five subordinates. The person can be employed at your college, or work in a business within your community, such as a bank, retail store, restaurant, car dealership, factory, service business, construction business, and so on.

2. **Or** you can go online and select a CEO from the list of the "Most Admired Businesses" compiled each year by *Fortune Magazine*.

3. Prepare a list of questions to use in the interview. In researching the CEO online, try to find answers to the same questions. The questions should focus on:
   a. What are the duties and responsibilities of the manager? In other words, what does the leader do?
   b. What kinds of managerial skills does the manager need to successfully do his/her job?
   c. What leadership skills does the manager need to do his/her job?
   d. What kind of leadership behaviors does the leader possess?
   e. What kind of assumptions does the leader make about his/her subordinates and how does that affect the culture of the organization?
   f. What is your assessment about the type of leadership the manager uses— charismatic or transformational?
   g. In the interview, ask the manager, "What do I need to know to be a good leader?"

4. Compile your answers and prepare a written report reflecting what you learned about leadership from the interview or online research.

CASE
Making Some Necessary Changes

Helen Knighter and Sam Schwede are assistant store managers for a large retail department store chain located throughout the midwestern and southern parts of the country. The chain was started by Mel Robinson back in 1903. He opened his first store, a mercantile store, in Kansas. It supplied ranchers in the area and travelers going west.

After Jane got to work and before she started working on her project, she went to see her boss, Helen Knighter. Jane stated, "My son is graduating from high school next Friday evening, and I would like to have three days off starting Wednesday of next week. I know the deadline is Friday for completing all the work on this project, but can it wait until the following week?" Her boss thought for a moment and replied that she understood. Helen said, "I think it will be fine; we can finish the project when you get back on Monday."

Knighter began her career with the firm three years ago. The company was hiring people for its human resources department, and Knighter's degree in psychology helped her land the job. Although most of the new hires were put into training and development, Knighter was assigned to counseling. In this job, she talked to store people who were having a variety of personal problems, from drinking to failure to interact effectively with customers. Knighter's job was to provide them assistance and guidance in straightening out their lives. During her first six-week trial period, she was assigned a number of cases and performed well. Her performance ratings were always in the top 10 percent of the department. Although Knighter liked her job, she realized that there was a limited career track for people in counseling. If she wanted to succeed with the company, she needed to get a job in one of the company's retail stores.

At the end of her second year, she applied for a position as assistant store manager and was assigned to a unit four months ago. Since then, Knighter has worked very hard to learn her job. So far she is doing well. Her employees seem to like her. They are easy to work with and they all know their jobs. Knighter enjoys being with people and interacting with them, as well as customers. She has a natural way of getting support from people. While her store's performance has been acceptable, it has not been within the top 10 percent of all the stores in the chain. That doesn't seem to bother her.

Last week, she attended a managerial training program. During one of the sessions, the participants measured their leadership style. Before interpreting this style, the trainer asked each of the participants to identify the style that he or she thought would be most effective for getting his or her particular jobs done. Knighter chose the 9,9 style. When her test results were interpreted, however, it turned out that Knighter was using the 1,9 style.

Sam Schwede was sitting next to her during the training program. Schwede has been with the company for only four months. He was hired directly out of college, where he majored in management and minored in marketing. Because Schwede has had little experience in retail management, his store manager sent him to the training program. Like Knighter, Schwede identified the 9,9 style as the one that would be ideal for him in managing the store personnel. However, his leadership style test indicated that he was using a 5,5 style.

Sam encourages his employees to do their best and to meet deadlines. He feels that if employees know what to do, they will do it willingly. Sam is comfortable in his job and really has no aspirations of becoming a regional manager. One thing that concerns Sam, however, is that on several occasions, three of his department managers failed to report to work and did not let Sam know. Sam feels they are taking advantage of him, but he really does not know what to do. When the department managers returned to work, Sam did not say anything to them for fear they would quit. Sam does not want his store's performance to fall below the acceptable range as set by the president of the company. So far, Sam's store is doing OK. Its performance always seems to fall within the acceptable range. Therefore, Sam does not focus on trying to reach a higher performance level.

When the trainer discussed the results of the test with both Knighter and Schwede, he pointed out that both will have to make changes to bring their current styles more into line with their desired style. "This won't be as hard as it seems," he told them, "but it will take some work on your part."

Case Questions
1. Describe the five basic styles on the managerial grid.
2. What changes will Knighter need to make? Give specific examples and tell why. How easy will it be for Knighter to change from her people-oriented counseling approach to having more concern for increasing sales and meeting sales quotas? What must she do? Be specific, and give examples.
3. What specifically must Schwede do to move his style of management into the 9,9 group? Explain. Give examples.
4. Will it be easier for Schwede or Knighter to make changes? Why? Which one will achieve his or her goals first?
5. How easy will it be for each one to maintain the 9,9 style of leadership?

Developing, Appraising, and Rewarding Employees

An effective leader develops productive subordinates. From a human relations viewpoint, every employee is affected by the way the organization recruits, develops, appraises, and rewards its personnel. In this chapter, the techniques, practices, and tools for completing these processes are explored, along with ways for linking performance and rewards, while dealing with discipline issues and methods.

LEARNING OBJECTIVES

1
Identify and describe the stages in the process for developing employees.

2
Discuss the performance appraisal cycle.

3
Identify four performance appraisal tools and tell how each can be used in appraising employees.

4
Describe four major problems associated with performance appraisal.

5
Explain ways of dealing with appraisal problems.

6
Identify ways for rewarding performance.

7
Examine the link between performance and rewards.

8
Describe the types of discipline used when performance is inadequate.

9
Discuss how time management can enhance your career.

A Diversified Workforce: The 55-and-Over Group—Productive and Still Going!

According to research, the organizations that are most successful in beating the competition are those that have adopted innovative human resource strategies that help them deal with myriad new human relations challenges. Among other things, these companies hire people regardless of age, religion, or sexual preference, and more importantly, senior management in these companies makes a commitment to meeting diversity challenges. As a result of their leading-edge recruiting, developing, appraising, and rewarding programs, they are able to outperform the competition.

The baby boomer generation is getting older and closer to retirement. "By 2015, the number of workers aged 55 and older will hover around 30 million, or 20 percent of the total labor force." About 76 percent of the baby boomers want to continue working after retirement, but only on their terms, reported a Merrill Lynch survey. These mature workers are well trained and can provide a wealth of experience to fill the void created by a shortage of younger workers. According to the U.S. Bureau of Labor Statistics, The sixteen to twenty-four aged group is projected to decline to 14.4 percent in 2050, down from 16.2 percent in 2005. The pool of the prime-age workforce, aged twenty-five to fifty-four, is projected to decline until 2020 and to grow slowly after that date.

After taking a hard look at the demographics of its customer base, Borders discovered that 50 percent of its books were bought by consumers over the age of 45. To reach these customers, Borders created a formal hiring and retention initiative aimed at older workers. Today, 16 percent of Borders' workforce is over the age of 50.

One benefit Borders has found to hiring older workers is that the turnover rate for workers over 50 is ten times less than those under 30. Older workers have a great passion to be connected to the community, which Borders provides. To attract and to retain these part-time workers, Borders has also added medical and dental benefits. Another program called "passport" allows employees to work half-time in one store in one part of the country and the other half at a different store. For example, during the winter months, they work in a warm climate, and in the summer months, they move across country and work in a cooler climate.

Another good example is McDonald's, which has developed special strategies for recruiting a diversified group of employees, especially the older employee. Many retired people who have an interest in working for McDonald's end up in units run by college graduates who are still in their 20s. When these managers interview older applicants, they are taught not to ask such standard questions as "What are your career goals?" Instead, interviewers focus on talking about how older candidates can share their skills and experiences with others, and they sell McDonald's as a career opportunity based on scheduling flexibility and the fact that older employees will not jeopardize their own social security earnings. Additionally, to minimize older workers' fears of moving into the workforce, McDonald's has set up a buddy system so that each older worker has someone to help him or her acclimate to the way things operate in the company. Workers can choose one restaurant position in which they are particularly interested, or they can choose to learn a variety of positions.

Do older employees make better employees? Statistics show that often they do. For example, only 3 percent of workers older than 50 change jobs in any given year, in contrast to 10 percent of the workforce at large and 12 percent of those between the ages of 25 and 34. Additionally, older workers are more careful: Studies show that although workers 50 years of age or older now make up 26.9 percent of the workforce, they suffer only 10 percent of all workplace injuries. They are also healthier. Research from the University of Southern California has found that people older than 50 tend to use less health care benefits than do workers with school-age children. This helps to explain why such employers as McDonald's actively seek the well-seasoned employee.

Companies like to retain their older employees because these people are extremely productive. For example, consider the case of Fort Worth–based Texas Refinery Corporation. Among its sales force of more than three thousand, the company employs more than five hundred people who are 60 years of age or older. The company works hard to retain these people for purely selfish reasons: They are productive. As the president says, "Age is immaterial to us. We put a great deal of value on life experience, and we think that in relationships, often an older, more experienced person probably has a distinct advantage." Many of the company's salespeople are hired as independent contractors who receive commission and benefits based on their sales. One employee, now in his 70s, has worked as a sales representative for over twenty years. He averages fifty hours per week, drives one hundred miles per day, and still climbs ladders to inspect roofs of industrial buildings.

Web sites to help older workers find employment are popping up on the Internet. Web sites such as www.alumniintouch.com, www.Selectminds.com, www.yourencore.com, www.retiredbrains.com, and www.Retireecareers.com are playing matchmaker between companies and retirees. More than 155 companies have established Alumniintouch databases, which let former employers identify suitable candidates from their own alumni for both short-term and permanent positions. These sites are proving to be popular. Retirees are posting résumés that focus on their skills, and companies are finding skilled workers. For example, for the past ten years, Chevron Corporation has been operating an alumni Web site, called Alumni and Bridges, where its retired employees can network. When Chevron needs to fill a position, the company will post the job opportunities and needs at the Web site, and then interested persons can post their résumés. Job applicants often can negotiate the number of days they want to work per week or the number of hours. Bringing former employees back brings value to the company through their prior knowledge and also sends the message to its current employees that it values work–life balance and shows the company is flexible. Though Chevron will not disclose the number of former employees it has brought back, former employees are found in positions at almost all levels within the company. Chevron feels that bringing back former employees is more cost effective than going through traditional recruiting channels. Southwest Airlines is another company that has created a Web site for employees and retirees. It is called "About Me."

Why are companies that hire older workers so productive? One reason is that these workers have excellent attendance. Another is that they are committed to quality. Other key reasons are solid performance records, practical knowledge, the ability to get along with others, solid experience, and emotional stability. All these assets add up to profit for the firm.

Identify and describe the stages in the process for developing employees.

Developing Employees

The development of employees begins when individuals enter the organization and does not end until they leave. From a human relations standpoint, this subject is important because every person in an organization will be affected by the ways in which the enterprise recruits and develops its people. This overall process typically involves:

1. Recruiting
2. Screening
3. Selecting
4. Orientation
5. Training
6. Appraising
7. Rewarding

Recruiting

Recruiting is the process of attracting qualified applicants to apply for available positions. Applicants can come from internal sources—employees who want to change positions or be promoted within the organization—and from external sources—those outside the organization. Examples of external sources are résumé databases, ads in newspapers and industry journals, job fairs, employee referrals, the firm's Web site, cold calls, recruiting firms, Internet job/career sites, and social networks such as Facebook, Twitter, and LinkedIn.

By developing a job profile that accurately defines the duties, responsibilities, and skills required for the job, the recruiter can begin the search for the person who has the appropriate technical and personal skills to do the job and can fit into the culture of the firm. "Recruiters need more than just a list of job skills to find candidates. They need to understand the culture and environment," says the senior vice president of human relations and employee relations at Adecco North America, an international employment firm headquartered in Melville, New York. "What you want is for the recruiter to find people who fit into your environment," says Cathy Fyock, president of Innovative Management Concepts, Crestwood, Kentucky.[1]

Technology, social networks, and the changing workforce have impacted the way companies currently recruit applicants. While the traditional methods of recruiting are still viable and used by most companies, many companies are relying more heavily on recruitment technology that has significantly evolved over the past ten years. These customer relationship management (CRM) tools use an applicant tracking system that can simultaneously post the requirements on hundreds of job boards and provide overnight search capabilities through defined criteria for increased efficiency to pinpoint the right talent.

As the economy slowed down during the last recession, businesses began looking for more cost-effective ways to recruit. They found that social media such as Twitter and LinkedIn can provide a source of applicants and also are inexpensive ways to recruit. For example, Organic, an advertising agency, places more than three-fourths of its job requirements solely on social media sites such as Twitter, LinkedIn, and Facebook and the company's Web site and posts the rest of its job requirements on traditional job boards such as Monster. By using a social network, recruiters can tap into a group of people who already are engaged in the company. Just how popular are social networks? An AfterCollege survey recently found that more than 82 percent of the 670 college students surveyed use social networks on a regular basis.[2]

Gen Yers will soon become the largest generation in the workforce; so, if the company wants to recruit and retain them, it is important to understand them. For example, one aspect is that salary is not the biggest bargaining tool for Gen Yers, time is more important. Research has revealed that many Gen Yers plan to remain engaged in work after they retire. Most of them do not want to work full time; they want part-time or contract work, and they want a flexible work schedule. Talent acquisition must be treated as a strategic part of the company's business plan. With the composition of the workforce changing, recruiters in the next decade will be challenged to look beyond the traditional sources of applicants. Getting a diversified and qualified pool of applicants is the job of the recruiter.

Finding the right recruiter is important. Recruiters must understand a company's value system and understand its intangible needs in order to fill positions with people who will fit into a company's culture and who can work effectively with other employees, creating good human relations within the company. This is not an inexpensive process. Each year, companies spend a vast amount of money on recruiting and staffing.

Screening and Selecting

Screening is the process of eliminating applicants who are unlikely to be successful on the job. **Selecting** is the process of determining which applicants will be offered jobs. The challenge is to screen the pool of applicants and select accurately the best individuals.

Organizations do this in a number of ways. One example is checking an applicant's education, previous employment, credit history, driving record, and criminal record.

Although this process can cost anywhere from $50 to $200 per applicant, a growing number of firms are finding that this is money well spent, because it reduces the likelihood that they will hire the wrong person.[3]

Job Interviews. Another useful screening and selecting tool is the *job interview*. Recruiters often use a number of human relations techniques in this process. One is the *structured interview*, in which all applicants are asked the same questions. This approach allows interviewers to make comparisons among job candidates based on responses to identical questions. The second is the *unstructured interview*, which focuses on specific objectives but allows the interviewer to determine the direction that the interview will take, thereby permitting interviewers to judge a wide range of candidate abilities.

In the interview process, not only should applicants be interviewed, but also applicants should ask their own questions to learn more about the job and firm. Figure 10.1 lists some common questions often asked of hiring managers. How many of these questions have you used in your past job interviews?[4]

Regardless of the type of interview used, in recent years, interviewers have begun relying more and more heavily on situational questions. A situational question describes a scenario—typically a problem likely to occur on the job—and asks applicants what they would do in that situation. These questions are designed to help evaluate how well applicants can express themselves, examine problem situations and offer recommendations, and think on their feet. Situational questions often are very effective in distinguishing those who have true self-confidence from those who merely express bravado in the interview situation.[5]

Attitude Testing. Attitude, and not a fixed set of skills or experiences, is what Southwest Airlines is looking for in applicants. The company needs employees with a "perfect blend of energy, humor, team spirit, and self-confidence to match Southwest's famously offbeat and customer-obsessed culture." Often applicants participate in group testing where applicants are graded on a scale ranging from "passive" to "active" to "leader."[6]

Nordstrom, a clothing retailer, and Planned Cos., a real estate services company, both use a hire-for-attitude and train-for-skills approach in selecting candidates. As a result, Planned Cos. has reduced its turnover rate to only 20 percent and has increased client retention rate to 95 percent. After much research, CEO Robert Francis of Planned Cos. designed a plan called IPLAN that measures five qualities of applicants. They are integrity, passion, longevity, positive attitude, and knowledge of tasks that are relevant to the job and the company's mission and role. Francis states that "a lot of people talk the talk, but don't have the attitude we are looking for." On the average, out of fifteen candidates, only one will be hired.[7]

Screening Tests. Another common approach is the use of *screening tests*. Various types of screening tests are available. One general category is the *demonstration test*, which is used to identify proficiency in a specific job-related skill, such as the ability to use a word-processing program to produce monthly reports. Another general category is the professional test, used to select individuals for such areas as managerial positions by identifying the individual's knowledge and familiarity with the technical and managerial aspects of a position. For example, at the Ritz-Carlton Hotel, customers pay a premium for the perfection they receive. To accomplish this perfection, employees must be hospitable, quality oriented, and attentive to detail, just to name a few requirements. The Ritz has been successful at selecting employees with these qualities by using a psychological test to determine the ideal profile for each job. The Ritz strives to not only meet but also to exceed customer expectations.[8]

Figure 10.1 Common Questions to Ask Hiring Managers

1. Could you explain the company's organizational structure?
2. What is the organization's plan for the next five years, and how does this department or division fit in?
3. What specific skills from the person you hire would make your life easier?
4. Will we be expanding or bringing on new products or new services that I should be aware of?
5. What are some of the problems that keep you up at night?
6. What are some of the skills and abilities you see as necessary for someone to succeed in this job?
7. What would be a surprising but positive thing the new person could do in the first ninety days?
8. What challenges might I encounter if I take on this position?
9. How does upper management perceive this part of the organization?
10. What are your major concerns that need to be immediately addressed in this job?
11. What do you see as the most important opportunities for improvement in the area I hope to join?
12. What are the attributes of the job that you'd like to see improved?
13. What are the organization's three most important goals?
14. What is your company's policy on attending seminars, workshops, and other training opportunities?
15. How do you see this position impacting the achievement of those goals?
16. What is the budget this department operates with?
17. What attracted you to working for this organization?
18. What committees and task forces will I be expected to participate in?
19. What have you liked most about working here?
20. How will my leadership responsibilities and performance be measured? By whom?
21. What are the day-to-day responsibilities I'll be assigned?
22. Are there any weaknesses in the department that you particularly want to improve?
23. What are the department's goals, and how do they align with the company's mission?
24. What are the company's strengths and weaknesses compared with the competition? (name one or two companies)
25. How does the reporting structure work here?
26. What are the preferred means of communication?
27. What goals or objectives need to be achieved in the next six months?
28. Can you give me an idea of the typical day and workload and the special demands the job has?
29. What are the forces that suggested the need for this position (if it is a new position)?
30. What areas of the job would you like to see improvement in with regard to the person who was most recently performing these duties?

In another example, the Bubba Gump Shrimp Company, a restaurant franchise, has implemented an employee development program for combating turnover and to groom top performers for leadership roles. Recruitment and selection are integrated functions of that program. During the behavioral-based interviews, the candidates are assessed on personality and aptitude. Related job experience is secondary to a person's attitude. The firm feels it can train people to do the jobs in a restaurant, but they cannot train employees to be kind, thoughtful of each other, or to interact well with guests.[9] Regardless of the type of screening test used, however, the company must be careful that it does not discriminate against an applicant.

Discriminatory Practices.   Inquiries that invade privacy provide a good example of discriminatory practices in hiring. Job applications and job interviews cannot delve into areas that are not job related. For example, the U.S. Supreme Court has ruled in *Shelton v. Tucker* that requiring public school teachers to disclose all organizations in which they have held membership in the previous five years is a violation of their right to association. In *Shuman v. City of Philadelphia*, a federal court found that inquiry into people's sexual conduct was a violation of their right to privacy. At the same time, however, there are forms of inquiry that do not violate privacy. For example, in *McKenna v. Fargo,* a federal court held that personality testing of firefighter applicants was designed to determine whether they could stand the pressures of the job and that, therefore, the city's interest in ensuring public safety outweighed the privacy rights of the applicant.[10]

Orientation

Orientation is the process of introducing new employees to their work group, their superior, and their tasks. Some of the most common items on an orientation agenda are a brief discussion of the company's history and general policies, a description of its services and products, an explanation of the organizational structure, a rundown of personnel policies, an explanation of general regulations, and a formal introduction to the group in which the individual will be working. In small organizations, much of this is handled orally; in large organizations, new employees typically are given booklets or brochures that explain and elaborate on the oral presentation.

Many important advantages are associated with an effective orientation. Among them are:

1. A reduction in the costs of instruction.
2. A lessening of anxiety regarding job failure.
3. A reduction in employee turnover.
4. A saving in time spent on assistance.
5. An increase in the employee's job satisfaction.

Numerous studies have been conducted on the benefits of orientation programs. For example, one group of new employees in a manufacturing firm was given a standard orientation and another group a more detailed, comprehensive orientation. It was found that the latter group exhibited 50 percent less tardiness and absenteeism, required 50 percent less training time, and had 80 percent less scrap work. Well-designed orientation programs do indeed pay off.

Training

Training of employees can take many forms. The first step, however, is to identify the objectives of the training: What does the individual need to know? The answer to this question will determine the appropriate training method.

Types of Employee Training.   The basic principal types of employee training are apprentice, vestibule, on-the-job, off-the-job, and virtual training.

- **Apprentice training** is given to people who are new to a job. The training is designed to teach them the rules for getting the work done and to provide an opportunity for applying these procedures. Apprentice training is done both on and off the job.

- **Vestibule training** takes place in an environment that simulates the actual workplace. For example, a trainee who is being taught to run a lathe will be sent to a special area of the plant where a trainer will provide close supervision. Once the trainee learns the job, he or she will then be sent to the shop floor and assigned to a lathe.

- **On-the-job training** is provided by the immediate superior and by fellow workers. It can be formal or informal in nature and usually consists of coaching the individual in the most effective ways of getting the job done. The major benefit of on-the-job training is that it teaches the individual the right way to do the job, bypassing the inefficiencies of trial and error.

- **Off-the-job training** is done away from the workplace. Often, it is used when people need to be trained in activities or ideas that are nontechnical in nature, such as effective communication, motivation, and leadership. Trainers who teach both theory and practice can best handle these instructional areas.

- **Virtual training** uses a computer and a well-designed learning program, more commonly known as e-learning. Self-paced components are often combined with computer-driven components.

These training methods help an individual to learn a job quickly and correctly. They assist in matching an individual to a job and improve a person's chance of receiving a good performance appraisal.

Training Developments.   A number of interesting developments have occurred in the training arena in recent years. One is the increased scope and depth of training that companies now offer to their employees. According to the American Society for Training & Development (ASTD) in Alexandria, Virginia, the average company spent $1,068 in 2008, which was down 3.8 percent from 2007, on training per eligible employee. This drop in training expenditures reflected the slowed economy of 2008. Even in one of the worst economic conditions in the United States, organizations have spent $137.07 billion on employee learning and development in 2008. Employees received 36.3 hours of formal learning in 2008, a drop from 37.4 hours in 2007.[11] In 2009, nearly 60 percent of employee training took place in traditional instructor-led physical classrooms.[12]

Another development is the growing gaps in skills among workers, which is resulting in new challenges for companies. Training and learning professionals are expected to take the lead in redeveloping skills in the gap areas. If this fails to happen, businesses will find themselves ill-equipped to grow because the skills required to meet demand for growth are in short supply. The role of training has become critical and it must deliver expected results.[13]

Many companies are waking up to the fact that employee skill gaps are getting wider. For example, Caterpillar Inc., a company that makes tractors, earthmovers, and other heavy construction equipment, realized that its management needed more training if the company was going to fend off domestic and foreign competitors. While it has been in business for over eighty-two years, its managers are being held accountable like never before. The company realized that identifying and developing leaders are key to its growth and survival.[14]

Yet, another development is the use of diversity training, which is designed to teach managers how to deal with America's changing workforce. Demographic data projected by the U.S. Bureau of Labor Statistics show that the number of women in the workforce will remain about the same from 2010 to 2020, and will drop slightly by 2030. Women are an important part of the labor force, but many managers are still not comfortable managing women. Many managers are also accustomed to older workers retiring. Now that mandatory retirement is a thing of the past in most organizations, managers must learn how to supervise older workers. The same is true for people of color. African American, Hispanic, and Asian American employees are entering the workforce in unprecedented numbers. Managers must be better trained to understand, motivate, and lead these employees.

Over the past few years, there has been an increase in the number of systems developed for training managers and workers. Some companies integrate several systems to create a whole new training system that better meets the needs of that company. The combination training programs described later in this section speak to that idea. A few of the many systems on the market are described in the next few paragraphs.

Virtual Classroom.   After the events of 9/11 and again during the recession of 2008, the economy slowed down and budgets became tight. Money budgeted for training was cut, and companies had to find new ways to train employees. The virtual classroom, commonly known as e-learning, gained momentum and is predicted to be the vehicle for training in the future. Advantages of e-learning are flexibility learning and cost effectiveness, provided the program is designed correctly. "The content must be measurable and performance based. People have to know going in what they are expected to learn, how they are expected to apply that on the job, and how the experience will benefit them and the company."[15] Grant Thornton, a global accounting, tax, and business advisory firm in Chicago, believes that training is a strategic tool for achieving business results. Its management believes that "daily learning is a key to competitiveness and profit." The firm focuses on building a continuous learning culture. Through the Grant Thornton University, a Web-based corporate learning portal, employees have "access to more than one thousand hours of self-paced training, live Webcasts, and virtual-classroom courses." The learning paths are broken down by competencies and skill requirements, and then tied to job performance. The firm believes the blended model of combining self-paced modules with live virtual-classroom components is critical for learner success.[16]

Pathfinder Training Program.   Cisco Systems, a producer of hardware and software for routing traffic on the Internet, "is changing, experimenting, and rethinking the way it recruits, hires, and trains its employees and how it will maintain its winning culture." Cisco is using a computer software program called Pathfinder to fill positions within the firm. "The software allows Cisco employees to search for jobs that interest them and contact the supervisors directly to set up interviews." This program allows Cisco to shift its talent to the most promising places within the firm and to develop skills that facilitate Cisco's goal of relying on internally nurtured talent.[17]

The Saba System.   Honeywell, one of the largest companies in America, is challenged to find talented employees. The company rolled out what may be the world's learning management system, which serves about 111,000 employees on five continents. The corporate director of learning technology and operations stated the system helps Honeywell "make sure we have the right people with the right skills doing the right jobs at the right times." The Saba system can help measure, track, and deliver the training. For example, the system helps transfer the knowledge needed for the "20- to 30-something crowd" to fill positions of retired employees.[18]

Communities of Practice.   Communities of practice, a training system used by the American soldiers while training the Afghan and Iraqi armies, is fast becoming a vital training tool for businesses. It allows employees with similar jobs or interests to get advice and to share best practices. In business, it is a way to capture the knowledge about processes, customers, or corporate culture possessed by employees who are nearing retirement so they can pass it along to younger employees. Interaction and discussion are key factors to its success. The communities of practice system must be integrated into what employees already are using, such as training and networking, and it must be contextually relevant. The communities must be nurtured and facilitated; places where people can put something out and also receive something back. The communities must be easy to use and be designed for engagement. "It is a way to share knowledge and build networks among people who might otherwise never connect."[19]

Human Capital (Talent) Management Systems.   "Under talent management systems, HR managers can access which skills and training a new hire needs, sign the employee up for live or online classes, check test scores, create training and other goals for performance reviews and monitor whether they are being met, and, finally, evaluate if and when the employee is ready for promotion." For example, Pitney Bowes, a postage and mailing company, has implemented a human capital management system that integrates learning, performance management, succession planning, and knowledge management. The change toward more integrated learning and performance management is being driven by technological advances, competition, vendors, suppliers, and industry analysts.[20]

Moodle Learning Management System.   Moodle is an open-source learning management system that can be downloaded free and operates with most other training-related software systems on the market. Subaru of America has embraced this system for training its management. Moodle allows the company to develop online course content and deliver it to its dealers via the company's intranet. Subaru has incorporated an interactive communities-of-practice system within the Moodle platform. The dealers love the system because they can talk and share information and develop best practices.[21]

In-House Training Programs.   Another development in the training arena is the creation of in-house programs. In many cases, enterprises rely on colleges and universities for assistance, although some of the larger firms are now becoming self-reliant. For example, Walmart ended its training relationship with a major university and took its Walton Institute in-house. Company personnel now train all new store managers. Walmart has implemented a twenty-week training program for all managers, assistant managers, and new management trainees. A designated store in each district conducts the training. Likewise, Mervyns, a retail chain store, and McDonald's a fast-food restaurant, both have their own universities for training personnel.

Combination Training Programs.   More common, however, are firms that combine in-house and university-linked training for their people. As Motorola's corporate change agent and a world-renowned corporate university, Motorola University brings time-tested and highly refined business improvement practices to leading organizations around the world. Motorola University has full-time professionals who provide annual training to employees. At the lower levels of the company, these programs extend from one day to fifteen days and include a wide range of topics from technical (manufacturing, operations, and engineering) to behavioral (time management, effective communication, and leadership). At the upper levels, Motorola has a senior executive program that is conducted annually for top managers worldwide. Topics range widely and, in the past, have dealt with the challenge of Asian competition, rethinking offshore manufacturing strategies, and developing more effective customer-driven programs. At the same time, Motorola has a formal agreement with Northwestern University's Kellogg School of Management to deliver a two-week development program for senior executives, and it has licensed community colleges to teach Motorola courses.

The learning philosophy at Motorola University reveals the commitment Motorola has made to training and to its employees.

> Motorola has a time honored and valued tradition of commitment to the growth and development of its people. Continuous learning is a strategic investment that represents one of the only remaining sustainable sources of competitive advantage. To maximize our investment, employee development and learning must be aligned with our business strategies and needs. All Motorola managers have a clear obligation to budget strategic development funds in areas that yield the greatest return for our business and in employees they wish to attract, develop, and retain.

> Motorola managers and employees are in a crucial developmental partnership to select the developmental opportunities that best meet the unique needs of the business and the associate. Employees have an essential responsibility to ensure that their personal competence and capability is growing to meet the increasing performance challenges of our changing business environment. To achieve this end they must create and enact development plans that align with business needs, meet their personal development goals, and are financially supported by the business. Managers have a duty to evaluate, approve, plan, and budget for the development and learning needs in their respective business units.[22]

The whole purpose of training is to increase employee performance by ensuring that all employees know what is expected of them and how they can progress and develop. A firm must design its training system to meet both the employee's and the employer's needs in the most cost-effective way possible. In many cases, as in Coca-Cola, the workers learn by doing. Workers are assigned to task forces where they develop their problem-solving skills.[23]

Ill-Prepared Workforce.   A recent report compiled by the Society for Human Resource Management, the American Society for Training & Development, and Corporate Voices for Working families revealed that half the employers surveyed provide remedial training to improve the employees' writing, math, and problem-solving deficiencies. The survey indicated, however, that the majority report less than desirable results. The low scores may be linked to a mismatch between the employees' needs and the employers' needs. The survey also found sizeable gaps in training for critical thinking and creativity skills, which are crucial to companies' ability to compete in the global marketplace. Another gap appeared in training programs designed to increase awareness of ethics and social responsibility, with less than one-fourth of the companies offering it. The research also found that some companies have decided not to hire and train new entrants who are unprepared. For example, for customer service positions, American Express uses a detailed hiring profile based on skills in math, computing, reading, and memory retention, as well as applicants' aptitude for teamwork and communication skills. "By eliminating the need for remedial training, American Express can focus on career development instead."[24]

What can business do to improve workforce readiness? If business wants a better prepared workforce, it needs to communicate to the public that new workers must come prepared with both basic and applied skills, and business must work closely with educators on developing workforce readiness skills through mentoring, internships, and other learning opportunities.[25]

Training That Should Never Be Cut.   Training is more important than ever. Many employers have come under attack by government enforcement agencies because they have done a poor job of training their employees on the laws and what type of behavior is acceptable in the workplace. To alleviate this crisis in the future, companies should include in their training such topics as the prevention of unlawful harassment and discrimination, prevention of workplace violence, prevention of wage-and-hour law violations, and adherence to the organization's code of conduct.[26]

Appraising Subordinates

Every effective organization wants to reward its best performers and ensure that they remain with the enterprise. How does one separate the best from the average or poor performers? The answer is through a well-designed performance appraisal process. If this process is carried out properly, and the employees realize that management intends to be equitable in its reward system, employee morale will be high and teamwork can be both developed and nurtured by the enterprise.

To understand fully the performance appraisal process, we must:

1. Examine the performance appraisal cycle, which describes how the entire evaluation process should be conducted.
2. Examine the appraisal tools that can be used in carrying out the evaluation.
3. Compare the attributes of appraisal techniques.
4. Learn to recognize the problems that can accompany a performance appraisal and the ways to reduce or avoid them.

 CHECK YOUR UNDERSTANDING

In developing employees, what is the most important factor in each phase of the process?
a. Recruiting _____
b. Screening and selecting _____
c. Orientation _____
d. Training _____
e. Appraising subordinates _____

Discuss the performance appraisal cycle.

The Performance Appraisal Cycle.   Performance appraisal is a four-step process known as the **performance appraisal cycle**.

First, there must be some *established performance standards* that specify what the worker is supposed to be doing. These standards are often quantified; that is, the machinist is supposed to process twenty-five pieces an hour or the administrative assistant is expected to type an average of sixty words per minute. Such performance standards establish a basis against which to evaluate the individual.

Second, there must be *a method of determining individual performance.* To say "Barry does a good job" or "Kathleen is an asset to the department" is not a sufficient measure of individual results. The organization needs appraisal instruments that measure desired performance. In the case of the machinist, we would want to consult daily output records to determine whether his or her average is twenty-five pieces per hour; or in the case of the administrative assistant, he or she is expected to key an average of sixty words per minute or produce a specific number of pages in a typical day.

Figure 10.2 Performance Appraisal in Action

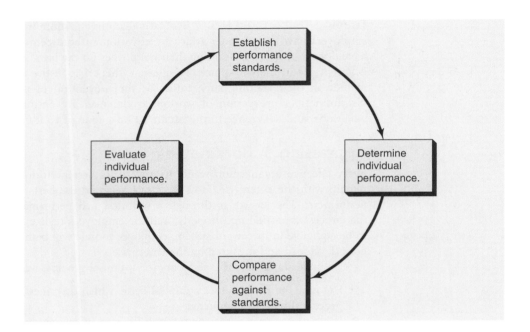

Of course, appraisals will not be conducted on a daily basis, but if proper evaluation instruments are designed, output can be recorded periodically and evaluated later.

Third, there must be some *comparison of performance against standards.* At some point, usually once annually, the individual's work record should be compared with the standards set for the job.

Fourth, an *evaluation of performance* should be made on the basis of the comparison. This process can take several forms. Sometimes, the boss meets with the subordinate, reviews progress in general terms, and then announces the basic direction for the upcoming year. At other times, the manager has a detailed work report on the subordinate and is able to pinpoint strengths and weaknesses in great detail. In either case, this step is not finished before the manager has told the subordinate how well he or she is doing. The more definitive the manager is, the more useful the feedback will be in directing and motivating the subordinate. Once this fourth step is completed, the manager and the subordinate are ready to establish performance standards for the next evaluation period. Building on current successes (and sidestepping failures), the two can determine the department's needs and the subordinate's abilities and then work to mesh them. This overall performance appraisal cycle, presented in Figure 10.2, provides the primary basis for any evaluation program.

 ## CHECK YOUR UNDERSTANDING

What is the correct order in the performance appraisal cycle? Put number 1 in front of the first step and 2 in front of the second step, and so on.

_____ Evaluate individual performance
_____ Determine individual performance
_____ Establish performance standards
_____ Compare performance against standards

Identify four performance appraisal tools and tell how each can be used in appraising employees.

Performance Appraisal Tools. Many kinds of appraisal tools can be used to evaluate employee performance. Four common appraisal tools are:

1. Graphic rating scales
2. The paired comparison method
3. Management by objectives
4. 360-degree evaluations

Graphic Rating Scales. The most widely used of all performance appraisal tools are **graphic rating scales**. One major reason is undoubtedly the ease with which they can be developed and applied. Figure 10.3 illustrates such a scale. In the chart, the factors on which the employee is to be evaluated are identified and the degrees of evaluation are spelled out. The rater, usually the subordinate's boss, has merely to read each of the factors and then check the appropriate box. By totaling the value associated with every factor degree (i.e., from 1 for unsatisfactory up to 5 for exceptional), the rater can obtain a total score for the subordinate.

Figure 10.3 Illustration of a Graphic Rating Scale (Partial Form)

Employee _____ Date _____

Department _____ Rater _____

Rating / Factor	1 — **Unsatisfactory** Totally inadequate	2 — **Fair** Meets minimal requirements	3 — **Good** Exceeds minimal requirements	4 — **Superior** Always does above the basic job requirements	5 — **Exceptional** Is consistently outstanding
Quantity The volume of output produced					
Quality The accuracy and thoroughness of the output					
Supervision The need for direction, correction, and/or advice					
Attendance Dependability, regularity, and promptness					

Table 10.1
A Comparison of
Rating Levels

Five Levels

Advantages	Disadvantages
Provide for the finest distinctions in performance	May be harder for supervisors to communicate how to attain higher performance levels
More consistent with bell-curve distribution	Typically only four levels are used
Most managers believe they can discriminate among five levels of performance	Middle rating usually perceived negatively—as average, or mediocre, or a "C" student
Consistent with familiar "A–F" school-grading model	May encourage central tendency
Most familiar rating scheme; less training required	

Four Levels

Advantages	Disadvantages
Do not include a middle rating that may be perceived as "average"	May not provide a way to distinguish between those who can improve and those who should be terminated
Eliminate "central tendency" rating error	May skew raters in a positive or negative direction
May skew raters in a positive or negative direction	Typically, only three levels are used
Provide for finer distinctions than a three-level scale	

Three Levels

Advantages	Disadvantages
Supervisors find it easy to categorize performance into three categories	May not provide fine-enough distinctions in performance
Supervisors tend to be more consistent if given fewer choices; higher reliability	Managers frequently alter system by adding pluses and minuses
Some jobs may be better appraised on a "pass/fail" basis	Do not distinguish between those who can improve and those who should be terminated
Only three levels of performance can be proved empirically	Typically only two levels are used
Middle rating implies expected performance, not average performance	Do not allow for identifying the truly exceptional 2–5 percent
More consistent with TQM principles	

Each rating level communicates a different message and has a different outcome, so what is the best number of rating levels to use on a rating scale? To illustrate the differences among the levels, Table 10.1 gives some advantages and disadvantages for five levels, four levels, and three levels.

Figure 10.4 Paired Comparison Method for Rating Employees

On the Basis of Work Quantity

	Employees Being Rated				
As compared to:	**Anderson**	**Brown**	**Carpenter**	**Davis**	**Evans**
Anderson		−	+	−	+
Brown	+		+	+	+
Carpenter	−	−		−	+
Davis	+	−	+		+
Evans	−	−	−	−	

↑

Evans has the highest
ranking for work quantity.

On the Basis of Work Quantity

	Employees Being Rated				
As compared to:	**Anderson**	**Brown**	**Carpenter**	**Davis**	**Evans**
Anderson		−	+	+	+
Brown	+		+	+	+
Carpenter	−	−		+	+
Davis	−	−	−		−
Evans	−	−	+	+	

↑

Davis has the highest
ranking for work quality.

Note: A plus (+) indicates higher than and a minus (−) indicates lower than (the coworker against whom an individual is being compared). The individual with the greatest number of pluses is the one with the highest ranking.

The Paired Comparison Method.   Many managers regard the **paired comparison method** as superior to the graphic rating scale because it is more discriminating in its approach. Rather than just providing an overall evaluation of a person, in which each worker might end up receiving an exceptional score, this method compares each employee to every other one in the group with respect to a number of factors (see Figure 10.4). In this way, although everyone may be doing good work, it is still possible to determine who is best and who is poorest. It is no longer simply a matter of how well a person is performing the job but of how the individual compares with all the other workers. In Figure 10.4, work quality and quantity are measured. A rater may end up with five to ten paired comparison forms before compiling the scores and getting an overall evaluation for each employee. Regardless of the number of factors rated, however, only one person ranks at the top of the list when all the ratings are completed.

Management by Objectives: Management by objectives (MBO) is an overall appraisal system used at all levels of the employment hierarchy. Many organizations prefer MBO because it is systematic, all encompassing, and easy to understand. Because of its great popularity, we shall study it in much greater depth than we have the other appraisal tools. Before doing so, however, let us define the term. **Management by objectives** is a process in which the superior and the subordinate jointly identify common goals, define the subordinate's major areas of responsibility in terms of expected results (objectives), and use these measures as guides for operating the unit and assessing the contribution of each member. It is a goal-setting process initiated by Peter Drucker, a management guru.

How MBO Works. The MBO process consists of six basic steps. Figure 10.5 illustrates the typical cycle employed in implementing it.

First, the manager identifies the goals that his or her unit should pursue over the next evaluation period. These goals can often be expressed in terms of profit, revenues, margins, competitive position, or employee relations.

Second, the organization must be clearly described. Who is in the department? What does each person do? Having answered these questions, the manager then reviews each individual's work, noting what can be expected of each person.

Third, the manager establishes objectives for each worker for the next evaluation period. This is achieved by:

1. Asking each subordinate to list the objectives that he or she wants to complete in the next year and setting a date for discussing them.
2. Making a personal list of objectives that the manager would like to see the subordinate attain.

Figure 10.5 The Basic MBO Cycle

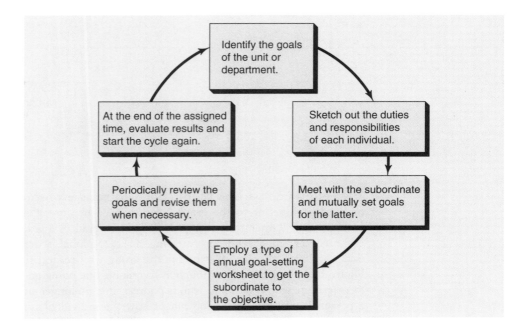

3. Reviewing both lists and then jointly agreeing on a final set of objectives for the subordinate.

4. Typing two copies of the final draft of objectives, one each for the superior and the subordinate.

5. Making oneself available to help the subordinate accomplish the assigned goals.

Fourth, an annual goal-setting worksheet is designed to help the subordinate reach his or her objectives. Figure 10.6 is an example. As can be seen in the figure, the worksheet is divided into three parts: objectives, major steps for achieving the planned objectives, and the way in which progress is to be evaluated—in short, what is to be done, how it will be accomplished, and the methods that will be used to show how well it is being accomplished.

Fifth, during the year, each subordinate's goals are checked to determine whether the objectives are being reached. In particular, the manager needs to know how close the person is coming to attaining these targets, whether any of the goals need to be amended, and what kinds of assistance the person requires to reach the goals.

Sixth, results are measured against goals. Near the end of the MBO cycle, which commonly coincides with the budget year, the superior asks each subordinate to prepare a brief statement of performance. Then the two meet to review how well the subordinate has done and to establish objectives for the next budget year.

Advantages of MBO.   MBO has proved to be a very popular approach because it is both comprehensive and easy to understand. One *of its primary advantages is the attention given to the subordinate in the goal-setting process.* Rather than the individual being told what goals he or she should pursue, the manager and subordinate now engage jointly in a give-and-take process.

Another advantage of this approach is that *MBO places a strong emphasis on quantifiable objectives that are tied to a time dimension.* For example, performance standards are stated in specific, measurable terms, such as percentages, dollars, ratios, costs, and quality. If a manager is going to reduce tardiness, this goal will be stated in a percentage: "We will cut tardiness by 18 percent." In addition, a period will be set for the attainment of the objective. Expanding the foregoing statement, then, we can bring together the quantifiable goal and the time dimension in this way: "We will cut tardiness by 18 percent within the first six months of the upcoming fiscal year." Some of the following might be objectives for other major areas of organizational performance:

- Raise return on investment to 15 percent within the next four operating quarters.
- By December 31, complete the management control reporting system for all operating decisions.
- Install a new computerized information system by April 30.

Note that each objective is written in such a way that what is to be attained (the goal) and when it is to be attained (the time dimension) are clearly stated.

A third advantage of MBO is *that there is a concentration on the organization's key goals.* Each manager ties his or her unit's objectives to the goals of the organization at large. As a result, all units are working in the same direction.

In the MBO approach, emphasis is given to working with a small, manageable number of objectives. The number of objectives assigned to each person usually is limited to five or six. The accomplishment of these objectives will satisfy the key goals assigned to the manager in a specific work area. When these objectives are accomplished, the manager is effective. Limiting subordinates' objectives makes it easier for employees to channel their energy toward accomplishing the objectives that fit into the goals assigned to their specific work area and for the superior to monitor progress and to review performance.

Figure 10.6 An Annual Goal-Setting Worksheet (Partial Form)

NAME Hal Lymer	DATE January 2, 2014

POSITION Superintendent of Engine Manufacturing	SUPERVISOR Les Rodgers

Objectives	Major Steps for Achieving Planned Objectives	The Way in Which Progress Will Be Evaluated
Increase the number of production hours in the engine departments from 30,000 to 40,000.	Conduct a study to determine the causes for the bottleneck operations in engine assembly and make necessary changes.	Progress will be measured in terms of shipments reported on the monthly cost control report.
	Reduce machining time on the planer type mill by employing an assistant operator during peak periods.	
	Add three floating supervisors to give round-the-clock supervision to the bottleneck operations.	
Reduce supervisory overtime by cross-training supervisors.	Cross-train supervisors in the large-machine, small-machine, and engine assembly departments.	In the first 6 months of last year, forepersons and assistant forepersons in engine manufacturing worked an average of 20 of 26 Sundays. The target for the first 6 months of this year is to reduce this to no more than 15 of 26 Sundays.
	Determine how general supervisors can be used as substitutes for forepersons and assistant forepersons. Use these general forepersons on at least four Sundays per calendar quarter.	
Reduce scrap cost from 4 percent to 3 percent of production.	In conjunction with quality assurance, have manager conduct a study to identify the specific causes of scrap losses. Determine ways to measure scrap and rework costs by shift.	Measure progress in terms of scrap and rework costs reported on the monthly cost control report.
	Determine ways to measure scrap and rework costs by shift.	
	Put together a task force for determining alternative ways to reduce this scrap.	
	Develop an incentive plan for rewarding the shift with the best scrap record.	
	Determine the feasibility of disciplining employees who cause major scrap losses.	

MBO helps to coordinate the activities of the units by linking each with those above, below, and on the same level. For example, Mary is in charge of department B. When, to determine her objectives, she meets with her boss, Ted, who is in charge of a group of departments, Ted integrates her objectives with his own. He will do the same for the other departments, A and C, that report to him, as will Mary with the subordinates in her department who report to her.

Another advantage of MBO is that *it encourages the manager to delegate time-consuming activities and to devote his or her energies to overall planning and control.* Using MBO, the manager knows what everyone is supposed to be doing. The initial delegation of authority is very systematic. Additionally, MBO helps the manager to evaluate subordinates and to learn what each can do well and what each does poorly. With this information, the manager can then determine what work to delegate to each subordinate in the future. Who does job A well? Who is best assigned to job B? Who is the best performer on job C? In delegating these tasks, the manager is able to pass off much of the busywork that he or she has performed in the past, because now the manager knows better the strengths of the subordinates. Additionally, the manager's boss will encourage such delegation. One of the primary benefits of MBO is its philosophy of delegating busywork and concentrating one's time on "think-work." An effective top manager will not let the subordinate manager delegate work that should be handled personally while hanging on to time-consuming activities.

Overall, MBO has been accepted in many organizations. In particular, managers like its systematic approach and the emphasis it gives to the key managerial functions of planning, organizing, and controlling. In both public and private sectors, it holds a great deal of promise for the future.

360-Degree Evaluation Reviews.   In recent years, a growing number of companies have begun using 360-degree evaluation reviews.[27] These companies are Alcoa, Bank of America, Hewlett-Packard, Johnson & Johnson, Procter & Gamble, and Shell Oil.[28] These reviews are carried out not just by the individual's superior but also by the person's subordinates, peers, work group, and others with whom he or she comes in frequent contact.[29] One of the biggest fears people have about 360-degree feedback is that a group of anonymous people will determine their raises, promotions, and standing. Therefore, companies must be diligent about designing an appropriate approach to implementing a 360-degree feedback process. The steps in a 360-degree process are:

1. The employee and manager agree on the list of individuals who will be used to evaluate the employee, and each of these individuals receives an evaluation form.
2. The evaluators complete the forms and return them to the managers.
3. The manager collects and summarizes the data.
4. The manager and the subordinate meet and discuss the results and agree on a developmental plan of action that will help the employee address any problems as well as expand his or her knowledge, experience, and other job-related skills and abilities.
5. The 360-degree summary and action plan are used to evaluate the individual, and these become part of the employee's personnel file.
6. The action plan is used as a guide in providing the individual with overall leadership direction and serves as a basis for the next 360-degree evaluation.

A key part of the evaluation process is the determination of how well the individual has performed during the measurement period. The focus is on what the person accomplished, and this result is expressed in terms of a 1, 2, or 3 rating:

1 = excellent performance

2 = fully satisfactory performance

3 = significant improvement needed

Coupled with this is an evaluation of the means that were used in accomplishing these goals. This part of the evaluation is based on how others view the person's company business values, including vision, accountability, receptivity to change, teamwork, empowerment, involvement, energy, and speed. In this case, there are three evaluations—A, B, and C:

A = significant strength

B = some development needs exist

C = significant development is required

The two sets of ratings (1, 2, or 3 and A, B, or C) then are brought together in a nine-block matrix. Figure 10.7 provides an illustration. This matrix is used to summarize an individual's strengths and identify development needs.

As noted earlier, the final step in the 360-degree evaluation review is the creation of a development action plan. This consists of a dialogue between the manager and the employee regarding long- and short-term development needs and the options available for meeting these needs. This overall development process is linked very closely to the firm's business strategy so that all new skills, knowledge, and training will help the

Figure 10.7 General Electric's Nine-Block Matrix

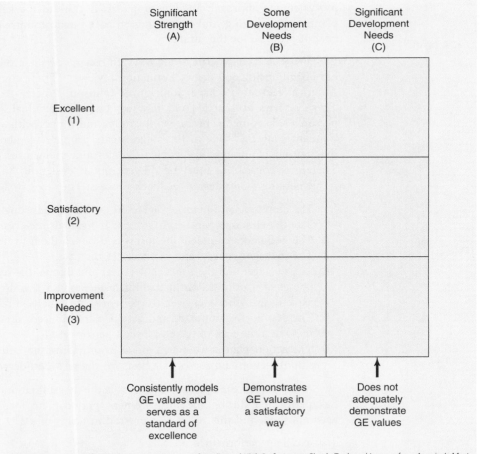

Source: Adapted from Richard M. Hodgetts, *Measures of Quality and High Performance: Simple Tools and Lessons from America's Most Successful Companies* (New York: American Management Association, 1998), chapter 6.

individual do a better job of meeting both personal and team goals. In turn, these goals will assist the operating unit in attaining its goals.

On the basis of the development meeting, an action plan is formulated. This plan is a result of agreement between the employee and the manager regarding the performance areas (outputs and competencies) that need improvement or that hold high payoff potential for the employee's long-term career goals. The two individuals also discuss ways in which the employee can obtain any assistance that is needed. Examples are coaching, one-to-one instruction, assignment changes, task-force work, project leadership, classes, courses, workshops, and personal reading assignments of books and articles.

Once the action plan has been formulated, it is the employee's responsibility to take charge and begin implementing the agreed-on steps. The manager, of course, remains available to assist, but it is the employee who ultimately is responsible for his or her development. Then, at the end of the agreed-on time, the 360-degree evaluation process begins again.[30]

One reason that 360-degree reviews have proven to be so popular is that they help organizations more effectively deal with performance evaluations. For example, a Korn/Ferry–Columbia Business School study found that minority executives report that they are often treated harshly or unfairly by whites,[31] which can negatively affect their career opportunities. The objectivity of 360-degree reviews can help to eliminate this problem.

Coaching and goal setting are important components of the 360-degree feedback process. Research by DecisionWise, Inc., indicates that some form of coaching should accompany the 360-degree feedback process in order for it to be effective. For example, 92 percent of those who received coaching felt that the 360-degree feedback process was effective, whereas only 34 percent of those who did not receive coaching felt the feedback process was effective. Two-thirds of those who did not receive coaching did not set goals, while 87 percent of those who set goals felt the 360-degree process was effective. Overall, 94 percent of those who received coaching and set goals felt the 360-degree feedback process was effective. The research concluded that coaching greatly increases the effectiveness of the 360-degree feedback process, creates a personal development plan, and allows employees to receive regular follow-up leading to real improvement.[32]

 ## CHECK YOUR UNDERSTANDING

Match the appraisal rating tool with its description.

Appraisal Rating Tool	Description
1. Graphic rating scales	_____ The results of several evaluators culminate in a development action plan.
2. Paired comparison method	_____ The factors and rating levels are defined.
3. Management by objectives	_____ Employees are compared to others in the group.
4. 360-degree evaluations	_____ A system of goal setting that includes all employees.

Performance Appraisal Problems

Performance appraisal helps the manager to identify those who should be rewarded for adequate or superior performance and those who should not. However, such an approach can yield erroneous results if the appraisal form is designed improperly or if the rater is biased.

Clarity of the Appraisal Form.   One of the most common appraisal problems relates to clarity of the form. If every appraiser does not have an identical interpretation of what the factors and their ratings mean, uniformity is impossible. In Figure 10.3, for example, quantity, quality, supervision, and attendance are defined briefly, as are the ratings for each. But how does the appraiser determine when a person should get a rating of fair and when he or she should be rated as good? Unless the factors are defined precisely and this information is made available to the evaluator, an employee might be rated fair by one manager and good by another. The situation is even worse if the factors or their ratings are not described at all. If each manager is using only his or her own judgment, performance evaluations will not be uniform throughout the organization.

To overcome this problem, it is necessary to describe on the evaluation form the factors on which the employee will be evaluated and to what degree and to ensure that the appraisers apply a uniform interpretation. When is an individual's performance to be considered good? When is it to be rated superior? Many organizations find it very helpful to schedule a meeting of all the people who are rating a particular group of employees, such as salespeople, to discuss the evaluation form and determine the ground rules for the appraisal. In this way, all employees doing similar work can be rated in uniform terms.

The Halo Effect.   A **halo effect** occurs when the appraiser gives a worker the same rating on all factors, regardless of actual performance. For example, the manager has noticed that Paul is occasionally late for work. The manager believes that Paul does not care much for his job, and this impression carries over to the manager's rating of Paul. Regardless of how much work Paul does or how high the quality of the work output is, he continually receives a fair rating. Conversely, Mandy is always on time for work and has a very pleasant personality. This biases the manager's rating of her, and she is always rated excellent in all categories. Many firms find that a training program can alleviate this problem by helping the manager to identify these built-in biases and work to correct them.

Central Tendency.   A second common rater-generated problem is that of **central tendency**, in which everyone receives an average rating, regardless of how effective he or she has been. For example, Andy is one of the department's poorest workers and Karl is one of the best, yet their performance ratings are always identical. The manager continually rates both as good. Such an approach helps Andy, who should be given a rating of fair, but it punishes Karl, who should be given a rating of superior.

One of the greatest problems faced by managers who rate their people this way is that the best workers begin looking for new jobs. After all, their chances for increased salary or promotion are being severely limited. Another problem is that the evaluations are now useless. The organization cannot rely on them to identify those who should be advanced and those who should be terminated. One way of overcoming this problem is to use a paired comparison evaluation or an MBO approach, in which results are quantified or described in such terms that the manager is required to give each person a more precise rating.

Leniency.   A third common rater-generated problem is that of **leniency**, in which managers give all their people the highest possible rating. Here again, failure to distinguish between those doing an outstanding job and those doing a poor job results in inaccurate ratings. Many organizations in recent years have worked around this problem through the use of a paired comparison evaluation.

Lonnie Harvey, Jr., of the Jesclon Group in Rock Hill, South Carolina, has identified five primary causes that can affect grade inflation when completing appraisals.

1. The organization has not clearly defined to managers and employees what "good" or "expected" behavior looks like.
2. Neither managers nor employees are properly trained on how to measure and report performance results.
3. It is not unusual for both managers and organizations to make the mistake of viewing and using a performance appraisal process as a means of rewarding employees and staying in their good graces.
4. Managers have not experienced a model of proper performance appraisal as a step in a comprehensive employee development system.
5. The final results are not challenged. Appraisals should be reviewed by another party and/or compared with other employees.[33]

 CHECK YOUR UNDERSTANDING

Match the term with the statement.

Term	Statement
1. Halo effect	_____ Everyone receives an average rating.
2. Central tendency	_____ Everyone receives the highest possible rating.
3. Leniency	_____ All evaluation factors receive the same rating.

Explain ways of dealing with appraisal problems.

Dealing with Appraisal Problems

The rating form or the rater is generally the cause for appraisal problems. By investigating the various advantages and disadvantages of each rating approach, an organization can determine which one best meets its needs. Additionally, training the raters in how to use the selected form can eliminate many bias problems.

Remember, two major issues must be dealt with in performance appraisal: validity and reliability. By **validity**, we mean that the instrument measures what we want it to measure. If work quantity is important, then this factor should be on the rating form. If cooperation with others is of no value because the individual works alone, it should not appear on the form. By **reliability**, we mean that the instrument measures the same factor repeatedly. If we are interested in work quality but not work quantity, we want to be sure the raters understand this. Otherwise, the way a person is rated by two managers might differ.

A wealth of research has shown that validity and reliability continue to be problems when appraising individuals. For example, one study of interview panels of police officers found that race was an influencing factor when screening officers for promotion. People on interview panels tended to give a higher evaluation to candidates who were the same race as themselves.[34] In another study, which examined the impact of both physical attractiveness and gender, researchers found that individuals who were above average in attractiveness tended to receive higher evaluations than those who were below average.

IN ACTION

CONDUCTING AN EFFECTIVE PERFORMANCE APPRAISAL

Managers need to know many things about carrying out an effective performance appraisal. The following five guidelines present much of this information in abbreviated form.

1. *Be familiar with the jobs being evaluated.* The best way to make an effective appraisal is to know what the person has been doing. Some people can look productive while performing simple or meaningless tasks. They could be overrated. Conversely, an effective worker might be underrated by someone unfamiliar with the job. There is no substitute for work familiarity.

2. *Know the factors to be evaluated.* Criteria that can be used in deciding how well the individual is performing the job are: work quantity, work quality, speed, accuracy, ability to get along with others, and communication effectiveness. These factors should be job-related so that individuals who do well on the job also receive high ratings.

3. *Let employees know the factors being evaluated.* This has a number of advantages. One is that the workers are aware of what they need to do to receive a good evaluation. A second is that the amount of tension and anxiety often associated with being evaluated tends to decline. A third is that it lets the workers know that the evaluation is job-related and not tied to such personal factors as the ability to get along with the boss.

4. *Measure the evaluation criteria appropriately.* Some jobs can be measured on a daily or weekly basis. For example, office workers often handle short-term assignments. Progress can be evaluated from week to week. In contrast, salespeople often experience certain seasons of the year that are better than others, and so their overall performance cannot be evaluated until you see how well they have done during the best sales months.

5. *Use the evaluation to help people perform better.* Evaluations should not be punitive instruments. Using them to show people where they have made mistakes creates anger and resentment. Instead, evaluations should be used as learning tools for showing people where their performance needs to be improved. An effective evaluation can serve as a basis for employee training and development.

Additionally, women tended to be ranked lower than men, and those women who were of below-average attractiveness did poorest of all. However, the researchers also found that the extent of bias was less among experienced managers than among those who were less experienced.[35] Still another study found that the accuracy of performance evaluations often is influenced by how well the manager remembers subordinate performance, and when memory is inaccurate, so too is the evaluation.[36]

Fortunately, there are ways of dealing with appraisal problems. Some are presented in the "Human Relations in Action" box. Another is to require managers to justify their evaluations. Researchers have found that when people are required to explain why they gave the evaluation they did, they are more careful about how they carry out the process, and their evaluations tend to be more accurate.[37] Still other useful ways are the following:

1. Involve employees in the design, development, and administration of the appraisal process. Participation creates ego involvement and a sense of commitment.

2. Invest time and effort in training managers to use the system for evaluation purposes, and teach them how to communicate this information effectively to those being rated.

3. Create an environment in which performance information is viewed as a resource that managers can use in developing their subordinates rather than as a method for punishing them.

4. Make performance appraisals the responsibility of the ratee—not the rater—by teaching employees how to use feedback on their job performance to help them manage their own careers and to rely less on their superior in determining their progress.

5. Reduce reliance on just one reviewer by building a system that allows multiple raters to provide input. This reduces bias and helps to provide a clearer, more complete picture of the ratee's strengths and weaknesses.[38]

CHECK YOUR UNDERSTANDING

1. Validity means ___instrument used to measure performance___
2. Reliability means ___can the measurement be used time after time again___
3. Ways to deal with appraisal problems are: involve ___ratee___, invest in ___LED___, create an ___appraisal resource platform___, make appraisal the responsibility of the ___rater___, and build a ___reliance___ of raters.

Identify ways for rewarding performance.

Rewarding Performance

The manager is in a position to reward, or not reward, a subordinate on the basis of the performance appraisal. In determining the type and degree of reward to give, it is necessary to examine three important areas: extrinsic and intrinsic rewards; performance and rewards; and discipline. The practical side of rewards was discussed in Chapter 2, but here we want to apply them directly to performance rewards. Discipline is important because sometimes the manager must give out negative rewards.

Extrinsic and Intrinsic Rewards. **Extrinsic rewards** are external and physical, taking such forms as money, increased fringe benefits, and use of a company car. **Intrinsic rewards** are internal and psychological, taking such forms as a feeling of accomplishment, increased responsibility, and the opportunity to achieve.

Money is both an extrinsic and an intrinsic reward. In and of itself, money is extrinsic, but with it often comes psychological rewards, such as esteem ("I'm important; look how much the organization is paying me"), a feeling of accomplishment ("Well, I did it: I finally made $75,000 in one year"), and a sense of achievement ("I'm good at what I do, a real achiever; that's why I'm being paid so much").

Intangible rewards and recognition are much more powerful motivators than money. A nationwide survey sponsored by Katzenbach Partners LLC found "that employees—by a more than three to one margin—would rather feel proud of their work than receive a higher salary." The study found that slightly more than half of the employees strongly agreed or mostly agreed with the following statement: "Feeling proud of your work is more important to you than getting a raise."[39]

The effective leader realizes that a mixture of extrinsic and intrinsic rewards is needed. Which mix will be best depends on the subordinate, and to be more definitive in our answer, we must apply expectancy theory to the specific situation.

Remember that expectancy theory can be expressed as: motivational force = valence × expectancy. **Valence** is the individual's preference for an outcome; for example, John may prefer a $100-per-week raise to a company car. **Expectancy** is the perceived probability that a particular act will be followed by a particular outcome: If John has the highest sales in the region, he will be given a one-week, all-expenses-paid trip to San Francisco. Knowing a person's valence and expectancy is no easy task. However, effective leaders understand their people and soon learn to know which rewards will motivate them.

For example, Maureen Wilson is the head of advertising for a large cosmetics firm. Maureen is making more than $100,000 annually in salary and 50 percent more in bonuses tied directly to sales. The more effective the advertising program, the more likely that sales, and her bonus, will rise.

Realizing that money will not motivate Maureen very much, her boss has scheduled her to go to sales meetings in London, Paris, and Rome during the next month. The boss knows Maureen likes to travel and that her husband, who owns a successful retail store, can get away any time he wants. The two often can spend three weeks in Europe, and the cosmetics firm will pay most of their expenses. Next year, Maureen will be going to the Far East.

It is obvious that Maureen's boss knows how to motivate her. The reward schedule is designed to meet Maureen's specific needs. The boss gave her a combination of extrinsic and intrinsic rewards. The free travel saved her the cost of going to Europe on her own. Her income tax bracket is very high; so if the cost of her trip were $8,000, she would have to make around $12,000 to have this amount after taxes. It also shows her how much the firm appreciates her talents.

On the other hand, some people want extrinsic rewards and are little influenced by psychological payoffs. This is especially true for people just starting their careers and raising a family at the same time.

For example, Tony Farino is a middle manager in a manufacturing plant. He is married and has three children. He recently bought a house for $180,000, and his car is two years old. Tony's salary is $55,500, but with overtime, including Saturday and occasional Sunday work, he can gross $67,500. Last month, there was an opening for a manager in the purchasing department. This department has had more than its share of problems. The company's sales are growing so quickly that the department is in a constant state of turmoil trying to check on orders, verify deliveries, and see that suppliers are paid promptly.

When the department manager resigned, Tony was offered the job. The salary was $65,000, with the opportunity of making another 25 percent through overtime. Tony accepted and so far has been very happy. Although he is working harder than ever before, he feels the higher pay more than compensates. Also, with the increased salary, he and his wife are planning to take the family on a week's vacation, something that would have been impossible with his former salary. Tony realizes he is working long hours and not seeing very much of his family, but he feels that within 12 to 18 months, things will turn around. The car will be paid for, and the cost-of-living increase that management gives the employees will raise his salary enough to ease the burden of the house payments. Then he will be able to relax and spend more time with the children. For the time being, however, he is willing to sacrifice his leisure time for increased extrinsic rewards.

In both our illustrations, the manager knows how to motivate the subordinate, offering each what he or she wants. Involved in the two cases was the issue of equity, something that merits closer attention.

CHECK YOUR UNDERSTANDING

1. What type of rewards mean the most to you: extrinsic rewards or intrinsic rewards? Explain why.
2. Give examples of extrinsic rewards that motivate you to be a better performer.
3. Identify some examples of intrinsic rewards that motivate you?

Examine the link between performance and rewards.

Linking Performance and Rewards

One of the most important questions in modern compensation theory is: How closely should performance and rewards be linked? This question is particularly critical because dozens of studies show how people who expect to receive a reward for completing a task successfully often perform no better than those who expect no reward at all. Therefore, management must carefully design its reward system. The compensation system can offer three types of rewards: wages, incentive programs, and benefit programs. Recognition programs also can provide important rewards, especially during a weak economy.

Wages. Wages are agreed-on or fixed rates of pay. For an hourly employee making $12 per hour, we need merely multiply the number of hours worked by $12 to determine the person's pay for the period under consideration. Most people, however, do not work for an hourly wage; they are salaried. Managerial personnel, in particular, are paid an annual amount, such as $52,000 per year. This salary then is broken down by pay period—that is, $1,000 per week before taxes and other deductions.

Incentive Programs. Some organizations also have **incentive payment plans**. When offered on an individual basis, they typically take the form of production or sales incentive plans. In a production incentive plan, a worker is paid a higher rate for producing output over and above an established level. For example, a firm might pay $2.00 per manufactured piece per week up to two hundred pieces and $2.25 for any output in excess of two hundred pieces. In a sales incentive plan, the salesperson's pay is tied to sales dollars generated. Often the individual receives a guaranteed draw, such as $100 per week, and a percentage of sales, such as 5 percent of all receipts generated. In recent years, these incentive plans have begun to gain popularity. Hiring bonuses and retention bonuses, which are used to attract and keep talented people, also are becoming more popular.

One of the best examples of the use of individual incentive plans is Lincoln Electric, the Cleveland-based manufacturer of arc-welding equipment. More than seventy-five people on the shop's floor have been able to earn in excess of $100,000 annually because of the firm's incentive program.

Group incentive programs can also be found in many organizations. In these cases, the program is similar to the individual incentive plan. For example, the production output of the group, or the sales of the unit, are combined in determining how much of an incentive has been earned by these employees.[40] In the case of Lincoln Electric, every year there is a bonus pool that is shared by the employees at large. For example, on December 12, 2008, Lincoln Electric distributed profit sharing bonuses totaling $89 million to employees at its major operations in Northeast Ohio. The distribution marked the 75th consecutive year the 113-year-old company has paid a profit-sharing bonus.

Some organizations have found they can save money by instituting an organizationwide incentive program. In this case, everyone in the enterprise participates. The logic is simple. Management believes that, with a joint worker–management effort, increased efficiency and cost savings can be effected. Table 10.2 provides a comparison of these three different types of incentive plans.

Benefit Programs. Benefit programs also come in many different versions. Some of the most common are life, health, and accident insurance; sick leave; workers' compensation; pension plans; and unemployment insurance. An increasing number of organizations are also making use of "cafeteria benefits," in which each worker can pick and choose the benefits he or she wants within the dollar limit established by the firm. This allows people to tailor the benefit package to meet their particular needs.

Recognition Programs. Research shows that companies do benefit from good employee recognition programs. A direct link between employee satisfaction, customer satisfaction, the organization's bottom line, and good recognition programs was found by the Forum for People Performance Management and Measurement at Northwestern

Table 10.2
A Comparison of Individual and Group and Organization-wide Incentives

Individual Incentive Plans	Group and Organization-wide Incentives
Typical Characteristics of the Plan	
Rewards are based directly on what the individual produces.	Rewards are based on group performance.
Performance is determined by the individual worker.	A committee typically determines performance standards.
Rewards are provided every payday.	Performance is only indirectly controlled by employees.
Individuality and competitive spirit are encouraged.	Rewards are paid on a monthly, quarterly, semiannual, or annual basis.
The incentive relies heavily on monetary rewards.	Teamwork and unity are encouraged.
Commonly Cited Advantages	
There is a strong sense of individualism.	The incentive motivates a large number of employees.
Rewards are in direct proportion to output.	The approach can be used for a wide variety of tasks.
	All employees in the organization can be included.
	Group cooperation is encouraged.
Commonly Cited Disadvantages	
Seldom are all the employees included in the plan.	Employees are not all rewarded according to their own productivity.
This incentive tends to be restricted to mass-produced and relatively simple operations.	Individual initiative and effort often are discouraged.
The incentive cannot be easily adapted to high-quality jobs.	
Employee grievances are a continual headache.	

University. The trend is shifting away from giving recognition for years of service or retirements to giving recognition for doing good work. The program should reinforce "the mission, the goals, and the values of the company," says the director of performance recognition at O. C. Tanner Company. John Putzier, president of FirStep Inc., a performance improvement company in Prospect, Pennsylvania, says "it's impossible to give too much praise as long as the sentiment is genuine." If done correctly, reward and recognition programs should create more net revenue for the company.[41] Recognition programs should complement the rewards program and help to boost employee commitment and increase employee retention.

Linking Pay to Performance. Research by Towers Watson, a consulting firm, reveals that high-performance companies more closely link pay to performance than do their less-effective counterparts. For example, the firm found that 79 percent of the high-performing companies it studied use merit increases for hourly nonunion workers, as compared to 58 percent for other firms.[42] Thus, the first step is to institute the proper rewards system At Chicago-based Ameritech, for example, all employees are compensated with a variable pay approach. Some part of their pay is tied to performance, and if the employees do not meet the established level of performance, they will not receive their variable pay percentage. At Taco Bell, managers are given moderate salaries, and the rest of their income is based on the unit's performance; effective store managers can earn as much as 10 percent to 20 percent of their base pay in performance-related bonuses.[43]

More and more CEOs are finding performance targets attached to their pay. In 2005, thirty out of one hundred major U.S. corporations based a portion of the CEO's pay on performance targets, up from twenty-three in 2004 and seventeen in 2003, according to an analysis done by Mercer LLC, a human resource consulting firm. The reason is to keep executives from reaping rich rewards for reasons unrelated to their leadership skills. Because performance targets are often not revealed, it is not always easy for stockholders to determine if the boss is earning his keep. Performance-linked equity targets "need to be meaningful," with targets investors can understand.[44]

Many of these pay-for-performance plans make use of what are called *nontraditional rewards*, such as profit sharing, bonuses, individual incentives, gain-sharing programs that divide cost reductions among all members of the organization, small-group incentives, payment for knowledge, the granting of earned time off in lieu of a monetary reward, stock options, and employee stock purchase plans (ESPP).

Business Week reported that stock options and ESPP are often misunderstood and underutilized as employee benefits. They "are available at more than 4,000 companies, including Cisco Systems, Southwest Airlines, and Starbucks." These benefits allow employees to buy shares of company stock at a discount of 10 percent to 15 percent. Often, employers fail to educate employees about these benefits.[45]

Another interesting trend is taking place among service companies. Organization structures are being flattened, positions are being removed, and everyone is being given a greater opportunity to share in the reward system. For example, at the Hard Rock Cafe, as many as three times annually, the company president will walk into a unit and ask the managers to nominate and the staff to vote for the best employee of the quarter. The winner is given an all-expense-paid, one-week trip to Hawaii. In most service-driven organizations, however, incentives are not spontaneous. They are a result of a plan that has been communicated to the employees. For example, at the Peasant Restaurants, headquartered in Atlanta, the general manager of the year award winner receives a trip for two to Europe. To win the incentive, the individual must meet the demands of the company's five-part formula. According to this formula, the employee must have:

1. The five highest scores overall on regional inspections.
2. The highest scores on dining experience as rated by the corporate staff.
3. A superior training program.
4. An accurate and timely administrative record.
5. A positive sales growth.

Meanwhile, at Wendy's, the company gives quarterly cash bonuses to managers who meet a variety of performance goals related to sales, profits, and cost control. In addition, there are six levels at which agents can redeem points for prizes ranging from a Disney vacation to a gift.[46]

Offering the right rewards and benefits is crucial to hiring, motivating, and retaining employees. However, over time, employees' needs change and they want different types of rewards and benefits. For example, in January 2007, Accountemps, a staffing firm, conducted a survey of office workers and found that "frequent recognition of accomplishments" was the top non-monetary compensation followed by "regular communication." The survey results revealed a list of 25 ways to reward employees without breaking the bank.[47] Ten of the suggestions are:

1. Flex those hours—Implement flexible schedules.
2. Send a handwritten note—Write a personal note to employees who deserve recognition.
3. Make work fun—Plan different fun activities during the month.
4. Help them connect—Introduce employees to key suppliers, customers, or someone in senior management who might help their career.
5. Lose the shoes—Let employees take off their shoes at work.
6. Send them to the showers—Every birth and wedding deserves a shower, let employees go early, and no need to make up the time.
7. Reward effort as well as success—Even if employees' ideas fail, you want to keep them producing.
8. Give them a free pass—Allot a certain number of days that employees can use at their discretion.
9. Dole out cream and sugar—Serve drinks and refreshment to employees.
10. Blow out the candles—Have the CEO host a monthly hour-long birthday breakfast for any employee with a birthday that month. Employees can ask the CEO anything.

In closing our discussion, it is important to remember that an organization can link rewards and performance only when four conditions are present. First, individual performance can be measured objectively. Second, there is a low degree of interdependence among the individuals in the system. Third, it is possible to develop measures for all the important aspects of the jobs. And finally, effort and performance are closely related over a relatively short period.

In establishing this link, many managers find it helpful to focus on actions that reward people for work well done. Some of the specific suggestions in this process are as follows:

1. **Reward solid solutions instead of quick fixes.** Specifically identify what people are to do and then evaluate their performance over the long term rather than every three to six months.
2. **Reward risk taking.** Encourage people to take well thought-out, calculated risks and be willing to encourage those who fail and those who succeed.
3. **Reward applied creativity.** Give people bonuses and other forms of monetary payment when their creative ideas result in profits for the organization.
4. **Reward decisive action.** Encourage people to set deadlines and make decisions within this period rather than continually procrastinating and doing more thinking and research, thus falling victim to "paralysis by analysis."
5. **Reward people for working smarter rather than merely harder.** Give people the information and tools they need to get the job done right, correct poor work habits, and let them go home when they have attained their goals rather than making them sit around and wait until closing time.

IN ACTION

MAINTAINING A DIVERSE WORKFORCE

More women are now in management positions, and additionally, a growing number of women are breaking through the glass ceiling and making it into the executive suite. Examples are Indra Nooyi, chairman and CEO of PepsiCo; Irene Rosenfeld, chairman and CEO of Kraft Foods; Pat Woertz, chairman, CEO, and president of Archer Daniels Midland; Angela Braly, president and CEO of Wellpoint; Andrea Jung, chairman and CEO of Avon Products; Oprah Winfrey, chairman, Harpo; Ellen Kullman, CEO of DuPont; Carol Bartz, CEO of Yahoo; Ginni Rometty, SVP, Global Sales and Distribution of IBM; and Safra Catz, co-president of Oracle, just to name ten women on *Fortune Magazine's* 2009 list of the "50 Most Powerful Women." These women range in age from 47 to 61, the majority being in their 50s. Women still, however, have a long way to go. This is true for a number of reasons, including the fact that many women feel that if they are going to get ahead, they must switch jobs. What can organizations do to stem this exodus? In addition to financial rewards, companies are finding the following to be extremely effective tools:

1. Demonstrate a commitment to workforce diversity throughout the organization.

2. Use affirmative action as a tool to ensure that all qualified individuals have equal access and opportunities to compete based on ability and merit.

3. Prepare minorities and women for senior positions, not just staff positions.

4. Provide formal training at regular intervals to sensitize and familiarize all employees about the strengths and challenges of gender, racial, ethnic, and cultural differences.

5. Initiate work/life and family-friendly policies that balance work and family responsibilities that impact the lifelong career paths of all employees.

6. Provide opportunities for employees to gain skills and experience in line jobs across the organization, qualifying them for advancements.

7. Provide career planning for women and support networks for women.

8. Establish mentoring programs that link senior professional women (or men) with new female managers.

9. Change the preconceptions, stereotypes, and negative assumptions held by those in power about women and their abilities and commitment to careers.

10. Stop the subtle and blatant discrimination and sexual harassment toward women.

Sources: "The 50 Most Powerful Women," *Fortune Magazine*, March 25, 2010, www.fortune.com; and Dayle M. Smith, *Women at Work* (Englewood Cliffs, NJ: Prentice-Hall, 2000) pp. 13–17.

6. **Reward simplification.** Encourage people to use direct communications, such as calling on the phone rather than writing a memo, to avoid creating bureaucratic red tape.

7. **Reward quietly effective people.** Do not let the squeaky wheel get all the attention and rewards, but rather seek out and reward the quiet heroes who are responsible for getting things done.

8. **Reward quality.** See that people are well trained, encourage them to improve their techniques and methods, and give recognition and monetary rewards to those who produce the highest-quality output.

9. **Reward loyalty.** Providing job security, promoting from within, keeping communication lines open, offering fair pay and benefits, and providing people continuous education, training, and development are ways to reward loyalty.

In recent years, organizations have been finding it particularly challenging to develop reward systems that help attract and retain women. The "Ethics and Social Responsibility in Action" box spells out some of these problems and the solutions firms are using to solve them. At the same time, firms are instituting penalties for executives who leave the company to go elsewhere. At General Motors, for example, a special committee now determines how and when bonuses are awarded to top managers, and the committee can hold back a large percentage of this bonus until the person retires. If the individual leaves the firm, of course, the retirement portion of the bonus is forfeited.

✔ CHECK YOUR UNDERSTANDING

1. How can wages, incentive programs, and benefit programs be linked to performance?
2. Identify the steps in rewarding performance. Which of these steps are most important to you and your current job?

Discipline

Sometimes, instead of giving rewards to employees, the leader must discipline some of them. Often, this is known as a *negative reward*. The use of this approach will depend on the employee and the situation. For example, as seen in Table 10.3, problem employees can be divided into four categories. In dealing with people in each category, the manager must consider the primary and secondary goals to pursue. For purposes of human relations, the manager must integrate this information with an understanding of both the types of discipline and the manner in which discipline should be administered.

Types of Discipline.   Most formal disciplinary processes employ what is called **progressive discipline**, beginning with a verbal warning and, if there is no improvement, terminating with firing (see Figure 10.8). If an employee breaks a rule, especially a minor one, the first step usually is a clear **oral warning**, pointing out that repetition of the act will result in discipline. At this point, the manager hopes that the worker will refrain from breaking the rule in the future. If the employee breaks the rule again or if the first offense was a major one, some firms issue **written warnings**. These become part of the employee's records and can be cited as evidence if it is decided to terminate the individual's employment in the future.

A **disciplinary layoff** is the next most severe form of discipline. In this case, the employee is required not to come to work for a specified period and to forfeit pay for that period. A layoff varies in length from one day to two weeks. Some organizations, however, do not use disciplinary layoffs because of their inability to find a replacement for a few days or weeks. Instead, they simply fire the employee.

Discharge is the ultimate penalty. In recent years, this approach has been used less and less, principally because the penalty often is regarded as too harsh. The effective leader strives to avoid this situation by preventing rule violations. When such violations

Table 10.3
Types of Problem Employees

Type	Primary Goal	Secondary Goal
Type I does not intentionally violate the rules but does so unintentionally and infrequently.	To correct the behavior and to inform and train	To maintain the individual's motivation
Type II will violate the rules when he or she considers some treatment unfair and does so only occasionally.	To correct the behavior and to avoid discipline problems with others	To identify and deal with why the person feels unfairly treated, so that future problems can be avoided
Type III will violate the rules whenever he or she can get away with it, generally creates problems, and often is disciplined.	To avoid discipline problems with others	To document the use of discipline (toward eventual termination)
Type IV is not so much a problem employee as an employee with a problem.	To get help for the individual and to provide a reason to use that help	To document whether the individual is unwilling to seek help or the problem recurs

Source: John Seltzer, "Discipline with a Clear Sense of Purpose," *Management Solutions*, February 1987, p. 34.

Figure 10.8 Progressive Discipline Process

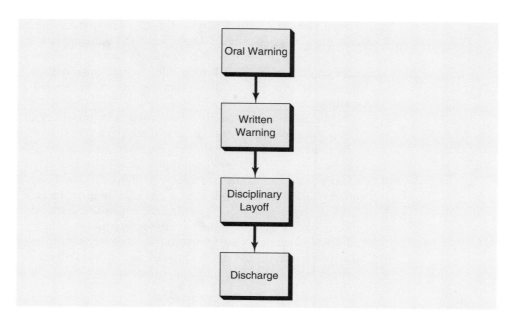

do occur, the leader must be consistent and impersonal in employing discipline. In discharging someone, Suters recommends the following six guidelines:

1. Be firm and unemotional and present the decision as irrevocable.
2. Give straight, honest reasons for the dismissal.
3. Do not be drawn into an argument or counterproductive discussion over the reasons for the termination.
4. Ease the blow by pointing out that the action is a mutual disappointment.
5. Do not terminate anyone's employment when you are upset.
6. Do not blame the decision on anyone else.[48]

Administering Discipline. One of the most effective methods of employing discipline is the **red-hot-stove rule**. This rule draws an analogy between touching a red-hot stove and receiving discipline. When someone touches a red-hot stove, the burn is *immediate*. There was *advance warning* in the form of heat emanating from the stove, which should have alerted the person to the danger. Anyone who touches the stove is burned, and this *consistency* holds for everyone else who touches it. The burn is *impersonal* in that everyone touching the stove is burned, regardless of who they are. These four characteristics can be applied to discipline.

Discipline Should Be Immediate.   As soon as the manager knows that a worker has broken a rule, discipline should follow. If the manager waits, the worker may not associate the disciplinary action with the violation of the rule, and bitter feelings are likely to result.

By immediate discipline, we do not mean hurried action. The facts of the case should be clear, and only if there is an obvious infraction of the rules should discipline be given. In many organizations, a worker is suspended until the investigation is complete. If the worker is found innocent, he or she is reinstated and given back pay for the suspension period. Conversely, if the worker is found guilty of the offense, the prescribed discipline is carried out.

There Should Be Advance Warning.   The organization should make its rules clear, and the employees should know what the penalties are for breaking them. One of the most common ways of doing this is to familiarize workers with the rules during the orientation period. Any future rule changes should then be communicated by the immediate superior or, if workers are unionized, should be included in the union contract.

Management must follow two important guidelines in giving advance warning. Never have too many rules. If people are given five rules to follow, they will generally adhere to them. However, if they are asked to abide by 105 rules, they will generally ignore them. The degree of importance tends to decline as the number of rules increases. Clearly state and uniformly apply the penalties for infractions. If management does otherwise, the workers will protest disciplinary procedures. For example, if Paul, a new worker, sees people walking around the construction site without hard hats, he will feel discriminated against if the supervisor disciplines him for not wearing his hat. In addition, when such cases go to arbitration, it is likely that the company will lose because disciplinary action has not been taken for previous offenses. "Why," the arbitrator will reason, "should the firm suddenly decide to start enforcing the rule now?"

Discipline Should Be Consistent.   If two people commit the same offense, each should be given the same discipline. The biggest problem for the manager is that of identifying everyone who breaks the rules. If the manager can catch only 20 percent of the workers who violate a particular rule, those who are caught often are angry because discipline seems to be more a matter of chance than anything else.

Discipline Should Be Impersonal.   The manager should make it clear to the workers that they are all on the same team but that this does not mean the workers can violate the rules with impunity. Some workers are more productive than others. Some are informal group leaders and others are followers. Obviously, the manager would want to cultivate the friendship of the more productive or leading workers. However, this cannot be done at the expense of either the other workers or the organization.

On the other hand, the manager should not be excessively harsh when disciplining a worker. After ensuring that the worker has indeed broken the rule, the effective manager should try to learn why and then to work with the individual to prevent another violation.

If the manager handles the situation properly, it is often possible to prevent feelings from being hurt. To a large degree, the manager's success in handling the disciplinary matter will be determined by his or her negotiating ability. In fact, appraising, rewarding, and disciplining employees requires effective negotiating skills. Before proceeding, take the accompanying "Time Out" quiz to rate your effectiveness in reward–discipline situations, as measured by your negotiating ability.

Dismissal and the Law.   Over the last few years, a new dismissal-related problem has arisen. Employees who have been discharged by their firms now are suing their former employers, and many have been winning large settlements. One reason is because the employees can prove discrimination.[49]

At the heart of the matter are the issues of **employment at will**, which means that the organization has a right to dismiss an employee at any time, regardless of cause, and the right of employees to expect fair and equitable treatment from the employer. Sometimes, these two issues are in conflict. A good example is when a loyal long-time employee is fired for a minor rule infraction or is summarily dismissed even though he or she has been receiving very good performance evaluations. Do employees have the right to continued employment, or is this provided at the discretion of the employer?[50]

How Great Is Your Negotiating Ability?

Performance appraisal, the allocation of rewards, and the effective use of discipline require a manager to be, among other things, a skilled negotiator. The individual must be able to evaluate performance diplomatically and effectively and withstand the pressures that come about when subordinates complain that they are being treated unfairly. How great is your negotiating ability? Decide whether each of the following sixteen statements is basically true or basically false in describing you.

	Basically True	Basically False
1. I really like to be liked.	_____	_____
2. I am not a very good listener, but I am an excellent talker.	_____	_____
3. I try not to do formal preparation for any performance appraisal because it detracts me from my spontaneity and creativity; I prefer to play things by ear.	_____	_____
4. I am not really much of a compromiser; I know what I want and I fight to get it all.	_____	_____
5. Under pressure, I can really handle myself well.	_____	_____
6. People who know me well find me to be both tactful and diplomatic.	_____	_____
7. I find that most things in life are negotiable.	_____	_____
8. No matter what salary increase is offered to me, I try to get more.	_____	_____
9. I take what people say at face value.	_____	_____
10. Whenever possible, I try to avoid conflict and confrontation.	_____	_____
11. I do not care how the other side feels about the results of my negotiation efforts; that is their problem, not mine.	_____	_____
12. I do not like to haggle with people over salaries; I pay what is asked or walk away from the negotiation.	_____	_____
13. A person's facial expressions often tell me more about what is being said than do the words.	_____	_____
14. I am not particularly adept at expressing my point of view.	_____	_____
15. In most cases, I am not willing to compromise on issues.	_____	_____
16. I find it easy to smile even when engaged in a serious discipline situation.	_____	_____

The interpretation of your self-assessment can be found at the end of the book.

Most states currently give employees the right to sue for "wrongful discharge." This means that if an employee believes that he or she has been fired without just cause, he or she can bring a lawsuit. In an effort to deal with this emerging social phenomenon, Montana has passed a law that requires employers to submit these cases to arbitration and limits the damages that can be awarded to four years' back wages. The law also prohibits firing anyone who has completed a probationary period, unless there is just cause for such action.

Many firms are now developing procedures for handling these situations. One is to institute lawsuits of their own, asking the courts to throw out the cases.[51] However, the most popular is an arbitration procedure that relies on neutral outside arbitrators to listen to the facts and then make a ruling. The Northrop Grumman Corporation has used this procedure for decades. Bank of America, NBC, Aetna Life Insurance, and Chrysler Corporation have followed suit. Coors has taken this idea a step further and developed a peer-review appeals process for handling appeals of grievance decisions. All appeals are referred to a small group of workers and managers who are chosen by an employee relations manager. The group reviews a grievance appeal and decides what to do. The company and the employees are both pleased with the program because they believe that it provides a balanced, equitable approach to resolving grievances.

Employers mostly do not win in discharge cases filed by employees. George W. Bohlander in his article, "Why Arbitrators Overturn Managers in Employee Suspension and Discharge Cases," concluded that five reasons accounted for more than 71.5 percent of the cases in which the arbitrator ruled on behalf of the employee. The first reason is lack of supporting evidence. The employer did not provide sufficient persuasive evidence to support the disciplinary action. The second reason is mitigating circumstances. The third reason is that employers committed procedural due process errors. Fourth, the punishment was too harsh for the rule infraction. And fifth, management was partly at fault. Bohlander concluded that supervisors need adequate training, and employers need to improve their investigatory skills in disciplinary matters.[52]

Some employers are beginning to fight back by having their employees sign statements that indicate they can be dismissed at the discretion of the company. However, except in the case of new employees who sign these forms at the beginning of their employment, the courts are setting them aside and allowing wrongful-discharge suits, which, in many cases, are proving to be costly to employers. Consequently, a continued trend toward impartial arbitration is likely in handling these matters.

✔ CHECK YOUR UNDERSTANDING

1. Give an example to illustrate each step in the progressive discipline process.
2. List the four characteristics of administering discipline.
3. How great is your negotiating ability? Analyze the differences in your answers in the "Time Out" exercise. What do you need to do to become a better negotiator?

© Ben Blankenburg, iStock

Discuss how time management can enhance your career.

Career Advisor

Manage Your Time Well

Successful people know how to manage their time. They are focused and know what they want out of life, what they need to do to advance in their career, and what they need to do in their job to be successful. People who use time wisely get more things done and experience fewer daily pressures.

One of the first things you need to know in managing time more effectively is exactly how you currently spend your time each day. To gain a clear understanding, you should record your activities over a period of a week or two and then analyze the results. Only then can you begin to make changes in the areas where you are wasting time. If you know where the problems are, you can fix them, get more accomplished, and be a more productive employee, resulting in greater personal recognition and rewards.[53]

For some people, knowing how their time is spent is not enough. They need to prepare a "to do" list each day, regularly checking schedules and updating calendars.

"To Do" Lists.   One approach to managing time more effectively is to start the workday by preparing a list of all the things that need to be done that day. It is highly unlikely that everything can be accomplished that day; therefore, you must make some choices on what is most important. Prioritize the items on the list into three groups, which can be called A, B, and C or top priority, medium priority, and low priority. The titles do not matter as long as the items fall into one of the following categories:

A. Critical things that need immediate attention.
B. Important things that need to be done.
C. Things that can be delegated or postponed.

Then, of course, focus your energy on completing the critical things first. A sense of accomplishment can be gained by marking off the finished items. People who use time wisely are not afraid to delegate work, while they focus their attention on matters that require their personal attention. Prioritizing activities helps managers lead more effectively.

When a person must carry out a number of different tasks, it is essential to use "to do" lists. The list keeps a person focused and in control of what needs to be done, resulting in less time wasted. Fewer things are forgotten and stress is reduced. "To do" lists provide a powerful means of staying organized. Sometimes, what needs to be done is overwhelming and creating a "to do" list seems impossible. At those times, what you need to do is to divide a monumental job into tasks, and then prioritize the tasks to find out what is most critical. Of course, as time passes, some items in the second and third categories will need attention. They will surface and you will need to deal with them. This usually occurs after receiving a follow-up notice by phone or by e-mail saying that action is needed. Instead of preparing "to do" lists, some people use goal setting.

Goal Setting.   Goal setting allows employees to decide what to achieve and how to move step by step toward the achievement of the objectives. With clearly defined and measurable objectives, employees gain a sense of confidence and a feeling of wanting to accomplish higher goals each time they achieve another objective. Managing one's time has taken on special importance in today's fast-paced global workplace, and goal setting is an important strategy. Moreover, when you have goals and know what you need to do, you can better utilize those blocks of time that would otherwise be wasted to complete a thirty-minute or even a ten-minute task on one of your major goals. This will move you closer to completion of the goal. When you take the time to visualize exactly what, when, and where you want to do something, it is more likely that you will accomplish the goal.

Researchers have found a strong correlation between a firm's financial performance and its goal-setting process. Just as critical is the alignment of your goals with the firm's goals. If this is not working for you, a change in employment may be the answer.

Generally, it takes a number of **objectives** to accomplish each goal. **Goals** are general statements of what you want to accomplish, such as receive a bachelor's degree in management, whereas objectives are clear statements of what you must do to accomplish the goal. Your objectives must be *S.M.A.R.T.*

- **Objectives must be *specific.*** They must be specific to let people know exactly what is to be accomplished. Specific includes identifying who is responsible, what is to be accomplished, when it is to be done, which requirements or constraints are involved, and why it is important or beneficial.
- **Your objectives must be *measurable.*** Specific criteria must be set so that measurement can occur. Measurement keeps you on track and provides ongoing motivation.
- **Your objectives must be *attainable.*** Your objectives must be realistic and achievable.
- **Your objectives must be *relevant.*** The objectives must be important to you, and in the case of your employment, you must be able to understand how objectives connect to your company's objectives.
- **Your objectives must be *timely.*** Objectives must be structured around a timeframe to provide a sense of urgency.[54]

Working Smarter, Not Harder.   Being better organized and utilizing good work habits can help you work more wisely and use time more efficiently. For example, one way to utilize time more effectively is to combine compatible activities whenever possible. Another example is to cut down on the number of times you handle paperwork or read e-mails. Always take action immediately by passing it along to someone who can take action, filing it for future reference, throwing it away, or deleting it. A third example is having a set time during the day or the week to do certain tasks, such as returning calls, writing reports, conducting meetings, or reading professional material. You can save time by doing similar tasks in one block of time.[55]

Time Management Principles.   Effective leaders learn how to make every moment count regardless of whether they are in the office or visiting a client. They constantly devise ways to get more done in a shorter period of time. These leaders use time management principles. Donna J. Abernathy has compiled a list of ten rules for managing time.[56] The rules are:

1. Carry a "to do" list with you; jot down notes on those things you have to do and cross out those that you have completed.
2. When reading memos, mail, or short reports, do so standing up. You read faster in this position.
3. As you read e-mails and letters that call for a reply, answer each as you go along. Otherwise, you will have to read each again later when you get around to formulating a response.
4. Concentrate your efforts on one thing at a time.
5. Give your primary attention to those tasks that are most important and work at delegating minor jobs to your subordinates.
6. If you have an appointment to visit someone, bring work with you so that if you are forced to wait, you can put the time to good use.
7. After you complete a particularly important or difficult task, give yourself time off as a special reward.
8. Try not to work on weekends.
9. Examine your work habits for ways of streamlining your current procedures and saving time.
10. If you do not get all you wanted accomplished in a given day, tell yourself you will get to it the next day. Do not feel guilty over any failure to meet your daily work plan. As long as you are doing your best, tell yourself that this is good enough.

 CHECK YOUR UNDERSTANDING

1. Do you have enough time to get everything done?
2. Prepare an activity log of how you spend your time each day for a week.
3. Analyze the results and make changes where needed.
4. What did you learn and what have been the results?

Summary

1 Identify and describe the stages in the process for developing employees.

In this chapter, we addressed the issues of employee development, performance appraisal, and performance rewards. Employee development should begin with an effective recruiting, screening, selecting, and orientation program. After the candidate is hired, training and developing the employee become important. The basic types of training are apprentice, vestibule, on-the-job, off-the-job, and virtual. Appraising and rewarding help keep employees motivated.

Qualified candidates must be made aware of available positions. This process is called *recruiting*. Recruiters can use internal sources—postings on bulletin boards, e-mail, newsletters, and meetings—or external sources—advertisements in the classified section of newspapers, cold calls, or recruiters. *Screening* is the process of eliminating applicants who are unlikely to be successful on the job, whereas selecting is the process of determining which applicants will be offered jobs.

Several strategies are used in this process. (1) By checking the applicant's education, previous employment, credit history, driving records, and criminal record, the possibility of hiring the wrong person can be reduced. (2) The interview gives the interviewers a chance to judge a wide range of the candidate's abilities. Two types of interviews are used. One is the *structured interview* where all applicants are asked the same questions, and the other is the *unstructured interview* where candidates are placed in decision-making scenarios. This allows the interviewer to determine how the applicant might behave in a similar situation. (3) Screening tests are another common approach to selecting the right applicant. One type of test is the *demonstration test*, which identifies proficiency in certain skills. Another test is the *professional test*, used to screen candidates for managerial positions. Regardless of the type of screening and selection device used, it must not invade privacy issues.

Orientation is the process of introducing new employees to the company, their work group, and their tasks. Some items covered are the company history, policies, procedures, structure, and benefits.

Training focuses on teaching new knowledge, skills, or improving skills. *Apprentice training* focuses on teaching employees a new job with an opportunity to apply the procedures. The training is done both on and off the job. *Vestibule training* is conducted in a similar setting away from the employee's actual work site. The immediate supervisor and fellow workers provide *on-the-job training*, whereas *off-the-job training* is done away from the workplace, usually in workshops, seminars, or class courses. *Virtual training*, more commonly called e-learning, uses a computer and a well-designed learning program. Several trends in training are an increase in training budgets; an increase in diversity training; an increase in the creation of in-house programs, namely, e-learning programs, and a combination of in-house and university-linked training.

Appraising performance is the process of monitoring, comparing, and correcting weaknesses. Employees with positive results are *rewarded*, whereas employees who fail to improve, even with training, are generally fired.

2 *Discuss the performance appraisal cycle.*

The four-step process of performance appraisal is as follows: (1) performance standards are established, (2) individual performance is determined, (3) a comparison of individual performance and performance standards is made, and (4) overall performance is evaluated. When the fourth step is completed, the cycle begins again.

3 *Identify four performance appraisal tools and tell how each can be used in appraising employees.*

Many kinds of appraisal tools can be used to evaluate employee performance. The simplest is the *graphic rating scale*, in which all the factors (and degrees of each factor) on which the employee is to be evaluated are listed. The manager's job then is to check the appropriate degree of every factor and to total the value associated with each to arrive at an overall score for the individual.

The *paired comparison method* of evaluation requires the manager to compare each employee in the group with every other. Often, there are five to ten factors on which all employees are compared. On the basis of the comparisons on all factors, the manager is able to rank the workers from the best to the poorest.

Management by objectives can be used at all levels of the employment hierarchy. The process consists of six steps: (1) identifying the goals of the unit or department, (2) describing the duties and responsibilities of the personnel, (3) meeting with the subordinate and mutually setting goals for this individual, (4) employing a goal-setting worksheet to help the subordinate work toward the objective, (5) periodically reviewing the goals and revising them as necessary, and (6) evaluating the results and starting the cycle anew.

The advantages of MBO are the attention given to the subordinate in the goal-setting process, a strong emphasis on quantifiable objectives that are tied to a time dimension, and a concentration on the organization's key goals. The number of objectives assigned to each person is usually limited to five or six.

The *360-degree evaluation review* gathers input from an individual's superior, subordinates, peers, work group, and others with whom the individual comes into frequent contact. The purposes of the evaluation are to determine the person's performance and to serve as a basis for creating a developmental action plan for improvement. This evaluation and the results of the action plan then serve as the basis for the next 360-degree review.

4 Describe four major problems associated with performance appraisal.

In every performance appraisal, the manager must be aware of problems. The most common problems are attributable to (1) *lack of clarity* of the form itself, (2) the *halo effect*, (3) *central tendency*, and (4) *leniency*. On the rating form, the levels on which employees are rated should be clearly defined. When employees are given the same rating on all factors regardless of performance, the halo effect occurs. Central tendency occurs when all ratings are marked average; when all ratings are marked high, a leniency problem occurs.

5 Explain ways of dealing with appraisal problems.

In noting the ways of dealing with appraisal problems, we stressed the need for validity and reliability in performance appraisal instruments. A testing instrument that measures what we want it to has *validity* and when the instrument repeatedly measures the same factor, it has *reliability*. Other ways of dealing with appraisal problems are: involving employees in the design, development, and administration of the appraisal process; investing time and effort in training managers to use the system; creating an environment in which performance information is viewed as a resource in developing employees; making performance appraisals the responsibility of the ratee; and reducing reliance on just one reviewer by building a system.

6 Identify ways for rewarding performance.

The most common ways of rewarding performance are extrinsic rewards—wages or salary—and intrinsic rewards—increased responsibility and feeling of accomplishment. *Extrinsic rewards* are external and physical and are administered from others, whereas *intrinsic rewards* are internal and psychological and are a result of how one feels about the reward. Money is both an extrinsic and intrinsic reward. It depends on how money is viewed by the employee. Money may be a motivator to one employee and a satisfier to another employee. It depends on what the employee expects. *Valence* is the worker's preference for an outcome. *Expectancy* is the perceived probability that a particular act will be followed by a particular outcome. Some people are more motivated by extrinsic rewards, while other employees are more motivated by intrinsic rewards. Managers must determine the best system to use.

7 Examine the link between performance and rewards.

The question is how closely should performance and rewards be linked? The compensation system can offer three types of rewards: wages, incentive programs, and benefit programs.

Wages are fixed rates of pay based on the number of hours worked in a pay period and salary is a fixed payment made periodically to a person based on an annual amount for regular work. *Incentive payment* plans include receiving a higher rate for production beyond a stated amount, hiring bonuses, retention bonuses, and group bonuses. *Benefit programs* come in many versions. They usually include life, health, and accident insurance; sick leave; workers' compensation; pension plans; and unemployment insurance. Most people, however, want extrinsic rewards. Research shows that high-performance companies more closely link pay to performance than do their less-effective counterparts. It is important to implement the proper rewards system.

Pay-for-performance plans make use of nontraditional rewards, such as profit sharing, bonuses, individual incentives, and gain-sharing programs. The needs and wants of employees change over time. Therefore, it is important to keep abreast of current changes in employees' needs and be ready to change the system or it will no longer provide the needed motivation to keep up performance and retain employees.

Research has shown that successful companies more closely link pay to performance than their less-successful competitors. Offering the right rewards and benefits is crucial to hiring and retaining employees. For one employee, ongoing training opportunities may be more important than flextime or child care. Specific suggestions include: rewarding solid solutions, not quick fixes; risk taking; creativity; decisive action; working smarter, not merely harder; simplification; quietly effective people; quality; and loyalty.

8 Describe the types of discipline used when performance is inadequate.

The manager must also exercise discipline, sometimes labeled as a negative reward. Most formal disciplinary processes employ *progressive discipline*, beginning with an oral warning and moving to a written warning, a disciplinary layoff, and, ultimately, discharge. In carrying out discipline, many managers use *the red-hot-stove rule*: that effective discipline should be (1) immediate, (2) preceded by advance warning of discipline penalties, (3) consistent, and (4) impersonal. If dismissal is required, just cause should be provable in case the dismissed person files a discrimination suit. At times, the notion of *employment at will*—an organization's right to dismiss an employee at any time, regardless of cause—and the right of employees to expect fair and equitable treatment can come into conflict. To deal with these issues, companies are using arbitration and mediation procedures.

9 Discuss how time management can enhance your career.

Successful people know how to manage their time. They know how they spend their time and where they waste time. They develop strategies to utilize time more effectively to accomplish the things that are important to them. Successful people know what it takes to advance in their career and how to get there. Ineffective people waste a lot of time contemplating what they want, in life as well as in a career, and wondering why others are so successful.

"To do" lists serve as a powerful guide in focusing attention on what is important and knowing what needs to be accomplished. Goal setting is another strategy that clearly defines what needs to be done to accomplish your objectives and ultimately your final goals. Being organized (combining activities) and using good work habits (doing similar work in a block of time) can help you use time more efficiently. Increasing an employee's productivity can make the employee more valuable to the company. Other principles for using time more effectively are responding immediately after reading a request, concentrating only on one thing at a time (multitasking does not always save time), giving attention to critical tasks first, taking reading material to appointments, taking time off after a difficult task, regularly examining your work habits, and not feeling bad if you fail to accomplish everything planned in a day.

Follow the S.M.A.R.T. plan in developing objectives for each goal. Objectives must be stated in *specific* terms and must be *measurable*, *attainable*, *relevant*, and *timely*, or they will never be accomplished.

Key Terms in the Chapter

Recruiting	Recruiting is the process of attracting qualified applicants to apply for available positions
Screening	Screening is the process of eliminating applicants who are unlikely to be successful on the job.
Selecting	Selecting is the process of determining which applicants will be offered jobs.
Orientation	Orientation is the process of introducing new employees to their jobs.
Apprentice training	Apprentice training is done both on and off the job to teach new rules for getting work done.
Vestibule training	Vestibule training takes place in an environment that simulates the actual workplace.
On-the-job training	On-the-job training can be formal or informal. Coaching by the supervisor is the most common method of on-the-job training.
Off-the-job training	Off-the-job training is done away from the workplace; usually it is nontechnical in nature.
Virtual training	Virtual training uses a computer and a well-designed learning program, such as e-learning.
Performance appraisal cycle	The performance appraisal cycle helps managers to set cycle goals and evaluate subordinate performance.
Graphic rating scales	Graphic rating scales evaluate personnel on the basis of predetermined factors.
Paired comparison method	The paired comparison method compares each person against all others being evaluated.
Management by objectives	MBO is a process by which superior and subordinate jointly set goals that then are used for evaluating the individual.
Halo effect	A halo effect occurs when the appraiser gives a worker the same rating on all factors, regardless of actual performance.
Central tendency	With central tendency, everyone receives an average rating.
Leniency	With leniency, the highest possible ratings are given out to all.
Validity	Validity means that the instrument measures what it is designed to measure.

Reliability	Reliability means that the instrument measures the same factor repeatedly.
Extrinsic rewards	Extrinsic rewards are external and physical.
Intrinsic rewards	Intrinsic rewards are internal and psychological.
Valence	Valence is an individual's preference for an outcome.
Expectancy	Expectancy is the perceived probability that a particular act will be followed by a particular outcome.
Incentive payment plans	Incentive payment plans tie rewards directly to output.
Progressive discipline	Progressive discipline is a formal disciplinary process that starts with an oral warning, followed by a written warning, and punishment.
Oral warning	An oral warning involves orally pointing out an infraction of a rule.
Written warning	A written warning is a warning that is placed in an employee's personnel file.
Disciplinary layoff	A disciplinary layoff involves sending a person home without pay for a predetermined time.
Discharge	Discharge is the separation of the individual from the organization.
Red-hot-stove rule	The red-hot-stove rule applies discipline immediately, consistently, and impersonally.
Employment at will	Employment at will means that the company has a right to dismiss an employee at any time, regardless of cause, and the right of employees to expect fair and equitable treatment from the employer.
Goals	Goals are general statements of what you want to accomplish.
Objectives	Objectives are specific statements that can be measured, and are attainable, relevant, and timely.

Review and Study Questions

1. What are the stages of the employee development process? Identify and define them.
2. How is recruiting an important part of the development process?
3. What are the differences between internal recruiting and external recruiting?
4. Why is a well-designed screening and selection program critical to organizational effectiveness? How is it a critical part of the employee development process?
5. How is a structured interview different from an unstructured interview? Give examples.
6. What are some examples of the most common screening tests?
7. Of what value is an orientation program? What are some benefits it offers?
8. Identify five basic types of training and describe each type.
9. What are some developments/trends in training in the past several years?
10. How can a business use communities of practice?
11. How does the performance appraisal cycle work? Be sure to discuss all four steps.

12. How does the graphic rating scale help managers appraise subordinates?

13. How does the paired comparison method work?

14. Why is MBO so popular? How does it work? What are some advantages?

15. How does a 360-degree evaluation work?

16. What are four major performance appraisal problems? Describe each.

17. What is meant by validity? Reliability? Which is more difficult to attain? Why?

18. When it comes to rewarding performance, which is more important: extrinsic rewards or intrinsic rewards? Why?

19. How can performance and rewards be linked?

20. What are the conditions that dictate a link between rewards and performance?

21. What are the steps in the progressive discipline process? Identify and define each.

22. If an individual must be discharged, what guidelines should the manager follow? Discuss at least four of the guidelines.

23. According to the red-hot-stove rule of discipline, what are four characteristics of appropriate behavior? Explain each.

24. Can an employer dismiss an employee regardless of cause? Why or why not?

25. How can time wasters be identified?

26. What is the importance of using "to do" lists? How does the priority system work?

27. How can goal setting be a time saver?

28. What does working smarter, not harder mean?

29. What is S.M.A.R.T? How can it be used with setting goals and objectives?

Connecting to the Real World

Getting Your Degree!

The purpose of this exercise is:

1. To understand how the goal/objective setting process works.
2. To construct a goal/objective setting worksheet using Figure 10.6 as a guide.

Situation: Your *goal* is to graduate in two years with a degree in business management and to seek employment. How will you accomplish this?

1. Write four to five measurable objectives for each of the following areas: Use S.M.A.R.T.
   a. Completing your studies successfully
   b. Financing the last two years of study
   c. Selecting an industry for employment
2. Tell how each objective will be measured.
3. Prepare a written paper discussing the key points you learned from using the goal/objective setting guide.

CASE
Following the Rules!

The Space-Management Company manufactures display racks and integrated shelving units for commercial and industrial use. The company was started in 1942 by Tom Eiland. It was unionized in the late 1970s by employees who felt that they were not being treated fairly regarding pay and benefits.

Fred Winslow is a shop steward in the New York City branch, who is well liked by management and the workers. Management feels that Winslow is particularly helpful in working out union–management grievances before they reach arbitration. Several times, Winslow has served as an intermediary and has always been able to establish harmony between the disagreeing factions. Winslow has worked for the company for the past twelve years and has a reputation for being friendly and fair, and his job skills are well above average. He has received excellent scores on his last five appraisals. His coworkers look to him for leadership, despite his lack of an official leadership title.

Adam Scott has worked as a supervisor for Space-Management for less than a year. So far, he has gained a reputation for rule enforcement and exhibits excellent budgetary skills. By streamlining office procedures, he has already saved the company over $500,000.

Last month, Bob, one of the unionized employees was charged with stealing some supplies. The supervisor, Adam Scott, laid Bob off immediately and recommended that he be fired. Winslow, as the shop steward, came to the man's defense and said that the punishment was too great for "accidentally" walking off the job with $10 worth of supplies. After talking to the man and getting his side of the story, Winslow approached the supervisor and suggested a compromise. The worker would admit that he accidentally took some supplies from the premises and would submit to punishment of five days off without pay. The supervisor agreed that the compromise was fair, and everyone was pleased.

In the last two weeks, however, Adam Scott, who also happens to be Winslow's boss, has encountered another problem. A company rule states that anyone who comes in late must be docked an hour's pay for any tardiness of less than sixty minutes, two hours' pay if the lateness extends into the second hour, and so on. In addition, a worker who is late twice in one week is laid off for one week. If a worker is late three times in a four-week period, the penalty is a layoff of two weeks. Finally, if the worker is late four times in any four-week period, he is dismissed.

Two weeks ago, Winslow was late thirty minutes one day and was docked an hour's pay. He said that the train had been delayed. Earlier this week, Winslow was again late by thirty minutes and was docked an hour's pay. The supervisor is worried, however, because Winslow was late again today. He came in at 8:15 A.M. and immediately went to his workstation. The supervisor noticed this, because he had been waiting since 7:30 A.M. to talk to Winslow. At 7:55 A.M., when he had gone to check for Winslow's timecard, it had not yet been punched.

When the supervisor finally saw Winslow enter the work area, he immediately went over to talk to him. The supervisor said nothing about Winslow's tardiness, although Winslow said he was sorry he was late getting to his workstation but that he had been talking to one of the men in another part of the plant about a union matter.

What has Adam Scott concerned is this: Winslow must clock in by 8:00 A.M., regardless of union activities, although he then is allowed to go to other parts of the plant on union business. If he is late, the supervisor feels, Winslow should be penalized, regardless of his position in the union and his value to management in helping solve union–company problems. The actual proof, of course, is the timecard, which should have Winslow's actual arrival time on it. After talking to Winslow, the supervisor went over to check the card, which showed a clock-in time of 7:58 A.M. Now the supervisor is unsure of what to do, for he is certain that Winslow was not in the building before 8:15.

Case Questions
1. What rules has Winslow broken? If so, what is the proof?
2. What specifically should Adam Scott do regarding Winslow's actions?
3. Was the disciplinary action of Adam Scott toward Bob justified? Explain.
4. How does the disciplinary action of supervisors, toward their employees, impact company–employee relations? What are the legal ramifications?
5. Is there anything Adam Scott can do to prevent employee theft, accidental or otherwise, employee tardiness, or time card discrepancy from occurring again? Explain.
6. What management skills should Adam Scott focus on as a learning objective? If you were Adam's boss, how would you mentor him?

PART 5

BEHAVIORAL EFFECTIVENESS

CHAPTER 11
Communicating for Effectiveness

CHAPTER 12
Managing Conflict and Change

In this part of the book, we examine two important areas for ensuring behavioral effectiveness: communication and change.

The goals of this Section are to:

1. Explore how modern organizations go about using technology for communicating effectiveness, describe the communication process, discuss the selection of a medium appropriate to the intended communication, examine some common barriers to effective communication, investigate ways to achieve effective communications in today's technological workplace, discuss guidelines for developing effective listening habits and for improving writing skills, and explore how to more effectively manage stress.

2. Study the management of conflict and change, discuss the nature of conflict and ways to manage it, describe the nature of change and how to manage change and examine how both processes work, discuss the role of participation and communication in the change process, explain organizational development interventions, and explain how to find a mentor.

When you have finished reading this part of the book, you should have a solid understanding of the communication process and of how modern organizations attempt to manage change. You should also understand the importance of behavioral effectiveness and know how communication and the management of change help to ensure this result. You will have a better understanding of how to manage stress and how to find and use a mentor in advancing your career.

© Marcin Balcerzak, Shutterstock Images LLC

CHAPTER **11** | # Communicating for Effectiveness

One of the most common causes of organizational inefficiency is poor communication. In this chapter, we study ways that managers can communicate effectively.

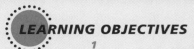

LEARNING OBJECTIVES

1
Describe how technology impacts communication.

2
Describe how the communication process works.

3
Discuss how to choose the appropriate communication medium.

4
Explain how perception, inference, language, and status can lead to communication breakdown.

5
Identify eight ways to overcome barriers to communication and achieve effective communication.

6
Describe how the four steps in the communication process can help improve a manager's communication skills.

7
Describe the importance of using simple, repetitive language; empathy; and body language in achieving effective communication.

8
Discuss ten guidelines for developing effective listening habits.

9
Identify four ways for improving writing skills.

10
Explain the four parts of PLAN for improving speaking skills and discuss how gender can make a difference.

11
Explain how to manage stress more effectively.

Making Communication Pay Off

Many organizations are finding that effective communication is the key to their overall ability to compete. One reason is that the frequency with which changes occur makes it necessary continually to inform employees about what is going on—and why. Consider the case of Wright Builders, a custom home builder based in Temple, Texas. Steve Wright, president and owner of Wright Builders, began his business as a framing contractor in 1976, and his company soon became a premier framing source in the Central Texas area.

Innovative ideas supported by a solid reputation for dependability directed the company to expand into a diversified profile of custom and commercial building along with versatile remodeling services. Currently, the company is expanding into speculative home building. Each home will have its own specialty feature. To meet consumer demands, Wright depends on a team of employees who research market pricing and site locations, and then communicate that information to develop plans and to estimate building costs.

The goal of Wright Builders is total customer satisfaction. Steve Wright stated:

> We believe that the pursuit of excellence in every aspect of our business enables us to meet this goal. This pursuit, which has been a thirty-year endeavor, begins with craftsmanship, the exceptional ability to produce a quality product with distinction. Attention to detail is the hallmark of this level of workmanship. The process continues by providing superior service to our customers, attained by striving to meet the individual needs of each client.

Over the years, Steve Wright has been the recipient of many awards and recognitions for his excellent work in the building industry. His latest awards are the President's Award of Excellence and the Builder of the Year Award from the Temple Area Builders Association. He was president for three years of the Temple Economic Development Corporation board and serves as president of the Temple Independent School District board.

So why is Wright Builders so successful? You only need to ask his staff. They will readily tell you, "It is organization and communication." Every associate and staff member on his team feels a part of the building process—from the time a potential client enters the front door of the office until the project is completed. To make this work, Wright and his team meet regularly to gather input from all phases of operations and to keep everyone posted on the progress of the project; in fact, he calls them "brainstorming" sessions. No one in particular handles each meeting; everyone shares in a roundtable fashion. By keeping his team informed, questions from clients, suppliers, vendors, bankers, carpenters, plumbers, electricians, and roofers can be answered quickly and accurately by whomever answers the phone, which builds rapport and results in excellent working relations. Because his team is knowledgeable about each phase of the project, no task in the office is left undone; anyone can jump in and finish uncompleted tasks on any project. Even though each staff member has specific duties, it is the participation of all staff members that enables this process to work effectively and efficiently. Each member has the authority to make decisions when needed. This professionalism, along with a positive attitude, is the true key to success.

Since the team concept is working at Wright Builders, how is it affecting the firm's organization structure? The structure looks like a bubble of concentric circles interconnecting with communication lines flowing between the circles (Figure 11.1). For example, Steve Wright is in the A circle. His associates and office staff fill the B circles. The clients, vendors, subcontractors, suppliers, and lending institutions fill the C circles whereas city inspectors, state regulators, or other government agents fill the D circles. This structure allows open communication to flow in all directions throughout the firm.

"Communication is the most essential key to providing the best customer service available," states Wright, who works hard at establishing a relationship with each client and with all subcontractors. This enables the decision-making process to be as easy as possible. When he interviews clients, he listens to what they want and the effect they want to achieve. Wright follows a printed outline listing an array of questions that guides him through the process. Pictures, illustrations, and samples of products may also be used to clarify points. By spending quality time in the first phase of the project, both the client and Wright's team have an understanding of the project. Estimating and monitoring the cost of the project are critical communication issues. Here is where Wright Builders depends on technology to give an accurate projection of the cost of the project. Jobs are entered into an estimator software program, which tracks the project for job costing and variance. Changes can be spotted immediately and communicated to the appropriate party for adjustments. This eliminates overrun cost surprises at the end of the project and makes for happier clients.

Wright can be described as a walking communication machine—constantly meeting face-to-face with clients, subcontractors, and suppliers on-site or keeping in touch by cell phone or e-mail. Close monitoring, follow-up, and communication build a high level of trust between his company and all partners in the project. All partners are continually informed about what is going on, which makes them feel important; therefore, they build a quality product. Communication is what makes Wright Builders successful.

Burlington Northern Santa Fe Railway Company is another example of how firms are making communication pay off. The company is currently using new technology that integrates communication systems with global-positioning satellites and onboard computers that can control speeds and even bring a train to a stop. The ultimate goal for Burlington is to reduce the train crew to one person—an idea "championed by the railroads and vigorously opposed by labor unions."

Technology is playing an increasing role in how communication occurs. For example, a new safety feature has been developed by Nissan Motor Company that causes the car's gas pedal to lift by itself, communicating to the driver a possible collision. The Raider Link Internet Café at Fort Hood, Texas, is an example of how communication is changing in the military. The café allows family members and friends to videoconference, send e-mails, video greeting cards, and instant messages to their soldiers who are deployed in Iraq. In another example, the Eye Institute at Scott and White Hospital in Temple uses an IOL (intraocular lens) Master machine to communicate to the doctor the size of lens to implant during cataract surgery.

Even in times of disasters, like an ice storm that brought down telephone poles and power lines across much of Kentucky, one small-town mayor pulled out his iPhone and began tapping away, posting updates on Facebook to let his constituents know what was going on. Down the road, another used his OnStar service to summon help when fallen trees blocked the road. The killer storm forced many people to get creative just to communicate. More than 1.3 million homes and businesses were left without power in several states. Through Facebook, people were able to keep themselves updated. As technology expands and changes in the next decades, so will communication.

Describe how technology impacts communication.

Technology's Impact on Communication

Technology is changing the way **communication** works in firms and affecting the way people interact. Technology speeds up communication and gives immediate access to information that was not available before. For example, on January 13, 2003, Shannon Syfrett, a fifteen-year-old ninth-grader at Central Academy in Macon, Mississippi, launched a chain letter over the Internet for her science fair project. The objective was to learn where and how fast information travels. She sent out twenty-three e-mails and expected to get two thousand to three thousand replies in six weeks, but got 160,478 e-mails from 189 countries and fifty states in twenty-five days, after which she had to pull the plug due to the volume of replies. "Shannon's first e-mail reply arrived two hours after lunch, and her first overseas reply arrived eleven hours after that from Schleswig-Holstein, Germany."[1]

Regardless of the technology used to exchange information, the basics of the communication process remain constant and are important to its effectiveness. It is the communication networks and electronic machines and gadgets that are changing. They impact how we communicate and how we interact in the workplace and in our job. For example, employees today are linked to a computer in the office, a laptop they take on the road, and a computer at home. Employees carry an array of handheld digital devices, such as mobile and smart phones; iPods; iPads; digital cameras; GPS devices; PDAs; iPhones; and pagers. These handheld devices use satellites to transmit messages and employees can engage in instant messaging in real time from any location.

As technology advances and environmentalists push to preserve trees, will the e-reader soon replace the newspaper industry? What will happen to the printing press? Are people who are currently accustomed to getting news articles free in the paper be willing to pay for individual articles? E Ink Corporation of Cambridge, Massachusetts, is fast at work moving the e-reader technology from black and white to color with greater screen visibility. E-reader usage is rapidly gaining acceptance.

Mobile Phones

Mobile, cell, and smart phones; personal computers; and the Internet have revolutionized ways of connecting and empowering people. Information can be sent to anyone, anyplace, and be received from almost anywhere in the world nonstop, twenty-four hours a day, seven days a week. The number of people who own mobile phones is growing rapidly, as is the number of workers in the industry. The world's worker population in the mobile industry will pass the 1-billion mark in 2010 and grow to nearly 1.2 billion people by 2013. The United States has the highest percentage of mobile workers in its workforce, with 72.2 percent of the workforce mobile in 2008. This number is expected to rise to 119.7 million workers being mobile in 2013.[2]

Mobile phones are not only changing the way we communicate with one another; they are changing behavior at work and at home. The mobile phone has upended existing social rules and created a new culture that worships mobility, modifying many long-held social rules that governed the use of landline phones. In today's rapidly evolving culture, people think nothing of engaging in a mobile phone conversation in almost anyplace, from a bathroom to a dining table located in an upscale restaurant. Conversations cover topics from business to sex, seemingly with no regard for privacy.

A study by the University of Michigan's Institute for Social Research found that 83 percent of the respondents said mobile phones have made life easier, but found them somewhat irritating when used in public. Of the respondents, 76 percent found that the Internet made their lives easier. The mobile phone clearly inspires mixed feelings for many people, although it has proven to be useful in some ways. For example, in a study by Sprint, almost two out of every three people used their cell phone backlights to look for something in the dark, mostly keyholes and walkways, while 7 percent used their mobile phones to cheer at a band concert, and 4 percent have used them to light up their face to tell a ghost story.

In an *ABC News* poll, 87 percent of the respondents said that the bad behavior they observed was annoying mobile phone calls, which falls third behind overall rude behavior and bad language usage. Other survey data show that people are still trying to figure out the socially acceptable limits for mobile phone use. Many of the previously accepted behaviors are no long accepted; for instance, the acceptance of using a mobile phone in a movie or theater has dropped to only 2 percent from 11 percent in 2000. It is suggested that the way we use our mobile phones may indicate how others perceive us. A BBDO Worldwide study suggests that the way a mobile phone is used reveals as much about a person as the car he or she drives.[3]

In a survey conducted in 2009 of two thousand NSA members, the National Safety Council found that 23 percent of the firms prohibit their employees from using both handheld and hands-free devices while driving. Several companies have paid dearly for injuries caused by a company employee using a mobile phone during an accident. Over half (58 percent) of the respondents said their companies had a mobile phone policy of some kind, and over a third of the companies without any policy expected to implement one within the year.[4] While the numbers may be low, the literature indicates that employers are implementing mobile phone policies in all industries and sectors—private corporations, nonprofits, government agencies, educational institutions, mass transit—not only their fleets and commercial drivers, but also for all employees. To protect the company and the employees from lawsuits and injury, all firms should consider preparing written policies covering employee use of mobile phones while on the job.

Should employers give employees access to company data systems through their cell phones and BlackBerrys? This issue must be carefully considered, boundaries must be set, and policies should be in place before giving access. Once access is permitted, employees can communicate instantly with customers, friends, family, and, quite literally, everyone else connected to the Internet. Policies must be reviewed as technology advances. Employers must act to protect proprietary and confidential information, or they could lose the ability to protect against its public use. Monitoring the access and use of the information may be a necessary step in proving that information was confidential.[5]

Camera Phones

As the technology for cellular camera phones explodes, employers must become more knowledgeable about the risks relating to the workplace. The new camera phones are equipped with technology that can expose companies to possible breaches of data security and employee privacy. Although businesses that rely on trade secrets are most exposed, the threat includes client lists, product formulas, marketing strategies, and proprietary information. The use of camera phones also can lead to harassment claims. Camera phones have many positive uses in the corporate world, as well as in the medical field. For example, camera phones can be used in surgery for getting help during an operation because the surgeon can send a picture of the patient's x-ray to another specialist across the world and receive a solution. Camera phones also help capture criminals in action.

Video surveillance equipment is another technology that can communicate employee actions and behaviors, which may result in disciplinary action and, in some instances, have ended in lawsuits. In some cases, the legal decision was to limit the use of video surveillance equipment in some companies. Often, insurance companies use video surveillance techniques to capture daily actions of persons on medical disability payments to determine if they are actually disabled and cannot work even in a sedentary job. The use of video surveillance equipment has its benefits and problems that must carefully be weighed by management prior to installation.

Have companies addressed the need for written policies concerning the use of camera phones and video surveillance equipment? A survey by the Society for Human Resource Management indicated that nearly 77 percent of the companies surveyed lacked a written policy addressing the use of camera phones at work, while 40 percent of the companies have a policy covering mobile phones. "Acts of industrial espionage are a real problem, costing companies globally up to $300 billion a year," says Richard Isaacs, senior vice president at Lubrinco Group, a risk management consultancy in New York. At DaimlerChrysler Corporation, cameras were banned almost thirty-five years ago. Dallas-based Texas Instruments also has a written policy prohibiting camera phones.[6]

What might be an even greater risk to employers is the possibility of harassment by employees who impulsively take inappropriate photos, which can land the company in court. To prevent abuse and limit an employer's legal liability, companies should develop a workplace policy concerning camera phones and the use of video surveillance equipment. Other companies suggest that sensitive things be placed in special areas of extreme security and that employees be better trained to watch for behavior that should not be going on.[7]

Workplace and Behavioral Changes

Communication technology is changing the workplace. Managers today must be computer and Internet literate. They are expected to take advantage of real-time information and to retrieve their own information and not depend on an office assistant. The Internet, intranet and extranet networks, e-mail, and instant messaging are the standard for businesses, even small businesses of 250 employees. To help enhance communication, firms are also increasing their use of voice recognition systems and videoconferencing systems. The number of Internet users has grown exponentially over the past several years. By the end of September 2009, the total number of global Internet users had surpassed 1.73 billion, an increase of 18 percent over 2008. China has the largest population of Internet users followed by the United States, Japan, India, Brazil, and Germany. In 2009 alone, over 90 trillion e-mails were received or sent by Internet users. Also, there were 126 million blogs, 273 million daily tweets with 57 percent of the twitters living in the United States, and 350 million Facebook users, plus all the millions of pictures being shared around the world in Flicker and YouTube, just to name two sources. The Internet is a tool by which communication flows immediately and quickly. When an event of importance occurs somewhere in the world, the news is spread around the world almost instantly by digital technology.[8]

E-Mail

Workforce Week wanted to know if e-mail was overused. It asked its online readers to respond to the question: Is e-mail overrelied-upon as a method of communicating with employees? The results from 865 respondents showed that 62 percent voted *yes*, 33 percent voted *no*, and 7 percent voted *depends/not sure*.[9] E-mail overload is now considered a workplace problem. Part of the problem is that too many people click on the "reply to all" button for trivial messages, resulting in colleague spam. The number of corporate e-mails sent and received per person per day was 142 in 2007, and expected to grow to 228 in 2011, causing some employees to spend almost half their time processing e-mails.[10]

Another question often asked is, "Is e-mail considered communication?" For instance, John sends an e-mail to his employees about a policy change. The records show the message was successfully sent and was received and that every employee opened the e-mail. Would you say that John had communicated successfully? According to a federal court case in Boston, e-mail does not qualify as communication. The courts say a company must go beyond the steps taken by John to ensure that workplace policies have been received and reviewed by its employees. John should have required each employee to indicate by return e-mail that he or she had read the e-mail and attachments, if any, and that he or she had understood the implications. Each employee should have been required to reply by stating, "I accept." It simply is not enough to distribute a policy electronically without applying further safeguards to ensure that employees actually receive, read, and understand the message.[11]

Should hourly workers be paid for time spent responding to work calls or e-mails while off the clock? Work was much easier to define when the federal Fair Labor Standards Act was passed than it is today. The Act states that employees must be paid for work performed off the clock, even if the work was voluntary. Lawsuits have been springing up around the country by employees claiming that they were required to use company-issued smart phones and cell phones to receive and respond to work messages after office hours without pay. As communication technology advances, firms must address these issues by adopting policies to regulate mobile phone use outside the office.[12]

E-mails are a way for businesses to keep in touch with customers. It is a means of providing customer service, along with the social networks, Facebook, MySpace, Twitter, and other social media, including the telephone. It is a way to get feedback and to stay abreast of changes in the marketplace. By monitoring these communication systems, businesses can get valuable feedback on their products, business services, or operations. If something negative is being spread, a business can respond and try to turn it into something positive. For example, Southwest Airlines reacted to negative feedback about its boarding process and changed the procedure from first-come, first-served to a more orderly numbered system based on the order of check-in. These communication systems allow employers to develop a more personal, emotional connection with customers and employees.

Seven rules that can make communicating by e-mail more effective are:

1. **Keep it to one screen or less**. If the message covers more than one screen, readers tend to just scan it.
2. **Write in bullet points**. Bullet points are easier to read and retain when read from a computer screen.
3. **Give the "meat" of the message in the subject line**. The subject line should grab the reader and tell exactly what the message is about.
4. **If you are sending e-mails from a wireless device, let people know**. If you are using a BlackBerry, include a tagline telling people you are using one of those devices or you may come across as rude.
5. **Spell-check your e-mails**. Preserve your credibility.
6. **Encourage questions via e-mail**. The true strength of e-mail is its interactive nature.
7. **Send e-mails only when necessary:** Remember that you are not the only one sending e-mails to your staff. Do your best to e-mail only when you need to so you do not add to inbox clutter.[13]

E-mail Netiquette.   Network etiquette is called netiquette. In writing, sending, and responding to e-mail, netiquette is the set of rules for conduct or behavior that should be followed. It is amazing that today some companies still do not realize how important their e-mail communications are. For example, e-mails are sent late or not at all and often the replies fail to answer the questions asked. If a company can deal professionally with e-mail, it can have an important competitive edge and convey a professional image. E-mails that get to the point are much more effective than poorly worded e-mails, and they allow the employees to use their time more efficiently. Moreover, by educating employees as to what can and cannot be said in an e-mail, the company can protect itself from awkward or costly liability issues.[14] There are many etiquette guides and many different rules of etiquette, which are influenced by the nature of the business and the corporate culture. Review the etiquette rules for effective e-mail replies shown in Table 11.1. How many of these rules do you follow in using e-mail?

E-Mail Etiquette Enforcement.   The first step in enforcing e-mail etiquette is to create a written e-mail policy. It should include all the do's and don'ts and should be distributed to all employees. The second step is to train all employees to fully understand the importance of e-mail etiquette. And finally, e-mail management software and e-mail response tools can be used to monitor the implementation of the rules.[15]

Wireless Networks

Another rapidly expanding communication technology is Wi-Fi networks. Wi-Fi stands for wireless fidelity, better known as *hot spots*. The technology was originally intended to be used for mobile devices, but is now being used for gaining access to the Internet. Wi-Fi allows employees to do their work and to communicate with the office regardless of where they are. For wireless services, WiMax is the new generation of technology. It is more powerful, can cover a larger area, is faster, and is a more efficient service to customers. Wireless services are being used to communicate throughout business operations, in retail stores, and within hospitals. Wireless services are a vital part of a firm's communication system that should be managed.

Table 11.1
E-Mail Etiquette: Rules for Effective E-Mail Replies

1. Be concise and to the point (reading an e-mail is harder than reading printed material).
2. Answer all questions, and preempt further questions (failure to answer questions requires more e-mails and wastes time; include additional information the sender will need to complete the request).
3. Use proper spelling, grammar, punctuation, structure, and layout.
4. Do not write in CAPITALS (too difficult to read and it appears to be shouting).
5. Answer swiftly, address the e-mail personally, and include customized content.
6. Do not attach unnecessary files (some e-mail systems cannot accept files).
7. Do not overuse the high-priority, urgent, or important options (when they are really needed, they may not work).
8. Include the message thread (reply to the e-mail so the recipient can recall the original message, instead of starting a new e-mail).
9. Always read the e-mail before sending it (use spell-check to find misspelled words).
10. Add disclaimers to your e-mails (for example, the recipient must check each e-mail for viruses and you cannot be held liable for any transmitted viruses).
11. Do not overuse "Reply to All" (use only when everyone needs to see the response).
12. Take care with abbreviations and emoticons (the recipient may not understand).
13. Be careful with rich text and HTML messages (not everyone can receive them).
14. Do not forward chain letters or request delivery and read receipts.
15. Do not ask to recall a message (instead, send another e-mail admitting your mistake).
16. Do not copy a message or attachment without permission (it may infringe on copyright laws).
17. Do not use e-mail to discuss confidential information (never make any libelous, sexist, or racially discriminating comments in e-mails, even if they are meant to be a joke).
18. Use a meaningful subject (be as specific as possible).
19. Use active instead of passive language and avoid long sentences (maximum of 15 to 20 words).
20. Do not send or forward e-mails containing libelous, defamatory, offensive, racist, or obscene remarks (court cases may result in multimillion-dollar penalties).
21. Do not forward virus hoaxes or reply to spam.
22. Keep the language gender neutral (he, she, and they are acceptable).
23. Use cc: field sparingly (use only when recipients know why they are receiving the e-mail).

Source: www.emailreplies.com.

Opportunities for free access to the Internet are being offered by more types of businesses and in more locations. For example, free wireless is becoming more available in restaurants and cafés all over. None have the national reach of Panera Bread, a chain of "bakery-cafés" famous for its artisan breads and cozy hangouts. Customer usage hours are increasing, which means selling more coffee and cookies.[16]

Global Positioning Systems

A Global Positioning System or GPS is a navigational system consisting of satellites that orbit the Earth, sending information to a device mounted on a vehicle or to a mobile phone. It is a communication system that pinpoints the recipient's exact location, but can be used for much more. For example, Roto-Rooter's GPS is linked to a series of mobile printers that generate invoices at client sites. It can detect when a technician is near completion of a job and automatically notifies the dispatch center. In addition, it directs the workers to the next assignment, saving time and creating a more efficient job-dispatching system, allowing technicians to serve 20 percent more customers. And at the same time, it can locate workers who are goofing off and not doing their work. A GPS can quickly direct a driver to the correct location for delivery of merchandise and save time and money. The SuperShuttle, which provides door-to-door ground transportation to and from twenty-three U.S. airports, uses GPS to assign routes based upon the real-time location and status of drivers. GPS gives the driver a summary of the routes, the total fares for all the pickups in the route, and the number of passengers.[17] By more efficiently utilizing employees and resources, GPSs save businesses and governmental agencies money every year.

Patterns of Communication

As the workplace becomes more mobile, new patterns of communication emerge. The traditional systems of downward, upward, and horizontal communication are no longer the dominant patterns of communication. New patterns are emerging, allowing all group members to have greater access to receiving and sending information across the organization. The way information flows changes with the technology used. For example, the flow of information among workers in remote locations is different from that used by employees working in an office. Teleworkers must depend on some kind of electronic communication device to talk with or send information to their bosses and to the home offices. Although employees in the office are able to meet face-to-face to share information and discuss problems and issues, they also have access to electronic communications devices. To be effective, each group forms its own unique system of communication, often following nontraditional lines of communication.

As communication systems become more complex, it is not unusual for a company to hire a COC, chief of communications, to be in charge of the company's communication systems. The COC is a highly responsible administrative, managerial, and supervisory position involving all phases of planning and directing the internal communication systems, as well as communicating with governmental agencies. The job may also include preparing new releases, communication counseling, and monitoring compliance with regulatory standards.

Organizational Structure

Changes in organizational structure also affect patterns of communication. For the past one hundred years, rank has equaled authority. The old hierarchy business structure placed people and functions in boxes, and some even developed a pyramid with the

Figure 11.1 Wheel of Fortune

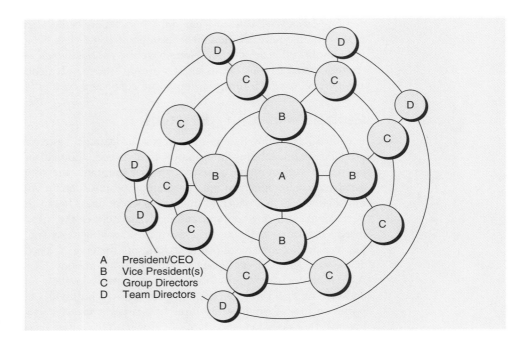

A   President/CEO
B   Vice President(s)
C   Group Directors
D   Team Directors

CEO sitting on the top, keeping watch over his workforce. In the past decade, massive changes in global competition, technology, philosophy, and leadership have forced organizations to transform their structures. The old way of doing business did not work anymore, as Frances Hesselbein, editor-in-chief of *Leader to Leader*, president and CEO of the Drucker Foundation, and former chief executive of the Girl Scouts of the USA, learned when she worked for the Girl Scouts organization. She developed "a new organizational structure where people and functions move across three concentric circles, with the CEO in the middle looking across, not at the top looking down." It is known as "the bubble chart" or "the Wheel of Fortune." In this organization, people communicate across the circles of the organization. See an illustration in Figure 11.1.[18] As discussed in the opening vignette, Steve Wright uses this type of structure with his staff at Wright Builders, a home construction business. He strongly believes that the "Wheel of Fortune" organization structure and the nontraditional communication system are keys to the success of his business.

Researchers at Hewlett-Packard have "developed a way to use e-mail exchanges to build a map of the structure of an organization. The map shows the teams in which people actually work, as opposed to those under which they were hired. Employees are often assigned to work on special projects involving people from all parts of the company, and they must exchange information with others in the firm. This tends to divide employees organically into informal collaborative networks, called "communities of practice," which was discussed in the previous chapter. This information is used to "construct a communications graph in which lines—each denoting a direct e-mail exchange—link nodes that correspond to individuals." At Hewlett-Packard, the researchers found sixty-six communities.[19]

Using Color in Communication

Hewlett-Packard has released a study conducted by the Color Association of the United States that featured tips on using color to increase the effectiveness of daily business communications. The report emphasizes the beneficial effects of color as an organizational and motivational tool for both customers and employees. "Color not only motivates and communicates key messages, but it also denotes a certain level of pride and energy."[20] Key findings from the study were:

- A color's brightness and intensity are key factors in eliciting reactions and motivating employees or customers to act.
- Although the essence of effective communication is simplicity, color connects a viewer far more directly than words or numbers.
- Contemporary color trends—such as pinks, water-based blues, and a variety of greens—create a fresh approach to corporate design.
- Multicolored graphic design adds credibility to a business and the use of provocative colors within multicolored designs signal that a business understands the needs of today's consumers and is flexible to their desires.
- Mixing and matching papers and textures in marketing collateral is an important consideration to achieve maximum impact.

Communication Challenges

When technology is used to communicate information, there are some drawbacks that managers must address. For example:

- *Information-security problems*. The wrong party can intercept the communication and use the information in the message to its advantage, such as during the Iraq War when the U.S. military intercepted messages among members of Saddam Hussein's regime. A disgruntled former employee can use your Web site or e-mail system for revenge or he or she can walk off the premises with a computer storage device loaded with sensitive information or with documents describing proprietary information. Information security has long been an issue, and firms are working hard to remedy the problem. One solution is to teach all levels of the workforce "security awareness" and to emphasize the importance of following the procedures.
- *Privacy issue concerns*. Most firms are doing a better job of protecting private information and convincing consumers that their personal information is protected on their Web sites, but still some companies have not adequately addressed the issue As a result, consumers must be cautious when shopping online. According to the U.S. Department of Commerce, online retail sales are up and e-shops are growing at a faster pace than their brick-and-mortar counterparts.
- *Extended workdays*. Communication can occur anytime and anyplace, not just during office hours, creating opportunities for employees to work from home. While this practice may have its advantages for both the company and the employees, it may not always be in the best interest of either the company or the employees.
- *Missing nonverbal clues*. Facial expressions and gesturing that provide clues to a receiver's level of understanding are missing. Voice inflection is the only thing that can sometimes give the sender a clue.
- *Increased multitasking*. People can make a phone call and send an e-mail at the same time or work on another message.
- *An overwhelming volume of information*. Processing e-mails can take a large block of time and reduce an employee's work time for other duties and responsibilities. Some feel e-mails have gotten out of control. The ePolicy Institute, a Columbus, Ohio, consulting firm, says 48 percent of all office workers spend one to two hours a day on e-mail. In some cases, employees spend more than half the day processing e-mail.[21]

- *Changes in interaction among team members*. Team members who are not located in the same location may not participate in face-to-face meetings or interact on a regular basis.
- *Reduced social interaction*. People using technology tend to get to the point and not engage in small talk, as they might in a face-to-face meeting People are social beings, and they have social needs.[22]

✔ CHECK YOUR UNDERSTANDING

1. Explain how mobile (cell) phones and camera phones are changing behavior in the workplace.
2. Describe ways you can improve your e-mail etiquette.
3. How does the "Wheel of Fortune" organizational structure work?
4. Discuss how color impacts communication. Give examples.
5. Identify several challenges that technology presents to managers.

Describe how the communication process works.

The Communication Process

In a study, Towers Watson surveyed eighteen thousand employees of multinationals, mostly in the United States. The results showed that 63 percent of the employees said that their senior leaders effectively communicated the company's progress in meeting business goals, which is an improvement over the 54 percent found in the previous year. Employees were unhappy, however, with the level of information they get on competitors and customers.[23] Another study of two thousand employees in Great Britain found that nearly half have never had a conversation with the big boss, and about 25 percent do not even know the names of top executives, including managing directors or CEOs. Moreover, if relationships with their bosses were better, 60 percent of the employees say they would be more loyal, and 58 percent say they would be better motivated.[24] So what is this saying about the communication process in these companies? Let us take a look at the process of communicating.

Communication is the process of transmitting meanings from sender to receiver. These meanings are conveyed through a medium such as e-mail, a phone call, a fax, a printed letter or memorandum, or a conversation. Regardless of the medium used, the **communication** process entails five essential elements: (1) the sender, (2) the message being transmitted, (3) the medium used to carry the message, (4) the receiver of the message, and (5) the interpretation given to the message. In conveying meanings from sender to receiver, three functions (described in Figure 11.2) must be performed.

Figure 11.2 The Communication Process in Action

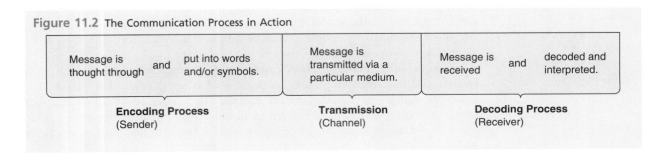

- First, the *message must be encoded*, or put into a form that will be understood by the receiver.
- Second, it must be conveyed through the *proper medium* or channel.
- Third, it *must be decoded*, or interpreted properly, by the person to whom it was directed.

Process of Encoding.   Before a message can be sent from one person to another, it must undergo **encoding**, or be expressed in a code (words, facial expressions, and gestures) that is intelligible to the receiver. For example, when Americans agree with something that is being said and they want to encode this response, they often will smile and nod their heads. This tells the speaker that the listener understands and is supportive of the idea that is being communicated. In contrast, Japanese often will smile and nod their heads to indicate politeness, but this does not mean that they either understand or agree with the speaker. Unfortunately, because many Americans are unaware of the differences in the encoding process between the two cultures, they erroneously believe that their Japanese listeners are supportive of their ideas. Another example of encoding is that when Steve Wright, a custom home builder, interviews clients he must translate technical building terms into words the client understands. Effective encoding requires an understanding of the receiver's level of knowledge. In another case, Barbara Moses, an international speaker, author, and consultant, received a letter with seven acronyms in a couple of paragraphs. She stated, "It had as much meaning as alphabet soup." She continued to say, "I frequently receive such incomprehensible notes. I always wonder if the senders have any idea of how ridiculous they sound, and how their communication style seriously undermines how they are seen by others."[25]

The encoding process involves two important steps: (1) the sender thinks through the ideas to be communicated, and (2) the sender translates these ideas into some code or symbol, such as the combination of words, facial expressions, and gestures described in the previous paragraph.

Selecting a Medium.   The second function is choosing the medium. In describing the encoding process, we have already noted three common forms of communication: words, facial expressions, and gestures. Other forms are conversation, pictures, diagrams, and charts. For example, when one is advertising a product, one frequently uses pictures to convey the idea, as in newspaper ads and billboards. Diagrams and charts are often used when managers communicate with one another. Large amounts of business data are conveyed in these forms. For example, Steve Wright uses pictures, house plans, and blue prints to communicate with his clients.

In addition, we need to consider nonverbal forms of communication. Body language is one example. People transmit meanings by their facial expressions, eye movements, and how close (or far away) they sit or stand in relation to other people. Even the way they walk tells us something about them.

The physical environment in which people live has an influence on their communication. For example, dentists' offices have comfortable chairs and pleasant decor in the waiting rooms so that patients will be less nervous. Restaurants offer dim lighting and soft music, which encourage people to talk softly and stay longer. Even the colors of the room can have an effect on people's mood, resulting in a particular communication pattern. Table 11.2 lists the moods commonly associated with certain colors. If the boss is going to communicate important news to an employee and has the employee wait in an orange room, the employee may surmise that the news is bad (orange tends to create a distressed,

Table 11.2
The Association of Moods with Colors

Mood	Color
Exciting, stimulating	Red
Secure, comfortable	Blue
Distressed, disturbed, upset	Orange
Tender, soothing	Blue
Protective, defending	Red
Despondent, dejected, unhappy, melancholy	Black
Calm, peaceful, serene	Blue
Dignified, stately	Purple
Cheerful, jovial, joyful	Yellow
Defiant, contrary, hostile	Red
Powerful, strong, masterful	Black

Source: Lois B. Wexner, "The Degree to Which Colors (Hues) Are Associated with Mood-Tones," *Journal of Applied Psychology*, December 1954, pp. 433–434.

disturbed mood), but if the employee is waiting in a yellow room, the employee might begin to expect good news (yellow tends to create a cheerful, jovial mood).

Finally, we must consider that the medium used could also direct the message toward certain people and away from others. It must be decided how the communication is to be delivered. For example, will it be delivered face-to-face, over a phone call, or in an e-mail message; printed in a letter or memo; posted on a bulletin board; sent by instant messaging; or delivered through some other medium? The medium selected can deliberately bypass certain people, while focusing on others.

Process of Decoding. The last phase of the communication process involves **decoding**, or interpreting of the message by the receiver. In understanding how this decoding process works, we must consider three areas: the sender's meaning, the receiver's interpretation, and the degree of overlap between them. Let us consider an exaggerated example of very little overlap.

Eddie Jones spent two weeks in South America consulting for the local branch office. The branch manager assigned him an office assistant and an office. A few days before his assignment was over, Jones told the branch manager that he wanted to show his gratitude to his office assistant for a job well done. He planned on getting her a small present on his last day there. The branch manager told Jones the office assistant would appreciate such a gesture. Following up on his promise, Jones brought the office assistant a dozen roses.

Imagine his surprise when the office manager came by to tease him later. "When you said you were going to get her a gift, I thought you were going to buy her something for her home. I should have asked you beforehand what you wanted to get. You see, giving flowers in this country is a sign of romantic interest!"

In this example, we can see that the office manager sent too little information for Jones to decode the message accurately. The office manager assumed Jones knew the customs of gift giving in the country. When senders make assumptions about receivers, problems in communication can occur. Receivers decode from their base of knowledge and experience and may not know enough to ask the proper questions. Even though Jones decoded the message accurately, the message failed to contain sufficient information for Jones to act appropriately, which resulted in an embarrassing situation for Jones and his office assistant. The branch manager should have questioned Jones about the type of gift he planned to buy. It is also the responsibility of the receiver to be forthright in offering clarification and meaning to communiqués.

 CHECK YOUR UNDERSTANDING

Match the term with the statement:

Term	Statement
a. Encoding	_____ Interpreting the message
b. Medium	_____ Thinks through ideas
c. Decoding	_____ Transmission occurs

Discuss how to choose the appropriate communication medium.

Choosing a Medium

In communicating effectively, it is important to choose the proper medium, and there is a wide range of choices. Two important considerations are associated with determining which medium to use. One is information richness, and the other is complexity.

The Matter of Information Richness.   The best choice of medium is the one that provides the appropriate degree of richness and that helps the parties to the communication deal with the complexity of the situation or problem. **Information richness** has been defined as "the potential information-carrying capacity of data."[26] If the medium carries a great deal of information, it is high in richness; if it conveys very little information, it is low in richness. Hence, alternative media can have varying degrees of information richness.

This richness can be measured by four factors.

1. Feedback, which can range from immediate to very slow.
2. The channel that is used to convey the information, which can range from a combination of audio and visual to limited visual.
3. The type of communication, such as personal versus impersonal.
4. The language source that is used, including body language, natural, or numeric.

Table 11.3 categorizes the information richness of five types of media in terms of these four factors.

The richest form of communication is face-to-face. It provides immediate feedback and is a check on how well the information has been comprehended. In addition, this form permits the communicating parties to observe language cues, such as body language and voice tone. Another form that is high in richness is the telephone, both landline and cell phone, although it is not as rich as face-to-face communication. On the other hand, formal numeric media, such as quantitative computer printouts or video displays, have low richness. These forms provide slow feedback, limited visual information, and impersonal data.

Table **11.3** Information Richness for Different Media

Information Richness	Medium	Feedback	Channel	Type of Communication	Language Source
High	Face-to-face	Immediate	Visual, audio	Personal	Body, natural
High–Moderate	Telephone	Rapid	Audio	Personal	Natural
Moderate	Personal written	Slow	Limited visual	Personal	Natural
Moderate–Low	Formal written	Very slow	Limited visual	Impersonal	Natural
Low	Formal numeric	Very slow	Limited visual	Impersonal	Natural

Source: Adapted from R. L. Daft and R. H. Lengel, "Information Richness: A New Approach to Managerial Behavior and Organization Design," in B. M. Staw and L. L. Cummings, eds., *Research in Organizational Behavior* (Greenwich, CT: JAI Press, 1984), p. 197.

The Issue of Complexity.   In communicating information for the purpose of passing on data or discussing problem situations, managers must match their choice of media with the complexity of the issue. For example, the communication of a decision to downsize some of the company's divisions is a complex situation. Those who are going to be affected by the message will have questions, concerns, and fears that must be addressed. Therefore, the company will have to communicate this situation in a deliberate, detailed way. In contrast, low-complexity situations are routine and predictable and can be handled through the use of rules or standard operating procedures. An example is a communiqué to all salespeople reminding them that their expense reports are due by the fifteenth of the month. The challenge for the manager is to choose the appropriate medium. Daft and Lengel have suggested that there are three zones of communication effectiveness.[27]

1. The *most effective zone* is the one in which the complexity of the problem or situation is matched appropriately with the richness of the medium. For example, when faced with a simple situation, a manager should choose a medium that is low in richness. Conversely, if a problem is very complex, the manager should opt for a medium that is high in richness. If the individual does not correctly match the situation and the medium, the individual will be in one of the other two zones, the overload zone or the oversimplification zone.

2. The *overload zone* is one in which the medium provides more information than is necessary. An example is the use of face-to-face communication to convey a simple, routine matter such as reminding someone to attend a weekly meeting; an e-mail or voice mail can easily accomplish this.

3. The *oversimplification zone* is one in which the medium does not provide the necessary information. For example, posting on the bulletin board a memo that relates that management has decided to downsize and terminate 10 percent of the workforce is going to cause a great deal of concern and anxiety. The employees will want to know more about the decision, who will be affected, and how management intends to handle the matter. A more detailed, medium-rich approach is needed.

Research studies have revealed that media usage is significantly different across organizational levels.[28] Senior-level managers tend to spend much more time in face-to-face meetings than do lower-level managers. Given that these executives are far more likely to be dealing with ambiguous and complicated situations, these results are consistent with those noted here regarding the importance of matching the situation and the media richness.

✔ CHECK YOUR UNDERSTANDING

Check the correct answers:

1. Information richness can be measured by which four factors: _____ feedback, _____ perception, _____ the channel used, _____ inference, _____ type of communication used, _____ language, _____ status.
2. The overload zone is one that: _____ matches appropriately with the richness of the medium, _____ provides more information than is necessary, _____ fails to provide the necessary information.
3. The oversimplification zone is one that: _____ provides too much information, _____ matches complexity to richness, _____ requires more information.

Explain how perception, inference, language, and status can lead to communication breakdown.

Barriers to Communication

All communication flows are subject to barriers that prevent the receiver from getting the sender's meaning. Some of the most common barriers are perception, inference, language, and status.

Perception

Cultural Barriers.   People are constantly bombarded with information that the mind has to organize into a mental map that represents his or her **perception** of reality. In no case is the perception of a certain person the same as the world itself, and no two maps are identical. As a person views the world, his or her mind absorbs experiences in a unique and personal way. Because perceptions are unique, the ideas a person wants to express differ from other people's, even when two people have experienced the same event.[29] People from different age groups, educational levels, economic positions, cultural backgrounds, temperament, religions, political beliefs, and values have different perceptions that can create a barrier to communications in the workplace.[30] Perceptions that men have about women and that women have about men can create gender barriers in the workplace. Women continue to work hard to prove they can successfully fill top management positions. This is evidenced by reviewing Fortune Magazine's 2009 list of the "50 Most Powerful Women in Business."

Secret Salaries.   A factor that can influence perception is secret salaries. When the amount of money that employees are being paid remains a secret, many people have the perception that they are being paid less than others who are doing the same work.[31] Conversely, when salary information is made available to everyone, it often results in higher employee satisfaction because the workers realize that they are not being shortchanged and that their perception was incorrect.[32]

Knowledge of Listener.   Another perception-related problem is the common belief that the listener has the same knowledge as the communicator. However, often this is not true, and so the listener is unable to follow the conversation because he or she lacks the necessary information. The result is communication breakdown.[33] Noise can even affect perception. Consumers expect a vacuum cleaner to be loud because they believe that there is a relationship between noise and how well the unit is working.

Figure 11.3
A Communication
Continuum

Value of Lifestyle. Lifestyle is another example. Americans perceive those who work long hours as being hardworking and responsible, whereas many Germans place greater value on leisure, work about 20 percent fewer hours than Americans, and find it difficult to perceive why people in the United States are so committed to work.[34] Clearly, when communicating with others, one's perception can influence the outcome.

Sufficient Information. Nonetheless, to communicate effectively, people do not need to have identical perceptions. It is necessary only that one party transmit sufficient information for the other party to take appropriate action. The major question for the manager is, "What constitutes 'sufficient' information?" Some messages may be well thought out and may still be misunderstood by the receiver. Other messages may be vague, but the receiver may have no trouble understanding them.

Clear and *vague* are two ideas that can be placed on a communication continuum, as shown in Figure 11.3. The messages on the left deal with ideas that are easily understood and do not involve matters of opinion or issues that are open to interpretation. For example, "George, beginning tomorrow you are to occupy Ralph's office. He is being transferred to the Denver office, and you are next in line in seniority, so the office is yours." This is a clear message. We can expect George to clean out his desk and move the contents into Ralph's office the next day. We would be surprised if we found that George moved into his boss's office, because that would indicate quite a deviation from the originally transmitted message.

"George, if you do well in your current position, you can expect a promotion to the Denver office as well." This message is much vaguer than the previous one. Note that the sender of the message does not make clear what is meant by "if you do well." It is implied that George knows, but does he?

As one moves across the communication continuum in Figure 11.3, there is a point at which the messages become extremely difficult to comprehend. However, it is erroneous to believe that all clear communiqués are error-free. Often people see and hear what they want or expect to see and hear. When this happens, communication breakdown can occur. Let us take an example. After this paragraph, there is a sentence containing all capital letters. Read the sentence slowly and carefully so you understand its entire meaning. When you are finished, go on to the paragraph that follows.

FINISHED FILES ARE THE RESULT OF YEARS OF SCIENTIFIC STUDY COUPLED WITH THE EXPERIENCE OF MANY YEARS.

Before reading further, you may read the foregoing sentence one more time. When you have finished, and only when you have finished, continue reading down this page. The capitalized sentence that you have read consists of seventeen words. It is a somewhat long, although not particularly difficult, sentence containing a handful of ideas. Within this sentence are a number of different letters: fourteen Es, four As, and so on. Adhere to the following ground rules and count the number of times another letter appears in the displayed sentence.

You may not use your finger, pen, or pencil in rereading the capitalized sentence; you may use only your eyes.

You are to read the sentence as quickly as possible, taking no more than ten seconds to do so. (If possible, time yourself.) When you have finished reading the sentence, you may continue to the next paragraph. Ready? Okay. Begin reading the capitalized sentence and count the number of times the letter F appears. Go!

How many times did you find the letter F in the sentence? The most common answers are two, three, four, five, six, and seven. Was your answer one of these? One of these numbers is correct. Regardless of the number you arrived at the first time, go back to the sentence and read it slowly and deliberately, counting the number of Fs very carefully.

If you have counted three—no more, no less—you are typical of most people. Actually, there are six Fs in the sentence (finished, files, scientific, and the three ofs). Most people miss these last three because they are accustomed to reading past short words, skimming over them too quickly to notice the spelling. This exercise demonstrates that even when it comes to "clear" messages, people make errors because they do not perceive what actually is there.

Let us take another illustration, this time using a vague message. Following this paragraph are nine dots. After studying them for a minute, connect all nine dots with four straight lines. Here are the rules:

1. You may not take your pen or pencil off the paper.
2. If you retrace a line by, for example, going from left to right and then back again to the point of departure, you have used two lines.

The lines must indeed be straight; do not curve them in any way.

After you have finished this exercise (take no more than five minutes with it), you can check your answer with the solution given at the end of the chapter. As you will see, going outside the perimeter formed by the nine dots is the only way to solve the puzzle. If you try to stay within this square area, you cannot solve the problem without using at least five straight lines.

When managers communicate, they often believe their messages are clear. Often, however, they are vague, and the receiver ends up asking, "What did the boss mean by that?"

Inference

Another common communication problem, closely associated with perception, is inference. An **inference** is an assumption made by the receiver of a message. Inferences are most often present in messages that are very long or that involve a large number of facts. In interpreting their meaning, the receiver often is forced to make assumptions, because the facts are not all clearly transmitted. The "Time Out" (A Matter of Inference) quiz is an illustration. How well did you do? Check your answers with those at the end of the book. Most people get no more than eight correct answers.

Inference occurs whenever the sender of the message fails to communicate clearly and completely. In face-to-face communication, many of these problems can be overcome, as the listener can quickly stop the conversation and ask a question. However,

A Matter of Inference

Instructions

Read the following story very carefully. You may assume that everything it says is true, but be aware that parts of the story are deliberately vague. You can read the story twice if you desire, but once you start reading the statements that follow, do not go back to either the story itself or any previous statements. Simply read each statement and decide whether it is true (the story said so), false (the story said just the opposite), or inferential (you cannot say whether it is true or false; you need more facts). Write your answer (T for true, F for false, and I for inferential) on the line before the statement. When you are finished, check your results with the answers given at the end of the book.

The Story

Bart Falding is head of the research and development (R&D) department of a large plastics firm located in New England. Bart has ordered a crash R&D program in hopes of developing a new process that will revolutionize plastics manufacturing. He has given five of his top R&D people authority to spend up to $250,000 each without consulting him or the R&D committee.

He has sent one of his best people, Mary Lou Rasso, to a major midwestern university to talk to a Nobel Prize winner there who has just applied for and received a patent that Bart believes may provide the basis for a breakthrough in the plastics field. Three days after Mary Lou left for the university, Bart received a call from her. Mary Lou was very excited, and said she and the scientist were flying in to see Bart the next day, although she declined to discuss the matter over the phone.

Bart believes he will have very good news for the company president when they meet for their biweekly lunch early next week.

The Statements

___ 1. Bart is head of the R&D department of a large plastics firm.
___ 2. The company is located in Los Angeles, California.
___ 3. Bart received orders from the president to engage in a crash R&D program.
___ 4. Bart's R&D budget is in excess of $1 million.
___ 5. Bart assigned five of his best people to work on developing a new process for revolutionizing plastics manufacturing.
___ 6. Mary Lou was sent to talk to a Nobel Prize-winning professor.
___ 7. Mary Lou works for the plastics manufacturing department.
___ 8. Mary Lou was authorized to spend up to $250,000 without approval from the R&D committee.
___ 9. Bart's company wants to buy the patent from the university professor.
___ 10. Bart believes that Mary Lou has already offered the professor a deal and the latter is prepared to accept it, but Mary Lou first wants to discuss the matter with top management.
___ 11. Mary Lou has agreed to pick up all the scientist's expenses if the latter will consent to come and talk to Bart in person.
___ 12. The scientist must be interested in some type of financial or business arrangement with Bart's firm, or the scientist would not have agreed to fly in and meet with Bart.
___ 13. The scientist received the Nobel Prize for work he did in the area of plastic processes.
___ 14. Bart and the company president have lunch on a biweekly basis.
___ 15. Bart believes he will have good news for the president, for he is sure the scientist will agree to sell the patent to the company if the firm makes a sufficiently high offer.

with written messages, this is more difficult because the receiver is forced to use his or her own best judgment in deciding what the message actually means.

Language

Language is used to convey meaning in the communication process. This is as true in written as in spoken communications. However, sometimes language proves to be a communication barrier. One of the most common reasons is that people are unfamiliar with some of the words that are being used or associate different meanings with them. For example, in recent years, a number of new words have become part of many people's lexicon, for example, *blogs* and *web logs*. Even the terms *telecommuting* and *teleworking* are used and defined in many different ways. Another example is words that have technical meanings. For example, in engineering firms, the word *burn* often means "to photocopy." Imagine the surprise of a manager when he or she tells a new office assistant to burn a copy of the original blueprints and then finds that they must be redrawn! Every profession has its own meanings for words.

Communications theorists like to point out that meanings are not resident in words but in the people who use them. When we employ language for communication purposes, we sometimes do not associate the same meaning with a word as does the receiver, and so communication breakdown is all but inevitable.

Another common language-related problem is reading. Many schools no longer teach students to read and write properly. Grammar, sentence construction, and reading skills are not stressed. Students now enter the workforce unprepared to communicate effectively.

Status

As defined in Chapter 4, **status** refers to the relative ranking of an individual in a group. In the formal organization, those at the top tend to have much higher status than those at the bottom. When people communicate, status affects the process, because they often monitor what they say or write on the basis of who is going to receive the message, and they distort what they hear by judging its accuracy according to who said it. For example, many people do not share good news or useful ideas with their boss because they believe their information will be ignored, or if it has any practical value, the boss will use the information for his or her personal gain. Peter Lilienthal, president of InTouch Management Communication Systems, has reported that surveys conducted by his firm reveal that 90 percent of employees believe they have good ideas for improving the effectiveness of their firms but only 50 percent of them ever share these ideas with the company.[35]

Another example involves status between management and union members. Management may regard a complaint it receives from the union as nothing more than union rhetoric. However, if a member of management tells the president that the complaint is accurate, the union's message takes on a higher degree of credibility. Conversely, if a union employee is late for work and is laid off for three days, the shop steward may fight to have the punishment reduced. However, if people in the employee's area tell the steward that the employee is always late for work, is unproductive in assignments, and altogether is more of a hindrance than a help, the shop steward may not argue the employee's case very hard.

One way to motivate people is to give them status symbols. Employees may want equality, but most people want to be just a little more equal than others. In short, status is important. We all want to feel special. As a result, the organization cannot remove status symbols; so it must learn to adjust to the problems that accompany them, including communication breakdown.

 CHECK YOUR UNDERSTANDING

Match the term to the statement:

Term	Statement
a. Perception	_____ Involves making assumptions.
b. Inference	_____ Gives a feeling of importance.
c. Language	_____ Provides a view of reality.
d. Status	_____ Conveys meaning.

Identify eight ways to overcome barriers to communication and achieve effective communication.

Achieving Effective Communication

The barriers we have just examined can prevent the sender from conveying his or her meaning to the receiver, but this need not happen. There are ways to overcome the barriers and achieve effective communication. Some of the most useful are:

1. Knowing the steps in the communication process.
2. Using simple, repetitive language.
3. Using empathy.
4. Understanding body language.
5. Learning how to receive and give feedback.
6. Developing effective listening habits.
7. Improving writing and speaking skills.
8. Understanding gender differences.[36]

Describe how the four steps in the communication process can help improve a manager's communication skills.

Knowing the Steps in the Communication Process

If a manager knows the steps in the communication process, many of the breakdowns we have just discussed can be avoided. The four steps in the communication process are:

1. Attention
2. Understanding
3. Acceptance
4. Action

Attention.   The sender must gain the **attention** of the receiver before communication can occur. Listeners may need to screen out distractions before they can focus on the message, hear, and understand it. Likewise, senders of e-mails and written communications must capture the reader's attention by highlighting the message's key points in the subject line or within the first paragraph of the communiqué. If the sender does not keep the message interesting and informative, there is a good chance that the receiver will begin to daydream or ponder on some of the other messages competing for his or her attention.

Understanding.   Comprehension of the message results in **understanding**.[37] The receiver must grasp the meaning. In trying to accomplish this step, many managers ask their people, "Do you understand what I'm saying?" However, this is the wrong approach. One should never ask people whether they understand because the pressure is on them to answer *yes*. Rather, the manager should ask them what they understand. In this way, the listeners are forced to restate the message in their own words, and the manager can judge the accuracy of their understanding.

The "Cultural Diversity in Action" (A Black Hole in Corporation Communication in Action) box offers additional insights to the area of understanding and provides an example of what happens in the absence of real information.

Acceptance.   When the receiver is willing to go along with the message, **acceptance** occurs. Only in rare cases do subordinates refuse to comply with directives from the boss. They usually obey without giving the matter much thought. However, people balk if they think that the order is detrimental to their best interests.

IN ACTION

A BLACK HOLE IN CORPORATE COMMUNICATION

I was in New York last week with my friend Ray, who works for a multinational financial services firm. He and his coworkers from around the country had gathered in the city for a week to review marketing plans and revenue goals, which they did. But during the meetings, the Pooh-Bahs in his division also cryptically mentioned the possibility of a divisionwide restructuring: something they called a "re-org."

After the second day of meetings, I returned to the Embassy Suites to find Ray sitting on the couch, staring into space, his shirt rumpled and untucked. This worried me. Ray is never rumpled. I asked if he was okay.

"What do they mean by re-org?" he asked, still staring straight ahead. "I'll tell you what they mean. They mean job cuts. I think I'm okay—but maybe not. Maybe I'm not okay. Do you think I'm okay?" He didn't wait for an answer. "I should've talked more during the meeting today," he said. "I should've gone to the dinner last night. I should've worn black shoes. I looked too casual."

I told him I thought layoffs were rarely decided on the basis of shoe color.

"YOU don't know these people," he shouted, as red blotches bloomed across his neck. "I just don't understand why they're doing this."

Ray crossed his arms over his chest and began rocking back and forth, clearly on the edge of a gale-force panic attack. I tiptoed from the room and shut the door. From down the hallway, I could hear him repeating the phrase "re-org, re-org, re-org."

At the time, I felt that Ray's behavior was a tad extreme. After all, his company's restructuring was far from certain—and besides, no one knew what it would entail. But the next day, I went to an exhibit on Albert Einstein at the American Museum of Natural History and experienced, firsthand, the panic and conjecture that come from not knowing how to interpret information. Physics will do that to you.

The exhibit started off well enough. I entered the hushed museum and learned about Einstein as a young boy. I reviewed a copy of his report card, which refutes the myth that he was not a motivated child. I saw a replica of the compass that launched Einstein's fascination with the forces of nature. And, in something that belongs in the "who knew?" category, I read one of the many love letters he wrote to one of his many mistresses. Apparently, Einstein was a hottie in his day, a babe magnet with a large romantic appetite.

But then, as I began to read about Einstein's theories, my sunny enjoyment of the day disappeared behind a dark cloud of ignorance.

I read about his general theory of relativity, which overturned the classic Newtonian view of gravity, which said that apples never fall far from the tree, or some such thing.

I read about the imaginary gravity of projected black holes, which helps to explain why SUVs plow into sinkholes on rainy days.

I learned about Einstein's search for a grand unified theory that would explain everything about everything, including, I presume, why Michael Jackson thought he was Peter Pan.

See, the more I read about Einstein's work, the less I understood it. And the less I understood it, the more I felt compelled to fill in the gaps with my own interpretation. Even though I listened to the curator's talk, watched a film narrated by Alan Alda, and reviewed the seventy-two handwritten pages that make up Einstein's theory of relativity, I couldn't grasp what his theories really meant.

I started to get agitated and sped through the exhibit. Gravitational warps? The space–time continuum? Yeah, yeah, whatever.

By the time I hit the gift shop at the end of the exhibit, I had a massive headache, caused, no doubt, by an unprecedented cerebral failure. I sped past the wall of books on Einstein and picked up a souvenir writing pen. Ahhhh. This was something I could understand. So simple. So elegant. I held it to my chest until my breathing returned to normal.

And when it did, I thought about my friend Ray and his company's re-org. I began to understand his panic over the proposed restructuring. He didn't understand why it was necessary. He didn't understand how it could affect him. He didn't understand why he'd been told that information. And in the absence of all that understanding, he filled in the black holes with his own warped view of the outcome.

As Einstein might explain it, Ray was suffering from an extreme case of $E = MC^2$, which I believe means that expectations are driven by management communication—or the lack thereof.

Source: Shari Caudron, "A Black Hole in Corporate Communication," Workforce Management, April 2003, p. 24.

Manager: Jane, I've just gotten a phone call from Morris, and they're shipping over the supplies we ordered last week. They'll be here in about forty minutes. I'd like you to wait, sign for the supplies, and put them in the storeroom.

Jane: I've got a night class at the university that starts at 6:00 P.M. If I don't leave right now, I'll miss it.

Obviously, the manager can try to force Jane to stay. However, if the boss reads the feedback signs, he should be able to see that Jane's acceptance will at best be slow in coming. The manager must be aware of these negative vibrations and either press for acceptance or ask someone else to wait for the supplies. In this case, asking someone else appears preferable.

Action. The final step in the communication process, **action**, requires the receiver to follow up and do what was requested. A purchase order may have to be placed, a report filed, or a meeting held. It would appear that, if the sender gets to this action stage, the communication process would attain completion with no further problems. However, this is not always so. Sometimes the receiver will encounter unforeseen difficulties. The purchase order may not be filled because the supplier is temporarily out of raw materials; an executive assistant may be on vacation so a particular report may have to wait to be filed until she returns; a vice president may be on an extended business trip so a meeting may have to be delayed until he or she returns. In all these cases, the message will not get through the action stage.

Another cause for inaction can be found in the receiver, who may be incapable of carrying out the order. For example, if Mary tells Bob to fill out Report A and send it to the comptroller but Bob has never been told how to perform this task, the report may be completed incorrectly or it may not be filled out at all. The message may not reach the stage of completed action. Alternatively, if Bob asks Mary for help and she is too busy to see him, he will fill out Report A as best he can, with the same result.

If the action stage is to be completed, the sender must be available to answer questions and provide assistance to the receiver. If a problem develops, the receiver then has someone to whom he or she can turn. The action stage ensures that there is feedback in case of trouble. Remember, the sender's communication responsibility does not end until the desired action is completed.

 CHECK YOUR UNDERSTANDING

Match the steps in the communication process to the statements:

Steps	Statements
a. Attention	_____ The receiver willingly goes along with the message.
b. Understanding	_____ Follow up to the message is required.
c. Acceptance	_____ A reduction in noise is necessary.
d. Action	_____ Tell me how you are going to proceed with the job.

Describe the importance of using simple, repetitive language; empathy; and body language in achieving effective communication.

Using Simple, Repetitive Language

The simpler a message, the more likely it is to be understood and acted on properly. Consider the advertisements you see in the daily newspaper. Research shows that the shorter the ad, the higher the reader rate, and the greater the likelihood that the material will be remembered.

Unfortunately, many people do not carry this simple rule to the workplace with them. They tend to communicate long messages in a hurried fashion. The receivers are unable to follow everything that has been said, but because the sender is in such a rush, they are afraid to interrupt either to ask questions or to get the sender to repeat the more difficult portions of the message. If the message is in writing, the sender tends to use vague terms and incorporate too many ideas into one sentence. When the receiver has read the memo, only part of the message has been properly decoded.

Effective senders know that every message should be understandable. If the subject matter is complex, the communication should be done in "small bites," giving the receiver the opportunity to ask questions or seek clarification. In addition, the sender should, from time to time, review part of the message so that the receiver finds it easier to follow the flow of information. We illustrate how this can be done later in this chapter.

Using Empathy

Putting oneself, figuratively, in another person's place is termed **empathy**. In so doing, one begins to see things as the other person does. Barker has put it this way:

> Empathy means deep understanding of other people, identifying with their thoughts, feeling their pain, sharing their joy. Such empathy is typical of strong, healthy relationships. Indeed, empathetic communicators know each other so well that they can predict the responses to their messages. For example, Travis says to himself, "I know if I tell Michelle that I'm not crazy about her new dress, she'll be hurt. So instead I'll say 'Michelle, that dress looks great on you, but I think the green one is even more becoming.'"[38]

We know that successful managers empathize with their subordinates. They know when to be task oriented and when to be people oriented, because they are capable of putting themselves in a subordinate's place and answering the question, "What kind of direction does this person need?"

Empathy is particularly important at two stages of the communication process: acceptance and action. When the manager gives an order that the subordinate is reluctant to accept, the manager should be tuned in to pick up the hesitancy. Apparently, the subordinate does not understand how important the matter is and how significant his or her role will be. The manager needs to clarify the situation further and explain why the subordinate is being asked to handle the task. If a manager lacks empathy, it is likely that he or she will ignore the hesitancy. The astute manager knows that the problem or issue should be dealt with immediately and laid to rest.

Empathy also helps in the action stage. When the subordinate has trouble carrying out a directive, empathetic managers are quick to give assistance. They realize immediately that help is needed and do not let their employees down.

Conversely, the manager who lacks empathy does not check on worker progress and, on learning that an employee is having trouble, lets the employee work it out alone. Research shows that empathetic managers are more effective than managers who lack empathy.

Empathy is also important in knowing how to talk to people. A training and consulting executive has noted that when speaking to the boss, for example, it is important to understand the individual's preferred communication style. Here are some examples of bosses and the style that works best with them:

- **The direct, results-oriented person:** This person has a short attention span, processes information very quickly, and is interested in only the bottom line. Therefore, it is best to present this individual with a bulleted list of conclusions and forget all the background information. This is a no-nonsense person who is a "give it to me straight" kind of communicator.
- **The free-spirit enthusiast:** This person is expressive, dramatic, and loves new ideas. This type of communicator is a creative, big-picture type of person who likes to consider alternative approaches to doing things but is not very good on follow-through. In dealing with this individual, it is important to be patient and to be prepared for changes in direction. This person often likes to assimilate what is being told and to consider several alternatives before making a decision.

- **The humanist, relationship communicator:** This person thrives on connecting with and caring for people and likes everyone to be happy and is very concerned with the feelings of others; so any suggestions or recommendations that are given will be passed around the entire department for full consensus before any action is taken. In dealing with this person, patience and tact are very important. Take time to find out something about this person's family. Once an alliance is made, relationship communicators are fabulously loyal.
- **The historian:** This person likes to know the complete picture and thrives on details. This type of communicator wants to be given a thorough analysis and background information, especially if it is presented in linear fashion. The individual does not jump from subject to subject but instead remains focused on the topic under consideration until it has been exhaustively reviewed and a decision has been made.[39]
- **The analyzer:** This person revels in facts and figures and will not do something for you simply out of loyalty, because this type of communicator is driven by logic. This individual needs details, specifics, and well thought-out reasons why you want the person to engage in an activity with you. An excellent tip is to provide the individual with printed pages or files of facts and statistics that can be reviewed and evaluated at his or her leisure.[40]

Understanding Body Language

Body language is one of the most important forms of nonverbal communication. People use this communication form to pass messages to one another, although in many cases, they are unaware that they are doing so. Common examples of body language are the way a person moves his or her eyes, where an individual stands in a room in relation to others, the way a person shakes hands or touches another on the shoulder, and the way a person dresses.

Eye Movement.   In regard to eye movement, many managers believe that if people are lying, they will not look the listener in the eye. This is untrue. Effective liars often do look their listeners right in the eye; they know such eye contact increases their credibility. However, there are things managers can learn by looking at the other person's eye movements. In particular, it is possible to tell when the other party is under stress or emotional strain. For example, right-handed people tend to look to the left when they are trying to deal with an issue on an emotional level, and they tend to look to the right when they are unemotional or rational. The reverse is true for left-handed people.Research by Daniel Casasanto, Stanford University, found that left-handers tend to associate the left with nice and good things and the right with ugly and bad things. In an experiment, Casasanto found that the right-handed people located good things in the box on the right while left-handers placed them in the box on the left.[41]

Posture.   A second important body language sign is posture. Slouching, looking down, or hanging back in the crowd are typical examples of individuals who are unsure of themselves. Mehrabian, a communications expert, has discovered a relationship between how near a person stands to another and how relaxed the individual is.[42] Some of Mehrabian's findings are as follows:

1. A high degree of relaxation generally indicates a lack of respect or a dislike of the other person, whereas a lesser 'degree of relaxation indicates a liking for the other person.

2. An absence of relaxation indicates the person feels threatened by or is being threatening to someone else.

3. Relaxation is related to status, with higher-status people being generally more relaxed than their lower-status counterparts.

4. Women consistently demonstrate greater immediacy and consequently deliver more positive feelings.

Touch. Another important body language sign is touch. When American businesspeople shake hands, a vigorous or firm handshake often is regarded as a sign of self-assurance. This type of touching is used to define power relationships. Casual touching or unwanted touching in the office can lead to lawsuits for sexual harassment. Some countries are regarded as "touch-oriented" countries where touching between men, such as holding hands while walking down a street, is a sign of great friendship and respect, not being homosexual as Americans might think. The Middle East, Italy, and the Latin countries are examples of touch-oriented countries, whereas Japan is not regarded as a touching society. As business operations become more global, cultures are colliding over this dilemma of "to touch or not to touch." This is an issue managers confront while working with diversified groups of employees. For example, a manager who wants to emphasize an order must know how an employee feels about touch before grasping the employee's arm while issuing the order, or if the manager wants to congratulate the employee, he or she should know it is alright to pat the person on the back.[43]

Physical Location. A fourth important form of body language is physical location. This subject is known as **proxemics** and deals with the way people use physical space to communicate. The quiz on physical location and body language in the "Time Out" box illustrates this idea. Take a moment to complete the exercise.

The physical location where people sit or stand in relation to one another also communicates a message. For example, when communicating personal information, individuals often stand within two feet of each other. When conveying general or social information, the parties generally stand two to six feet apart. When the message is less personal, the distance will be greater between the people. Of course, these cultural guidelines only hold in the United States and other Western countries. When dealing with Arabs or other people from the Middle East, for example, it is customary to conduct general business discussions within a few feet of one another. This nearness often makes Americans feel uncomfortable, but if they back away and try to establish a greater distance, they will usually find their Arab counterparts coming closer. The use of proxemics is culturally determined. Figure 11.4 draws together many of these comments about empathy and body language. As you examine the figure, notice the differences between the two groups: aggressivians (Americans being a good example) and passivians (most other countries of the world).

Learning to Receive and Give Feedback

Managers can improve their communication ability primarily by learning when their messages are being transmitted poorly and by working to overcome the breakdown. One way to do this is to solicit feedback. Let's look at some effective openers:

- "Could you give some more information about...?"
- "You've given me something to think over. I'd welcome any other ideas you might have about...."
- "I think the proposed reorganization plan is a good one. What do you think?"

Physical Location and Body Language: A Quiz

Assume you are Person A. You would like very much to be cooperative and open to Person F. Are you seated in a correct chair or should you switch chairs with someone else? Think about this for a minute and then compare your answer to that at the end of the book.

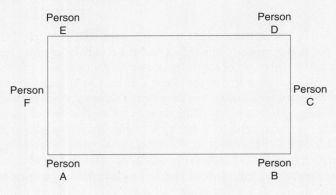

Person
E

Person
D

Person
F

Person
C

Person
A

Person
B

Figure 11.4 Culture Behavior Characteristics: Aggressivian versus Passivian

AGGRESSIVIAN	PASSIVIAN
Body Language	
Frequently uses gestures and facial expressions when speaking	Never uses gestures or facial expressions when speaking
Enjoys prolonged eye contact; stares intently at others when engaged in conversation	Avoids eye contact as much as possible
Smiles constantly	Never smiles
Stands and sits erectly	Slouches when standing and sitting
Personal Space	
Likes closeness; requires little personal space	Likes distance; requires much personal space
Stands and sits as close as possible to others	Stands and sits at a distance from others whenever possible
Touches others frequently	Never touches others
Concept of Time	
Believes time is money	Believes time is relatively unimportant
Believes decisions should be made within strict deadlines	Believes making a sound decision is more important than meeting deadlines
Is always in a hurry	Never rushes

Figure 11.4 Culture Behavior Characteristics: Aggressivian versus Passivian *(Continued)*

AGGRESSIVIAN	PASSIVIAN
Wants to discuss only the facts	Wants to discuss all aspects of a problem and how various decisions affect others involved
Wants to reach a decision as soon as possible	Wants to reach a decision only after all evidence has been thoroughly discussed and carefully evaluated
Vocal Qualities	
Speaks loudly	Speaks softly
Speaks rapidly	Speaks slowly
Speaks with exaggerated vocal inflections	Speaks in a monotone
Personality	
Is extremely self-centered	Is extremely group oriented
Frequently uses I, me, my, and mine	Frequently uses we, us, and ours
Is rarely willing to help others unless a personal benefit results	Is always willing to cooperate and help others
Constantly fosters his or her personal rights at the expense of others	Frequently relinquishes personal rights in deference to those of others
Never tries to understand the views of others	Always tries to understand the views of others
Always feels better than or more important than others	Never feels better than or more important than others
Negotiating Style	
Is brutally frank	Frequently uses euphemisms to avoid hurting others
Demonstrates no concern for the feelings of others	Is extremely concerned about the feelings of others
Likes to argue for the sake of arguing	Always avoids arguments and conflict
Talks at rather than with people	Talks with rather than at people
Always assumes he or she is right and others are wrong	Listens carefully and never interrupts others
	Accepts the fact that others may think differently and that there may be more than one correct viewpoint

Source: Jack E. Hulbert, "Overcoming Intercultural Communication Barriers," *The Bulletin*, March 1994, p. 42.

Notice that in each of these opening remarks the sender is encouraging the receiver to give feedback. The channel is being opened.

In discouraging feedback, the sender closes the channel by either threatening or belittling the receiver. In those cases, the receiver is likely to say nothing. The following are illustrations:

- "Let me say straight off that there is no way that I'll go along with any recommendation other than the one that J. R. proposed yesterday."
- "While you may not be aware of all the constraints I'm working under...."
- "Of course, that may be the way you see it, but let's look at the facts."

In each of these statements, the sender is closing down the feedback channel. In the first example, the sender is apparently backing up a top manager and daring the receiver to argue the point. In the second, the sender seems to be saying that he or she is overworked and does not want any disagreement or argument from the receiver. In the last example, the sender appears to be labeling the receiver as stupid. Unless the receiver is looking for an argument with the manager, there is little chance that he or she will say anything in response.

Once the manager starts getting feedback, it is important to sustain the flow of information. Numerous stock phrases or statements can be used for this. Here are some of the most effective:

- "Could you tell me more about ...?"
- "I see."
- "Right, right. Go on."
- "I appreciate your saying that."
- "Am I going into sufficient detail?"
- "What else?"

Finally, we must consider the subject of giving feedback. Sometimes, the subordinate will not ask questions about matters that merit further discussion or explanation. At these times, the effective manager needs to know how to introduce feedback into the process. Some of the best opening lines are these:

- "Would you be interested in my reactions to ...?"
- "You may be at a good point right now for me to give you some feedback on...."
- "I like what you did. What sets it apart is...."

In each of these instances, the sender (manager) has approached the feedback issue from the standpoint of the receiver (subordinate). Each comment conveys something of help or value to the receiver. For example, in the first opening, the manager is going to give reactions to some matter that apparently involved the subordinate. Note, however, that the manager did not attempt to give these reactions unsolicited. The manager asked if the subordinate would be interested in them. If the subordinate feels feedback will be of little value, he or she can say so, but the opportunity for feedback is there if the subordinate wants it. In the second and third openings, it is obvious that the subordinate is going to be given feedback that is important and, in the last case, laudatory.

These effective openers contrast significantly with ineffective openers that commonly lead the subordinate to tune out the message. Some common examples follow:

- "You really ought to know better than to...."
- "How many times do I have to tell you not to...?"
- "Now, Bob, you're just too critical of...."

In each case, the listener is not really being given feedback as much as being criticized for a particular behavior. The most common response is to ignore it. How does a manager overcome these common pitfalls and learn how to both receive and give feedback? The answer rests in analyzing one's messages and putting oneself in the receiver's shoes (empathizing). Communication serves as a critical aspect in building rapport, ensuring consistency, encouraging change, and receiving feedback.[44]

Handling Negative Feedback.   It is never easy to deal with negative feedback, such as a bad performance review or an unexpected scolding from the boss. Negative feedback usually hits workers squarely in the ego. It is hard to hear that something is wrong with your work, your behavior, or both. Becoming angry or argumentative, which many people do, will only make matters worse.

B. J. Gallagher, workplace consultant and author, says that when people get negative feedback, one of the first things they are likely to do is to protect or defend themselves. The key is to avoid those emotions. Going on the defensive will only make you look uncooperative, get your boss angry, and stop you from getting anything accomplished. Gallagher recommends that you "throw a circuit breaker" on your emotions and attend the meeting with your boss with the intent to learn. Gallagher's suggestions are:

1. Try to just take in the information and assess it.
2. Ask questions and make sure the boss gives examples of the times when performance was not up to par.
3. Say thank you. (Often, a complaint can be a gift.)
4. Give the boss your mission statement that shows your commitment to improving your performance.
5. Schedule another meeting. Asking for a chance to review your work again shows initiative and lets the boss know you want to do better.[45]

 CHECK YOUR UNDERSTANDING

1. Match the style of the communicator with each statement:

Style of Communicator	Statement
a. Direct, results oriented	_____ Driven by logic.
b. Free spirit enthusiast	_____ Thrives on details.
c. Humanist, relationship oriented	_____ Loves new ideas.
d. Historian	_____ Strives on connecting with people.
e. Analyzer	_____ Interested in the bottom line.

2. Give an example of how eye movement, posture, touch, and physical location are used in communicating.
3. How would you give feedback to a person who failed to follow instructions? Write down the statement you would make in giving that person feedback. Write another statement of what you would say if you were receiving the feedback from your boss.

Discuss ten guidelines for developing effective listening habits.

Developing Effective Listening Habits

Listening is difficult business. Research reveals that most people speak at a rate of approximately 125 words per minute but are capable of listening to more than 600 words per minute. This leaves a listener's brain a great deal of slack, which can be used for daydreaming or thinking up responses to issues the speaker raises. Instead of really listening to what the person is saying, the listener is trying to formulate a response. This is unfortunate, because effective human relations are based heavily on good listening skills. For example, individuals who are poor listeners are typically also poor negotiators. As a result, they are unable to learn what the other party wants or is willing to settle for, and so they end up with a less-than-ideal settlement. Poor listeners are also ineffective in crisis situations. During this period, these individuals need to gather as much information as possible in determining how to handle the situation. However, they often shut out incoming signals and make decisions that are based on incomplete information. A Maritz Poll revealed that almost one-fourth of American workers—23 percent—do not think that their company listens to or cares about them, and 28 percent disapprove of the ways that their organizations communicate with them.[46]

Fortunately, a number of techniques can be used to improve one's listening skills. One is to ask questions that will help provide feedback and increase understanding. Another is to remain objective and not get upset by what the other person is saying. A third is to empathize, put yourself in the other person's shoes, and try to see things from that individual's point of view. These suggestions are designed to encourage the listener to hear what the other person has to say and to put the information into proper perspective before saying anything. Further suggestions are discussed in the "Human Relations in Action" box. Other useful guidelines for developing effective listening habits are:

1. Do not label the speaker as either boring or uninteresting merely because you dislike his or her delivery. Listen to what is being said rather than how it is being said.
2. Tell yourself that the speaker has something to say that will be of value or benefit to you. Give the speaker a chance to communicate.
3. If the speaker starts talking about something you find boring, ask a pertinent question to influence the speaker toward more interesting subject matter.
4. If the presentation becomes too technical or difficult to understand, fight the tendency to tune out the speaker by increasing your determination to listen, learn, and remember.
5. Note the techniques used by the speaker to determine whether you should adopt any of them yourself. Did the speaker use a lot of facts? Was an emotional appeal ever employed? When? Was either of these approaches effective in presenting the message? Could you use these techniques to improve your own communication skills?
6. Evaluate the relevance of what is being said. Are any new or useful data being communicated that can be of value to you?
7. Listen for intended meanings as well as for expressed ideas. Are there any hidden messages that the speaker is trying to convey?
8. Integrate in your mind what the speaker is saying so that it all fits into a logical composite. If any information does not fit into this overall scheme, place it on the sidelines but seek to integrate it later.
9. Be a responsive listener by maintaining eye contact with the speaker and giving the speaker positive feedback, such as nods and facial expressions.

IN ACTION

HOW TO BECOME AN ACTIVE LISTENER

Effective listening involves more than just paying attention. It includes active, empathetic, and supportive behaviors that tell the speaker, "I understand. Please go on." This is the way an active listener behaves. However, watch out for four other types of listeners: directing, judgmental, probing, and smoothing. Here is a brief description of each.

The *directing listener* leads the speaker by guiding the limits and direction of the conversation. This individual likes to use such phrases as "If I were you I'd ..." and "Don't worry about it, everybody agrees that ..." The directing listener really does not listen; he or she takes control of the situation.

The *judgmental listener* introduces personal value judgments into the conversation. This individual offers advice or makes statements regarding right or wrong conduct. Some of the most common statements he or she might use are: "Well, you're just going to have to understand that ..." or "You're right to say that Bill is tough to get along with because ..." Rather than hearing the speaker out, the judgmental listener tends to impose his or her own personal values.

The *probing listener* asks a lot of questions in an effort to get to the heart of the matter. In the process, this person attempts to satisfy his or her personal needs rather than those of the speaker. A probing listener will ask such questions as, "What has this person done to you that prevents your getting along with him?" or "When did all of this start?" The probing listener tends to be inquisitive to the point of frustrating the speaker.

The *smoothing listener* adopts a strategy designed to reassure the speaker. The individual often says such things as, "Don't let that worry you because ..." and "I understand exactly how you feel about ..." This individual believes that conflict is bad and should be avoided at all costs.

The *active listener* tries to encourage the speaker to express himself or herself. This listener creates an environment in which the speaker feels free to develop his or her thoughts. The active listener commonly says such things as, "You sound upset about ..." or "It seems that you are willing to go ahead and implement your ideas regarding ..." The active listener gives the speaker neutral summaries of what is being said. These summaries encourage the other party to continue speaking.

The most effective listener is the active listener because this person maintains the role of listener. The other four types of listeners are characterized by their attempts to influence or dominate the speaker. Work on avoiding the habits of these ineffective listeners and strive to become a more active listener.

---

10. Be willing to accept the challenge of effective listening by telling yourself that it is a skill that you need to develop.[47]

Active Listening. Another way to improve one's listening skills is to become an active listener. How do you rate in terms of being an active listener? One way of finding out is by taking the "Time Out" quiz entitled "Are You a Good Listener?"

It is not always easy to follow the ten guidelines for effective listening. In fact, many effective managers report that when they first decided to become better listeners, they had to force themselves to follow these guidelines. Effective listening is not simply doing what comes naturally. Listening is a developed skill.

Companies That Listen. Cabela's, the largest tourist attraction stores that sell outdoor-recreation items, listens to its employees. Through an extensive loaner program, employees are encouraged to borrow a product for a month or so. Employees fill out a form detailing the product's pros and cons and give a talk to other employees or customers explaining what they learned. The information is then fed into a vast knowledge-sharing system, called "Item Notes," that can help answer customers' questions. In turn, customers' comments are also recorded in the system. Listening to its employees has helped make Cabela's and its 245,000 products a success.[48] Build-A-Bear Workshop is an example of a company that listens to its customers. To gain ideas, it taps its "virtual cub advisory council," a community of children on an e-mail list. Their suggestions, from bear accessories like miniscooters to mascot bears sold at sports stadiums, then make their way onto the shelves, resulting in happy customers.[49]

More than anything else, the first thing a speaker must do is give the listener a reason to listen right from the start. Get to the point, demonstrate that you care about the message, and quickly involve the listener. These points apply to written communication as well.

Are You A Good Listener?

Read the statements in this section and rate yourself on each by using the following scale:

A = Always

B = Almost always

C = Usually

D = Sometimes

E = Rarely

F = Almost never

G = Never

_____ 1. Do you let the speaker completely express his or her ideas without interrupting her or him?

_____ 2. Do you become upset or excited when the speaker's views differ from your own?

_____ 3. Are you able to prevent distractions from disrupting your ability to listen?

_____ 4. Do you make continuous notes on everything the other person says?

_____ 5. Are you able to read between the lines and hear what a person is saying even when hidden messages are being conveyed?

_____ 6. When you feel that the speaker or the topic is boring, do you find yourself tuning out and daydreaming about other matters?

_____ 7. Are you able to tolerate silence by sitting quietly and allowing the speaker time to gather his or her thoughts and go on with the message?

_____ 8. As you listen, do you find yourself trying to pull together what the speaker is saying by thinking of what has been said and what seems to be coming?

_____ 9. As you listen to the speaker, do you note that person's body language and try to incorporate this into your interpretation of the message?

_____ 10. If you disagree with what the speaker is saying, do you provide immediate feedback by shaking your head no?

_____ 11. Do you move around a great deal when listening, changing your posture, crossing and recrossing your arms or legs, and sliding back and forth in your chair?

_____ 12. When you listen, do you stare intently into the speaker's eyes and try to maintain this direct contact throughout the time the person is speaking?

_____ 13. When the other party is finished speaking, do you ask pointed and direct questions designed to clarify and amplify what was said?

_____ 14. If the speaker has been critical of you, do you try to put down that person before addressing the substantive part of the message?

The interpretation of your answers appears at the end of the book.

 CHECK YOUR UNDERSTANDING

1. Are you a good listener? Which items listed in the "Time Out" quiz do you need to improve to be a better listener?
2. Select three guidelines for effective listening. Practice them during the next two weeks.

Identify four ways for improving writing skills.

Improving Your Writing Skills

Whenever communication is discussed, talk usually centers on reading, speaking, and listening; writing typically is given a low priority. Why is this so? Perhaps the main reason is that most managers do not write well, and they hate to be reminded of it. Yet written communication is an important part of their job, as evidenced by the fact that managers are always writing and answering e-mails, preparing reports, conducting evaluations, and so on. In fact, because of electronic mail and facsimiles, written communication is becoming increasingly important. How can you improve your writing skills? There are a number of steps you can take.

- Force yourself to _write and rewrite material_. If you do this frequently enough, your writing will become much more effective.

- Make it a point to *write at least three drafts* of everything you do. The first draft is for gathering ideas. The second draft is for assuring that the material is accurate. The third draft is for polishing and making the material read smoothly and interestingly.
- See if you can get someone in your organization to *review your written work and comment on it*. There may be four or five problems that account for 90 percent of your inability to write effectively. Once you identify the problems, you can correct them in your writing.
- If possible, *sign up for a college course* and force yourself to learn more effective writing skills. Or put together your own checklist of the most important things to look for in written communiqués and compare your written work with this checklist.

What is most troubling to employers is that over the past several years, there has been a glaring deficiency in reading and writing skills among new entrants in the American workforce. Workers who cannot read or write well earn less and have higher unemployment rates. Interesting enough Linda Barrington, former managing director of the Conference Board found that among recent four-year college graduates, new hires were unable to write effective business communication, read analytically, or solve problems. Employers are being forced to invest in additional training or look for skilled workers offshore.

Improving Your Speaking Skills

Explain the four parts of PLAN for improving speaking skills and discuss how gender can make a difference.

Research among managers reveals that speaking skills are one of the basic shortcomings of many college graduates. Speaking skills, however, can be improved. One way is through what is called a PLAN approach.[50] The acronym stands for purpose, logistics, audience, and nonverbal communication:

P = Purpose: What is the reason for your message, presentation, or speech? Why are you sending a message? Make the purpose clear at the beginning of the message, presentation, or speech.

L = Logistics: When and where will the meeting be held? Is the time length appropriate? Is the meeting scheduled at a convenient time for your audience or on a convenient day with minimum conflict? What is the physical layout of the room—stage, tables, or chairs? What type of computer assistance or electronic assistance is needed, and what type of personnel assistance is needed?

A = Audience: Who will be present? What is the level of knowledge of the audience? How will you encode your message so the audience can understand what you are saying?

N = Nonverbal communication: How can the room layout and the presentation tools—PowerPoint, charts, and other audiovisual equipment—be used effectively? What will your behaviors say to the audience—your attitude, your smile, your dress, your tone of voice, your acceptance of questions, and so on?

To improve their speaking skills, managers and employees can enroll in a speech course at a local community college or university, which generally offers evening courses. Or they can join a local Toastmasters International club, or if a club is not available in the area, they can ask the company to charter a club that would meet at a convenient time, such as the lunch hour. Members learn the art of speaking, listening, and thinking skills by speaking to groups and working with others in a supportive environment of twenty to thirty people. The club's vision is to empower people to achieve their full potential and realize their dreams. It appears that American managers are making an effort to improve their speaking skills.

Table 11.4 Some Communication Differences between Men and Women

Linguistic Characteristic	Men	Women
Asking questions	Not very likely to do so	More likely to do so than men
Giving feedback	Tend to be blunt and direct	Tend to be tactful and to temper criticism with praise
Offering compliments	Restrictive with their praise	Fairly generous with their praise
Showing confidence	Not very likely to indicate when they are unsure about something	More likely to indicate uncertainty about an issue
Making apologies	Tend to avoid saying they are sorry because it makes them "look bad"	More likely to say "I'm sorry" when they make a mistake
Taking credit	More likely to take credit for achievements ("I did that")	More likely to share credit ("We did that")
Use of indirectness	More likely to be indirect when admitting they do not know something or admitting that they made a mistake ("The report was late" rather than "I was late submitting the report")	More likely to be indirect when telling others something that needs to be done ("This is what needs to be done" rather than "This is what I want you to do")

Source: Deborah Tannen, "The Power of Talk: Who Gets Heard and Why," *Harvard Business Review*, September–October 1995. Reprinted by permission. Copyright, Harvard Business School Publishing Corporation. All rights reserved.

Understanding Gender Differences

Regardless of the reasons, research reveals that men and women communicate differently in a number of ways.[51] Men like to boast about themselves by giving blunt feedback, withholding compliments, and not admitting weaknesses or faults. Women are more likely to give carefully worded feedback, share credit for success, ask questions for clarification, and tactfully tell others what to do. Table 11.4 provides some examples of these and other contrasts. However, it is important to remember that these generalizations do not extend to all men and women. At the same time, they do point out the need for both groups to understand better how to communicate with the other. Many men need to be more patient and less dominant; many women need to speak up and be more forceful in presenting their ideas and opinions. Simply put, communication between the sexes can be improved by realizing that both groups have different ways of communicating the same ideas.

Career Advisor

Managing Stress Effectively

Stress is found in all aspects of life, including the workplace. Although research shows that stress can help people work more efficiently, too much stress can result in absenteeism, diminished productivity, employee turnover, accidents, medical problems, burnout, and even death. In other cases, stress is both cause and effect of workplace violence and harassment. The U.S. National Institute for Occupational Safety and Health reports

Explain how to manage stress more effectively.

stress-related disorders are fast becoming the most prevalent reason for worker disability. With the billions of dollars that businesses invest in health insurance each year, as well as the loss of productivity due to absenteeism and its negative effect on revenue, reducing stress should be a crucial focus for any organization.

Stress. So what is job stress? It can be defined as the harmful physical and emotional responses that occur when the requirements of the job do not match the capabilities, resources, or needs of the worker. Richard S. Lazarus, a former psychologist at the University of California, Berkeley, argues in his book, *Stress, Appraisal and Coping*, written with Susan Folkman, that when people lack the resources to deal with difficult events, they will suffer stress, but that they do not suffer stress if they believe that they have such resources Thus, stress and coping are intimately related to each other.[52] Another way to define stress is the "wear and tear" our bodies experience as we adjust to our continually changing environment; it has physical and emotional effects on us and can create positive or negative feelings. "As a positive influence, stress can help compel people to action."[53]

Cavanagh in his research found that stress can evoke feelings of frustration, fear, conflict, pressure, hurt, anger, sadness, inadequacy, guilt, loneliness, or confusion. For example, people who are fired feel stress; so do people who are promoted. Avoiding all stress is unrealistic because without stress we would be dead.[54]

Work Environment. People who work in poor work environments have reported more stress. Likewise, people in ongoing work situations that are negative or stressful have a higher potential for negative health consequences. On the other hand, scientists have found that people engaged in their work have much lower self-reported stress than those who are disengaged. So how stressed is work making us?

Harter states that in the United States, 30 percent of the working population reports that there have been three or more days in the last month when the stress of work has caused them to behave poorly with family or friends. Among actively disengaged employees, an alarming 54 percent agreed that work stress has caused them to behave poorly with family or friends, while only 17 percent of engaged employees reported that stress had caused them to behave poorly. The percentages are similarly high in other countries.[55]

Findings from a study conducted by the Families and Work Institute, a nonprofit research group in New York, revealed that Baby boomers are the most stressed out from their jobs and the most likely to feel that their health is suffering as a result. Additionally, Baby Boomers are stressed by having to report to Generation Xers moving into upper management, as well as having to care for both children and parents. Patricia Farrell, a clinical psychologist, states that roughly half of the disability claims she evaluates each month are related to on-the-job stress, mostly filed by Baby Boomers.[56]

Researchers argue that the "sick building syndrome," a term used to describe a range of physical symptoms suffered by employees, is not caused by poorly designed facilities but from another common cause, workplace stress. Employees who have demanding jobs, low levels of support, and little or no decision-making power are especially vulnerable to workplace stress.[57]

According to another school of thought, differences in individual characteristics, such as personality and coping style, are most important in predicting whether certain job conditions will result in stress. In other words, what is stressful for one person may not be a problem for someone else. This viewpoint leads to prevention strategies that focus on workers and ways to help them cope with demanding job conditions.

Ways to Eliminate Stress

The goal is not to totally eliminate stress, but to learn how to manage it and how to use it. The challenge is to find the optimal level of stress that will motivate but not over- whelm you. What causes stress in your life? One of the first areas you must analyze is the balance between your work and family life. Then look at the things in the workplace that cause stress. New research by careers Web site CollegeGrad.com suggests that young people entering the workforce seek out companies willing to invest in their future. "Sev- enty percent of those surveyed said they would rather work for smaller growth compa- nies that offer competitive benefits and emphasize a balance between work activities and their personal lives." In fact, 18 percent of U.S. workers are seeking new jobs that offer an improved work–life balance.[58]

Personal Life Stressors. Are there things that you could do differently? Can you eliminate some activities or reduce your expectations of others? For example: get up earlier to exercise in the morning instead of the evening and still get to work on time, hire someone to help with cleaning the house, or carpool the children to after-school activities. If you care for an elderly parent, analyze how you spend your time and then establish a schedule that is less stressful, which may mean hiring someone to help you. Women in particular believe they can do it all, bringing on more pressure and stress. It is OK to ask for help and not do everything perfectly. You must set priorities and strive to do well those things that are most important to you. Sometimes, things have to be set aside to be dealt with at a later date. That does not mean they are not important; you simply need to get better control of your time by reducing the number of things you are expected to do.

Learning to say "no" is very difficult for some people, especially when others have high expectations of you. By setting priorities and knowing what is important to you, you can rid yourself of guilty feelings when you need to say "no."

Workplace Stressors. To reduce stress in the workplace, you must recognize your stressors—the things that cause you stress. By recognizing your stressors, you can begin to make changes. First, you can discuss your concerns with your supervisor and try to create a more desirable work situation. In other instances, it may mean changing jobs, seeking employment in another firm, or enrolling in a college program to gain new skills. Some job conditions that lead to stress and ways the organization can prevent job stress are:[59]

- **The design of tasks.** The design of work tasks can lead to stress. For example, some employees are tied to their computers, allowing little time for flexibility, self- initiative, or rest. Jobs need to be designed to provide meaning, stimulation, and opportunities for workers to use their skills. Also, the workload must be in line with workers' capabilities and resources. Engagement in the job gives satisfaction, reducing stress.
- **Management style.** The lack of participation in the decision-making process can lead to stress. This includes poor communications in the organization and the lack of family-friendly policies. Employees must be given opportunities to participate in decisions and actions affecting their jobs.
- **Interpersonal relationships.** A poor social environment and a lack of support or help from coworkers and supervisors lead to stress. Implementing effective interper- sonal relationships reduces stress. Organizations must provide opportunities for social interactions among workers.

- **Work roles.** Conflicting or uncertain job expectations lead to stress. Employees who have too much responsibility or wear too many hats, such as trying to satisfy both the customer's needs and the company's expectations, can feel overwhelmed with stress. Work roles need to be clearly identified and defined. Work schedules must be established that are compatible with demands and responsibilities outside the job. Increased workloads must be adjusted to better fit the employee's job description.

- **Career concerns.** Job insecurity and the lack of opportunity for growth, advancement or promotion, or rapid changes for which workers are unprepared can cause stress. A study found that 33 percent of executives from around the world who were surveyed cited a lack of challenges or opportunities for career growth as the top reason for leaving a job and 20 percent cited ineffective leadership.[60] Communication must be improved to reduce uncertainty about career development and future employment prospects. Career development and training programs must be enhanced.

- **Environmental conditions.** Unpleasant or dangerous physical conditions, such as crowding, noise, air pollution, and ergonomic problems, can cause stress. Greater attention must be given to the safety of employees, resulting in reducing stress and retaining valuable employees.

Managing stress in your job requires an understanding of your stressors, what you can do to reduce the stress, and who you are. What is your personality type? Are you a Type A or Type B person? Take the "Time Out" quiz to find out.

- **Burnout.** According to the Merriam-Webster's Collegiate Dictionary, burnout is "exhaustion of physical or emotional strength or motivation usually as a result of prolonged stress or frustration." Burnout is a particular problem for individuals with Type A personalities, characterized by a desire to get more and more done in less and less time. This is in contrast to Type B personalities, who are evenly paced and do not constantly feel overly pressed by time constraints.

How to Deal with Stress

In dealing with stress, some of the most effective steps are:

1. Staying alert for signs of stress.
2. Maintaining a positive mental attitude at all times.
3. Making time in your daily work schedule to put everything aside and just relax for ten to fifteen minutes.
4. Being prepared to make changes in your work routines or career if stress becomes too great.

Other things you can do to reduce stress are listening to uplifting music, reading inspirational books, keeping company with positive-thinking people, practicing affirmations, practicing positive self-talk, replacing negative statements with positive statements, replacing self-limiting statement, such as: "This is impossible!" with "How is this possible?" and exercising.

There is an array of activities you can do to reduce stress. They include getting a massage, taking yoga lessons, engaging in visualization and imagery, practicing meditation, being hypnotized, and breathing exercises conducted at your workstation. Exercising relaxes the body and allows positive ideas and thoughts to work.

Are You a Type A or Type B Person?

Here are ten combinations of statements related to your work and personal habits. In each case, read the A and B statements and decide which is most descriptive of you. If A is totally descriptive of you and B is not at all descriptive, give 10 points to A and none to B. If both statements are descriptive of you, divide the 10 points between A and B based on their degree of descriptive accuracy. If B is totally descriptive of you and A is not at all descriptive, give 10 points to B and none to A. An interpretation of your score is provided at the end of the book.

Points

_____ 1. A Even when it is not necessary I find myself rushing to get things done.

B I seldom rush to get things done, even if I am running late.

_____ 2. A I often get upset or angry with people, even if I do not show it.

B I seldom get angry with people if there is no real reason for it.

_____ 3. A When I play a game or compete in an event, winning is my primary objective.

B When I play a game or compete in an event, my greatest enjoyment comes from the social interaction with others.

_____ 4. A I am a tense, anxious person, but I try to cover this up by smiling a lot and trying to be social.

B I am basically a relaxed, easygoing individual; I seldom get tense or uptight.

_____ 5. A Even when I am sitting down watching TV, I am usually moving about, checking my nails,

tapping my foot, or carrying out some similar physical activity.

B When I sit down to watch TV, I get totally involved in the program and seldom move about or change position.

_____ 6. A I set high goals for myself and become angry if I fail to attain them.

B I set reasonable goals for myself, and if I fail, I try not to let this get me down.

_____ 7. A I write down how I intend to spend my day, and I rigidly stick to this schedule.

B I note objectives that I want to attain during the day but try to remain flexible; if something is not finished today, I will get to it tomorrow morning.

_____ 8. A I hate to wait for people; it makes me edgy and nervous.

B If I have to wait for others, I try to spend the time doing something relaxing such as reading, talking to others, or quietly walking around.

_____ 9. A Meals interrupt my schedule, and I often find myself doing work while I am eating.

B I enjoy meals and eat them slowly and in a relaxed fashion; if there is any work to do, it can wait until I am finished eating.

_____ 10. A At the end of the day, I often find myself extremely tired and run down.

B I like to get things done but not at the cost of physical exhaustion.

Your attitude, confidence, and self-image all play an important role in how you handle stress and will impact the level of stress you have in your life. By improving your coping skills, you can reduce your stress levels.

Reducing stress is an ongoing process that requires being alert to the things that are causing you stress, realizing you can change, taking the initiative to change, and designing a plan to reduce the stress and eliminate the stressors causing a negative effect on your body.

 CHECK YOUR UNDERSTANDING

In your career journal, outline what you have learned about stress.
1. Discuss how you can reduce stress in your life by identifying things you can change at work, as well as at home.
2. Prepare three to five basic rules that you can live by that will help keep your stress level at a manageable level.
3. Post these rules on the front of your refrigerator.

Summary

1 Describe how technology impacts communication.

Technology is changing the way people communicate in firms and affecting the way people interact. The increase in communication networks and electronic machines (mobile, cell, smart phones; computers; BlackBerrys; and the Internet) have people connected twenty-four hours a day, seven days a week—at work, on the road, and at home—extending the day to anytime, anyplace.

Communication technology is changing the workplace and the way people behave in the workplace. Camera phones are creating risks for some businesses that rely on trade secrets, creating opportunities for harassment, and threatening employee privacy. Using text messaging is becoming standard practice. E-mail does not always count as communication. Certain policies must be followed to ensure that e-mail qualifies as a business communiqué. E-mail netiquette is an important communication behavior. Rules are given for e-mail etiquette. Wireless networks and GPSs are expanding the workplace and reducing business costs.

New patterns of communication are emerging, forcing some traditional downward, upward, and horizontal organizational structures to become bubble charts or wheels. Communication flows across the lines, creating systems of webs. Firms can use technology software to detect functioning teams versus assigned teams by studying e-mail transmissions and analyzing patterns of communication within the firm. Color is used as a means of communication. Colors communicate different things to people.

There are challenges in using technology to communicate information. They are: (1) information-security problems, (2) privacy issue concerns, (3) extended workdays (4) missing nonverbal clues, (5) increased multitasking, (6) an overwhelming volume of information, (7) changes in the interaction among team members, and (8) reduced social interaction among employees.

2 Describe how the communication process works.

One of the best ways to achieve behavioral effectiveness in the workplace is to communicate properly. In this section, we reviewed the communication process of transmitting meanings from sender to receiver. Five essential elements make up this process: (1) the sender, (2) the message, (3) the medium, (4) the receiver, and (5) the interpretation given to the message. In conveying the message, three functions must be performed: *encoding the message*—translating the message into words or symbols that the receiver can understand; choice of a communication medium—*transmitting the message* so the receiver will get it; and *decoding the message*—interpreting the message.

3 Discuss how to choose the appropriate communication medium.

To communicate effectively, the proper medium must be chosen. Two important considerations are associated with determining which medium to use. The first is the matter of *information richness*—the potential amount of information-carrying capacity of data. Four factors measure richness: (1) feedback, (2) the channel used to convey the information, (3) the type of communication—personal or impersonal, and (4) language source used, including body language, natural, or numeric. The richest forms of communication are face-to-face and the telephone. Computer printouts and video displays provide low richness and are impersonal.

The second consideration is the *issue of complexity*. There are three zones of communication effectiveness. If the message is simple, a medium that is low in richness can be selected; whereas when a problem is complex, a medium that is high in richness should be used. Media usage is significantly different across organizational levels.

4 Explain how perception, inference, language, and status can lead to communication breakdown.

We learned that many barriers can prevent effective communication, including perception, inference, language, and status. *Perception* is a person's view of reality. Because no two people have the same experiences and training, no two people see things in exactly the same way. For this reason, there are degrees of perception, and what is crystal clear to the sender may be very vague to the receiver. *Inference* is an assumption made by the receiver of a message. Whenever messages are long, involved, or nonspecific, there is a good chance that an inference will be made. *Language* is a barrier whenever two people associate different meanings with the same word. *Status* is a problem whenever people modify messages according to who is receiving or sending them.

5 Identify eight ways to overcome barriers to communication and achieve effective communication.

Eight of the most helpful ways to overcome barriers that can lead to communication breakdown are (1) knowing the steps in the communication process, (2) using simple, repetitive language, (3) using empathy, (4) understanding body language, (5) learning how to receive and give feedback, (6) developing effective listening habits, (7) improving writing and speaking skills, and (8) understanding the impact of gender differences on communication style. Of these, the two that warrant most consideration are the first and the sixth. By knowing the steps in the communication process, it is possible for the manager to be aware of breakdowns and to work to overcome them. By being an effective listener, the manager ensures a closed loop in the communication process. The subordinate sends back a message to the manager, and the manager can use it to correct any problems that have occurred in the communication process.

6 Describe how the four steps in the communication process can help improve a manager's communication skills.

Many breakdowns in communication can be avoided when the following four steps in the communication process are followed: (1) attention, (2) understanding, (3) acceptance, and (4) action. A sender must get the *full attention* of the receiver, who must block out any competition for attention. *Understanding* involves comprehension of the message. Asking appropriate questions helps to reveal levels of understanding. *Acceptance* means compliance—going along with the message. The final step, *action*, requires the receiver to follow up and do what was requested.

7 Describe the importance of using simple, repetitive language; empathy; and body language in achieving effective communication.

The *simpler a message*, the more likely it will be understood and acted upon. Shorter messages have higher reader rates and are more likely to be remembered. Complex messages should be broken down into small bites, giving listeners more opportunities to ask questions or seek clarification. In addition, parts of the message should be repeated and reviewed.

Empathy means putting oneself in another person's place. You can identify with his or her thoughts, feelings, and joys because you have been there yourself. Empathy is especially important in the acceptance and action stages of the communication process.

Empathy determines how quickly the receiver will respond and the degree of importance the receiver attaches to the message. Empathy is important in knowing how to talk to people. The style of communication should fit the type of person to whom you are communicating. Five types of communicators are: (1) direct, results oriented, (2) free-spirit enthusiast, (3) humanist, relationship communicator, (4) historian, and (5) analyzer.

People use *body language* to pass messages to others, but in some cases, they are not aware they are doing it. Common examples of body language are eye movements, where a person stands or sits in relation to others, handshakes or touches, and the way a person dresses. Posture gives off language signals; for example, a high level of relaxation indicates a lack of respect. The type of grip in the handshake sends signals, as does a pat on the back. **Proxemics** deals with the way people use physical space to communicate.

Communication can improve by learning how to analyze poorly transmitted messages and learn why they did not work effectively. Learn to ask sufficient questions for clarification. Another way is to put oneself in the receiver's shoes (empathizing).

8 Discuss ten guidelines for developing effective listening habits.

Listen to what the speaker is saying, not how it is being said. Tell yourself that the speaker has something to say that will be of value or benefit to you. If the speaker gets boring, ask a pertinent question. Increase your determination to listen in times when the presentation gets technical or difficult to understand. Note the techniques of the speaker to determine whether you should adopt any of them. Evaluate the relevance of what is being said—any new or useful data. Listen for intended meanings as well as for expressed ideas. Integrate in your mind what the speaker is saying. Be a responsive listener by maintaining eye contact and giving positive feedback—nods or facial expressions. Be willing to accept the challenge of effective listening by telling yourself that it is a skill that you need to develop.

9 Identify four ways for improving writing skills.

Four steps for improving writing skills are: (1) Force yourself to write and rewrite material. (2) Make it a point to write at least three drafts of everything you do. (3) See if you can get someone in your organization to review your written work and comment on it. (4) If possible, sign up for a college course in writing and force yourself to learn more effective writing skills.

10 Explain the four parts of PLAN for improving speaking skills and discuss how gender can make a difference.

The parts of the PLAN are: P = the *purpose* for the presentation or speech, L = *logistics* is when and where the meeting will be held, A = *audience*, or who will be present, and N = *nonverbal communication*, which involves the layout of the room and the effective use of presentation tools—PowerPoint, charts, samples, and so forth.

By enrolling in a college course or joining a Toastmasters International club, you can improve your speaking skills. Research indicates that men and women communicate differently in a number of ways. Men like to boast about themselves by giving blunt feedback, withholding compliments, and not admitting weaknesses or faults. Women give more carefully worded feedback, share credit for success, ask questions for clarification, and tactfully tell others what to do. Men need to be more patient and less dominant. Women need to speak up and be more forceful in presenting their ideas. Communication improves when both sexes understand that they communicate the same ideas in different ways.

11 Explain how to manage stress more effectively.

Stress is found everywhere. Although some stress is good, other stress can make you sick. In some instances, stress has led to workplace violence and harassment. Effective organizations should focus on reducing stress in the workplace, as it is becoming a reason for worker disability. Stress can be defined in many ways—as the harmful physical and emotional responses that occur when the requirements of the job do not match the capabilities, resources, or needs of the worker. It is the wear and tear our bodies experience as we adjust to our continually changing environment; it has physical and emotional effects on us and can create positive or negative feelings. Stress causes people to have a wide array of feelings, ranging from anger to happiness. To live is to have stress.

A poor work environment causes stress. Differences in individual characteristics such as personality and coping style can determine different levels of stress. The goal is to manage stress and use it to help us. The first step in managing stress is to identify the stressors that are causing various levels of stress within our personal lives, as well as our work lives. Actions must be taken to make the necessary changes to reduce or eliminate the stressors. The design of tasks, management style, interpersonal relationships, work roles, career concerns, and environmental conditions all offer stressors that produce stress in employees. Some effective ways to deal with stress are: staying alert for signs of stress, maintaining a positive mental attitude at all times, making time to relax, and being prepared to make changes in your work routine.

Key Terms in the Chapter

Communication	Communication is the process of transmitting meanings from sender to receiver.
Encoding	Encoding is translating a message into an intelligible code.
Decoding	Decoding is interpretation of the message by the receiver.
Information richness	Information richness is the potential information-carrying capacity of data.
Perception	Perception is a person's view of reality.
Inference	An inference is an assumption made by the receiver of a message.
Language	Language is used to convey meaning in the communication process.
Status	Status is a person's relative rank.
Attention	Attention is the overcoming of message competition.
Understanding	Understanding involves comprehension of the message.
Acceptance	Acceptance means compliance.
Action	Action requires that the receiver do what was expected.
Empathy	Empathy means putting oneself in another person's place.
Proxemics	Proxemics deals with the way people use physical space to communicate.

Review and Study Questions

1. How has technology changed communication in the workplace over the past decade?
2. Explain how cell phones provide greater efficiency in the workplace.

3. Identify several risks created by using camera phones in the workplace.

4. Discuss etiquette rules for e-mail. Why are these rules important?

5. What are several rules for making communicating by e-mail more effective?

6. How have wireless networks and GPSs improved communication?

7. How has technology changed the patterns of communication in businesses?

8. Describe how the "Wheel of Fortune" communication structure differs from the traditional bureaucratic structure—top to bottom.

9. How are communities of practice integrated into organizational structure?

10. What impact does color have on communication? Give examples.

11. What are some challenges facing communication systems in this decade and in the future?

12. What are the five essential elements in the communication process? Explain each.

13. Describe what happens in the encoding process. Include two basic steps.

14. Explain how the decoding process works.

15. How does the "matter of information richness" differ from the "issue of complexity" in the communication process?

16. In choosing a communication medium, when is face-to-face the most effective choice? When is it a poor choice? Explain.

17. In what ways can perception be a communication barrier?

18. What is an inference? In what way is it a communication barrier?

19. How can status create a communication barrier?

20. What are the four steps in the communication process? Describe each.

21. In what way can simple, repetitive language lead to more effective communication? Explain.

22. How can managers use empathy to achieve effective communication?

23. What does a manager need to know about body language? Cite some specific examples.

24. What are some of the most effective ways of getting feedback? Giving feedback? Handling feedback? Give some examples.

25. What are some of the important ways to develop effective listening habits? List at least six.

26. How can managers improve their writing skills? Offer at least three useful suggestions.

27. How can PLAN be used to improve speaking skills? Explain PLAN.

28. How do men and women differ in the way they communicate?

29. What is stress?

30. How can stress be reduced and/or eliminated in your personal life, as well as in your job?

31. What is burnout? What does your personality type have to do with burnout?

32. Identify four steps that are helpful in dealing with stress.

Connecting to the Real World

Was the message communicated effectively?

The purpose of this exercise is to communicate effectively both in writing and orally.

Procedures

1. Draft an e-mail message requesting a term paper extension from a seasoned professor, age 60–70. Use professional language, tone, and appropriateness of content. What barriers would you encounter? How would you deal with them?

2. How would the content of your message change if your professor was in the age bracket of 25–35? Rewrite the message.

3. How would the message change if you were making the request in person? What factors would you take into consideration? What barriers might you encounter?

4. How would encoding, decoding, perception, inference, language, and status be used differently in the two situations—written and oral?

CASE
Getting Prepared

Sandra Shelby was a top-notch student in college. She graduated with honors from the University of Texas with a degree in management. Upon graduation, she was immediately hired to manage the inventory in a local distribution warehouse. Shelby found she really enjoyed the training aspect of her job. After three years, she decided to make a career change and move into training.

Sandra Shelby was hired on as a training officer for a large metropolitan city. The city spends approximately $400 million per year on a variety of services, including transportation, garbage collection, and police and fire protection. The training and development department has a budget of $7 million and is responsible for providing orientation to new city employees as well as ongoing training to all public employees.

Each year, the board of commissioners of the city enacts a budget. Because funds are limited, each department within the city must present and defend its budget requests. An effective presentation can result in a department getting all the funds it requests, whereas a poor presentation can result in a department getting as little as 60 percent of its request.

Shelby has been chosen to make this year's presentation. The talk is to run twenty minutes, followed by approximately ten minutes of questioning by the commissioners. The presentation last year resulted in the department getting only 75 percent of the funds requested. Shelby feels she can do much better. She has given a lot of thought to what she needs to do to get the support of all the commissioners. One of the first things she plans to do is to interview the manager and assistant manager of her department to find out which programs they feel are critical. She then intends to compare this year's proposed budget with last year's proposed budget in order to ensure that she has not left out any requests.

It is a known fact that the six commissioners have very fixed views regarding the area of training and development. Two of the commissioners believe that the city is not spending enough money on training, while two feel that too much is spent, and the remaining two tend to listen to the arguments that are made at the meeting and vote accordingly. Shelby believes that it would be wise to talk to the two commissioners who support training and development and get some information from them regarding what might be included in the report. She would also like to talk to the two who do not make up their minds until the meeting itself to determine whether she can learn from them some of the key facts that would influence their decision. The commissioners are easily approachable, and Shelby knows that she will have no trouble getting into see the four of them.

Shelby intends to take all this information and condense it into a twenty-minute talk. She believes that the easiest way to present the information will be on a point-by-point basis. She intends to use a PowerPoint presentation projected onto a large screen that can be easily seen by all the commissioners. "It will help the commissioners clearly focus on the points I want to make," she told her assistant. "In addition, I need to be prepared to answer their questions. So I am going to run through my talk with you as my only audience. When I am finished, we will critique the presentation and see how it can be strengthened. Then, after we finalize the talk, I want you to make up twenty questions that you believe they will ask me, and we will discuss the proper responses."

Shelby believes this approach will be effective in ensuring that her department gets its budget request. However, she is remaining flexible in her approach, and if anyone in the department has constructive ideas, she intends to incorporate them into her presentation.

Case Questions

1. In handling this assignment, how can the PLAN approach help Shelby? Explain how Shelby can incorporate each phase of PLAN.

2. How can Figure 11.4 be of value to Shelby? Prepare a list of suggestions for Shelby to follow in giving her presentation. Give at least one suggestion for each of the six factors.

3. Is using PowerPoint the best use of technology? Discuss your ideas.

4. What other things would you recommend that Shelby do in preparing for her presentation?

5. What techniques is Shelby using to manage stress in preparing this presentation?

6. Would you characterize Shelby as a Type A person or as a Type B person? Why?

7. Is Shelby making a mistake by not getting input from all six commissioners prior to her presentation? Explain.

8. What should Shelby's nonverbal language communication skills be when dealing with the two commissioners who feel that too much money is already being spent on the training budget? How should she act toward these commissioners?

9. How will Shelby's body language change from interviewing the commissioners individually to presenting before the entire group?

Managing Conflict and Change

CHAPTER 12

As discussed in Chapter 11, one of the most important duties of the manager for achieving behavioral effectiveness is to communicate well. However, this alone will not ensure overall effectiveness. Two of the most common reasons are conflict and change, topics that are the focus of this chapter.

Survival Requires Change

Change is inevitable and is a reality of any successful company. If businesses want to survive in today's global marketplace, they must change by using new and innovative ideas that meet today's customers' needs and wants. Companies must cultivate a management approach that will encourage a continuous flow of innovation, which is a recognized cornerstone of all high-performance businesses. An example of one of these businesses is Whole Foods Market IP, L.P., a fast-growing chain based in Austin, Texas. It was started in 1980 and since has grown to 270 stores in North America and the United Kingdom with over fifty-four thousand team members. Today, Whole Foods is the world's leader in natural and organic foods. It maintains the strictest quality standards in the industry and has an unshakeable commitment to sustainable agriculture. Whole Foods caters typically to the food buyer who is concerned about health issues and eating healthier.

Whole Foods offers the customer a shopping experience. Some of the store's features are cooking stations, prepared foods, and tasting stations. Another feature is to allow authors to set up promotional tables to talk about their books. For years, the Whole Foods' stores were located only in stand-alone buildings with their own parking lots. This is now changing; they are finding new locations to serve customers' needs. With the resurgence of urban living, luxury-condo towers and apartments have sprouted up around the country, particularly in downtown areas. These buildings typically attract professional people who have more sophisticated tastes. To give their buildings a greater appeal to this market, Ron Shuffield, president of Esslinger Wooten Maxwell., Inc. Realtors, a Miami-based company, sought out Whole Foods to build a store within one of its complexes. That innovative idea resulted in a huge number of people buying into the condo towers, a trend that has continued in other similar projects around the country. Likewise, Whole Foods saw an opportunity to expand its operations and meet the needs of a new market, which proved to be a successful change for Whole Foods. The chain's profits continue to soar in tandem with its growth.

The Home of the Whopper has had its share of problems. When the sales at Burger King Corporation plummeted, causing some restaurants to close and others to file for bankruptcy protection, the owners hired a new chief executive, Greg Brenneman, to make changes and turn around the company. During visits to the Burger King restaurants, Brenneman noticed that employees did not talk with each other, a large amount of the restaurant's space was not being used, and the menu was not competitive with Burger King's competition.

So where did Brenneman begin? His first challenge was to change the culture. He set out to improve morale at the headquarters, fix how employees perceived each other in the restaurants, and improve relationships with franchisors. His visits revealed that the company had abandoned the slogan "Have it your way," which at one time created success for Burger King. Customers liked the slogan because they could ask for their food to be prepared how they like it. The slogan was brought back.

After identifying its customers and their needs, Brenneman had the menu changed to reflect what the customers wanted instead of what the company thought the customers needed. For example, Burger King introduced the popular Enormous Omelet Sandwich—760 calories of eggs, bacon, and sausage on a bun—as well as more salads to satisfy other customers. By understanding and listening to their best repeat customers, known as "Super Fans," Burger King has become a more profitable company. Brenneman has also changed the size of the restaurants, making them more cost efficient. Unused space is no longer a drain on the budget.

Some of Brenneman's tips for fixing a troubled company are focusing on giving customers what they want (not what you think they need), challenging conventional thinking (smaller restaurants are more cost effective), indulging your best repeat customers with new products that cater to their wishes (not your wishes), communicating constantly with employees (giving them weekly updates on progress), and making employees feel proud of what they are doing (regularly giving employees feedback on their goals). With these changes, Burger King is once again a competitive company. Brenneman has since resigned, turning the reigns over to John Chidsey, who was Burger King's president and chief financial officer. During the eight quarters that Brenneman was CEO, he increased sales every quarter and 14.5 percent systemwide. Net profit rose from $5 million to $47 million in one year. Change definitely paid off at Burger King.

The recession of 2008 brought more changes to Burger King. In competition with McDonald's, Burger King reduced the cost to $1 for the Whopper Jr., and later as the ingredients became more expensive, reduced the size of the patty to 2 ounces a piece from 2.2 ounces. Burger King also pulled a slice of cheese from its $1 double cheeseburger. As the economy improved, the prices of the hamburgers moved slowly upward. At the same time, through what some called its irreverent, sexy ads, the reputation of Burger King was damaged, creating the need for more changes to repair its brand image. To stay ahead of its competition, Burger King in the coming months promoted its value offerings and moved toward promoting "round the clock" purchases, like more breakfast items. McDonald's is still the number one leader in breakfast offerings in the fast-food industry.

To stay ahead of its competition, McDonald's is also making changes. The growing coffee bar market has McDonald's installing machinery to serve lattes, mochas, and frappés in competition with Starbucks. McDonald's has upgraded its drip coffee and its interiors, and at the same time, Starbucks has added drive-through windows and hot breakfast sandwiches. It seems that convenience is the dominating force shaping the food-service industry. Change is a reality at Burger King, McDonald's, and Starbucks, as well as at other businesses, if they want to stay competitive and survive.

The Nature of Conflict

Define conflict and explain some of the major types of conflict.

Conflict is opposition or antagonism toward other individuals or things. For example, Sara has beaten out Travis for a promotion, and now there is conflict between the two because Travis feels he was better qualified and should have gotten that job. Similarly, Tim and Tina believe the new monthly cost control report is a waste of time and have decided to file their reports late and incomplete. Both have a conflict with this new report.

In overall terms, two types of conflict are important in the study of human relations. One is conflict at the individual level. The other is conflict at the organizational level. Each type of conflict has its own characteristics.

Individual Conflict

Whenever the needs of individuals in the organization are at odds, conflict can develop. Two of the most common reasons are frustration and interpersonal conflict.

The result of a blocked need is **frustration**. In the example just given, Travis was frustrated because his need to reach a desired goal (the promotion) was blocked by a barrier (only one person could receive the promotion). Figure 12.1 provides an illustration of Travis's frustration. Another good example is provided by the worker who is unable to accomplish a task because of interference by other employees or because of a failure in the equipment that is provided for doing the job.

What a manager needs to realize is that the stronger the worker's motivation to reach a desired goal, the greater the person's frustration with failure. Because a manager wants to encourage high motivation, it is imperative that some form of assistance be provided in helping the individual deal with this frustration. For example, in many cases, a manager can intervene and remove the roadblocks that are preventing goal attainment. An example is to give an employee access to the information needed to complete the task in a timely manner or to find the resources needed to get the job done.

Another common cause of frustration is unfair or discriminatory treatment in the workplace. In some organizations, minorities are not accorded the same treatment as others. For example, research shows that blacks and women, on average, have lower

Figure 12.1 Blocked Need Drive and Frustration

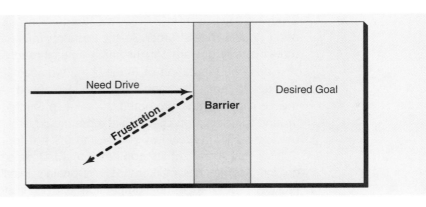

IN ACTION

DEALING WITH SEXUAL HARASSMENT

Many people in the workplace feel they are sexually harassed. In the past, involvement in this problem was confined to the person claiming to be harassed and the person who was doing the harassing. This no longer is true. The U.S. Supreme Court has ruled that it is sexual harassment to create a "hostile environment" in which individuals are subjected to such behaviors as sexually suggestive comments, mental abuse, and obscenities. In response, many organizations have created formal policies that specifically forbid sexual harassment in all forms. These policies must, however, be continually updated to stand up in court. Under Title VII, the employer is also liable for harassment from customers, as well as independent contractors. Even users of e-mail have been victims of harassment.

Managers should know how to deal with this problem when it arises. In particular, they should adhere to five guidelines:

1. *Know the organization's policy on sexual harassment.* If you do not have a copy of the rules, get one and read it.
2. *If there is a formal policy, ensure that everyone in your work unit knows about it and understands it.* If there is no formal policy, tell your employees that sexual harassment will not be tolerated and urge those who feel they have been victims to report the matter to you.
3. *Take all complaints seriously.* Meet with the complaining employee, take notes, and ask any questions that will help you to get a better understanding of what has happened. Also make it clear that the organization does not tolerate sexual harassment in any form and that you will not allow it in your work unit. It is important to convey the seriousness with which you approach this matter. If it ever gets into court, one of the first things the prosecution will attempt to prove is that you knew of the situation and treated it lightly.
4. *Act immediately.* Call in whoever has been named in the sexual harassment charge and talk to the person. Try to resolve the situation at this point. Make it clear that any remarks that can be misconstrued as sexual harassment can get an individual into serious trouble. If, in your view, the matter is sufficiently serious, have the person who brought the charge present at your meeting with the worker who has been accused and make it clear to both of them that you expect no further problems along this line.
5. *Follow up on your actions.* After a week has gone by, check with the person to be sure he or she is not being subjected to further harassment. Let him or her know that you have not forgotten the matter and that, if it arises again, you want to know about it at once.

It is unlikely that you can stamp out sexual harassment in the workplace. However, you can reduce its occurrence and its negative impact by following these five guidelines.

---

salaries than do their white male counterparts. In July 2010, the U.S. Bureau of Labor Statistics reported that white males earned $838 per week while black males earned $632 per week. White females earned $682 per week and black women earned $585. White males continue to be the highest paid.[1] Additionally, women sometimes are subjected to sexual harassment. The "Ethics and Social Responsibility in Action" box describes some of the steps that organizations are now taking to ensure that this practice is terminated.

Closely related to the idea of frustration is that of **interpersonal conflict**, which arises when disagreements occur among employees. For example, when Daimler-Benz acquired Chrysler, its objective was to establish a strong foothold in the American auto market and to give Chrysler greater entry into the European market. Within a short period, however, the senior-level German managers were engaged in interpersonal conflict with their American counterpart regarding how Chrysler should be run. The Germans felt that the American executives were paid too much money, and the Americans felt that the Germans did not understand how the U.S. auto market operated. As a result, when Chrysler began losing money, the German executives began replacing the senior American staff with their own executives. This, in turn, created interpersonal conflict and resulted in even further deterioration of relations between the two groups.[2]

Organizational Conflict

When viewed from an organizational level, conflict can be categorized into two groups: institutionalized and emergent.

Institutionalized conflict results from organizational attempts to structure work assignments. For example, three major departments are fighting for increased budgets, but insufficient monies are available for all to receive their requests. Each department fights to gain increases at the expense of the others. In the end, at least one department will not get its request, and possibly, none of them will end up with what they want. Ultimately, conflict often ensues, with each department harboring a grudge against the others.

Another example of institutionalized conflict occurs when employees refuse to share information because it results in their losing informal power. For example, when Buckman Laboratories International, Inc., a specialty chemical company, implemented an electronic network to enable knowledge sharing by all employees so that complex customer problems could be quickly resolved, the new system faced institutional conflict. In particular, it threatened many employees who had developed a great deal of informal power by hoarding their valuable expertise. Therefore, when employees tried to make use of the electronic network to obtain necessary information, those who could provide the data refused to do so while offering a variety of reasons, including "You don't need to know this information."[3]

Emergent conflict arises from personal and social causes. For example, there may be disagreement between the formal and informal organizations regarding how much work the employees should perform. Another example is conflict that emerges when subordinates feel they know a great deal more than their boss regarding how to improve efficiency. Although the boss has the formal authority to run the department and make decisions related to work assignments, the employees are in conflict with these decisions because they feel the boss lacks the necessary knowledge and experience to do the job as well as they can.

 CHECK YOUR UNDERSTANDING

1. **Individual conflict:** An example of frustration is _____. An example of interpersonal conflict is _____.
2. **Organizational conflict:** An example of institutionalized conflict is _____. An example of emergent conflict is _____.

Relate some of the most effective ways of managing conflict.

Managing Conflict

Conflict can be managed in a number of ways. One of the most common is general counseling. However, in some cases, such as that of troubled employees or individuals who are drug abusers, the approach must be more carefully planned. Other approaches to managing conflict are mutual problem solving, expansion of resources, smoothing, and compromise. The following sections examine these ways of managing conflict.

General Counseling

Counseling is the discussion of an emotional problem with an employee for the purpose of eliminating or reducing the problem. Many people in the workplace need counseling because the demands of their jobs create emotional problems for them. The overall purpose of counseling is to provide emotional support for employees. In this function, the manager's job is to increase the employee's understanding, self-confidence, and ability to work effectively as a member of the team. Managers typically use four approaches in carrying out this function: advice, reassurance, release of emotional tension, and reorientation.

Advice.   When the manager advises a subordinate, he or she lays out a course of action to be followed. The manager takes the lead, and the subordinate follows. Some professional counselors have pointed out the dangers in trying to understand another person's complicated emotions and to recommend a path of action. Despite the possible dangers, however, this approach to counseling is widely used because managers believe they should provide such guidance and workers expect them to do so. Many employees admit that they would rather have the manager suggest a course of action (even if it might be wrong) than to plan one themselves.

Reassurance.   Closely related to advice is reassurance. Some people, for example, encounter stress because they are unsure of how well they are performing their jobs. The manager may tell a subordinate that he or she is doing fine and may encourage him or her to keep it up. To a worker who is experiencing job stress, the manager may point out, "This is all temporary. Our busy season ends next week, and everything will return to normal." Sometimes, reassurance is just what the person needs to reduce frustration or stress. In other cases, the individual needs to be assured that organizational rules will be enforced. A good example is sexual harassment on the job. Managers not only need to be aware of this form of behavior, they also must be prepared to take action as soon as they learn about it.

Release of Emotional Tension.   Many times, all a worker needs is a sympathetic ear. The tension declines once he or she pours out what has been bottled up inside. Of course, this may not solve the problem, but it often removes mental blocks and permits the worker to face the problem squarely. Few people can resolve their problems when seething with anger and tension. This counseling function can help to alleviate such emotions.

Reorientation.   Sometimes employees need to be reoriented. They require additional training for a new job, a revision of their aspirations so that they are more in line with their abilities, or a rethinking of their current goals and values vis-à-vis those of the organization. Managers can sometimes handle these problems, but, if the problems are severe, professional help must be engaged. If, for example, an employee is an alcoholic, helping him or her become reoriented may be beyond the ability of most managers. When one's subordinate has a problem like this, it is best to let professional counselors take over.

Dealing with More Serious Problems

Sometimes, employees' problems are serious and troubling, and they need more than general counseling. Their problems could be a result of alcohol or drug abuse.

Troubled Employees.   Sometimes, employees will be troubled over job-related or home-related problems. If the manager feels the problem is best handled by letting it go, of course, no action is required. However, if the manager believes that some action is needed, three courses are available:

1. Tell the employee to shape up or ship out.
2. Discipline the person.
3. Discuss the problem with the employee in an effort to work out a solution.

This last approach requires effective counseling or coaching by the leader. Some of the most useful guidelines that can be employed are the following:

- Talk to the employee early in the workweek rather than just before the weekend. In this way, you can follow up the next day if additional coaching or counseling is needed.
- Talk to the employee early in the day rather than just before quitting time. This will allow you ample time to at least cover your main points and give the worker a chance to respond.
- Talk to the individual privately, away from other workers and managers. Let the person know that just the two of you are involved—at least at this stage.

- Get to the point immediately. Describe the problem situation or behaviors you have been noticing and present them from your point of view rather than from someone else's. The following are some examples.

  Example 1:
  Say: I am becoming concerned about the number of accidents you are having.
  As opposed to: Your nervousness is causing you to have too many accidents.
  Example 2:
  Say: I am upset over your failure to follow my instructions.
  As opposed to: You make me mad by failing to follow my instructions.
  Example 3:
  Say: I have some concerns about your work.
  As opposed to: Some concerns have been voiced about your work.

- If the worker finds it difficult to talk, provide reassurances and let the individual proceed at his or her own pace. Acknowledge what the person says without passing judgment or giving advice.

- When the employee is done talking, discuss how he or she can improve his or her work performance. Let the person know you are available if assistance is needed.

- If the individual's problem requires professional counseling, do not offer it yourself. The problem is beyond your training. Help to identify the problem and then have the organization's counseling service handle the matter. If no such service is available, prepare a list of community referral services to which the worker can turn. Typical examples of problems for which referrals should be made are:

  Recurring bouts of anger, sadness, or fear

  Feelings of loneliness, isolation, moodiness, or depression

  Suicidal thoughts

  Inability to concentrate or sleep

  Lack of self-confidence

  Family problems

  High stress levels

  Constant anxiety

- Respect the employee's confidentiality. Do not discuss his or her situation with coworkers or others who have no need to know about the matter.

Alcoholism.   Frustration and stress are very common in modern organizations. In dealing with these problems, some people turn to alcohol because they believe that it helps them to unwind. The unfortunate fact is that alcoholism in industry has now become a major problem resulting in accidents, absenteeism, wasted time, ruined materials, and premature job termination. For example, the rate of alcohol use was 63.0 percent for full-time employed adults age 18 or older in 2008, higher than the 55.5 percent of unemployed adults. Among the 17.3 million heavy drinkers aged 12 or older, 29.4 percent were current illicit drug users. Alcohol consumption levels were also associated with tobacco use.[4]

Research, according to the University at Buffalo's Research Institute on Addictions, shows that just over 7 percent of American workers drink during the workday, mostly during lunch. And more interestingly, 9 percent have nursed a hangover in the workplace. In nearly 19 percent of on-the-job-fatalities, the person dying tested positive for alcohol, drugs, or both.[5]

How does a manager know when a worker is drinking too much? Answering this question is difficult, but there are some signs for which a manager can remain alert (see Figure 12.2). Among white-collar workers, these include such things as elaborate and often bizarre excuses for work deficiencies, pronounced and frequent swings in work pace, avoidance of the boss and associates, and increased nervousness. Among blue-collar workers, the clues are a sloppy personal appearance, signs of a hangover, frequent lapses of efficiency leading to occasional damage to equipment or material,

Figure 12.2 Observable Behavior Patterns of Alcohol Abuse

(Alcohol Addiction Line)

Stage	Absenteeism	General Behavior	Job Performance
I Early	Tardiness Quits early Absence from work situations ("I drink to relieve tension")	Complaints from fellow employees for not doing his or her share Overreaction Complaints of not "feeling well" Makes untrue statements	Misses deadlines Commits errors (frequently) Lower job efficiency Criticism from the boss
II Middle	Frequent days off for vague or implausible reasons ("I feel guilty about sneaking drinks"; "I have tremors")	Marked changes Undependable statements Avoids fellow employees Borrows money from fellow employees Exaggerates work accomplishments Frequent hospitalization Minor injuries on the job (repeatedly)	General deterioration Cannot concentrate Occasional lapse of memory Warning from boss
III Late middle	Frequent days off; several days at a time Does not return from lunch ("I don't feel like eating"; "I don't want to talk about it"; "I like to drink alone")	Aggressive and belligerent behavior Domestic problems interfere with work Financial difficulties (garnishments, etc.) More frequent hospitalization Resignation; does not want to discuss problems Problems with the laws in the community	Far below expectation Punitive disciplinary action
IV Approaching terminal stage	Prolonged unpredictable absences ("My job interferes with my drinking")	Drinking on the job (probably) Completely undependable Repeated hospitalization Serious financial problems Serious family problems; divorce	Uneven Generally incompetent Faces termination or hospitalization

Source: Gopal C. Pati and John I. Adkins, Jr., "The Employer's Role in Alcoholism Assistance," *Personnel Journal*, 1983.

increased nervousness, and increased off-the-job accidents. Perhaps the biggest problem managers must face in dealing with alcoholics is that they are skillful in denying the problem, especially when confronted by the boss.

Alcoholic employees have an uncanny knack for manipulating the feelings of supervisors. In many cases, they sense the onset of angry outbursts and know how to play for the counterfeelings that will block supervisory urges to act decisively. A favorite ploy is the "whipped child" syndrome, characterized by the hangdog look and the "I can't do anything right" verbalizations. Almost invariably, these behaviors tug at parental heartstrings, and suddenly, a supervisor finds himself or herself comforting and supporting the alcoholic employee rather than confronting the individual. At other times, outbursts of righteous indignation by an employee will frighten the supervisor and cause him or her to back off. Alcoholics have a great deal of experience at playing these games. Unless they know what is going on, supervisors do not have a chance.[6]

Regardless of how effective they are in initially hiding their problem, it eventually becomes obvious. This is particularly true if the organization has trained its managers in how to identify the excessive drinker. At this point, the problem worker should be sent either to the firm's medical department or to the human resources department for counseling or further referral. Because the manager is not likely to be an expert on alcohol rehabilitation, he or she must be careful about what is said. For example, it is a mistake for the manager to moralize to the employee about the dangers of drinking or to try to diagnose why the person has become a problem drinker. Instead, the manager should stress that the problem will be handled confidentially and that alcoholism can be successfully treated. From here, it is a matter of providing assistance to the person in getting the necessary treatment. Many organizations have their own programs designed to deal with alcoholism; this is the ideal situation.

Some firms have found that managers do not like to be the ones to confront a subordinate about a drinking problem. The confrontation can be awkward, and the manager is often defensive about having to take the action. As a result, some firms are now using a team approach, in which a subordinate's associates and peers are involved in the evaluation process. It is easier to fool the boss than it is to hide the problem from coworkers and peers who have daily contact with the employee and can observe the employee's work behavior.

Drug Abuse.   Employee drug use is widespread in industry, and its impact on the bottom line can be significant. Employers are rightfully worried about substance abuse by their employees. The Sam M. Walton College of Business at the University of Arkansas has found that methamphetamine abusers cost companies in Benton County, with a population of 150,000 people, about $21 million a year related to absenteeism of addicted workers. In neighboring Washington County, employers absorbed direct costs of $24 million associated with meth abuse. This has caught the eye of Tom Siebel, founder of Siebel Software, who launched the Montana Meth Project to combat the problem in his adopted state.[7] Other statistics, for example, reveal that:

1. Absenteeism is 66 percent higher among drug users than nondrug users.
2. Almost half of workplace accidents are drug related.
3. Disciplinary actions are 90 percent higher among drug users.
4. Employee turnover is significantly higher among drug users.[8]

In addition, the U.S. Department of Health & Human Services reports that 77 percent of drug users are employed full-time. An estimated 6.5 percent of full-time and 8.6 percent of part-time workers are current illicit drug users.[9] Various reasons account for this rise in drug use. Generally, people take drugs at work to reduce the boredom, tension, or anxiety that accompanies the work.

Table 12.1
Signs of Drug Abuse in the Workplace

Changes in attendance (i.e., missing work, tardiness)
Changes in job performance
Changes in overall attitude or personality
Sudden outbreaks of anger
Changes (deterioration) in physical appearance or grooming
Money or equipment missing from the workplace
Complaints from coworkers or customers about the employee's attitude or behavior
Missing work deadlines
Shying away from responsibility

Source: "Signs of Drug Abuse in the Workplace," www.drugtestcenter.com.

The symptoms of drug abuse are similar to those of alcoholism: slurred speech, dilated eyes, unsteady walk, lack of dexterity, and uncontrollable laughter or crying. Additional signs are listed in Table 12.1.

Also, like alcoholism, programs have been developed for dealing with drug abusers. A typical program, in a large organization, can be designed and implemented in four stages:

1. A committee is formed. If the firm is unionized, the union will be adequately represented. One representative in the group will be from the firm's medical department, if such a department exists.
2. A policy statement expressing the philosophy of the organization toward the effect of drug abuse on job performance will be developed.
3. If the firm is unionized, a joint labor–management policy statement recognizing the effect of drug abuse on health and behavior will be developed.
4. Supervisors and management personnel will be trained in identifying drug-related problems and the proper ways to deal with them most effectively, including monitoring rehabilitation progress as measured by job performance.

Those found to be using drugs are removed from the workplace and often provided with assistance. If they accept this help and overcome their drug dependency, no disciplinary action is taken. Otherwise, they are dismissed.[10]

Drug Testing.   In recent years, disagreement has arisen regarding the use of drug testing and what to do when people test positive. Testing often is conducted before employment, randomly and for cause, as in the case of someone involved in a job-related accident.[11] Research indicates that drug testing has increased over the past decade. Part of this increase is a result of state and local drug testing ordinances that permit preemployment and random testing and, if there is reason to suspect the use of drugs, testing "for cause" as well. At the same time, it is important to remember that testing can result in false positive results; some experts contend that the error rate in drug testing can be as high as 30 percent. For example, evidence shows that the ingestion of codeine can produce positive results for heroin, some brands of aspirin have resulted in people testing positive for marijuana, and some cough medicines have resulted in individuals receiving positive test results for the use of amphetamines.[12] Clearly, drug testing has its limitations. This undoubtedly helps to explain the current move toward relying less on drug testing and more on educating employees about the dangers of drugs and encouraging them to be intolerant about substance abuse by other employees.

Employee Assistance Programs.   How else should drug testing be handled? Many experts recommend that an employee assistance program (EAP) be created that offers confidential and professional help to those employees who are drug abusers. Many firms have an alcohol-related EAP, so it is merely a matter of expanding the program's focus. Rather than putting the emphasis on catching drug users and firing them, however, attention is devoted to prevention and rehabilitation. This is a frontline defense for many organizations in their fight to deal with drug abusers in the workplace.[13] Firms, however, need to do a better job of informing employees about these programs. Recently, the Office of Applied Studies in the Substance Abuse and Mental Health Services Administration (SAMHSA) reported about 53 percent of workers were aware of substance use EAPs at their workplaces. Those workers in administrative support occupations were more likely than workers in other occupations to be aware of written workplace policies about employee substance use. Workers in the transportation, communication, and other public utilities industries were more likely than workers in other industries to be aware of substance use testing at their workplaces.[14]

Implementing workplace substance abuse programs can save a company a lot of money. For example, Turfscape Landscape Care, Inc. of Chandler, Arizona, saved more than $50,000 per year, just four years after implementing a drug-free workplace program. Quaker Furniture of Catawba County, North Carolina, is another firm that has a drug-free workplace program.[15]

Drug use among workers is related to a series of workplace outcomes dealing with health, productivity, and performance. For example, a survey conducted by the National Survey on Drug Use & Health revealed that, compared to those not using drugs, employees using drugs were more likely to have worked for three or more employers in the past year, skipped one or more days of work in the past month, or have voluntarily left an employer in the past year.[16] Other studies reveal that substance abusers are more likely to have extended absences from work, show up late, be involved in a workplace accident, and file a workers' compensation claim. The bottom line is that "substance abusers in the workplace significantly contribute to increased health care costs, disability insurance costs, absenteeism rates, employee theft, and accidents, as well as decreased productivity, product quality, and employee morale."[17] SAMHSA has a wealth of information on its Web site concerning issues that are alcohol and drug related. This source can help managers learn more about these issues.

Other Common Approaches

Counseling is an important method of resolving conflict. However, other approaches are also commonly used. Four of these are examined below, and some useful guidelines offered. The four approaches are mutual problem solving, expansion of resources, smoothing, and compromise.

Mutual Problem Solving.   The process of bringing together all the parties to a conflict to discuss the issues face to face is called **mutual problem solving**. For example, if two groups in the department are having a problem working together, the manager will sit down with both groups and discuss the matter jointly. Each group will be given the opportunity to explain why it is having trouble with the other. Then the manager will work to create ground for common understanding, will discuss how the current conflict can be resolved, and will often require the two groups to determine mutually how they will resolve their own conflict. Through this process of sharing concerns and communicating with each other, mutual problem solving often brings about intergroup harmony.

Expansion of Resources.   Sometimes, conflict can be resolved through an *expansion of resources*. For example, the department may need five computers but has a budget for only three. However, by talking the finance people into delaying the purchase of other equipment, there will be more money left for departmental computers. Alternatively, the company may be reorganized and some people given early retirement, thus freeing up funds for computer equipment. An expansion of resources involves a reworking of the budget for the purpose of determining how additional funds can be found.

Smoothing.   **Smoothing** is the process of playing down the differences between individuals and groups while emphasizing their common interests. This approach often is useful only in the short run, as it involves ignoring or overlooking the major reasons behind the conflict. However, smoothing can be important in that it provides a temporary respite from the bickering and backbiting that often accompany conflict. Then, after all parties have had a chance to cool off, the problem can be reviewed and readdressed.

Compromise.   When each side gives up something, such that neither side emerges as the big winner, the approach is called **compromise**. Compromise is an important conflict resolution approach because it often allows each side to gain at least some of what it is seeking. In union–management negotiations, compromise is commonly used. If each side is able to feel that it did better with a compromise than it would have done with a prolonged conflict, the problem may be resolved permanently. However, if one side to the conflict feels that it gave up far too much, then the conflict is likely to reemerge.

Additional Useful Guidelines

Research in the area of conflict has generated a series of practical suggestions for managers.[18]

1. A suggestion is not to promote conflict as "healthy competition." No empirical data support this assumption, and firms that do so often invite trouble for themselves.
2. A suggestion is to remember that it is better to avoid conflict from the beginning than to determine how to manage it when it appears.

 CHECK YOUR UNDERSTANDING

How Can Conflict Be Resolved?
Match the term with the statement:

Term	Statement
a. Counseling	_____ Playing down or overlooking reasons for conflict
b. Mutual Problem solving	_____ Each side gives up something important
c. Expansion of Resources	_____ A discussion to reduce or eliminate a problem
d. Soothing	_____ Reworking the budget and reorganizing
e. Compromise	_____ All parties discuss the issues

3. A suggested guideline is to realize that when conflict cannot be averted, it is extremely important to address some of its effects (distrust, anxiety, and escalation of feelings) and to accept the fact that sometimes the elimination of conflict is not feasible.

4. A suggestion is to identify, if possible, the major reasons for the conflict. The manager should then try to set up trades in which each side acquiesces on issues that have low costs for it and relatively high payoffs for the other side(s).

5. A suggestion is that managers adopt a pragmatic approach to managing conflict by using techniques that are reasonable and, when possible, also inexpensive.[19]

Discuss how change occurs.

The Nature of Change

Any modification or alteration of the status quo is **change,** and in recent years, virtually every organization has had to deal with rapid and often unpredictable changes. Often people are clueless about what is causing the change and how it affects them. Companies are not fine-tuned machines that can be copied easily; they are "living, breathing, changing organisms that interact with millions of other living, breathing, changing organisms."[20] Commenting on the nature and severity of change, one expert wrote:

> *Change is sudden, nonlinear, and constant. Its amplitude and direction can't be forecast. Killer apps can come from anywhere; new competitors are lurking everywhere. Markets emerge, flourish, inspire imitators, breed competitors, and disappear seemingly overnight. Brands, which once took years to establish and which, once established, seemed unassailable, now burst on the scene like a new strain of virus, finding competitive spaces and market niches that were previously invisible. Internet buzz can make a product overnight—or break it. There is more choice than ever, more challenge than ever—and more change than ever. As a result, products and markets are continuously morphing, so organizations that want to prosper over the long term need to practice the art of continuous change.[21]*

Before examining the importance of change in the field of human relations, let us look at the nature of change by studying how it occurs and by answering the question, "Is resistance to change always a bad thing?" (Before continuing, take the "Time Out" quiz.)

How Change Occurs

When change takes place, three things happen:

1. There is a movement from one set of conditions to another.
2. Some force(s) causes the change to come about.
3. A consequence results from the change.

Many forms of work-related technology provide a good example of consequence. The introduction of a new software system can frighten employees. The employees like the old system, and they do not feel it is necessary to change the system. Since the new system is more complex, they may feel that it will take more time and effort to get their work completed. The same is true for some types of machinery, from production equipment to photocopiers. Another major reason for resistance is that employees do not know how to use the new equipment or do not understand its value to them. As long as people do not know how to use the new technology or how to use a software program, resistance is likely. Companies can reduce employee resistance by implementing a training program that addresses these issues.

How Much Do You Know about the Change Process?

Before studying the management of change, take a minute to examine how well you understand the change process. Presented here are a dozen statements that relate to change. Read each carefully and then check whether it is basically true or basically false. Answers are given at the end of the book.

	Basically True	Basically False
1. Because change is so much a part of everyday life, most modern workers like new work procedures and policies.	___	___
2. Most work changes lead to an immediate increase in productivity.	___	___
3. Many employees like the status quo; change scares them.	___	___
4. If a computer designed to help them do their work were available, most employees would try to learn how to use the machine as quickly as possible.	___	___
5. Most organizational changes that are introduced are truly designed to increase efficiency.	___	___
6. If their friends at work are opposed to a change, most workers will also oppose the change.	___	___
7. Most people who resist change do so because they enjoy giving the organization a hard time.	___	___
8. People prefer to be told about new changes just before they are to be implemented.	___	___
9. People tend to be more supportive of changes they helped to fashion than of those forced on them.	___	___
10. Most managers tend to overrate the time needed to implement changes effectively.	___	___
11. Change always results, if only in the short run, in an increase in work output.	___	___
12. Unions tend to reject new work changes.	___	___

Is Resistance Bad?

Some people believe that resistance to change is inevitable. In many cases, this is true, for when an organization's employees weigh the benefits associated with the status quo against those that they believe will result from the change, they opt for maintaining things the way they are. "Change, as it is usually orchestrated, creates initiative, overload and organizational chaos, both of which provoke strong resistance from the people most affected."[22] As a result, they resist alteration of the status quo.

Such resistance is not necessarily bad. Several important functions are served by it. First, resistance forces those supporting the change to build a case against the status quo, thereby providing management a chance to weigh the pros and cons. Here is an example.

A public library located in a mid-size city houses more than 700,000 volumes. When the city council voted to appropriate the necessary funds to upgrade the computerized system, many of the staff were delighted with the news. But some opposed the new system, claiming it would be very difficult to implement and would make exorbitant demands on their time. However, after a general meeting in which both sides had the opportunity to air their concerns, it was agreed that everyone would work together to implement the new computerization system. After the meeting, one of the employees, who initially had opposed the move, said, "After hearing the pros and cons, I now realize the new computerization system would not increase our workload or threaten our jobs. So I'm all for it."

A second benefit of resistance to change is that it encourages the organization to look before it leaps. This is particularly important when implementation of the change will be expensive and, if wrong, could mean major problems for the enterprise. In dealing with resistance and ensuring that change is properly implemented, the first place to begin is with careful planning. This involves consideration of three issues:

1. Whether there should be a change
2. If so, what type of change is needed
3. How the change should be implemented

In many cases, change is good for the entire organization. For example, many technological innovations, from personal computers to cellular telephones to handheld computers, as well as e-mail and social networks, are making it easier and cheaper to communicate information. Nonetheless, employees will not necessarily go along with a

Figure 12.3 Stimulus–Response–Outcome—Effect Brought on by Change

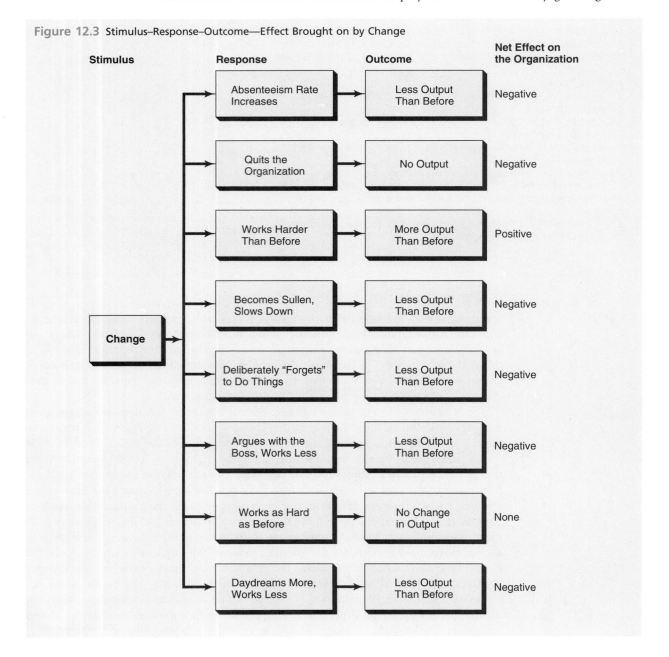

change. Change calls up many different responses. Some are a result of rational reasoning; others can be a result of unjustified concerns or biases brought about by fear, prejudice, or lack of trust.[23] Whatever the reason, it is important to realize that the response to change can take numerous forms.

Responses to Change

Explain four common responses to change—rejection, resistance, tolerance, and acceptance.

People's reactions to change will depend on the benefits they think will result from it. If people believe they will profit from the change, they will support it; if people feel they will lose status, prestige, earning power, or the job itself because of change, they will fight it. If employees think of change as a stimulus, they will make numerous responses, with varied outcomes and effects on the organization. For example, in Figure 12.3, eight workers are being subjected to the same change. As you can see, there are many responses: increase in absenteeism, resignation, working harder than ever, slowing down, arguing with the boss, and so on. Overall, however, there is a negative effect on the organization. In this case, we may conclude that most of the workers do not like the change or that it was not properly introduced.

In examining the situation further, we need to take a closer look at the stimulus (change) and response (outcome) relationship. We can view the change or stimulus as a causal variable and the response or outcome as an end-result variable. For human relations purposes, however, we need to investigate why different people respond in different ways to the same stimulus.

Some psychologists believe the answer can be found in an individual's attitude toward the stimulus. A person's attitude is a reflection of psychological, personal, and social factors. These factors will result in a particular evaluation of the change. In turn, the evaluation will lead to one of the four reactions: rejection, resistance, tolerance, or acceptance (Figure 12.4).

Figure 12.4
Analysis of Response to Change

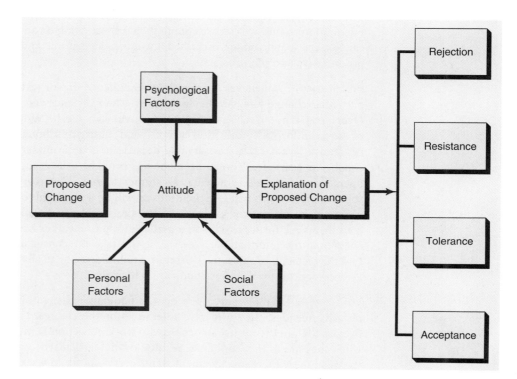

One of the most important *psychological factors* affecting attitudes is the individual's reaction to stress, a topic discussed earlier in the text. Some workers are rather comfortable under stressful or high-anxiety-producing conditions, but other employees shun stress and seek a calm environment.

One of the most important *personal factors* is experience: People who have encountered similar changes in the past draw on the results of those changes to evaluate the current or pending change. For example, if the last time it changed work procedures a company tried to increase output requirements by 15 percent, the workers probably will fight the management's new attempt to change work procedures again. They are likely to believe that if they give in, management will once more increase output requirements.

Conversely, we can take the example of the organization that introduced a new hospitalization plan to save the employees money: The next time the company announces a change in the hospitalization plan, there is likely to be warm support for the move because the employees had a good experience with a similar change.

The *social factors* refer to the group in which the individual works. If there is a great deal of cohesion in the group, all members will tend to stick together. If the proposed change conflicts with the norms and values of the informal group, members will not go along with management's attempt to introduce change. Conversely, if the change is supportive of its norms and values, the group will accept the change. Keep in mind that when we talk about group acceptance, one of the primary norms is always group unity. If management makes any reorganizational changes that will break up the group, the members will oppose the plans.

As a result of psychological, personal, and social factors, an employee will form an attitude regarding the change. This attitude will assist him or her in evaluating the impact of the change to determine whether it is acceptable. On the basis of this evaluation, the employee will reject, resist, tolerate, or accept the proposed change.

Rejection.   When the change is perceived as potentially destructive, **rejection** occurs. Those being subjected to the change view it as totally unacceptable. In this case, it is not uncommon to find workers resigning their jobs or going on strike. At best, management can expect to encounter increased turnover, alienation, and dramatic reductions in productivity and job satisfaction.

Resistance.   Whenever workers feel threatened by or extremely anxious about a particular change, they are likely to resist. The resistance can be either overt or covert. **Overt resistance** is observable; management can see it. Work slowdown, the setting of lower informal production norms, and outright sabotage are examples. **Covert resistance** is not readily observable because it is done under the guise of working as usual. For example, the management has brought in a group of consultants to study operations and make efficiency recommendations. The workforce is concerned that some of the workers will lose their jobs or will be transferred to other departments. In an effort to thwart the consultants' efforts, the workers use **veiled resistance**. When the consultants ask for some data on a particular topic, a worker hands them a massive report containing the information. However, it will take the consultants two or three hours to find the material. In short, the workers are not refusing to go along; they are simply making it more difficult for the consultants to do their jobs.

Tolerance.   If the workers are neutral about the change or have equal positive and negative feelings, they will have **tolerance** for the change. For example, management decides that, in the future, all people who work in Section D must wear safety equipment when they are in the work area. Because of the particularly high noise factor created by the machinery there, management wants every worker to wear plastic earmuffs that will screen out the noise and prevent damage to hearing. Many of the workers admit they are not particularly eager to wear the earmuffs, but they can understand management's point of view, so they will go along with management's request. They have no particularly strong feelings either way.

Acceptance.   Sometimes, the positive factors favoring the change are weighed much more heavily than the negative ones. In these cases, the workers' **acceptance** of the change is likely. For example, instead of asking workers to wear regular plastic earmuffs, the management has a set of earmuffs specially wired for each person. Music can be piped through the set so that workers can listen to music and do their jobs at the same time. Changes such as this have been widely accepted in many industrial settings. Printing companies, especially large newspaper firms, often give these earmuffs to their press operators, who, according to research, like the changed environment.

 CHECK YOUR UNDERSTANDING

Match the change behavior with the statement.

Change Behavior	Statement
a. Rejection	_____ Employees wear their ear plugs.
b. Resistance	_____ Workers feel neutral about the change.
c. Tolerance	_____ Workers slow down their work pace.
d. Acceptance	_____ Employees resign their jobs.

Why Is There Resistance to Change?

In most cases, workers do not reject change outright nor do they accept it. Rather, they tend to either resist it or tolerate it. In our study of human relations, resistance is the reaction of greatest interest to us. After all, if the workers tolerate a particular change, there is really nothing for the manager to be concerned about. However, if they resist, the manager should find out why and then should determine how this resistance can be reduced or eliminated. Let us discuss in detail nine of the most common causes of resistance to change.[24]

1. Obsolescence of Job Skills.   A bookkeeper who has worked for the same company for twenty years and finally learned a software program is going to fight a change to another software program. An assembly-line welder who learns that the company has just bought automatic welding machinery that will weld faster and more efficiently than can be done by hand will oppose the change. Additionally, whereas organizations will attempt to find these people other positions in the firm, the meaningful alternative jobs require special training that the displaced workers lack.[25] These people have been on the job for so long doing the same thing day after day that their knowledge about other work is obsolete. Also, they do not qualify for the jobs being given to college-educated engineers and business specialists. In short, they have no real marketable skills, so they fight for the status quo.

2. Fear of the Unknown.   Fear can create a great impasse for change. The unknown brings uncertainty and, for some individuals, a natural resistance. For example, conservative individuals tend to resist change. Introducing technology into a firm brings fear and uncertainty, especially for older workers. As a result, they may develop a negative attitude toward their work.

3. Fear of Economic Loss. Another reason for resistance to change is fear of economic loss. Sometimes, workers are replaced or fired or find themselves in dead-end jobs. Technology often plays a key role here, turning rather demanding jobs into simple ones that can be done by anyone. When this occurs, the lower demands of the job often are reflected by a new lower pay rate, and the workers now find that salary raises are much lower than before. After all, who needs highly paid people if the job is automated so that anyone can do it?

4. Ego Defensiveness. Sometimes, a change will make a person look bad, so he or she will fight it. For example, Roberta has an idea for expanding the marketing effort out of the eastern part of the country and into the western states. If things go well there, the effort will then be expanded to the national market. However, her boss, Chuck, is reluctant to go along with her suggestion because it will make him look bad with his colleagues, who will all realize that Roberta was the one who thought up the new sales effort. Rather than allow this to happen, Chuck continually claims that he needs to develop the market in the east more fully before considering expansion.

5. Fear of Loss in Status Quo. Change is disturbing to many people. They feel more comfortable working in established routines and procedures than taking risks by entering into new ventures or undertakings. Any attempt to alter this status quo meets with resistance.

6. Shortsightedness. Many people know what is going to happen in the short run but not in the long run. Therefore, they look only at the short-run effects of any change. We can illustrate this through an analysis of the impacts of autocratic and democratic, or participative, leadership. In the short run, if a manager changes from autocratic to participative leadership, his or her department often will suffer short-term decreases in productivity (Figure 12.5). This will not last indefinitely, however; long-term increases eventually will follow. Research reveals that it takes time for such a change to bring

Figure 12.5 From Autocratic Leadership to Participative Leadership—An Illustration

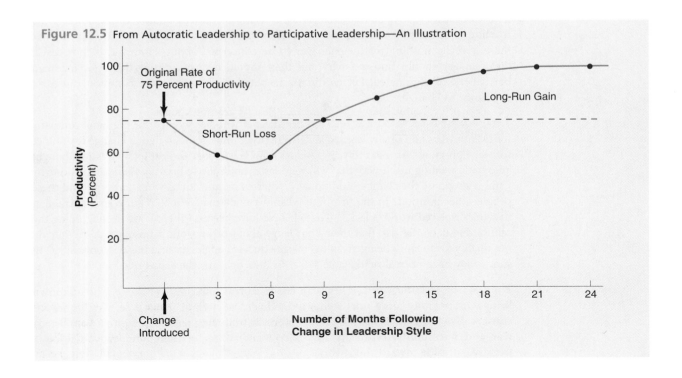

about increased productivity. Unfortunately, many managers are not interested in riding out the short-run declines to reap long-run benefits and so are not willing to change their leadership style.

7. Peer Pressure. Many times, people refuse to accept change because their peers are unwilling to go along with it. Remember, as noted in the discussion of group cohesiveness, if there is high cohesion, the group will stay together. If a change is introduced, therefore, the group may collectively agree to resist it.

8. Lack of Information. Whenever people do not know what is going to happen, they are likely to resist the change. The unknown scares them. Consider how you would feel if a doctor told you that you were very sick and had to have an immediate operation. Not knowing what is wrong with you, what kind of operation you need, or what the effect of the operation will be, you would probably be very nervous, and unless you were convinced that the operation was indeed warranted, you would resist the doctor's advice.

9. Social Displacement. Whenever changes are introduced, it is possible that work groups will be broken up and social relationships will be disturbed. People usually enjoy working with their fellow employees and, when these friendships are interrupted, a psychological letdown occurs. Research shows that in combat situations, soldiers often fight the tendency to make friends among the other members of their platoon because, if one member is killed or injured, the effect on the others can be disastrous. They would not be totally prepared to do their jobs and could be injured or killed themselves. When social relationships have been developed, people tend to want to maintain them and to fight social displacement.

 CHECK YOUR UNDERSTANDING

Why Do People Resist Change?
Match the reason for resistance to change to the statement.

Reason for Resistance	Statement
a. Obsolescence	_____ It will make a person look bad.
b. Fear of unknown	_____ High cohesion is the problem.
c. Fear of economic loss	_____ Results are not known.
d. Ego defensiveness	_____ Enjoy working with my friends.
e. Change in status quo	_____ A new technology is implemented.
f. Shortsightedness	_____ The new job has a lower salary.
g. Peer pressure	_____ A manager's title changes to leader.
h. Lack of information	_____ The long-term vision is missing.
i. Social displacement	_____ Plans are not shared with workers.

Managing Change

Until now, we have been discussing how people respond to change and why they often resist it. Managers, however, should introduce and manage change properly. Admittedly, change causes problems. Yet, if the manager analyzes the situation properly, follows some basic steps, and remains aware of the important areas of implementation, he or

Figure 12.6
Dimensions of Change

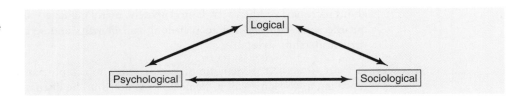

she can effect many changes to the benefit of both the employees and the organization.[26] In particular, the manager needs to:

1. Understand the three dimensions of change.
2. Know the basic steps in the change process.
3. Understand the characteristics of change leaders.
4. Be aware of the importance of participation and communication.

Identify three dimensions of change.

The Dimensions of Change

The first things a manager must know are the three dimensions of change (see Figure 12.6).

1. First is the **logical dimension**, which is based on technological and scientific reasons. Why is the change needed from an organizational standpoint? The logical answer is found in such responses as increases in profit, productivity, or efficiency and decreases in cost, worker fatigue, monotony, or machine downtime.
2. The **psychological dimension** is the logic of the change in terms of the workers who would be affected. Do these people feel the change will be good for them? Is it in line with their values? If the answer is affirmative, the psychological dimension has been satisfied.
3. Finally, there is the **sociological dimension**, which refers to the logic of the change in terms of the work group. Will the change be consistent with the norms of the group? Will it help to maintain teamwork? Will the group members be able to live with it?

Unless the manager considers all three of these dimensions, implementation of the change will be less than ideal.

 CHECK YOUR UNDERSTANDING

Draw a line between the change dimension and its corresponding question.

a. Logical dimension	Will the change help maintain teamwork?
b. Psychological dimension	Why is the change needed?
c. Sociological dimension	Is the change in line with employees' values?

Describe the five basic steps in the change process.

The Basic Steps in Change

If the three dimensions of change have all been adequately considered, attention can then be focused on the basic steps in change. There are five basic steps in securing effective change, and each is vital to maximum effectiveness.

First, the manager must answer the question, "*Is this change truly necessary*?" The benefits and costs must be weighed. If the manager has examined the dimensions of change that we have discussed, the answer to this question must be affirmative before further consideration of the change process is undertaken.

Second, the manager must consider *whether the proposed change is the right one*. In many cases, alternative changes exist, any one of which might accomplish the desired result. The manager must choose one that will provide the best results for both the organization and the personnel.

Third, and often most important, *the impact of the change must be evaluated*. What will be the effect of the change in the short run and in the long run? These may be difficult questions to answer, but the manager should attempt some investigation to compare the impact of various proposed changes. Collect questions generated by employees and answer them in a clear, concise manner that the employees can understand.

Fourth, the manager must *work to secure acceptance of the change*. In this case, workers most directly affected by the change hold the key to success. Their anxieties and fears must be calmed if the company hopes to effect a successful change. Address what people fear the most and get resistance to change out in the open. Ask each person to be a change agent, starting with top managers. Be honest and realistic about how people's roles will change, and most of all, keep a positive attitude. Set clear priorities and establish accountability. Keep morale up by asking for employees' opinions and then respond quickly to their issues. An important factor in getting acceptance is to be a careful listener.[27]

Fifth, there must be some *follow-up*. After the change is implemented, the manager must obtain information on how well things are going. Has the change been accepted and implemented properly? More important, is it doing what was desired or was it a waste of time?

Describe the characteristics of a change leader.

Leading the Change

Many organizations lead change from the top. For example, senior-level management may decide to expand operations into Canada and Mexico and set a goal of achieving 20 percent of all revenue from these two locales by the year 2015. Then all members of the management team cooperate in helping to gain support for the new program throughout the enterprise.

Researchers have found that change can also be effectively initiated and led from lower levels of the hierarchy. Moreover, there are seven characteristics that are common to these lower-level change leaders.

1. The first characteristic is that such leaders are easily *identified by their actions*. These people are not afraid to stand up, challenge the status quo, and suggest ways that change can be constructively implemented.
2. A second characteristic is that these *individuals often are not on the company's "high potential" list*. They have not been identified as people who are likely to be the senior leaders and managers of the future. In fact, many of them come from the firm's rank and file.
3. A third characteristic is that these change agents *are loyal to the enterprise but are willing to go beyond their current job* and take the initiative to perform additional tasks that will help to carry the changes forward.
4. A fourth characteristic is that these *people are willing to learn new ideas and skills* in order to make the change successful.

5. A fifth is that they are *internally driven to make a difference* and are unwilling to be chained to their desks and simply carry out their day-to-day routines.
6. A sixth is that they are *action oriented and have a sense of urgency* for accomplishing changes. As a result, they do not wait for approval; they simply move forward and implement the changes they feel are needed.
7. Researchers have found that people with this personal initiative *tend to focus far more on results than on teamwork.* They do not wait for others to agree to join them in getting things done; they are willing to move forward on their own, if this will ensure that the necessary results are achieved.[28]

Leading change is an important managerial responsibility. Several important recommendations for managing change initiatives are (1) accepting the fact that change is nonlinear; (2) involving more people in the process; and (3) paying closer attention to the pockets of resistance. For these initiatives to be successful, managers need an organized framework that clarifies the reasons for a change, or they will fail.[29]

Getting Employees to Change

One of the main mistakes that leaders make in trying to get employees to change is that they fail to present a vision of what is to occur or what the change should look like. The first mistake is not using language that employees understand. The leader must not only use appropriate language, but must also present a vision so that employees can see how they will benefit from the change. Chip Heath and Dan Heath have set forth ideas on how to get people to change in their 2007 bestseller, *Made to Stick: Why Some Ideas Survive and Others Die*, and their 2010 book, *Switch: How to Change Things When Change is Hard.*[30]

Some people are going to be stubborn and will not want to change. Do not argue with them, but try to find their feelings that would make them empathize with others and build on them. The Heaths feel it is best to stick to small changes at a time, rather than making drastic changes at once. Usually, small changes are easier to make, more readily accepted by employees, and often less expensive. Changing the environment, not the employee, can make a difference in employee behavior. For example, to encourage people to use an open-door policy, arrange the office into an inviting warm environment, not one dominated by a computer screen filled with distracting messages. Peer pressure can be a strong motivator for change. Therefore, the leader should build on the positive social influence of the employees. Instead of stressing the negative that a certain percentage of workers are not making the change, state the positive and give illustrations of how employees are accepting the change. Fear is short lived, so it is important to find feelings of hope and optimism. Look for the bright spots. To learn more about dealing with change, refer to Chip and Dan Heath's books.[31]

✔ CHECK YOUR UNDERSTANDING

1. What is the first basic question a person must ask in securing effective change?
2. Discuss what a manager must do to secure acceptance of the change.
3. Identify several characteristics that are common to lower-level change leaders.
4. Recommendations for managing change initiatives are: accepting the fact that change is _____, involving _____ people in the process, and paying closer attention to the pockets of _____.

THE JAPANESE WAY

Manufacturing plants opened by the Japanese in the United States have proven to be some of the most productive in the industry. Why? One of the primary answers is that the Japanese know how to use participative management and communication in introducing and managing change. Some of the basic principles that Japanese firms use are the following:

1. Japanese managers identify closely with the workers and spend a great deal of time interacting with them. This allows the managers to understand the workers' concerns and needs better, and when change is introduced, the managers have excellent insights regarding how the change will be perceived and what types of barriers will have to be overcome.

2. Japanese firms get the workers actively involved in the change process. By gathering employees' ideas and opinions, management learns the concerns and fears of the personnel and then develops an effective strategy for dealing with them.

3. In dealing with change, Japanese managers carefully examine what needs to be done and what problems are likely to result. They spend much more time analyzing the situation than do their American counterparts. This has led some observers to note that Japanese managers follow the cliché, "Don't do something … stand there!" which is the direct opposite of the way American managers do things. As a result of the Japanese approach, although formation of a change may take a great deal of time, implementation often proceeds smoothly.

4. If something does go wrong, management does not blame the workers; it blames the system. The viewpoint is that there must have been an error in the way the change was handled. Management will accept that it did not do its job properly.

5. Japanese firms use much flatter organizational structures than do American firms. This reduces bureaucratic red tape and encourages open communication on the part of the personnel.

Sources: Richard M. Hodgetts and Fred Luthans, *International Management*, 4th ed. (Burr Ridge, IL: Irwin/McGraw, 2000), chapters 5–7; Noboru Yoshumura and Philip Anderson, *Inside the Kaisha* (Boston, MA: Harvard Business School Press, 1997); and Philip R.Harris and Robert T. Moran, *Managing Cultural Differences*, 4th ed. (Houston, TX: Gulf Publishing, 1996), pp. 267–273.

Participation and Communication

Explain how participation and communication can help the manager implement change and how structural changes and organizational development interventions can be used as change interventions.

In most cases, personal initiative is not the primary way that change is implemented. Typically, management announces the changes that are to be made, often including them as part of the annual strategic plan or performance evaluation criteria. In such a case, participation and communication by the leaders of the change are critical. Participation is important in the change process because, as we know from research, people will be more supportive of changes that they helped bring about than of changes that were either assigned to them or forced on them. Additionally, if some problem occurs with the implementation of a change with which they have assisted, the workers will help to eliminate or work around the problem. However, if they have had no input regarding the change, they will sit on the sidelines and let management figure out how to solve the problem.[32]

For example, when a company decides to make a major organizational change by expanding its product lines and look for more lucrative markets, employees may resist these changes because they believe the company is doing well. To bring about the change, senior-level managers must develop a plan that includes input from lower-level managers and employees. By communicating with employees and getting them to participate in the change process, the negative effects that typically accompany change can be overcome.

Another good example is provided in the "Human Relations in Action" box, which shows that one primary reason for the success of Japanese firms in the United States is their ability to promote participation and communication in the change process.

Using Organizational Structural Interventions

Reorganizing, implementing new reward systems, and making cultural changes are all examples of how organizations make changes.[33]

Reorganization

Many factors dictate when and why firms reorganize. The most common factor is the state of the economy. When the economy is weak, firms cut costs by eliminating unnecessary functions, resulting in reorganizing the operations to be more cost effective. This was evident during the last recession. Many people lost their jobs, while others worked shorter hours or flexible hours. Work duties and responsibilities were changed. Remaining employees were expected to perform additional tasks, and retirees were brought back into the workforce to cover the busy times. A permanent part-time workforce was created.

Reward System

The purpose of a reward system is to attract talented people and motivate them in their jobs. The best-designed reward system of one company may not work in another firm. For example, too much emphasis may be placed on the wrong rewards, the wrong behavior is being rewarded, there is too much time between the performance and receiving the reward, or one reward is expected to fit everyone.

Many reward systems are out of step with the times and preferences of today's employees. For example, years of service recognition, employee of the month, and attendance awards no longer motivate employees. Employees do not want more mugs, T-shirts, or clocks. What they want is some form of sincere thanks. According to the Gallup Organization, 61 percent of those polled claimed they had not received any meaningful "Attaboy!" in the past year.[34] Of the top most desired forms of recognition, communication in the form of personal, written, electronic, or public acknowledgment, given in a timely, sincere, and specific manner, is what they want. Employees want support from their leaders, especially when they make a mistake. They want to be involved in the decisions that affect them and to have the autonomy required to decide how best to do their work. Managers must design a reward program that provides greater personalized forms of recognition. The success of the program will be dictated by the amount of direct input the employees have in the program.[35] Research indicates that formal recognition programs are being replaced with informal recognition programs. Changing the reward system to fit employees' needs can result in improved individual performance, resulting in greater productivity for the firm. Everyone wins: the employees as well as the firm.

Recognition should occur continuously, in some instances on a daily basis, and not be an annual or even a semiannual event. For some employees, instituting a casual-clothes day or allowing a more flexible schedule is more important than giving a small monetary award. More importantly, recognition and rewards should be suited to individual employees to be meaningful.[36]

Cultural Changes

An organization's culture reflects the value systems and the norms preferred by the organization. It is important to reevaluate the culture periodically to determine if it in essence reflects what the firm values. Is the culture focusing on the main goals of the organization? By more directly aligning the company's culture with the goals and values of the firm, employees have a greater identification with the organization and will generally make a greater commitment to the firm. Changing an organization's culture is another way to effect change in an organization.

In a climate where coworkers encourage and recognize each other's accomplishments, employees contribute more. For example, the Container Store, a Dallas-based retailer that has made *Fortune* magazine's "100 Best Companies to Work For" list for four years in a row, believes in celebrating its employees' accomplishments throughout their tenure, instead of only at retirement. Every year the five-, ten-, fifteen-, and twenty-year anniversaries are celebrated. Their employee turnover of 15 percent to 25 percent is incredibly low for a retail establishment.[37]

A climate where employees are highly motivated and committed to giving their best performance is one where employees are engaged in their work, are satisfied with their jobs, and are effective in doing their jobs. So what does a fully engaged employee look like? Engaged employees do their best, are constantly learning, take calculated risks, and feel stretched beyond their comfort zone. They take personal pride in their quality of work and find that work can be stressful at times, but also rewarding and fun. They basically love their jobs.[38]

Because organizational cultures, attitudes, and behavior flow from senior executives, it may not be easy to change the climate, but that does not mean a manager should not try. Before going to top management to discuss changes that are needed in the culture of the company, a manager must first gather the relevant facts and data to support the needed cultural changes. One way for the manager to get his or her point over to the CEO is to be well prepared and to be committed to the course of action. A good persuasive argument can get the attention of the senior executive who can help make changes. The CEO should appreciate that the manager cares enough about the company to help to solve problems and to prevent valuable employees from leaving out of frustration. But if that CEO denigrates employees, it becomes a risky venture.[39]

The change journey begins by educating employees regarding the need for the changes and involving them every step of the way. Employees must understand the reason for change, whether it's competition, regulations, the economy, or poor performance, and that the existing situation is no longer acceptable. Identify early adopters of the change and have them champion change throughout the organization. Encourage employees to take responsibility without the risk of failure or the loss of their jobs and the culture will begin to change. Communication and employee involvement are essential.[40]

In the new global environment, Western freedoms and Islamic traditions are beginning to clash in the business world, creating another challenging situation for the workforce management world. How will managers deal with these cultural differences? How effectively can a firm's existing culture deal with employees of different beliefs or with customers of different beliefs? For many firms, changes in their cultural climate must be made to ensure that employees, as well as customers, are treated with respect without imposing cultural norms on each other.[41]

Using Organizational Development Interventions

Getting employees to change their behavior is a frustrating, challenging, and confounding task. "Employees often do not see the value of performing their jobs differently or taking on new roles, or they don't trust the reasons for change in the first place," says Chris Butler, president of the Performance Engineering Group. "If they don't support the change, they won't alter their behavior and the project can't succeed."[42]

Sometimes, change can be created through the use of organizational development interventions, which are typically conducted by an outside behavioral expert. Outside consultants are used to avoid political agendas and biases from within the organization.

Organizational development (OD) is an effort to improve an enterprise's effectiveness by dealing with individual, group, and overall organizational problems from both a technical and a human standpoint. "For OD to work, its users must believe that people are important, not mere 'human resources' to be used and discarded. By bringing out the best in their people, organizations can reach optimal effectiveness and increase profits."[43] The methods used in this process are called **OD interventions**, and they take such forms as role playing, team building, and survey feedback. The individual who carries out or leads the intervention is called an **OD change agent**. This person's job is to introduce the intervention, get the personnel involved, and show them how the particular intervention can help them deal with the problems they face. People can affect systems as much as systems affect people.

Role Playing

One of the most common forms of training used in OD is **role playing**. It consists of the acting out of a realistic situation that involves two or more people. The purpose of the training is to acquaint one or more of the participants with the proper way of handling a given situation. For example, one person may be told that he or she is a plant supervisor and that absenteeism and tardiness at the plant have been increasing dramatically. The supervisor's job is to reduce these irregularities by sending everyone home who arrives late, thereby penalizing the latecomer a day's pay. Another person is to play the role of a late worker who is trying to talk the supervisor out of sending him or her home. As the two people begin acting out their roles, the rest of the participants watch. When the scene is over, the trainer and the participants all have the opportunity to give their analysis of what each said and did. Then the trainer gives the participants and the other members of the group some do's and don'ts for handling similar situations.

The benefit of role playing is that it puts the participants in a situation that they are likely to face in the future, gives them a chance to react to the situation, and then provides feedback on performance. When these people return to the real work environment and face a similar situation, they experience less tension and anxiety regarding how to handle the matters because, for all practical purposes, they have been in that situation before.

Team Building

Currently, the most popular form of OD consists of approaches directed toward improving the effectiveness of regular work groups. The overall term given to these approaches is **team building**. A number of different team-building interventions exist. Some focus on intact, permanent work teams, and others are directed toward special teams or newly constituted work groups. The following are some common objectives pursued by team-building interventions:

1. Increasing task accomplishment by improving the group's problem-solving ability, decision-making skills, and goal-setting approaches, or defining the roles and duties of the individual managers.
2. Building and maintaining effective interpersonal relationships, including boss–subordinate relationships and peer relationships.
3. Understanding and managing group processes and intergroup relations.
4. Improving intergroup relations and resolving interpersonal or intergroup conflict.
5. Developing more effective communication, decision-making, and task-allocation skills, both within and between groups.

One of the most popular methods of team building consists of asking two work groups who are having trouble working with each other to adjourn to separate rooms and draw up a list of those things that each group dislikes about the other group and a list of those things that each believes the other group will say it dislikes about them. Then the two groups are brought together, and each reads its first list. The only questions permitted are those that allow the person reading the list to clarify what the group means by a listed item. When both groups are finished, each then reads its second list (what it believed the other group would say about it).

Having now identified their real and imaginary problems, the two groups begin discussing the issues. Some issues are disposed of very quickly because they had been caused by lack of communication or simple misunderstandings. From this point, a list of the major problems that still exist between the two groups is constructed, and ways of solving the problems are identified. Then the groups put together a timetable for solving the problems and list the specific steps that will be taken in problem solving. Having developed an action plan, the two groups then work together and follow the timetable to overcome their mutual problems. In most cases, the OD change agent checks back with the two groups to determine whether they are making progress in resolving the problems or whether further meetings are needed to revitalize their efforts.

Most OD practitioners have great faith in team building, which undoubtedly helps to account for the approach's current popularity. However, some problems are common to this intervention. The major difficulty is that one work group may fail to be honest with the other group, holding back feelings because it is afraid of being too forthright with people it has learned to distrust. However, this problem can be overcome early in the intervention if the change agent keeps everyone honest.

The early stages of these interventions—making lists and sharing them—lead the participants to experience feelings of success in dealing with the other group. Feelings of anxiety, apprehension, and hostility start to give way to feelings of competence and success as the early stages of the interventions produce better communication and understanding than the participants had expected. Nothing succeeds like success, and both groups usually perceive the early stages as a successful experience. This leads to the optimistic realization that "We can work together with those people."

Participants watch for subtle cues of defensiveness, resistance to the data, stubbornness, and the like, and the controlled nature of the process makes most of these unnecessary. This starts building momentum for feelings of competence and success.[44]

If carried out competently, team building can be very beneficial to both the employees and the organization. For more information on building effective teams, see Chapter 4.

Survey Feedback

Another important and widely used intervention is that of **survey feedback**, a comprehensive OD intervention. The technique entails three distinct steps:

1. A systematic collection of data on the current state of the organization, usually obtained through questionnaires, interviews, or both.
2. A feedback of the findings to the organizational personnel.
3. The development of an action plan for dealing with the problems that have been identified.

Gathering the Data.   Data in the survey feedback intervention are often gathered by means of an objective–subjective questionnaire such as the one illustrated in Figure 12.7. The survey usually is designed by a specialist in attitude measurement and is administered to the total organization, to a department, or to a representative sample of either.

Feeding Back the Information.   After the information is collected and analyzed, the results are revealed to the survey participants. In a nutshell, the OD change agent says, "Here's an overall view of what you told me about the organization. These are the things that everyone seems to like. These are the things that most people feel need to be corrected. Let us look at this information and decide what should be done about the situation."

Figure 12.7 Sample Survey Feedback Questions

	Strongly Agree	Agree	Undecided	Disagree	Strongly Disagree
There is a lot of teamwork in my work group.	_____	_____	_____	_____	_____
Very few people in this organization listen to one another.	_____	_____	_____	_____	_____
Management is as interested in the people as it is in the work.	_____	_____	_____	_____	_____
Most important decisions are made by management and then announced to the workers without any input from the latter.	_____	_____	_____	_____	_____
This organization is a good place to work.	_____	_____	_____	_____	_____

In your opinion, what are the three biggest problems currently facing the firm? Write your answers in the spaces, and use the back of the page if necessary.

Developing an Action Plan.   The last phase of the survey feedback intervention involves the development of an action plan. This plan is formulated by individuals at all levels of the group(s) who participated in the original survey. Often included in the action plan is a time limit for following up to see that the proposed plan is implemented. The follow-up prevents the OD effort from becoming only a short-lived, interesting experience.

When the results are communicated back to employees, survey feedback has proven to be an effective change technique. Otherwise, employees become frustrated and feel their input was never really wanted. Telling people the results of the survey builds respect and cooperation. However, more than knowing the results, employees want to know what real changes have been made to improve the organization.[45] Bowers, for example, has reported that a study evaluating the effects of different change techniques in twenty-three organizations revealed that survey feedback was more effective than many other types of change strategies.[46] However, to keep these results in perspective, we should note that these survey feedback programs may have been better rated because they were more comprehensive than other programs. The positive results may reflect the superiority of more comprehensive programs to less comprehensive ones. On the other hand, some researchers have also noted that survey feedback is a cost-effective means of implementing a comprehensive program, making it a highly desirable change technique.[47]

 CHECK YOUR UNDERSTANDING

1. Define organizational development (OD).
2. How can role playing change behavior? Give an example.
3. Identify some objectives of using team-building interventions to change behavior.
4. What are the three steps in using surveys as an OD?

© Daniel Laflor, iStock

Explore ways of using a mentor to enhance your career.

Career Advisor

Using a Mentor

Another important aspect of getting ahead is to find a mentor. A **mentor** is a person who coaches, counsels, teaches, or sponsors others. Although it is possible to succeed in a large organization without having a mentor, it is easier to succeed if you have one. Studies since the 1970s have repeatedly indicated that mentoring is the single-most valuable ingredient in a successful career for both men and women. "Mentors are not fairy godmothers; they cannot and should not be expected to make all your dreams come true."[48] One of the fifty-four best practices associated with companies that people most want to work for is to "create a strong mentoring culture that will provide career advancement and growth opportunities."[49]

What, in particular, makes a mentor so useful? The primary answer is the mentor's willingness to share knowledge and understanding with younger managers, helping them to develop into effective leaders. "Mentors can help you see things in a way you might not have thought about," says Mack Tilling, cofounder and CEO of Instill Corp., a business-to-business technology company.[50] The mentoring process is particularly important to individuals who are in the learning and growing period of their careers. To be effective, mentoring should be tailored to a mentee's individual development process.

Mentoring comes in many forms. In many companies, it is a matter of an individual finding his or her own mentor; other firms support formal mentoring programs using teams, groups, or matchmaking software. Also, Web-based matchmaking mentoring programs are available on the Internet. Even e-mail, the phone, and written communications can be used as mentoring vehicles.

Informal Mentoring.   Although it is possible to learn through trial and error, new hires can develop more confidence and learn more if they get things right the first time around. Mentors can help them succeed the first time. Finding a mentor is usually an informal affair that requires approaching people with whom you can cultivate a personal and professional chemistry. A good mentor believes in the business.[51] Once you have identified a potential mentor, it is best to ask the person for feedback on some idea and follow up with how you applied the results rather than asking the potential mentor outright: "Will you be my mentor?" Thank the person and propose another meeting. Hopefully, this approach will lead to an ongoing relationship.[52]

Formal Mentoring Programs.   Many firms have established formal mentoring programs where senior-level managers are matched with junior-level managers. When Diana McGinnis of Cigna Inc., an employee benefits company, was thrust into the world of management, she was assigned a vice president as a mentor. The mentor met with McGinnis every month and was at McGinnis's beck and call whenever she needed to discuss managerial issues. McGinnis stated, "Without the program, I don't know if I would have had the confidence to know that management was a possibility I could aspire to."[53]

Group Mentoring Programs.   In some firms, teams, groups, or sponsors are used for mentoring. For example, the mentoring process at W. L. Gore & Associates, a diversified manufacturing company that continues to be placed on the list of "100 Best Companies to Work For," by *Fortune* magazine, has changed from informal conversations about associates' performance and prospects to a more structured system called the Fall Development Process. Team sponsors meet to discuss whether the associates under their guidance are in the roles that best utilize their skills, and they discuss what other opportunities might be available in the company.[54] Chubb Group of Insurance Companies is another company that has added a more formalized mentoring program to its Chubb's Partnership for Women program. The formal program groups seven women with a person who monitors the group's progress. The group members meet monthly to discuss a wide range of topics on personal development and career advancement.[55]

Web-matching Software Mentoring Programs. After having little success at finding a mentor, Michael Witt, a product stewardship specialist at Dow Chemical Company, used a Web-matching software system that connects individuals looking for a mentor with a person wanting to serve as a mentor.[56] Companies like Fast Company have listings of mentors on their Web sites. Recently, IBM established a cross-border information sharing and collaboration system, which makes mentoring a tool for transferring knowledge globally. Any IBM employee can give or receive advice by filling out a profile in a Web-based employee directory called Blue Pages. IBM has "broken new ground in using the Internet to develop global relationships."[57]

Other Mentoring Sources. Mentoring can come by e-mail, phone, and letters, not just in face-to-face encounters. The mentors need to be knowledgeable and have the experience required to provide guidance and encouragement to mentees without a having a formal meeting.

Finding the Right Mentor

One of the greatest hurdles with mentoring is finding the right mentor. Some rules of the mentoring game are set forth by Margaret Heffernan and Saj-nicole Joni.[58]

1. Find someone who is committed to the relationship, will give time to the relationship, wants to see you thrive, and does not need to compete with you. The mentor must be someone you can learn from. The mentor must give you honest feedback, not just moral support, and you must be ready to listen to hard truths.

2. If the company has a formal mentoring program, sign up. You can learn a great deal about corporate policies, politics, and fault lines just by engaging in discussions with a mentor who understands your aspirations and expectations.

3. You can learn a great deal by watching experts do their job. These people may work at any level within the company. Informally, you may view this person as a mentor. In fact, the Mentoring Group, worldwide mentoring services, recommends that employees not select their bosses as their mentors, but seek formal mentors from outside your group, who do not have your agenda.[59]

4. To help stretch your professional and intellectual ambition, find a leader in your discipline, either inside or outside the firm, to be a mentor. Engage the person in stimulating discussions.

5. People at the top level of an organization who may have a hard time finding a mentor will generally look for a "thinking partner" from outside the firm who has no vested interest in the company. Top-level people need someone who can look for answers with them.

6. Work is just one part of your life. A software executive at General Electric argues that you need mentors for each part of your life—family, financial security, community, spiritual—and they should be thought of as your personal board of directors. Having access to several mentors can enrich your life and can take the burden off any one mentor.

Personal Vision

A compelling "personal vision" can help you get more out of your life. It can help you succeed, be more satisfied with your life, and get more out of a mentoring relationship. A powerful vision can move you beyond where you would be without one. Your vision also can inspire those around you to reach their dreams. Peter Senge defines vision as what you want to create of yourself and the world around you.

Before identifying your personal vision, several questions need to be answered. What does your vision include? Does it include working in a particular job or company; changes in some aspect of your life—health, wealth, environment, and friends; traveling; raising a family; or retirement plans? What are you good at? What do you love to do? What are some weak areas that you would like to change? In other words, a "personal vision" is what or who you want to be, do, feel, think, own, and associate with by some date in the future.[60,61]

To successfully find an effective mentor who is a good match, you need to know what you want out of life and know your strengths and weaknesses. Your personal vision statement is a testimony of who you are. It can be used as an instrument for comparing the strengths and weakness of a potential mentor. A mismatched mentor will be a waste of your time. A mentor should understand your needs and have the ability and expertise to help you move ahead in your job and in your career.

Trends

Today, the trend toward mentoring continues, with approximately 75 percent of all executives younger than forty having a mentor. As these people continue their climb up the career ladder, they eventually lose their need for a mentor but begin taking on protégés of their own. Hence, mentoring begets mentoring.

To a large degree, this process is inevitable. Given today's complex and rapid-paced environment, increased demands are being put on managers. One of the best ways to meet these demands is by seeking out individuals from whose experience one can learn. Of course, you can succeed in any organization without a mentor, but it will help if you have one or more who can provide you with assistance and advice along the way. A mentor cannot guarantee that you will succeed, but he or she can give you that extra push that will help you move out from the pack.

 CHECK YOUR UNDERSTANDING

In your career journal, outline the things you need to know to help find and use a mentor successfully.

Summary

1 Define conflict and explain some of the major types of conflict.

Conflict is opposition or antagonism toward other individuals or things. Conflict can exist at the individual level in such forms as frustration and interpersonal conflict. It can also exist at the organizational level in such forms as institutionalized and emergent conflict.

Frustration is the result of a blocked need. Managers must understand that the stronger the worker's motivation to reach a desired goal, the greater will be the individual's frustration with failure. Unfair and discriminatory treatment in the workplace creates frustration. Interpersonal conflict arises when disagreements occur among employees. If not handled properly, it can deteriorate relations between the parties involved.

Institutionalized conflict occurs when assignments, resources, and information are not fairly distributed and shared among personnel and departments. Personal and social issues can cause emergent conflict; for example, differences between formal and informal groups, the boss and workers, and authority of the boss and the boss's lack of knowledge.

2 Relate some of the most effective ways of managing conflict.

Managers often try to manage conflict through general counseling, such as providing advice, reassurance, release of emotional tension, and reorientation. If the problem is more serious, as in the case of troubled employees or individuals suffering from alcoholism or drug abuse, more carefully structured counseling may be necessary, including the use of outside professional assistance. With troubled employees, three courses of action are needed: (1) tell the employee to shape up or ship out, (2) discipline the person, or (3) discuss the problem with the employee in an effort to work out a solution.

Some employees turn to alcoholism to help them deal with frustration and stress on the job. They are skillful at denying the problem, making it difficult for managers to confront these people. Drug abuse causes absenteeism, accidents on the job, and an increase in employee turnover, resulting in costs to the firm. These problems contribute to increased health care costs, disability insurance costs, employee theft, as well as decreased productivity, product quality, and employee morale. People take drugs to reduce boredom, tension, and anxiety that accompany work. More companies are developing programs to deal with both alcoholism and drug abuse. Drug testing also has increased.

Methods for resolving conflict are numerous. Four of the most common are mutual problem solving, expansion of resources, smoothing, and compromise. Mutual problem solving brings the parties in a conflict together face to face to jointly resolve the issues. Reorganization and budget increases can make available additional resources. Smoothing is the process of playing down the differences between the parties in conflict, while emphasizing their common interests, whereas compromise involves each side giving up something. If one side feels it gives more than the other side, the conflict may rise up again.

3 Discuss how change occurs.

Change is any modification or alteration of the status quo. When change takes place, three things occur: (1) there is movement from one set of conditions to another, (2) some force(s) causes the change to come about, and (3) a consequence results from the change. Some people believe that resistance to change is inevitable. Although this may be true, there are some very good reasons for resistance. One is that it compels the prochange forces to build a case against the status quo. Another is that it encourages the organization to look before it leaps. Change is generally good for the entire organization. In dealing with resistance and ensuring that change is properly implemented, begin with planning (1) whether there should be a change, (2) what type of changed is needed, and (3) how the change should be implemented.

4 Explain four common responses to change—rejection, resistance, tolerance, and acceptance.

How do most people react to change? People's reactions to change will depend on the benefits that they think will result from it. People will react in a variety of ways to the same stimulus. Some psychologists believe the answer can be found in an individual's attitude toward the stimulus. A person's attitude is a reflection of psychological factors, such as reaction to stress; personal factors, including experience; and social factors like group makeup.

People respond to change in different ways, but most can be categorized as rejection, resistance, tolerance, or acceptance. Of these, the most common is resistance to change. Rejection is simply refusing to accommodate a change. Resistance can be either readily observed or not so readily observed, depending on the individual worker. Tolerance is a condition of putting up with the change when the worker is neutral about the change. Acceptance is the response of going with the change.

More reasons for resistance to change are: obsolescence of job skills, fear of the unknown, fear of economic loss, ego defensiveness, the comfort of status quo, shortsightedness, peer pressure, lack of information, and social displacement.

5 *Identify three dimensions of change.*

Despite the various pressures and tendencies to resist change, it is possible to alter the status quo if the change is introduced and managed properly. One of the first things the manager must do is to be aware of the three dimensions of change: logical, psychological, and sociological.

The logical dimension of change is based on scientific reasons—productivity, decreases in cost, worker fatigue, or machine downtime. The psychological dimension of change is based on how the individual will be affected. Will the worker feel the change is good? The sociological dimension of change is based on how the change will affect the group— work group members, teamwork, and group norms.

6 *Describe the five basic steps in the change process.*

The manager should know the five basic steps in the change process. Answers to the following questions provide the key: (1) Is this change necessary? (2) Is the change the right one? (3) What will be the impact of the change? (4) How will the manager get acceptance of the change? (5) Has the change been accepted and implemented properly?

7 *Describe the characteristics of a change leader.*

Change leaders are (1) identified by their actions, (2) not on the company's "high-potential" list, (3) loyal to the company and willing to go beyond their current job, (4) willing to learn new ideas and skills in order to make the change successful, (5) internally driven to make a difference, (6) action oriented and have a sense of urgency for accomplishing changes, and (7) focused far more on results than on teamwork.

8 *Explain how participation and communication can help the manager implement change, and how structural changes and OD interventions can be used as change interventions.*

Participation is important in the change process because people will be more supportive of changes if they have helped bring about the change. If problems occur, workers will be more eager to assist and help eliminate the problems. Effective communication is critical in the change process. Workers have a need to be informed of what is going on that will affect them and why.

Organizations can use reorganization, new reward systems, and culture change as change interventions. Reorganizing is necessary when the company is no longer cost effective. Reward systems should reward performance, meet the expected needs of the employees, and motivate employees to continue to perform excellent work. The culture of an organization reflects the values and purpose of the business. When employees feel an identity with the organization, they are more committed. A climate where employees are highly engaged results in greater motivation and commitment. Employees take greater pride in their work and basically love their jobs. A change in climate should come from senior-level management. Employees must be educated about the change and understand the reason for change. As the workplace becomes more global, the values and traditions of employees can clash with American values and traditions, creating a challenging situation.

OD is an effort to improve an enterprise's effectiveness by dealing with individual, group, and overall organizational problems from both a technical standpoint and a human standpoint. At the heart of OD is a concern for improving the relationships among the organization's personnel. This often is accomplished through OD interventions. The person who carries out or leads the intervention is called the OD change agent.

Many kinds of OD interventions exist. Some relate exclusively to the individual and seek to improve behavioral skills. One such intervention is role playing. Other OD interventions, such as team building, are designed to improve intragroup and intergroup performances. Finally, there are overall or comprehensive interventions. One of the most popular is survey feedback.

9 Explore ways of using a mentor to enhance your career.

A mentor is a person who coaches, counsels, teaches, or sponsors others. Effective mentors can play a very valuable role in a successful career for both men and women. What do mentors do? They share knowledge about corporate policies, politics, and work. Mentoring comes in many forms, from informal relationships to formal company-sponsored programs. E-mail, phone, and written communications can serve as vehicles for mentoring. There are Web sites that offer lists of names of mentors over the Internet.

For a successful relationship, the match between mentee and mentor is crucial. The personality, chemistry, desire to teach, yearning to learn, and the willingness to take the time necessary are all ingredients to consider in finding the right mentor. Commitment to the relationship is important. Employees can learn a great deal about the job and industry, as well as stretch their professional and intellectual ambitions by interacting with the right mentor. Some firms use Web-based software programs in matching employees with mentors; others use groups or teams.

Before searching for a mentor, an employee must have an idea of what he or she wants out of life, and understands his or her strengths and weaknesses. Without having a personal vision, the relationship will go nowhere and both parties' time will be wasted. Research indicates that mentoring is on the increase. As time goes on and employees move up the ladder, they eventually become mentors. You can succeed in an organization without a mentor; however, a good mentor can help you move ahead of the pack.

Key Terms in the Chapter

Conflict	Conflict is opposition or antagonism toward other individuals or things.
Frustration	Frustration is the result of a blocked need.
Interpersonal conflict	Interpersonal conflict is a result of disagreement between personnel.
Institutionalized conflict	Institutionalized conflict results from organizational attempts to structure work assignments.

Emergent conflict	Emergent conflict arises from personal and social causes.
Counseling	Counseling is the discussion of an emotional problem with an employee for the purpose of eliminating or reducing the problem.
Mutual problem solving	Mutual problem solving involves bringing together all the parties to a conflict and discussing the issues face-to-face.
Smoothing	Smoothing is the downplaying of differences between individuals and groups while emphasizing their common interests.
Compromise	Compromise involves each side giving up something such that neither side emerges as the big winner.
Change	Change is any modification of the status quo.
Rejection	Rejection is the refusal to accommodate a particular condition or change.
Overt resistance	Overt resistance is observable.
Covert resistance	Covert resistance is not readily observable.
Veiled resistance	Veiled resistance occurs when information is given in greater quantity than needed to make it more difficult for the person to do a job
Tolerance	Tolerance involves putting up with a change.
Acceptance	Acceptance occurs when the positive factors are weighted more than the negative ones.
Logical dimension	The logical dimension of change is based on scientific reasons.
Psychological dimension	The psychological dimension of change is based on how the individual will be affected.
Sociological dimension	The sociological dimension of change is based on how the change will affect the group.
Organizational development (OD)	OD is an effort to improve an enterprise's effectiveness by dealing with individual, group, and organizational problems.
OD intervention	An OD intervention is a method used in carrying out the OD process.
OD change agent	An OD change agent is a person who carries out or leads on OD intervention.
Role playing	Role playing is the spontaneous acting out of a real-life situation.
Team building	Team building is an OD intervention for resolving group problems.
Survey feedback	Survey feedback is an OD intervention based on the collection of data and the feeding back of this information to the organizational personnel.

Review and Study Questions

1. What is the meaning of conflict?

2. Identify and describe two common forms of conflict at the individual level.

3. What are two common forms of conflict at the organizational level? Describe each.

4. What is the overall purpose of counseling? Describe four basic approaches managers can use in carrying out counseling.

5. How should a manager counsel a troubled employee? Describe at least five useful guidelines.

6. What do managers need to know about alcohol- and drug-related employee problems?

7. What are the four stages in designing a program for dealing with drug abusers? Identify and describe each stage.

8. How can each of the following approaches help to resolve conflict: mutual problem solving, the expansion of resources, smoothing, and compromise? Give an example for each approach.

9. Describe three things that happen when change occurs.

10. Is resistance to change bad for the organization? In your answer, be sure to make a case both for and against resistance.

11. How do employees behave as they engage in each response to change: rejection, resistance, tolerance, and acceptance? Describe the behavior in each situation.

12. One of the primary reasons for resistance to change is the fear of economic loss. What does the statement mean?

13. How does the lack of information impact a resistance to change?

14. What are the three dimensions of change? Why are they important to the manager in the change process?

15. What are the five basic steps in the change process? Describe each.

16. How do participation and communication play important roles in the introduction of change?

17. How can reorganization, reward systems, and culture changes be used as change interventions?

18. Role playing is one of the most common forms of training used in OD. How does role playing work? What is the purpose of using role playing?

19. How does team-building intervention work? Why is this intervention so well liked by OD practitioners?

20. What are five common objectives pursued by team-building interventions?

21. What are three distinct steps in survey feedback?

22. How effective is the survey feedback approach as a change technique? Why?

23. What is the role of a mentor?

24. How does informal mentoring differ from formal mentoring programs?

25. What can a Web-matching software mentoring program provide?

26. Discuss rules for finding the right mentor.

27. What is a personal vision, and why is it important in finding a mentor?

28. Describe the trend in mentoring. What is happening?

Connecting to the Real World

Change Happens!

The purpose of this exercise is to understand the importance of introducing change appropriately and in a timely manner.

Situation: Marcy, the manager of the advertising department of a major retail outlet, has just announced that all employees working in the department are required to work on Saturdays. The employees are expected to work at least two Saturdays per month. This news has not been well received by the employees.

Questions

1. What steps might Marcy have taken to insure acceptance of the new policy?
2. How will Marcy deal with the resistance to this new policy?
3. What are the psychological, personal, and social factors that the employees will experience?
4. Suggest a recognition and reward plan that Marcy can implement to smooth this transition. Is your plan appropriate? Why?
5. What have you learned from this exercise about implementing change?

CASE
What Did Paul Do Wrong?

Nine months ago, a privately owned hospital was taken over by the county. The population in the local area had grown by approximately 125 percent in the last five years, and the hospital was unable to keep up with local needs. Its owners felt that too great an investment was needed for additional emergency care, patient rooms, and equipment. The owners proposed that the county buy and run the hospital, and the county agreed.

Since the takeover, the number of hospital employees has increased by almost 50 percent, and the costs of operating the hospital have increased by 44 percent. As a consequence, the county has implemented a number of new cost controls. Also, a number of prominent citizens, as well as the local newspaper, have questioned the purchase of the hospital and are saying that it will cost millions of dollars more each year to run a county hospital than it would to have the hospital run by a private group. In response to these charges, the county wants to ensure that the hospital is run as efficiently as possible.

One of the changes introduced was a monthly cost control report. This report is specially designed to provide information to central accounting, as well as feedback to the various departments.

Now that the reports have been in use for three months, it has become evident that some departments understand them, fill them out completely, and use them as a source of feedback in controlling their costs and expenditures. Other departments seem confused about the report, do not know what to put into it, and do not appear to be using the data to control their costs and expenditures.

Phil Albright, head of central accounting, decided to check out the situation for himself by visiting one of the departments that was filling out the form properly and one that was not. The first department is run by Pat Rogers, and after talking to both Rogers and her employees, Albright confirmed that Rogers's people are familiar with the form, know the kinds of information that are supposed to go into it, and are aware of how to use the data for control purposes. Much of their understanding stems from a meeting that Rogers had with her employees at which they discussed the report at length. By the end of the meeting, everyone in the department was familiar with the format of the report and was prepared to provide the necessary data.

Conversely, Paul Heckman's department is having all sorts of problems with the report. All three times it was submitted, it was both incomplete and late. In addition, Heckman's department is currently 21 percent over budget. In talking to the employees, Albright learned that Heckman had not discussed the report with his department. Rather, he had e-mailed the form to each person, stating that the report was to be submitted monthly to accounting, the employees should decide what they thought should go into the report, and then they should e-mail the information to his secretary. He then would incorporate the data into his monthly cost control report. Albright realizes that this way of introducing the report undoubtedly accounts for most of the problems that Heckman's department is having.

Albright also learned that Paul has not always been available for feedback during the implementation period. Several employees have reported that he takes long lunch breaks with many of the female staff who were recently hired. Paul justifies these lunch meetings as business expenses, and established employees are concerned about the appropriateness of this behavior. On several occasions, the employees have noticed alcohol on his breath upon his return. The employees have been afraid to report this behavior due to his position in the hospital.

Albright realizes that there is more than one issue regarding Paul Heckman, but he is unsure of how to begin discussing the matter with Heckman.

Case Questions

1. How important is participation and communication in effecting change? Give examples from this case.
2. How has Rogers's approach helped to reduce the anxiety that often accompanies change?
3. What did Heckman do wrong? Explain. Discuss at least four managerial errors presented in this case.
4. What would you recommend that Albright say to Heckman to change the situation? Why?
5. Which problem would you recommend that Heckman address first. Why?
6. How should Heckman have handled change with his employees?
7. How can Albright get Heckman to accept his own behavioral changes?

PART 6

LOOKING TO THE FUTURE

Thus far in this book, we have studied the entire field of human relations, which, as you will remember from Chapter 1, we defined as a process by which management brings workers into contact with the organization in such a way that the objectives of both groups are achieved. Now we consider two important questions:

1. How can human relations work in the global marketplace?
2. What are the future challenges of human relations?

We answer these questions by first examining some of the developing trends that have a major impact on human relations. These include the growth of international business; the need for a greater focus on innovation, creativity, and imagination; commitment to quality using engaged employees; changing social values; and the need to examine human relations practices in the best-managed firms.

The goals of this section are to:

1. Define a multinational enterprise; discuss why firms become multinational companies; study the nature of international culture, with a particular emphasis given to the four dimensions of culture; examine the impact of international culture in the workplace, paying specific attention to work attitudes, motivation, and the way people deal with time; describe the process of outsourcing in globalization; study the types of cross-cultural training used by multinational enterprises; discuss major global human resource challenges; explain ways of developing a global perspective; and discuss how to effectively organize your office.

© Emin Ozkan, Shutterstock Images LLC

2. Examine the area of innovation and the ways in which organizations are trying to nurture and sustain creativity; look at how the nature of work is changing and the implications that this will have for human relations during the next decade; discuss the importance of imagination, entrepreneurial spirit, and reengineering; examine employee engagement; study the ways in which businesses are meeting the diversity challenge, examine world-class organizations that are leading the way in the twenty-first century, and explore the possibilities of switching careers.

CHAPTER 13 | Human Relations in Global Business

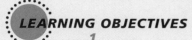

LEARNING OBJECTIVES

1

Discuss the major reasons businesses become multinational companies.

2

Identify the term culture *and relate four basic dimensions of international culture.*

3

Discuss the value of cultural dimensions in understanding the impact of culture in the global arena.

4

Relate the ways in which culture affects work attitudes, motivation, and how people deal with time.

5

Discuss outsourcing in globalization.

6

Describe several major global human resource challenges.

7

Explain ways of developing a global perspective.

8

Discuss how an organized office can enhance your career.

Telecommunications technology is rapidly changing how business is done around the world, and global competition is expanding the marketplace and the workplace. Today's marketplace comprises firms doing business in many countries around the world. China and India are fast emerging as markets for establishing partnership businesses that manufacture products, as well as places to market foreign goods and services. China, for example, has always been known for its Great Wall, but today it's becoming known for its great malls, such as the South China Mall that opened in 2005 in Hong Kong. Every year, more and more organizations begin conducting business in a foreign country. As a result, human relations in global business is emerging as a major area of study for managers.

Mickey Has a Human Relations Problem

The Walt Disney Company is one of the world's premier entertainment firms. Disneyland in Anaheim, California, and Walt Disney World in Orlando, Florida, have been immensely successful. Hence, when the company decided to create EuroDisney, everyone was sure it would be another success. The company opened a park in April 1992 near Paris, France, and drew record opening-day crowds. However, by 1993, EuroDisney had lost $1 billion, and by 1994, the operation had to be totally overhauled. What went wrong? Disney had its share of financial and marketing problems, but it failed to understand the values, attitudes, customs and traditions of the people in France. As a result, Disney experienced problems related to poor human relations. Here are some examples:

1. Management had been very successful with its American theme parks and went into the EuroDisney deal believing that its approach would transfer directly to Europe. This attempt to run a European venture with American values and attitudes led to a series of operating mistakes.

2. Disney got carried away with its desire to build a high-quality park. As a result, the firm spent exorbitant amounts of money to ensure that the facility was not a carbon copy of Disneyland or Walt Disney World, by constructing larger and more detailed buildings. The outcome was a venture that cost millions of

dollars more than expected, resulting in the need to charge increased admission prices—at which many European customers balked.

3. The company discovered that it had built far more hotel rooms than were needed. In the United States, most visitors stay at Disney theme park hotels for three or more days. However, at EuroDisney, the park is smaller and can be seen in one or two days. Many guests arrive at their hotel early in the morning, rush to the park, come back late at night, then check out the next morning before heading back to the park.

4. Disney failed to realize that many Europeans are economical. A room at the EuroDisney Hotel costs about $340 per night—the same as a premiere hotel in Paris. As a result, most visitors find accommodations elsewhere or stay only one night at the Disney hotel.

5. The firm failed to realize that many Europeans enjoy walking. Therefore, the trams that were built to take guests from their hotels to the park went unused, resulting in a needless investment of approximately $250,000.

6. Disney misunderstood the eating habits of Europeans. The policy of serving no alcohol in the park (which has since been changed) caused astonishment in a country where a glass of wine with lunch is common. Management also thought that Europeans did not eat breakfast, so restaurants were downsized. However, the demand for breakfast was often ten times the restaurants' seating capacity, and waiting lines were extremely long.

7. Disney management underestimated the number of people who would be arriving by bus. In the United States, most people come to the parks by car. As a result, the parking space for buses was far too small to accommodate the two thousand buses that arrived on peak days.

8. The company failed to realize that peak days in Europe are different from those in the United States. Disney was used to having a light Monday crowd but a very heavy Friday crowd. However, just the opposite occurred at EuroDisney.

Since opening EuroDisney in 1992, which has since been renamed Disneyland Paris, the Walt Disney Company was forced to make a number of important human relations changes designed to better address the needs of its European customers to avoid a disaster. After addressing the issues and making changes in its operations, Disneyland Paris began to earn a profit. Despite some early concerns from stockholders and some ongoing geopolitical uncertainties, the company forged ahead with its plan to incorporate two theme parks, seven theme hotels, three selected hotels, and a range of dining and entertainment options. The result is that revenues of Disneyland Paris have continued to increase each year.

Did the Walt Disney Company learn anything from its EuroDisney experiences? The real test was whether Disney would be able to transport the magic of the Disneyland brand into Asia in its Hong Kong Disneyland Park. The Disney Company was successful. It opened the Hong Kong Disneyland Resort at Lantau Island, China, in late 2005. Hong Kong Disneyland has become a beacon to millions of people in Hong Kong, mainland China, and throughout Southeast Asia. The Walt Disney Company has tried very hard to be culturally sensitive to the Chinese people. Examples of these efforts are: being sensitive to language by using printed signs in English and Chinese, accepting the serving of wine in parks, moving the main entrance gate by twelve degrees, with cash counters placed close to corners or along walls, using lucky numbers like eight that abound versus unlucky ones like four that do not appear, and serving food that is authentic to the Chinese people versus American cotton candy and hot dogs, and pricing the food reasonably for the Chinese market.

Although it was not easy, Disneyland Paris survived and will celebrate its twentieth birthday in 2012. Critics, however, wondered whether the park ever would prove to be a sound business investment or whether the Disney management was trying to superimpose an American strategy on a European market, which presents a variety of significantly different human relations challenges. The Walt Disney Company, however, was quick to use innovative and creative ways to correct the problems in Paris. These lessons were applied in China in the Hong Kong Disneyland project. The challenge for the Walt Disney Company was being sensitive to a different culture and not duplicating Paris.

The Walt Disney Company continues to expand. In 2007 Disney purchased twenty-one acres in Hawaii on the island of Oahu to build a luxury family resort called Aulani, scheduled to open in late 2011. It will be the home of Disney's first mixed-use family resort outside of its theme park developments. It will have more than eight hundred units including hotel rooms and villas. Disney continues to engage in other endeavors internationally. For instance, in 2009, Adventures by Disney, a luxury tour operator, began offering exciting new global itineraries to Africa, Switzerland, China, Australia, Peru, Germany, England, Italy, Ireland, and Costa Rica. And in 2011 and 2012, Disney will double its fleet with the launch of two new cruise ships.

Discuss the major reasons businesses become multinational companies.

A Multinational Enterprise

A **multinational company** is headquartered in one country but has operations in two or more countries. Every year, more American and foreign companies are entering the global marketplace and are ranking among the top most admired companies. Table 13.1 lists the twenty multinational companies that were ranked in 2010 by *Fortune* as the world's most admired companies. Table 13.2 lists *Fortune's* top twenty American multinationals in terms of revenue. In the top twenty companies, there are five companies that are listed on both lists—Walmart, General Electric Company (GE), Berkshire Hathaway, IBM, and J. P. Morgan Chase. This illustrates that the largest companies are not always the most admired companies. Today, international business operations touch almost every enterprise—hence, the importance of global human relations.

Reasons for Becoming a Multinational Company

One reason a company goes multinational is *to protect itself from the risks and uncertainties of the domestic business cycle.* By setting up operations in another country, a firm often can secure a hedge against economic volatility in its home country. For example, General Motors (GM) produces a small car in China for its local market through its joint venture, Shanghai General Motors (SGM) with SAIC (Shanghai Automotive Industry Corporation), one of three automotive corporations in China. SGM had sales of over 2.72 million vehicles in 2009, with a revenue of over $24.88 billion. Although the GM's share of the American auto market has declined in recent years, it is profiting from this new emerging market. GM is expected to boost its annual sales in China to more than three million vehicles in 2015 as the country's automobile market continues to grow

Rank	Company
1	Apple
2	Google
3	Berkshire Hathaway
4	Johnson & Johnson
5	Amazon.com
6	Procter & Gamble
7	Toyota Motor
8	Goldman Sachs Group
9	Walmart Stores
10	Coca-Cola
11	Microsoft
12	Southwest Airlines
13	FedEx
14	McDonald's
15	IBM
16	General Electric
17	3M
18	J.P. Morgan Chase
19	Walt Disney
20	Cisco Systems

Source: *Fortune*, March 22, 2010, p. 121

faster than that in the United States.[1] In the Main Show at the World Expo 2010 Shanghai, GM-SAIC presented a holistic experience, a revolutionary mobility and transportation concept that looked ahead to the year 2030. It is a vision of future driving that is free from petroleum, free from emission, free from crashes, free from congestion, and, at the same time, fun and fashionable. The vision showed how electrification, networking, and autonomous driving will enable humans to coexist harmoniously with the natural environment, bringing people and personal transportation closer together.[2]

A second, and complementary, reason is *to tap the growing world market for goods and services.* For example, many foreign multinational companies have targeted the United States because of its large population and per capita income. Americans have both a desire for new goods and services and the money to buy them. Currently, India and China, with their growing economies, are countries whose citizens also are eager to buy the latest in consumer goods. The same is true for many other industrialized nations, which helps to explain why American multinational companies have been targeting Europe and Asia as

Table 13.2
Fortune's List of the Top Twenty Largest Global Corporations in the United States in 2010

Country Rank	Company	Global 500 Rank	Revenues ($ millions)	City
1	Walmart	1	408,214	Bentonville
2	Exxon Mobil	3	284,650	Irving
3	Chevron	11	163,527	San Ramon
4	General Electric	13	1566,779	Fairfield
5	Bank of America Corporation	15	150,450	Charlotte
6	ConocoPhillips	17	139,515	Detroit
7	AT&T	21	123,018	Dallas
8	Ford Motor	23	118,308	Detroit
9	J.P. Morgan Chase & Co.	25	115,632	New York
10	Hewlett-Packard	26	114,552	Palo Alto
11	Berkshire Hathway	28	112,493	Omaha
12	Citigroup	33	108,785	New York
13	McKesson	34	108,720	San Francisco
14	Verizon Communications	35	107,808	New York
15	General Motors	38	104,589	Detroit
16	American International Group	41	103,189	New York
17	Cardinal Health	43	99,612	Dublin
18	CVS Caremark	45	98,729	Woonsocket
19	Wells Fargo	46	98,636	San Francisco
20	International Business Machines	48	95,758	Armonk

Source: "Fortune Global 500 World's Largest Corporations," *Fortune Magazine*, July 26, 2010, p. F-1

primary expansion areas. For example, in recent years, Walmart has been opening stores in China, as well as in many other countries. As of 2008, Walmart had opened thirty outlets across China, and in 2009, it opened its first outlet in India. By 2009, Walmart had 3,400 stores in its International Division, which account for over one-fourth of its revenue. But Walmart stores have not been successful in every country. It missed its mark in Germany and Japan where the Walmart model did not work. One reason is that the people in those countries are more willing to pay top prices for exclusive goods of the highest quality and not "always low prices."[3]

Home Depot is another company contemplating opening operations in China. The home improvement market in China, however, is a lot trickier to navigate. In China, newly constructed homes do not have rooms inside the exterior walls. The home owners fix up the shells themselves. The home improvement stores provide the workers. In contrast to the U.S. market, Home Depot must train thousands of its staffers to do the floor-to-ceiling installations, as well as face stiff competition from the Chinese home improvement stores. Chinese people like to handle the merchandise before buying, meaning the displays must accommodate the customers.[4] Today, Home Depot maintains an office in Shanghai, China, but has yet to establish an official store. Home Depot, however, has gone global with stores in Mexico and Canada.[5]

A third reason is *to respond to increased foreign competition*. Using a follow-the-competitor strategy, multinational companies set up operations in the home countries of competitors. This strategy serves a dual purpose: It takes business away from competitors, and it lets other firms know that, if they attack the multinational company in its home market, those firms will face a similar situation. This strategy is particularly important when multinational companies want to communicate the conditions under which they will retaliate.

A fourth reason is the desire *to reduce costs*. By setting up operations close to the customer, multinational companies can eliminate transportation costs, avoid the expenses associated with having intermediaries handle the product, develop a more accurate and rapid response to customer needs, and take advantage of local resources. A good example is Ford Motor Company, which is now building small, economic cars—Ikon, Figo, Fiesta, and Endeavour—in India. After conducting a great deal of research, the company was able to determine the features that were most appealing to buyers in India. As a result, sales have more than met projected forecasts. Ford has since moved into other markets in Europe. In March 2010, Ford was number one in sales in Europe. Ford is expanding its European market and is introducing over twenty new models in 2010. These are class-leading fuel economy, quality, safety, and technology-driven vehicles. What is important in determining affordability for a new car buyer is the initial price of the car, fuel efficiency, and the cost of maintenance. Sales increases indicate that Ford is listening to its customers and building what the customers want.[6]

A fifth reason is *to overcome tariff walls by serving a foreign market from inside*. The European Union (EU) provides an excellent example.[7] Firms exporting their goods to France are subject to tariffs, but those that are producing the goods in France can transport them to any other country in the EU without paying tariffs. The same is true in North America, where the North American Free Trade Agreement (NAFTA) binds Canada, the United States, and Mexico into an economic bloc that has almost as much purchasing power as that of greater Europe. The Central America Free Trade Agreement (CAFTA) is an example of another economic trade agreement. It comprises the countries of Costa Rica, the Dominican Republic, El Salvador, Guatemala, Honduras, Nicaragua, and the United States. As a result of the EU, NAFTA, and CAFTA, more and more businesses are now finding it profitable to do business in other nations as well as to enter into partnerships or joint venture agreements with foreign firms that conduct business locally.

The Nature of International Culture

Identify the term culture and relate four basic dimensions of international culture.

Culture is the acquired knowledge that people use to interpret experience and to generate social behavior.[8] This acquired knowledge forms values, creates attitudes, and influences both individual and group behavior. Culture is learned through education and experience and is shared, so that members of a group, an organization, or a society have a common culture. Moreover, culture is passed from one generation to another, so

IN ACTION

WOMEN IN INTERNATIONAL MANAGEMENT

Many American businesses are surprised to find that human resource practices that are commonplace in the United States are frowned on or ignored in overseas markets. A good example is the hiring of women for management positions. In the United States, companies that hire and promote women are viewed as role models and are held up for emulation. Currently, women represent over 40 percent of the global labor force. Approximately 70 percent of women in developed countries and 60 percent in developing countries are engaged in paid employment. According to the International Labour Organization, U.S. women hold nearly 46 percent of managerial and administrative jobs, a higher percentage than nearly any other country. Another striking difference at the top executive level is that women in the United States have 13.6 percent of the board seats, compared with 8.2 percent in Australia, 8 percent in Germany, and less than 5 percent in France. More women are completing higher levels of education. For example, women in the United States are getting Masters of Business Administration (MBAs), making up approximately one-third of the graduating class, versus 20 percent of the graduating class in France. To broaden their experience, many American women seek international jobs and are filling vacancies overseas.

With increased global trade, Jordanian women, for example, are benefiting from greater job opportunities than ever before. Employment opportunities for women have increased in the textile and garment-making industries. More women are beginning to gain economic independence and freedom of mobility. They are receiving a secondary level education. Having a job outside the home is a significant achievement for these women. But because women are considered unskilled cheap labor, they are offered few career development opportunities.

However, research reveals that gender equality is still inadequate for women in top management positions, as well as in pay benefits and in what is called the "sticky floor" (women in the lowest paid jobs). In the last few years, many of these issues are being addressed at the global level. One reason for this change is that multinational companies realize that to be successful they must judge people based on their worth to the organization and not on social customs alone. Firms such as IBM Europe have long espoused equality for women in the workplace, and if only to prevent this company from getting a big jump on them, other computer multinational companies have followed suit. For example, the Campbell Soup Company has initiated a successful program for promoting women called, "Winning in the Workplace, Winning in the Marketplace, Winning with Women." In addition, governments in Europe and Asia now are enacting and enforcing legislation to promote equality in the workplace.

Although this is a step in the right direction, the challenge for many American multinational companies is to realize that social values in the United States often differ from those in other countries, and some cultures have difficulty dealing with female managers or company representatives. The firm must be careful not to present itself as aggressive and unconcerned about local custom. To ease the way, many American multinational companies first promote a woman into the upper ranks of the overseas subsidiary and then, after the local business community is accustomed to dealing with this person, into the top job. In some cases, multinational companies are finding that women are able to open doors that are closed to men, because foreign managers are impressed by the fact that a multinational company would send a woman rather than follow the usual procedure of appointing a man. In many cases, women report that top managers are willing to give them appointments, whereas their male counterparts have never been able to get in to see these managers. Women also report that many of these foreign managers believe that women are better listeners and more receptive to the needs of their enterprise. They view the women as putting the client's needs ahead of their own company's profit. These recent findings help to explain why more and more American women are willing to accept overseas assignments. They realize that international cultures are different, but they also know that excellent opportunities exist in the international arena.

Sources: Janet Guyon, "Worldly Women," *Fortune*, October 18, 2004; "Facts on Women at Work," International Labour Organization, www.ilo.org.; "World of Work Report 2009: The Global Jobs Crisis and Beyond," www.ilo.org; and Nicki Gilmour, "Gender Parity in the Workplace: Is it Only a Matter of CEOs Believing the Business Case for Change?" April 1, 2010, www.theglasshammer.com.

it is enduring. At the same time, cultures undergo change as people adapt to new environments. As a result, in most countries, the culture of the first decade of this millennium is different from that of the 1980s, although, as seen in the "Ethics and Social Responsibility in Action" box, a wide variety of biases still exist.

Two major human relations problems associated with culture arise for those doing business in the global marketplace: first, understanding the cultures of other countries and, second, learning how to adapt to the cultures.[9] It is a known fact that "few managers are trained in how to motivate workers and provide the kind of environment that supports optimal performance."[10] These failures often are a result of ethnocentrism and misconceptions.

Ethnocentrism is the belief that one's way of doing things is superior to that of others. Ethnocentric behavior can be found among both people and organizations. In the case of individuals, it often takes the form of "we're better than anyone else." In the case of organizations, it is typified by a multinational company that uses the same strategies abroad that it employs at home because it is convinced that the way business is done in the home country is superior to that used by the competition overseas.

A second major reason for people's lack of understanding of international culture is the misconceptions that they hold regarding these other people. A good example is provided in the case of the United States and Russia. Before the thaw in international relations, many Russians believed a large percentage of Americans not only lived in poverty but were street people who roamed the cities and slept on park benches and in subways. As a result, most Soviets concluded that life in America was much worse than that in Russia. Americans also have misconceptions about other countries.

Some misconceptions occur because of differences in gestures of the eyes, the face, and the hands. For example, in the United States, when listening to a speaker, it is customary to look at the speaker's mouth, and when speaking, to make intermittent eye contact with the listener; however, in China, a speaker maintains unbroken eye contact. In North American and northern European cultures, eye contact displays openness, trustworthiness, and integrity, whereas in Arab cultures, intense eye contact and concentration on the eye movement is used to read intentions, and in the Japanese culture, people do not make direct, intense eye contact; in fact, it is an intimidating gesture—one to be avoided. Handshaking is a way to greet and to depart from people. How it is done varies among cultures. For example, in Austria, the handshake is firm, with direct eye contact and with women first; in Germany, the handshake is firm, with one or two pumps the custom among men and with women offering their hand first; in Spain, the handshake is accompanied with a pat on the back with a slight embrace; in Saudi Arabia, the handshake is light, with the left hand touching the forearm, elbow, or the shoulder; and in Mexico, the handshake is gentle, and women friends embrace and kiss the cheek. General gestures of the hand can vary by geographic locations, as well. Gestures made by people living in the southern part of the United States can mean something very different from the same gesture made by people living in the north.[11]

To show respect, business meeting etiquette should be followed. Here again, each country has its own set of rules. For example, in China, businesspeople should be at least ten minutes early to a business meeting. While in Egypt, be early, but expect the Egyptians to be late. Always expect to be kept waiting. In Sweden, businesspeople should be punctual; being "fashionably late" is not appropriate. In Turkey, be on time but expect to wait. Appointments should be made at least one to two weeks in advance by telephone, and prearrangements are necessary. Punctuality is very important in all business situations in the United Kingdom and especially in Scotland. In Japan, it is considered rude to be late.[12]

Table 13.3 illustrates a comparison of cultural values by priority among Americans, the Japanese, and the Arabs. For example, the most important value for Americans is "freedom," whereas for the Japanese people, it is "belonging" and for the Arabs, "family security" is the most important value.

The most effective way of dealing with misconceptions is by learning about international culture. Before doing so, however, take the "Time Out" quiz to determine how much you currently know about Japanese business.

Cultural Dimensions

In recent years, researchers have attempted to develop a composite picture of culture by clustering or grouping these differences. This has been accomplished in two ways. First, attention has been focused on finding cultural dimensions that help to identify similarities and differences between cultures. Second, researchers have attempted to integrate

TIME OUT

Doing Business in Japan

Here are nine statements about Japanese business. Read each carefully and decide whether it is true or false. Answers are provided at the end of the book.

T/F 1. The Japanese produce better-quality products than do the Americans.

T/F 2. Japanese productivity per worker is higher than that of the American worker.

T/F 3. Under Japanese management approaches, workers have higher work satisfaction than do their American counterparts.

T/F 4. Japanese employees work harder than do American employees.

T/F 5. The Japanese management approach is more humanistic than the American approach.

T/F 6. The Japanese have a technological advantage over the Americans.

T/F 7. The Japanese are better educated than Americans and thus are able to be trained more quickly in sophisticated operations.

T/F 8. The Japanese provide their personnel with better orientation and training than do Americans.

T/F 9. Japanese companies make better use than do American companies of modern human resources management techniques, such as quality circles and cooperative union relationships.

Source: Richard M. Hodgetts and Fred Luthans, "Japanese HR Management Practices: Separating Fact from Fiction," *Personnel*, April 1989, pp. 42–45.

Table 13.3
Comparison of Cultural
Values by Priority

Americans	Japanese	Arabs
Freedom	Belonging	Family security
Independence	Group harmony	Family harmony
Self-reliance	Collectivity	Parental guidance
Equality	Age/seniority	Age
Individualism	Group consensus	Authority
Competition	Cooperation	Compromise
Efficiency	Quality	Devotion
Time	Patience	Patience
Directness	Indirectness	Indirectness
Openness	Go-between	Hospitality

Source: Carolena Lyons Lawrence, "Teaching Students How Gestures Communicate across Cultures," *Business Education Forum*, February 2003, p. 39. Reprinted with permission from Business Education Forum © 2003 by the National Business Education Association, 1914 Association Drive, Reston, VA 20191.

these findings and to group countries into clusters that contain nations with similar cultures.

Geert Hofstede, a Dutch researcher, has found four cultural dimensions that help to explain how and why people from various cultures behave as they do:

1. Power distance
2. Uncertainty avoidance
3. Individualism
4. Masculinity[13]

Power Distance. **Power distance** is the degree to which less powerful members of organizations and institutions accept the fact that power is not distributed equally. People in societies in which orders are obeyed without question live in a high power distance culture. Many Asian and Latin countries, such as Malaysia, the Philippines, Panama, Guatemala, Venezuela, and Mexico, are typified by high power distance. In contrast, the United States, Canada, and many European countries (such as Denmark, Great Britain, and Austria) have moderate to low power distance.

In countries demonstrating high power distance, managers make autocratic and paternalistic decisions and the subordinates do as they are told. Close control of operations and a fairly weak work ethic usually are extant. Organization structures tend to be tall, and managers have a fairly small number of subordinates reporting directly to them. In countries with moderate to low power distance, people put a high value on independence, managers consult with subordinates before making decisions, and the work ethic is fairly strong. Organizational structures tend to be flat, and managers directly supervise more subordinates than their counterparts in high-power-distance enterprises.

Uncertainty Avoidance.   **Uncertainty avoidance** is the extent to which people feel threatened by ambiguous situations and have created institutions and beliefs for minimizing or avoiding these uncertainties. Countries with high uncertainty avoidance try to reduce risk and to develop systems and methods for dealing with ambiguity. There is strong uncertainty avoidance in Greece, Uruguay, Guatemala, Portugal, Japan, and Korea but weak uncertainty avoidance in such countries as Singapore, Sweden, Great Britain, the United States, and Canada.

Countries with high uncertainty avoidance tend to structure organizational activities and depend heavily on rules to ensure that everyone knows what he or she is to do. There often is high anxiety and stress among these people, they are very concerned with security, and decisions are often a result of group consensus. Low-uncertainty-avoidance societies offer less structuring of activities and encourage more risk taking by managers. People tend to take things as they come, have more acceptance of dissent and disagreement, and rely heavily on their own initiative and ingenuity in getting things done.

Individualism.   **Individualism** is the tendency of people to look after themselves and their immediate family only. This dimension is in direct contrast to **collectivism**, the tendency of people to belong to groups where members look after each other in exchange for loyalty. Economically advanced countries tend to place greater emphasis on individualism than do poorer countries. For example, the United States, Great Britain, the Netherlands, and Canada have high individualism. In contrast, Ecuador, Guatemala, Pakistan, and Indonesia have low individualism.

Countries with high individualism expect all workers to take care of themselves. The strong emphasis is on individual initiative and achievement. Autonomy and individual financial security are given high value, and people are encouraged to make individual decisions and not rely heavily on group support. In contrast, countries with low individualism place a great deal of importance on group decision making and affiliation. No one wants to be singled out for special attention, even if it is praise for an outstanding job. The workers believe they collectively account for all success and that to praise one person more than the others is embarrassing to that individual because it implies that he or she is better than the others. Countries with low individualism emphasize belonging and draw strength from group affiliation.

Masculinity.   **Masculinity** is the degree to which the dominant values of a society are success, money, and material things. This is in contrast to **femininity**, which Hofstede perceives as the degree to which the dominant values of a society focus on caring for others and on the quality of life. Countries with high masculinity are Japan, Austria,

Venezuela, and Mexico. Countries that have low masculinity (or high femininity) are Norway, Sweden, Denmark, and the Netherlands. The United States has a moderate to high masculinity score, as do other Anglo countries.

Countries with high masculinity scores place a great deal of importance on earnings, recognition, advancement, and challenge. Achievement is defined in terms of wealth and recognition. These cultures often favor large-scale enterprises, and economic growth is viewed as very important. In school, children are encouraged to be high performers, and boys are expected to think about work careers where they can succeed. Less emphasis is given to careers for girls because there are fewer opportunities for women in upper-level jobs. Countries with low masculinity scores place great emphasis on a friendly work environment, cooperation, and employment security. Achievement is defined in terms of human contacts and the living environment. There is low stress in the workplace, and workers are given a great deal of freedom.

 CHECK YOUR UNDERSTANDING

Match the term with the statement.

Term	Statement
a. Culture	_____ Dominant values are money and material things.
b. Ethnocentrism	_____ People feel threatened by ambiguous situations.
c. Power distance	_____ Acquired knowledge used to generate social behavior.
d. Uncertainty avoidance	_____ People accept that power is not distributed equally.
e. Individualism	_____ We are better than anyone else.
f. Collectivism	_____ Groups look after each other in exchange for loyalty.
g. Masculinity	_____ Dominant value is caring for others.
h. Femininity	_____ Tendency to look after one's self and family.

Discuss the value of cultural dimensions in understanding the impact of culture in the global arena.

Integrating the Dimensions

The four dimensions just described influence the overall culture of a society and result in a unique environment. No culture is identical to another; however, some similarities exist among most cultures. For example, the United States has high individualism and moderate power distance. American culture is characterized by a desire to do things personally, and individuals in authority do not overly impress people. Other Anglo cultures that fit a similar pattern are Australia, Great Britain, Canada, Sweden, Switzerland, Denmark, and Ireland. Western European countries, including Italy, Belgium, France, and Spain, have cultures similar to those of their European neighbors.

Latin countries, Asian nations, East and West African countries, and Arab nations are characterized by moderate to low individualism and moderate to high power distance. It is particularly interesting to note that of all the Asian nations, Japan is most similar to the United States, indicating that technology and affluence may well have an impact on a culture and make it more like other nations with these same characteristics.

American culture encourages uncertainty avoidance, and moderate emphasis is placed on masculinity. Once again, some of the countries similar to the United States are Anglo nations characterized by similar religious leanings, history, economic development, and language. Latin and Asian nations are characterized by high uncertainty avoidance and varying degrees of masculinity. Japan is characterized by high uncertainty avoidance and high masculinity.

In recent years, other researchers have taken Hofstede's work and used it to study attitudinal dimensions.

Attitudinal Dimensions

Using Hofstede's findings, researchers have been investigating the similarities and differences in work values and attitudes between countries. Early work by Simcha Ronen and Allen Kraut led these researchers to conclude that "countries could be clustered into more or less homogeneous groups."[14] Ronen and Kraut sought to cluster countries by using a mathematical technique that allowed them to identify how close countries were to one another in terms of overall culture. They identified five different country clusters: Anglo, Nordic, South American, Latin European, and Central European. Since the time of their research, additional multicultural studies have been conducted, and the number of countries and clusters has been expanded.

The most integrative analysis to date has been offered by Ronen and Shenkar, whose review of the literature revealed that eight major cluster studies had looked at four major cultural areas:

1. The importance of work goals
2. Need deficiency, fulfillment, and job satisfaction
3. Managerial and organizational variables
4. Work role and interpersonal orientations[15]

The problem with the studies was that each examined different countries and regions. However, after carefully reviewing the studies, Ronen and Shenkar were able to identify eight country clusters and four countries that were independent and did not fit into any of the clusters. Their findings are presented in Figure 13.1.

In Figure 13.1, each country shares values, attitudes, and beliefs with the other countries in its' cluster. Additionally, the closer to the center of the overall circle that a country is located, the higher is its gross national product (GNP). Those nations with similar GNPs will not necessarily have intercluster similarity, but to the degree that GNP influences values and culture, they will have converging cultural values.

Not everyone agrees with the data in Figure 13.1; some researchers have formulated different international clusters. However, the figure does provide a basis for investigating the international cultural environment, and it is particularly useful to the study of global human relations. In particular, multinational enterprises can benefit from knowledge of the impact of local culture on business attitudes and practices.

④

Relate the ways in which culture affects work attitudes, motivation, and how people deal with time.

The Impact of International Culture at Work

Culture directly affects the way people work. It influences their attitudes, motivation, and even the way they deal with time. The following sections examine the impact of culture in each of these areas.

Work Attitudes

Work attitudes can influence both the quality and quantity of employee output. Americans are taught to believe in the work ethic, but this ethic is not unique to the United States.

Figure 13.1
A Synthesis of Country
Clusters

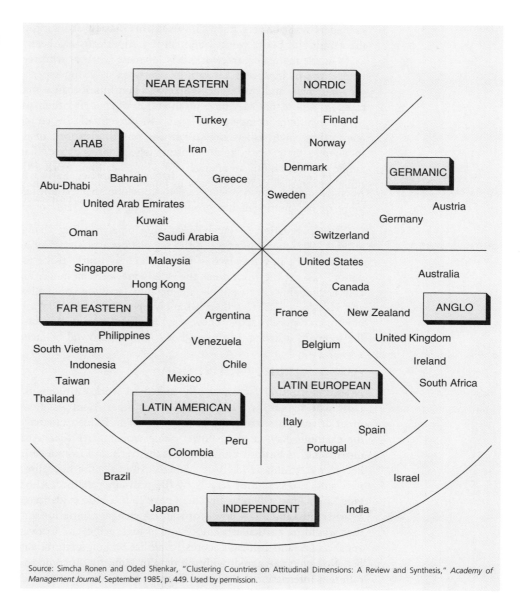

Source: Simcha Ronen and Oded Shenkar, "Clustering Countries on Attitudinal Dimensions: A Review and Synthesis," *Academy of Management Journal*, September 1985, p. 449. Used by permission.

Many people around the world believe in hard work, and it shows in their attitudes. In many Asian countries, job attendance is viewed as a major responsibility, and everyone comes to work every day. Another common cultural work attitude among Asians is that they remain on the job for the entire workday, in contrast to many Americans who believe that if people can get their work done early, they should be allowed to go home.

However, there must be a limit to what people do or they will collapse from stress and overwork, and many managers report that they face these conditions on a daily basis. In fact, a survey of managers in twenty-four countries found that British managers, in particular, are more heavily stressed than those from any of the other countries where managers were surveyed. Long working hours and the lack of job security were the major reasons for this condition.[16] The study also reported that stress among American managers was not very high. However, this may be changing given that, in recent years, the number of hours worked annually by Americans has been continually increasing.[17]

On the matter of overwork, it is Japanese workers who seem to suffer most. In particular, the incidence of karoshi, or overwork, is rising especially among forty- to fifty-year-old men, and this trend is likely to continue because many employees in this age category report that they have no intention of changing their work habits. In a poll taken by an insurance company in Japan, 40 percent of the employees surveyed said they feared they might fall victim to karoshi, but almost none of them said they were going to change their work habits. Fortunately, signs indicate that younger managers and employees are willing to change and adopt healthier work attitudes. However, multinational enterprises doing business in Japan will have to remain aware of the dangers presented by karoshi and be prepared to encourage the employees to slow down and take more days off.

The population of Japan is growing older, causing changes in the workplace. "By around 2007, the proportion of the population over sixty-five jumped to 20 percent from 10 percent in just twenty-one years, which is nearly twice as fast as any other major nation." To get the work done, the elderly are working longer and harder. The work available is changing. For example, major auto Japanese companies, such as Nissan, Toyota, and Honda, are shifting their assembly operations out of Japan and are not opening any new operations in Japan. These actions affect pension benefits, consumption levels, and the standard of living. In time, other countries also will be facing this problem.[18]

Achievement Motivation

A second cultural factor, closely linked to work attitudes, is achievement motivation. How achievement-driven are people from other countries? Research reveals that achievement drive in Eastern Europe is not very high. Industry managers in the Czech Republic, for example, have a much lower achievement drive than American managers. On the other hand, as Eastern Europe makes the transition from a command economy to a market economy, this is likely to change. After all, the need for achievement is a learned need and is determined largely by the prevailing culture. Another good example is provided by China, where researchers have found little evidence of high achievement drive. Workers in China have low scores on challenge, promotion, and earnings, all work goals that would be particularly important to high achievers. Conversely, whereas high achievers would not give high scores to affiliation- or safety-related goals, such as security, benefits, physical working conditions, or time for nonwork activities, Chinese workers rate these variables as very important.

These results help to illustrate why culture is so important to multinational companies as they formulate their strategic plans. Multinational companies are looking for countries and geographical regions that encourage economic activity and achievement drive. In places such as Eastern Europe and China, the company would have to plan on sending its own managers to head the enterprise, if only in the short run, and would have to look for ways of creating and nurturing high achievement drive among the employees it hires.

Time and the Future

A third element of culture that will affect a multinational company is the society's view of time and how it should be spent. In some areas of the Far East, people believe they will be reincarnated, so they do not worry about whether they will get something done in this lifetime. In some African cultures, time is not a constraint. In fact, lateness is an acceptable behavior. As noted earlier in the text, the same is true in many Latin cultures of both South America and Europe, although in countries such as Spain, the traditional siesta is now being radically modified and, in some cases, eliminated by companies.[19]

In follow-up research on culture, Hofstede has added a fifth dimension: long-term orientation.[20] This dimension was a result of work by both Hofstede and a colleague in Hong Kong, who measured basic values through the use of an instrument known as the *Chinese values survey*. This survey clearly indicated that Asians have a long-term orientation. Hofstede believes that this cultural dimension may help account for such developments as the willingness of Asians to save greater amounts of their income and invest it in economic growth, thus helping spur the rise of such economies as Japan, Hong Kong, Korea, Taiwan, Singapore, and China. However, the long-term orientation does not end here. It can also be extremely useful in helping companies to make decisions.

For example, Asians are known to take a long time making up their minds to do something. However, once they have decided on a plan of action, implementation usually follows in short order. This is in direct contrast to many Western cultures, where decisions to proceed are made quickly but implementation is extremely slow. Thus, among firms that value rapid implementation, Asian cultures can be ideal.

American multinational companies have also found that firms in the Far East, especially Japanese companies, are more long range in their planning efforts and do not expect to generate a fast return on their investment. These firms are willing to invest today and wait five to ten years to make an adequate profit. This makes them particularly attractive to U.S. firms looking for investors. A good example is the Walt Disney Company, which raised almost $1 billion from Japanese investors in the last decade. In return, the investors are limited partners in movies made by Disney and will share in the future profit of these films. The arrangement is ideal for both sides. Disney gets interest-free capital that it can use to make films, and the investors have future earnings that, if the movies are successful, as are most Disney films, will provide a handsome return on investment.

 CHECK YOUR UNDERSTANDING

Give an example of how each element in an international culture impacts how work gets done.
a. Work attitudes
b. Achievement motivation
c. Time constraints

Discuss outsourcing in globalization.

Outsourcing in Globalization

Outsourcing is the concept of sending upscale jobs offshore, such as basic research, chip design, innovation, engineering, and even financial analysis. It is a trend in globalization that is saving costs for U.S. companies. Outsourcing is "one of the biggest trends reshaping the global economy. The driving forces are digitization, the Internet, and high-speed data networks that girdle the globe."[21] Currently, cost is not the only important benefit of outsourcing. A survey by Hewitt Associates found three more reasons: gaining outside expertise, improving service quality, and being able to focus on the core business.[22]

How did outsourcing start? Jack Welch, then CEO of GE, was instrumental in developing the concept of outsourcing in 1989. He had gone to India on a sales call in hopes of selling products like airplane engines and plastics. But during the sales meeting with the top government officials of India, Welsh was the one who got the sales pitch.

India needed business for its high tech sector. In 1990, GE formed a joint venture to develop and market its medical equipment in India. In 1997, GE formed Gecis to handle backroom work and market analytics, and then in 1999, Gecis set up its first international call center in India.[23] Other contributing factors were the liberation of India's economy in 1991 after decades of restrictive regulation. Multinational companies began looking at India as a huge market of talent for outsourcing, as well as a growing middle class consumer market for their products. The competitive edge comes in serving customers better than the competition.

Knowledge work of all kinds can be done anywhere in the world through outsourcing. Analyst Paul Roehrig of Forrester Research, Inc., has stated that the worldwide IT and applications outsourcing market in 2007 was worth about $120 billion per year. Because multiyear outsourcing deals are common, even a conservative estimate is that outsourcing agreements comprise more than half a trillion dollars of total contract value.[24] Intel, Inc., and Texas Instruments, Inc., for example, are using engineers from India and China, and Hewlett-Packard has employed more than three thousand engineers in India. For United Parcel Service, the world's largest package carrier, outsourcing has allowed the company to focus on its core competencies. Whereas the rise in a globally integrated knowledge economy is helping developing nations, it is unclear what it means for the United States. "IBM, Microsoft, and Nokia outsource chunks of their research and development (R&D) and product development work to Symbio, a global product development firm with seven R&D centers in Finland and Sweden and five offshore development centers in mainland China, Taiwan, and Bangladesh."[25] For Americans, outsourcing is an emotional issue that is hard to deal with especially when jobs that were traditionally handled by Americans are now going to places like India, where they can be done more cheaply. The outsourcing boom is evidence that the global supply chain is changing, evolving, and becoming much more efficient."[26] By tapping the world's best talent, "companies like American Express, Dell Computer, and Eastman Kodak can offer round-the-clock customer care while keeping costs in check."[27]

Effects of Global Outsourcing.   Global outsourcing is causing the financial industry to undergo a major change. For example, processing insurance claims, selling stocks, and analyzing companies can all be done by workers in Asia. In the meantime, India, China, and the rest of South Asia have developed one of the fastest-growing consumer bases for credit-, debit-, and cash-card services for Visa, MasterCard, and American Express. Their economies are growing, and consumers are buying homes and consumer goods at an ever increasing rate. In India and China, the number of wealthy households with accounts in private banks has grown at a new rate, which in turn is fueling Asian offshore private banking.[28] The process of outsourcing has rapidly changed the world of financing into a global operation.

Think of it as a new twist: "offshoring in reverse." Indian companies are now hiring aggressively in the United States instead of sending their own people to work in the States. The work that Wipro (other Indian companies are Tata and Infosys) is doing, for example, requires more and more knowledge of the customers' businesses, and it wants local people to do the work. Wipro acknowledges that the trend might ease tensions as the U.S. Senate mulls over regulations concerning immigration and temporary working papers for foreigners. India is becoming a major employer in the United States. It is actively recruiting at campus job fairs and is seeking experienced vets who have worked at American companies.[29]

One of the reasons for using outsourcing is to save costs, which may not always prove to be true. Casauri, which designs laptop cases and travel bags, found that outsourcing did not work. After customers continued to call with complaints that they had received the wrong color, the wrong style, or the wrong number of bags, Emily McHugh, CEO, started looking for another alternative. After doing research, she figured out that she could do the job in-house for about half of what she was paying for outsourcing. Other costs also can run up the bill. McHugh outlines three often overlooked costs: (1) Entrepreneurs can underestimate the cost of researching vendors and vetting choices. The process may take weeks or even months and may require an on-site visit. (2) Failing to define the details in the contract can blow the budget. (3) Failing to get communication lines open can be costly in time and revenues.[30]

The Right Time to Outsource.

When a company is looking for new innovative ideas, should it look inside the company or should it consider outsourcing? A study, conducted by three professors in the field of marketing, of the sourcing habits and innovative performance of 359 companies based in the United States revealed four situations that call for outsourcing.[31]

1. When companies need to add lots of new knowledge to innovate, such as figuring out how to work with an unfamiliar chemical compound to make a different line of pharmaceuticals.
2. In the early stages of a project, when there are lots of technical hurdles to be overcome and the outcome is far from certain.
3. When intellectual property is not well protected in the industry. In such cases, since new ideas spread quickly from company to company, it may not be possible to differentiate products with innovations. So, businesses turn to outsourcing to limit spending.
4. When companies have had lots of experience with outsourcing. Let's say all the factors above are equal—it's basically a toss-up between working on a project in-house and outsourcing it. In such cases, companies with a long track record of contracting tend to hand off the job to outsiders—three times as often as businesses with average levels of experience in the practice. The costs and benefits of outsourcing are more certain for experienced firms, and they can better manage the situation to produce effective results.

Drawbacks of Outsourcing.

The professors in their research found two drawbacks to outsourcing. The first is that companies that outsource can end up with generic products, especially when contractors are dealing with multiple clients that had similar needs. The second is turning to outsourcing too late in the development of a product, forcing the contractor to learn more about the work that had already been done in-house.

Outsourcing is expected to continue in greater volume in the next decades. Companies must remember that human relations is always at the heart of international business transactions. As companies work out the bugs in their systems and develop standards, they must also address issues concerning the welfare of their people. There are a number of challenges facing these issues.

CHECK YOUR UNDERSTANDING

1. What is outsourcing?
2. How did outsourcing get started?
3. What have been some of the effects of global outsourcing?
4. How does "offshoring in reverse" work?
5. Identify several situations where outsourcing is feasible.

Describe several major global human resource challenges.

Global Human Resource Management Challenges

In today's global marketplace, companies face a host of human resource management challenges, including selection of personnel, training of employees, dealing with culture shock, and ethics and proper behavior.

Selection of Personnel

One of the current global human relations challenges facing organizations is that of choosing the appropriate personnel for international assignments. Should the company send people from the home office or select local managers? In recent years, a growing number of enterprises have been opting for local managers, although the top positions often are reserved, if only in the beginning, for home office employees. Sometimes, this is done because there is a shortage of talented senior-level managers in the other country.[32]

Today, powerful corporations are tapping talent wherever they can find it and are building a truly integrated global workforce. In other cases, management simply wants to have someone in charge who understands what headquarters wants done and is able to communicate effectively with those at the home office. For example, in China, Ford owns 35 percent of Changan Ford Mazda, Chinese partner Chongqing Changan Automobile holds 50 percent, and Japan's Mazda the other 15 percent. Although this venture has been successful over the years, it is expected to split up by 2012. Affective communication among personnel in three different countries has played an important role in its success. At Mazda Motors of Japan, Ford has assigned one of its own managers to oversee the relationship between Mazda and Ford.[33]

To protect themselves, global companies are finding that preemployment screenings are critical. By hiring people without a criminal record and with the education and experience advertised on their résumé, companies can limit their exposure to crime and fraud. Applicants for all jobs are being screened. For example, First Advantage, a prescreening firm, has 3,700 employees, with 500 employees in India, China, Hong Kong, Singapore, and Australia. Another prescreening firm, Kroll, has 275 employees outside the United States serving the United Kingdom, South Africa, Poland, and India. Global employment prescreenings are expected to double.[34]

Workforce Optimization. Currently, IBM is no longer reliant on great hardware; instead, it depends on great talent and on exceptional systems for managing that talent. IBM invests heavily in tools for deploying people. Its primary focus is **workforce optimization**, which is the process of ensuring that IBM has the right number of people with the right set of skills. The right people must be recruited and provided with the proper development and training and assigned to the right projects.[35] It also means letting employees go who no longer fit the organization's goals.

After Lenovo, one of China's largest companies, bought IBM's personal computing division, making it the world's third-largest seller of PCs, Bill Matson, then senior vice president of human resources, launched an extensive communications program to transition Lenovo's employees into a new organization driven by the global integration of its offices around the world. Lenovo immediately "quadrupled its revenue, doubled the size of its workforce and adopted the new model of optimal workforce management: buying up top talent on a global scale." One of Lenovo's greatest challenges was unlocking the power of the talent within the global organization. The focus is on people who can operate effectively on a global scale, regardless of their birth country. Currently, a global mindset is taking place—more Europeans than Americans are managing multinational enterprises.[36]

Selection Criteria.   In choosing the best people to fill overseas positions, a growing number of companies have focused on identifying criteria that can be used to select the people most likely to do the best job.[37] Typically, both technical and human skills are evaluated. Some of the most common criteria are:

1. The ability to adapt personally to an overseas assignment
2. Technical competence
3. The ability of one's family to adapt
4. Human relations skills
5. Previous overseas experience[38]

In addition, many firms use interviews as part of the screening process. In the case of managers, these interviews typically are held with both the candidate and the candidate's spouse. The objective of this screening is to ensure that there is a strong fit between the person's abilities and talents and the demands of the position.

Training of Employees

In many cases, those who are selected for overseas assignments are given special types of training prior to their departure. The two most common are cultural training and language training. *Cultural training* is designed to familiarize the individual with the ways life is lived in the country and typically includes a wide array of considerations, from social customs to business practices.[39] Some of this training is generic and is designed to provide general information about how things are done in that country. For example, the overall cultural highlights and specific guidelines that often are provided regarding how to do business in China are as follows:

- The Chinese place a great deal of emphasis on trust and mutual connections, so it is important to spend time building good relationships with those with whom you will be doing business.
- Business meetings typically start with pleasantries such as tea and general conversation about your trip to the country, local accommodations, and family. In most cases, the host will have already been briefed on your background.
- When it's time to begin a meeting, the Chinese host will give the appropriate indication. Similarly, when the meeting is over, the host will indicate that it is time for you to leave. Be alert for these signs.
- Chinese businesspeople tend to be slow in formulating a plan of action, but once they decide what they want to do, they generally proceed at a fairly good rate. When the plan begins to be implemented, it is important to be fully prepared to do your part.
- In negotiations, reciprocity is important. If the Chinese make concessions, they expect something in return. Additionally, it is common for them to slow down negotiations in order to take advantage of Westerners (Americans, in particular) who are eager to conclude a deal. The objective of this tactic is to extract further concessions. Therefore, be patient in your negotiations.
- Because negotiating can involve a loss of face, it is common to find Chinese carrying out the process through intermediaries. This allows them to convey their ideas without fear of embarrassment.[40] As a result, you typically will find that no one in the negotiation has the authority to sign off on the deal.

Each country has its own way of doing business. For example, doing business in Spain differs from doing business in China. Some business behaviors in Spain are:

- As with most Latin cultures, the Spanish tend to stand very close in both social and business situations. They may even rest their hand lightly on your forearm or elbow.
- Spanish businesspeople enjoy vigorous discussion that may, to our ears, sound strongly argumentative.
- Where the "old boy's network" may exist in other countries, in Spain, an exclusive network of leading families prevails. And it is the men of those families who compose this special network.
- Pride, bordering on arrogance, is often cited as a common trait among Spanish businessmen.
- Spanish men tend to converse quickly and expressively. They may interrupt you, but by their standards, it would be impolite for you to do the same to them.
- Eye contact will be a special challenge. Holding eye contact during a conversation shows sincerity; lowering the eyes signals respect. Yet, as in the United States and Canada, prolonged contact by a woman could send a wrong message.[41]

Information concerning business behaviors is often provided in two ways. One is through the use of cultural assimilators and the other is by individuals who have been stationed in the country and can speak from firsthand experience.

Cultural Assimilator. A **cultural assimilator** is a programmed learning technique that is designed to expose members of one culture to some of the basic concepts, attitudes, role perceptions, customs, and values of another culture. Cultural assimilators are developed for pairs of cultures, such as to familiarize managers from the United States with the culture in Germany. The approach almost always takes the same format: The person being trained is asked to read a short episode of a cultural encounter and then to choose an interpretation of what has happened and why. If the person's response is correct, the individual goes onto the next episode. If not, the person is asked to reread the episode and make another choice. Table 13.4 provides an illustration.

Table 13.4 A Cultural Assimilator Situation

Sharon Hatfield, a schoolteacher in Athens, Greece, was amazed at the questions that were asked of her by Greeks whom she considered to be only casual acquaintances. When she entered or left her apartment, people would ask her where she was going or where she had been. If she stopped to talk, she was asked questions such as, "How much do you make a month?" or "Where did you get that dress you are wearing?" She thought that the Greeks were very rude.

Page X-1

Why did the Greeks ask Sharon such "personal" questions?

1. The casual acquaintances were acting like friends do in Greece, although Sharon did not realize it.

Go to page X-3

2. The Greeks asked Sharon the questions to determine whether she belonged to the Greek Orthodox Church.

Go to page X-4

3. The Greeks were unhappy about the way in which she lived, and they were trying to get Sharon to change her habits.

Go to page X-5

4. In Greece, such questions are perfectly proper when asked of women but improper when asked of men.

Go to page X-6

Page X-3

You selected 1: The casual acquaintances were acting like friends do in Greece, although Sharon did not realize it.

Correct. It is not improper for in-group members to ask these questions of one another. Furthermore, these questions reflect the fact that friendships (even casual ones) tend to be more intimate in Greece than in America. As a result, friends generally are free to ask questions that would seem too personal in America.

Go to page X-1

Page X-4

You selected 2: The Greeks asked Sharon the questions to determine whether she belonged to the Greek Orthodox Church.

No. This is not why the Greeks asked Sharon such questions. Remember, whether or not some information is personal depends on the culture. In this case, the Greeks did not consider these questions to be too personal.

Why? Try again.

Go to page X-1

Page X-5

You selected 3: The Greeks were unhappy about the way in which she lived, and they were trying to get Sharon to change her habits.

No. There was no information given to lead you to believe that the Greeks were unhappy with Sharon's way of living. The episode states that the Greeks were acquaintances of Sharon.

Go to page X-1

Page X-6

You selected 4: In Greece, such questions are perfectly proper when asked of women but improper when asked of men.

No. Such questions are indeed proper under certain situations. However, gender has nothing to do with it. When are these questions proper? Try to apply what you have learned about proper behavior between friends in Greece. Was Sharon regarded as a friend by these Greeks?

Go to page X-1

Source: Reprinted from Fred E. Fiedler, Terence Mitchell, and Harry C. Triandis, "The Cultural Assimilator: An Approach to Cross-Cultural Training," *Journal of Applied Psychology*, April 1971, pp. 97–98. Copyright © 1971 by the American Psychological Association. Reprinted by permission.

Cultural assimilators use critical incidents as the basis for training, and these incidents typically are provided both by managers who have served in the particular country and by members of the host nation. Once the incidents are written, they are tested on people who have had experience in that country in order to ensure that the responses are realistic and that one choice is indeed preferable to the others. Typically 150 to 200 incidents are developed, and then the list is pruned to 75 to 100 incidents that eventually are included in the assimilator booklet.

Assimilators can be expensive to create. However, for multinational companies that are continually sending people to a particular overseas location, the cost can be spread over many trainees, and the assimilator package can remain intact for a number of years. For example, a $100,000 assimilator package that is used by five hundred people over a five-year period will cost the company only $200 per person and the cost of revising the program often is very small. Thus, over the long run, cultural assimilators can be cost effective as well as being extremely helpful in developing effective global human relations-oriented personnel.

Training Costs. Overall spending on training and development continues to increase, a reflection that companies are preparing their employees to provide them with a competitive edge. In-house training still continues to be the preferred method of training. The growing need for better-trained and better-developed workers has led companies to hire chief learning officers, a standard feature in many large corporations. The rapidly changing and global nature of today's corporate world is putting increased demands on training and development.[42] What does this mean? It means that there is a need for more outside vendors who are familiar with the language and training needs in specific countries. Not only is globalization changing the workplace, technology, market forces, and an aging workforce, just to name a few, are also impacting training programs.

Language Training. Language training is another area that often is regarded as important for those who are going to work in the global arena. During the 1980s, when Japan was the most competitive nation in the world and its economy was booming, a number of major multinational companies with operations in that country began encouraging their people to learn Japanese. Certainly, to the extent that it can help multinational managers interact more effectively with the local personnel, the ability to speak the local language is a benefit. It is also useful in learning about the culture of the country, because it allows the individual to read the newspapers and listen to local radio and television and thus get a very good grasp of what is going on in the country. Other benefits of knowing the language are that it helps one interact socially with both the employees and the clients, and it can be particularly useful in recruiting local talent. On the other hand, the recent trend has been toward minimizing language training for American managers, because English is so dominant and, for all intents and purposes, has become the primary language of the business world. One expert in the area explained the new trend this way:

> By happy coincidence, English has become the lingua franca of international business. It would be quite impossible, after all, for all the people in the world to learn all the languages of the people they do business with. When Germans and Japanese meet to strike a deal, the chances are the negotiations will take place in English.
>
> An increasing number of people in the business world speak English. Many European companies require their employees to speak English as a condition of employment. In most parts of the world, children learn English in elementary school. Generally speaking, as you go higher in the corporate hierarchy of a foreign company, more people speak English and speak it better. But even at lower levels, speaking English is an important skill in many foreign firms.[43]

Language and culture training are not just for the people assigned to work in a foreign country; they are also beneficial to the employees working in the United States who engage in foreign business transactions. Knowing something about the history of the country, its customs, its traditions, and communication behaviors gives insight in how to adjust one's behavior and communication style. For example, employees in Asia copy all executives on local e-mails and it is considered the polite thing to do, whereas, in the United States, it contributes to e-mail overload. Also, getting to know the customer on a personal level is crucial to doing business in Asia.[44] A number of sources are available for educating employees about language and culture in foreign countries. They range from courses taught within the company to Web-based courses, such as GlobeSmart, a cross-cultural training product.

Dealing with Culture Shock

Leaving one's home country to work in a new country can be a stressful experience, even though the person has planned and prepared for the move. "People usually experience many emotions while adapting to a foreign culture, changing from excitement and interest in the new culture to depression and fear of the unknown."[45] The difficulties a person experiences can be called **culture shock**. The term *culture shock* was first introduced in 1958 to describe the anxiety produced when a person moves to a completely new environment. It is the lack of direction, the feeling of not knowing what to do or how to do things in a new environment, and not knowing what is appropriate or inappropriate. Culture shock is a state of impaired ability to function. To understand culture shock, it helps to understand what culture is. Culture is made up of the common things that members of a community learn from each other, their families, the media, and literature, for example. These things influence how we act and communicate.[46]

Early in the assignment to a new country, a person generally feels that everything is going great and he or she may even be having a wonderful time. This is called the **honeymoon stage**, which usually does not last long. The **culture shock stage** begins to set in when the differences increase to the point that they become overwhelming and a person does not know how to deal with them. Some of the symptoms of culture shock are feeling angry over minor inconveniences, irritable, withdrawn, extreme homesickness, overeating or loss of appetite, boredom, headaches, and depression. To survive, a person must rely on the preassignment training that the company provided and learn how to deal with the issues. This is called the **negotiation stage**. The final stage is the **acceptance stage**. This occurs when a person is able to live with the differences in the culture and accepts the customs of the new country as just another way of living. Over time, most people can make the adjustment and adapt to the differences. The fact is that the environment does not change; it is a person's attitude that changes toward the differences in the culture.[47]

Selecting people with the proper personality, experiences, social support systems, familiarity with the language, education, mental health, and attitude makes a difference in how well they can deal with culture shock.[48] Along with engaging in a well-designed training program and having proficient language skills, a person can become active in the community, make friends who can teach the customs and traditions of the country, read to gain knowledge of the culture, continue studying the language, and most of all have patience. The home company should also help a person through culture shock by giving easy access to home via e-mail, fax, and interoffice mail and by providing support. Working in a foreign country can be frustrating and stressful at times; therefore, to meet these challenges, a person must stay healthy by making time for relaxation, exercising, and eating healthy meals. It may be helpful to understand that culture shock is a normal experience that does not have to last long.

Cross-cultural knowledge is crucial. "People who are responsible for hundreds of millions of Intel's wealth and prosperity need to understand how to work well on a global basis," says Kevin Gazzara, who developed the Leading Through People program for Intel. Its program makes firsthand exposure to different cultures a cornerstone. Intel set up a training program for its midlevel managers. Of those who attended, Intel has noticed a difference in the way these managers deal with customer relationships around the globe. Gazzara travels internationally to gain firsthand knowledge of the culture in the countries where Intel does business. The information is used to develop a new leadership program for that country. During the training week, the participants are divided into groups of six to nine people from different geographical areas. Each group must create a new-product business proposal by the end of the week. The key to the program's success is exposing the managers in a learning environment with colleagues from around the world. The diverse participant makeup and experiential approach make this program different and one suited for a global business climate.[49]

Ethics and Proper Behavior

It is scary that most companies appear to be unaware of their obligation to provide ethics and compliance training to all their employees. Out of two thousand legal, ethics, and human resources professionals surveyed, more than seventy were unaware that such training is mandated by federal law.[50] A company that integrates ethics along with diversity, environment, social responsibility, and more in its training program is the Xerox Corporation.[51]

It appears Americans have a problem. According to people from other countries, Americans have a long way to go to become sensitive to the world outside their borders and to promote the importance of world citizenship. After the 9/11 terrorist attacks, Keith Reinhard, an advertising executive, decided to do something about Americans' lousy image abroad. He launched a group called Business for Diplomatic Action. Its purpose was to better the image of the American by improving the behavior of Americans abroad. Reinhard surveyed two hundred international offices in seventeen countries asking: "If you could advise Americans what they could do to be better global citizens and reduce resentment, what would you say?" While the respondents lauded Americans for their "can-do" spirit, cultural diversity, land of opportunity, and country filled with youthful enthusiasm, they felt Americans were arrogant, self-serving, insensitive, exploitive, and quick to take but slow to give back. Their perception is, "How can they (Americans) lead the world when they don't know anything about the world?" From the information gathered in the survey, a booklet called *World Citizens Guide for Americans* was prepared in 2004. The booklet has tips on how to become better world citizens. The Business for Diplomatic Action group wants the booklet in the hands of all American travelers. Companies such as AMR Corporation's American Airlines, Loews Hotels, and Novell, Inc., are promoting the program. See Table 13.5 for suggestions from the booklet.[52]

Know Before You Go. U.S. expatriates and their families expect an overseas assignment to be a wonderful adventure. However, this may not always be the case. Not only will culture shock set in, but the living conditions may not be comparable to those in the States. A major challenge for companies sending an employee overseas is educating the entire family about the customs and traditions of the country, the living conditions, and educational and social opportunities. Failure to provide the proper predeployment training will impact an expatriate's success. For example, family issues are cited by the majority of the human resource managers surveyed worldwide as the main reason for an expatriate's failure.

 CHECK YOUR UNDERSTANDING

1. Describe what happens in each stage of culture shock.
   a. Honeymoon Stage _____
   b. Culture Shock Stage _____
   c. Negotiation Stage _____
   d. Acceptance Stage _____
2. What is the purpose of the *World Citizens Guide for Americans*?

Table 13.5
Suggestions from the
World Citizens Guide

Think big. Act small. Be humble. No bragging, please.

1. Be patient and slow down. In many other countries, life moves at a slower pace.

2. Try the language. At least master some basic greetings and words, including "please."

3. Be quiet. In many cultures, a loud voice is considered a bragging voice.

4. Be a traveler, not a tourist. Learn a little bit about where you're going.

5. Read a map. Familiarize yourself with the local geography to avoid making insulting mistakes.

6. Dress up. In some countries, casual dress is a sign of disrespect.

7. Talk small. Talking about wealth, power, or status—corporate or personal—can create resentment.

8. No slang. Even casual profanity is unacceptable.

9. Listen as much as you talk. Ask people you're visiting about themselves and their way of life.

10. Religious restraint. In many countries, religion is not a subject for public discussion.

11. Political restraint. Steer clear … if someone is attacking U.S. politicians or policies. Agree to disagree.

Source: Business for Diplomatic Action.

*Explain ways of
developing a global
perspective.*

Development of a Global Perspective

During the past decade, American businesses, as well as foreign businesses, have entered the global marketplace at an accelerated rate. In most cases, this has been accomplished by setting up overseas operations in conjunction with a *local partner*. In most foreign countries, this is the only way an American business can establish an international operation.

Another way that multinational enterprises have expanded their operations is through the use of *mergers and acquisitions*. "The merger boom that characterized the 1990s is back, with the total worldwide deal volume reaching a whopping $2.8 trillion in 2005." The countries most affected are Brazil, Russia, India, and China. These are fast-growing economies that are competing for worldwide consumer goods. A study by the Economist Intelligence Unit, on behalf of Accenture, confirmed that cultural fit is critical for the success of a merger or acquisition. In fact, large cultural differences are the main reasons for merger failures. In cross-border mergers, the opportunities for misunderstanding between the companies are vast.[53] Dealing effectively with cultural issues provides one of the greatest challenges for global managers. An example of a global *merger* was Daimler-Benz merging with Chrysler. The merger of these two highly recognized automobile companies, however, has since dissolved. An example of an *acquisition* is Unilever, the Anglo-Dutch consumer products company, purchasing Bestfoods, the maker of Skippy Peanut Butter and Hellmann's Mayonnaise.[54]

A third way companies are expanding their operations is through the process of *outsourcing*, which continues to grow and change the global supply chain. For many Americans, outsourcing remains an emotional issue, especially when it comes to the issue of losing jobs. Outsourcing goes to those countries where the work can be done more cheaply. To remedy this situation, Americans must place more emphasis on learning math, science, and computer science. Globalization is here to stay, and the outflow of work is just another adjustment that globalization brings.[55]

In each of these instances, the companies found themselves having to adjust to a new culture. After. all, the way Daimler did business in Europe was somewhat different from the way Chrysler carried out business in the United States. In an effort to ensure that all of their operations, domestic and foreign, were working together, multinational companies now are developing and refining a global perspective. In particular, they are blending the overall corporate culture with the local culture of their global operations. The following are some representative examples:

- At Costco's warehouse in Korea, employees dine at the corporate cafeteria. As this is traditional in other companies in Korea, Costco is following local customs.
- Siemens of Germany has a feedback tool called *management dialogue* that is used to judge the effectiveness of managers. Once annually, employees provide feedback about their supervisor. However, this tool is not used in China because that culture has a strong respect for hierarchies, and employees do not feel comfortable making comments about their bosses.
- Walmart offers stock options to its American employees in order to build morale. However, the company uses different forms of motivation in Germany, because stock options violate local laws.[56]

Simply put, multinational enterprises are working to strike a balance between creating a unifying corporate culture and addressing local differences.[57] A goal of Omron, a Japanese electronics sensing and control technology manufacturer headquartered in Kyoto, Japan, is to make itself a multi-local company by promoting business operations that meet the particular characteristics of the local market in which it operates, that contribute to the local community, and, at the same time, that must be unified on a global scale. In some cases, a company will insist that its overseas subsidiaries do things the way they are done in the home country because there must be a uniform culture in these areas. A good example is language: More and more firms now are insisting that everyone communicate in English. Omron has designated English as the company's official language, and all international meetings are conducted in English. The company believes that the use of one language reinforces the global nature of its business. Omron has also standardized its software to eliminate compatibility issues and to ensure a smooth exchange of information among its offices worldwide. To set the course for the future and at the same time maintain a balance, the company formulated three key management concepts for its "Grand Design 2010" plan—Omron's long-term management vision:

- **Self-reliance**—to encourage each internal business company to operate more autonomously.
- **Coexistence**—to maintain harmony with individuals, countries, environment, and society.
- **Creativity**—to offer higher added value and enhance Omron's corporate value by strategically combining hardware production.[58]

Omron's motto is: "At work for a better life, a better world for all." The core value of this motto is "working for the benefit of society." In today's global marketplace, the values that society demands of companies have changed significantly over the last decade. They have moved from emphasizing economic values to focusing on social values. In Omron's expanding global operations, the stakeholders, including customers, business associates, shareholders, employees, and local communities, are growing in

Table 13.6
The Omron Principles

Corporate Core Value	Working for the benefit of society
Management Principles	Challenging ourselves to always do better
	Innovation driven by social needs
	Respect for humanity
Management Commitments	Respect for individuality and diversity
	Maximum customer satisfaction
	Relationship-building with shareholders
	Awareness and practice of corporate citizenship
Guiding Principles for Action	Quality first
	Unceasing commitment to challenging ourselves
	Integrity and high ethics
	Self-reliance and mutual support

Source: www.omron.com.

scope and diversity, each with its own set of values and expectations. To address the new value perceptions, in 2006 Omron reorganized the platform of its corporate philosophy and established the Omron Principles (see Table 13.6).[59]

Knowledge Sharing.   In addition, multinational companies are beginning to develop systems for sharing information worldwide. For example, Ernst & Young, an international consulting firm, has its people share knowledge and discuss different approaches to doing business in other countries. One reason for knowledge sharing is that a solution that worked well in India may be of value to a consulting team in the United Kingdom. A second reason is that this information can help company consultants understand the culture of other countries. The Ernst & Young consulting team can then modify its approach to address the local culture. In particular, understanding cultural nuances and how they shape customers' behaviors can help multinational companies plan business operations to better suit customer requirements. Skoda Automobilova, a Czech Republic car maker, has trained its managers in Western management techniques so that they are better able to work with the firm's multinational partner. At the same time, Skoda has taught its partner, Volkswagen, how business is conducted in the Czech Republic. The result is that both groups now work together more productively.

Another example is provided by Walmart, which has found that some facets of its corporate culture can be easily exported to foreign operations, whereas others require modification or do not work at all and must be abandoned. For example, when the company entered the German market in 1997, it brought along the culture that it had successfully used in the United States. One of these cultural activities was the company "cheer," in which a person stands in front of the associates and yells, "Give me a W!" and everyone shouts "W." The individual then continues with the Walmart cheer by saying, "Give me an A!" and so on until the company's name is spelled out. The German employees had no problem participating in this activity. However, other Walmart activities were not well received. One is the Ten-Foot Rule, which states that an employee must greet any customer who is within a ten-foot radius. Neither the employees nor the customers felt comfortable with this custom, so it is not used in Germany.

Cultures differ from country to country, and too often, culture expectations are mismatched. For example, McDonald's will fail if it expects consumers in a country where cows are sacred to eat American beef-centric products. Likewise, in China consumers think that starting the day with something cold, like milk on cereal, is a shock to the system and warm milk makes the cereal taste like wet paper. Understanding and accepting differences are keys to success in international transactions.

Multinational companies are working very hard to ensure that their corporate culture and the culture of both their business partners and their customers fit together. This is particularly important given that in one investigation of the reasons that business alliances fail, 75 percent of the companies said it was a result of an incompatibility of their corporate culture and the other firm's culture.[60] In dealing with this challenge, many multinational companies now are developing their own in-house programs. At Nokia, for example, all new employees must attend the firm's "cultural awareness" class.

Virtual Work Spaces.   With employees spread across the world, not only is sharing knowledge important, having virtual shared workstations that allow real-time communication and exchange of documents is equally important. Virtual technology software is growing. In fact, CorasWorks says it is closing thirty new deals a month, up from only eight a month just a year ago.[61] The most competitive companies will be those that do the best job of getting their people to work together and solve problems.

Developing Global Perspective.   Companies are also reinforcing the development of a global perspective at salary review time. At Gillette, managers consider an employee's commitment to corporate culture as part of the individual's overall performance. At Siemens, when evaluating people for salary raises and promotions, managers look carefully at how well employees are working in accordance with the firm's core beliefs. Developing a culture of unifying corporate beliefs is important for a company to become a major global player regardless of the country in which the company is located. The process of developing global perspective begins with developing a culture that promotes the company's values.

Building Cultural Compatible Alliances.   The value of this is going to be even more important in the future, because of the growing number of alliances that are taking place between multinational companies. For example, Airbus, the aircraft manufacturer, is allied with more than one hundred partners with whom it works in designing and building planes; and Sprint, Deutsche Telekom, and France Telecom, members of the Global One joint venture, serve seventy-five countries and work to function as one firm in addressing the global telecommunications needs of corporations. Unless the group can develop a uniform global perspective, the venture is likely to flounder.[62] Deutsche Telekom, one of the world's leading telecommunications and information technology service providers, is setting international standards of quality, efficiency, and innovation.

Innovation.   Innovation is the ingredient that produces successful companies, grows a prosperous economy, and allows companies to compete in a fierce global marketplace. For example, innovation in relationships keeps the company ahead of its competition. Innovation in information processes provides a competitive edge. It improves productivity and is even required in penetrating global markets. It is a necessary part of developing a global perspective.

As indicated in earlier chapters, technology is changing the world and how things get done. To stay abreast of technology requires constant attention and study. An understanding of how technological changes impact multinational companies and their international operations must be included in one's global perspective. As a result, human relations will continue to be an important consideration in the global marketplace.

 CHECK YOUR UNDERSTANDING

1. Describe three major ways an American business can expand its operations into foreign countries.
2. Why is knowledge important to a multinational company?
3. What is the role of innovation in the global marketplace?

© Sean Locke, iStock

Discuss how an organized office can enhance your career.

Career Advisor

Organize Your Office Properly

Another important success variable that can enhance your career is the way you organize your office. Several psychological principles can be employed to help arrange your office most effectively.

The Desk and Computer Station.   The first rule is that, no matter how small it is, make your office look spacious and less crowded by arranging the furniture appropriately. The desk should be given initial priority. If the office is small, keep the desk fairly small or it will crowd the rest of the room. Conversely, if the office is spacious, get a fairly large desk that takes up more room. If at all possible, have a wooden desk or one that looks like wood. In contrast to metal desks, wood connotes power and authority and will help to increase your status. Your own physical dimensions will dictate the size of the desk chair. If you are a tall or large person, a small chair will make you look like an ogre. If you are a short or slender person, a large chair will dwarf your appearance. Choose a chair proportional to your size and, if possible, one that has a back that comes up to the back of your head.

Place the computer station convenient to the desk, at an angle either to one side or to the other side. Placing the computer station behind the desk is not the best choice of locations. To use the computer requires turning your back to the front of the office. If you have a visitor and need to check something on the computer, you must turn your back to the visitor, which is not a polite thing to do. Also, the visitor will have a full view of the computer screen, which is a security risk to the company.

Appropriately placed equipment saves time and money and improves the look and feel of a business office. Utilizing ergonomics in selecting your desk and computer station will help your office work more effectively.

Other Furniture.   If you have your choice of style of visitors' chairs, get two that match your desk chair. Some of the most acceptable colors for these chairs are natural leather in rich brown or deep maroon. Black, the most commonly manufactured color, is not as effective, because it lacks the richer look of these other colors.

The chairs should be placed in front of your desk. Do not put any of them on the side of your desk because this reduces your power and authority in relation to other people.

If space allows, you can place a couch, a coffee table, or easy chairs in a grouping separate from your work area. That will divide the room in two sections. The area with the desk is for day-to-day business, whereas the part with the couch or easy chairs is for small-group work or conferences.

Focal Point. Finally, for maximum psychological results, you must try to set up the office so that it draws attention to you. You must "frame" yourself so when people enter your office, they are directed toward you, the central person there. This can be accomplished in one of two ways: by placing your desk in front of a window or by placing a picture on the wall directly behind your chair. In either case, the desk should be positioned symmetrically in front of the window or picture. Otherwise, visitors will feel that your desk is off center or the picture is askew.

A final test of your office's effectiveness is to take a picture of it and take pictures of several friends' offices who are in the same line of work. Give these pictures to other managers outside your organization and ask them to rate the importance of the officeholder based on the office arrangement. This will give you a good idea of how your office compares.

Paperwork, Magazines, and Books. In order to work at maximum efficiency, you must handle paper and information effectively. The amount of paperwork, magazines, and professional books you have will dictate the amount of storage space you need. Although a certain amount of paperwork is needed on one's desk at any given time, the rest should be filed for easy access or thrown away. The accumulation of paper and magazines—piles stacked high on your desk, in a corner, or on the coffee table—make you look messy and inefficient. In passing your office, one might wonder if you ever meet a deadline or if the product of your work looks the same way. The way your office looks can implant a stereotype of you in a viewer's mind that may be hard to overcome; therefore, a clean, organized office can make a difference in your career path.

Take the time to set up a filing system that is manageable. Your old system may no longer be working efficiently. In addition to paper, the seemingly endless stream of e-mail and electronic files need to be managed today.[63] Take the time to purge all those unnecessary files. Think about how you want to use your files, set up new labels, and print a copy of the file names, so you can easily find what you or your boss needs.

Are you a pack rat and need to clean up your clutter? If you have a weakness of hanging onto old papers, you need to face your weakness and develop a strategy to address the problem. You may need to hire a professional to help you. First, you will need to set priorities, then create a filing system and stick to it. Whenever possible, go paperless.[64]

Clearing out clutter also means getting rid of any office supplies you have not used in the past year. You can return them to the store for credit or donate them to your favorite charity. Do not forget to update your rolodex, whether it is on your desk or on your computer. Clear out old cards and place them in a file labeled "may be I'll call them one of these days."[65]

Working at a desk with appropriate ergonomic specifications and keeping your desk and office area clean of unnecessary items benefits not only you, but the business as well. "Disorganization reduces office efficiency, is also not visually appealing, can depress employees, and also reflects poorly on the business when customers or others tour your office."[66]

 CHECK YOUR UNDERSTANDING

In your career journal, make notes on how you can organize your office to give it a professional look. Discuss how this can enhance your career.

Summary

1 Discuss the major reasons businesses become multinational companies.

A multinational company is headquartered in one country but has operations in two or more countries. More and more firms are expanding into the international arena for a number of reasons, including protecting themselves from the risks in the domestic business cycle, tapping the growing world market for goods and services, responding to foreign competition, reducing operational costs, and overcoming tariff walls by serving a foreign market from inside.

2 Identify the term culture *and relate four basic dimensions of international culture.*

Culture is the acquired knowledge that people use to interpret experience and to generate social behavior. Culture creates two major problems for those doing business internationally: understanding the cultures of other countries and learning how to adapt to these cultures. *Ethnocentrism* is the belief that we are better than anyone else and our way is the right way. Lack of understanding occurs because of one's misconceptions about another country or the people within that country. Behaviors that are different from one's own behaviors cause misunderstandings.

The four dimensions of culture are: power distance, uncertainty avoidance, individualism, and masculinity. *Power distance* is the degree to which less powerful members of organizations and institutions accept the fact that power is not distributed equally. Some countries have a greater power distance than other countries. *Uncertainty avoidance* is the extent to which people feel threatened by ambiguous situations and create ways of dealing with the uncertainties. *Individualism* is the tendency of a person to look after himself or herself, whereas *collectivism* is the tendency for people to belong to groups that look after each other. *Masculinity* represents the dominant values of success, money, and material things, while *femininity* focuses on caring for others and on the quality of life.

3 Discuss the value of cultural dimensions in understanding the impact of culture in the global arena.

In recent years, researchers have attempted to develop a composite picture of culture by clustering or grouping people based on these differences. Another way in which clustering has been performed is through an analysis of work values and attitudes between countries. Originally, five different country clusters were identified: Anglo, Nordic, South American, Latin European, and Central European. Since then, more clusters have been identified.

4 Relate the ways in which culture affects work attitudes, motivation, and how people deal with time.

Multinational companies are particularly interested in the effect of country and geographical cultures on their international operations. In particular, they are concerned with the ways in which work attitudes, achievement motivation, and the society's view of time will affect the productivity and performance of the unit. They are also interested in taking steps to ensure that their company is able to deal effectively with other cultures.

Work attitude is an element of culture that impacts the quality and quantity of output, job attendance, stress levels, and work habits. Achievement motivation is an element of culture closely linked to work attitudes. Research shows that the level of achievement motivation varies among countries. Society's view of time and how it should be spent is another element of culture.

5 *Discuss outsourcing in globalization.*

Outsourcing is the process of sending jobs overseas. It was started by Jack Welch, then CEO of GE, back in 1989. The driving forces for outsourcing are digitization, the Internet, and high-speed data networks. Reasons for outsourcing are cost reductions, gaining outside expertise, improving service quality, and being able to focus on the company's core business. Outsourcing has exploded in the last few years and has changed the way business is done, particularly in the financial industry and for projects involving R&D. "Offshoring in reverse" is the opposite of outsourcing. It is the concept of foreign companies hiring people of expertise from the United States to work in foreign countries. Companies should use outsourcing when they need to add lots of new knowledge to innovate, in the early stages of a project, when intellectual property is not well protected in the industry, or when companies have had a lot of experience in outsourcing. Two drawbacks are: (1) a company may end up with a generic product versus a unique innovative product or (2) turning to outsourcing too late in the project.

6 *Describe several major global human resource challenges.*

Four major challenges facing global management are: the selection of personnel, training of employees, dealing with culture shock, and using proper ethics and personal behavior. Choosing the right people for international assignments is critical. Pre-employment screenings are necessary to protect the company. Global prescreening firms can help with this process. *Workforce optimization* is the process for ensuring that the right people are hired into the right positions. Employees must be able to work effectively on a global scale.

Some of the criteria for selecting the right person are: the ability to adapt personally to an overseas assignment, having the technical competence needed for the job, the ability of the family to adapt, possessing human relations skills, and having previous overseas experience, if possible.

The most common training provided for employees who have been selected for overseas assignments is cultural training and language training. An array of teaching methods is used, from cultural assimilators and technology driven in-house training programs to formal training programs. Language training is regarded as important. Speaking the native language will help the expatriate to interact more effectively with local personnel.

Employees given overseas assignments must understand that culture shock will probably set in and they need training in how to deal with each stage in the culture shock process. There are four stages to culture shock: the honeymoon stage, culture shock stage, negotiation stage, and the acceptance stage. The **honeymoon stage** is described as the initially happy period when a person moves into a completely new environment. **Culture shock stage** sets in when the differences increase to the point of being overwhelming and the person does not know how to deal with it. **Negotiation stage** sets in when the person must deal with the overwhelming differences in order to survive. And the **acceptance stage** is the point at which the person is able to live with the differences.

Ethics and compliance training, as well as proper personal behavior, are needed. The World Citizens Guide for Americans is a current source for learning proper etiquette in the international arena. Educating personnel before sending them on an international assignment is a must and failure to do so is asking for trouble and possible failure.

7 *Explain ways of developing a global perspective.*

Entering into the global marketplace can be done by entering a partnership with a foreign company, by using mergers and acquisitions, and outsourcing. In each case an adjustment to the new culture is necessary. Both groups must work together to redefine their perspective. In blending the cultures, measurements must be established to determine how the company is doing. Society has expectations of companies, and companies, therefore, must adhere to society's principles.

Multinational companies are beginning to establish systems for sharing knowledge around the world. Cultural expectations must be matched or the expatriate or the product introduced in a foreign country will fail. Virtual technology is allowing shared virtual workstations to operate in real time and to share documents across space and time. Salary considerations are another global perspective that is gaining attention. The goal is to develop a meeting of the minds that distinguishes the company from all others, not just transplant a culture into the foreign company. This is becoming an important global perspective. Innovation is the ingredient that produces successful companies. Innovation in all aspects of business operations is the driver for a profitable company.

8 *Discuss how an organized office can enhance your career.*

The way your office is organized reflects who you are. Your office should always look spacious and not crowded or messy. The furniture should be arranged so the desk is given initial priority. Keep the size of the desk and computer station compatible to the size of the room. Wooden desks, in contrast to metal desks, connote power and authority and can help increase your status. The desk and matching chairs should meet ergonomic specifications. Your office should frame you as the focal point in the room.

Process paperwork immediately and do not let it pile up or ask for more storage space. Accumulated, high paper stacks give the impression you never meet deadlines or that the quality of your work looks the same way. Take time to file your paperwork and to purge your electronic files.

Clear out clutter. Get rid of things you do not need. Disorganization reduces office efficiency, can depress employees, and reflects poorly on the business when customers visit your office.

Key Terms in the Chapter

Multinational company	A multinational company is headquartered in one country but has operations in two or more countries.
Culture	Culture is the acquired knowledge that people use to interpret experience and to generate social behavior.
Ethnocentrism	Ethnocentrism is the belief that one's way of doing things is superior to that of others.
Power distance	Power distance is the degree to which less powerful members of the society accept the fact that power is not distributed equally.
Uncertainty avoidance	Uncertainty avoidance is the extent to which people feel threatened by ambiguous situations and have created institutions for minimizing or avoiding these uncertainties.
Individualism	Individualism is the tendency of people to look after themselves and their immediate family only.
Collectivism	Collectivism is the tendency of people to belong to groups that look after each other in exchange for loyalty.
Masculinity	Masculinity is the degree to which the dominant values of a society are success, money, and material things.

Femininity	Femininity is the degree to which the dominant values of a society focus on caring for others and on the quality of life.
Cultural assimilator	A cultural assimilator is a programmed learning technique that is designed to expose members of one culture to the values of another culture.
Workforce optimization	Workforce optimization is the process of ensuring that the right number of people are selected to do the right job with the right set of skills.
Culture shock	Culture shock is the anxiety produced when a person moves to a completely new environment.
Honeymoon stage	Honeymoon stage occurs early in an assignment when everything seems to be going great.
Cultural shock stage	Cultural shock stage sets in when the differences increase to the point they become overwhelming and the person does not know how to deal with them.
Negotiation stage	Negotiation stage is when preassignment training is used to deal with the differences.
Acceptance stage	Acceptance stage occurs when a person is able to live with the differences in the culture and accepts the customs of the country.
Outsourcing	Outsourcing involves sending upscale jobs overseas, such as basic research, design work, engineering, and financial analysis.
World Citizens Guide for Americans	*World Citizens Guide for Americans* is a guide giving tips on how Americans can be better world citizens.

Review and Study Questions

1. Why are so many firms now expanding internationally? Identify and discuss three reasons.
2. Explain what is meant by culture in the global marketplace?
3. In what ways are ethnocentrism and misconceptions about other cultures major problems for those doing business internationally?
4. In what ways do power distance and uncertainty avoidance influence how people in different cultures behave? What implications does this have for the study of human relations? In your answer, be sure to define each term.
5. In what ways do individualism and masculinity influence the way that people in different cultures behave? What implications does this have for the study of human relations? In your answer, be sure to define each term.
6. Of what value is clustering countries in understanding international human relations? In your answer, compare and contrast two different clusters.
7. In what way does culture influence work attitudes? How do work attitudes in the United States differ from those found in Asia? What does your answer relate about the importance of understanding international human relations?
8. In what way does culture influence achievement motivation? Give two examples.
9. In what way is time a cultural element that is of interest to multinational companies? Explain.
10. What is outsourcing? Of what value is outsourcing to the multinational company?
11. Describe the expected trend in outsourcing for the next few years.

12. Explain "offshoring in reverse."

13. What are some challenges in selecting personnel for overseas assignments?

14. How does workforce optimization impact training?

15. Identify several common criteria for selecting personnel for international assignments.

16. What are two basic types of training for expatriates? Tell how each benefits the employee.

17. Why is language training so useful in preparing people for overseas assignments?

18. How does a cultural assimilator work? Of what value is it in helping people to understand international human relations? Explain.

19. What is culture shock? Describe the four stages of culture shock.

20. What roles do ethics and behavior play in multinational companies? Give several examples of how Americans should behave when interacting with foreign businesspeople.

21. Discuss three ways a company can gain a greater perspective in the global marketplace.

22. What is the value of knowledge sharing?

23. How do virtual work spaces operate and why are they important?

24. What is the value of building cultural compatible alliances?

25. Why is it important to properly organize your office? How can it influence your career?

26. Discuss several ideas on how to arrange your office furniture and computer workstation.

27. How can a focal point be created in the office?

28. What should you do with piles of paper, magazines, and books? Clutter?

Connecting to the Real World

Going Overseas: How Can I Prepare?

The purpose of this exercise is to identify elements in the culture of a foreign country that would impact the success of opening a business in that country and selling industrial machinery directly to customers.

Procedure

1. Select two clusters from Figure 13.1. Select one country from each cluster. Research and prepare a written report on your findings.

2. Gather information on the cultural problems you would face in opening a business in each country and selling your machinery (see following situation). Use the Internet to facilitate your research. Also, you are encouraged to interview foreign students and professors who have knowledge of your selected country.

3. After identifying the major cultural problems that your company will face, discuss how your firm can deal with these problems in order to be successful.

4. Note the cultural differences and similarities between the two countries selected.

5. What are your own aspirations about working overseas? Why or why not? What barriers would you face and how would you overcome them?

Situation You are working for a firm that plans to open an overseas branch to sell its industrial machinery directly to customers in this foreign country. Your firm has never before directly sold its products outside the United States. You are to present your boss with a list of the major cultural barriers that must be surmounted if this sales effort is to be successful.

CASE
Look Out World, Here We Come!

Roxling, Inc., a consumer appliance firm, plans on expanding internationally. The company designs and manufactures small, lightweight appliances, such as mixers, toasters, coffee pots, blenders, electric skillets, and slow cookers. The organization has many patents on its products and is widely considered to be one of the foremost firms in this growing industry.

In the past, a number of companies from other countries have approached Roxling and asked for the right to manufacture or distribute its products overseas. Roxling has refused because it wanted to maintain total control of both the production and the distribution of its products. Six months ago, the firm concluded that it is now in a position to begin expanding internationally. The company would like to move into three countries—England, China, and Saudi Arabia—within the next six months.

Roxling's initial plan is to train salespeople for the overseas market. These people will operate out of small offices in these countries and will send their sales reports back to headquarters. These orders then will be shipped from the United States to the overseas customers. Over the next two years, this approach will be modified, with the company opening up manufacturing plants in both Europe and the Far East. This strategy will reduce both delivery time and transportation costs.

Some members of Roxling's board of directors have suggested that the company spend more time preparing for this overseas expansion. While working for other companies, several members of the board have been involved with overseas expansion, which has given them some degree of experience. They are familiar with some of the problems that might be encountered. "You really don't know much about these overseas countries," one of them explained. "You are going to have to find out a lot more about the culture and methods of doing business there than we know currently. Doing business in Saudi Arabia, for example, is a lot different from doing business in Chicago. We can't assume that our methods are going to fit in overseas and that we can simply send people over and have them go out and get orders."

The company president agrees with these comments but is unsure of the specific types of training to give his salespeople.

However, he has budgeted $250,000 on training. Due to their success in the United States, he plans to send his top three salespeople. "We are going to be selling products that have worldwide appeal," he explained. "This is going to help overcome a lot of the cultural barriers that most firms have to deal with. Also, there is no better way to learn the culture of a country than to go and live there, and this is exactly what we are going to have our salespeople doing. They are going to be within a day's drive of their customers, and if there are any problems, they can quickly resolve them."

The firm intends to start its sales training program within the next three weeks. After completing the training program, the salespeople will be scheduled for their overseas locations. Roxling intends to have a sales force in the field within six months.

Case Questions

1. When it comes to such dimensions as power, distance, and individualism, how similar are England, China, and Saudi Arabia? Give an example.
2. When comparing the degree of uncertainty avoidance and masculinity in these three countries, how similar are they?
3. For the personnel being sent overseas, what types of cultural adaptation would you recommend for these managers? Explain your answer.
4. How can this company minimize the cultural shock of the employees going overseas?
5. Would you recommend entering all three of these markets at the same time, or what would your recommendation be and why?
6. What type of language training should the company implement?
7. How can a cultural assimilator be useful? Explain.
8. How can the Internet help prepare these employees to face a new culture?
9. How successful do you think the president's plans will be with his preconceived ideas on how things will be in those countries? Explain.

CHAPTER 14 | Human Relations Challenges of the Future

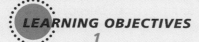
Myriad human relations challenges will confront managers in the next decade. The overriding objective of this chapter is to identify and examine some of the major challenges.

Human Relations Ideas Continue to Work

Jack Welch, former CEO of General Electric Company (GE), was instrumental in coining the phrase "boundaryless organization." Welch wanted to create an environment in which no internal boundaries existed among the people in the company. Ideas and suggestions would flow up and down the enterprise, as well as across departments. The objective was to create an internal team that was able to work as a cohesive unit and focus all its energies on addressing external problems, such as customer needs and competitive strategies. This idea revolutionized the way successful organizations now manage their people.

One way in which GE began developing its boundaryless organization was by establishing "work-out" sessions, during which forty to fifty people would meet for three days at a local hotel. There they would divide into three or four groups, each of which would be asked to identify low-value work that could be eliminated or streamlined. Each group, led by an outside facilitator, would focus on ways in which reports, approvals, meetings, policies, and practices could be streamlined. After each group had identified its list of improvements, action plans were developed and a champion was assigned for each plan. On the last day of the session, the manager of the business would come in with four to six assistant managers, and they would listen to these ideas. The managers would then either approve or disapprove each proposed change on the spot. As a result of the work-out sessions, GE was able to simultaneously downsize and increase productivity.

Today, GE continues to use work-out sessions. However, instead of two- to three-day meetings at a local hotel, the sessions now are carried out at the job site. In contrast to years past, when senior-level management would insist that all managers attend these work-out sessions, today, the sessions are held on a regular basis in-house because everyone realizes they are useful. The sessions cut down on bureaucratic red tape, and they provide motivation for employees. As they say at GE, "In the past, work-out sessions used to be orchestrated; today they are spontaneous."

GE's CEO Jeff Immelt continues to look for ways to bond with his team. He calls the last decade the "decade from hell. He attributes this to the changes that many businesses went through after the disaster of 9/11 and followed by an economic recession." Jeff Immelt is actively searching for ways to shape and to measure GE's leaders. Currently, during a couple of Fridays each month, he hosts sleepovers with a different officer. The officer is invited to Immelt's home for dinner, drinks, and a few laughs, before going to lodging at the GE headquarters in nearby Fairfield. The next morning, Immelt meets the officer, and they continue their discussions on getting to know each other, their careers, their strengths, and their weaknesses. Immelt is trying to establish the "personal connection" with his officers, something he took for granted in the past. "These sleepovers are part of a major rethink by Immelt." The current and past managers say that for years too much of Immelt's warmth, wit, and attention was beamed outside the GE family. After all, he was the traveling salesman, the thought leader, and the motivational speaker. Leaders in the future will need new traits to manage in a more complex global world. To meet this challenge, GE is currently searching for leaders who have the traits that will help them thrive in the years to come, while at the same time, the company is working on defining the 'twenty-first century' attributes and discarding the twentieth century model that was so prevalent during the Jack Welch days at GE. Immelt feels that the "one-on-one sessions will help drive new ideas and strengthen his connections with his top team."

Empowering individuals is another human relations approach used by GE. The company believes that decision making should take place at the lowest level "where a competent decision can be made." This last qualifying phrase is emphasized by GE because the company wants to point out that empowerment is not a process of turning a company into a democracy; rather, it is a way of ensuring that the best decisions are made at the lowest possible levels and that individuals who have no need to be involved in the process are systematically excluded. This process requires GE managers to ask themselves three questions: What value am I adding by making a decision? What information keeps me from letting my subordinate make this decision? What factors keep me from giving that information to subordinates and letting them make the decision?

A third human relations strategy is the introduction of wide banding, a process of decreasing the pay grades so that it is easier to give people salary raises. With narrow banding, the pay grade for a particular job might range from $9 to $14 per hour. Earlier, a boss who wanted to give someone an increase that would put their wage rate in excess of $14 per hour would first have to get the person assigned to a new pay grade, which took time. Today, as a result of wide banding, there are fewer pay grades at GE, and the grades cover greater ranges. Hence, a particular pay grade might encompass a number of jobs and range from $9 to $30 per hour. If a boss wants to raise an employee's wage from $14 to $15 per hour, he or she now has authority to do so. In this way, GE has empowered its bosses and given them more opportunities for motivating their workers.

Are these human relations ideas paying off? According to recent reports, GE is one of the most competitive companies in the world, and in most markets it is growing faster than its major competitors. A large degree of this success can be tied directly to the firm's ability to build a boundaryless organization in which everyone works together as a team. In today's environment, people must react much more quickly to any situation. Employees need access to information that flows in a boundaryless way within the organization. Boundaryless does not mean without boundaries; it means boundaries that are effective and appropriate to promote business operations. It is a human relations model that many other organizations are seeking to develop in order to compete effectively in the next decades. It will only be accomplished through the use of innovation and creativity.

Describe the character-istics of creative people.

Greater Focus on Innovation and Creativity

Innovation

During the next decade, organizations must do more than merely try to understand how innovation works; they must focus their attention on using human relations ideas to help their people be more innovative. "To create long-lasting advantage, produce dramatic shifts in competitive position and cross new performance thresholds, companies must do more than brainstorm; they must cultivate a management approach that will encourage a continuous flow of innovation, a recognized cornerstone of all high-performance businesses." Apple, a computer company, is an example of a business that uses the power of relentless innovation to achieve enduring market leadership. Continuous product innovation allows it to stay ahead of the curve.[1]

Companies often fail because of their attitude toward innovation. Because of their successes, they believe they are invincible and lose sight of opportunities for growth that may be lurking around the corner. Executives must be astute enough to overcome obstacles that may confront them in the innovation process. Company leaders must take responsibility to help everyone in the organization to understand how to get beyond the obstacles and move toward success. Innovation is a philosophy, and for it to succeed, it must have top management's support and commitment. When innovation is driven from top management, it cuts through internal politics and nails down resource priorities. "Innovation is a journey, not a destination."[2]

Some companies are just better at using innovation to generate growth. UPS is an example. "Innovation is the company's lifeblood; continuous improvement is part of the company DNA," observes Robert J. Thomas, executive director of Accenture Institute for High Performance Business. UPS uses a potent mix of management-led and customer-driven innovation philosophies to address innovation constraints. UPS continuously seeks ways to produce customer-tailored solutions—moving packages to the correct location at the right time.[3] Innovation involves thinking creatively through problems to create the best solutions that will generate growth for the business.

Creativity

Most people are a great deal more creative than they believe. Additionally, most organizational jobs do not tap the full potential of the employee; therefore, the employee does not use all of his or her creative potential. Figure 14.1 illustrates this idea. Notice that the job requires only a fraction of the employee's ability. The organization must learn to tap this asset. One way of doing so is to make employees aware of how creative they truly are. Most people believe that only geniuses are creative. However, this ability is much more widespread than is believed, and individuals in the general population possess

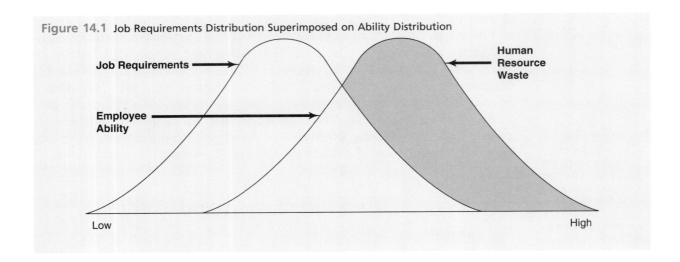

Figure 14.1 Job Requirements Distribution Superimposed on Ability Distribution

varying degrees of creativity. The following are some characteristics of creative people. They:

- Tend to be bright rather than brilliant.
- Have a youthful curiosity throughout their lives.
- Are open and responsive to feelings, emotions, and the world around them.
- Tend to have a positive self-image.
- Have the ability to tolerate isolation.
- Frequently are nonconformists.
- Enjoy finding imaginative solutions to problems.
- Are persistent.

Explain how creativity in an organization setting can be both encouraged and nurtured.

Encouraging Creativity.   One reason people are not creative is that they approach creativity in the wrong way. For example, many have erroneous, preconceived ideas about innovation that actually stifle their creativity. Here are some illustrations of these myths:

Myth 1: ***Innovation is planned and predictable.*** In truth, innovation is highly unpredictable and can be introduced by anyone from a scientist in the research and development laboratory to a clerical worker who has discovered a better way to file invoices.

Myth 2: ***Innovation is the result of exaggerated daydreaming.*** Actually, most accomplished innovators are practical people who base their ideas on realistic, down-to-earth developments, such as piggybacking on someone else's invention and generating a smaller, cheaper, higher-quality, or faster-working model.

Myth 3: ***Innovation is the result of carefully drawn technical specifications.*** In most cases, this approach takes too long. Successful innovators often rely on a try–test–review approach. Sometimes, this is jokingly addressed as "ready, fire, aim." Only after innovators have seen the quality of their completed work do they make the necessary modifications.

Myth 4: ***Large projects produce more innovative results than do small ones.*** This is untrue; research reveals that small project teams working with limited budgets typically produce better results because the participants have an opportunity to share their ideas, brainstorm, and quickly implement modifications and changes. There is no bureaucratic red tape that exists in larger projects.

TIME OUT

Improving Your Creativeness

There are many ways to improve personal creativeness. One is by engaging in mental exercises that stir the imagination. This creativity test requires you to think of two rhyming words that describe a specific definition. Write your answer to the right of each definition. Answers are provided at the end of the book.

Definition	Examples	Answers
1. Highest-ranking officer in the police department	Top	cop
2. A fat porker	Big	pig
3. The amount of difference between two very similar points of view	Fine	line
1. An angry father	___	___
2. A happy young boy	___	___
3. A person who steals from a library	___	___
4. A cloak worn by a gorilla	___	___
5. An obese feline	___	___
6. A beverage with very little alcohol	___	___
7. A heavy crying spell	___	___
8. A quick meal	___	___
9. Food with very few calories	___	___
10. A sickly escargot	___	___

Myth 5: *Technology is the driving force behind innovation and success.* Although technology is one source for innovation, the most important ingredient is people who are able to modify new discoveries so the market accepts them. In production work, for example, American firms have spent billions of dollars annually to improve the quality of their output, yet they have been unable to close the gap between this country and Japan. Why? Part of the answer is that American businesspeople have not focused enough attention on the human element.[4]

If individuals were aware of these myths, it would help to improve their creativity. Organizations can also help by implementing time-proven principles. These are:

1. Employees must be encouraged to search actively for new ideas, opportunities, and sources of innovation.
2. Ideas that are pursued should have practical application.
3. Projects should be small and well focused.
4. An initial schedule of events or milestones should be drawn up even if the project falls behind and does not meet all these deadlines.
5. Participants should be encouraged to learn from failures.
6. Employees should remember that innovation requires hard work and persistence.
7. Participants should follow a try–test–review approach.
8. Innovative activity should be rewarded.

Another way of improving creativity is to engage in mental games that require clever or imaginative solutions. (The "Time Out" quiz provides an example.) Often, creativity and innovation are a result of improving on the ideas of others both inside and outside the organization. In past years, many of the highly creative products produced and sold by the Japanese, for example, were nothing more than modifications of goods that were produced initially by American firms. This practice is known as *creative swiping* and is practiced widely by many organizations located in many countries. One Japanese professor explained the idea this way:

When we want to do something, we just try to learn and absorb all the possible answers, alternatives, and developments not only in Japan but in Europe, in developing

559

countries, and in the U.S. Then, by combining and by evaluating the best of all this, we try to come up with the optimum combinations which are available ... we are very sophisticated copycats.[5]

Jim Clifton, chairman and CEO of Gallup, believes that "the future belongs to the best ideas, not the best products, and to stay competitive, we have to lead the world in per-person creativity." As globalization grows in the marketplace, businesses will face greater competition. To expand in this environment will take creativity—"one good idea after another to make the business better, faster, richer, and harder to trounce." Companies that are more creative than their competitors will have value in tomorrow's marketplace. Having an idea is not enough; it also involves figuring out what the idea will do for the efficiency of the company and how the company will implement the idea. This process begins with leadership that encourages creativity throughout the organization and makes generating ideas a part of everybody's job. Some of the best ideas come from employees who are directly involved in getting jobs done. For example, when Sam Walton was confused or needed an answer to a problem, he went to Walmart employees for the answer.[6]

Innovation and Human Relations

In addition to helping their employees become more creative, a growing number of organizations now are working to ensure that their own human relations programs are innovative. In fact, the most successful enterprises, according to the latest research, are leaders in human relations programs, and this is as true at the top of the organization as at lower levels. One group of researchers, for example, found that high firm performance is associated with placing strong emphasis on innovation and creativity when selecting top managers.[7] Those at the executive level must be prepared to think "out of the box" in meeting the organization's emerging challenges. These findings were echoed by Philip Mirvis, based on his analysis of the data provided in the well-known Labor-Force 2000 study. Mirvis found that companies that are human relations leaders tend to develop innovative ways of managing people.[8]

Firms that are leaders in human relations programs and efforts are also more likely than other organizations to invest in training and development. This is particularly true for entry-level employees, many of whom begin work straight out of high school and have poor math, science, and communication skills that are critical for effective job performance. Human relations leaders take on the responsibility of providing remedial education and basic skills training. Additionally, these firms focus a great deal of attention on redesigning the workplace, launching employee involvement programs, introducing total quality management tools and techniques, and retraining those employees whose skills need updating.

The three primary factors that have been found to influence human relations innovativeness are customers, new technologies, and changes in the demographics of the workforce. Leading firms are acutely aware of what customers want and the types of programs that are needed to address these desires. They also tend to be on the cutting edge in terms of acquiring, mastering, and using state-of-the-art equipment. Perhaps most important, however, is that they show evidence of a stick-to-it philosophy. This cultural mindset is reflected in their belief that people make the difference in an organization's success. Attention to these three factors—customers, new technologies, and demographic changes in the workforce—is proving critical in helping leading firms to sustain their competitive advantage. At the same time, these changes are creating a challenge, and a possible problem, for organizations that are not on the human relations cutting edge.

Table 14.1
The World's Top Ten Most Innovative Companies

Company Name	Ranking in 2009
Facebook	15
Amazon	9
Apple	4
Google	2
Huawei	New in 2010
First Solar	18
PG&E	New in 2010
Novartis	New in 2010
Walmart	33
HP	12

Source: "The World's Most Innovative Companies 2010," www.fastcompany.com

As a result, these companies may be placed at a crucial competitive disadvantage. As the marketplace becomes more global in nature, a greater emphasis will be placed on innovation and creativity in all aspects of the business.

Fast Company Magazine's list of the "World's Most Innovative Companies" for 2010 covers a wide range of companies as seen in Table 14.1 These companies have integrated customer needs, new technologies, and demographic changes in their workforces to make their companies new and different to meet the challenges of today's marketplace. Three new companies appear in the top ten companies—from the fields of utilities, research and development, and telecom equipment. It is interesting to see how the companies have changed position on the list from the previous year. For example, Facebook moved into first position from fifteenth and Walmart moved into ninth position from thirty-third. Walmart is currently the largest company in the world, and yet, it continues to be innovative.

 CHECK YOUR UNDERSTANDING

1. How creative are you? Which characteristics do you possess?
2. How can you become more creative? Give several ideas.
3. Identify three factors that influence human relations innovativeness. Why are they important?

Discuss some of the reasons the nature of work is changing and the role that imagination, entrepreneurial spirit, engaged employees, and hiring practices are playing in this process.

The Changing Nature of Work

On September 11, 2001, a group of nineteen Internet-savvy fundamentalists humbled the world's only superpower.[9] These terrorists brought American businesses to their knees and forever changed the way work is done. It started a work revolution in which employees now perform their jobs differently. Also, the recession in the last decade added more leadership challenges. As a result, managers are being challenged to learn how to lead in this new environment. The strategies with which organizations are meeting this new challenge are:

- Imagination and the entrepreneurial spirit
- Engaged employees
- Hiring and retaining the best talent

Imagination and the Entrepreneurial Spirit

Technology is changing how we work and do business. For example, banking transactions conducted electronically cost pennies, transactions done by telephone cost dollars, while face-to-face transactions cost tens of dollars. Eventually, all the processes of a company will be subject to some form of digitization. Imagination and ideas are what generate change. "All big ideas share at least one of three business objectives: improved efficiency, greater effectiveness, or innovations in products or processes." Simply put, "you do things right, you do the right thing, or you do something new."[10]

Reengineering is a concept that was introduced in the early 1990s by Michael Hammer and James Champy.[11] It required rethinking and redesigning to achieve improvements in performance. Reengineering did not simply modify a process; it redid the process from the ground up. Reengineering could have been truly a big idea, which held all three idea objectives, but people used it solely for gaining efficiencies, limiting its power and value. Because technology is now in place to fundamentally change the way the world works, Tom Peters believes that what is needed is not reengineering, but reimagining every facet of the way a company does its operations. To grow in the next decade, he states that organizations must use their imagination and outthink their competitors. Peters believes that only the imaginative, the entrepreneurial, and the well-educated are going to thrive.[12]

As demographics change, leaving fewer people in the labor force, there is going to be a battle for the best professional jobs. What do we need to do? Philip Bobbitt states that we need to arm our people with education and with an entrepreneurial spirit.[13]

What is an entrepreneurial spirit? The **entrepreneurial spirit** comes from deep down inside a person. It is often associated with venturesomeness or being creative. The entrepreneurial spirit is what makes entrepreneurs successful. They think outside the box and can find the resources needed to build and grow a business. An entrepreneur can create something of recognized value from scratch, overcome the obstacles that would stop most people, see the project to completion, and perceive opportunities that others would miss or only see in retrospect.

The entrepreneurial spirit is truly a pioneer spirit. A person with the entrepreneurial spirit does not want to be locked into a job. Steve Jobs, who started Apple Computers and Pixar Animation Studios, is one of the most successful entrepreneurs of our generation. In a commencement address at Stanford University, he told the graduates to "find your true passion, do what you love to do, and make a difference. Your time is limited, so don't waste it living someone else's life. Don't be trapped by dogma—which is living with the results of other people's thinking."[14]

The entrepreneurial spirit is more than dreams; it is following through to make things happen. Entrepreneurs love what they do, have perseverance, are open to change, are flexible, have the power to make things happen, and are knowledgeable about what it is they want to accomplish. Imagination and the entrepreneurial spirit are what will be needed to help businesses grow in the next decade and help them to successfully compete in the ever expanding global marketplace.[15] When employees are not allowed to use their entrepreneurial talents, the company loses. For example, many stories are given in the literature of women who have risen to the top ranks in a company, but are never promoted into a CEO position.[16] Frustrated, they leave the company and use their entrepreneurial skills to open their own businesses, becoming their own CEOs. Businesses need to find ways to capture this spirit and use it to their advantage.

Although ideas generally come from the frontlines, it is top management that sets the tone. Top managers must be receptive to new ideas, understand that business-improvement initiatives are vital to a company's success, and be passionate advocates of new ideas. Unless ideas are supported and communicated, they will be short lived. Back in May 2005, GE launched its ecomagination commitment to imagine and build innovative solutions that benefit customers and society at large. "It is both a business strategy to drive growth at GE and a promise to contribute positively to the environment in the process."[17] GE wants to develop cleaner technologies, increase revenues on products and services that provide significant and measurable environmental performance advantages to customers, reduce emissions, and improve energy efficiency.

An idea is successful when everyone does it without thinking about it. If businesses expect to succeed in the future, they will need to use greater imagination and more entrepreneurial spirit.

Engaged Employees

Employees today want "to do meaningful work or intellectually stimulating work, in a pleasant environment where efforts are recognized, while still allowing time for a life."[18] In a study, the Gallup Organization found that "employees who are more engaged in their work take greater pride in the companies they work for, are more likely to build their careers within their companies, are happier with their compensation, and have more fun at work." Engaged employees are not only more productive, they are more positive, profitable, safer, create stronger customer relationships, and stay longer with their companies. So who are engaged employees? **Engaged employees** have a strong emotional connection with the organization—a connection that causes employees to exert greater discretionary effort at work. They work with passion and feel a profound connection to their company. Engaged employees drive innovation and move the organization forward.[19]

There is a real link between employee engagement and the bottom line. For example, at Best Buy, the average annual increase in sales rises when employees are found to be engaged. Research shows that companies with highly engaged employees experience significantly higher employee retention rates, as well as a dramatic improvement in overall effectiveness and profitability. It is interesting to note that the employees who leave companies are not from the high-engaged group or the low-engaged group, but are from the average-engaged group. They leave because they are looking for something better. Out the door goes their knowledge and abilities, at a very high cost to the company. The most highly engaged employees are the ones least likely to leave the company.[20] Gallup has also discovered that better employee engagement means better health. People who are engaged feel less stress, and the stress they feel is offset by a lot more happiness, enjoyment, and interest. Conversely, disengaged people feel more stress and have fewer sources of pleasure at work.[21]

Engaging Employees. How can management provide the stimulus to engage employees? The Gallup Organization in its studies found that engagement varies greatly among work groups and departments, but it has learned that issues such as employee development, retraining, and work–life balance are important matters that have a bearing on employee engagement levels. The studies revealed that companies that want to promote engaged employees need to pay particular attention to certain employee needs.[22]

- *Role clarity:* Employees need to know what is expected of them at work.
- *Resource availability:* Employees should have the tools they need to do their jobs right.
- *Talent utilization:* Workers need opportunities to use their talents in their roles everyday.
- *Recognition:* Employees need to receive recognition regularly and feel cared for.
- *Communication:* Workers must receive ongoing feedback on their performance and have regularly scheduled progress discussions.
- *Bonding:* Employees need a strong bond with their coworkers.
- *Development:* Employees should have opportunities to learn and grow.

Leaders and managers play a major role in lifting engagement levels; therefore, if a company wishes to increase employee engagement, it must look closely at ways that employees are managed. The Gallup research found that when the supervisor treated the employees like bosses, engagement levels doubled and when employees were treated as partners rather than subordinates, disengagement was cut in half. So, how can you learn how to engage an employee?

At all times, but especially during a turndown in the economy, leaders must win the trust and confidence of their employees. To foster engagement, leaders would well be advised to (1) communicate, communicate, and communicate, (2) be transparent and (3) enlist supervisors. When employees are let go, the work does not diminish; it stays the same. Therefore, attention must be given to reorganizing the work structure and environment. Training and career development, coaching, and regular performance feedback must continue. Organizations need to ensure that performance ratings translate in differentiated rewards and that reward philosophies are clarified—both tangible and intangible rewards.[23] Appropriate recognition at the appropriate time is a best practice that ultimately improves the performance in any organization. A survey conducted by Gallup found that 82 percent of employees say that the recognition or praise they receive at work helps them to be more engaged and motivated to improve their performance. Also flexible work schedules are very important in helping to keep employees engaged.[24]

Using Survey Results.   A well-crafted survey can help increase employee engagement. Too often, however, managers do not know what to do with the survey results. Two things need to happen: inclusive impact planning and effective changes. Gallup has conducted extensive research on the benefits of impact planning as part of the employee engagement process It has found that when managers and work groups openly discuss and explore each item in the survey and discuss their ideas about how to improve the workplace, the company benefits. When the results are not discussed, employee engagement plummets. Generally, it is best to select two or three key items to work on over a given period of time. Brainstorm follow-up actions and complete a plan for improvement. Regular follow-up is crucial to gauging the employee's feelings on the progress toward his or her goal. Problems can occur when work teams are too small or when they are separated geographically; their survey results may not be meaningful. The managers also must know how to facilitate the planning process.[25]

Research by CLC Genesee shows that by shifting from low engagement to high engagement, discretionary effort can increase by 60 percent and employee performance can improve by up to 20 percent. Google's annual survey gathers feedback on what is working and what can be improved. The company has created a two-way dialogue called "Thank goodness it's Friday" to have active conversations and answer questions. Google involves employees in solving problems, not just in raising problems. Employees and management actively work together to solve problems and to create a culture where employees like to work. Google believes that a culture of involvement drives employee engagement and success.[26]

In another example, Douglas R. Conant, president and CEO of the Campbell Soup Company, was hired to turn around a wounded company. He believed that engagement created trust and inspiration and that inspired employees can accomplish extraordinary things. Conant was right; his strategy boosted engagement, productivity, and profitability, just as he had expected. When the employees became engaged, they got engaged in more than just their departments. They started getting engaged in the company, holding conversations with each other on how the company could move forward. The employees began to feel accountable to each other, and they did not want to let anyone down. With everyone on the same page, actions became more aligned, and the company became more effective in the marketplace. It was not an easy task and it took time to turn around the company.[27]

Defining Employee Engagement.   Employee engagement is not easily defined. It can mean different things to different people. For example, to one company, it means commitment, work ethic, and loyalty, whereas in another company, employee engagement is a combination of perceptions including satisfaction, commitment, pride, loyalty, sense of personal responsibility, and willingness to be an advocate of the organization. Another company defines engagement as "an individual sense of purpose and focused energy, evident to others in their display of personal initiative, effort and persistence that is directed toward organizational goals." A manager of organizational effectiveness states that employee engagement is the mortar that sticks together the building blocks: attract, develop, and retain employees. Therefore, it is important for managers to communicate to employees what is expected of them and how their engagement will be measured.[28]

Hiring and Retaining the Best Talent

When a professional baseball player signs a multimillion-dollar contract to play baseball with the Texas Rangers, the baseball enthusiasts note that exceptional talent now commands huge salaries. The same is true in industry, as more and more companies realize that skilled employees are in great demand and that, to attract and retain these people, new motivation packages must be developed. Unlike baseball, however, the motivational part of these packages is heavily geared to the nonfinancial side. The logic of this approach is that when people like working for an organization, they are unlikely to leave merely because they are offered more money by another organization. They like their coworkers; the job is challenging; the prerequisites (perks, for short) are extremely good; and they are happy with their work. Russell Campanello, chief people officer at Nervewire, Inc., which was acquired by Wipro Limited of Bangalore, India, put it this way: "The number-one reason why people leave their jobs is to pursue personal development—the chance to learn something new. If you want to hold on to your best people, you've got to make sure that they're learning, growing, and changing."[29] The challenge, of course, is to develop the appropriate environment for making this happen, and a growing number of firms are doing just that.

Although some companies use perks to recruit and retain top-notch workers in a competitive industry, other companies use them to reward commitment to the company. Perks vary widely among companies. They range from personal favors to recognition, which must come in a form that meets the needs of the employee—not just the needs of the company, the department, or even the supervisor. Examples of perks offered by companies are company fitness centers that remain open around the clock, basketball and racquetball courts, swimming pools, bowling alleys, saunas, hot tubs, and game rooms. When these companies recruit people, one of the first things they do is take the recruit on a tour of the firm's facilities. No one goes away unimpressed. The strategy is to show that, although employees work very hard, they are compensated with a more peaceful, relaxed environment. It is about trying to create the right atmosphere.

For example, BeFree Inc., a subsidiary of ValueClick, located in Marlborough, Massachusetts, offers a variety of cost-effective and measurable ways to attract customers and increase online sales using partner marketing and an automated merchandising assistant. The company maximizes return and eliminates waste, turning limited online marketing dollars into quality customers and sales. Some of the perks the company has provided are a popcorn machine, fresh fruit delivered twice weekly, a well-stocked ice cream freezer, a pool, and on-site auto oil changes. In addition, when someone did something that merited attention, the person received a check and an e-mail that was copied to all of his or her coworkers. The company has also sponsored monthly lunches with the chief executive, giving employees an opportunity to share ideas and discuss matters of concern.[30]

Another company, Altru Health System, through its "Worklife Center" helps employees with personal errands during the workday, such as tending to oil changes for personal vehicles, taking care of dry cleaning, and even procuring concert tickets. Phillips International, Inc., a publishing house in the Washington, D.C. area, has taken its full- and part-time employees and their families on three-day cruises.[31]

Applied Creative, Inc., a graphic design, advertising, and marketing communications agency in Scottsdale, Arizona, has created a stimulating work environment by using creative art, bright color, and open office space. The kitchen is stocked with snacks and drinks so employees can fuel their energy at any time. A satellite television provides a temporary escape, and a quiet room with a futon is provided for a quick nap.[32] Perks are important incentives, but they must be offered in a climate in which employees are comfortable.

Barbara Moses, an organizational career management expert, states that the corporate culture must reflect what employees want if the company expects to retain employees. The climate must promote a collegial work environment and the effort–reward ratio must be in line with employees' needs. Today's new employees are ambitious, and they have high expectations that they should be happy all the time and should be treated with nurturing care. They want work to be fun, want to interact with other young people, want to be provided with lots of learning opportunities, and want to be treated with sensitivity. On the other hand, older workers are more interested in doing meaningful work.[33]

Hiring practices are changing and will change even more in the next few years. Because companies will compete for the same talent, they must look beyond the old traditional ways of recruiting employees. Competencies will become more important as the search goes outside their industry. People who can articulate what they need will be the most attractive potential employees.

In addition to the examples just cited, companies can offer an array of other perks. The number of perks a company may offer will depend on several factors such as the state of the economy and the financial condition of the company. Examples of company perks are leasing BMWs for all full-time employees, offering free flying lessons, providing dry cleaning pickup and delivery, setting up hammocks in the lounge so that employees can take midday naps, providing day-care services and elder care on location, and keeping a supply of cold drinks in the break room. These perks are all designed to make the company a place where people like to work. As a senior director of human resources put it, "You have to pay people competitively, but people don't leave a

IN ACTION

HUMAN RELATIONS IN ACTION

MANAGING EFFECTIVELY WITH LESS Downsizing can be traumatic, especially on the remaining employees, who often must work longer hours with less control of what is going on around them. The remaining employees become stressed and sometimes come close to psychological exhaustion. What can organizations do to help overcome these negative effects of downsizing? Experts recommend the following steps.

Increase the value of the employees. As long as the reductions in force continue, people will be nervous and concerned that they are on the "hit list." One way of removing these fears is by eliminating work that does not contribute to overall productivity and moving these people to other jobs where they can make a substantive contribution. In many cases, this means retraining, but most people will go along with this approach as long as they can remain with the firm. At the same time, the organization is less likely to cut someone who has just been retrained for more productive work.

Communicate...communicate...communicate. During a reduction in force (RIF), the rumor mills grind out new messages at a rapid rate. To combat these rumors and put everyone at ease, it is necessary to let employees know why the company is cutting back and where these cuts are likely. If

employees realize that the company is losing money every month, they also will understand why RIFs are necessary. They are even likely to support the effort and to determine how they might help.

Give employees extra attention. Survivors of a cutback need much reassurance and support. This means telling each person why he or she is valued, letting each employee know his or her unique contributions, and discussing each employee's future with the organization. It also means keeping in touch with employees on a regular basis, giving them time to talk about their feelings and concerns, and encouraging them to be open and frank about anything that is troubling them. This concern for their well-being often results in growing trust and increased productivity.

Attend to your personal well-being. Managers are not above feeling the same concerns and fears as do their subordinates. Employees look to their managers for guidance, but they also look to them for cues regarding how they should react to situations that arise. If the manager's morale is low, the subordinates' morale will suffer. If the manager appears not to trust higher-level management, they will not trust this group either. The manager must serve as a positive role model whose behavior says, "I'm not worried about the future of this organization, and you shouldn't be either."

company because of salary. They leave because they don't like working for you; they don't enjoy the environment."[34]

Another challenge facing managers is managing with fewer employees. As the marketplace changes, companies must also change to survive. Often, this means reducing the workforce. For hints on how to effectively manage with fewer employees, read the information in the "Human Relations in Action" box.

✔ CHECK YOUR UNDERSTANDING

1. How does reimagining differ from reengineering?
2. What is an entrepreneurial spirit? How important is the entrepreneurial spirit in expanding a business into the global marketplace? Describe your own entrepreneurial spirit?
3. Describe an engaged employee. Be specific. How engaged are you as an employee? Why? Or why not?
4. How important is creating an appropriate environment to the retention of employees? Give a couple of examples.
5. How important are perks in hiring and retaining the best talent?

Review the current state of diversity in the workplace.

Meeting the Cultural Diversity Challenge

The demographics in the United States are shifting and so are the demographics in the workforce. According to the U.S. Census Bureau, the Hispanic population has accounted for nearly half the 2.8 million people added to the U.S. population from July 2004 to July 2005, more than any other group. The Hispanic/Latino group is growing five times faster than the general population. The African American group that was about equal to the Hispanics a few years ago now trails by more than 6 million. The White race accounted for less than 67 percent of the overall population in 2005, down from 70 percent in 2000. It is predicted to become the minority race sometime in this century. It is expected that by 2050, the population will increase by 80 million immigrants—two-thirds of the U.S. population increase.[35]

There is a greater range of ages in the workforce than ever before. More young people (age 25 and under) are entering the workforce, and more older people (age 65 and over) are staying on the job.[36] In addition, women, African Americans, Hispanics, and Asian Americans are entering the workforce in record numbers. The result is a major diversity challenge for companies everywhere. Among the reasons for this are the following:

- Many of today's managers are accustomed to supervising Anglo men and have limited experience leading a diverse workforce.
- Women and other nontraditional managers often are not given the necessary organizational support for developing their skills.
- Many businesses have failed to develop the talents of their nontraditional employees, thus denying both them and the enterprise an opportunity to succeed.
- Many firms have failed to examine the career and family needs of their employees and to work out plans for helping employees balance both these demands. Such concerns are particularly evident given the current status of women and minorities in today's workforce.

Women and Minorities

Women and minorities in the workforce continue to remain largely untapped resources. In an effort to change this condition and to achieve equality in the workplace, companies will need to take a number of steps. Let's examine some of these challenges.

Pay for Women.   Although some progress has been made in recent years, women are still being paid less than men. According to the July 20, 2010 Usual Weekly Earnings Summary, prepared by the U. S. Bureau of Labor Statistics, women's median weekly earnings were $672, which is 83 percent of the men's median weekly earnings of $810, among full-time wage and salary workers. Women made up only 31 percent of the highest earnings category and made up a slight majority of the lowest earnings category compared to men. The report concluded that more women than men were in the lowest earnings category, and women were underrepresented among the highest earners.[37] The industries in which women and men worked differed. Although women are more likely than men to work in professional and related occupations, they are not as well represented in the higher paying job groups within this broad category. In 2008, only 9 percent of female professionals were employed in the high-paying computer and engineering fields, compared with 45 percent of male professionals. Sixty-eight percent of professional women were more likely to work in the education and health care occupations in which pay was generally lower, compared with 29 percent of male professionals.[38]

Upper Management Positions.   Women also have a more difficult time securing management positions. For example, in 2008, women held 4.5 million positions while the men held 6.7 million positions. In the finance industry, a report from the U.S. Equal Employment Opportunity Commission (EEOC) showed that women and minorities remain underrepresented. Although women represent 48.6 percent of all officials and managers at banking and credit firms, African American women hold only 7 percent of such jobs, Hispanics hold 5 percent of such jobs, and Asians hold 4.3 percent of such jobs.[39,40] If employers in the future expect to engage women and to retain them in their workplace, they must pay closer attention to this problem and find a way to correct it.

On the other hand, before the number of women in management positions can increase, women must begin to internalize themselves as strong leaders who have the attributes to succeed in management. Countless surveys over the past decades have proven that there is very little difference between the leadership styles of successful men and women bosses. Men feel that women are roughly equal when it comes to team building, mentoring, consulting, and networking, with higher marks for supporting and rewarding. Men said they were superior to women at problem solving, inspiring, delegating, and having an impact on the people above them.[41] Women must see themselves as strong team builders, problem solvers, mentors, motivators, and relationship builders at all levels in the organization.

Harassment, Discrimination, and Retaliation.   Many women report they are subjected to harassment, discrimination, and retaliation actions. In response, a number of lawsuits have been filed in recent years, and in some cases, significant settlements have resulted. For example, in June 2001, six former and current female hourly workers and managers accused the world's largest retailer, Walmart, of systematically denying women workers equal pay and opportunities for promotion (*Dukes v. Walmart*). Finally in April 2010, a federal appeals court ruled that the gender discrimination lawsuit can go forward as a civil rights class-action case. The case is the largest such action in U.S. history, covering potentially one million women or more. It is estimated that Walmart may have to pay the women more than $1 billion in back pay alone. Walmart's defense attorney said the company plans to appeal to the U.S. Supreme Court.[42]

Every year hundreds of discrimination cases are filed with the EEOC. For many of these cases, it will take several years to settle. The cases deal with a wide array of discrimination issues, such as race, gender, national origin, religion, disability, age, pregnancy, reverse discrimination, employment practices, retaliation, and the list goes on and on. To learn more about the lawsuits, go on the Internet to www.eeoc.gov. The following cases are examples of cases filed between 2008 and 2010.[43]

1. Allied Aviation Services, Inc. paid nearly $2 million for harassment of African American and Hispanic workers who were subjected to a racially hostile work environment consisting of verbal and other abuse by their co-workers on a daily basis.
2. U-Haul Company of Mississippi paid $140,000 for discriminating on the basis of race when it hired the son of a selecting official rather than a veteran African American manager, to serve as the company's marketing company president.
3. West Front Street Foods, LLC, d/b/a/ Compare Foods settled a $30,000 lawsuit alleging that it fired a White, non-Hispanic meat cutter based on his race and national origin and replaced him with a less-qualified Hispanic employee.
4. John Wieland Homes and Neighborhoods Inc. settled a case for $378,500, alleging the company unlawfully discriminated by assigning Black sales employees to neighborhoods based on race, failing to promote African Americans or women to management, and harassing an employee who complained.
5. Professional Building Systems of North Carolina, LLC, settled its lawsuit for $118,000 and significant non-monetary relief after it identified at least 12 Black employees who had been subjected to racial harassment.
6. Worldclass Automotive, d/b/a/ Planet Ford, a North Houston new and used car dealership and service center, settled a lawsuit for subjecting a Caucasian male over age 40 to unlawful harassment based on his race, age, and sex by his African American male supervisor causing the Caucasian male to resign.

7. Spencer Reed Group, a Kansas-based national employment staffing firm settled a case for $25,000 on behalf of a White, 55-year-old former employee who allegedly was treated less favorably than younger Black colleagues and fired when she complained.

8. Starbucks in Russellville, Arkansas paid $80,000 to settle a disability discrimination lawsuit for failing to hire Chuck Hannay because of his multiple sclerosis.

9. Bobby Goldstein Productions, Inc. and Cheaters II, Ltd. paid $50,000 to settle a sexual harassment lawsuit for subjecting two female office assistants to sexually explicit remarks and unwelcome touching from the companies' owner and upper management staff for the duration of their employment.

10. Area Temps, Inc. of Greater Cleveland, Ohio, agreed to pay $650,000 to settle an employment discrimination lawsuit that alleged the temp agency violated federal law by matching workers with companies' requests for people of a certain race, age, gender and national origin and illegally profiling applicants according to their race and other demographic information using code words to describe its clients and applicants.

Retaliation complaints have increased. They now make up 30 percent of the allegations filed with the EEOC. One reason is that these claims are easier to prove in court than outright discrimination charges. For example, in 2006, a $2 million consent decree was filed against Cracker Barrel Old Country Store "after 51 employees charging racial and sexual harassment and retaliation at three restaurants claimed they were later punished with cuts in hours and undesirable shift changes and table assignments."[44] In 2009, Mountaire Farms of North Carolina Corp, a poultry processor, engaged in unlawful retaliation when it gave an African American employee an unjustifiably negative performance evaluation shortly after she filed two internal complaints with management about her White supervisor's use of racially offensive language about her and in her presence and when Mountaire discharged her two weeks after she filed an EEOC charge because of her dissatisfaction with the company's response to her discrimination complaints.[45] One thing is clear; more management training is needed.

The next wave of employment discrimination class actions appears to be cases focusing on so-called *systemic discrimination*. The EEOC defines systemic cases as "pattern or practice, policy, and/or class cases where the alleged discrimination has a broad impact on an industry, profession, company, or geographic location." In such cases, the plaintiff must prove that differential treatment is the defendant's standard operating procedure. Several cases have been settled using this approach. Walgreen Company, for example, settled a race discrimination case involving promotions and assignments for $24.4 million.[46]

Other Forms of Discrimination

Although women and minorities often face discrimination in the workplace, they are not alone. Researchers have found that personal appearance often influences the way people are treated at work. This is particularly true for those who are overweight, which has led some experts in this area to conclude "weight may now draw more open and widespread discrimination than race or gender or age."[47]

People who are overweight agree with this statement, and many of them report they often are denied jobs or are ridiculed by their coworkers. These individuals are more likely to make less money than their counterparts. In fact, one study by Mark Roehling, a professor in the Department of Management, Western Michigan University, found that obese women earn 24 percent less than their thinner coworkers, and moderately obese women earn about 6 percent less. After reviewing twenty-nine studies of obese people in the workplace, Roehling found evidence for discrimination at every stage of the work

DEVELOPING DIVERSITY PROGRAMS

Many companies are developing diversity programs designed to ensure that women and other minorities are not just given equal employment opportunities but are provided with mentors and training so that their full potential can be tapped. At the same time, diversity training is given to all employees so that everyone is better able to work as a member of the organization's team. Diversity training is becoming more important as the nation's population becomes more ethnically and racially diverse. Building a diverse workforce makes good business sense. In fact, "some companies believe that having a diverse workforce facilitates their understanding of minority groups and provides a leg up on the competition when vying for market share." Here are examples of what several companies are doing.

Ryder System, Inc., a logistics, supply chain, and transportation giant, requires all thirty thousand employees to take its extensive diversity program. The program focuses on "respecting and valuing all aspects of employees' beliefs and backgrounds, not only differences of race, gender, ethnicity, and sexual orientation, but also individual talents, ideas, and experiences." Managers and supervisors go through an additional round of training "promoting skills for managing differences within heterogeneous groups and pushing employees toward quality performance." Litigation avoidance is taught using scenarios and describing behaviors that put the company at risk for lawsuits.

New York Life Insurance, the largest mutual life insurance company in the United States, focuses its extensive diversity program on recruitment and retention of minority candidates. For managers, diversity is one of the components in their performance appraisal. This is just one illustration of how serious the company is about its diversity program.

PriceWaterhouseCoopers, one of the world's largest accounting firms, sees diversity as a marketing imperative. If the company expects to win and sustain new business contracts, its diversity must reflect the diversity within their clients' organizations.

Finally, GTE Corporation, the telecommunications giant, actively pursues a diversity strategy because such a strategy is critical to its global efforts. Program items are minority recruitment, employee career advancement, training in managing and being part of a diverse workforce, and the celebration of multicultural awareness events. One of its specialized educational programs for minorities is its eighteen-month associate development program that gives "high-potential" individuals exposure to line and management positions and a chance to interview for appropriate positions within GTE. The company also regularly sponsors two-day seminars on managing diversity for all of its managers.

Source: Fay Hansen, "Tracking the Value of Diversity Programs," *Workforce Management*, April 2003, p. 31.

---

process: "selection, placement, compensation, promotion, discipline, and discharge. Overall the evidence of consistent, significant discrimination against overweight employees is sobering."[48]

Obesity is the "second leading cause of preventable death in the United States." It is a disease that affects one-third of America's adult population, causing at least 300,000 unnecessary deaths each year.[49] The number of obese people is increasing each year. Obese employees are victims of employment discrimination and are penalized for their condition despite many federal and state laws and policies.

Some of the reasons given for not hiring obese people are concerns about health insurance premiums and worries that customers will respond negatively to them. As a result, in the opinion of the company, operating costs will rise and revenues will decline. Moreover, although some obese people have argued that obesity is a disability, the courts have ruled that the Americans with Disabilities Act provides protection to them in some cases but not in others, depending on the circumstances.

What can be done to address these problems? Firms are taking a number of steps, one of which is tied to well-designed diversity training programs. One of the first things a company must do is to attract a diverse population and then provide diversity training to all its employees. Many firms also offer special diversity training to their managers. Ideas on how this can be done are described in the "Ethics and Social Responsibility in Action" box.

Generational Differences. Alison Brod, owner of a New York public relations firm, found that differences are emerging among female bosses from different generations. There are definite generation gaps between the Generation Xers (born between 1965 and 1979) and the Generation Yers (born between 1979 and 1990). Also, the baby boomers (1946 to 1964) and the Matures (born before 1945) have trouble relating to women born of the later generations. The challenge for these four generations of women is finding new ways of working together. For example, the "twenty somethings" were coddled as girls; now, they want to be coddled on the job. Some employees are less likely to work hard and put in long hours, while others expect it. Younger women often feel that older colleagues and bosses are not helpful. The reason is that older women do not feel comfortable being mentors when the younger women may get their jobs. Professor Barash conducted a study of five hundred women and found that 70 percent felt that male bosses treated them better than female bosses. Approximately 65 percent of the women over age 50 admitted they would rather mentor women in their 20s instead of women in their late 30s or 40s.[50]

Explain how awareness-based, skill-based, and integrated training programs are being used to deal with the challenge of diversity.

Diversity Training

Companies are developing diversity training programs to meet their human relations challenges in a number of ways. The focus of these programs tends to fall into three categories: making employees aware of the diversity issues, helping employees to develop skill-based approaches for dealing with such issues, and combining both awareness- and skill-based methods and objectives into an integrated approach.

Awareness-Based Diversity Training. **Awareness-based diversity training** helps participants to discover the nature and causes of diversity and helps them to understand their own assumptions and tendencies to stereotype. People typically judge the behavior of others by comparing their own cultural values to those of others. When others act differently, people may experience discomfort and anxiety. For example, researchers have found that men and women often think differently when it comes to situations, such as ethical dilemmas, that call for moral reasoning. Here are some contrasts:[51]

Women are likely to:	Men are likely to:
Respect the other person's feelings	Respect the other person's rights
Avoid being judgmental	Value the importance of being decisive
Search for a compromise	Seek a solution that is objectively fair
Rely on communication	Rely on rules
Be guided by emotion	Be guided by logic
Challenge authority	Accept authority

Awareness-based training increases employees' knowledge and sensitivity to diversity issues. Some of the specific objectives of this type of training are:

1. Providing participants with information about diversity.
2. Heightening awareness and sensitivity by uncovering hidden personal assumptions and bias.
3. Assessing participants' attitudes and values.
4. Correcting myths and stereotypes that these individuals may have.
5. Fostering an environment in which individual and group sharing of information can take place.

Awareness-based training also focuses on developing effective intercultural communication. In doing so, it works to achieve long-range goals, such as improving morale, productivity, and creativity, and contributing to the organization's competitive position. The training strives to promote feelings of unity, tolerance, and acceptance with the existing organizational culture and structure. Many different approaches are used in attaining these goals. Some programs focus on heightening diversity awareness by providing information on the cultures of the various ethnic groups in the workplace. Others are process oriented and uncover unconscious cultural assumptions and biases by using experiential exercises that help people to get in touch with their feelings about diversity.

One problem with awareness-based training programs is that they may make the participants more knowledgeable about their feelings but they do not always lead to a change in attitudes. This is why many organizations combine this approach with skill-based training.

Skill-Based Diversity Training. **Skill-based diversity training** is behavioral in nature and goes beyond consciousness-raising. It provides workers with a set of skills to enable them to deal effectively with a heterogeneous workplace setting.

Four common objectives of this type of training are:[52]

1. Gaining a better understanding of how and why culturally different team members act the way that they do.
2. Eliminating intercultural communication barriers, such as semantic difficulties and perception problems.
3. Creating facilitation skills that allow participants to mediate differences and negotiate misunderstandings.
4. Teaching participants to be more flexible and adaptable when working with others.

Some of the skills that are taught in this type of training typically are:

- *Self-awareness*—ability to recognize the assumptions one has about those who are perceived as different.
- *Clear-headedness*—ability to overcome stereotypes and rely on individual character and skills assessments when making job assignments, recommending promotions, or rendering other key decisions.
- *Openness*—willingness to share knowledge about the "rules of the game" with outsiders and to provide them with access to mentors who can help them to penetrate invisible barriers and move up in the organization.
- *Candor*—ability to engage in constructive dialogue about differences, whether they are individual, ethnic, cultural, or organizational.
- *Adaptability*—willingness to change old rules to allow the full benefits of diversity to the organization.
- *Egalitarianism*—a commitment to encourage employees to grow professionally and to participate fully in the success of the organization.

Integrated Diversity Training. **Integrated diversity training** combines both awareness- and skill-based methods and objectives. Some companies integrate their diversity training into existing training programs, such as management development, team building, and leadership training programs. This requires working with all appropriate groups within the company.

Regardless of the type, most diversity training addresses the same issues: race, gender, stereotypes, business objectives, work–family issues, age, sexual harassment, national demographics, disabilities, and sexual orientation.

Diversity training is not always successful. It takes more than requiring employees to attend classes. The program must be designed to fit the company, which starts with an assessment of the needs within the company. Some well-intentioned diversity training fails for several reasons, such as:[53]

1. The training is driven by equal employment opportunity or affirmative action.
2. The training is considered the moral thing to do.

3. Training is the only activity; appropriate interventions are not included.
4. There is management support, but no management commitment.
5. Training is "off the shelf" or "canned" and does not fit the organization.
6. Only external consultants are used.
7. Training is conducted without a needs assessment.
8. Training is only awareness based.
9. There are no internal resources after training.
10. There is no follow-up plan to training.

Diversity will continue to be a major issue for organizations; however, research indicates that many are willing to take the necessary steps to meet this challenge. More important, much of this desire is not a result of response to government mandates or social pressure. Rather, it is generated by senior management's belief that it is critical to the survival and growth of the enterprise. Such strategies certainly are going to help businesses meet this important human relations challenge. Diversity training will also play a major role in helping an enterprise become a world-class organization.

 CHECK YOUR UNDERSTANDING

1. Match the diversity training term with the statement:

Diversity Training Term	Statement
a. Awareness based	_____ Learn how to be open and to share knowledge.
b. Skill based	_____ May be included in management development.
c. Integrated	_____ Provides information about diversity.

2. As a manager responsible for diversity training, identify key factors you would include in your diversity training program. Tell why.

Identify the major pillars of world-class organizations and explain how organizations are using these pillars.

Becoming a World-Class Organization

Businesses cannot afford to stand still. They must improve their ability to deliver higher-quality goods and services at competitive prices, or they will soon cease to exist. This trend has resulted in the emergence of **world-class organizations**, enterprises that can compete effectively on a global basis. This does not mean that the organization must do business in an international setting. However, if a multinational enterprise sets up operations locally, the world-class organization must be able to compete effectively, or if it is a supplier, it must make a competitive bid to supply the multinational enterprise with the desired goods. Simply stated, businesses now use their competitive advantage to invade international markets, and local companies must meet that challenge. Just being a total quality or adaptive organization is no longer good enough. It means companies must learn how to anticipate and stay ahead of impending changes and continuously improve to maintain a competitive advantage. What do organizations need to do to become world-class organizations? There are six "pillars" that present human relations challenges.[54]

1. Customer-based focus
2. Continuous improvement
3. Flexible or virtual organizations

4. Creative human resource management
5. Egalitarian climate
6. Technological support

Customer-Based Focus

Being customer focused is the most important characteristic of a world-class organization. Although all businesses are designed to meet the needs of external and internal customers, a world-class business is the one that can deliver goods and services that the customer wants and at the time the customer needs them. A good example is Pitney Bowes, Inc., long known as an innovator in the postage meter business. Pitney has developed creative products that have made the firm indispensable to the U.S. Postal Service and to many domestic and international customers. Today, Pitney has expanded its focus from the postal business to the entire mailing business and has become a world-class organization in this niche because of its drive to go beyond serving its customers to creating new products and services for them. In doing so, Pitney has had to address important elements that support the customer-based pillar of the world-class organization, including:

1. Teaching its employees to share a single vision for customer service.
2. Redesigning its structure and jobs to better serve the customer.
3. Empowering teams to generate new ideas and approaches that result in improved customer service.
4. Designing compensation systems that reward and motivate its employees.

Continuous Improvement

World-class organizations are not content to be the best at what they do; they want to maintain their status and continue to grow. To do this, they create continuous improvement strategies that encourage employees constantly to strive to do better. The use of imagination, entrepreneurial spirit, engaged employees, and hiring and retaining the best talent are ways to create a world-class business. Another way is to implement the latest technology in the industry and to train the employees who will be using it.

World-class organizations maintain continuous improvement efforts in several ways, including:

1. Benchmarking the best-in-class companies, and copying or adapting their approaches.
2. Redesigning work processes and procedures.
3. Empowering employees to take actions that will cut through red tape and get things done faster and more efficiently.
4. Using outsourcing to purchase from vendors those goods and services that cannot be provided as efficiently in-house.
5. Developing innovation-based reward systems that encourage employees to keep up their continuous improvement efforts.

Flexible or Virtual Organizations

World-class organizations know the importance of getting things done efficiently and effectively. They do not build facilities when it is cheaper to rent them. They do not produce products that can be purchased for less from outside vendors. They do not develop a particular expertise when they can enter into a business alliance with a partner that already has such expertise. These strategies help to create what is called a **virtual**

organization. This term refers to an enterprise that lacks the facilities or the ability to produce large amounts of goods and services but acts as if this lack does not exist because it is able to compensate for it through its business arrangements with other firms. The company acts just as if it were a giant producer; hence, the term virtual.

A good example is Dell Inc., which relies on outside suppliers for just about everything that goes into its computers. Several strategies for creating flexible or virtual enterprises are to:

1. Train workers to employ multiple skills.
2. Rely heavily on cross-training and job rotation of employees.
3. Create multifunctional work teams.
4. Empower employees.
5. Use innovative approaches that reduce the time needed to deliver goods and services.

Creative Human Resource Management

Human resource management programs of world-class organizations are tailored to help employees provide state-of-the-art goods and services to customers. One way of accomplishing this goal is to teach employees to think and act creatively. Another is to help them develop empowered teams that work well together. A third is to create employee suggestion systems that encourage new ideas, which can be used by workers throughout the organization. To increase employee motivation, John Sullivan, a professor of management at San Francisco State University, suggests that a survey be used to learn what employees want. Four powerful questions that are just never asked are: What would you like more of? What would you like less of? How would you like to be managed? Why did you quit your last few jobs?[55] Identifying what motivates employees is crucial to developing a meaningful program. Education is the key to change and to success, and well-designed training programs are at the heart of these human resource management programs.

Many important factors are involved in bringing about creative human resource management. Some of these factors are:

1. Continuous training
2. Employee suggestions systems
3. Empowered teams
4. Promotion of risk takers
5. Reward systems that encourage teamwork and effort

Egalitarian Climate

Another key pillar of world-class organizations is an egalitarian climate in which everyone values the contributions of all employees and respects the people in the organization, as well as those the company services. This climate is critical in ensuring teamwork within the organization and proper response to the needs and expectations of those outside the enterprise's walls. World-class organizations promote an egalitarian climate in many ways, such as:

1. Developing open communication channels with all internal and external customers.
2. Sharing the organization's vision with everyone and ensuring their commitment to these same values and beliefs.
3. Developing an effective mentoring, coaching, and buddy system for creating the most effective employees possible.

4. Sponsoring community, wellness, and family programs.
5. Developing a code of business ethics and community citizenship and adhering strictly to these guidelines.

Technological Support

Many of the creative, innovative, and productive approaches of world-class organizations are a result of their ability to use the latest technology effectively: telecommunications networks, distributed database systems, interorganizational information systems, multimedia systems, and executive information systems. When organizations compete in the global market, where speed, information, and resilience are essential in developing a competitive edge, technological support is critical. The most important factor, of course, is not technology but the way that creative people use it. For example, American Express launched a new company, AmeriTax, which created an electronic link between the Internal Revenue Service and the tax preparation firm. Through the use of this interorganizational information system, AmeriTax not only offers tax return preparation service to its customers, but it has also developed a basis for offering a larger set of financial products and services, such as lending or borrowing billions of dollars. For the Internal Revenue Service, this system has reduced costs and improved overall accuracy. World-class organizations develop technological support in a number of ways by:

1. Offering continuous technical training to employees.
2. Modernizing all information and telecommunication systems.
3. Pushing decision making down to the lowest possible level in the organization.
4. Creating effective technology–human interfaces.
5. Encouraging information sharing so that everyone who needs the data has access to them.

A Final Word

The six pillars of world-class organizations are not new. They have been discussed throughout this book. However, by bringing them together here at the end, the objective has been to illustrate their value to organizations in the twenty-first century. Close analysis of these pillars shows how important human relations practices are to each of them. Regardless of the amount of technology needed to produce goods and services, an enterprise succeeds or fails based on its human resources, for it is the personnel who must use the organization's assets in achieving its goals. If employees are treated well and committed to the vision and objectives of the company, the business will succeed. If the employees feel they are being exploited and are not committed to the same vision and objectives as management, the business will fail. In the final analysis, it all comes down to human relations. Before we close our study of this topic, we want to look at some trends predicted for the next decade that will provide human relations managers with a variety of challenges.

 CHECK YOUR UNDERSTANDING

1. Identify the six pillars of a world-class organization.
2. Why is "customer-based focus" listed first? How do the other five pillars support the first pillar? Why does it take six pillars to create a world-class organization?

Describe several human relations challenges facing managers in the next decade.

Human Relations Challenges in the Future

After the disaster of the twin towers in New York City on September 11, 2001, businesses began to implement prevention and protection programs to cover their employees, customers, and operations. For many companies, their way of doing business changed. Focusing closer on business operations resulted in finding fraudulent operations caused by executives in the firm. For example, on Wall Street, a parade of corporate scandals put executives in handcuffs and led companies to restate billions of dollars on their balance sheets. A succession of bankruptcy cases made history. The downfall of Enron was just the beginning of uncovering many business scandals involving CEO greed, fraud, and creative accounting practices used to inflate earnings that misled shareholders.[56] Greed, however, continued to grow until the collapse of the housing market, financial markets, and automobile industry in late 2007 and 2008, causing a recession, which forced many businesses to drastically reduce their operations or close their doors resulting in people losing their jobs. To survive this aftermath, companies were forced to change the way they do business. For many companies, technology perpetuated the change, affecting decision making and how things get done. However, at the heart of this change is human relations management.

Tomorrow's leaders will face greater challenges in moving their companies forward in a rapidly evolving world. Leaders will experience a pace and volume of change unseen by their predecessors, and they will need the benefits of training and the tools of their trade. With walls crumbling around the world, leaders will need to appreciate and "to manage diversity in thought, language and cultural experience."[57] Leaders will need to embrace ethics and social responsibility, and to practice ethical business behavior internally and externally. Tunnel vision must be replaced with a broader way of thinking.

More powerful computers, for example, will build incredibly complex physical and biological phenomena that in turn will enable us to build nano-structures, bio-inspired machines, and medicines heretofore unthinkable. The speed of innovation is being pushed forth, not by researchers, but by passionate people who are tinkering on other people's ideas. John Seely Brown, former chief scientist at Xerox Corporation, in an interview with a high school student stated that new and creative "innovations will impact every aspect of how we live, work and play."[58] After all, where do new ideas come from? They come from rethinking, readjusting, integrating, and combining old ideas.

If the innovation agenda is to be filled in the United States, there must be an increase in the number of science, math, engineering, and information technology workers. This means more incentives must be granted to entice students to study in these fields and seek degrees. The National Association of Manufacturers released a study indicating that 80 percent of the employers surveyed were experiencing a shortage of qualified workers. According to 74 percent of the respondents, the most important factor determining business success will be a "high-performance workforce."[59]

Businesses continually face new trends in their business operations. The managers who are cognizant of these trends will make better decisions. The following list was compiled by forward-thinkers and trend-spotters, who make it their business to look into the future. These trends may serve to inform and intrigue all of us who manage people.[60]

1. ***Communication tools***. E-mail, cell phones, smart phones, Facebook, Twitter, and YouTube, for example, are changing how many firms do business. As more information-management and collaboration tools emerge, new capabilities will be added to make the job easier and faster.
2. ***Organized labor***. Despite declining membership and overwhelming odds, labor unions are not in danger of dying anytime soon. During the decade from 2000 to

2010, the vast majority of growth in union membership was among women, Latinos, and part-time employees. Future union membership movements are projected to attract the next generation of working women and younger workers.

3. *Business goes to kindergarten.* All signs indicate that corporate involvement in public schools—already redefining education in kindergarten through high school—will continue to increase over the next decade.

4. *Going Euro.* As American companies engage in more multinational activities, they may need to reverse their policies on workplace privacy and increasingly look to Europe as the standard. For example, in Europe, snooping at employees' e-mail is not only considered bad form, but is often flat-out illegal.

5. *Companies will not sleep.* In a quest to reach new customers in foreign time zones and to speed up production and services, many more companies in the future will be open for business around the clock, seven days a week The migration to a 24/7 workplace makes human resources managers' jobs far more complex.

6. *Artificial intelligence (AI).* As the Web and data warehouses grow, AI will solve problems that are beyond the reach of the human brain. The use of robots will become more widespread in businesses. AI's strength is that it can uncover patterns and spot problems amid a mountain of data.

7. *The simmering malaise.* Employers who ignore workplace discontent run the risk of periodic productivity slumps as skilled staffers depart for higher-paying positions whenever the labor market surges. Smart companies that make employees feel valued will gain a crucial competitive edge.

8. *Office design.* Human resource managers will be more actively involved in the design process. There is an office movement toward more shared workspace coupled with private desk areas. This promotes a more collaborative work environment.

9. **Defined benefit plans**. Attracting the best and brightest employees in the future will become nearly impossible without a defined benefit plan. Companies will have to offer retirement plans that provide a floor level of retirement income.

10. *Telework.* Telework will continue to be common in many more businesses. As communication technologies advance, the number of employees working from home will increase. Since some people need to stay connected, there will still be a central location where people come to work. Managing a dispersed workforce takes special managerial skills.

11. *Consumer-driven health care reigns.* The Internet and a push for greater openness about corporate finances will allow employees to see exactly what health care will cost them and the employees will be able to make comparisons to other plans. The critical pieces for the success of consumer-driven programs are "education, advocacy, and assistance." Time will determine how Obama's Federal Health Care and Education Reconciliation Act of 2010 will impact businesses.

12. *Child care.* Access to quality child care will continue to be a major issue for working moms and their employers. It is expected that a number of companies will offer backup-care arrangements that employees can use in the event of emergencies. Employees often are willing to pay a fee for the care, so all the company may have to provide is the space.

13. *Help wanted.* Declining birth rates and the decrease in the number of jobs will put pressure on baby boomers to remain in the workplace. Older workers will fill positions on a contract basis and the permanent part-time workforce created by the economic downturn during 2008–2010 will continue. This problem will be aggravated by the shortage of skilled, educated workers already occurring in manufacturing, health care, and various technical fields.

14. *Outsourcing.* Double-digit growth is expected in the multibillion-dollar outsourcing market, dramatically gobbling up traditional human resources tasks and significantly altering people management. Growing even faster will be the one-stop shopping market, where companies bundle different human resources management services into one large contract rather than serving it up piecemeal.

15. *Recruiting older workers.* With the graying of the workforce, American business is going to have to pay attention to what older workers want and how to recruit them. Companies must use terminology that better reflects age diversity, such as "experienced workers" and "age-diverse." Older employees work not only for money but also for enjoyment and a sense of purpose. They want time off and flexible schedules, health care benefits, insurance, and good pension benefits.

16. *Mergers.* In the coming years, people management will play a far more pivotal role in corporate mergers. One of the principal reasons mergers and acquisitions have failed in the past is that workforce management is not brought into negotiations until the deal is consummated.

17. *Freelancers and consultants.* The corporate workplace will evolve into a continually shifting mix of employees and freelancers, to the point where it will become difficult to distinguish one from the other. This may lead to profound changes in health care, retention, and career development and an increased freedom to move in and out of corporate positions.

18. *Pay for wellness performance.* Instead of waiting to pay for the treatment of sick employees, more and more employers will turn to the concept of wellness management. Employees are given financial incentives to participate, such as lower insurance premiums.

19. *Spirituality at work.* Americans eat too much and spend too much money. They are obese and in debt and worried about personal safety and job security—especially since 9/11 and the economic downturn. These are some of the reasons that they are increasingly looking for spiritual comfort. The biggest change in the workplace is the interest in spirituality. It is about doing the right thing. It is not about religion. It is about job satisfaction. Jobs in the future will have to be meaningful. Pay will not be as important as a good job.

20. *Women at work.* With steeply mounting numbers of educated women, glass ceilings are going to shatter in the coming years. More women than men are receiving four-year degrees. More women will be moving into management jobs, and more men will move into women's jobs such as nursing and teaching. The line between men's and women's work will blur and fade.

21. *Skills shortage.* A job-skills shortage is already a reality in the manufacturing industry and is likely to spread to other industries over the next ten to fifteen years as baby boomers retire. Well-trained workers will be needed in information technology and the global energy and electrical utility industries. Shortages are expected in the global competition for managers, engineers, technicians, skilled craftspeople, and frontline workers, mostly jobs requiring a college degree or technical education.

22. *Security versus privacy.* As technology becomes more sophisticated, the ability of those who administer company—and government—computer networks to monitor the comings and goings of workers will grow exponentially. In the future, the cat-and-mouse war between businesses and crooks will lead to more sophisticated surveillance, the standard use of data encryption, and sophisticated data mining techniques that spot potential problems and risks by analyzing patterns. The threat of terrorism is raising the stakes. We are living in a new era.

23. *Accounting for people.* More information will be printed in corporate publications about a company's most important assets—its people. More statistics will be printed

on turnover, absenteeism, and revenue per employee. The basis for competition in the twenty-first century is a person's ability to think through complex problems, serve the customers better, and be more creative. Wall Street analysts will want to see what corporations know about the people who are winning patents for the company and closing big deals.

24. *Universal health care.* As costs soar and the number of uninsured Americans—both employed and unemployed—rapidly expands, there are many predictions about where health care is headed. Some dramatic change is likely. The Federal Health Care Law of 2010 moved the country toward a system of universal health care, and it will change how the health care system works in the United States. Will medical costs be contained or will they soar? How it will work is yet to be determined.

25. *The end of HR as we know it.* Conventional wisdom says that human resources finally has achieved its sought-after seat at the table. But the ability of human resources to add value at a strategic level "is currently more promising than reality." Today's managers are still most comfortable with traditional human resources activities. Human resources must reinvent its self. The old approaches and models are not good enough.

Ethical Trends for the Future

Business and personal ethics have gone by the wayside over the past decade. Almost daily, the news reports fraud, cheating, and misconduct in all kinds of businesses and among people doing all kinds of work. Stephen M. Paskoff has devised a list of what he believes to be trends that organizations will be unfolding in and around their workplaces during 2010. Leader misconduct will become more public as employees publicize the actions of their leaders. Claims based on the Fair Labor Standards Act will grow and expand to include those who are not paid overtime, such as salaried associates. Unions will once again be on the increase. The Internet and social media will be used more extensively than before to track references and to find out about applicants. Learning will be differentiated from training with reinforcement going beyond the classroom or desktop. Of those in their 20s, many will start their own businesses, while others will seek stability in employment. An emphasis will be placed on seeking candidates who are analytical and have creative skills, as well as an ability to learn, to absorb new concepts and to think abstractly. Jurors will be sympathetic to virtually all claims of discrimination. And there will be a renewed focus on values such as integrity, replacing the "greed is good" mentality that was prevalent in many organizations over the past years.[61]

Workplace Changes Impact Human Relations Management

As the workplace changes, it will bring new issues before human relations managers, which are discussed in the following paragraphs.

Identity Management (IM). Identity management (IM), "the integrated set of processes, services, and architectures that provide secure and appropriate access to organization system assets," is growing in importance as security issues and risks get bigger and the challenges get more acute. Companies have a responsibility to protect their employees' identities, as well as the identities of their customers, lenders, vendors, and suppliers. As laptops, storing very sensitive information, are taken around the country from office to home to appointments across the country and back again, opportunities for theft grows. Breaking into a company's database can put many people and businesses in jeopardy. For example, when a laptop was stolen from the car of a Blue Cross and Blue Shield Association employee, the American Medical Association sent out a warning to physicians across the country about the possibility that their identities could be stolen. As technology advances, companies must be cognizant about security issues. All employees must be trained in what Mike Saylor, national security services director for Accretive Solutions, calls "security awareness." Employees should be trained in how to continually and proactively be on the lookout for attempts to steal information, whether it is by an outsider or by a coworker.[62]

Currently, another area of identity management that impacts the hiring process is that of showing empirical evidence for criminal screening. Workplace homicides and inflated vendor claims paint a dramatic picture of workforce criminality and criminal screening as an effective risk-reduction practice, but when the EEOC demands empirical evidence, companies have no empirical evidence to back up the statement. Criminal records and credit checks seem to carry more weight than direct job-related employment reference checks and skills evaluations. There is no evidence that criminal screening reduces theft or fraud. The growing trend is to require criminal screening for specific jobs, such as caregiver positions, and restrict screening in all others. This topic certainly will receive more attention in the next few years.[63]

Green Technology.   Many businesses are using green technology to reduce their carbon footprint and to minimize waste. "The field of "green technology" encompasses a continuously evolving group of methods and materials, from techniques for generating energy to nontoxic cleaning products." What does this mean for businesses? Companies must find ways to meet customers' needs without depleting our natural resources, create products that can be reclaimed or reused, reduce waste and pollution by changing patterns of production and consumption, and use innovation to develop alternatives to technologies that have demonstrated a damage to health and the environment. As green technology gains acceptance, it brings forth a whole set of new challenges for management and human relations issues.[64]

Office buildings, warehouses, and distribution centers are taking on a luxurious look, using more and more green technology. Green building encompasses everything from the choice of building materials to where a business is located. California has become the first state to establish a green building code called *CalGreen Code*, which stands for California Green Building Standards Code. The code will become mandatory on January 1, 2011. It will essentially revolutionize the way buildings are built. Green buildings soon will be the standard.[65]

Video Cameras and Privacy.   Employee monitoring is nothing new, and big brother will continue to watch. Many companies use surveillance cameras, Webcams, and closed-circuit TVs to monitor employees. These practices call for well-documented policies to be established and shared among the employees. Cameras placed in wrong locations are grounds for lawsuits, such as bathrooms or areas where employees change clothes. More and more people in the next decade will be carrying camera phones that will record activities and events as they occur. Video cameras already are recording activities in many places—retail stores, offices, manufacturing plants, street corners, police cars, and workplaces to name a few. Issues of protecting employee privacy will demand greater attention along with the need to prevent workplace violence. These activities all involve human relations management.

Cost-cutting Labor Practices.   In tight markets, such as during the last recession, employers find job seekers willing to accept lower salaries. Businesses make common cost-saving moves by swapping expensive labor with lower-paid workers. The position is not eliminated, but rather the higher-paid person in the position is eliminated. Deciding which employees to keep and which to discard involves human relations decisions that impact all employees in the company.[66]

 CHECK YOUR UNDERSTANDING

1. Select five trends that will make the greatest difference in the way business is done in the next ten years. Tell why you selected them.
2. How are changes in the world impacting the workplace? Describe changes you have seen in the workplace in the last three to five years.

Impact of Global Events.   Major events in the world can change the way business is done. For example, when Walmart was unable to send buyers to China because of an outbreak of Severe Acute Respiratory Syndrome (SARS), it had to come up with an emergency alternative to product-development trips. Buyers accustomed to doing business face-to-face on Asian soil had to improvise.[67]

Opportunities for Older Employees.   Another human relations issue concerns the lack of opportunities for advancement for managers in their 40s and 50s. These managers feel underutilized and are stuck in jobs they have mastered. The challenge is to find ways to motivate these workers.

Impact of Technology.   As technology grows, so do the opportunities to slack off at the office. Davis Wiskus, a Denver tech-support worker, "installed a program on his hand-held Handspring Visor that allowed him to manipulate the screen on his office computer from a booth at a local diner." New options and strategies allow diehard slackers to crack into program settings to make themselves appear perpetually available. Wiskus was eventually fired for habitual lateness.[68] Technology has allowed business to eliminate human contact. As more self-serve devices are added, what will it mean for human relations management? The travel industry, struggling for cost-cutting measures, is in the forefront of eliminating human contact. For example, you can book a plane ticket on the Internet, print your e-ticket, take a shuttle to the car lot, pick your vehicle, swipe your membership card and drive off, and then use a self-service machine at the hotel to check in and out faster.[69]

Collaboration Between Employees—Young and Old.   Fostering interaction between the younger and older workforces within a company is a necessary step in preparing younger workers for senior leadership roles while preserving valuable institutional memory," said Tom Silveri, ex-CEO , Drake Beam Morin. In a survey of human resource professionals, 40 percent felt their companies were unsuccessful in encouraging the collaboration of younger and older generations in the workplace. Some strategies that organizations should consider are:

- Educating employees of different age groups on what each contributes to the work environment and organizational goals.
- Motivating older workers to continue acquiring new skills.
- Enabling workers of all ages to recognize their transferable skills and to seek opportunities within the organization before taking their experience and knowledge elsewhere.
- Implementing a corporate mentoring program.
- Equipping employees of all ages to network across generations, forming connections internally and externally.[70]

As you can see, the job of human relations management is an ever-changing process that brings with it a multitude of challenges. Hence, we close our study of this topic as we opened it—by defining human relations, the process by which management and workers interact and attain their objectives.

Explore the possibilities of switching careers.

Career Advisor

Consider Career Switching

People switch careers for many reasons. Today, switching a career is not viewed as a negative thing as in years past. Often, it provides the path toward greater success. In most cases, people switch careers because they have not been as successful as they would like and they are looking for better opportunities.

Common examples are:

1. People who have been passed over for a promotion.
2. Those who believe their organization is falling behind the competition and who want to work for an industry leader.
3. Individuals who are being moved onto a career track that will not get them to their long-range goals.

Most people who switch careers do so because *there is no alternative*. A sales analyst who has been laid off because of cutbacks in the industry—especially during times of economy slowdown—may conclude that the only way to salvage a career is to change jobs and become a salesperson. A stockbroker who is laid off may look for a job in a bank or a real estate firm. Notice that in both of these illustrations, the individual is seeking new employment in a related field. This is the easiest, and often-times wisest, approach, because the person is entering an arena of which he or she has some knowledge or indirect experience. Businesspeople who decide to change careers often take jobs in business colleges, teaching subjects that they know firsthand.

A second common career switch is to *go into business for oneself*. Becoming self-employed has occurred with increasing frequency in recent years as middle- and upper-level managers have concluded that it is more profitable to break away from their large firms and set up their own operations. Many of these managers have been carrying out all the important functions needed to run a competitive company, so breaking away to start a new venture is not a high-risk decision. Similarly, many salespeople have found that by leaving their firms, they are able to take some of their customers with them and build successful businesses from this initial base.

A third common career switch is to *move to a job in an unrelated field*. This can be a risky decision, but for many people, it is the only available choice. A mechanic who dislikes his work may be willing to try a job as a salesperson for an insurance company. A social worker who dislikes the bureaucracy may be willing to start anew as a bank teller. Every year, millions of people begin new careers.

The important point to remember about career switching is that it typically requires additional training and education. This is particularly true when one is changing to an unrelated field. Not only is it necessary to learn new procedures and policies but also many jobs require the individual to know how to operate machinery and to learn how to interact effectively with customers and clients. As hiring practices change, just remember that after periods of economy slowdown and layoffs, companies try to upgrade their workforces by being very selective and bringing on better people. They want the

A-players, people who can add value to an organization. "You have to be ready to work 20% longer and 20% harder," says Tom Johnson, founding partner of executive search firm, WorldBridge Partners in Cleveland.[71]

Career Shift versus a Career Switch

Too often when a person says, "I'm sick of my job," "I want to do something different," or "I can't stand doing what I'm doing any more," it is not the job, but the pressures that surround the job, such as the need to increase revenue, the long required work hours, or the short turnaround times, or it could be the environment in which the person works or the people with whom he or she works. Barbara Moses, an international speaker and a work/life expert, advocates doing a self-assessment to find out the problems and what factors are the most bothersome. Does it involve the job itself, the environment, or the people? Sometimes it makes more sense to make a career shift rather than a career switch. Career shift means reconfiguring skills and knowledge and applying them in new ways. Always "evaluate the opportunity cost of your move, such as the cost of education and lost income, as well as the feasibility of putting your new skills to work in the face of younger competition. Be realistic about your prospects of success."[72]

In her work as a consultant, Barbara Moses has heard an array of reasons why people fail to quit their job when they are no longer satisfied. They like the idea of switching careers, but never do anything about it. In fact, most people cling to their jobs much too long. If you are in that position, it is time to start reappraising yourself. Some of the beliefs people come up with that get in the way of making a change are:

1. I can't afford to quit.
2. The economy is too risky.
3. I'll never find other work at this level.
4. I can turn this situation around.
5. Things will change.
6. My job is not really so bad.
7. Nobody else will hire me.
8. My partner says the timing isn't good.
9. I won't find something better, and I will look like an idiot.
10. It's not fair.
11. Nothing else interests me.
12. I'll become a nobody.
13. I'm afraid.

As you can see, the items on the list are negative statements and will do nothing to encourage you to take the necessary steps toward making a career shift or career switch. To be successful, you must rely on positive statements, not negative ones. This list, however, can be used as a checkoff list to find out where you are with your beliefs.[73]

Helpful Hints in Making a Successful Career Switch

Asset-Based Thinking.   We have all heard about positive thinkers and negative thinkers, but have you ever heard of an asset-based thinker? If you are thinking about switching careers, you may want to learn more about this concept. It can make you a more valuable employee. Kathryn Cramer, in her recently released book, *Change the Way You See Everything through Asset-Based Thinking*, states that asset-based thinkers see opportunities rather than problems, see strengths more than weaknesses, and focus on what is right rather than what is wrong. "When you increase your focus on what is right, not what is wrong, you build enthusiasm, energy, and strengthen relationships and move people and productivity to the next level. Asset-based thinking is a special way of viewing and interacting with everyday life." In the workplace, **asset-based thinking** includes personal assets, relationship assets, and situational assets. It starts with your own personal assets—purpose, passion, courage, confidence, integrity, analytical skills, emotional intelligence, ethics, and so on. *Relationship assets* cover compassion, empathy, mutual trust and respect, commitment to the welfare and growth of others, skills collaboration, and giving and receiving feedback. *Situational assets* are challenges that promote breakthrough solutions, setbacks that lead to new standards of performance, mistakes that offer new insights and learning, and opportunities that ignite innovation mastery and advancement. By improving your skills in these areas, you become an asset to the company, not a liability, and have a greater chance for success in your career.[74]

Sabbaticals.   Sabbaticals are attracting greater attention. It is a time to "stop-out" doing your present job, especially if you are working long hours day after day or working two or more jobs. About 16 percent of U.S. employers offer unpaid sabbaticals, and about 4 percent offer paid ones. Sometimes, it takes months to prepare to temporarily abandon a stressful job and have meaningful experiences away from the job. It takes courage and thoughtful planning to have a successful sabbatical, which also offers an excellent opportunity to explore new careers.[75]

Résumé Padding.   A form of "impression management" is one way to look better in someone else's eyes by inflating your educational credentials on your résumé. A significant number of applicants include fibs on their résumés. For example, ResumeDoctor.com, a résumé-writing business, found that 43 percent of one thousand resumes in a six-month period contained "significant inaccuracies." Companies find that a "falsified résumé can indicate a deeply rooted inclination toward unethical behavior." Companies are wising up and now approximately 96 percent of businesses conduct background checks. Employers are even conducting background checks on employees who are being considered for promotion. A word to the wise: Do not tell fibs on your résumé. Sometimes, it is more difficult to switch careers than get a job in your present field; therefore, you want to approach the process with all the integrity you can.[76]

Greener Grass on the Other Side.   You receive an offer from an outside company. What do you do now? Is the grass greener over there? Or do you negotiate with your current boss for more money or better benefits? This is a situation you may face in the future. "For most employees, this sounds like a dream scenario," but it can have its risks. If you take the "make-me-an-offer-I-can't-refuse" route, you should first consider the consequences. Career experts recommend giving your boss ammunition that will help him or her sell the improved compensation package to higher management. Spell out your value—contributions—to the company and why it would make sense to keep you. Be specific and clear by identifying two or three things you plan to work on in the next six months that will add to the bottom line of the company. It is important to let your boss know why you are seeking a counteroffer. If you stay, you do not want to be viewed with suspicion or your loyalty to the company be questioned. If a counteroffer is extended, do not rush to accept it. You should think about it before accepting. Usually, money is not the only reason for seeking another job. It is wise to think about the intangible qualities that make one employer more attractive than the other.[77]

Don't Burn Bridges.   Regardless of why you leave a job in one company for a job in another company, it is important not to burn any bridges when you leave. Use integrity and honesty in explaining your reasons for leaving. Always leave a company in good favor and under good terms. If you don't, it may come back to haunt you, especially if in the future you want, or need, to return and work for the company. More and more companies are creating Web sites where ex-employees can share leads and remain within reach. Keeping in touch with your knowledge may be the key to an opportunity for a future position with that same company.

One Recruiter or Two.   Many companies rely on executive recruiters to find management talent and to negotiate job offers; therefore, if you plan to work in upper management, it would be beneficial to start building relationships with several executive recruiters early in your career. Kimberly Bishop, senior client partner in the New York office of Korn/Ferry International, suggests that you start online. Another place to look is at your own professional network.[78] On the other hand, is it beneficial to talk with two recruiters about the same job? In some situations, this may be fine, but when an employer receives your résumé from two different recruiters, what kind of impression will you make on the employer? If you are hired, would the company need to pay both recruiters? How will the recruiters feel when they find out? You may have destroyed your relationship with the recruiters. Furthermore, "What would working for two recruiters simultaneously say about your character and honesty?" Needleman says that you could be labeled a serial networker, giving the appearance that you are approaching your search in a frenzied way. It is best to be honest up front because honesty is the best policy. Employers are becoming more critical and demanding greater integrity in the people they are hiring.[79]

Talking Too Much.   According to a survey conducted by Korn/Ferry International, a global executive search firm based in Los Angeles, 36 percent of the recruiters said the most common mistake job applicants make is talking too much. Talking too much is a signal for not listening very well. You will do yourself a service by listening more than you talk. When you talk, say something meaningful on the point being discussed. Employers are more interested in your skills than in how good you feel you are. Your answers should not sound too rehearsed. An additional question could throw you off guard letting the interviewer know what you are doing. Learning about the company prior to the interview will help prepare you for the interview.[80]

Follow-Up.   Follow-up is important whether it is to the potential employers, interviewers, or recruiters. In fact, failing to follow up on what you said you would do, such as providing additional information, is a common turnoff and could be the reason you are not hired. Following up is a common courtesy. Follow up every interview, and send a note thanking the interviewer for his or her time. If you are interested in the job, say that you look forward to hearing from them. Employers remember those who show common politeness. It is an indicator of how you would treat their customers.

 CHECK YOUR UNDERSTANDING

In your career journal, outline the key points for making a successful career switch.

Summary

1 Describe the characteristics of creative people.

The twenty-first century is bringing to light a number of important human relations challenges. One is a greater focus on innovation. Companies often fail because of their attitude toward innovation. Innovation is a philosophy that needs commitment from top management to succeed. Innovation involves thinking creatively. Most people are more creative than they believe themselves to be, and creativity is widespread in the population. Some characteristics of creative people are: they are bright, have a youthful curiosity throughout their lives, are open and responsive to feelings and emotions, have a positive self-image, have the ability to tolerate isolation, are nonconformists, enjoy finding imaginative solutions to problems, and are persistent.

2 Explain how creativity in an organization setting can be both encouraged and nurtured.

To encourage creativity, organizations must debunk some of the myths about innovations, such as innovation is planned and predictable, innovation is the result of exaggerated daydreaming, innovation is the result of carefully drawn technical specifications, large projects produce more innovative results than do small ones, and technology is the driving force behind innovation and success. They also must implement innovation principles, such as promoting the active search for new ideas, encouraging people to learn from their failures, and rewarding those who are most innovative. The future belongs to the best ideas, not the best products, and to lead the world, we have to have the greatest per-person creativity.

Many organizations are working to ensure that their own human relations programs are innovative. These organizations are more likely to invest in training and development. They provide remedial education and basic skills training. Additionally, these firms redesign the workplace, launch employee involvement programs, and implement total quality management tools and techniques. Three factors that affect human relations innovativeness are customers, new technologies, and changes in the demographics of the workforce. Attention to these factors can provide a competitive advantage.

3 Discuss some of the reasons the nature of work is changing and the role that imagination, entrepreneurial spirit, engaged employees, and hiring practices are playing in this process.

Technology and global competition are changing how we work and do business, creating major human relations challenges for companies. A few years ago, the answer seemed to lie in reengineering—a complete redo of the process from the ground up. Redesigning workplaces and restructuring how work gets done today require more than reengineering; they require imagination and an entrepreneurial spirit—a venturesome, pioneer spirit that allows a person to think outside the box. People with these characteristics do not like to be locked into a job. They take ownership and follow through to completion. Ideas must be supported and communicated, or they die. Greater imagination is needed in the future for businesses to survive in a global marketplace.

Today, employees want to do meaningful or intellectually stimulating work in a pleasant environment where efforts are recognized, while still allowing time for a life. This requires employees to engage in their work. Engaged workers are more productive, positive, profitable, safer, and stay longer with the company. Employee development, retraining, and work–life balance are important factors that have an effect on the level of employee engagement. Leaders and managers are key factors in increasing engagement levels. Companies in the future must look at the ways their managers manage and how they facilitate the process. To foster employee engagement, certain employee needs must be met such as: the employees should know what is expected of them, resources and tools must be provided to do the job right, employees need opportunities to use their talents in their roles every day, employees need to receive recognition regularly, workers must receive ongoing feedback on their performance, employees need a strong bond with coworkers, and employees should have an opportunity to learn and grow.

Companies must hire the best people to fill their required positions and must use incentives to retain employees. Perks can be used to recruit employees, as well as to reward them for quality work. Companies provide a wide array of incentives, ranging from simple recognition to elaborate cruises. Most important, for employees to remain, they must have opportunities to learn, grow, and change. The real challenge is to create an appropriate environment for making this happen. Hiring practices are changing and they are expected to change even more in the next decade. The greatest challenge will be managing with fewer employees.

4 Review the current state of diversity in the workplace.

As the number of women and other minorities in the workforce increases and the range of ages in the workforce widens, businesses will have to learn how to adapt to the needs of these individuals. At present, a great deal of discrimination against women and minorities still exists. To tap the full potential of the workforce, businesses must make major changes in the way that people are managed and led. Cases continue to be filed for gender, unequal pay, and sexual discrimination in the workplace. Larger and larger settlements are occurring. Obesity is another form of discrimination. It occurs in every stage of the work process: selection, placement, compensation, promotion, discipline, and discharge. One reason for not hiring obese people is the concern over health insurance premiums. Today, companies are beginning to address these issues in diversity training programs. As people become more sensitive to discrimination issues, tomorrow's managers must more than ever continue to remain cognizant of diversity issues.

5 Explain how awareness-based, skill-based, and integrated training programs are being used to deal with the challenge of diversity.

Awareness-based diversity training programs help participants to discover the nature and causes of diversity and help them to understand their own assumptions and tendencies to stereotype. They increase an employee's knowledge and sensitivity to diversity issues and focus on developing effective intercultural communication. The training strives to promote feelings of unity, tolerance, and acceptance within the existing organizational culture and structure.

Skill-based diversity training is behavioral in nature and provides participants with tools for effectively interacting in a heterogeneous work setting. It goes beyond consciousness-raising; it provides workers with a set of skills to enable them to deal effectively with workplace diversity. Some of the skills are self-awareness, clear-headedness, openness, candor, adaptability, and egalitarianism.

Integrated diversity training combines both awareness- and skill-based methods and objectives. This training is sometimes integrated into existing programs. Regardless of the type of training, it covers the same issues: race, gender, stereotypes, business objectives, work–family issues, age, sexual harassment, national demographics, disabilities, and sexual orientation.

6 Identify the major pillars of world-class organizations and explain how organizations are using these pillars.

A major challenge is that of becoming a world-class organization—or at least a sufficiently competitive organization locally to ensure the survival of the enterprise. The six pillars of a world-class organization help to ensure this: a customer-based focus, continuous improvement, the use of flexible or virtual organizations, creative human resources management strategies, development of an egalitarian climate, and proper technological support. Attention to these areas will ensure that organizations employ effective human relations, the process by which management and workers interact and attain their objectives.

Having a *customer-based focus* is the most important characteristic of a world-class organization. Employees must understand the single vision of customer service. The structure and jobs may need redesigning, teams must be empowered to generate ideas, and employees must be compensated and rewarded.

For *continuous improvement* in world-class organizations, the concepts of benchmarking, redesigning work processes and procedures, empowering employees, using outsourcing, and developing innovation-based reward systems must be used.

World-class organizations are *flexible, virtual organizations* that use partnerships and other combinations of business units. Workers are trained to employ multiple skills. Such organizations rely on cross-training, job rotation of employees, multifunctional teams, and empowerment, and use innovative approaches to reduce the time needed to deliver goods and services.

Employees in world-class organizations *think and act creatively*. Surveys can identify employee issues. Continuous training, suggestion systems, empowered teams, promotion of risk takers, and reward systems that encourage teamwork and effort are ways that human resources management tailors programs to employees.

World-class organizations develop an **e***galitarian climate* in which everyone values the contributions of all employees. They use open communication channels; share the organization's vision with everyone; use effective mentoring, coaching, and buddy systems; sponsor community, wellness, and family programs; and follow a code of business ethics.

World-class organizations *use the latest technology* effectively throughout the entire organization. They support technology efforts by offering continued training and modernizing all information and telecommunications systems, allow decision making at the lowest possible level, create effective technology–human interfaces, and encourage information sharing.

7 Describe several human relations challenges facing managers in the next decade.

Trends that will impact how business is done in the next decade include the use of e-mail and other electronically operated devices, forming new labor unions, businesses becoming involved in public schools, and privacy issues in the face of global transactions. There will be 24/7 operations, use of artificial intelligence, workplace discontent, office redesign, defined benefit plans, telework, consumer-driven health care and child care, older employees working longer and having different needs, outsourcing, using people management in mergers and acquisitions, more freelancers and consultants, pay for wellness performance, and spirituality at work—doing the right thing. In addition, there will be more women in management, skills shortage, issues of security versus privacy in a technology world, more information printed about employees in corporate publications, and universal health care, and HR as we know it today will have to reinvent itself.

Additional changes that are impacting human relations are: identity management (IM)—providing appropriate access to organization system assets, warehouse and distribution centers taking on a new luxurious look, video cameras being used everywhere—big brother watching, and high-salaried employees being replaced by lower-paid employees. Major events in the world are increasingly impacting business policies and practices in companies located around the globe. Companies must find ways to motivate older employees, where advancements are not possible. Technology not only helps conduct business faster and more efficiently but also allows employees to manipulate the system for their own pleasure.

8 *Explore the possibilities of switching careers.*

Generally, people switch careers because they have not been as successful as they would like or they want better opportunities. Some people have been overlooked for a promotion or believe their company is falling behind the competition. Others are on a career track that is going nowhere. Some people switch careers to a related field, while others switch to an unrelated field. Some go into business for themselves. Several hints for making a successful career switch are as follows: (1) Use asset-based thinking, that is, using your assets to your advantage. It is the concept of focusing on what is right, not what is the wrong way. (2) Take a sabbatical to get away from the stress. (3) Do not tell fibs on your résumé and try to look better than you are. That can come back to haunt you, maybe even cause you to lose your job. Employers are doing more background checks than ever. (4) It is not always greener on the other side of the fence. Before accepting an offer from another company, think about the reasons you want to leave the current company. (5) Regardless of the reason for leaving, use integrity in explaining your reasons. Don't burn any bridges. You may want to work for that company again. (6) It is best to work with only one recruiter at a time when seriously seeking a job. If more than one recruiter is involved, be honest with each one. (7) Listen more than talk in an interview. Talking too much can signal that you are not a good listener. Before going to the interview, do your homework by learning all you can about the company. (8) Follow up is crucial. After the interview, send a thank you note to the interviewer. Always respond in a timely manner to the people who have asked for information.

Key Terms in the Chapter

Reengineering	Reengineering involves the fundamental redesign of business processes to achieve dramatic results.
Entrepreneurial spirit	Entrepreneurial spirit is a venturesome feeling, invested interest, and ownership of an idea that operates outside the box.
Engaged employees	Engaged workers use their talents, are passionate, and have an interest in their work.
Awareness-based diversity training	Awareness-based diversity training helps participants to discover the nature and causes of diversity and to understand their own assumptions and tendencies to stereotype.
Skill-based diversity training	Skill-based diversity training is behavioral in nature and provides participants with tools for effectively interacting in a heterogeneous work setting.
Integrated diversity training	Integrated diversity training combines both awareness-based and skill-based diversity training.
World-class organization	World-class organization is a company that can compete effectively on a global basis.

Virtual organization	Virtual organization is an organization that lacks the facilities or the ability to produce large amounts of goods and services but acts like it does by using partnerships.
Asset-based thinking	Asset-based thinking starts with one's assets. It focuses on opportunities rather than problems, strengths more than weaknesses, and on what is right rather than on what is wrong.

Review and Study Questions

1. Why should companies focus more on innovation?
2. Why do innovation ideas fail?
3. What do most people believe about creative people?
4. Describe five characteristics of creative people.
5. What are some of the myths about creativity? Identify and discuss three of them.
6. Describe how organizations overcome the myths about creativity and improve innovation. Identify five useful ideas.
7. Identify three primary factors that have been found to influence human relations innovativeness. Describe each one.
8. Why is imagination becoming an important concept in businesses?
9. What is an entrepreneurial spirit? When would an organization use this approach? Give an example.
10. Describe an engaged employee. What role do engaged workers play in the bottom line of a company?
11. Identify several things that employers can do to increase an employee's engagement level.
12. What are some major challenges in retaining good employees?
13. Companies everywhere are facing a diversity challenge. What are some of the reasons for this challenge?
14. Personal appearance, particularly obesity, is becoming an issue in the workplace. How should the boss handle the topic of obesity?
15. What are the challenges facing managers in dealing with employees from different generations?
16. One of the most common forms of diversity training focuses on awareness-based objectives. How does this training work?
17. Another very common form of diversity training focuses on skill-based objectives. How does this training work?
18. What is integrated diversity training? How does it work?
19. What is a world-class organization? How do customer-based focus, continuous improvement, and creation of flexible or virtual organizations help to create a world-class organization?
20. How do creative human resource management, an egalitarian climate, and technological support help to create a world-class organization?
21. What are some things that will impact business in the future? Identify ten trends that will change the way business is done in the next decade.

22. What is identity management (IM)?

23. How will video cameras invade employee privacy?

24. Describe how employees are being treated in cost-cutting practices.

25. What are some negatives of using technology in the workplace?

26. Describe how managers can foster interaction between the younger and the older workforce.

27. What are several common reasons people switch careers?

28. What is asset-based thinking? Why is it important when switching careers?

29. How do applicants pad their résumés?

30. What do the statements "greener on the other side" and "don't burn your bridges" mean? How can they impact a career switch?

31. Why is talking too much in an interview not a good idea? What signal may it send to the interviewer?

Connecting to the Real World

How can one become a more creative thinker?

The purpose of this exercise is to show how interaction with others can result in more creative solutions than can working alone.

Procedure:

1. Examine each of the definitions or statements that follow and try to come up with two rhyming words that describe the definition. If you want to obtain more insights into how this works, review the "Time Out" box, Improving Your Creativeness, which appears in this chapter.

2. After you have finished writing down your descriptive words for each definition, ask a friend to complete the items. Compare your answers.

3. Create five new "Improving Your Creativeness" definitions and ask a friend to complete them.

4. Prepare a report summarizing your results. How creative are you?

Definitions:

1. A Super Sonic Transport (SST) has been caught in a torrential downpour: _____ _____

2. An ocular growth that prevents someone from seeing clearly: _____ _____

3. A light-red colored potable: _____ _____

4. An illegitimate business that takes cars and cuts them up for their parts: _____ _____

5. A police officer who stops all drivers who fail to obey a traffic light: _____ _____

6. An FBI agent who is secretly working for Russia: _____ _____

7. A location fifty yards outside an oasis on the equator: _____ _____

8. An auto located a great distance away: _____ _____

9. A man who badly needs a glass of water: _____ _____

10. A drop to the ground from the top of the Eiffel Tower: _____ _____

C A S E
After the Storm, What Next?

The Garrett Manufacturing Company has been in business for thirty-eight years. Much of its early success was a result of flexible manufacturing techniques that allowed the company to offer a wide array of products. As a result, Garrett became a supplier to a large number of well-known firms in the auto and computer industries.

Recently, however, the company has experienced a downturn. The company's primary customers have started giving their business to other suppliers. The primary reason is that Garrett's quality has not kept up with its competition. Once Garrett realized this, it began making dramatic changes. In particular, four strategies have been initiated in the last four months.

First, the company has completely overhauled its machinery and equipment and purchased twelve new high-tech units that can increase output by 40 percent while driving down costs by almost 50 percent. At the same time, Garrett scheduled 60 percent of its machinists for specialized training so that they can efficiently operate these new units. Now the company is completely redesigning the production area and revising work procedures and job assignments.

Second, the company has begun a diversity program for all its employees. The reason for this move is that more than 75 percent of the workforce consists of Hispanics and African Americans, although 90 percent of the managers are Anglo men. The president of the company, Ty Garrett, believes that, in order to increase productivity further, the firm must get everyone working as a team. "This means we have to learn to better understand and respect each other," he noted recently. "This is an area we have neglected until now, but I see a lot of world-class manufacturing firms moving in this direction, and I think we have to follow suit." Within the next month, Ty Garrett is offering two types of training to his people. The first program will deal with diversity awareness. The second will focus on skill-based diversity training.

The third strategy is to diversify management positions. Garrett is considering developing a managerial career ladder to promote minorities and women to management positions. A consultant has been hired to guide Garrett in this process in order to avoid discrimination or reverse discrimination issues.

The fourth strategy is to begin downsizing the company and letting go of approximately 25 percent of the workforce. The new technology and the need to be competitive are forcing the firm to cut its labor and overhead costs. Even with this reduction in staff, Garrett will be able to increase output and quality and generate a higher profit than it has in the past six years.

Ty Garrett's main concern now is implementing the strategy effectively. "I know what I'm doing is right, but I have to be careful about implementing these changes correctly," he explained to one of his senior-level managers. Feedback from two managers indicates that the workers are considering unionizing to ensure wages and job positions are not in jeopardy. Employee satisfaction with the work environment is critical. Ty Garrett would like to divert employee attention away from the need to unionize. "We've had to dig in and weather a competitive storm, and we've done that. Now we've got to take advantage of the situation and not drop the ball at the last minute."

Case Questions

1. How will redesigning the production area help the company? How can Garrett use imagination and an entrepreneurial spirit in the production area to improve quality? Be specific and give examples.
2. How can Garrett engage his employees to increase productivity and to improve the quality of products?
3. How can diversity training be of any practical value to the company? Explain.
4. Does the company need to have a stronger and more immediate approach to diversifying management at this time? Support your answer.
5. What can Garrett do to reduce the trauma that employees may be feeling as a result of the downsizing? Offer three suggestions.
6. Explain how Garrett is using the six pillars that define a world-class organization.
7. Are the strategies that Garrett is implementing enough to regain its market share and avoid the employees unionizing? Support your answer.

Time out Answers and Table Answers

Chapter 1

Human Relations in Organizations

1. **False**   Although money is certainly an important motivator, most workers place it only in the fourth or fifth position. The most commonly cited factors are recognition for a job well done, a chance to succeed, a feeling that the work is important, and an opportunity to contribute to the accomplishment of worthwhile objectives.

2. **False**   The work group with high morale will outperform the work group with moderate morale only if the first group's objectives or goals call for higher output than the second group's. If the first group sets low output goals because it is in conflict with the management, the group's output will be low.

3. **True**   Workers who do the same job, belong to the same union, or are members of the same unit are more likely to associate with one another than they are to associate with individuals who do none of these things.

4. **False**   The most efficient workers perform best when placed under moderate stress. Under high stress, their output slows because they have to adjust to job-related tension and anxiety.

5. **True**   Managers tend to use the grapevine far more than workers do in sending and receiving information.

6. **False**   Top managers tend to be more intelligent than their average-intelligence subordinates. Additionally, although personality is important, it is no substitute for intelligent problem solving and decision making.

7. **False**   Many managers do not get all their work done because they fail to establish priorities and do not delegate enough minor work to subordinates.

8. **False**   Although job-related stress increases as one goes up the hierarchy, it is greatest at the middle to upper-middle ranks. After this, it tends to decrease because the executive can delegate to subordinates many stress-creating tasks.

9. **False**   The major reason is that the organization's machinery is inefficient, the workers are not trained as well as they should be, and the rewards associated with high output are not sufficiently motivational to encourage personnel to maximize their output.

10. **True**   Research reveals that eight out of ten managerial communications are downward, whereas only one out of ten involves an upward flow of information.

Scoring — How many of your answers match the answers in the key?

9–10	Excellent. Your score is in the top 4 percent of all individuals taking this quiz.
8	Good. Your score is in the top 26 percent of all individuals taking this quiz.
7	Average. Your score is just about in the middle. Thirty-seven percent of all individuals taking this quiz received this score.
6 or less	Below average. Thirty-seven percent of all individuals taking this quiz received this score.

Regardless of your score, you should use this quiz only as an indication of the amount of general human relations knowledge you now have. You will be learning a great deal more as you read this book.

Chapter 2

What Motivates You

Remember that you gave a 10 to the most important factor and a 1 to the least important factor, so high scores indicate greater motivating potential than do low scores. With this in mind, fill in the number you assigned to each of the 10 factors and then add both columns.

Column A	Column B
_____ 1	_____ 2
_____ 4	_____ 3
_____ 6	_____ 5
_____ 8	_____ 7
_____ 10	_____ 9
_____ Total	_____ Total

If your total in Column A is higher than that in Column B, you derive more satisfaction from the psychological side of your job than from the physical side. Notice that the five factors in Column A are designed to measure how you feel about the job. These factors are internal motivators. If your score in Column A is higher than 30, you are highly motivated to succeed and achieve at your current job. Individuals who are most successful in their careers have jobs with higher psychological value than physical value. If your total in Column B is higher than that in Column A, you derive more satisfaction from the physical side of your job than from the psychological side. Notice that the five factors in Column B all relate to the environment in which you work or the pay you receive for doing this work. These factors are external, and you have limited control over them. A score of 30 or more indicates that you do not particularly care for the job, but you do like the benefits the company is giving you. Most people who have a higher total in Column B than in Column A rank good wages as one of their top two choices. If you are younger than 40, it is likely that either you will be promoted to a job with greater psychological value or you will leave the organization. If you are older than 40, you may find that your job mobility is reduced, the money is too good to pass up, and you will stay with the organization because of these financial rewards.

Answers to Table 2.2

As Ranked by	Workers	Supervisors
Job security	4	2
Full appreciation for work done	1	8
Promotion and growth with the company	7	3
Tactful disciplining	10	7
Good wages	5	1
Feeling in on things	2	10
Interesting work	6	5
Management loyalty to the workers	8	6
Good working conditions	9	4
Sympathetic under-standing of personal problems	3	9

Chapter 3

What Is Important to You?

Enter your average scores on the designated lines below.

Average Score	Interpretation
Group 1	Importance of control. This score measures your desire to take charge and control situations.
Group 2	Importance of fairness. This score measures the importance you assign to equity and fairness.
Group 3	Importance of material rewards. This score measures the extent to which you value money and other tangible rewards.

Chapter 4

What Type of Thinker Are You?

Circle your answers on the answer sheet. For example, if your first answer was an a and your second was a b, put a circle in Column I for Answer 1 and in Column II for Answer 2. Continue this for all sixteen answers and then total the number of circles you have in each column.

Answer	Column I	Column II
1.	a	b
2.	a	b
3.	b	a
4.	b	a
5.	a	b
6.	b	a
7.	a	b
8.	b	a
9.	b	a
10.	a	b
11.	a	b
12.	a	b
13.	b	a
14.	b	a
15.	b	a
16.	b	a
Total	_____	_____

Your answers in Column I indicate your preference for left-brain thinking. Your answers in Column II indicate your preference for right-brain thinking. Highly analytical people have higher scores in Column I; highly creative people have higher scores in Column II. Of course, these sixteen questions are not sufficient to determine whether you are left-brain dominant or right-brain dominant. However, they should provide you with insights regarding your preference. Most people's scores indicate they are more left-brain than right-brain dominant.

Chapter 5

The Informal Organization: Initial Appraisal

This quiz consists of two parts. Questions 1 through 7 measure your use of the informal organization. Questions 8 through 15 measure how much you really know about the informal organization.

Do you use the informal organization? The following key is for scoring your answers to Questions 1 through 7. For each answer you have that agrees with this key, give yourself a point.

1. False
2. True
3. False
4. True
5. False
6. True
7. False

The higher your score, the greater is the likelihood that you use the informal organization. However, if you have a score of 6 or 7, you must be careful that you are not simply ignoring the formal structure. A high score can indicate total disregard for organizational policies and procedures, but only you can determine this. Most effective managers have a score of at least 5 on this part of the quiz.

What do you know about the grapevine? Questions 8 through 15 are designed to measure your knowledge of the informal organization. For each answer you have that agrees with this key, give yourself a point.

8. False
9. True
10. True
11. True
12. False
13. False
14. False
15. False

If you currently know a great deal about the informal organization, your score here will be in the 6–8 range. In any event, as you read the material in this chapter, you will learn the logic behind each of the answers.

Chapter 6

Your Job and You

This quiz is designed to measure the effect that the technological surroundings of your job have on you. Keeping in mind the five possible responses to each statement, here is the way to score each:

	Highly Disagree	Disagree	Indifferent	Agree	Highly Agree
1.	−2	−1	0	1	2
2.	2	1	0	−1	−2
3.	−2	−1	0	1	2
4.	2	1	0	−1	−2
5.	2	1	0	−1	−2
6.	2	1	0	−1	−2
7.	2	1	0	−1	−2
8.	−2	−1	0	1	2
9.	−2	−1	0	1	2
10.	2	1	0	−1	−2

If you have a positive score, the impact of technology and stress on your job is not at all negative. In fact, you are doing well in beating the dysfunctional effects of technology and stress. A score of 4 or better is a very good sign. Conversely, a score of −4 or less indicates that technology and job-created stress are getting to you. A score of −7 or less is a sign that you should consider switching jobs.

Chapter 7

Is Empowerment Necessary?

If your answers are no, then either you are already empowering your employees or you aren't yet feeling the pressure to do so. If you answered yes to four or more on the checklist, you have just identified several reasons to empower your employees.

Are You an Intrapreneur?

Give yourself 1 point for each of the following answers.

1. No	8. Yes	15. No
2. Yes	9. No	16. No
3. No	10. Yes	17. Yes
4. Yes	11. Yes	18. Yes
5. Yes	12. No	19. No
6. Yes	13. No	20. Yes
7. Yes	14. Yes	

A score of 15 or more indicates that you have values and beliefs that are similar to those of successful intrapreneurs.

Chapter 8

How You View Your Work

This quiz is designed to measure the five core job dimensions discussed in the chapter. (Feedback has more questions associated with it because information on feedback from both the job itself and the personnel in the organization was obtained.) Here is how to obtain your score for each dimension: (1) Enter all six of your answers to Part A in the appropriate place on the answer sheet; (2) subtract from 8 each of your answers in Part B for numbers 1–4, 11, and 12, before entering the result in the appropriate place in the chart; and (3) enter answers in Part B for numbers 5–10 in the appropriate place. As you can see, the answers from Part B that have an asterisk were handled with reverse scoring; a low answer received a high score, and vice versa.

Skill Variety	Task Identity	Task Significance
A1. _____	A2. _____	A3. _____
B1.* _____	B6. _____	B4.* _____
B9. _____	B11.* _____	B7. _____

Autonomy	Feedback (from the job)	Feedback (from others)
A4. _____	A5. _____	A6. _____
B3.* _____	B8. _____	B2.* _____
B5. _____	B12.* _____	B10. _____

The largest total you can have for any of the foregoing job dimensions is 21 and the smallest is 3. Divide all your answers by 3 to determine your average score per job dimension. Average scores tend to be in the range of 4.3–6.0. If you score lower than 4.3, your job is low on this particular job dimension; if you score higher than 6, your job is high on this particular job dimension. If you do not like your current job, you can probably determine why this is so by examining your work from the standpoint of these job dimensions. The reverse is also true; if you like your current job, you should be able to determine why from your totals.

Chapter 9

Your Assumptions about People

This test measures your tendency to support Theory X and Theory Y beliefs. To determine your scores for each, fill in the answer sheet and then plot a graph by placing a dot at the point where your Theory X and Theory Y scores intersect.

Theory X Score	Theory Y Score
_____ (b)	_____ (a)
_____ (c)	_____ (d)
_____ (f)	_____ (e)
_____ (h)	_____ (g)
_____ (i)	_____ (j)
_____ (k)	_____ (l)
_____ (m)	_____ (n)
_____ (p)	_____ (o)
_____ (q)	_____ (r)
_____ (t)	_____ (s)

Look at the dot you have placed on the graph. Now draw a line from the origin through the dot and on outward to the end of the graph. At the end of this line, place an arrowhead. This line points the direction in which your beliefs about people move. Based on the direction of the arrow, you can determine whether you are basically a Theory X person, a Theory Y person, or a blend of the two.

Chapter 10

How Great Is Your Negotiating Ability?

Compare your answers to the self-assessment quiz to the answers that follow. For each answer that is identical to the scoring key presented here, give yourself one point.

1. Basically false	7. Basically true	13. Basically true
2. Basically false	8. Basically true	14. Basically false
3. Basically false	9. Basically false	15. Basically false
4. Basically false	10. Basically false	16. Basically true
5. Basically true	11. Basically false	
6. Basically true	12. Basically false	

Your total score, assuming your self-evaluation is correct, provides some insights regarding your ability to negotiate well. The following is a general breakdown regarding your negotiation effectiveness:

4–16	Excellent. You are a true negotiator.
11–13	Good. You have real negotiating potential.
8–10	Average. You do not see yourself as much of a negotiator.
0–7	Below average. You do not see yourself as a negotiator.

How can you improve your negotiating ability? The best way is by examining your incorrect responses and trying to change your behavior appropriately.

Chapter 11

A Matter of Inference

1. True.   The first sentence of the story says so.
2. False.   Although we are never told exactly where the firm is located, we do know that it is in New England.

3. Inference. We are never told who gave Bart the order to engage in the crash R&D program.

4. Inference. We are never told the size of Bart's budget. The $250,000 he has allowed his top R&D people to spend might be coming from a special fund created for this purpose by the president of the firm and so may not be included in his regular budget.

5. Inference. We do not know what the five people are supposed to be doing with the money. They may be working to develop a new process or they may be trying to buy the process from someone else. The story is unclear on this point.

6. Inference. We do not know that the individual to whom Mary Lou is talking is a professor. The story refers to the person as a scientist, who may not hold a professorial rank.

7. False. The story says Mary Lou is one of Bart's best people, so she is in the R&D department, not the plastics manufacturing department.

8. Inference. We do not know whether Mary Lou is one of the five people authorized to spend up to $250,000 or is a sixth member of Bart's department.

9. Inference. We do not know that the company wants to buy the patent. Even if the company does want it, it might be interested in giving the scientist stock in the firm and a position that pays about what the scientist currently is receiving but offering better fringe benefits. In short, it may want to trade for the patent, not to buy it.

10. Inference. Bart may believe this. However, he may believe the scientist is wavering and needs to be convinced by someone in higher authority who can spell out the terms of an agreement. Even this conclusion, however, is inferential.

11. Inference. We do not know why the scientist is coming with Mary Lou. Additionally, he or she may have decided not to accept any reimbursement of expenses so that there is no implied obligation to go along with the company's offer.

12. Inference. Again, we do not know for sure why the scientist is coming to see Bart. Could it be that Mary Lou has told him or her that the firm will build a special research facility far better than that at the university and that this is motivating the scientist to fly in and talk to Bart?

13. Inference. We do not know in what area the scientist received the Nobel Prize. We also do not know that the scientist is a man.

14. True. The story says Bart and the president have lunch on a biweekly basis.

15. Inference. We do not know the basis for Bart's belief that he will have good news for the president. Might it be that the president assigned Bart to another project, which is coming along so well that Bart knows that the president will be pleased?

Physical Location and Body Language

You are seated in a correct chair. Individuals seated at an angle to each other are more likely to engage in cooperative interaction than those seated either side by side or completely opposite each other. You and Person F can move closer to each other or further away, making the corner position the ideal one for the two of you.

Are You a Good Listener?

Using the scoring key given, determine the total number of points you earned for the answers that you gave.

| | Points earned for Answer | | | | | | | |
Question	A	B	C	D	E	F	G	Score
1.	7	6	5	4	3	2	1	____
2.	1	2	3	4	5	6	7	____
3.	7	6	5	4	3	2	1	____
4.	1	3	5	7	5	3	1	____
5.	7	6	5	4	3	2	1	____
6.	1	2	3	4	5	6	7	____
7.	7	6	5	4	3	2	1	____
8.	7	7	6	4	3	2	1	____
9.	7	6	5	4	3	2	1	____
10.	1	2	3	4	5	6	7	____
11.	1	2	3	4	5	6	7	____
12.	1	3	5	7	5	3	1	____
13.	7	6	5	4	3	2	1	____
14.	1	2	3	4	5	6	7	____
						Bonus point	+2	
						Grand total		

Scoring Interpretation

90–100	Excellent. You are an ideal listener.
80–89	Very good. You know a great deal about effective listening.
70–79	Good. You are an above-average listener.
60–69	Average. You are typical of most listeners.
Less than 60	Below average. You need to work on developing more effective listening habits.

Are You a Type A or Type B Person?

Add up your total points for the A statements and for the B statements.

If your total for A is:

| 80–100 | You exhibit strong Type A behavior. |
| 60–79 | You exhibit moderate Type A behavior. |

If your total for B is:

| 80–100 | You exhibit strong Type B behavior. |
| 60–79 | You exhibit moderate Type B behavior. |

Any other combination is a mixture of Type A and Type B behavior that does not exhibit a clear pattern.

Chapter 12

How Much Do You Know about the Change Process?

1. Basically false. Most changes scare people and they, at least initially, tend to dislike them.
2. Basically false. Most changes take time to be accepted so, if anything, there is an immediate decrease in productivity.
3. Basically true. Most changes scare people, as explained in number one.
4. Basically false. They would regard it with fear or concern, wondering if the machine would have them do more work or even replace them.
5. Basically true. This is usually the objective of all organizational changes.
6. Basically true. Workers tend to stick together, especially when change is involved.
7. Basically false. People resist because they are afraid of losing their jobs.
8. Basically false. Advance notice is crucial, and the greater the change, the more advance notice that should be given.
9. Basically true. Participation in the change process is one of the most effective ways of ensuring successful implementation of the change.
10. Basically false. They tend to underrate the time needed to implement change effectively and end up pushing the change too quickly. The result is resistance from the workers.
11. Either answer can be right here so take one point regardless of your response—if the change is a positive one, it often results in a short decline in work output before things turn around and vice versa.
12. Basically true. Unions usually fight change because they are afraid of the effect of the change on worker employment.

Total the number of your correct responses. How well did you do? Use the following to measure your current knowledge of the change process:

11–12	Excellent
9–10	Above average
7–8	Average
6 or fewer	Below average

Regardless of your score, you will find the answers to these questions in the chapter, so take heart and read on.

Chapter 13

Doing Business in Japan

1. Basically true, although, for some products, American quality is still regarded as superior (such as computers, telephone equipment, and commercial aircraft), and the Americans have greatly closed the quality gap in many consumer products.
2. False.   The American worker has had the highest productivity for well over a half century.

3. False.   Researchers have found that American workers tend to have higher work satisfaction than do their Japanese counterparts.

4. False.   Both groups work about equally as hard.

5. False.   Many Japanese admit that they work in an environment in which they are told what to do and in which failure to comply carries strong penalties. Democratic leadership is far less prevalent in the Japanese workplace than many people realize.

6. Partially true.   The Japanese tend to lead in areas in which applied concepts are important, but they are behind in areas in which theoretical knowledge is critical.

7. Partially true.   The Japanese provide a better basic education to their people, but at the university level, they are inferior to the United States, which is the acknowledged world leader in upper-division education. This is particularly evident given the number of Japanese students who come to the United States for university and graduate studies.

8. True.   The Japanese do an excellent job in providing their people with orientation and training.

9. True.   Japanese companies work hard at developing quality circles and cooperative company–employee teamwork, and they are very successful in their efforts.

Chapter 14

Improving Your Creativeness

1. mad dad	6. near beer
2. glad lad	7. deep weep
3. book crook	8. fast repast
4. ape cape	9. lean cuisine
5. fat cat	10. frail snail

Score Interpretation

8–10	Excellent
6–7	Above average
4–5	Average
1–3	Below average

Regardless of how well you click, remember that creativity can be improved. Individuals who like crossword puzzles or enjoy puns tend to do best on these rhyme-type tests. Your creative interests may lie in other areas, so do not be disheartened. This test is only one of many that can give you insights to your creativeness.

Notes

Chapter 1

1 Adapted from Rensis Likert, *The Human Organization* (New York: McGraw-Hill, 1967), pp. 4–10.

2 For a complete account of the program, see Alfred J. Marrow, David G. Bowers, and Stanley E. Seashore, *Management by Participation; Creating a Climate for Personal and Organizational Development* (New York: Harper & Row, 1967).

3 William F. Dowling, "At G.M.: 'System 4' Builds Performance and Profits," *Organizational Dynamics*, Winter 1975, pp. 23–28.

4 Sam Deep and Lyle Sussman, "Eight Management Principles You Can't Work Without," *Working Woman*, June 1991, pp. 61–63.

5 C. Northcote Parkinson, *Parkinson's Law* (Boston: Houghton Mifflin, 1957), p. 24.

6 Fred N. Kerlinger, *Foundations of Behavioral Research*, 2nd ed. (New York: Holt, Rinehart and Winston, 1973), p. 6.

7 For more on this, see B. F. Skinner, *Contingencies of Reinforcement* (New York: Appleton-Century-Crofts, 1969); Fred Luthans, *Organizational Behavior*, 8th ed. (New York: McGraw-Hill, 1998), Chapter 8.

8 For more information on personality and birth order, read Frank J. Sulloway, *Born to Rebel: Birth Order, Family Dynamics, and Creative Lives* (Vintage Books, Division of Random House, Inc., New York, 1997).

9 Karen E. Klein, "Younger Siblings, Better Entrepreneurs?" *Business Week Online*, June 1, 2006. For more information on personality and birth order, read Frank J. Sulloway, *Born to Rebel: Birth Order, Family Dynamics, and Creative Lives* (Vintage Books, Division of Random House, Inc., New York, 1997).

10 Michael Schrage, "Will Evolving Corporate Strategy Be Darwin-win-ian?" *Fortune*, June 21, 1999.

11 Allan Alter, "Knowledge Workers Need Better Management," *CIOInsight*, August 5, 2005.

12 To learn more about knowledge workers, read A. D. Amar's *Managing Knowledge Workers: Unleashing Innovation and Productivity*, Quorum Books, Westport, CT, 2002, Chapter 4, p. 61.

13 Louisa Wan, "Making Knowledge Stick," *Management Review*, May 1999, p. 25.

14 Amy Barrett et al., "Jack's Risky Last Act," *Business Week*, November 6, 2000, pp. 40–45.

15 Peter Coy and Jack Ewing, "Where Are All the Workers?" *Business Week*, April 9, 2007, p. 28.

16 Claudio Fernandez-Araoz, "The Coming Fight for Executive Talent," *Business Week*, December 7, 2009, p. 72.

17 Fay Hansen, "Where the Knowledge Workers Are," *Workforce Management*, July 2005.

18 Julie Forster and Ann Therese Palmer, "That's It, I'm Outta Here," *Business Week*, October 9, 2000, p. 96.

19 Mark Schoeff, Jr., "Appeal for Diversity," *Workforce Management*, July 14, 2008, p. 31–36.

20 Scott Reeves, "An Aging Workforce's Effect on U.S. Employers," *Forbes*, September 29, 2005.

21 Peter Coy, "Surprise! The Graying of the Workforce Is Better News Than You Think," *Business Week*, June 27, 2005, pp. 78–86.

22 Clare Ansberry, "Elderly Emerge as a New Class of Workers—and the Jobless," *Wall Street Journal*, February 23, 2009, p. A1.

23 "More Businesses Look at Diversity as an Obligation, Not a Choice," *HR Focus*, October 1993, p. 14.

24 See David A. Andelman, "Too Tight a Grip on Diversity," *Management Review*, June 1996, pp. 21–23.

25 Ann M. Van Eron, "How to Work with a Diversity Consultant," *Training and Development Journal*, April 1996, pp. 41–44.

26 Geresa Brady, "The Downside of Diversity," *Management Review*, June 1996, pp. 29–31.

27 Kris Maher, "More People Pushed into Part-Time Work Force," *Wall Street Journal*, March 08, 2008, p. A1, 6.

28 Peter Coy, Michelle Conlin, and Moira Herbst, "The Disposable Worker," *Bloomberg Businessweek*, January 18, 2010, pp. 33–39.

29 "Highlights of Women's Earnings in 2008," U.S. Department of Labor Statistics, July 2009, www.bls.gov.

30 Ibid.

31 Hewlett-Packard's homepage, Company Information, "Diversity & Inclusion" (accessed October 2005), www.hp.com.

32 Toddi Gutner, "The Rose-Colored Glass Ceiling," *Business Week Online*, September 2, 2002.

33 For more on the glass ceiling, see Debra E. Meyerson and Joyce K. Fletcher, "A Modest Manifesto for Shattering the Glass Ceiling," *Harvard Business Review*, January–February 2000, pp. 127–136.

34 Adrienne L. Mercer, "Breaking the Glass Ceiling: Women's Leadership Summit," University of Maryland, President's Commission for Women, March 1, 2006, www.umbc.edu/women.

35 Rhea Borja, "Breaking the Glass Ceiling," June 25, 2004, www.Washingtonpost.com.

36 "Raytheon Ranks among the Top 25 Best Places to Launch a Career," September 9, 2009; "Raytheon One of Top 50 Employees for Persons with Disabilities," January 5, 2010, www.raytheon.com.

37 "Diversity: Making All the Difference," www.xerox.com (accessed October 2005).

38 "Avon Selected as One of the Top Ten 'Best Corporate Citizens' by Business Ethics Magazine," press release, April 22, 2002, http://www.avon.com.

39 "Who's Up? And Who's Down?" *Fortune*, October 18, 2004, p. 181.

40 Linda Himelsteen and Stephanie Anderson Forest, "Breaking Through," *Business Week*, February 17, 1997, p. 66.

41 Jessica Marquez, "Workforce Management Q&A: Driving Opportunities for Women," *Workforce Management Online*, September 2008.

42 "Workplace Violence Statistics," *Workplace Management Strategies*, 2008, www.workplacevisions.com.

43 Eugene A. Rugala, "Workplace Violence: Issues in Response," monograph, FBI's National Center for the Analysis of Violent Crime, 2002.

44 Jeremy Smerd, "Yale Student's Death Cited as Case of Workplace Violence," *Workforce Management*, September 17, 2009, www.workforce.com.

45 Kelly Nolan and Veronica Dagher, "Workplace Shooting in St. Louis Leaves Four Dead," *Wall Street Journal*, January 8, 2010, p. A5.

46 "Most Accountable Companies," *Fortune*, November 24, 2008, CNNMoney.com.

47 Alex Altman, "A Brief History of: Ponzi Schemes," *Time*, January 19, 2009, p. 18.

48 Russell Gold, "Halliburton Ex-Official Pleads Guilty in Bribe Case," *Wall Street Journal*, September 4, 2008, p. A1.

49 "How to Avoid Cons That Can Lead to Identify Theft," *Wall Street Journal*, May 1, 2008, p. D1.

50 Joann S. Lublin and Kara Scannell, "Critics See some Good from Sarbanes–Oxley," *Wall Street Journal*, July 30, 2007, pp. B1, B3.

51 *Wall Street Journal*, October 17, 2005, p. R3.

52 Ibid.

53 Thomas J. Healey, "Sarbox Was the Right Medicine," *Wall Street Journal*, August 9, 2007, p. A13.

54 Diya Gullapalli, "Living with Sarbanes-Oxley," *Wall Street Journal*, October 17, 2005, p. R3.

55 Ron Crossland, "Scandalous," *Point E-Newsletter*, April 2008, www.bluepointleadership.com.

56 "The Interview," *Time*, January 6, 2003, p. 59.

57 Special Report, "The Whistle Blowers," *Business Week Online*, January 13, 2003.

58 Jennifer Devitz, "Whistleblowers are Left Dangling," *Wall Street Journal*, September 4, 2008, p. A3.

59 Q&A, "To Cure Fraud, Start at the Top," *Business Week Online*, October 18, 2002.

60 Andy Serwer, "The Decade from Hell," *Time*, December 7, 2009, pp. 30–38.

61 Adapted from Carl Pergola's interview, "To Cure Fraud, Start at the Top," *Business Week Online*, October 18, 2002.

62 William D. Hall, *Making the Right Decisions* (New York: John Wiley & Sons, 1993), p. 44.

63 Kelly Global Workforce Index, "Social Responsibility Key to Attracting Top Talent," Kelly Services, Troy, Michigan Office, October, 28, 2009, www.kellyservices.com.

64 Heesun Wee, "Corporate Ethics: Right Makes Might," *Business Week Online*, April 11, 2002, http://www. businessweek.com.

65 Full Text of President Bush's Speech at the Regent, *Wall Street Journal*, July 9, 2002.

66 Keith Naughton, "The CEO Party Is Over," *Newsweek*, January 6, 2003, p. 55.

67 Employee Code of Ethics, www.howardbank.com.

68 "Winning Through Talent in Times of Uncertainty," *SuccessFactors*, 2008, www.successfactors.com.

69 Age Bias Discrimination Case, December 11, 2002, http://www.eeoc.gov.

70 Linda Greenhouse, "Justices, in a Unanimous Decision, Make it Easier to Sue for Discrimination on the Job," *New York Times*, June 13, 2000, p. A21.

71 See, for example, Constance L. Hays, "Coca-Cola Reaches a Settlement with Some Workers in a Bias Suit," *New York Times*, June 15, 2000, section C, pp. 1, 6; Patrick McGeehan, "Morgan Stanley Is Cited for Discrimination against Women," *New York Times*, June 6, 2000, section C, pp. 1–2; and Charles Gasparino and Randall Smith, "U.S. Agency Calls Morgan Stanley Biased against Female Executive," *Wall Street Journal*, June 6, 2000, section C, pp. 1–2.

72 Jennifer Steinhauer, "If the Boss Is Out of Line, What's the Legal Boundary?" *New York Times*, March 27, 1997, pp. C1, C4.

73 Filed by Judy Greenwald, Business Insurance, News in Brief, "Vulgarity Justifies Hostile Work Environment Suit," *Workforce Management*, January 25, 2010, www.workforce.com.

74 Irwin Speizer, "Diversity on the Menu," *Workforce Management*, November 2004, pp. 41–45.

75 "Sears, Roebuck to Pay $6.2 Million for Disability Bias," September 29, 2009, www.dol.gov.

76 Tim M. Maiolo, "Are you Ready for the ADA Amendments Act of 2008?" *Workforce Management Online*, November 2008.

77 "Tim Dahle Nissan to Pay $455,000 for Sexual Harassment and Retaliation," October 29, 2009, www.dol.gov.

78 David Hancock, "Judge: Channel 10 Discriminated on the Basis of Age," *Miami Herald*, February 13, 1996, pp. 1B–2B.

79 Carey Goldberg, "Fat People Say an Intolerant World Condemns Them on First Sight," *New York Times*, November 5, 2000, p. 30Y; Wade Lambert, "Obese Workers Win On-the-Job Protection against Bias," *Wall Street Journal*, November 12, 1993, pp. B1, B7; and Tamar Lewin, "Workplace Bias Tied to Obesity Is Ruled Illegal," *New York Times*, November 24, 1993, p. A10.

80 Lucinda Harper, "Good Looks Can Mean a Pretty Penny on the Job, and 'Ugly' Men Are Affected More Than Women," *Wall Street Journal*, November 23, 1993, p. B1.

81 Antonio Regalado, Laurie McGinley, and Sarah Lueck, "Cloning Claim Spurs Ethics Debate," *Wall Street Journal*, December 30, 2002, p. A3.

82 Bernadine Healy, M.D., "To Create, or Not to Create?" *U.S. News and World Report*, March 21, 2005.

83 "Why Is Knowledge Management Important in Today's Business Climate?" Knowledge Management Library, www.about-goal-setting.com/ KM-Library1/knowledge-management-why-important.

84 "World Economic Forum Launches New 'Gender Gap Index' Measuring Inequality between Women and Men in 58 Countries," World Economic Forum, Geneva, Switzerland, May 16, 2005.

85 Daniel W. Drezner, "The Outsourcing Bogeyman," *Foreign Affairs*, May/ June 2004.

86 Arianne Cohen, "Scuttling Scut Work," *Fast Company*, February 2008, p. 43.

87 Pete Engardio and Arlene Weintraub, "Outsourcing the Drug Industry," *Business Week*, September 15, 2008, p. 49.

88 "Back in the U.S.A.," *Fortune*, September 28, 2009, p. 30.

89 "The Great Migration in Numbers," *Fast Company*, July 2000, p. 205.

90 William B. Johnston, "Global Work Force 2000: The New World Labor Market," *Harvard Business Review*, March–April 1991, pp. 115–116.

91 Howard W. French, "Women Win a Battle, But Job Bias Still Rules Japan," *New York Times*, February 26, 2000, p. A3.

92 Also see Richard M. Hodgetts and Fred Luthans, *International Management*, 4th ed. (Burr Ridge, IL: Irwin/McGraw, 2000), p. 76.

93 Cara Buckley, "Worldwide Music Piracy Costs Industry $5 Billion," *Miami Herald*, October 3, 2000, section C, p. 1; Craig S. Smith, "Piracy a Concern as the China Trade Opens Up," *New York Times*, October 5, 2000, p. W1.

94 Louisa Wah, "The Generation 2001 Workforce," *Management Review*, April 1999, p. 8.

95 For some examples, see "Sanity Tool Box," in Pamela Kruger, "Jobs for Life," *Fast Company*, May 2000, p. 250; Jean-Marie Hiltrop, "The Quest for the Best: Human Resource Practices to Attract and Retain Talent," *European Management Journal* 17, no. 4, 1999, pp. 422–430.

96 Anne Fisher, "How to Choose the Right Career for You," *Fortune*, October 10, 2005, Chapter 2.

Chapter 2

1 Bob Nelson, "Road to Recovery—Keeping Up in a Down Economy," *Workforce Management*, December 2009, www.workforce.com.

2 Warren R. Plunkett, Raymond F. Attner, and Gemmy S. Allen, *Management: Meeting and Exceeding Customer Expectations*, Cengage Learning, 9th ed., 2008, Chapter 12, pp. 390–425 Roy J. Blitzer, Colleen Petersen, and Linda Rogers, "How to Build Self-Esteem," *Training and Development Journal*, February 1993, pp. 58–60.

3 Paul Kirby and Dominic Di Mattia, "A Rational Approach to Emotional Management," *Training and Development Journal*, January 1991, pp. 67–70.

4 See David C. McClelland, J. W. Atkinson, R. A. Clark, and E. L. Lowell, *The Achievement Motive* (New York: Appleton-Century-Crofts, 1953); David C. McClelland, *The Achieving Society* (Princeton, NJ: Van Nostrand, 1961); and Richard Davidson, "Motivating the Underachiever," *Supervisory Management*, January 1983, pp. 39–41.

5 Srikumar S. Rao, "The Superachiever's Secret," *Success*, June 1991, pp. 28–31.

6 Abraham H. Maslow, "A Theory of Human Motivation," *Psychological Review*, July 1943, pp. 388–389.

7 Frederick Herzberg, Bernard Mausner, and Barbara Bloch Snyderman, *The Motivation to Work* (New York: Wiley & Sons, 1959).

8 For other examples of dissatisfiers, see Dean R. Spitzer, "The Seven Deadly Demotivators," *Management Review*, November 1995, pp. 56–60.

9 Dean R. Spitzer, "Power Rewards: Rewards That Really Motivate," *Management Review*, May 1996, p. 47.

10 Wendelien Van Eerde and Henk Thierry, "Vroom's Expectancy Models and Work-Related Criteria: A Meta-Analysis," *Journal of Applied Psychology*, 81, no. 5, 1996, pp. 575–586.

11 Victor H. Vroom, *Work and Motivation* (New York: Wiley & Sons, 1964).

12 Lyman W. Porter and Edward E. Lawler III, *Managerial Attitudes and Performance* (Homewood, IL: Richard D. Irwin, Inc. and Dorsey Press, 1968).

13 In some cases, however, pay for performance has not proven acceptable. See, for example, Dirk Johnson, "Teachers Reject Linking Job Performance to Bonuses," *New York Times*, July 16, 2000, p. A16.

14 Also see "Raises and Praise or Out the Door," *Wall Street Journal*, June 21, 1999, p. B1.

15 See, for example, Greg Winter, "Coke Issuing Widespread Pay Increases," *New York Times*, October 20, 2000, pp. C1–C2; "Soaring Salaries: It's Payback Time," *Business Week*, October 9, 2000, pp. F24–F30.

16 "The Big Picture," *Business Week*, July 31, 2000, p. 10.

17 George Paulin, "Changing the Economics of Executive Compensation," *Business Week*, October 13, 2009, www.businessweek.com.

18 Special Report, "Executive Pay Trends for 2010," *Business Week*, October 13, 2009, www.businessweek.com.

19 Hardy Green, "When Money Doesn't Talk," January 8, 2010, CNNMoney.com, money.cnn.com.

20 Ana Dutra, "How to Retain and Motivate Talent Now," *Business Week*, October 13, 2009, www.businessweek.com.

21 See *Business Week*, April 17, 2000, p. 16. Also see Gary McWilliams, "Dell to Cut Back on Stock Options, Pay Cash Bonuses," *Wall Street Journal*, May 6, 2003, p. A3.

22 "Working at Lincoln Electric," 2003, http://www.lincolnelectric.com.

23 Peter Burrows, "HP's $58,000-a-Day Interim CEO," *Business Week Online*, April 7, 2005.

24 Eric Wahlgren, "CEO Pay Tomorrow: Same as Today," *Business Week Online*, August 21, 2002.

25 Janet Wiscombe, "Can Pay for Performance Really Work?," *Workforce Management*, August 2001, pp. 28–34, www.workforce.com.

26 G. Karen Jacobs, "The Broad View," *Wall Street Journal*, April 10, 1997, p. R10.

27 "Broad Banding: A Management Overview," White Paper, Effective Compensation, Incorporated, Lakewood, CO, 2001.

28 "Broadbanding Programs," copyright 2010 Compensation Resources, www.Compensationresources.com.

29 "Market Pricing Broad Band Compensation System," October 22, 2008, www.bc.edu/offices/compensation/broadband.html.

30 Holly Ocasio Rizzo, "Guide to Cafeteria and Flex Plans for Small Business," www.work.com (accessed January 16, 2010).

31 Stephanie Hampton, "Marriott International Named One of the '100 Best Companies for Working Mothers' for the 15th Year," *Marriott News*, October 6, 2005.

32 Steven Kerr, "Practical, Cost-Neutral Alternatives That You May Know, But Don't Practice," *Organizational Dynamics*, Summer 1999, p. 68.

33 Michelle V. Rafter, "Special Report on Rewards and Recognition—Back in a Giving Mood," *Workforce Management*, September 14, 2009, pp. 25–29.

34 http://www.recognition.org (accessed June 2000).

35 Christi L. Gibson, "2005 NAER Best Practice Awards Announced in Los Angeles," news release, National Association for Employee Recognition, May 11, 2005.

36 Christi L. Gibson, "Trends in Employee Recognition 2005," Survey, WorldatWork and the National Association for Employee Recognition, May 2005.

37 http://www.recognition.org (accessed September 20, 2002).

38 Ryan Johnson and Jim Stoeckmann, "Sales Survey 2009," Interview, WorldatWork.org.

39 "Companies Are Working to Improve Recognition Programs," The Conference Board, p. 7. www.conference-board.org.

40 "2010 Recognition RX: Engaging Employees for Economic Recovery," A white paper prepared by Recognition Council, www.recognitioncouncil.org.

41 Judy Artunian, "Small Business Building Loyalty," *Chicago Tribune*, North Sports Final, 2002, pp. 7, 11–12.

42 Ibid.

43 "Benefits and Perks: What College Grads Most Desire," *Workforce Recruiting Online*, September 9, 2004.

Chapter 3

1 Milton Rokeach, *The Nature of Human Values* (New York: Free Press, 1973).

2 Gordon W. Allport, Philip E. Vernon, and Gardner Lindzey, *Study of Values*, test booklet (Boston: Houghton Mifflin, 1960).

3 In the Lead, "Managers Find Ways to Get Generations to Close Culture Gaps," *Wall Street Journal*, July 9, 2007, p. B1.

4 "Just What Do People Want in a Job, Anyway?" *Workforce Management*, January 7, 2008, www.workforce.com.

5 "Growth Occupations," *Workforce Recruiting Newsletter*, March 13, 2008, www.workforcerecruiting.com.

6 Garry Kranz, "Deloitte Reaches across Generations," *Workforce Management*, April 2008, www.workforce.com.

7 Roger O. Crockett, "How P&G Finds—And Keeps—A Prized Workforce," *Business Week*, April 20, 2009, p. 55.

8 Daniel Massey, "Recession's Seesaw: Older Workers Stay as the Younger Set Scrambles to Get a Foot in the Door," *Workforce Management*, June 2009, www.workforce.com.

9 News In Brief, "Study: Flexibility Programs Gain Ground in Hard Times," *Workforce Management*, July 23, 2009, www.workforce.com.

10 News in Brief, "Work-Sharing Programs Get a Closer Look, Could Help Stem Layoffs," *Workforce Management*, March 31, 2009, www.workforce.com.

11 Sally Roberts, "Sabbatical Programs Aid Work/Life Balance," *Workforce Management*, January 2009, www.workforce.com.

12 Susan Berfield, "Bridging the Generation Gap," *Business Week*, September 17, 2007, pp. 60–61.

13 Joann S. Lublin, "Memo to Staff: Stop Working," *Wall Street Journal*, July 6, 2000, pp. B1, B4.

14 Charlene Marmer Solomon, "Workers Want a Life! Do Managers Care?" *Workforce Management*, August 1999, pp. 54–58.

15 Edward L. Powers, "Employee Loyalty in the New Millennium," *SAM Advanced Management Journal*, Summer 2000, pp. 4–8.

16 Nicholas Kulish, "Postal Service Is Satisfying Its Customers," *Wall Street Journal*, May 15, 2000, p. A2.

17 Mark Larson, "Survey Reveals Alarming Lack of Generational Workplace Interaction," *Workforce Management*, July 2008, www.workforce.com.

18 Will Ruch, "How to Keep Gen X Employees from Becoming X-Employees," *Training and Development Journal*, April 2000, pp. 40–43.

19 Scott Hays, "Generation X and the Art of the Reward," *Workforce Management*, November 1999, p. 46.

20 "Three Ways to Find Generation Y," *Workforce Management Online*, September 2003.

21 Barbara Moses, "The Challenges of Managing Gen Y," *Globe & Mail* (Online Newsletter), March 11, 2005. Barbara Moses, Ph.D., is an organizational career management expert, speaker, and author of *What Next: Find the Work That's Right for You* (Dorling Kendersley, Ltd., Toronto, Ontario, 2006).

22 Tom Terez, "What Works: The Power of Nice," *Workforce Management*, January 2003, pp. 22–24.

23 "Employee Attitudes," 2002 Workplace, *CRN News*.

24 Lisa Bannon and Bob Davis, "Spendthrift to Penny Pincher: A Vision of the New Consumer," *Wall Street Journal*, December 17, 2009, p. A1.

25 Bob Nelson, "Taking Care of Business Starts with Taking Care of Employees," *Workforce Management*, November 2009, www.workforce.com.

26 Beverly Kaye and Sharon Jordan Evans, "'Wake Up, and Smell the Coffee: People Flock to Family-Friendly': Excerpts from *Love 'Em or Lose' 'Em: Getting Good People to Stay*," *Business Week Online*, January 28, 2000.

27 Unmesh Kher, "How to Sell XXXL," *Time*, January 27, 2003, pp. 43–46.

28 SCORE, "Good Employee Attitudes Help You Make Money," News & Information.

29 Jill Neimark, "The Power of Positive Thinkers," *Success*, September 1987, pp. 38–41.

30 Jack Stack, "Measuring Morale," *Inc.*, January 1997, pp. 29–30.

31 Samuel Greengard, "Employee Surveys: Ask the Right Questions, Probe the Answers for Insight," *Workforce Management*, December 2004, pp. 76–78.

32 Ibid.

33 Also see Stephen Fineman, ed., *Emotion in Organizations*, 2nd ed. (London: Sage, 2000).

34 Daniel Goleman, *Working with Emotional Intelligence* (New York: Bantam, 1998), p. 317.

35 Ibid., p. 19.

36 "Can You Answer the Real Question about Emotional Intelligence?" Emotional Intelligence at Work, http://eqatwork.com (accessed June 2003).

37 For more on EI in the workplace, see Tony Schwartz, "How Do You Feel?" *Fast Company*, June 2000, pp. 297–313; Jennifer Laabs, "Emotional Intelligence at Work," *Workforce*, July 1999, pp. 68–71; Scott Hays, "American Express Taps into the Power of Emotional Intelligence," *Workforce*, July 1999, pp. 72–73.

38 Daniel Goleman, *Emotional Intelligence*, Bantam Books, New York, 1995, p. 318.

39 Daniel Goleman, "Emotional Intelligence: Why It Can Matter More Than IQ," Bantam Books, New York, 1995, pp. 3–12.

40 Cary Cherniss, "The Business Case for Emotional Intelligence," 1999, Consortium for Research of Emotional Intelligence in Organizations, http://www.eiconsortium.org (accessed under Reports).

41 Helen Fisher, *The First Sex: The Natural Talents of Women and How They Are Changing the World* (New York: Random House, 2000).

42 Cynthia E. Griffin, "Vive La Difference!" *Entrepreneur*, November 1999, p. 52.

43 Psych Self-Help, "Methods for Developing Skills," *Mental Health Net*, http://www.mentalhelp.net.

44 Lynn Z. Bloom, Karen Coburn, and Joan Pearlman, *The New Assertive Woman* (New York: Dell, 1976), pp. 175–176.

45 Barbara Moses, *The Good News about Careers* (San Francisco, CA: Jossey-Bass, 2000).

46 For more on these profiles, see Barbara Moses, "Degrees of Motivation," *Black Enterprise*, November 2000, pp. 155–162.

47 Milton Moskowitz, Robert Levering, and Christopher Tkaczyk, "100 Best Companies," *Fortune*, February 8, 2010, pp. 75–80.

48 Kemba J. Dunham, "Wacky Resumes Get Attention—But a Job, Too?" *Wall Street Journal*, December 19, 2000, p. B16.

49 Joann S. Lublin, "College Students Make Job Hunting Tougher with Weak Resumes," *Wall Street Journal*, April 29, 2003, p. B1.

50 Michelle Conlin, "The Resume Doctor Is in," *Business Week*, July 14, 2003, pp. 116–117.

51 Molly Selvin, "Don't Lie On Resumes," *Temple Daily Telegram*, March 28, 2008, p. 2B.

52 Joann S. Lublin, "Job Hunters with Gaps in Their Resumes Need to Write around Them," *Wall Street Journal*, May 6, 2003, p. B1.

53 Cynthia Crossen, "Classified Ads Tell Tales of Social Change: Sober Need Not Apply," *Wall Street Journal*, April 16, 2003, p. B1.

54 Laura Morsch, "10 Ways to Get Your Resume Tossed," September 23, 2008, www.careerbuilder.com.

55 Douglas MacMillan, "The Art of the Online Resume," *Business Week*, May 7, 2007, p. 86.

56 Victor Godinez, "Recruiters Often Prefer Getting Resumes by E-Mail," *Miami Herald*, Business Section, December 25, 2000, p. 40.

Chapter 4

1   Bruce Crumley, "Air France: Climbing," *Time*, March 19, 2007, pp. G1-2.

2   For more on this, see John Beck and Neil Yeager, "Moving beyond Team Myths," *Training and Development Journal*, March 1996, pp. 51–55.

3   For more on this, see Joyce Ranney and Mark Deck, "Making Teams Work: Lessons from the Leaders in New Product Development," *Planning Review*, August 1995, pp. 6–13.

4   David Chaudron, "How to Improve Cross-Functional Teams," *HR Focus*, August 1995, pp. 4–5.

5   For more on virtual teams, see Leigh Thompson, *Making the Team* (Upper Saddle River, NJ: Prentice Hall, 2000), pp. 247–250; and Regina Fazio Maruca, "How Do You Manage an Off-Site Team?" *Harvard Business Review*, July–August 1998, pp. 22–26.

6   Charlene Marmer Solomon, "How Virtual Teams Bring Real Savings," *Workforce Management*, June, 2001, p. 62.

7   Lewis Brown Griggs and Lente-Louise Louw, "Diverse Teams: Breakdown or Breakthrough," *Training and Development Journal*, October 1995, p. 27.

8   Ellen van Velsor and Jean Brittain Leslie, "Why Executives Derail: Perspectives across Time and Cultures," *Academy of Management Executive*, November 1995, p. 65.

9   Griggs and Louw, "Diverse Teams."

10 For more on groups in this stage, see Susan A. Wheelan, *Creating Effective Teams* (Thousand Oaks, CA: Sage, 1999), pp. 28–30.

11 Ellen Hart, "Top Teams," *Management Review*, February 1996, pp. 43–47.

12 Wheelan, *Creating Effective Teams*, pp. 62–64.

13 Also see Margaret Coles, "Call in a Therapist to Boost Team Morale," *Sunday Times*, July 23, 2000, section 7, p. 24.

14 "Size Is the Key," *Fast Company*, November 2000, p. 118.

15 For more on this topic, see Robert F. Bales and Edgar F. Borgatta, "Size of Group as a Factor in the Interaction Profile," in A. P. Hare, Edgar F. Borgatta, and Robert F. Bales, eds., *Small Groups* (New York: Knopf, 1955), pp. 396–413; and Lyman W. Porter and Richard M. Steers, "Organizational, Work, and Personal Factors in Employee Turnover and Absenteeism," *Psychological Bulletin*, August 1973, pp. 151–176.

16 For more on the use of this organizational arrangement, see Douglas A. Saarel, "Triads: Self-Organizing Structures that Create Value," *Planning Review*, August 1995, pp. 20–25.

17 Bertram Schoner, Gerald L. Rose, and G. C. Hoyt, "Quality of Decisions: Individuals versus Real and Synthetic Groups," *Journal of Applied Psychology*, August 1974, pp. 424–432.

18 Dorwin Cartwright, "Risk Taking by Individuals and Groups: An Assessment of Research Employing Choice Dilemmas," *Journal of Personality and Social Psychology*, December 1971, pp. 361–378; Russell D. Clark III, "Group Induced Shift toward Risk: A Critical Appraisal," *Psychological Bulletin*, October 1971, pp. 251–270; and Dean G. Pruitt, "Choice

Shifts in Group Discussion: An Introductory Review," *Journal of Personality and Social Psychology*, December 1971, pp. 339–360.

19 Earl A. Cecil, Larry L. Cummings, and Jerome M. Chertkoff, "Group Composition and Choice Shift: Implications for Administration," *Academy of Management Journal*, September 1973, pp. 413–414.

20 Jill Rosenfeld, "Here's an Idea!", *Fast Company*, Issue 33, March 31, 2000, p. 100.

21 Michael A. West and Neil R. Anderson, "Innovation in Top Management Teams," *Journal of Applied Psychology*, December 1996, p. 691.

22 Cheryl Comeau-Kirschner and Louisa Wah, "Who Has Time to Think?" *Management Review*, January 2000, pp. 16–23.

23 Suzy Wetlaufer, "Common Sense and Conflict: An Interview with Disney's Michael Eisner," *Harvard Business Review*, January–February 2000, p. 119.

24 Bob Eckert, "Fear: The Great Innovation Killer," *Creativity Portal*, January 27, 2010, www.creativity-portal.com.

25 "Koinonia," *Creativity Portal*, January 27, 2010, www.creativity-portal.com.

26 Richard L. Priem, David A. Harrison, and Nan Kanoff Muir, "Structured Conflict and Consensus Outcomes in Group Decision Making," *Journal of Management*, Volume 21, No. 4, 1995, pp. 691–710.

27 Larry Armstrong, "Nurturing an Employee's Brainchild," *Business Week*, Special Issue, December 1993, p. 196.

28 Arthur B. Van Gundy, *Idea Power* (New York: American Management Association, 1992), Chapters 10 and 11.

29 Sue Barrett, "How to Brainstorm and Be Creative," *Workforce Management*, http:// www.workforce.com.

30 Dorothy Leonard and Jeffrey F. Rayport, "Spark Innovation through Empathic Design," *Harvard Business Review*, November–December 1997, pp. 102–103.

31 See, for example, Gary Hamel and C. K. Prahalad, *Competing for the Future* (Boston, MA: Harvard Business School Press, 1994).

32 Paco Underhill, *Why We Buy: The Science of Shopping* (New York: Simon & Schuster, 1999).

33 Millard Fuller, "A Hammer as a Way to Help People," *Fast Company*, November 2000, p. 130.

34 H. David Aycock, "Selfish People Spell Doom for a Team Effort," *Fast Company*, November 2000, p. 128.

35 Jeanie Duck, "Don't Shortchange Your Startup," *Fast Company*, November 2000, p. 142.

36 Ben Nagler, "Recasting Employees into Teams," *Workforce Management*, January, 1998, pp. 101–106.

37 Company overview, "Signs of the Time," Signicast, January 28, 2010, www.signicast.com.

38 Stephen P. Robbins, *Organizational Behavior*, 8th ed. (Englewood Cliffs, NJ: Prentice-Hall, 1998) pp. 290–293.

39 Author Hegar's personal interview with the director of Holland America's *Ryndam* cruise liner, September 2005.

40 IBM, Business Consulting Services, Cases: Ford Motor Company, January 10, 2006, www.ibm.com.

41 Michelle V. Rafter, "Microsoft Does a Benefits Tech Makeover," *Workforce Management*, December 2009, www.workforce.com.

42 Anne Fisher, "How to Build a (Strong) Virtual Team," *CNNMoney*, November 20, 2009, www.cnnmoney.

43 Ibid.

44 Diane Coutu, "Why Teams Don't Work," *Harvard Business Review*, May 2009, pp. 99–105.

45 Jena McGregor, "The Struggle to Measure Performance," *Business Week Online*, January 9, 2006.

46 Ron Crossland, "Voicing Opinions," *Point E-Newsletter*, August 2008, www.bluepointleadership.com.

47 Robbins, *Organizational Behavior*, pp. 294–300.

48 Norman Shidle, "Thoughts," *Tribune-Progress*, Holland, Texas, February 1, 2006, p. 12.

49 Douglas P. Shuit, "Monster's Competitors Are Nipping at Its Heels," *Workforce Management*, November 2004, pp. 37–44.

50 "The Job Bank," www.twc.state.tx.us and www.jobbankusa.com.

51 Steve Santiago, "8 Great Ways to Land a Job," Bankrate, Inc., April 27, 2009, www.bankrate.com.

52 Susan Ladika, "Blogs: A New Frontier in Online Recruiting," *Workforce Management Online*, May 2004.

53 Shuit, "Monster's Competitors," pp. 37–44.

54 Jennifer C. Berkshire, "A Controversial New Strategy for Employee Referrals," *Workforce Management Online*, November 2004.

55 Alison Stein Wellner, "The Pickup Artists," *Workforce Management Online*, July 2004.

56 Jobweb.com–Career development and job-search advice for new college graduates, Career Library. Copyright, National Association of Colleges and Employers.

Chapter 5

1 David Krackhardt and Jeffrey R. Hanson, "Informal Networks: The Company behind the Chart," *Harvard Business Review*, July–August 1993, p. 105.

2 Maryann Durland, "Understanding Sociograms: A Guide to Understanding Network Analysis Mapping," Durland Consulting, Inc., 2003.

3 Richard Rapaport, "How to Build a Winning Team: An Interview with Head Coach Bill Walsh," *Harvard Business Review*, January–February 1993, pp. 111–120.

4 K. Michele Kacmar and Gerald R. Ferris, "Politics at Work: Sharpening the Focus of Political Behavior in Organizations," *Business Horizons*, July–August 1993, pp. 70–74.

5 Bruce Fortado, "Informal Supervisory Social Control Strategies," *Journal of Management Studies*, March 1994, pp. 251–274.

6 Some of these ideas can be found in Ken Myers, "Games Companies Play," *Training*, June 1992, pp. 68–76.

7 David De Long and Patricia Seemann, "Confronting Conceptual Confusion and Conflict in Knowledge Management," *Organizational Dynamics*, Summer 2000, p. 39.

8 Dennis A. Gioia and Clinton O. Longenecker, "Delving into the Dark Side: The Politics of Executive Appraisal," *Organizational Dynamics*, Winter 1994, p. 50.

9 Herminia Ibarra, "Race, Opportunity, and Diversity of Social Circles in Managerial Networks," *Academy of Management Journal*, June 1995, pp. 673–703.

10 Glenn R. Carroll and Albert C. Teo, "On the Social Networks of Managers," *Academy of Management Journal*, April 1996, p. 433.

11 Also see Patricia A. Wilson, "The Effects of Politics and Power on the Organizational Commitment of Federal Executives," *Journal of Management*, Spring 1995, pp. 101–118.

12 Leigh Thompson, *Making the Team: A Guide for Managers* (Upper Saddle River, NJ: Prentice-Hall, 2000), p. 236.

13 Keith Davis, *Human Behavior at Work: Organizational Behavior*, 6th ed. (New York: McGraw-Hill, 1981), p. 339.

14 Jitendra Mishra, "Managing the Grapevine," *Public Personnel Management* (International Personnel Management Association–USA, 1990).

15 K. C. Desouza, "Barriers to Effective Use of Knowledge Management Systems in Software Engineering," *Communications of the ACM* 46, no. 1, 2003, pp. 99–101; and K. C. Desouza, "Facilitating Tacit Knowledge Exchange," *Communications of the ACM* 46, no. 6, 2003, pp. 85–88.

16 R. Cross, A. Parker, L. Prusak, and S. P. Borgatti, "Knowing What We Know: Supporting Knowledge Creation and Sharing in Social Networks," *Organizational Dynamics* 30, no. 2, 2001, pp. 100–120.

17 Yukika Awazu, "Informal Network Players, Knowledge Integration, and Competitive Advantage," *Journal of Knowledge Management* 8, no. 3, 2004, pp. 62–70.

18 Stephen Power and Neal E. Boudette, "Daimler Goes Its Own Way," *Wall Street Journal*, March 4, 2005, p. B2.

19 For more on setting goals, see Lynda McDermott, Bill Waite, and Nolan Brawley, "Putting Together a World-Class Team," *Training and Development Journal*, January 1999, pp. 47–51; and Dale Buss, "The Entitlement Generation Wants It All—And They Want It Easy. How Dare They?" *Wall Street Journal*, May 22, 2000, p. R23.

20 See, for example, Gordon W. Allport and Leo Postman, *The Psychology of Rumor* (New York: Holt, Rinehart and Winston, 1974), p. 33.

21 Julie Forster and Anne Therese Palmer, "That's It, I'm Outta Here," *Business Week*, October 9, 2000, pp. 96, 98.

22 Davis, *Human Behavior at Work*, pp. 337–338.

23 Also see Alan M. Webber, "Will Companies Ever Learn?" *Fast Company*, October 2000, pp. 275–282.

24 Amy Zipkin, "The Wisdom of Thoughtfulness," *New York Times*, May 31, 2000, p. C1.

25 Jay Knippen, "Grapevine Communication: Management Employees," *Journal of Business Research*, January 1974, pp. 47–58.

26 Cheryl Comeau-Kirschner, "The Sharing Culture," *Management Review*, January 2000, p. 8.

27 Kerry Sulkowicz, M.D., "Don't Breathe a Word," *Business Week*, July 23, 2007. p. 14.

28 Bill Radin, "The Power of Interview Preparation," Revised: 08/17/2001, www.recruitersnetwork.com.

29 Samuel Greengard, "Gimme Attitude," *Workforce*, July 2003, pp. 56–60, www.workforce.com.

30 Ibid.

31 Ibid.

32 George Anders, "Talent Bank," *Fast Company*, November 2000, p. 96.

33 Christina Binkley, "Tassels, Pantsuits, and Other Interview Don'ts," *Wall Street Journal*, January 17, 2008, p. D8.

34 Carole Martin, "Ten Interview Fashion Blunders: What Not to Wear to the Interview," Monster contributing writer. www.monster.com.

35 Carole Martin, "Nonverbal Communications: Escape the Pitfalls," Monster contributing writer, www.monster.com).

36 "Guide to Interviewing." Brandeis University, Hiatt Career Center, Student and Alumni Resources, www.brandis.edu/hiatt.

37 Deanna G. Kucler, "Interview Questions: Legal or Illegal?" *Workforce Management Online*.

38 Rachael King, "Chili's Hot Interview Makeover," *Workforce Management Online*, July 2003.

39 Stephen P. Sonnenberg, "Can HR Legally Ask the Questions That Applicants with Disabilities Want to Be Asked?" *Workforce Management*, August 2002, pp. 38–44.

40 Carol Hymowitz, "Managers Face Battle to Keep Salaries Fair in a Tight Job Market," *Wall Street Journal*, March 21, 2000, p. B1.

41 Bill Radin, "The Power of Interview Preparation," Revised: 08/17/2001, www.recruitersnetwork.com2; Jack Thomas, "Hiring in Times of Anger and Fear," *Career Journal of the Wall Street Journal*, http://www.careerjournal.com.

Chapter 6

1 Alvin Toffler, *Future Shock* (New York: Bantam Books, 1971).

2 Allen R. Myerson, "Superhuman Feats from a Subhuman Diver," *New York Times*, July 13, 1994, p. C4.

3 Jeremy Mullman, "Adidas Rewards Consumers for Sharing in Online Push," *Advertising* Age, February 4, 2010, www.adage.com.

4 "Newport Digital Technologies, Inc., Announces Participation in a $500 Million State and Federal Grant Program for Schools and Public Areas," Press Release, Source: Yahoo Finance, January 27, 2010.

5 Joe Mullich, "A Second Act for E-Learning," *Workforce Management*, February 2004, pp. 51–55.

6 Jonathan Pont, "Employee Training on iPod Playlist," *Workforce Management*, August 2005, p. 18.

7 Jessica Marquez, "Faced with High Turnover, Retailers Boot Up E-learning for Quick Training," *Workforce Management*, August 2005, pp. 74–75.

8 "Innovation: From Laboratory to Pharmacy Shelf," www.phrma.org, February 9, 2010.

9 Press release from American Honda Motor Co., Inc., February 6, 2003, http://www.honda.com.

10 Pete Engardio, "The Electric Car Battery War," *Business Week*, February 23, 2009, pp. 52–54.

11 "Rebel Forces Capture US Spy Plane," November 15, 2008, www.military.com.

12 Anne Marie Squedo, "21st Century Armor," *Wall Street Journal*, February 10, 2003, p. B1.

13 Alex Salkever, "Sports Gear Goes Geek," *Business Week Online*, July 16, 2002.

14 Peter Waldman, "Figure Skaters Blame Boot Design for Injury Plague," *Wall Street Journal*, February 17, 2006, pp. A1, A11.

15 Lindsey Tanner, "Doctors Use Wii for Rehab Therapy," *Temple Daily Telegram*, February 10, 2008, pp. 1E, 9E.

16 Steven Labadessa, "The Mind-Bending New World of Work," *Business Week*, April 2, 2007, pp. 46–54.

17 Patricia O'Connell, "The Bank of 7-Eleven," *Business Week Online*, February 6, 2003.

18 "The Boston Herald Chooses DTI's ContentPublisher and DTI Lightning," Pressroom, January 14, 2010, www.dtint.com/NewsEvents.

19 Jeffrey R. Young, "Beam Me to the Faculty Senate," *Chronicle of Higher Education*, October 18, 2009, http://chronicle.com.

20 Gentex Corporation, www.gentex.com.

21 Ibid.

22 Tom Becker, "Self-Healing Materials Aren't Far Off," *Wall Street Journal*, July 16, 2003, p. A10.

23 "News in Brief," *Workforce Week, Volume* 7, No. 9, February 26–March 4, 2006.

24 Heather Green and Steve Rosenbush, "Wi-Fi Means Business," Special Report, *Business Week*, April 28, 2003.

25 Green and Rosenbush, "Wi-Fi Means Business."

26 *Wall Street Journal*, May 4, 2000, p. 1.

27 Juli Ann Reynolds, "Culture is a Strategic Asset," *Tom Peters Times*, December 2007, www.tompeters.com.

28 Raymond Sokolov, "Googling Lunch," *Wall Street Journal*, December 1–2, 2007, pp. W1, W5; an e-mail documentation of Google benefits, November 12, 2009.

29 Jane Black, "The Battle to Streamline Business Software," *Business Week Online*, December 4, 2002.

30 Mark Jarvis, "At Oracle, Simplicity Rules All," *Business Week Online*, December 4, 2002.

31 News release, *Starbucks Newsroom*, January 7, 2008, www.news.starbucks.com.

32 Thomas M. Burton, "By Learning from Failures, Lilly Keeps Drug Pipeline Full," *Wall Street Journal*, April 21, 2004, pp. A1, A12.

33 Melanie Trottman, "Inside Southwest Airlines, Storied Culture Feels Strains," *Wall Street Journal*, July 11, 2003, pp. A1, A6; and February 12, 2010, www.southwest.com.

34 Ronald Alsop, "Scandal-Filled Year Takes Toll on Firms' Good Names," *Wall Street Journal Online*, February 12, 2003.

35 Kate Rockwood, "The Employee Whisperer," *Fast Company*, November 2008, pp. 72–74.

36 W. Mathew Juechter, Caroline Fisher, and Randall J. Alford, "Five Conditions for High-Performance Cultures," *Training and Development Journal*, May 1998, p. 65.

37 Julianne Pepitone, "U.S. Job Satisfaction Hits 22-Year Low," *Money*, January 5, 2010, www.money.cnn.com.

38 Jessica Marquez, "Halo Effect: The Myth of Employee Satisfaction," *Workforce Management*, July 2007, www.workforce.com.

39 Chris Grant, "Office Ergonomics Training: DeMystifying all Those Chair Adjustability Options," July 28, 2010, www.office-ergo.com.

40 Cheryl Powell, "When Workers Wear Walkmans on the Job," *Wall Street Journal*, July 11, 1994, pp. B1, B8.

41 Sarah Fister Gale, "Virtual Training with Real Results," *Workforce Management*, December 2009, www.workforce.com; Garry Kranz, "ASTD Reports that Learning Investments Held Steady in 2008," *Workforce Management*, November 2009, www.workforce.com; and Garry Kranz, "Downturn Prompts a Change in Learning Initiatives," *Workforce Management*, October 2009, www.workforce.com.

42 Charlotte Huff, "Training Adapts to the Downturn," *Workforce Management*, February 2009, www.workforce.com.

43 "Motorola, FedEx Develop Wireless, Pocket PC for Couriers to Enhance Customer Service," news release, November 26, 2002, http://www.federalexpress.com.

44 See Richard M. Hodgetts and Fred Luthans, *International Management*, 4th ed. (Burr Ridge, IL: Irwin/McGraw, 2000), p. 497.

45 "Motivating People," Toolpack Consulting, LLC, Teaneck, New Jersey.

46 Stacy Perman, "Baking Principles into the Business," *Business Week Online*, December 13, 2005; and Dancing Deer Baking Company's Web site, February 14, 2010, www.dancingdeer.com.

47 Workplace Violence, "OSHA Fact Sheet," www.osha.gov.

48 http://www.osha.gov/SLTC/workplaceviolence/index.html.

49 http://www.osha.gov.

50 Ibid.

51 George Henderson, *Human Relations Issues in Management* (Westport, CT: Quorum Books, 1996), pp. 147–148.

52 Henderson, *Human Relations Issues*, pp. 152–153.

53 "Seven Tips to Prevent Workplace Violence," Crisis Prevention Institute, Inc. February 15, 2010, www.crisisprevention.com.

54 Anusha Goonetilleke, Minter Ellison Lawyers, "Domestic Violence and Workplace Violence," *Australia's CEO Challenge*, December 2008 News, p. 3.

55 Anusha Goonetilleke, Minter Ellison Lawyers, "When Domestic Violence Becomes Workplace Violence," *Australia's CEO Challenge*, January 10, 2010, www.ceochallengeaustralia.org.

56 National Institute of Occupational Safety and Health, *Stress … At Work*, NIOSH Publication No. 99–101, 2000, p. 4, http://www.cdc.gov.

57 "Stress Prevention and Job Performance," www.cdc.gov/niosh/home page, March 25, 2005, Source in article: *Journal of Applied Psychology* p. 15.

58 Ibid. p. 15.

Chapter 7

1 Bradley T. Gale and Robert D. Buzzell, "Market Perceived Quality: Key Strategic Concept," *Planning Review*, March–April 1989, pp. 6–15, 48.

2 U.S. Bureau of Labor Statistics, February 21, 2010, www.bls.com.

3 Michael Mandel, "Why Rising Productivity is Cause for Worry," *Business Week*, May 14, 2009, www.businessweek.com.

4 Jason Bush, "Why is Russia's Productivity so Low?" *Business Week*, May 8, 2009, www.businessweek.com.

5 Miguel Bustillo, "Home Depot Undergoes Renovation," *Wall Street Journal*, February 24, 2010, p. B2.

6 Jeffrey Liker, "Toyota's Lost Its Quality Edge? Not So Fast," *Business Week*, January 28, 2010, www.businessweek.com.

7 Jay Hall, "Americans Know How to Be Productive If Managers Will Let Them," *Organizational Dynamics*, Winter 1994, pp. 39–44.

8 Joanne Wojcik, "Unhealthy Employees Cut Productivity, Study Finds," *Workforce Management*, May 2009, www.workforce.com; and Randy Dotinga, "Treating Workers' Mental Woes May Boost Productivity," *Business Week*, September 10, 2009, www.businessweek.com.

9 Joanne Wojcik, "Most Employers Aren't Combating Workplace Stress," *Workforce Management*, December 2009, www.workforce.com.

10 Dexter A. Hansen, "Total Quality Management (TQM)" Tutorial, July 29, 2010, www.flowhelp.com.

11 Richard M. Hodgetts, *Quality Measures in America's Most Successful Firms* (New York: American Management Association, 1998), p. 14.

12 "Hewlett-Packard Company," *Wall Street Journal*, March 7, 2003.

13 Alex Taylor III, "Chrysler: Is the Crossfire Just Another Sexy Sportscar?" *Fortune Online*, March 3, 2003.

14 "Services: Document Outsourcing," *Our Company, Our Capabilities, and Our Commitment*, July 29, 2010, www.xerox.com.

15 "Xerox Office Products Receive 14 Top Industry Awards," news release, March 4, 2003, http://www.xerox.com.

16 John Carey, "Making the Space Program Soar Again, *Business Week Online*, February 7, 2003.

17 "NASA – A Countdown of Countdowns: The Space Shuttle's Finale," February 22, 2010, www.nasa.gov.

18 Motorola's Learning Policy, Public Relations, Motorola Corporation, March 5, 2003.

19 Garry Kranz, "E-Learning Hits Its Stride," *Workforce Management*, February 2008, www.workforce.com.

20 Claudia H. Deutsch, "New Economy, Old-School Rigor," *New York Times*, June 12, 2000, pp. C1–C2; and Interview with Robert, Customer Service Department, General Electric Corporation, March 2, 2006.

21 Interview with Kaylene, Home Depot Store, Appliance Department, Temple, Texas, February 24, 2010.

22 Keith Bradsher, "The Long, Long Wait for Cars," *New York Times*, May 9, 2000, pp. C1, C29.

23 Also see Robert B. Handfield, Gary L. Ragatz, Kenneth J. Petersen, and Robert M. Monczka, "Involving Suppliers in New Product Development," *California Management Review*, Fall 1999, pp. 59–82; and Michael Useed and Joseph Harder, "Leading Laterally in Company Outsourcing," *Sloan Management Review*, Winter 2000, pp. 25–36.

24 See D. Keith Denton, "Eat or Be Eaten," *Industrial Management*, May–June 1999, pp. 20–22.

25 Jeffrey Pfeffer and Robert I. Sutton, "Knowing 'What' to Do Is Not Enough: Turning Knowledge into Action," *California Management Review*, Fall 1999, p. 88.

26 "FedEx Freight Improves Transit Times; Enhancements Support Fast Cycle Distribution," news release, March 5, 2003, http://www.fedex.com. Also see Richard M. Hodgetts, Donald F. Kuratko, and Jeffrey S. Hornsby, "Quality Implementation in Small Business: Perspectives from the Baldrige Award Winners," *SAM Advanced Management Journal*, Winter 1999, pp. 37–47.

27 Also see Richard M. Hodgetts, Donald F. Kuratko, and Jeffrey S. Hornsby, "Quality Implementation in Small Business: Perspectives from the Baldrige Award Winners," *SAM Advanced Management Journal*, Winter 1999, pp. 37–47.

28 Holly Treat, FedEx Corporation, e-mail correspondence with author, April 22, 2003.

29 News Room, news releases, "FedEx Couriers Play Cupid This Valentine's Day," February 14, 2010; "FedEx Delivers Longer Vase Life for Flowers for Valentine's Day," January 22, 2009; "China-Bound 'FedEx Panda Express' Takes Flight from Washington, D.C. with Precious Cargo on Board," February 4, 2010; "FedEx Introduces SenseAware, The Next Generation Supply Chain Information Platform," November 17, 2009; and "FedEx Named among FORTUNE Magazine's 2010 'Best Companies to Work For,'" January 21, 2010; www.fedex.com.

30 "Flex Time, The Workplace Challenge," http://www.semcog.org (Southeast Michigan Council of Governments, 2003).

31 J. Carroll Swart, "Clerical Workers on Flextime: A Survey of Three Industries," *Personnel*, April 1985, p. 44.

32 "Workers on Flexible and Shift Schedules in 2004: Summary," U.S. Bureau of Labor Statistics, July 29, 2010.

33 Jessica Marquez, "Flexible Hours for Nonexempt Workers May Be Next on Lobbyists' Agenda," *Workforce Management*, August 2009, www.workforce.com.

34 James E. Hall, Mark T. Kobata and Marty Denis, "Overtime Pay Plan for Flexible Workweek Approved," *Workforce Management*, November 2009, www.workforce.com.

35 Gina Ruiz, "Age Wave: Adapting to Older Workers," *Workforce Management*, March 27, 2006, pp. 32–36.

36 Jessica Toonkel Marquez, "The Future of Flex," *Workforce Management*, January 2010, p. 19.

37 Katelyn DeRogatis, "New Book Highlights 260 Ways Employees "Make Work Work" in a Down Economy," Families and Work Institute, August 12, 2009, www.familiesandwork.org.

38 Robert Webb, "Empowerment History," Motivational Tool Chest, 2000, http://www.motivation-tools.com.

39 Ibid.

40 "Customer Empowerment," Trends Report 2000, Trends Shaping the Digital Economy, http://www.trendsreport.net/2000/customer/4.html.

41 Newsmaker Q&A, "Meg Whitman on eBay's Self-Regulation," *Business Week Online*, August 18, 2003.

42 "What Is Empowerment?" *Empowerment Illustrated*, January 1, 2003, www.empowermentillustrated.com.

43 Tim Manners, "Controlling the Conversation," *Fast Company Online*, May 2005.

44 Sharon Jordan-Evans and Beverly Kaye, "The 'E' Word … Again," *Fast Company Online*, March 2005.

45 Mark Northern, "Everyone Loves Their Own Ideas," *Fast Company Online*, November 2004.

46 Donna Lipari, Xerox Corporation, e-mail correspondence with author, April 10, 2003.

47 "History of Intrapreneurship," Small Business Notes, http://www.smallbusinessnotes.com.

48 Steven C. Brandt, *Entrepreneuring in Established Companies* (Homewood, IL: Dow Jones-Irwin, 1986), p. 54.

49 "The Intrapreneur," Small Business Notes, http://www.smallbusinessnotes.com.

50 "The Intrapreneurial Organization," Small Business Notes, http://www.smallbusinessnotes.com.

51 "Art Fry and the Invention of Post-it Notes," http://www.3m.com.

52 Donald F. Kuratko and Richard M. Hodgetts, *Entrepreneurship*, 2nd ed. (Fort Worth, TX: Dryden Press, 1992), p. 99.

53 Chris Fox, "Some Thoughts on Intrapreneurship," http://www.ChrisFoxInc.com.

54 Gifford Pinchot III and Elizabeth S/ Pinchot, "The Intrapreneur's Ten Commandments," July 29, 2010, www.intrapreneur.com.

55 D. F. Twomey and D. L. Harris, "From Strategy to Corporate Outcomes: Aligning Human Resource Management Systems with Entrepreneurial Intent," *International Journal of Commerce and Management*, 10, 2000, pp. 43–55.

56 Ibid., p. 55.

57 Stephen J. Simurda, "There's a Word for It: Intrapreneurism," *Worldbusiness Magazine*, November/December 1996.

58 Fox, "Some Thoughts on Intrapreneurship."

59 Stacy Perman, "Intrapreneurs and Adaptive Persistence," *Business Week*, April 2, 2008, www.businessweek.com.

60 Carmine Gallo, "You: The Brand," *Business Week Online*, March 2, 2006; Linda Tischler, "The Good Brand," *Fast Company*, August 2004, p. 47; Tom Peters, "The Brand Called You," *Fast Company*, August/September 1997, p. 83; Scott Bedbury, "Nine Ways to Fix a Broken Brand," *Fast Company*, February 2002, p. 72; and Joanna Krotz, "How to Create a Brand," http://www.bcentral.co.uk.

61 Dan Schawbel, "Personal Branding 101: How to Discover and Create Your Brand," February 5, 2009, www.mashable.com.

Journal, April 1993, pp. 61–67; John H. Dobbs, "The Empowerment Environment," *Training and Development Journal*, February 1993, pp. 55–57; and David E. Bowen and Edward E. Lawler III, "The Empowerment of Service Workers: What, Why, How, and When," *Sloan Management Review*, Spring 1992, pp. 31–39.

3 For more on this, see Robert W. Renn and Robert J. Vandenberg, "The Critical Psychological States: An Underrepresented Component in Job Characteristics Model Research," *Journal of Management* 21 (2), 1995, pp. 279–303; Steven P. Brown and Thomas W. Leigh, "A New Look at Psychological Climate and Its Relationship to Job Involvement, Effort, and Performance," *Journal of Applied Psychology*, August 1996, pp. 358–368; and Greg R. Oldham and Anne Cummings, "Employee Creativity: Personal and Contextual Factors at Work," *Academy of Management Journal*, June 1996, pp. 607–634.

4 Geoffrey Colvin, "What Makes GE Great?" *Fortune*, March 6, 2006, p. 92.

5 "Southwest Airlines' Recognitions," www.southwestairlines.com.

6 Southwest Airlines, March 11, 2002, http://www.southwestairlines.com.

7 Linda Tischler, "Death to the Cubicle," *Fast Company*, June 2005, p. 29.

8 Compiled by the *Fast Company* staff, "Most Innovative Companies; Top 10 by Industry," *Fast Company*, March 2010, p. 106.

9 Chuck Salter, "Rethinking Work," *Fast Company*, April 2000, p. 262. Also see Chuck Salter, "Office of the Future," *Fast Company*, April 2000, pp. 273–286.

10 Tischler, "Death to the Cubicle."

11 Cases, "Butler Community College," February 28, 2010, www.hermanmiller.com.

12 Ibid.

13 Gary McWilliams and Ann Zimmerman, "Dell Plans to Peddle PCs inside Sears, Other Large Chains," *Wall Street Journal*, January 30, 2003, p. B1.

14 U.S. Bureau of Labor Statistics, released September 22, 2005, www.bls.gov.

15 Bernie Kelly and Bruce McGraw, "Traits of Successful Telecommuters," *Successful Management in the Virtual Office*, May 10, 1995, www.cognitive-technologies.com.

16 "How Can I Make Sure That My Teleworking Works for Both Me and My Agency?" U.S. Office of Personnel Management, General Services Administration, www.telework.gov.

17 U.S. Office of Personnel Management, www.telework.gov.

18 Elka Maria Torpey, "Flexible Work," *Occupational Outlook Quarterly*, Summer 2007, www.bls.gov.

19 Jessica Marquez, "Novel Ideas at Borders Lure Older Workers," *Workforce Management*, May 2005, p. 28.

20 John Zappe, "Temp-to-Hire is Becoming a Full-Time Practice at Firms," *Workforce Management*, June 2005, pp. 82–85.

21 Steve Hipple, personal communication, U.S. Bureau of Labor Statistics, March 24, 2006.

22 John F. Middlebrook, "Avoiding Brain Drain: How to Lock in Talent," *HR Focus*, March 1999, pp. 9–10.

23 David Woodruff, "Europe's Companies Coddle Employees," *Wall Street Journal*, August 4, 2000, pp. A7, A9.

24 Jill Greenwood, "Stew Leonard's Look at the Positive Impact Couples Have on Company Culture," news release, January 17, 2006, www.stewleonards.com.

25 "Company Background," www.stewleonards.com (March 24, 2006).

26 Amy Zipkin, "The Wisdom of Thoughtfulness," *New York Times*, May 31, 2000, pp. C1, C10.

27 Also see Melinda Ligos, "The Nicest Man on Wall Street." *New York Times*, May 31, 2000, p. C10.

28 Barbara Moses, "Career Planning Mirrors Social Change," www.bbmcareerdev.com.

29 Barbara Moses, "Mentor Match: Choose One Right for You," *Globe and Mail*, November 11, 2005, www.bbmcareerdev.com.

30 Garry Kranz, "More Firms Paying Mind to Mentoring," *Workforce Management*, January 2010, p. 10.

31 Barbara Moses, "Career Killers: Behavior to Change," *Globe and Mail*, July 15, 2005.

32 Article Resource Association, "Tips for Working Your Way Up," *Temple Daily Telegram: Career Supplement*, April 25, 2007.

Chapter 8

1 See "Autonomy Is In!" *HR Focus*, October 1993, p. 10.

2 Also see Robert Frey, "Empowerment or Else," *Harvard Business Review*, September–October 1993, pp. 80–94; Richard J. Magjuka, "The 10 Dimensions of Employee Involvement," *Training and Development*

Chapter 9

1 Ralph Stogdill, *Handbook of Leadership* (New York: Free Press, 1974), p. 81.

2 Bernard M. Bass, *Bass & Stogdill's Handbook of Leadership* (New York: Free Press, 1990), pp. 64–65.

3 Stogdill, *Handbook of Leadership*, pp. 80–81.

4 For more information on leadership skills, see Robert M. Fulmer and Stacey Wagner, "Leadership: Lessons from the Best," *Training and Development Journal*, March 1999, p. 31.

5 Jennifer Robinson, "Why Can't Women Be Leaders Too?" *Gallup Management Journal Online*, October 13, 2005. http://gmj.gallup.com.

6 Keith H. Hammonds, "The Secret Life of the CEO: Do They Even Know Right from Wrong?" *Fast Company Magazine*, October 2002, http://www.fastcompany.com.

7 Douglas McGregor, *The Human Side of Enterprise* (New York: McGraw-Hill, 1960).

8 Ibid., pp. 33–34.

9 Ibid., pp. 47–48.

10 Edmund L. Andrews, "No Apologies from Stuttgart," *New York Times*, December 2, 2000, pp. B1–B2.

11 Mark Landler, "Shake-Up at DaimlerChrysler; Incoming Chief Led Turnaround," *New York Times*, July 29, 2005, p. C1.

12 See "The Superior CEO: A Profile," *Fortune*, June 21, 1999, p. 78.

13 Ron Zemke, "Can You Manage Trust?" *Training*, February 2000, pp. 80–82.

14 "Things Leaders Do," *Fast Company Magazine*, April 2004, p. 96.

15 Fred E. Fiedler, *A Theory of Leadership Effectiveness* (New York: McGraw-Hill, 1967).

16 Fred E. Fiedler, "Style or Circumstance: The Leadership Enigma," *Psychology Today*, March 1969, p. 42.

17 R. R. Blake and J. S. Mouton, *The Managerial Grid* (Houston, TX: Gulf Publishing, 1964).

18 Gary McWilliams, "Dell Looks for Ways to Rekindle the Fire It Had as an Upstart," *Wall Street Journal*, August 31, 2000, pp. A1, A8.

19 Bernard M. Bass, *Bass & Stogdill's Handbook of Leadership*, 3rd ed. (New York: Free Press, 1992), p. 221.

20 "Transformational Leadership," Changing Minds Organization, www.changingminds.org (March 28, 2006).

21 Erik Rees, "Seven Principles of Transformational Leadership: Creating a Synergy of Energy," www.pastors.com.

22 Bernard M. Bass, "Is There Universality in the Full Range Model of Leadership?" *International Journal of Public Administration* 19 (6), 1996, p. 742.

23 John P. Kotter, "The Difference between Management and Leadership" *Leadership Insights: 15 Unique Perspectives on Effective Leadership*, (Harvard University Press, Cambridge, MA, 2001), p. 26.

24 Joan Peterson, "Leadership Lessons from Kate," *Bluepoint Leadership Development*, September 9, 2009, www.bluepointleadership.com.

25 Lee Iacocca with Catherine Whitney, *Where Have All the Leaders Gone?* "Nine Cs of Leadership" (Scribner, New York, NY, 2007).

26 Book excerpts, *Business Week Online*, June 13, 2002, Patrick J. McKenna and David H. Maister, *First among Equals*, chapter 4, "Dare to be Inspiring," The Free Press, 2002.

27 Bob Nelson, "1001 Ways to Reward Employees," http://www.fed.org.

28 Robert Whitehead and Robert Hertzberg, "When IT Success Taps Team Spirit," *Baseline Magazine*, September 9, 2002, www.baselinemag.com.

29 Bob Nelson, "Introduction," *1001 Ways to Reward Employees* (Workman Publishing Company Inc., New York, NY, 2005), p. viii.

30 Ibid.

31 "Virtual Company Advice," *Inc Magazine*, October 21, 1999, http://www.inc.com.

32 Alison Overholt, "The Art of Multitasking," *Fast Company Magazine*, October 2002, p. 118, www.fastcompany.com.

33 Julie Morgenstern, "Never Check E-Mail in the Morning," *Bottom Line/Personal*, January 1, 2006, p. 11.

34 Camille Noe Pagan, "Quit Multitasking (And Start Getting More Done)," *Forbes Woman*, January 21, 2010, www.forbes.com.

35 Stephen Rhinesmith, "Using Your Head, Heart, and Guts: Becoming a Complete Leader," *Workforce Management*, February 26, 2007, p. 9.

36 "Global Leader of the Future," *Management Review*, October 1999, p. 9.

37 Carol Hymowitz, "More Managers Allow Workers to Multitask as Job and Home Blur," *Wall Street Journal*, October 28, 2003, p. B1.

38 Ibid.

39 Maxine Neuhauser, "Oops, I Did It Again: Ten Most Common Managerial Mistakes That Lead to Litigation," *Workforce Management Online*, March 2005.

40 Scott Thurm, "How to Drive an Express Train," *Wall Street Journal*, June 1, 2000, pp. B1, B4.

41 John C. Maxwell, *The 21 Irrefutable Laws of Leadership* (Nashville, TN: Thomas Nelson, 1998), p. 208.

42 James Waldroop and Timothy Butler, "Managing Away Bad Habits," *Harvard Business Review*, September–October 2000, pp. 91–98.

43 Ibid., p. 96.

44 For additional insights regarding how leaders must act, see Nancy S. Ahlrichs, *Competing for Talent* (Palo Alto, CA: Davies-Black, 2000), pp. 173–175.

45 Brent B. Allred, Charles C. Snow, and Raymond E. Miles, "Characteristics of Managerial Careers in the 21st Century," *Academy of Management Executive* 10 (4), 1996, pp. 17–27.

46 "Knowledge and Livelihood: The Global Forces Reshaping Work," Trend: Power, 4Work Food for Thought, www.4work.com.

47 Kemba J. Dunham, "Executives Seek Career Boost from Writing, Speaking Stints," *Wall Street Journal*, August 22, 2000, p. B12.

48 Preston C. Bottger and Jean-Louis Barsoux, "Do you Really Want to Be a Leader," *Wall Street Journal*, November 30, 2009, p. R8.

49 Candice Choi, "How Much Slacking at Work is OK?" *Temple Daily Telegram*, March 29, 2009, p. 1D.

50 Barbara Moses, "Finding Your Footing in Shaky Times," *Globe and Mail*, January 7, 2009, www.bmoses.com.

51 Adele Scheele, "When You've Been Passed Over," *Working Woman*, April 1994, pp. 64–66, 90.

52 Pepi Sappal, "Should I Stay or Should I Go?" *Wall Street Journal*, April 18, 2000, p. B15.

Chapter 10

1 Cathy Fyock, "News from Cathy Frock and Innovative Management concepts," May 29, 2006, www.cathyfyock.com.

2 Jamie Minier, "Here Today, Gone Tomorrow: Keeping Up with the Current State of Recruiting," *Workforce Management*, July 2009, www.workforce.com.

3 Samuel Greengard, "Are You Well Armed to Screen Applicants?" *Personnel Journal*, December 1995, pp. 84–85.

4 "200 Questions Job Candidates May Ask Your Company: Questions for Hiring Managers" Reprinted from *201 Best Questions to Ask on Your Interview* by John Kador, 2002, McGraw-Hill Companies, Inc., *Workforce Management*, http://www.workforce.com.

5 Diann R. Newman and Richard M. Hodgetts, *Human Resource Management: A Customer-Oriented Approach* (Upper Saddle River, NJ: Prentice-Hall, 1998), pp. 166–167.

6 Peter Carbonara, "Hire for Attitude, Train for Skill," *Fast Company*, August 1996, http://www.fastcompany.com/online/04/hiring.html.

7 Fay Hansen, "Company's Customized Test Goes beyond Job Skills," *Workforce Management*, March 2010, www.workforce.com.

8 Scott Hays, "Exceptional Customer Service Takes the 'Ritz' Touch," *Workforce Management*, January 1999, www.workforce.com.

9 Garry Kranz, "A Menu for Management," *Workforce Management*, June 2007, www.workforce.com.

10 Jeffrey A. Mello, "Personality Tests and Privacy Rights," *HR Focus*, March 1996, pp. 22–23.

11 State of the Industry Report, American Society for Training & Development, 2009, pp. 4, 8.

12 Garry Kranz, "Downturn Prompts a Change in Learning Initiatives," *Workforce Management*, October 2009, www.workforce.com.

13 Jennifer Homer, "Growing Skills Gaps among Workers Result in New Challenges for Organizations," news release, American Society for Training & Development, April 13, 2005.

14 Garry Kranz, "A Higher Standard for Managers," *Workforce Management*, January 11, 2007, www.workforce.com.

15 Sarah Fister Gale, "Making E-Learning More Than 'Pixie Dust,'" *Workforce Management*, March 2003, pp. 58–62.

16 Sarah Fister Gale, "Blended Formats Engage All Learners," *Workforce Management*, March 2003, p. 60.

17 Patrick J. Kiger, "Cisco's Homegrown Gamble," *Workforce Management*, March 2003, p. 34, http://www.workforce.com.

18 "Honeywell's Director: Constant Challenges Thrown in Front of Us," *Workforce Week*, February 9–15, 2003, http://www.workforce.com.

19 Sarah Fister Gale, "The Power of Community," *Workforce Management*, March 2009, www.workforce.com.

20 Michelle V. Rafter, "Talent Management Systems Make Inroads with Employers," *Workforce Management*, January 2006, www.workforce.com.

21 Sarah Fister Gale, "Moodle Goes Corporate," *Workforce Management*, September 2008, www.workforce.com.

22 Jennifer Weyrauch, Motorola, Inc., e-mail correspondence with the author, April 25, 2003.

23 Patrick J. Kiger, "Task Force Training Develops New Leaders, Solves Real Business Issues and Helps Cut Costs." *Workforce Management*, May 2007, www.workforce.com.

24 "How Business Can Improve Workforce Readiness," A Conference Board Report, "The Ill-Prepared U.S. Workforce", *Workforce Management*, September 14, 2009, p. 33, www.workforce.com.

25 Ibid.

26 Lynn D. Lieber, "The Four Types of Training that Should Never Be Cut," *Workforce Management*, January 2010, www.workforce.com.

27 Mark R. Edwards and Ann J. Ewen, *360° Feedback: The Powerful New Model for Employee Assessment & Performance Improvement* (New York: American Management Association, 1996).

28 Francis J. Yammarino and Leanne E. Atwater, "Do Managers See Themselves as Others See Them? Implication of Self-Other Rating Agreement for Human Resources Management," *Organizational Dynamics*, Spring 1997, p. 36.

29 Richard Lepsinger and Anntoinette D. Lucia, *The Art and Science of 360° Feedback* (San Francisco, CA: Jossey-Bass, 1997), p. 6.

30 For more on this, see Richard M. Hodgetts, *Measures of Quality and High Performance: Simple Tools and Lessons from America's Most Successful Companies* (New York: American Management Association, 1998), chapter 6; Keith E. Morical, "A Product Review: 360° Assessments," *Training and Development Journal*, April 1999, pp. 43–47; Kenneth M. Nowack, Jeanne Hartley, and William Bradley, "How to Evaluate Your 360° Feedback Efforts," *Training and Development Journal*, April 1999, pp. 48–53; and Adrian Furnham and Paul Stringfield, "Congruence in Job-Performance Ratings: A Study of 360° Feedback Examining Self, Manager, Peers, and Consultant Ratings," *Human Relations*, April 1998, pp. 517–530.

31 Sharon Davis, "Minority Execs Want an Even Break," *Workforce Management*, April 2000, p. 52.

32 "360 Feedback and Leadership Coaching Lead to Development Success" Leadership Intelligence Report, August 5, 2010, www.decision-wise.com.

33 Lonnie Harvey, "How Do We Improve Our Evaluations?" *Workforce Management*, January 3, 2008, www.workforce.com.

34 Amelia J. Prewett-Livingston, John G. Veres III, Hubert S. Field, and Philip M., "Effects of Race on Interview Ratings in a Situational Panel Interview," *Journal of Applied Psychology*, April 1996, pp. 178–186.

35 Cynthia M. Marlowe, Sandra L. Schneider, and Carnot E. Nelson, "Gender and Attractiveness Biases in Hiring Decisions: Are More Experienced Managers Less Biased?" *Journal of Applied Psychology*, February 1996, pp. 11–21.

36 Juan I. Sanchez and Phillip De La Torre, "A Second Look at the Relationship between Rating and Behavioral Accuracy in Performance Appraisal," *Journal of Applied Psychology*, February 1996, pp. 3–10.

37 Neal P. Mero and Stephan J. Motowidlo, "Effects of Rater Accountability on the Accuracy and the Favorability of Performance Ratings," *Journal of Applied Psychology*, August 1995, pp. 517–524.

38 Steven L. Thomas and Robert D. Bretz Jr., "Research and Practice in Performance Appraisal: Evaluating Employee Performance in America's Largest Companies," *SAM Advanced Management Journal*, Spring 1994, pp. 33–34.

39 "Money Isn't Everything" *Workforce*, March 6, 2003. Source: August Vlak, principal at Katzenbach Partners LLC, New York, January 20, 2003.

40 See, for example, "Why Gainsharing Works Even Better Today Than in the Past," *HR Focus*, April 2000, pp. 3–5.

41 Todd Henneman, "State of the Sector Recognition and Rewards: What's the Payoff?" *Workforce Management*, October 10, 2005, pp. 41–44.

42 "What Distinguishes High Performing Company Pay Practices from the Pack?" *HR Focus*, May 2000, p. 4.

43 Interview with Jessie Torres, district manager, Taco Bell, March 31, 2003.

44 Joann S. Lublin, "Boards Tie CEO Pay More Tightly to Performance," *Wall Street Journal*, February 21, 2006, p. A1.

45 Lewis Braham, "A Perk for the Rank and File, Too," *Business Week Online*, March 10, 2003, http://www.businessweek.com.

46 Personal Interview with Debra Loftis, Assistant Manager, Wendy's Restaurant, Temple, Texas, August 5, 2010.

47 Dan Tynan, "25 Ways to Reward Employees (Without spending a Dime)." August 5, 2010, www.hrworld.com.

48 Everett T. Suters, "The Toughest Job Around," *Inc.*, November 1986, pp. 138, 140.

49 To see the number of discrimination cases and the extent of the cases being filed, go to the Web site, www.eeoc.gov.

50 For more on this, see Susan Gardner, Glenn M. Gomes, and James F. Morgan, "Wrongful Termination and the Expanding Public Policy Exception: Implications and Advice," *SAM Advanced Management Journal*, Winter 2000, pp. 38–44.

51 See Sara Siwolop, "Recourse or Retribution?" *New York Times*, June 7, 2000, pp. C1, C10.

52 A. Jonathan Trafimow, "What 'Employment at Will' Really Means to You," *Workforce Management*, January 2005, www.workforce.com.

53 James Manktelow, "How to Use Time Effectively: Time Management Skills," *The Mind Tools Ebook* (Wimbledon, London, UK: Mind Tools Ltd, 2005), pp. 153–164.

54 "Driving Success: The Incredible Power of Company-Wide Goal Alignment," *Success Factors*, HR Insider Series eGuide.

55 Leslie W. Rue and Lloyd L. Byars, "Managing Your Time," *Supervision: Key Link to Productivity*, 5th ed. (New York: McGraw-Hill/Irwin, 1996), pp. 82–91.

56 Donna J. Abernathy, "A Get-Real Guide to Time Management," *Training and Development Journal*, June 1999, pp. 22–26.

Chapter 11

1 June Kronholz, "How 23 E-Mails Sent by a 9th-Grade Girl Got 160,478 Replies," *Wall Street Journal*, February 13, 2003, p. A1.

2 Wireless Week staff, "By the Numbers—March 2010," *Aviat Network*, March 7, 2010, www.wirelessweek.com.

3 Ryan Kim, "The World's a Cell-Phone Stage," *San Francisco Chronicle Online*, February 27, 2006. http://sfgate.com.

4 Employer Policies, "NSC Member Survey: Employer Cell Phone Policies," April 6, 2010, www.nsc.org.

5 Zachary A. Hummel, "Their BlackBerries—Your Problem," *Workforce Management*, March 2008, www.workforce.com.

6 "Proliferation of Camera Phones Calls Up a Wide Range of Risks Relating to the Workplace," *Workforce Management Online*, May 2005. Based on an article from *Business Insurance*, May 23, 2005, written by Rupal Parekh.

7 Ibid.

8 Andromida, "Internet Usage Statistics—Global Net Users Number & Growth of World Traffic Trend," www.hubpages.com.

9 News Poll Results, *Workforce Week*, September 5–11, 2004.

10 Rebecca Buckman, "E-mail's Friendly Fire," *Wall Street Journal*, November 27, 2007, p. B1.

11 Brian E. Lewis, "Court Says Just Sending Employees an E-Mail Doesn't Qualify as Communication," *Workforce Management Online*, August 2004.

12 Michael Sanserino, "Suits Question After-Hours Demands of E-mail and Cell Phones," *Wall Street Journal*, August 10, 2009, p. B1.

13 "Communicating Electronically: What Every Manager Needs to Know," Sample Issue, *Communication Solutions*, www.managementresources. com.

14 www.emailreplies.com.

15 Ibid.

16 Jena McGregor, "High-Tech Runner-Up: Panera Bread," *Fast Company Magazine* (99), October 2005, p. 51.

17 Cindy Waxer, "Navigating Privacy Concerns to Equip Workers with GPS," *Workforce Management Online*, August 4, 2005.

18 Frances Hesselbein, "Managing in a World That Is Round," *Leader to Leader Institute Journal* (2), Fall 1996, pp. 6–8.

19 Philip Ball, "E-Mail Reveal Real Leaders," *Nature Science Update*, March 20, 2003, Nature News Service, Macmillan Magazines Ltd.

20 "HP Releases Tips to Increase Effectiveness of Everyday Business Communications," news release, Hewlett-Packard, October 18, 2005, Palo Alto, CA.

21 Marlon A. Walker, "The Day the E-Mail Dies," *Wall Street Journal*, August 26, 2004, p. B1.

22 Adapted from Debra L. Nelson and James Campbell Quick, "How Do Communication Technologies Affect Behavior?" *Organizational Behavior*, 4th ed. (South-Western College Publishers, 2003), pp. 277–278.

23 News in brief, *Workforce Week Online*, September 11–17, 2005.

24 News in brief, "Faceless CEO," *Workforce Week*, March 12–18, 2006.

25 Barbara Moses, "It's Not Just What You Say, It's How You Say It," *Globe and Mail*, December 2, 2009, bbm@bbmcareerdev.com.

26 R. L. Daft and R. H. Lengel, "Information Richness: A New Approach to Managerial Behavior and Organizational Design," in B. M. Staw and L. L. Cummings, eds. *Research in Organizational Behavior* (Greenwich, CT: JAI Press, 1984), p. 196.

27 Ibid., p. 197.

28 R. E. Rice and D. E. Shook, "Relationships of Job Categories and Organizational Levels to Use of Communication Channels, Including Electronic Mail: A Meta-Analysis and Extension," *Journal of Management Studies*, March 1990, pp. 195–229.

29 Martin Hahn, "Overcoming Communication Barriers Between People," *Ezine Articles*, December 29, 2005, www.ezinearticles.com.

30 Rupal Jain, "The Barriers to Effective Communication," Ezine Articles, August 7, 2010, www.ezinearticles.com.

31 Patricia Schiff Estess, "Open-Book Policy," *Entrepreneur*, March 2000, pp. 130–131.

32 K. Denise Bane, "Gaining Control by Losing It? The Dilemma of Entrepreneurial Information," *Academy of Management Executive*, May 1997, pp. 80–82.

33 Raymond S. Nickerson, "How We Know—and Sometimes Misjudge—What Others Know: Imputing One's Own Knowledge to Others," *Psychological Bulletin* 125 (6), 1999, pp. 737–759.

34 Daniel Benjamin and Tony Horwitz, "German View: You Americans Work Too Hard—and for What?" *Wall Street Journal*, August 14, 1994, pp. B1, B6.

35 Lin Grensing-Pophal, "Talk to Me," *HR Magazine*, March 2000, p. 70.

36 Also see Paul Sandwith, "Building Quality into Communications," *Training and Development Journal*, January 1994, pp. 55–59.

37 See Howard E. Butz Jr. and Leonard D. Goodstein, "Measuring Customer Value: Gaining the Strategic Advantage," *Organizational Dynamics*, Winter 1996, p. 72.

38 Larry L. Barker, *Communication* (Englewood Cliffs, NJ: Prentice-Hall, 1978), p. 151; and Larry L. Barker and Deborah A. Gaut, *Communications*, 7th ed. (Boston, MA: Allyn & Bacon, 1995).

39 "Speaking to the Boss," *Training*, February 2000, p. 28.

40 Carolyn B. Thompson and Robin Vance, "Communicate with Others the Way They Communicate Best," *Training Systems*, http://trainingsys.com.

41 University of Granada, "Right-Handed and Left-Handed People Do Not See the Same Bright Side of Things," *ScienceDaily*, February 2, 2010, www.sciencedaily.com.

42 Albert Mehrabian, *Nonverbal Communication* (Chicago, IL: Aldine-Atherton, 1972), pp. 25–30.

43 Roger E. Axtell, *Gestures: The DO's and TABOO's of Body Language around the World*, 2nd ed. (New York: John Wiley & Sons, Inc., 1991) pp. 42–45.

44 "Managing Employee Information and Communications," *Workforce Management*, January 3, 2008, www.workforce.com.

45 Associated Press, "How to Handle Negative Feedback," *Temple Daily Telegram*, November 10, 2009, p. 3B.

46 "In Brief: Employee Satisfaction," *Workforce Week* 3 (15), April 13–19, 2003, http://www.workforce.com.

47 For more on this topic, see "Listening Is a 10-Part Skill," *Nation's Business*, September 1987, p. 40.

48 Michael A. Prospero, "Leading Listener: Cabela's," *Fast Company* (99), October 2005, p. 53.

49 Lucas Conley, "Customer-Centered Leader: Maxine Clark," *Fast Company* (99), October 2005, p. 54.

50 Richard M. Hodgetts and Jane Whitney Gibson, "Building Effective Oral Presentations: The PLAN Approach," 1986 IEEE International Professional Communication Conference Proceedings, pp. 67–69.

51 See, for example, K. Hawkins and C. B. Power, "Gender Differences in Questions Asked during Small Decision-Making Group Discussions," *Small Group Research*, April 1999, pp. 235–256; and K. C. Gordon, D. H. Baucom, N. Epstein, C. K. Burnett, and L. A. Rankin, "The Interaction between Marital Standards and Communication Patterns: How Does It Contribute to Marital Adjustment," *Journal of Marital Family Therapy*, April 1999, pp. 211–223.

52 Richard S. Lazarus and Susan Folkman, "The Concept of Coping", **Stress, Appraisal and Coping**, Springer Publishing Company, New York, NY, 1984, pp. 117–139.

53 "Stress Management: What Is Stress?" Georgia Reproductive Specialists, www.ivf.com.

54 Suzanne M. Crampton, John W. Hodge, Jitendra M. Mishra, and Steve Price, "Stress and Stress Management," Questia Online Library.

55 "Your Job May Be Killing You," *Gallup Management Journal*, April 13, 2006.

56 Robert Schlesinger, "Is There Life after Work?" *AARP Bulletin*, May 2005, p. 3.

57 News in brief, "Stress," *Workforce Week*, April 16–22, 2006.

58 News in brief, "Career Growth," *Workforce Week*, April 9–15, 2006.

59 "Stress at Work," U.S. National Institute for Occupational Safety and Health, www.cdc.gov.

60 Jessica Marquez, "Executives Leaving? It's Probably Not the Money," *Workforce Management*, April 14, 2006.

Chapter 12

1 "Usual Weekly Earnings of Wage and Salary Workers, Second Quarter 2010," U.S. Bureau of Labor Statistics, August 8, 2010, www.bls.gov.

2 Edmund L. Andrews, "Daimler Says Chrysler's Problems Are Worsening," *New York Times*, December 19, 2000, p. W1; and Jeffrey Ball, "DaimlerChrysler Official Expects Restructuring, Change Next Year," *Wall Street Journal*, December 20, 2000, p. A4.

3 David de Long and Patricia Seemann, "Confronting Conceptual Confusion and Conflict in Knowledge Management," *Organizational Dynamics*, Summer 2000, p. 37.

4 "Result From the 2008 National Survey on Drug Use and Health: National Findings," *U.S. Department of Health and Human Resources*, August 8, 2010, www.oas.samhsa.gov.

5 News in brief, "Alcoholics," *Workforce Week*, January 29–February 4, 2006.

6 Donald A. Phillips and Harry J. Older, "Alcoholic Employees Beget Troubled Supervisors," *Supervisory Management*, September 1981, p. 5.

7 News in brief, "Methamphetamine," *Workforce Week*, February 12–18, 2006.

8 Becky Vance, "Drug Use and Abuse Remains a Serious Workplace Problem," *Houston Business Journal*, July 21, 2000, p. 49.

9 "Substance Abuse Facts and Figures," U.S. Department of Health & Human Services, Substance Abuse and Mental Health Services Administration, 2000, www.drugtestcenter.com.

10 Bill Oliver, "Ten Steps to a Near-Drug-Free Workplace," *HR Focus*, December 1993, p. 9.

11 Erica Gordon Sorohan, "Making Decisions about Drug Testing," *Training and Development Journal*, May 1994, p. 112.

12 "Drug Testing in the Workplace," ACLU Briefing Paper (5), July 26, 1997.

13 For more on EAPs, see Peggy Stuart, "Investments in EAPs Pay Off," *Personnel Journal*, February 1993, pp. 43–54.

14 March 19, 2003, www.oas.samhsa.gov.

15 "Saving Lives and Money: Solving Substance Abuse in the Workplace," U.S. Department of Health & Human Services, Substance Abuse and Mental Health Services Administration, www.drugtestcenter.com.

16 March 10, 2002, www.oas.samhsa.gov.

17 "Saving Lives and Money."

18 James A. Wall Jr. and Ronda Roberts Callister, "Conflict and Its Management," *Journal of Management*, Fall 1995, p. 395.

19 Also see Willem F. G. Mastenbroek, "Organizational Innovation in Historical Perspective: Change as Duality Management," *Business Horizons*, July–August 1996, pp. 5–14.

20 Seth Godin, "Survival Is Not Enough," *Fast Company*, January 2002 (54), p. 90.

21 Robert B. Reich, "Your Job Is Change," *Fast Company*, October 2000, p. 143.

22 Eric Abrahamson, "Change without Pain," *Harvard Business Review*, July–August 2000, p. 74.

23 See Kenneth P. de Meuse and Kevin K. McDaris, "An Exercise in Managing Change," *Training and Development Journal*, February 1994, pp. 55–57.

24 Alan M. Webber, "Will Companies Ever Learn?" *Fast Company*, October 2000, pp. 275–282.

25 For more on this topic, see Daniel C. Feldman and Carrie R. Leana, "A Study of Reemployment Challenges after Downsizing," *Organizational Dynamics*, Summer 2000, pp. 64–74.

26 Curt M. Thompson, "Preparation Is Key to Successful Change," *HR Focus*, April 1994, pp. 17–18.

27 Carl Nielson, the Nielson Group, Dallas, September 20, 2005, printed in Dear Workforce, *Workforce Management Online*, October 20, 2005.

28 Alan L. Frohman, "Igniting Organizational Change: The Power of Personal Initiative," *Organizational Dynamics*, Winter 1997, pp. 39–53.

29 "How Does Change Management Need to Change?" *Harvard Management* Update, January 2001, http://www. hbsp.harvard.edu.

30 Bobbie Gossage, "How to Get People to Change," February 1, 2010, www.inc.com.

31 Ibid.

32 Mary Buchel, "Accelerating Change," *Training and Development Journal*, April 1996, pp. 48–51.

33 Shikha Sharma, "Organizational Change" and "Structural Interventions," *Organizational Design*, 1995, Faculty of Information Studies, University of Toronto.

34 Jared Sandberg, "Been Here 25 Years and All I Got Was This Lousy T-Shirt," *Wall Street Journal*, January 28, 2004, D1.

35 Bob Nelson, "Everything You Thought You Knew about Recognition Is Wrong," *Workforce Management Online*, January 2004.

36 Kathryn Meyer, Capital H. Group, Milwaukee, February 11, 2005, printed in Dear Workforce, *Workforce Online*, March 3, 2005.

37 Joe Mullich, "They've Got the Gold Watch Blues," *Workforce Management*, November 2003, pp. 73–78.

38 "Employee Engagement—What's the Difference?" *DecisionWise*, April 2006, www.decision-wise.com.

39 Roger E. Herman, "How Do We Reserve a Culture of Hostility?" *Dear Workforce*, *Workforce Online*, March 17, 2005.

40 J. J. Thakkar, "How Do I Change Corporate Culture Diplomatically?" Capital H Group, the Woodlands, Texas, March 28, 2005. Printed in *Dear Workforce*, *Workforce Online*, May 5, 2005, www.workforce.com.

41 "Member Poll: When Cultures Clash," *Workforce Week*, February 5–11, 2006.

42 Sarah Fister Gale, "Incentives and the Art of Changing Behavior," *Workforce Management*, November 2002, pp. 80–82.

43 "How Organizational Development Works: Conceptual View," Toolpack Consulting, LLC, Teaneck, New Jersey.

44 Wendell L. French and Cecil H. Bell Jr., *Organizational Development*, 2nd ed. (Englewood Cliffs, NJ: Prentice-Hall, 1978), p. 137.

45 "Employee Surveys: A Tool for Change," White Paper, Toolpack Consulting, October 2001, Version 1.1b.

46 David G. Bowers, "OD Techniques and Their Results in 23 Organizations: The Michigan ICL Study," *Journal of Applied Behavioral Science*, January–February 1973, pp. 21–43.

47 For a complete account of the program, see Alfred J. Marrow, David G. Bowers, and Stanley E. Seashore, *Management by Participation* (New York: Harper & Row, 1967).

48 Margaret Heffernan and Saj-nicole Joni, "Of Proteges and Pitfalls," *Fast Company*, August 2005, p. 81.

49 "What Makes Some Employers So Desired," *Workforce Management Online*, January 2005.

50 Jennifer Reinfold, "Want to Grow as a Leader? Get a Mentor!" *Fast Company*, January 2001, p. 58.

51 Ibid.

52 Linda Phillips-Jones, "How Assertive Should I Be?" the Mentoring Group, www.mentoringgroup.com.

53 Eve Tahmincioglu, "When Women Rise," *Workforce Management*, September 2004, pp. 26–32.

54 Patrick J. Kiger, "Small Groups, Big Ideas," *Workforce Management*, February 27, 2006, pp. 1, 22–27.

55 "Group Mentoring: A Cost-Effective Option," *Workforce Management Online*, December 2004.

56 Eve Tahmincioglu, "Logging on to Link Mentors, Proteges; Keyword: Matchmaking," *Workforce Management*, December 2004, pp. 63–65.

57 Steve Hamm, "Match.com for Mentors," *Business Week*, March 23 and 30, 2009, p. 57.

58 Heffernan and Joni, "Of Proteges and Pitfalls."

59 Linda Phillips-Jones, "Mentoring Your Own Staff," the Mentoring Group, www.mentoringgroup.com.

60 For more information on personal vision, read Peter M. Senge, *The Fifth Discipline: The Art & Practice of the Learning Organization* (Random House, New York, NY, 1990), and "Business as a Human Community: An Interview the Peter Senge," *SGI Quarterly*, October 2006, www.sololine.org.

61 Linda Phillips-Jones, "Creating or Revising Your Personal Vision" and "Writing a Personal Vision Statement," the Mentoring Group, www.mentoringgroup.com.

Chapter 13

1 Esther Fung, "GM Expects Bigger Lift from China," *Wall Street Journal*, April 14, 2010, p. B1.

2 News release, "GM and SAIC Debut World Expo 2010 Pavilion—The Road to 2030," April 11, 2010, http://media.gm.com.

3 Miguel Bustillo, "New Chief at Wal-Mart Looks Abroad for Growth," *Wall Street Journal*, February 2, 2009, p. B1; and "Wal-Mart Wholesale Outlet Opens in India," *Temple Daily Telegram*, May 31, 2009, p. 1D.

4 Global Business, "Home Depot: One Foot in China," *Business Week Online*, May 1, 2006.

5 Home Depot Web site, www.homedepot.com, April 16, 2010.

6 www.india.ford.com and www.ford.com, April 16, 2010.

7 The EU consists of Austria, Belgium, Bulgaria, Cyprus, Czech Republic, Denmark, Estonia, Finland, France, Germany, Greece, Hungary, Ireland, Italy, Latvia, Lithuania, Luxembourg, Malta, the Netherlands, Poland, Portugal, Romania, Slovakia, Slovenia, Spain, Sweden, and the United Kingdom.

8 Richard M. Hodgetts and Fred Luthans, *International Management*, 4th ed. (Burr Ridge, IL: Irwin/McGraw, 2000), p. 108.

9 Esmond D. Smith Jr. and Cuong Pham, "Doing Business in Vietnam: A Cultural Guide," *Business Horizons*, May–June 1996, pp. 47–51; and Arvind V. Phatak and Mohammed M. Habib, "The Dynamics of International Business Negotiations," *Business Horizons*, May–June 1996, pp. 30–38.

10 "Now Solutions," *Workforce Management*, February 27, 2003, www.workforce.com.

11 Carolena Lyons Lawrence, "Teaching Students How Gestures Communicate across Cultures," *Business Education Forum*, February 2003, pp. 38–40.

12 Colleen A. Rickenbacher, *Be On Your Best Cultural Behavior*, Colleen Rickenbacher, Inc., USA, 2008.

13 Geert Hofstede, *Culture's Consequences: Differences in Work-Related Values* (Beverly Hills, CA: Sage, 1980), p. 420.

14 Simcha Ronen and Allen I. Kraut, "Similarities among Countries Based on Employee Work Values and Attitudes," *Columbia Journal of World Business*, Summer 1977, p. 90.

15 Simcha Ronen and Oded Shenkar, "Clustering Countries on Attitudinal Dimensions: A Review and Synthesis," *Academy of Management Journal*, September 1985, pp. 435–454.

16 Dominic Rushe, "UK Bosses Top World Stress Poll," *Sunday Times*, July 23, 2000, p. 2G.

17 Hodgetts and Luthans, *International Management*, p. 389.

18 Sebastian Moffett, "Going Gray: For Ailing Japan, Longevity Begins to Take Its Toll," *Wall Street Journal*, February 11, 2003, p. A1.

19 Suzanne Daley, "Spain Rudely Awakened to Workaday World," *New York Times*, December 26, 1999, pp. 1, 6.

20 Richard M. Hodgetts, "A Conversation with Geert Hofstede," *Organizational Dynamics*, Spring 1994, pp. 53–54.

21 Pete Engardio, Aaron Bernstein, and Manjeet Kripalani, "The New Global Job Shift," *Business Week Online*, February 3, 2003.

22 Todd Henneman, "Measuring the True Benefit of Human Resources Outsourcing," *Workforce Management*, July 2005, pp. 76–77.

23 Jay Solomon and Kathryn Kranhold, "In India's Outsourcing Boom, GE Planning a Starring Role," *Wall Street Journal*, March 23, 2005, p. A1.

24 Andrew Bartels, "Global IT 2008 Market Outlook," Forrester Research, Inc., February 11, 2008, www.forrester.com.

25 Fay Hansen, "R&D Sent to China," *Workforce Management*, December 14, 2009, p. 27, www.workforce.com.

26 John Hollon, "Outsourcing: Get over It," *Workforce Management*, March 13, 2006, p. 58.

27 Engardio et al., "The New Global Job Shift."

28 Isabelle Sender, "Cashing in on India's Banking Boom," *Business Week Online*, February 23, 2006.

29 Steve Hamm, "Guess Who's Hiring in America," *Business Week*, June 25, 2007, p. 47.

30 Strategy, "Managing Outsourcing to Save Money? Be Careful, or Your Plan May Backfire," *Inc.*, January/February 2009, pp. 96–97.

31 Michael A. Stanko, Jonathan D. Bohlmann, and Roger J. Calantone, "Outsourcing Innovation," *Wall Street Journal*, November 30, 2009, p. R6.

32 John Varoli, "It's a Free Market, But Who's Fit to Manage?" *New York Times*, December 26, 1999, pp. 1, 6.

33 "Ford Joint Venture in Asia to be Dissolved: 3-way deal is with Mazda, Chongqing," January 18, 2010, www.istockanalyst.com.

34 Mark Larson, "Background Checking Goes Global," *Workforce Management Online*, April 2006.

35 David Creelman, "IBM Optimizes Its Workforce to Address New Business Goals," *Workforce Management Online*, July 2005.

36 Fay Hansen, "International Business Machine," *Workforce Management*, July 2005, pp. 36–46.

37 Margaret Linehan and James S. Walsh, "Recruiting and Developing Female Managers for International Assignments," *Journal of Management Development* 18 (6), 1999, pp. 521–530.

38 Hodgetts and Luthans, *International Management*, p. 433.

39 Suzanne Daley, "A Spy's Advice to French Retailers: Politeness Pays," *New York Times*, December 26, 2000, p. A4.

40 For more on culture and negotiations, see Philip R. Harris and Robert T. Moran, *Managing Cultural Differences*, 5th ed. (Houston, TX: Gulf Publishing, 2000); and Richard D. Lewis, *When Cultures Collide* (London, UK: Nicholas Brealey, 1999).

41 Roger E. Axtell, Tami Briggs, Margaret Corcoran, and Mary Beth Lamb, *Do's and Taboos around the World for Women in Business* (New York: John Wiley & Sons, 1997), pp. 92–93.

42 Irwin Speizer, "The State of Training and Development: More Spending, More Scrutiny," *Workforce Management*, May 22, 2006, pp. 25–26.

43 Sheida Hodge, *Global Smarts: The Art of Communicating and Deal Making Anywhere in the World* (New York: John Wiley & Sons, 2000), pp. 152–153.

44 Ed Frauenheim, "Custom-Fit Communication," *Workforce Management*, November 21, 2005, p. 30.

45 "Culture Adjustment," The World at Your Fingertips, www.cie.uci.edu.

46 Reviewed by Richard S. Kingsley, MD, "Culture Shock," August 11, 2010, http://kidshealth.org.

47 Katherine Schneider, "Cultural Differences," University of Wisconsin Eau Claire Counseling Services, www.uwec.edu.

48 Guanipa, "Culture Shock."

49 Ed Frauenheim, "Crossing Cultures," *Workforce Management*, November 21, 2005, pp. 1, 26–32.

50 News in brief, "Ethics," *Workforce Week*, June 4–10, 2006.

51 "Xerox North America President Addresses Value of Corporate Citizenship; Keynote Presented at Financial Executives International Conference," June 2, 2006, press release, www.csrwire.com.

52 Scott McCartney, "Do Americans Traveling Abroad Need Tips on Behaving Better?" *Wall Street Journal Online*, CareerJournal.com; Joann Klimkiewicz, "Everyone's an Ambassador," *Hartford Courant Newspaper Online*, www.kentucky.com; "Engaging Americans in World Citizenship," Business for Diplomatic Action, www.businessfordiplomaticaction.org; and Scott McCartney, "Teaching Americans How to Behave Abroad," *Wall Street Journal Online*, CareerJournal.com, April 13, 2006.

53 Peggy Anne Salz, "Merger Ahead: A Three-Prong Strategy Smooths the Path to Profitable M&As," *Wall Street Journal*, June 2, 2006, p. A8.

54 Andrew Ross Sorkin, "The Year That European Corporate Acquirers Invaded America," *New York Times*, December 18, 2000, p. C14.

55 John Hollon, "Outsourcing: Get over It," *Workforce Management*, March 13, 2006, p. 58.

56 Jenny C. McCune, "Exporting Corporate Culture," *Management Review*, December 1999, p. 55.

57 Andrew Rosenbaum, "Testing Cultural Waters," *Management Review*, July–August 1999, pp. 41–43.

58 Yoshio Tateishi, representative director and CEO, "Meeting the Challenges of the 21st Century," GD2010, May 28, 2003, http://www.omron.com.

59 The Corporate Profile, "The Omron Principles," www.omron.com.

60 Larraine Segil, Intelligent Business Alliances (New York: Random House, 1996).

61 Jessica Marquez, "Virtual Work Spaces Ease Collaboration, Debate among Scattered Employees," *Workforce Management*, May 22, 2006, p. 38.

62 Cyrus F. Freidheim Jr., "The Battle of the Alliances," *Management Review*, September 1999, p. 47.

63 Office Organization, "Organize Now for Better Productivity Later," June 1, 2006, www.lexmark.com.

64 Paige Arnof-Fenn, "Organizing Your Home Office," *Entrepreneur*, December 19, 2005, www.entrepreneur.com.

65 Leslie Jacobs, "10 Quick Tips for Getting Organized," *Entrepreneur*, January 12, 2006, www.entrepreneur.com.

66 "About Office Efficiency and Ergonomics," www.ergoindemand.com.

Chapter 14

1 Peggy Anne Salz, "High Performance: The Key to Sustainable Success Is Unfettered Innovation," *Wall Street Journal*, May 8, 2006, p. A10.

2 Ibid.

3 Ibid.

4 For more on entrepreneurial myths, see Donald F. Kuratko and Richard M. Hodgetts, *Entrepreneurship: A Contemporary Approach*, 5th ed. (Orlando, FL: Harcourt, 2001), pp. 71–72.

5 Tom Peters, *Thriving on Chaos* (New York: Knopf, 1987), p. 229.

6 "Is Your Organization Creative Enough?" A *Gallup Management Journal* interview with Jim Clifton, chairman and CEO of Gallup, *Gallup Management Journal*, May 11, 2006.

7 Kathryn Martell and Stephen J. Carroll, "Which Executive Human Resource Management Practices for the Top Management Team Are Associated with Higher Firm Performance?" *Human Resource Management* 34 (4), 1995, pp. 497–512.

8 Philip M. Mirvis, "Human Resource Management: Leaders, Laggards, and Followers," *Academy of Management Executives*, published by the Academy of Management, May 1997, p. 49.

9 Interview between Tom Peters, the author of *Re-imagine! Business Excellence in a Disruptive Age*, and Michael Slind, a former *Fast Company* editor, July 28, 2003.

10 Bill Breen, "Hidden Asset," *Fast Company*, March 2004, p. 93.

11 Michael Hammer and James Champy, *Reengineering the Corporation* (New York: HarperCollins, 1993), p. 32.

12 An interview between Tom Peters and Michael Slind about *Re-imagine! Business Excellence in a Disruptive Age* (West Tinmouth, VT), July 28, 2003, Archives: www.tompeters.com.

13 Tom Peters references Philip Bobbitt in the interview with Michael Slind. Philip Bobbitt is the author of *The Shield of Achilles: War, Peace, and the Course of History* (New York: Alfred A. Knopf, 2002), Archives: www.tompeters.com.

14 Vadim Kotelnikov, "The Entrepreneur," Ten3 Business e-Coach – Innovation Unlimited, www.1000ventures.com.

15 Joe Love, "The Entrepreneurial Spirit," *Ezine Articles*, October 24, 2005, www.ezinearticles.com.

16 Linda Tischler, "Where Are the Women?" *Fast Company*, February 2004, p. 52.

17 GE Imagination at Work, "Ecomagination," www.ge.com.

18 Barbara Moses, "Employers: Dangle the Right Carrots to Entice Workers," *Globe and Mail Online Newsletter*, February 17, 2006.

19 Dear Workforce, "How Do We Determine the Meaning behind Our Employee Engagement scores?" *Workforce Management*, January 2010, www.workforce.com.

20 DecisionWise, Inc., "Employees that Quit and Stay," info@decwise.com, August 15, 2007.

21 Jennifer Robison, "Disengagement Can Be Really Depressing," *Gallup Management Journal*, April 2, 2010, www.gmj.gallup.com.

22 Ashok Gopal, "Worker Disengagement Continues to Cost Singapore," *Gallup Management Journal*, May 11, 2006, gmj.gallup.com.

23 Mark Royal and Rebecca Masson, "Employee Engagement in Tough Times, Part Two," *Workforce Management*, May 2009, www.workforce.com.

24 Recognition Council, "The Time for Employee Recognition and Rewards Programs Is Now," April 7, 2009, www.recognitioncouncil.org.

25 Joanne Earl and Melissa Dunn Lampe, "You've Gotten Employee Feedback, Now What?" *Gallup Management Journal*, May 11, 2006, www.gmj.gallup.com.

26 Corporate Executive Board, "Involve Your Employees, Says Google, CEB," *Business Week*, December 11, 2009, www.businessweek.com.

27 Jennifer Robison, "When Campbell Was in the Soup," *Gallup Management Journal*, March 11, 2010.

28 Rachele Williams, "Employee Engagement: Define It, Measure It and Put It to Work in Your Organizations," *Workforce Management*, January 2010, www.workforce.com.

29 Press release from Wipro Limited, April 24, 2003, http://www.nervewire.com and http://www.wipro.com.

30 http://www.befree.com, April 27, 2010.

31 www.phillips.com, April 27, 2010.

32 www.appliedcreative.com, 2010.

33 Anne Robertson, "Employee Perks and Comforts Keep Creative Juices Flowing," *Business Journal*, Phoenix, February 17, 2003.

34 Barbara Moses, "Employers: Dangle the Right Carrots."

35 Jane Shealy, "Playing for Keeps," *Success*, December–January 2001, p. 63.

36 June Kronholz, "Hispanics Gain in Census," *Wall Street Journal*, May 10, 2006, p. A6; and Kenneth N. Wexley and Gary P. Latham, *Developing and Training Human Resources in Organizations*, 3rd ed. (Englewood Cliffs, NJ: Prentice-Hall, 2002), p. 325.

37 Katharine Q. Seelye, "Future U.S.: Grayer and More Hispanic," *New York Times*, March 27, 1997, p. A18.

38 http://www.bls.gov, April 2010.

39 "Women Still Underrepresented among Highest Earners," U.S. Bureau of Labor Statistics, www.bls.gov (March 2006).

40 http://www.bls.gov, April 2010.

41 Joi Preciphs, "Finance Firms Still Lag on Hiring," *Wall Street Journal Online*, CareerJournal.com, April 28, 2006.

42 Ann Zimmerman and Nathan Koppel. "Bias Suit Advances Against Wal-Mart," *Wall Street Journal*, April 27, 2010, p. A1.

43 "Significant EEOC Race/Color Cases," "E-Race and Other EEOC Initiatives," and "Newsroom Press Releases," August 17, 2010, www.eeoc.gov.

44 Sue Shellenbarger, "Supreme Court Tackles Employee Harassment," *Wall Street Journal Online*, CareerJournal.com, April 14, 2006.

45 "Significant EEOC Race/Color Cases" August 17, 2010, www.eeoc.gov.

46 A. Craig Cleland, "The Next Wave – Systemic Discrimination Class Actions," *LexisNexis*, July 14, 2008, www.martindale.com.

47 Carey Goldberg, "Fat People Say an Intolerant World Condemns Them on First Sight," *New York Times*, November 5, 2000, p. 30Y.

48 Ibid.

49 American Obesity Association, www.obesity.org (July 14, 2003).

50 American Obesity Association, www.obesity.org (May 16, 2006).

51 Jeffrey Zaslow, "Differences Are Emerging among Women Employees," *Wall Street Journal*, www.careerjournal.com (May 5, 2006).

52 Shari Caudron, "Learning to Understand Each Other by 'Genderflexing,'" *Personnel Journal*, May 1995, p. 54.

53 Linda Gravett, Ph.D., SPHR, "Why Diversity Training Fails," http://www.e-Hresources.com.

54 Fred Luthans, Richard M. Hodgetts, and Sang M. Lee, "New Paradigm Organizations: from Total Quality to Learning to World-Class," *Organizational Dynamics*, Winter 1994, p. 15.

55 John Sullivan, "Personalizing Motivation," *Workforce Management*, March 27, 2006, p. 50.

56 Laura Saunders Egodigwe, John C. Long, and Nima Warfield, "A Year of Scandals and Sorrow," *Wall Street Journal*, January 2, 2003, Section R.

57 Noel Fahey, Irish Ambassador, Speaker at the 2006 Bentley Leadership Forum, Bentley College, April 26, 2006, quoted in *Time*, May 15, 2006, p. 60.

58 Jason Madara, "Full Text: The Future's So Bright," *Fast Company*, March 2006, p. 144.

59 Mark Schoeff Jr., "Democrats Push to Add Workers in Science Fields," *Workforce Management*, January 16, 2006, p. 12.

60 The list appearing in the following article was updated on August 18, 2010. "Fast Forward: 25 Trends That Will Change the Way You Do Business," *Workforce Management*, June 2003, pp. 43–56.

61 Stephen M. Paskoff, "10 Ethics Trends for 2010," *Workforce Management*, December 2009, www.workforce.com.

62 Patrick J. Kiger, "HR Information Insecurity—Steal Our Data, Please," *Workforce Management*, February 2010, www.workforce.com.

63 Fay Hansen, "Special Report on Background Checking—Burden of Proof," *Workforce Management*, February 2010, www.workforce.com.

64 "Green Technology – What is it?" April 30, 2010, www.green-technology.org.

65 Racquel Palmese, "Game Changer: California's Green Building Code," *Green Technology Magazine*, April 30, 2010, www.green-technology.org.

66 Carlos Tejada and Gary McWilliams, "New Recipe for Cost Savings: Replace Expensive Workers," *Wall Street Journal*, June 11, 2003, p. A1.

67 "In Age of SARS, Wal-Mart Adjusts Global Buying Machine," *Wall Street Journal*, May 28, 2003, p. B1.

68 Jane Spencer, "Shirk Ethic: How to Fake a Hard Day at the Office," *Wall Street Journal*, May 15, 2003, p. D1.

69 Kortney Stringer, "How to Have a Pleasant Trip: Eliminate Human Contact," *Wall Street Journal*, October 31, 2002.

70 "DBM Survey Finds Companies Have Not Prepared Younger Workers for Senior Leadership Roles," Drake Beam Morin, http://www.dbm.com (July 14, 2003).

71 News Analysis, "Hiring Outlook '03, Part One," *Business Week Online*, January 2, 2003.

72 Barbara Moses, "Career Change: Look Before You Leap," *Globe & Mail*, May 29, 2009.

73 Barbara Moses, "Even in Uncertain Times, Quitting is an Option," *Globe & Mail*, October 3, 2008.

74 The Cramer Institute, assetbasedthinking.com. An interview between Tom Peters and Kathryn Cramer, Archives: www.tompeters.com, posted March 28, 2006.

75 Joann Lublin, "How One Executive Used a Sabbatical to Fix His Career," *Wall Street Journal*, January 8, 2008, p. B1.

76 Lisa Takeuchi Cullen, "Getting Wise to Lies," *Time*, May 1, 2006, p. 59.

77 Gaston F. Ceron, "The Grass May Not Be Greener," *Wall Street Journal*, April 10, 2006, p. R3.

78 Sarah E. Needleman, "Reaching out to Recruiters as You Work Your Way Up," *Wall Street Journal Online*, CareerJournal.com, March 30, 2006.

79 Perri Capell, "Is It OK to Talk to Two Recruiters about the Same Job Opening?" *Wall Street Journal Online*, www.careerjournal.com (May 15, 2006).

80 Andrea Coombes, "Avoid Being a Chatterbox During Job Interviews," The *Wall Street Journal Online*, www.careerjournal.com (May 10, 2006).

Index